T0135021

Communications
in Computer and Information Science 1616

More information about this series at https://link.springer.com/bookseries/7899

Filippo Sanfilippo · Ole-Christoffer Granmo ·
Sule Yildirim Yayilgan ·
Imran Sarwar Bajwa (Eds.)

Intelligent Technologies and Applications

4th International Conference, INTAP 2021
Grimstad, Norway, October 11–13, 2021
Revised Selected Papers

 Springer

Editors
Filippo Sanfilippo 🄳
University of Agder (UiA)
Grimstad, Norway

Ole-Christoffer Granmo 🄳
University of Agder (UiA)
Grimstad, Norway

Sule Yildirim Yayilgan 🄳
Norwegian University of Science
and Technology (NTNU)
Gjøvik, Norway

Imran Sarwar Bajwa 🄳
The Islamia University of Bahawalpur (IUB)
Bahawalpur, Pakistan

ISSN 1865-0929   ISSN 1865-0937 (electronic)
Communications in Computer and Information Science
ISBN 978-3-031-10524-1   ISBN 978-3-031-10525-8 (eBook)
https://doi.org/10.1007/978-3-031-10525-8

This Springer imprint is published by the registered company Springer Nature Switzerland AG
The registered company address is: Gewerbestrasse 11, 6330 Cham, Switzerland

Preface

The present book includes accepted papers of the 4th International Conference on Intelligent Technologies and Applications (INTAP 2021), held in Grimstad, Norway, during October 11–13, 2021, organized and hosted by the University of Agder (UiA) and by Oslo Metropolitan University (OsloMet) with the support of the Top Research Centre Mechatronics (TRCM), UiA; the Center for Artificial Intelligence Research (CAIR), UiA; and the Artificial Intelligence Research Group (AIRG), Islamia University of Bahawalpur (IUB), Pakistan. INTAP 2021 was supported by the Institute of Electrical and Electronics Engineers (IEEE) Norway Section.

The conference was organized in thirteen simultaneous tracks: Intelligence [6 papers], Internet of Things (IoT) [1 paper], Smart Electrical Energy Systems [4 papers], Decision Support Systems [1 paper], Intelligent Environments [1 paper], Social Media Analytics [2 papers], Robotics [8 papers], Artificial Intelligence (AI) and Machine Learning (ML) Security [1 paper], ML in Energy Sectors and Materials [4 papers], Applications of Intelligent Technologies in Emergency Management [1 paper], ML and AI for Intelligent Health [2 papers], ML and AI for Sensing Technologies [2 papers], and Miscellaneous [6 papers].

INTAP 2021 received 243 submissions from authors in 27 countries and districts in six continents. After a single-blind review process, only 39 submissions were accepted as full papers based on the classifications provided by the Program Committee, resulting in an acceptance rate of 16%. The selected papers come from researchers based in several countries including Australia, Belgium, Chile, China, Denmark, Finland, France, Germany, Greece, India, Italy, Japan, Lithuania, Malaysia, the Netherlands, Norway, Pakistan, Palestine, Philippines, Portugal, Romania, South Africa, Spain, Sweden, the UK, the USA, and Vietnam. The highly diversified audience gave us the opportunity to achieve a good level of understanding of the mutual needs, requirements, and technical means available in this field of research. Papers coauthored by members of the conference committees were handled so that there were no conflicts of interest regarding the review process.

The selected papers reflect state-of-the-art research in different domains and applications of artificial intelligence and highlight the benefits of intelligent and smart systems in these domains and applications.

The high-quality standards of research presented will be maintained and reinforced at future editions of this conference.

Furthermore, INTAP 2021 include six plenary keynote lectures given by Domenico Prattichizzo, Shugen MA, Deepak Khazanchi, Stephan Sigg, and Valeriya Naumova. The talk by Valeriya Naumova was supported and sponsored by the European Association for Artificial Intelligence (EurAI). We would like to express our appreciation to all of them and in particular to those who took the time to contribute a paper to this book.

On behalf of the conference Organizing Committee, we would like to thank all participants, the authors, whose high-quality work is the essence of the conference, and the members of the Program Committee and all reviewers, who helped us with their eminent expertise in reviewing and selecting the quality papers for this book. As we know, organizing an international conference requires the effort of many individuals. We also wish to thank all the members of our Organizing Committee, whose work and commitment were invaluable. Finally, we thank Springer for their trust and for publishing the proceedings of INTAP 2021.

October 2021

Filippo Sanfilippo
Ole-Christoffer Granmo
Sule Yayilgan Yildirim
Imran Sarwar Bajwa

Organization

General Co-chairs

Filippo Sanfilippo	University of Agder (UiA), Norway
Ole-Christoffer Granmo	University of Agder (UiA), Norway
Sule Yildirim Yayilgan	Norwegian University of Science and Technology (NTNU), Norway
Imran Sarwar Bajwa	The Islamia University of Bahawalpur (IUB), Pakistan

Program Co-chairs

Michael Rygaard Hansen	University of Agder (UiA), Norway
Geir Grasmo	University of Agder (UiA), Norway
Athar Mehboob	The Islamia University of Bahawalpur (IUB), Pakistan

Organizing Committee

Filippo Sanfilippo	University of Agder (UiA), Norway
Elisabeth Rasmussen	University of Agder (UiA), Norway
Kjell G. Robbersmyr	University of Agder (UiA), Norway
Martin Marie Hubert Choux	University of Agder (UiA), Norway
Naureen Akhtar	University of Agder (UiA), Norway
Ole-Christoffer Granmo	University of Agder (UiA), Norway
Pål Grandal	University of Agder (UiA), Norway
Mohamed Abomhara	Norwegian University of Science and Technology (NTNU), Norway
Imran Sarwar Bajwa	The Islamia University of Bahawalpur (IUB), Pakistan

Program Committee

Ahmed Abouzeid	University of Agder (UiA), Norway
Ajit Jha	University of Agder (UiA), Norway
Alex Alcocer	Oslo Metropolitan University (OsloMet), Norway
Andreas Klausen	University of Agder (UiA), Norway
Andrii Shalaginov	Norwegian University of Science and Technology (NTNU), Norway

Bjørn Erik Munkvold	University of Agder (UiA), Norway
Christian Walter Peter Omlin	University of Agder (UiA), Norway
Dariush Salami	Aalto University, Finland
Deepak Khazanchi	University of Nebraska Omaha, USA
Domenico Prattichizzo	University of Siena, Italy
Erjon Zoto	Norwegian University of Science and Technology (NTNU), Norway
Evi Zouganeli	Oslo Metropolitan University (OsloMet), Norway
Filippo Sanfilippo	University of Agder (UiA), Norway
Frank Reichert	University of Agder (UiA), Norway
Gionata Salvietti	University of Siena, Italy
Hima Vadapalli	University of the Witwatersrand, South Africa
Hira Nazir	The Islamia University of Bahawalpur (IUB), Pakistan
Hossein Baharmand	University of Agder (UiA), Norway
Hugo Pedro Proença	University of Beira Interior, Portugal
Ibrahim A. Hameed	Norwegian University of Science and Technology (NTNU), Norway
Ilya Tyapin	University of Agder (UiA), Norway
J. Radhakrishna Pillai	University of Ålborg, Denmark
Jaziar Radianti	University of Agder (UiA), Norway
Johnson Agbinya	Melbourne Institute of Technology, Australia
Kiran Raja	Norwegian University of Science and Technology (NTNU), Norway
Kjell G. Robbersmyr	University of Agder (UiA), Norway
Kristian Muri Knausgård	University of Agder (UiA), Norway
Le Nguyen	Aalto University, Finland
Lei Jiao	University of Agder (UiA), Norway
Linga Reddy Cenkeramaddi	University of Agder (UiA), Norway
M. Sabarimalai Manikandan	Indian Institute of Technology, Bhubaneswar, India
Martin Wulf Gerdes	University of Agder (UiA), Norway
Mette Mo Jakobsen	University of Agder (UiA), Norway
Mohamed Abomhara	Norwegian University of Science and Technology (NTNU), Norway
Mohammad Poursina	University of Agder (UiA), Norway
Mohan Lal Kolhe	University of Agder (UiA), Norway
Morten Goodwin	University of Agder (UiA), Norway
Morten Kjeld Ebbesen	University of Agder (UiA), Norway
Muhammad Faisal Aftab	University of Agder (UiA), Norway
Muhammad Muaaz	University of Agder (UiA), Norway
Nadeem Sarwar	Bahria University, Pakistan

Nadia Saad Noori · Norwegian Research Centre (NORCE), Norway
Nico Vandaele · Katholieke Universiteit Leuven, Belgium
Nils Jakob Johannesen · University of Agder (UiA), Norway
Nurilla Avazov · University of Agder (UiA), Norway
Petar Sarajcev · University of Split, Croatia
Peter Hugh Middleton · University of Agder, Norway
Rafaqut Kazmi · Universiti Teknologi Malaysia, Malaysia
Raghavendra Ramachandra · Norwegian University of Science and Technology (NTNU), Norway
Rajesh Kumar Tripathy · Birla Institute of Technology and Science, India
Ricardo Da Silva Torres · Norwegian University of Science and Technology (NTNU), Norway
Rohitash Chandra · University of New South Wales (UNSW), Australia
Rym Hicheri · University of Agder (UiA), Norway
Siva Mouni Nemalidinne · Indian Institute of Technology, Hyderabad, India
Stefan Stieglitz · University of Duisburg-Essen, Germany
Stephan Sigg · Aalto University, Finland
Surya Teja Kandukuri · University of Agder (UiA), Norway
Tim Majchrzak · University of Agder (UiA), Norway
Tomas Blažauskas · Kaunas University of Technology (KTU), Lithuania
Vahid Hassani · Oslo Metropolitan University (OsloMet), Norway

Invited Speakers

Domenico Prattichizzo · University of Siena, Italy
Shugen Ma · Ritsumeikan University, Japan
Deepak Khazanchi · University of Nebraska Omaha, USA
Stephan Sigg · Aalto University, Finland
Valeriya Naumova · Simula Research Laboratory, Norway

Contents

**ML and AI for Intelligent Health, Applications of Intelligent
Technologies in Emergency Management**

Smart Electrical Energy Systems, AI and ML in Security

Miscellaneous

Intelligence, Decision support systems, IoT

Dense Nearest Neighborhood Query

Hina Suzuki[1]([✉]), Hanxiong Chen[2], Kazutaka Furuse[3], and Toshiyuki Amagasa[2]

[1] Degree Programs in Systems and Information Engineering, University of Tsukuba, Tsukuba, Japan
`suzuki.hina.ss@alumni.tsukuba.ac.jp`
[2] Department of Computer Science, University of Tsukuba, Tsukuba, Japan
`{chx,amagasa}@cs.tsukuba.ac.jp`
[3] Faculty of Business Administration, University of Hakuoh, Oyama, Japan
`furuse@fc.hakuoh.ac.jp`

Abstract. A nearest neighbor (NN) query is a principal factor in applications that handle multidimensional vector data, such as location-based services, data mining, and pattern recognition. Meanwhile, a nearest neighborhood (NNH) query finds neighborhoods which are not only dense but also near to the query. However, it cannot find desired groups owing to strong restrictions such as fixed group size in previous studies. Thus, in this paper, we propose a dense nearest neighborhood (DNNH) query, which is a query without strong constraints, and three efficient algorithms to solve the DNNH query. The proposed methods are divided into clustering-based and expanding-based methods. The expanding-based method can efficiently find a solution by reducing unnecessary processing using a filtering threshold and expansion breaking criterion. Experiments on various datasets confirm the effectiveness and efficiency of the proposed methods.

Keywords: Nearest neighborhood query · Spatial database · Information retrieval · Grid index

1 Introduction

In multi-dimensional vector data such as spatial databases, a nearest neighbor (NN) query is a fundamental and important query in many fields, such as data mining and information retrieval, and it is widely used in various applications, such as services using pattern recognition, facility information, and map and navigation services using location information.

Many neighbor searches have been developed from the NN search. Sometimes users want to search a "dense group" of neighboring points quickly. Examples are as follows:

– A tourist who wants to visit several stores without moving too much
– A user who wants to find a social networking community whose hobbies and interests match his own

© The Author(s), under exclusive license to Springer Nature Switzerland AG 2022
F. Sanfilippo et al. (Eds.): INTAP 2021, CCIS 1616, pp. 3–16, 2022.
https://doi.org/10.1007/978-3-031-10525-8_1

– A user who wants to identify an accident-prone area near a school

Figure 1 shows an example for some neighbor points from a given query q. In (b), four points nearest to the query are searched, which are obtained by repeating the single neighbor point search four times. As indicated in this example, searched points may be scattered in the data space. In (c), a dense group including four points is searched. This paper addresses the latter type of searches.

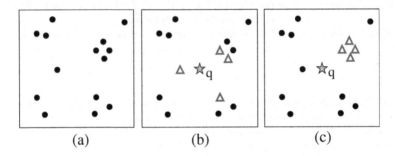

(a)   (b)   (c)

Fig. 1. (a) Data Points, (b) 4-NN of query q (data points that are emphasized as triangles), (c) A Dense neighborhood of q

Among the many studies on the efficiency and extension of the NN query, the most relevant queries for this type are the nearest neighborhood (NNH) query [1] and balanced nearest neighborhood (BNNH) query [6], which are explained in detail in Sect. 2. The BNNH query is an extension of the NNH query that solves the query of the empty output owing to the strong constraints. However, the remaining constraints of the BNNH query interfere with users obtaining the desired output.

In this paper, we propose a novel flexible query, **dense nearest neighborhood (DNNH)**, releasing the above constraints, and three algorithms for solving the query. One is an intuitive method that uses clustering techniques, and the other two algorithms provide faster search by exploiting the filtering thresholds and expansion breaking criteria for group retrieval. To verify the usefulness and the efficiency of the proposed methods, we conducted experiments on a large dataset and compared the performance of the proposed methods.

2   Related Work

The neighborhood search query starts with the most basic (k-)NN query, which searches for the (k) points closest to the query point, and has been studied in many ways to improve its efficiency and extension [2,5,7,8]. Intuitively, clustering the dataset and find the nearest cluster answers DNNH query. However, it is inefficient to run the clustering algorithm whenever a single datum changes.

To compare, we still implement an algorithm based on x-means and believe that using other clustering algorithms makes no fundamental difference.

The queries that are most relevant to the search for dense neighborhood groups are the NNH query [1] and BNNH query [6]. When each of these queries is applied to the dataset in Fig. 1(a), the candidate groups are as shown in (a), (b) and (c) of Fig. 2.

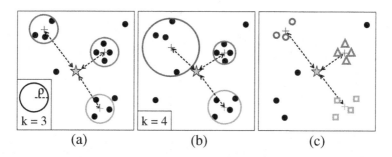

Fig. 2. (a) NNH, specifying $k = 3$ and a fixed radius ρ. Circles with a smaller ρ may not guarantee 3 points contained (b) BNNH, specifying $k = 4$ and ρ is changeable. May enlarge the circles to guarantee 4 points contained and gives up the density. (c) DNNH

NNH Query. The NNH query [1] outputs the smallest distance between the center of a circle and a query point among the circles that contain more than a specified number (k) of points within the circle of a specified radius (ρ).

As shown in Fig. 2(a), it is possible to obtain the desired group (triangle mark points in Fig. 1(c)) by specifying the appropriate parameters. However, in reality, it is not always the case that more than k points are found within the circle of fixed ρ, which implies that the query obtains an empty result if the appropriate parameters cannot be specified. Estimating the appropriate parameters in advance is particularly difficult for large datasets.

BNNH Query. The BNNH query uses a circle of variable radius to guarantee that it contains the specified number (k) of points. This is implemented by finding the circles minimizing the evaluation $\Delta(C, q)$ expressed by the following equation:

$$\Delta(C, q) = \alpha\|q - c(C)\| + (1 - \alpha)\rho$$

Here, $c(C)$ is the center of C, and ρ is the radius of C. $\|q - c(C)\|$ is the Euclidean distance between q and $c(C)$. α is a value for $0 < \alpha < 1$, where the closer the value to 0, the greater the cohesion, and the closer it is to 1, the greater the distance to q. Unlike NNH queries, BNNH queries allow to enlarge the circle to guarantee k data in the answer.

However, there is still the problem that the group circle will not be dense unless an appropriate k is specified. For example, the candidate groups in the sample dataset (Fig. 2(b)) by BNNH with varying parameters are shown in Fig. 3. The best dense nearby group is group C with parameter $k = 4$, as shown in (a). However, in (b), for parameter $k = 5$, it returns group C', which is neither dense nor close to the query q.

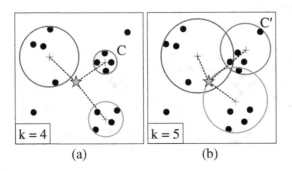

Fig. 3. The candidate groups by BNNH with varying parameters. (a) $k = 4$, (b) $k = 5$

Therefore, the BNNH query strongly depends on the parameter k, and there is a high possibility that the desired dense nearby group cannot be obtained if the appropriate value is not given. Nevertheless, it is difficult to estimate the value depending on the dataset and query location in advance. To address the problem that neither NNH nor BNNH guarantees that the answer groups found are dense, we propose DNNH, which finds a dense group without specifying the parameters k and ρ. DNNH queries are more flexible than BNNH queries because they compare dense groups that were retrieved regardless of the number of points in the group.

3   Dense Nearest Neighborhood Query

Definition 1. *(Dense nearest neighborhood query, DNNH). Given a set of points P and a query point q, the DNNH query returns a group C that minimizes the value of $\Delta(C, q)$.*

The total degree of approximation Δ is defined by the following equation[1]:

$$\Delta(C, q) = \|q - c(C)\| + \mathrm{sd}(C) \tag{1}$$

Here, $c(C)$ is the centroid of C, and $\mathrm{sd}(C)$ is the standard deviation of C. Compared with the previous studies that used the center and radius of a circle, this method can accurately represent the variation of points in a group. Moreover, DNNH overcomes the disadvantage of BNNH such that the searched groups are not necessarily dense, because it does not require the number of points in each group.

---

[1] Note that the definition of Δ is not same as the one of BNNH.

The most difficult part of solving a DNNH query is to efficiently retrieve dense groups. For example, if we consider how to find a dense group to which a point p may belong, in the case of the BNNH query, because the number of data in the group k is specified, we can find it only by performing a number of NN searches based on k for p. Meanwhile, in a DNNH query, the number of data in a group is not specified; thus, we must find a dense group from a large number of combinations including p, and it is NP-hard to find the optimal solution. We propose three approximate solutions by heuristics—the one is by clustering and the others are by expanding—for implementing efficient DNNH search.

3.1   Clustering-Based Approach

As the simplest approach for solving DNNH queries, we propose calculating Δ after clustering all the points. It is important to note here that the DNNH query is parameter free; therefore, clustering should not take redundant parameters as well.

X-means is an extension of k-means and is characterized by the fact that it can estimate the number of clusters and perform clustering simultaneously without the need to specify the number of clusters in advance, by using the recursive 2-means partitioning and the stopping criterion based on the information criterion BIC. BIC is calculated by the likelihood function and the size of a dataset, intuitively telling whether it is likely to split a set into two. In this study, we used an algorithm improved by Ishioka [4]. This algorithm differs from the original one by Pellog and Moore in that it considers the possibility that the variance differs among clusters, and it uses approximate computation for some calculations to enhance the efficiency. The pseudocode is shown in Algorithm 1.

3.2   Expanding-Based Approach

Clustering of large datasets used in the abovementioned approach is time consuming. To avoid this, our another approach attempts to retrieve groups from nearby the query q. Intuitively, points located near the query are more likely to form the result group. In this approach, we retrieve groups from the query's neighborhood and filter points that cannot be answers using the current degree Δ_e as a threshold. Using this approach, we briefly repeat the following: (1) Extract the query neighbor from the dataset, (2) retrieve the dense group to which the extracted point belongs (Sect. 3.2.1, 3.2.3), (3) update the threshold for filtering and remove the points that cannot be answers from the dataset (Sect. 3.2.2).

3.2.1   Evaluation Metric for Retrieving a Cluster

In this section, we explain how the retrieval of a dense group C_p to which a point p belongs is performed. In this study, this is achieved by selecting a dense preferred group from among the groups obtained by expansion using an NN

Algorithm 1. X-means Clustering-based Algorithm

Input: P, q, k_0
Output: C
1: $C, \mathbb{C} \leftarrow \phi$
2: $C_1, C_2, ..., C_{k_0} \leftarrow k\text{-means}++ (p, k_0)$ // partition P into k_0 clusters
3: **for each** $C_i \in \{C_1, C_2, ..., C_{k_0}\}$ **do**
4:     splitClusterRecursively(C_i)

5: **for each** $C_i \in \mathbb{C}$ **do**
6:     **if** $\Delta(C_i, q) < \Delta(C, q)$ **then**
7:         $C \leftarrow C_i$
8: **return** C

9: **function** splitClusterRecursively(C)
10:    $C_1, C_2 \leftarrow k\text{-means}++(C, 2)$
11:    **if** $BIC(C) > BIC'(C_1, C_2)$ **then**
12:        **for each** $C_i \in \{C_1, C_2\}$ **do**
13:            splitClusterRecursively(C_i)

14:    **else**
15:        Insert C into $\mathbb{C}$

---

search. The problem is to select a group from the enlarged ones based on the criteria, which we address by designing and using the enlargement index Δ_e.

The Δ_e is calculated by

$$\Delta_e(C, p_{next}) = \Delta(C, q) \cdot \pi_e(C, p_{next})$$

where $\pi_e(C, P)$ denotes the expandability of group C in dataset P and is defined by the following equation:

$$\pi_e(C, p_{next}) = \frac{pd_{mean}(C)}{pd_{mean}(C) + nd_{mean}(C, p_{next})}$$

$$pd_{mean}(C) = \frac{1}{\binom{|C|}{2}} \sum_{p_i, p_j \in C} \|p_i - p_j\|$$

$$nd_{mean}(C, p_{next}) = \frac{1}{|C|} \sum_{p \in C} \|p_{next} - p\|$$

$$p_{next} = arg \min_{p \in P - C} \|c(C) - p\|$$

pd_{mean} and nd_{mean} represent the average distance between the samples in the group and the average distance between the candidate points (p_{next}) and the samples in the group, respectively. The candidate point p_{next} is the point that has the smallest distance to the center $c(C)$ among the points not in C.

3.2.2   Bounding the Expanding Group

In this section, we explain the conditions under which a point p is removed using Δ of an already retrieved group C. Let C_p denote the group to which p belongs. If $\min \Delta(C_p, q) > \Delta(\exists C, q)$ holds, the group to which p belongs will not be preferred to the existing groups, and no further processing of p is necessary. Therefore, if we can derive $\min \Delta(C_p, q)$ from the information of p, we can determine whether the group is removed by filtering using $\Delta(C, q)$. However, in a DNNH query where the number of data in a group is not specified, Δ may be as small as possible depending on the distribution of the data, and it is difficult to determine the exact filtering threshold. Evidently, it makes no sense to find dense groups in a uniform distribution; therefore, we assume that the data of C_p follow a normal distribution.

Based on the assumption that the data of C_p follow a normal distribution, $arg \min \Delta(C_p, q)$ as C_p^{min}, we can approximate its centroid and standard deviation. In this case, $\min \Delta(C_p, q)$ can be calculated as follows:

$$\min \Delta(C_p, q) = \|q - c_p^{min}\| + sd(C_p^{min}) = \frac{\|q - p\|}{2} + \frac{\|q - p\|}{2\alpha} = \frac{\alpha + 1}{2\alpha}\|q - p\|$$

The α indicates the sigma rule coefficient, and all points in group C_p are assumed to be within the radius $\alpha \cdot sd(C_p)$ from the centroid. According to the 68-95-99.7 rule of the normal distribution, about 95%, 99.7% of the points of C_p are within the radius $2sd(C_p)$, $3sd(C_p)$ from the centroid. Therefore, $\alpha = 2$ or 3 seems to be effective. Substituting this into $\min \Delta(C_p, q) \leq \Delta(C, q)$, we obtain $\|q - p\| > \frac{2\alpha}{\alpha+1}\Delta(C, q)$. This leads to the following conclusion.

Theorem 1. *A point p locating further than a bound, that is, p which holds the following in equation:*

$$\|q - p\| > \frac{2\alpha}{\alpha + 1} \min_C \Delta(C, q) \tag{2}$$

can be removed in the filtering process.

3.2.3   Expansion Breaking Criteria

The bound given above is inefficient because it works only in the second and subsequent retrieval of clusters. For the computation of pd_{mean}, nd_{mean}, the first group retrieval always continues to expand until the entire dataset is included, and $\mathcal{O}(|P|^2)$. This is a problem because the DNNH query does not specify the group size, which affects the efficiency.

By the definition of Δ_e, we know that p of small Δ_e suggests that the corresponding group is desired so that we can stop the enlargement process, thereby reducing the computational cost. Then, we determine that Δ_e is small enough. Under the assumption that C to which p belongs follows a normal distribution, and they exist within the radius $\alpha \cdot sd(C)$ from the centroid c, when Eq. 3 holds for the expansion point p_{next}, we can conclude that further expansion is meaningless.

$$\|p_{next} - q\| \geq \alpha \cdot sd(C) \tag{3}$$

In addition, in the latter half of the cluster retrieval, where the solution is less likely to be obtained, we aim to further speed up the process by terminating the expansion when the cluster is found to be less preferable than the current most preferable cluster C_{best} among the retrieved clusters. However, as mentioned in Sect. 3.2.2, because the DNNH query does not specify the group size, Δ may be as small as possible depending on the distribution of the data. For C of a certain size, it is reasonable to assume that $sd(C)$ monotonically increases with each expansion. Let C' be the cluster of C expanded an arbitrary number of times; then, $sd(C') > sd(C)$ holds by the assumption. Here, if

$$sd(C) > \Delta(C_{best}) \tag{4}$$

holds, then by the definition of Δ, $\Delta(C') > sd(C') > sd(C) > \Delta(C_{best})$ holds. This means that Eq. 4 can be used as expansion breaking criteria to stop expanding C.

3.2.4   Basic Expanding Algorithm

The basic method is shown in Algorithm 2. In this method, the points of dataset P are first sorted in order of their distance from the query point q. The points are extracted from the sorted dataset in order from the top (line 3), and groups are retrieved as described in Sect. 3.2.1, 3.2.3 (lines 4, 10–18). After the retrieval is finished, the points in the group are removed from P as processed (line 5), the threshold *bound* is updated and filtered (lines 6–8), and if there are still unprocessed points, the group is retrieved again (line 2). The process is terminated when there are no more unprocessed points.

3.2.5   Grid Expanding Algorithm

The problem of the basic method is that the entire process, from indexing to filtering of the dataset, is point-based, which is inefficient. Therefore, we propose a grid-based method for preferential search from the neighboring points of query points and further reduction of the search space in the NN search. The images are presented in Fig. 4. The figure shows an example of a grid that divides the space into 4×4 cells. The grid structure allows us to directly refer to the points in the cells, thereby enabling us to achieve a more efficient refinement of the search space in the NN search and coherent filtering process for each cell. The pseudocode is shown in Algorithm 3.

4   Experiments

We conducted experiments to verify the efficiency of the proposed methods. All algorithms for the solutions presented were implemented in C++. The experiments were conducted on a Windows operating system with the following specifications: Windows 10 Home, with a 2.9 GHz 8-Core Intel Core i7 processor and

---

Algorithm 2. Basic Expanding Algorithm

Input: P, q, α, k_{min}, k_{max}
Output: C_{best}
 1: $bound \leftarrow \infty$
 2: **while** P is not empty **do**
 3:     $p \leftarrow$ nearest point $\in P$ from q that is nearer than $bound$ in Eq. 2
 4:     $C \leftarrow$ RetrieveCluster(p, k_{min}, k_{max})
 5:     $P \leftarrow P - C$
 6:     **if** $\Delta(C) < \Delta(C_{best})$ **then**
 7:         update $bound$ of Eq. 2
 8:         $C_{best} \leftarrow C$
 9: **return** C_{best}

10: **function** RetrieveCluster(p, k_{min}, k_{max})
11:     $C \leftarrow \{p\}$, $C_{best} \leftarrow C$
12:     **while** P is not empty $\wedge$ Eq. 4 is not satisfied **do**
13:         $p_{next} \leftarrow$ nearest point $\in P$ from c
14:         **if** Eq. 3 is not satisfied **then break**
15:         **if** $|C_{best}| = 1 \vee \Delta_e(C, p_{next}) < \Delta_e(C_{best}, p_{next}{}^{best})$ **then**
16:             $C_{best} \leftarrow C$
17:         $C \leftarrow C \cup p_{next}$
18:     **return** C_{best}

---

memory of 64 GB 1466 MHz MHz DDR4. The real data NE (123,593 data), RR (257,942 data), and CAS (196,902 data) were provided by the U.S. Census Bureau's TIGER project[2]. In addition, to measure the correspondence to the datasets with various distributions, we prepared uniform random data UN (10000–200000 pts) and a cluster dataset RN. RN is a composite dataset of random numbers that follow the standard normal distribution and are scaled and arranged equally in space as clusters. All these datasets were two-dimensional and normalized to $[0, 1]$. Experiments compare the performance of the three proposed methods (x-means clustering-based, basic expanding, and grid expanding) on real data, scalability, changes in cluster size $|C|$, α, and distance between clusters. In the grid expanding algorithm, we vary the grid size n and investigate the appropriate value of n. q was selected randomly from the dataset. Unless otherwise stated, $\alpha = 2$, $n = 100$, the distance between clusters $= 1.0$, and the cluster size lower limit $k_{min} = 10$. All results are reported as the average processing time for conducting DNNH queries 10 times.

4.1   Experimental Results

Performance for the Real Datasets. The results are presented in Fig. 5. The results of the x-means clustering-based algorithm are "xmeans"; basic expanding and grid expanding algorighm are "basic" and "grid," respectively; and "U100"

---

[2] http://chorochronos.datastories.org/?q=user/15/track.

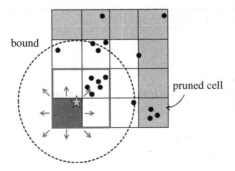

Fig. 4. Grid-based algorithm

and "U500" indicate that the cluster size upper limit k_{max} is set to 100 and 500, respectively. First, it can be observed that the x-means clustering-based algorithm is the slowest, and the basic expanding and grid expanding algorithms are the fastest for all datasets. This is especially true for RR, where even the basic expanding algorithm ($k_{max} = 500$), which is the slowest among the basic expanding and the grid expanding algorithms, is 10 times faster than the x-means clustering-based algorithm. The fastest algorithm is the grid expanding algorithm, which is up to three times faster than the basic expanding algorithm.

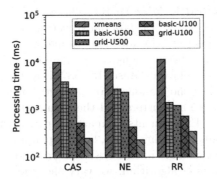

Fig. 5. Performance for the real datasets

Effect of Dataset Size. The results are shown in Figs. 6 and 7. First, the experimental results for the UN dataset (Fig. 6) show that the x-means clustering-based algorithm is the fastest when the data size is 10000. However, after 50000, the basic expanding and the grid expanding algorithms are reversed and become faster. A linear or gradual increase in the execution time is observed in all algorithms. The fastest algorithm is the grid expanding, which shows a higher performance than the basic expanding, as the data size increases. The experimental results for the RN dataset (Fig. 7) show that the basic expanding and the grid

---

Algorithm 3. Grid Expanding Algorithm

Input: P, q, k_{min}, k_{max}, α
Output: C_{best}
 1: $bound \leftarrow \infty$, $P_{cur} \leftarrow \phi$
 2: $cells \leftarrow$ get surround cells of q
 3: **while** $cells$ locate in $bound$ **do**
 4:     $P_{cur} \leftarrow$ points in $cells$
 5:     **while** P_{cur} is not empty **do**
 6:         $p \leftarrow$ nearest point $\in P_{cur}$ from q that is nearer than $bound$ in Eq. 2
 7:         $C \leftarrow$ RetrieveCluster(p, k_{min}, k_{max})
 8:         $P \leftarrow P - C$
 9:         **if** $\Delta(C) < \Delta(C_{best})$ **then**
10:             update $bound$ of Eq. 2
11:             $C_{best} \leftarrow C$
12:     $cells \leftarrow$ the next round of $cells$
13: **return** C_{best}

14: **function** RetrieveCluster(p, k_{min}, k_{max})
15:     $C \leftarrow \{p\}$, $C_{best} \leftarrow C$
16:     $cells \leftarrow$ get surround cells of p
17:     **while** $cells$ locate in $bound$ **do**
18:         $P_{cur} \leftarrow$ points in $cells$
19:         **while** P_{cur} is not empty $\wedge$ Eq. 4 is not satisfied **do**
20:             $p_{next} \leftarrow$ nearest point $\in P_{cur}$ from c
21:             **if** Eq. 3 is not satisfied **then break**
22:             **if** $|C_{best}| = 1 \vee \Delta_e(C, p_{next}) < \Delta_e(C_{best}, p_{next}{}^{best})$ **then**
23:                 $C_{best} \leftarrow C$
24:             $C \leftarrow C \cup p_{next}$
25:         $cells \leftarrow$ the next round of $cells$
26:     **return** C_{best}

---

expanding algorithms are clearly faster than the x-means clustering-based algorithm when the cluster size $|C| = 50$ and the increase in the execution time was also slow. Again, the fastest algorithm is the grid expanding algorithm, which performed about 100 times faster than the x-means clustering-based algorithm.

Effect of Cluster Size. The results are shown in Fig. 8. From 10 to 200, the basic expanding and the grid expanding algorithms are from 10 to 1000 times faster than the x-means clustering-based algorithm. However, the execution time of the basic expanding and the grid expanding algorithms increased with an increase in the cluster size and reversed when the cluster size was 500. For the x-means clustering-based algorithm, the decrease in execution time as the cluster size increases can be attributed to the fact that the number of clusters in the entire dataset decreases owing to the fixed data size, which reduces the number of divisions by k-means and the amount of BIC computations.

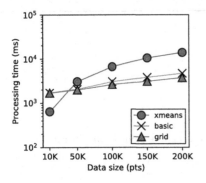

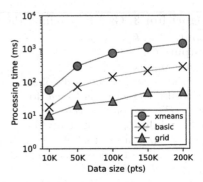

Fig. 6. Effect of data size (UN) ($k_{max} = 500$)

Fig. 7. Effect of data size (RN) ($k_{max} = 1000$; $|C| = 50$)

Effect of the Cluster Distance. The results are shown in Fig. 9. If the distance between clusters is x, there is an interval of x clusters between the clusters. Consequently, while the basic expanding and the grid expanding algorithms are from 10 to 100 times faster than the x-means clustering-based algorithm in many cases, the performance of the basic expanding and the grid expanding deteriorated rapidly when the distance of the clusters was 0.0. This is because the expansion breaking criteria can no longer function due to the loss of distance between clusters, but it does function after 0.5, indicating that the proposed expansion breaking criteria is effective even for small intervals.

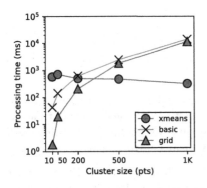

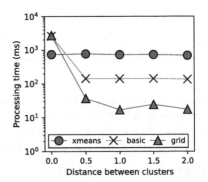

Fig. 8. Effect of cluster size ($|P| = 100000$; $k_{min} = 5$; $k_{max} = 1000$)

Fig. 9. Effect of distance of clusters ($|P| = 100000$; $|C| = 50$; $k_{max} = 500$)

Effect of sigma rule coefficient α. The results are shown in Fig. 10. Consequently, it is the fastest when $\alpha = 2$ or 3 especially in the grid expanding algorithm. The slowest speed is obtained when $\alpha = 1$ or 5 because it is quite small or large value that the expansion breaking criteria or filtering no longer works.

Effect of Grid Size n. For example, because the datasets are two-dimensional, when $n = 100$, the maximum number of cells is $n^2 = 100000$. The results are shown in Fig. 11. The cluster size of RN is fixed at 50 (RN-50P) and 200 (RN-200P). Hence, the fastest execution time was obtained when $n = 10, 30$ or 50, and the execution time increased slowly. This is because, when the grid size becomes quite large, the cells become smaller than necessary, and the amount of search and the expansion processing of each cell increases.

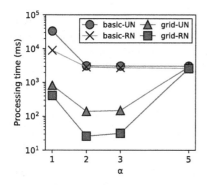

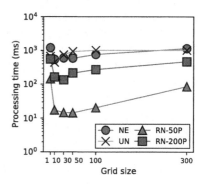

Fig. 10. Effect of α ($|P| = 100000$; $|C| = 50$; $k_{max} = 500$)

Fig. 11. Effect of grid size n ($|P| = 100000$ (UN, RN); $k_{max} = 300$)

4.2 Evaluation of the Proposed Methods

Overall, the grid expanding algorithm is the fastest. In particular, in comparison between the basic expanding and the grid expanding algorithms, the grid expanding algorithm is faster in all results, unless the data size is small or inefficient parameter settings (such as $\alpha = 5$) are used. Therefore, the grid expanding algorithm should be chosen unless there is concern about memory usage or the small overhead of building the cellular data. Depending on the distribution of the data, a grid size of approximately 10–50 is considered the most suitable for achieving a good balance between memory usage and processing efficiency.

However, depending on the distribution of the dataset and the purpose of the search, the x-means clustering-based algorithm may be a better choice. For example, the dataset may be sparsely distributed or the cluster size may be larger than 200. However, in this study, we consider finding a set of nearby facilities in a location-based service using a spatial database, or finding a set of objects with attributes similar to those of a particular user in a social network service (SNS). In these situations, the basic expanding or the grid expanding algorithm is preferable because it can rapidly detect small- to medium-sized neighborhood clusters.

5   Conclusion and Future Work

In this paper, we proposed a DNNH query, which finds dense groups without severe constraints, and the efficient methods for solving the query: x-means clustering-based algorithm, basic expanding algorithm, and grid expanding algorithm. The DNNH query can flexibly find more desirable groups for users, which cannot be achieved by strongly constraining existing problems. Among the proposed methods, the grid expanding algorithm is the fastest, and it can contribute to many applications that deal with large datasets.

For future work, we are going to investigate the effect of the expansion breaking criteria in distributions with overlapping clusters. We will also extend the grid based method to high dimension data. For example, we can consider an approach using density-based clustering methods such as DBSCAN [3] for group retrieval. It is also under consideration to parallel our algorithms and apply multi-threaded solution.

References

1. Choi, D., Chung, C.: Nearest neighborhood search in spatial databases. In: 2015 IEEE 31st International Conference on Data Engineering, pp. 699–710, April 2015. https://doi.org/10.1109/ICDE.2015.7113326
2. Deng, K., Sadiq, S., Zhou, X., Xu, H., Fung, G.P.C., Lu, Y.: On group nearest group query processing. IEEE Trans. Knowl. Data Eng. **24**(2), 295–308 (2012). https://doi.org/10.1109/TKDE.2010.230
3. Ester, M., Kriegel, H.P., Sander, J., Xu, X.: A density-based algorithm for discovering clusters in large spatial databases with noise. In: Proceedings of the Second International Conference on Knowledge Discovery and Data Mining, KDD, vol. 96, no. 34, pp. 226–231 (1996)
4. Ishioka, T.: Extended K-means with an efficient estimation of the number of clusters. Data Min. Finan. Eng. Intell. Agents (2000). https://doi.org/10.1007/3-540-44491-2_3
5. Jang, H.-J., Hyun, K.-S., Chung, J., Jung, S.-Y.: Nearest base-neighbor search on spatial datasets. Knowl. Inf. Syst. **62**(3), 867–897 (2019). https://doi.org/10.1007/s10115-019-01360-3
6. Le, S., Dong, Y., Chen, H., Furuse, K.: Balanced nearest neighborhood query in spatial database. In: 2019 IEEE International Conference on Big Data and Smart Computing (BigComp), pp. 1–4, February 2019. https://doi.org/10.1109/BIGCOMP.2019.8679425
7. Malkov, Y.A., Yashunin, D.A.: Efficient and robust approximate nearest neighbor search using hierarchical navigable small world graphs. IEEE Trans. Pattern Anal. Mach. Intell. **42**(4), 824–836 (2020). https://doi.org/10.1109/TPAMI.2018.2889473
8. Stanoi, I., Agrawal, D., Abbadi, A.E.: Reverse nearest neighbor queries for dynamic databases. In: ACM SIGMOD Workshop on Research Issues in Data Mining and Knowledge Discovery, pp. 44–53 (2000). https://www.semanticscholar.org/paper/Reverse-Nearest-Neighbor-Queries-for-Dynamic-Stanoi-Agrawal/cb60aef9f2187d4052b36f99aba6e1b8eca9f4ca

Explainable Nonlinear Modelling of Multiple Time Series with Invertible Neural Networks

Luis Miguel Lopez-Ramos[1,2,3]([envelope]) [ID], Kevin Roy[1,2,3],
and Baltasar Beferull-Lozano[1,2,3] [ID]

[1] SFI Offshore Mechatronics Center, University of Agder, Grimstad, Norway
luis.m.lopez.ramos@gmail.com
[2] Intelligent Signal Processing and Wireless Networks (WISENET) Center,
Grimstad, Norway
[3] Department of ICT, University of Agder, Grimstad, Norway

Abstract. A method for nonlinear topology identification is proposed, based on the assumption that a collection of time series are generated in two steps: i) a vector autoregressive process in a latent space, and ii) a nonlinear, component-wise, monotonically increasing observation mapping. The latter mappings are assumed invertible, and are modeled as shallow neural networks, so that their inverse can be numerically evaluated, and their parameters can be learned using a technique inspired in deep learning. Due to the function inversion, the backpropagation step is not straightforward, and this paper explains the steps needed to calculate the gradients applying implicit differentiation. Whereas the model explainability is the same as that for linear VAR processes, preliminary numerical tests show that the prediction error becomes smaller.

Keywords: Vector autoregressive model · Nonlinear · Network topology inference · Invertible neural network

1 Introduction

Multi-dimensional time series data are observed in many real-world systems, where some of the time series are influenced by other time series. The interrelations among the time series can be encoded in a graph structure, and identifying such structure or topology is of great interest in multiple applications [7]. The inferred topology can provide insights about the underlying system and can assist in inference tasks such as prediction and anomaly detection.

There is a plethora of applications where topology inference is relevant and its successful application has a potential practical impact. Examples of real-world

The work in this paper was supported by the SFI Offshore Mechatronics grant 237896/O30.
L. M. Lopez-Ramos and K. Roy—Equal contribution in terms of working hours.

applications include inference of connectomes in neuroscience to detect different conditions from multiple EEG signals, discovery of hidden logic causation links among sensor variables in industrial environments (e.g. network of Oil & Gas separators), identification of spread patterns of an infectious disease in a certain population, or inference of dependencies among different types of stocks, among others. In most of these applications, the signal interrelations are often inherently nonlinear [3, 6, 17] due to the nature of the underlying interactions. In these cases, using linear models may lead to inconsistent estimation of causal interactions [20]. We propose deep learning based methods by applying feed-forward invertible neural networks. This project proposes a low-complexity nonlinear topology identification method that is competitive with other nonlinear methods explaining time series data from a heterogeneous set of sensors.

1.1 State of the Art and Contribution

The use of linear VAR models for topology identification have been well-studied. A comprehensive review of topology identification algorithms was recently published [7], where the issue of nonlinearity is discussed together with other challenges such as dynamics (meaning estimating time-varying models).

In [22], an efficient algorithm to estimate linear VAR coefficients from streaming data is proposed. Although the linear VAR model is not expressive enough for certain applications, it allows clear performance analysis, and is subject to continuous technical developments, such as a novel criterion for automatic order selection [15], VAR estimation considering distributions different to the Gaussian, such as Student's t [23], or strategies to deal with missing data [9, 22, 23].

The use of invertible neural networks for analyzing inverse problems is discussed in [1] and references therein, where a mapping is sought between an observation space and an underlying space where some real variables (and possibly some latent unknowns) lie. Invertibility is required because the mapping has to be evaluated in one direction for training and in the reverse direction for prediction. However, to the best of the authors' knowledge, such an idea has not been investigated with a VAR process in the latent space.

Regarding non-linear topology identification based on the VAR model, kernels are used in [13, 18] to linearize the nonlinear dependencies by mapping variables to a higher-dimensional Hilbert space. The growth of computational complexity and memory requirements (a.k.a. "curse of dimensionality") associated with kernel representations is circumvented in [13, 18] by restricting the numeric calculation to a limited number of time-series samples using a time window, which results in suboptimal performance. A semiparametric model is proposed for the same task in [5].

A different class of nonlinear topology identification methods are based on deep feedforward or recurrent NNs [19, 20] combined with sparsity-inducing penalties on the weights at one layer, labeled as "Granger-causality layer". An additive model based on NN is proposed in [2] for nonlinear VAR processes.

Recent work [14] considers a nonlinear VAR framework where the innovations are not necessarily additive, and proposes estimation algorithms and identifiability results based on the assumption that the innovations are independent.

All the aforementioned nonlinear modeling techniques are based on estimating nonlinear functions that predict the future time series values in the measurement space, which entails high complexity and is not amenable to predicting multiple time instants ahead. The main contribution of our work is a modeling assumption that accounts for mild nonlinear relations that are independent from the latent linear structure, and reduces the model complexity in terms of the number of parameters and reduces the overfitting risk at long-horizon predictions. The model complexity will be explained in detail in Sect. 3.2.

2   Background

2.1   Graph Topology Identification

Estimating the topology of a system means finding the dependencies between network data time series. These dependencies may not be physically observable; rather, there can be logical connections between data nodes that are not direcrly connected in a physical sense due to, e.g. control loops. Topology inference has the potential to contribute to the algorithmic foundations to solve important problems in signal processing (e.g. prediction, data completion, etc.) and data-driven control.

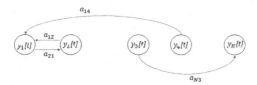

Fig. 1. Illustration of an N-node network with directed edges

While the simplest techniques such as correlation graphs [10] cannot determine the direction of interactions in a network as illustrated in Fig. 1, one may employ to this end structural equation models (SEM) or Bayesian networks [21]. However, such methods account only for memory-less interactions. On the other hand, causality in the Granger [8] sense is based on the idea that the cause precedes the effect in time, and knowledge about the cause helps predicting the effect more accurately. The way Granger causality is defined makes it interesting, from a conceptual point of view, for understanding data dependencies; however, it is often computationally intractable. Thus, alternative causality definitions, such as those based on vector autoregressive (VAR) models [8,22] are typically preferred in practical scenarios. The simplest possible VAR model is a linear VAR model.

Consider a collection of N sensors, where $y_n[t]$ denotes the measurement of the n-th sensor at time t. A P-th order linear VAR model can be formulated as

$$y[t] = \sum_{p=1}^{P} A_p y[t-p] + u[t], \qquad P \leq t \leq T \tag{1}$$

where $y[t] = [y_1[t], \ldots\ldots, y_N[t]]^T$, $A_p \in R^{N \times N}$, $p = 1, \ldots, P$, are the matrices of VAR parameters (see Fig. 2), T is observation time period, and $u[t] = [u_1[t], \ldots\ldots, u_N[t]]$ is an innovation process typically modeled as a Gaussian, temporally white random process. With $a_{n,n'}^{(p)}$ being the (n, n') entry of the matrix A_p, the r.h.s above takes the form:

$$y_n[t] = \sum_{n'=1}^{N} \sum_{p=1}^{P} a_{n,n'}^{(p)} y_{n'}[t-p] + u_n[t], \qquad P \leq t \leq T \tag{2}$$

for $n = 1, \ldots, N$, The problem of identifying a linear VAR causality model reduces to estimating the VAR coefficient matrices $\{A_p\}_{p=1}^{P}$ given the observations $\{y[t]\}_{t=0}^{T-1}$. The VAR causality [12] is determined from the support of the VAR matrix parameters and can be interpreted as a surrogate (yet not strictly equivalent) for Granger causality[1].

2.2   Nonlinear Function Approximation

The main advantages of linear modeling are its simplicity, the low variance of the estimators (at the cost of a higher bias compared to more expressive methods), and the fact that linear estimation problems often lead naturally to convex optimization problems, which can be solved efficiently.

However, there are several challenges related to inferring linear, stationary models from real-world data. Many instances such as financial data, brain signals, industrial sensors, etc. exhibit highly nonlinear interactions, and only nonlinear models have the expressive capacity to capture complex dependencies (assuming that those are identifiable and enough data are provided for the learning). Some existing methods have tried to capture nonlinear interactions using kernel-based function approximators (see [13,17] and references therein). In the most general non-linear case, each data variable $y_n[t]$ can be represented as a non-linear function of several multi-variate data time series as:

$$y_n[t] = h_n(y_{t-1}, \ldots, y_{t-P}) + u_n[t], \tag{3}$$

where $y_{t-p} = [y_1[t-p], y_2[t-p], \ldots, y_N[t-p]]^T$, and $h(\cdot)$ is a non-linear function.

---

[1] Notice that VAR models encode lagged interactions, and other linear models such as structural equation models (SEM) or structural VAR (SVAR) are available if interactions at a small time scale are required. In this paper, for the sake of simplicity, we focus on learning non-linear VAR models. However, our algorithm designs can also accomodate the SEM and SVAR frameworks without much difficulty.

However, from a practical perspective, this model is too general to be useful in real applications, because the class of possible nonlinear functions is unrestricted and, therefore, the estimators will suffer from high variance. Notice also that learning such a model would require in general an amount of data that may not be available in realistic scenarios, and requiring a prohibitive complexity. A typical solution is to restrict the the modeling to a subset of nonlinear functions, either in a parametric (NN) or nonparametric (kernel) way.

Our goal in this paper is to learn nonlinear dependencies with some underlying structure making it possible to learn them with limited complexity, with an expressive capacity slightly higher than linear models.

3 Modelling

The linear coefficients in Eq. (1) are tailored to assessing only linear mediating dependencies. To overcome this limitation, this work considers a non-linear model by introducing a set of node dependent nonlinear functions $\{f_i\}_{i=1}^N$. In previous work on nonlinear topology identification [2,13,17,20], nonlinear multivariate models are estimated without necessarily assuming linear dependencies in an underlying space; rather, they directly estimate non-linear functions from and into the real measurement space without assuming an underlying structure. In this work, we assume that the multivariate data can be explained as the nonlinear output of a set of observation functions $\{f_i\}_{i=1}^N$ with a VAR process as an input. Each function f_i represents a different non-linear distortion at the i-th node.

Given data time series, the task is to jointly learn the non-linearities together with a VAR topology in a feature space which is linear in nature, where the outputs of the functions $\{f_i\}_{i=1}^N$ belong to. Such functions are required to be invertible, so that sensor measurements can be mapped into the latent feature space, where the linear topology (coefficients) can be used to generate predictions, which can be taken back to the real space through $\{f_i\}_{i=1}^N$. In our model, prediction involves the composition of several functions, which can be modeled as neural networks. The nonlinear observation function at each node can be parameterized by a NN that is in turn a universal function approximator [4]. Consequently, the topology and non-linear per-node transformations can be seen in aggregation as a DNN, and its parameters can be estimated using appropriate deep learning techniques.

The idea is illustrated in Fig. 2. The green circle represents the underlying latent vector space. The exterior of the circle is the space where the sensor measurements lie, which need not be a vector space. The blue lines show the linear dependency between the time series inside the latent space. The red line from each time series shows the transformation to the measurement space. Each sensor is associated with a different nonlinear function. Specifically, if $y_i[t]$ denotes the i-th time series in the latent space, the measurement (observation) is modeled

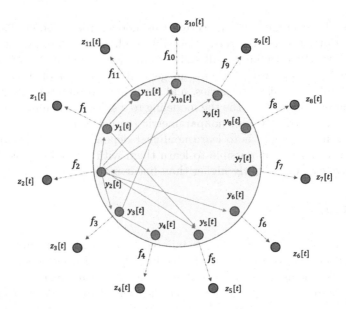

Fig. 2. Causal dependencies among a set of time series are linear in the latent space represented by the green circle. However, the variables in the latent space are not available, only nonlinear observations (output of the functions f_i) are available. (Color figure online)

as $z_i[t] = f_i(y_i[t])$. The function f_i is parameterized as a neural network layer with M units, expressed as follows:

$$f_i(y_i) = b_i + \sum_{j=1}^{M} \alpha_{ij} \sigma(w_{ij} y_i - k_{ij}) \qquad (4)$$

For the function f_i to be monotonically increasing (which guarantees invertibility), it suffices to ensure that α_{ij} and w_{ij} are positive $\forall j$. The pre-image of f_i is the whole set of real numbers, but the image is an interval $(\underline{z}_i, \overline{z}_i)$, which is in accordance ro the fact that sensor data are usually restricted to a dynamic range. If the range is not available a priori but sufficient data is available, bounds for the operation interval can be easily inferred.

Let us remark three important advantages in the proposed model:

- It is substantially more expressive than the linear model, while capturing non-linear dependencies with lower complexity than other non-linear models.
- It allows to predict with longer time horizons ahead within the linear latent space. Under a generic non-linear model, the variance of a long-term prediction explodes with the time horizon.
- Each non-linear nodal mapping can also adapt and capture any possible drift or irregularity in the sensor measurement, thus, it can directly incorporate imperfections in the sensor measurement itself due to, e.g. lack of calibration.

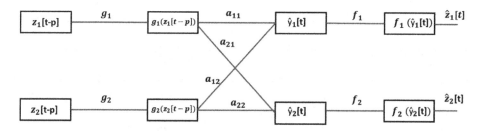

Fig. 3. Schematic for modeling Granger causality for a toy example with 2 sensors.

3.1   Prediction

Given accurate estimates of the nonlinear functions $\{f_i\}_{i=1}^N$, their inverses, and the parameters of the VAR model, future measurements can be easily predicted. Numerical evaluation of the inverse of f_i as defined in (4) can easily be done with a bisection algorithm.

Let us define $g_i = f_i^{-1}$. Then, the prediction consists of three steps, the first one being mapping the previous samples back into the latent vector space:

$$\tilde{y}_i[t-p] = g_i \left(z_i[t-p]\right) \tag{5a}$$

Then, the VAR model parameters are used to predict the signal value at time t (also in the latent space):

$$\hat{y}_i[t] = \sum_{p=1}^{p} \sum_{j=1}^{n} a_{ij}^{(p)} \tilde{y}_j[t-p] \tag{5b}$$

Finally, the predicted measurement at each node is obtained by applying f_i to the latent prediction:

$$\hat{z}_i[t] = f_i \left(\hat{y}_i[t]\right) \tag{5c}$$

These prediction steps can be intuitively visualized as a neural network. The next section formulates an optimization problem intended to learn the parameters of such a neural network. For a simple example with 2 sensors, the network structure is shown in Fig. 3.

3.2   Model Complexity

To analyze the model complexity in terms of the number of parameters, observe a single nonlinear function f_i as defined in (4). If f_i is modeled using M neurons or units, $3M+1$ parameters are needed. Given a collection of N time series, a P-th order VAR model without an intercept needs N^2P parameters. Assuming that each of the nonlinear functions f_i is modeled with the same number of neurons M, the complexity of the proposed model is $(3M+1)N + PN^2$. Whenever $N >> M$, the dominant term is PN^2, meaning that the complexity of the proposed model is practically the same as that of a linear VAR model for high dimensional time series.

4   Problem Formulation

The functional optimization problem consists in minimizing $\|z[t] - \hat{z}[t]\|_2^2$ (where $z[t]$ is a vector collecting the measurements for all N sensors at time t), subject to the constraint of f_i being invertible $\forall i$, and the image of f_i being $(\underline{z}_i, \bar{z}_i)$. The saturating values can be obtained from the nominal range of the corresponding sensors, or can be inferred from data.

Incorporating Eq. (1), the optimization problem can be written as:

$$\min_{f,A} \ \left\| z[t] - f\left(\sum_{p=1}^{p} A^{(p)} \left[g(z[t-p]) \right] \right) \right\|_2^2 \tag{6a}$$

$$\text{s. to: } \sum_{j=1}^{M} \alpha_{ij} = \bar{z}_i - \underline{z}_i \ \forall i \tag{6b}$$

$$b_i = \underline{z}_i \ \forall i \tag{6c}$$

$$\alpha_{ij} \geq 0 \ \forall i,j \tag{6d}$$

$$w_{ij} \geq 0 \ \forall i,j \tag{6e}$$

The functional optimization over f_i is tantamount to optimizing over α_{ij}, w_{ij}, k_{ij} and b_i. The main challenge to solve this problem is that there is no closed form for the inverse function g_i. This is addressed in the ensuing section.

5   Learning Algorithm

Without a closed form for g, we cannot directly obtaining gradients with automatic differentiation such as Pytorch, as is typically done in deep learning with a stochastic gradient-based optimization algorithm. Fortunately, once $\{g_i(\cdot)\}$ is numerically evaluated, the gradient at that point can be calculated with a relatively simple algorithm, derived via implicit differentiation in Sect. 5.2. Once that gradient is available, the rest of the steps of the backpropagation algorithm are rather standard.

5.1   Forward Equations

The forward propagation equations are given by the same steps that are used to predict next values of the time series z:

$$\tilde{y}_i[t-p] = g_i(z_i[t-p], \theta_i) \tag{7a}$$

$$\hat{y}_i[t] = \sum_{p=1}^{p} \sum_{j=1}^{n} a_{ij}^{(p)} \tilde{y}_j[t-p] \tag{7b}$$

$$\hat{z}_i[t] = f_i(\hat{y}_i[t], \theta_i) \tag{7c}$$

$$C[t] = \sum_{n=1}^{N} (z_n[t] - \hat{z}_n[t])^2 \tag{7d}$$

Here, the dependency of the nonlinear functions with the neural network parameters is made explicit, where

$$\theta_i = \begin{bmatrix} \alpha_i \\ w_i \\ k_i \\ b_i \end{bmatrix} \text{ and } \alpha_i = \begin{bmatrix} \alpha_{i1} \\ \alpha_{i2} \\ \vdots \\ \alpha_{iM} \end{bmatrix}, w_i = \begin{bmatrix} w_{i1} \\ w_{i2} \\ \vdots \\ w_{iM} \end{bmatrix}, k_i = \begin{bmatrix} k_{i1} \\ k_{i2} \\ \vdots \\ k_{iM} \end{bmatrix}.$$

5.2   Backpropagation Equations

The goal of backpropagation is to calculate the gradient of the cost function with respect to the VAR parameters and the node dependent function parameters θ_i.
The gradient of the cost is obtained by applying the chain rule as following:

$$\frac{dC[t]}{d\theta_i} = \sum_{n=1}^{N} \frac{\partial C}{\partial \hat{z}_n[t]} \frac{\hat{z}_n[t]}{\partial \theta_i}$$
$$\text{where } \frac{\partial C}{\partial \hat{z}_n[t]} = 2(\hat{z}_n[t] - z_n[t]) = S_n \tag{8}$$

$$\frac{\partial \hat{z}_n[t]}{\partial \theta_i} = \frac{\partial f_n}{\partial \hat{y}_n} \frac{\partial \hat{y}_n}{\partial \theta_i} + \frac{\partial f_n}{\partial \theta_n} \frac{\partial \theta_n}{\partial \theta_i} \tag{9}$$

$$\text{where } \frac{\partial \theta_n}{\partial \theta_i} = \begin{cases} I, n = i \\ 0, n \neq i \end{cases}$$

Substituting Eq. (8) into (9) yields

$$\frac{dC[t]}{d\theta_i} = \sum_{n=1}^{N} S_n \left(\frac{\partial f_n}{\partial \hat{y}_n} \frac{\partial \hat{y}_n}{\partial \theta_i} + \frac{\partial f_n}{\partial \theta_n} \frac{\partial \theta_n}{\partial \theta_i} \right). \tag{10}$$

Equation (10) can be simplified as:

$$\frac{dC[t]}{d\theta_i} = S_i \frac{\partial f_i}{\partial \theta_i} + \sum_{n=1}^{N} S_n \frac{\partial f_n}{\partial \hat{y}_n} \frac{\partial \hat{y}_n}{\partial \theta_i}. \tag{11}$$

The next step is to derive $\frac{\partial \hat{y}_n}{\partial \theta_i}$ and $\frac{\partial f_i}{\partial \theta_i}$ of Eq. (11):

$$\frac{\partial \hat{y}_n[t]}{\partial \theta_i} = \sum_{p=1}^{P} \sum_{j=1}^{N} a_{nj}^{(p)} \frac{\partial}{\partial \theta_j} \tilde{y}_j[t-p] \frac{\partial \theta_j}{\partial \theta_i}. \tag{12}$$

With $f_i'(\hat{y}) = \frac{\partial f_i(\hat{y}, \theta_i)}{\partial (\hat{y})}$, expanding $\tilde{y}_j[t-p]$ in Eq. (12) changes (11) to:

$$\frac{dC[t]}{d\theta_i} = S_i \left(\frac{\partial f_i}{\partial \theta_i} \right) + \sum_{n=1}^{N} S_n \left(f_n'(\hat{y}_n[t]) \sum_{p=1}^{P} a_{ni}^{(p)} \frac{\partial}{\partial \theta_i} g_i (z_i[t-p], \theta_i) \right) \tag{13}$$

Here, the vector

$$\frac{\partial f_i\left(\hat{y}, \theta_i\right)}{\partial \theta_i} = \left[\frac{\partial f_i\left(\hat{y}, \theta_i\right)}{\partial \alpha_i} \frac{\partial f_i\left(\hat{y}, \theta_i\right)}{\partial w_i} \frac{\partial f_i\left(\hat{y}, \theta_i\right)}{\partial k_i} \frac{\partial f_i\left(\hat{y}, \theta_i\right)}{\partial b_i}\right]$$

can be obtained by standard or automated differentiation via, e.g., Pytorch [16].

However, (13) involves the calculation of $\frac{\partial g_i(z, \theta_i)}{\partial \theta_i}$, which is not straightforward to obtain. Since $g_i(z)$ can be computed numerically, the derivative can be obtained by implicit differentiation, realizing that the composition of f_i and g_i remains invariant, so that its total derivative is zero:

$$\frac{d}{d\theta_i}\left[f_i\left(g_i\left(z, \theta_i\right), \theta_i\right)\right] = 0 \tag{14}$$

$$\Rightarrow \frac{\partial f_i\left(g_i\left(z, \theta_i\right), \theta_i\right)}{\partial g\left(z, \theta_i\right)} \frac{\partial g\left(z, \theta_i\right)}{\partial \theta_i} + \left.\frac{\partial f_i\left(\tilde{y}, \theta_i\right)}{\partial \theta_i}\right|_{\tilde{y}=g_i(z,\theta_i)} = 0 \tag{15}$$

$$\Rightarrow f_i'(g_i(z, \theta_i))\frac{\partial g\left(z, \theta_i\right)}{\partial \theta_i} + \left.\frac{\partial f_i\left(\tilde{y}, \theta_i\right)}{\partial \theta_i}\right|_{\tilde{y}=g_i(z,\theta_i)} = 0 \tag{16}$$

Hence $\displaystyle \frac{\partial g_i\left(z, \theta_i\right)}{\partial \theta_i} = -\left\{f_i'(g_i(z, \theta_i))\right\}^{-1}\left(\left.\frac{\partial f_i\left(\tilde{y}, \theta_i\right)}{\partial \theta_i}\right|_{\tilde{y}=g_i(z,\theta_i)}\right).$ $\tag{17}$

The gradient of C_T w.r.t. the VAR coefficient $a_{ij}^{(p)}$ is calculated as follows:

$$\frac{dC[t]}{da_{ij}^{(p)}} = \sum_{n=1}^{N} S_n \frac{\partial f_n}{\partial \hat{y}_n} \frac{\partial \hat{y}_n}{\partial a_{ij}^{(p)}} \tag{18}$$

$$\frac{\partial \hat{y}_n[t]}{\partial a_{ij}^{(p)}} = \frac{\partial}{\partial a_{ij}^{(p)}} \sum_{p'=1}^{P} \sum_{q=1}^{N} a_{nq}^{(p')} \tilde{y}_q[t - p]$$

where $\displaystyle \frac{\partial a_{nq}^{(p')}}{\partial a_{ij}^{(p)}} = \begin{cases} 1, n = i, p = p', \text{ and } q = j \\ 0, \text{otherwise} \end{cases}$ $\tag{19}$

$$\frac{dC[t]}{da_{ij}^{(p)}} = S_i f_i'\left(\hat{y}_i[t]\right) \tilde{y}_j[t - p]. \tag{20}$$

Even though the backpropagation cannot be done in a fully automated way, it can be realized by implementing Eqs. (17) and (13) after automatically obtaining the necessary expressions.

5.3   Parameter Optimization

The elements in $\{A^{(p)}\}_{p=1}^{P}$, and $\{\theta_i\}_{i=1}^{N}$ can be seen as the parameters of a NN. Recall from Fig. 3 that the prediction procedure resembles a typical feedforward NN as it interleaves component-wise nonlinearities with multidimensional linear mappings. The only difference is that one of the layers computes the inverse of a given function, and its backward step has been derived. Moreover, the cost function in (6) is the mean squared error (MSE).

The aforementioned facts support the strategy of learning the parameters using state-of-the-art NN training techniques. A first implementation has been developed using stochastic gradient descent (SGD) and its adaptive-moment variant Adam [11]. Constraints (6b)–(6e) are imposed by projecting the output of the optimizer into the feasible set at each iteration.

The approach is flexible enough to be extended with neural training regularization techniques such as dropout or adding a penalty based on the L1 or L2 norm of the coefficients, to address the issue of over-fitting and/or promote sparsity. The batch normalization technique can be proposed to improve the training speed and stability.

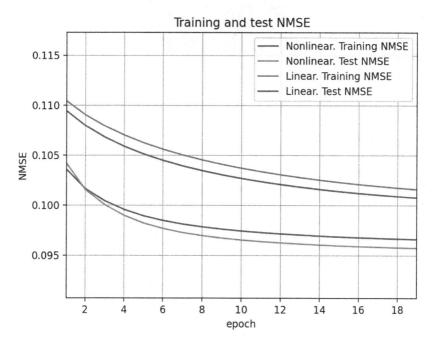

Fig. 4. Comparison of the proposed method (M = 12, P = 2) vs. a linear VAR model.

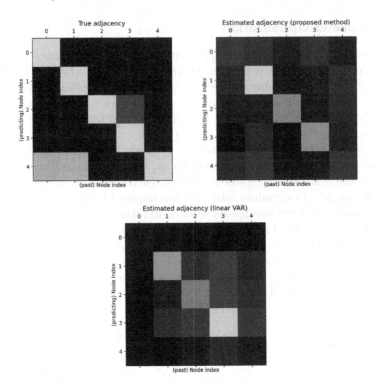

Fig. 5. Comparison between the generating (target) topology and its estimates via the nonlinear and linear methods.

6   Experiments

The experiments described in this section, intended to validate the proposed method, can be reproduced with the Python code which is available in GitHub at https://github.com/uia-wisenet/explainable_nl_var.

A set of $N = 10$ sensors is simulated, and an underlying VAR process of order $P = 2$. The VAR parameter matrices are generated by drawing each weight i.i.d from a standard Gaussian distribution. Matrices $\{A^{(p)}\}_{p=0}^{P}$ are scaled down afterwards by a constant that ensures that the VAR process is stable [12].

The underlying process samples $\{y[t]\}_{t=1}^{T}$, where $T = 1000$, are generated as a realization of the aforementioned VAR process, and the simulated sensor observed values $\{z[t]\}_{t=1}^{T}$ are obtained as the output of nonlinear observation functions that are also randomly generated.

The proposed nonlinear VAR estimator is analyzed in a stationary setting, and compared to the VAR estimator of the same order. The training and test curves are shown in Fig. 4. It can be observed that the proposed nonlinear model can explain the time series data with significantly lower error.

Topology Identification. An experiment ($N = 5$) where the proposed method attempts to identify a sparse topology (i.e. support of the matrix of VAR parameters) is illustrated in Fig. 5. To this end, an adjacency matrix W is calculated such that

$$[W]_{ij} = \left\| \left[[A_1]_{ij}, [A_2]_{ij}, \ldots [A_P]_{ij} \right]^\top \right\|_2$$

Unfortunately, the algorithm in its current form could not identify the topology (despite the error metric on the test set was lower). This undesired effect could be because this implementation does not incorporate any mechanism to avoid local minima or saddle points, which will be subject of future work.

7 Conclusion

A method for inferring nonlinear VAR models has been proposed and validated. The modeling assumes that the observed data are the outputs of nodal nonlinearities applied to the individual time series of a linear VAR process lying in an unknown latent vector space. The number of parameters that determine the topology does not increase, so that the model complexity remains similar to VAR modeling, making the proposed model amenable for Granger causality testing and topology identification. The optimization method, similar to that of DNN training, can be extended with state-of-the-art tools to accelerate training and avoid undesired effects such as convergence to unstable points and overfitting.

Acknowledgement. The authors would like to thank Emilio Ruiz Moreno for helping us manage a more elegant derivation of the gradient of $g_i(\cdot)$.

References

1. Ardizzone, L., et al.: Analyzing inverse problems with invertible neural networks. arXiv preprint arXiv:1808.04730 (2018)
2. Bussmann, B., Nys, J., Latré, S.: Neural additive vector autoregression models for causal discovery in time series data. arXiv preprint arXiv:2010.09429 (2020)
3. Chen, Z., Sarma, S.V. (eds.): Dynamic Neuroscience. Springer, Cham (2018). https://doi.org/10.1007/978-3-319-71976-4
4. Cybenko, G.: Approximation by superpositions of a sigmoidal function. Math. Control Signals Syst. **2**(4), 303–314 (1989)
5. Farnoosh, R., Hajebi, M., Mortazavi, S.J.: A semiparametric estimation for the nonlinear vector autoregressive time series model. Appl. Appl. Math. **12**(1), 6 (2017)
6. Fujita, A., Severino, P., Sato, J.R., Miyano, S.: Granger causality in systems biology: modeling gene networks in time series microarray data using vector autoregressive models. In: Ferreira, C.E., Miyano, S., Stadler, P.F. (eds.) BSB 2010. LNCS, vol. 6268, pp. 13–24. Springer, Heidelberg (2010). https://doi.org/10.1007/978-3-642-15060-9_2
7. Giannakis, G.B., Shen, Y., Karanikolas, G.V.: Topology identification and learning over graphs: accounting for nonlinearities and dynamics. Proc. IEEE **106**(5), 787–807 (2018)

8. Granger Clive, W.: Some recent developments in a concept of causality. J. Econom. **39**(1–2), 199–211 (1988)
9. Ioannidis, V.N., Shen, Y., Giannakis, G.B.: Semi-blind inference of topologies and dynamical processes over dynamic graphs. IEEE Trans. Signal Process. **67**(9), 2263–2274 (2019)
10. Jin, M., Li, M., Zheng, Y., Chi, L.: Searching correlated patterns from graph streams. IEEE Access **8**, 106690–106704 (2020)
11. Kingma, D.P., Ba, J.: Adam: a method for stochastic optimization. arXiv preprint arXiv:1412.6980 (2014)
12. Lütkepohl, H.: New Introduction to Multiple Time Series Analysis. Springer, Heidelberg (2005). https://doi.org/10.1007/978-3-540-27752-1
13. Money, R., Krishnan, J., Beferull-Lozano, B.: Online non-linear topology identification from graph-connected time series. arXiv preprint arXiv:2104.00030 (2021)
14. Morioka, H., Hälvä, H., Hyvarinen, A.: Independent innovation analysis for nonlinear vector autoregressive process. In: International Conference on Artificial Intelligence and Statistics, pp. 1549–1557. PMLR (2021)
15. Nassif, F., Beheshti, S.: Automatic order selection in autoregressive modeling with application in eeg sleep-stage classification. In: ICASSP 2021–IEEE International Conference on Acoustics, Speech and Signal Processing (ICASSP), pp. 5135–5139 (2021). https://doi.org/10.1109/ICASSP39728.2021.9414795
16. Paszke, A., et al.: Pytorch: an imperative style, high-performance deep learning library. In: Wallach, H., Larochelle, H., Beygelzimer, A., d' Alché-Buc, F., Fox, E., Garnett, R. (eds.) Advances in Neural Information Processing Systems 32, pp. 8024–8035. Curran Associates, Inc. (2019). http://papers.neurips.cc/paper/9015-pytorch-an-imperative-style-high-performance-deep-learning-library.pdf
17. Shen, Y., Giannakis, G.B., Baingana, B.: Nonlinear structural vector autoregressive models with application to directed brain networks. IEEE Trans. Signal Process. **67**(20), 5325–5339 (2019)
18. Shen, Y., Giannakis, G.B.: Online identification of directional graph topologies capturing dynamic and nonlinear dependencies. In: 2018 IEEE Data Science Workshop (DSW), pp. 195–199 (2018). https://doi.org/10.1109/DSW.2018.8439119
19. Tank, A., Covert, I., Foti, N., Shojaie, A., Fox, E.B.: Neural granger causality. IEEE Trans. Pattern Anal. Mach. Intell. (01), 1 (2021). https://doi.org/10.1109/TPAMI.2021.3065601
20. Tank, A., Cover, I., Foti, N.J., Shojaie, A., Fox, E.B.: An interpretable and sparse neural network model for nonlinear granger causality discovery. arXiv preprint arXiv:1711.08160 (2017)
21. Yanuar, F.: The estimation process in Bayesian structural equation modeling approach. J. Phys: Conf. Ser. **495**, 012047 (2014). https://doi.org/10.1088/1742-6596/495/1/012047
22. Zaman, B., Lopez-Ramos, L.M., Romero, D., Beferull-Lozano, B.: Online topology identification from vector autoregressive time series. IEEE Trans. Signal Process. **69**, 210–225 (2020)
23. Zhou, R., Liu, J., Kumar, S., Palomar, D.P.: Parameter estimation for student's t VAR model with missing data. In: Acoustics, Speech and Signal Processing (ICASSP) 2021 IEEE International Conference on Acoustics, Speech and Signal Processing, pp. 5145–5149 (2021). https://doi.org/10.1109/ICASSP39728.2021.9414223

Iterative Learning for Semi-automatic Annotation Using User Feedback

Meryem Guemimi[1(✉)], Daniel Camara[1], and Ray Genoe[2]

[1] Center for Data Science, Judiciary Pôle of the French Gendarmerie, Pontoise, France
{meryem.guemimi,daniel.camara}@gendarmerie.interieur.gouv.fr
[2] Center for Cybersecurity and Cybercrime Investigation, University College Dublin, Dublin, Ireland
ray.genoe@ucd.ie

Abstract. With the advent of state-of-the-art models based on Neural Networks, the need for vast corpora of accurately labeled data has become fundamental. However, building such datasets is a very resource-consuming task that additionally requires domain expertise. The present work seeks to alleviate this limitation by proposing an interactive semi-automatic annotation tool using an incremental learning approach to reduce human effort. The automatic models used to assist the annotation are incrementally improved based on user corrections to better annotate the next data. To demonstrate the effectiveness of the proposed method, we build a dataset with named entities and relations between them related to the crime field with the help of the tool. Analysis results show that annotation effort is considerably reduced while still maintaining the annotation quality compared to fully manual labeling.

Keywords: Semi-automatic annotation · Natural language processing · Named entity recognition · Semantic relation extraction · Incremental learning · Criminal entities

1 Introduction

The explosion of digital data in the last decades resulted in an exponential increase in structured and unstructured information with a massive growth for the latter. Unstructured data either does not have a predefined data model or is not organized consistently, contrary to structured data that presents a format, which improves its usability. According to Computer World [15], unstructured information may account for more than 70% to 80% of all data in corporations. For many organizations, appropriate strategies must be developed to manage such volumes of data. The Central Service for Criminal Intelligence (CSCI) of the French Gendarmerie receives and processes multiple documents per year such as criminal reports, signaling from citizens and companies. Only in terms of formal complaints the CSCI receives ~1.8 Million each year. These documents, sent by heterogeneous and voluntary sources, come mostly in unstructured form, making it impossible to impose or even control the reports format. However, having structured information is crucial for investigators and intelligence analysts who spend a considerable amount of time analyzing this data. Hence it is crucial to develop techniques that automatically organize text in a structured way such that the information obtained can be directly analyzed, classified, and used by other, higher-level information management tools.

State-of-the-art text mining tools are based on Deep Learning techniques that require sufficiently large corpora of labeled data. The unavailability of such resources and the prohibitive cost of creating them are addressed in this paper. Today we may find different frameworks proposing generic pre-trained models. However, the lack of domain-specific knowledge makes them unsuitable for certain fields. Law enforcement is not an exception. The vocabulary of the analyzed documents and information of interest vary significantly from those proposed by the regular frameworks. In this situation, transfer learning or even the full retraining of available models may be required which implies the annotation of a substantial number of documents.

This paper describes our efforts to build a system that simplifies and speeds up annotation. We propose a semi-automatic tool for textual information annotation that combines the efficiency of automatic annotation and the accuracy of manual annotation. We investigate the validity of the proposed method on Named Entity Relation extraction (NER) [17] and Semantic Relations Extraction (SRE) [20]. Many other tasks could be used within the annotator framework, but they are not the focus of this work. We use state-of-the-art pre-trained models capable of extracting general named entities and relations between them. As the user provides domain-specific text and corrects model predictions by modifying or adding missing elements, a background training process launches. A transfer learning strategy with fine-tuning is utilized to enable injecting user knowledge into models. After several iterations, the model's accuracy becomes high enough that we switch from an annotation mode to a reviewing mode, which reduces the amount of manual labor and level of expertise required to annotate domain-specific texts.

The remainder of this paper is organized as follows: Sect. 2 gives a brief overview of some related work. In Sect. 3, we outline our pipeline proposal, frameworks used, and experimental setup. Section 4 analyses the results and Sect. 5 concludes the paper.

2 Related Works

As manual labeling of data is a costly, labor-intensive, and time-consuming task, researchers have been exploring techniques to derive better annotation systems that minimize human effort. Different techniques have been proposed to partially or fully automate the annotation process. In this section, we present a selection of these studies, to compare and contrast these with our efforts.

2.1 Semi-automatic Approaches

Semi-automatic text annotation combines automatic system predictions with human corrections by asking a human annotator to revise an automatically pre-tagged document instead of doing it from scratch.

In their study, Komiya et al. [14] show that this approach can significantly improve both annotation quality and quantity. They compare manual annotation to a semi-automatic scheme where non-expert human annotators revise the results of a Japanese NER system. This method reveals that the annotation is faster, results in a better degree of inter-annotator agreement and higher accuracy. Following this line of work, Akpinar et al. [1] conduct a series of experiments to measure the utility of their tool and conclude that this approach reduces by 78.43% the labeling time, accelerates the annotators learning curve, and minimizes errors compared to manual tagging. Ganchev et al. [9] take a similar approach but with a different implementation that only allows binary decisions (accept or reject) from the human annotator. They conclude that this system reduces the labeling effort by 58%.

Halike et al. [11] point out the utility of this approach for low resource languages. Their work expands an existing Uyghur corpus with Named Entities and Relations between them using a semi-automatic system. Their method enables rapidly building a corpus and training a state-of-the-art model tackling the deficiency of annotated data.

Cano et al. [6] present BioNate-2.0, an open-source modular tool for biomedical literature that comes with a collaborative semi-automatic annotation platform allowing the combination of human and machine annotations. Their pipeline includes corpora creation, automatic annotation, manual curation, and publication of curated facts.

Semi-automatic approaches are generally found helpful by most annotators; however, they still require human intervention and are not efficient when applied to specific domains far from which the automatic model was trained [14]. Thus, requiring an initial manual annotation to help increase efficiency.

2.2 Semi-automatic with Iterative Learning Approaches

Other researchers take this idea one step further by proposing a semi-automatic approach with an interactive system that incrementally learns based on user feedback. The component used to tag the data automatically is updated at regular rounds based on user corrections to increase its efficiency and reduce the number of annotator updates.

Wenyin et al. [19] use this strategy for Image Annotation via keyword association for image retrieval. Their strategy is to create and refine annotations by encouraging the user to provide feedback while examining retrieval results. When the user indicates which images are relevant or irrelevant to the query keywords, the system automatically updates the association between the other images based on their visual similarity. The authors conclude that through this propagation process, image annotation coverage and quality are improved progressively as the system gets more feedback from the user.

Bianco et al. [4] develop an interactive video annotation tool integrating an incremental learning framework on the object detection module. Results demonstrate that the system reduces the average ratio of human intervention. The authors also highlight the utility of such systems for large-scale annotated dataset generation.

This paper proposes a similar method to annotate general and crime-related entities and relations in free text. We present a semi-automatic text annotation tool that iteratively updates auxiliary Natural Language Processing (NLP) models based on user feedback. Unlike the previously described studies, we additionally evaluate the impact of the model update frequency on the annotation and compare the intermediate models to a traditionally trained model, i.e., once with all the labeled dataset. Even though these studies were not applied to textual information, they provided some valuable guidelines for the development of our work, such as the suggestion to keep the ontology simple and the need to support annotators with interactive GUIs.

2.3 Fully Automatic Approaches

While semi-automated techniques require a significant amount of human labor, less than manual annotation but still considerable, other studies focused on fully automatic annotation.

Laclavik et al. [16] present Ontea, a platform for automated annotation based on customizable regular expression patterns for large-scale document annotation. The success rate of the technique is highly dependent on the definition of the patterns, but it could be very powerful for enterprise environments where business-specific patterns need to be defined and standardized to identify products. Similar to this work, Teixeira et al. [23] and Hoxha et al. [12] propose methods to construct labeled datasets without human supervision for NER using gazetteers built from Wikipedia and news articles. The evaluation results show that the corpora created can be used as a training set when no other is available but still are considered of silver quality and may lead to low performance trained models.

Canito et al. [5] make use of data mining algorithms to annotate constantly flowing information automatically. They test their approach on classification, clustering, and NER. They conclude that this approach is suitable for scenarios where large amounts of constantly flowing information are involved, but the results are poor compared to manual and semi-automatic techniques.

These fully automatic methods considerably reduce manual labor but have a lower precision or recall compared to other techniques.

3 Our Pipeline Proposal

3.1 Proposed Strategy

This paper presents an NLP annotator platform that automatically identifies and tags entities and relations between them in the input text. The human annotator then corrects the model prediction instead of annotating the text from scratch. The strategy is to iteratively update and refine the inference models via fine-tuning, until the whole corpus is annotated. The goal is to change the task from a manual annotation to a manual reviewing by using corrections introduced, making the annotation process much faster and more pleasant.

The motivation behind retraining the model is to propagate the knowledge gained from the corrected documents to the following ones. This helps increase models precision on known tags while learning new classes identified by users. If annotators identify during the annotation process, a new class that is of interest, model's architecture is adapted accordingly. After a few examples, as models learn, the new class will naturally start appearing on the next pre-annotated documents. Additionally, this method allows to revise or correct possible flaws in the annotation guidelines early rather than at the end as in traditional linear annotation methods [2].

3.2 Tool

The tool is based on a lightweight Web interface using a REST API to enable communication between the client and the server. When the server receives a request to annotate plain text, it returns a JSON object with the entities and relations automatically detected with the trained models. The interface is designed to be intuitive and user-friendly. It displays the input text highlighting detected entities on the annotation view alongside a relational graph constructed with the recognized relations. With simple mouse clicks, the user can manually create or remove entities and relations from the annotation view. The update is automatically detected and saved in the dataset.

3.3 Annotation Process

A typical user scenario goes as follows. First, the user prepares a dataset in the supported format and uploads it to the tool. The system automatically sends an annotation request to the server and displays the results. The user can review and correct the pre-annotated document and move to the next one. The system sends, in the background, a train request to the server with the last document manually corrected. The server finetunes the automatic models based on user feedback. Once it is complete, the server stores the updated models to the system, and uses them for the following inference round. The inference and training requests are treated asynchronously which avoids adding any possible overhead due to model retraining, making the training process transparent to users during the daily use of the system.

3.4 Training Process

The system uses generic NLP models pre-trained on large corpora for curation assistance. Different scenarios may arise during this process. The models may be applied to a domain unknown by the generic models. New use cases or even new classes of tags may be identified. This novelty should be captured by the models to better fit with the data in hand and keep up with changes introduced by the user.

This is made possible through transfer learning. However, this approach may suffer from a performance degradation on old tasks, also known as catastrophic forgetting [8–10]. When trained on one task, then trained on a second task, models may "forget" how to perform on the first one. Different fine-tuning adaptation techniques have been studied to reduce this effect and train models on new tasks while preserving their original capabilities [18].

In our case, the goal is to perform model expansion while still using the original network's information. Ideally, the new tasks could be learned while sharing parameters from the old ones without retraining on the whole original dataset. For this reason, we preserve the original weights of the previous architecture and add new task-specific nodes with randomly initialized parameters fine-tuned at a later stage instead of training a new model from scratch. The fine-tuning operates at the classifier nodes as low layers' weights are frozen. To tackle the possible catastrophic forgetting, at each training call, we retrain the model on the latest corrected texts mixed with a random sample of previously reviewed documents. On average, it is expected that the training set contains a fair distribution of most of the classes recognized previously by the model along with the newly introduced ones. As the model requires a few examples to learn a completely new class, we use a heuristic for training data construction that ensures an upsampling of the latest documents. The idea is to give a higher weight to the last batches of received documents. It can be seen as a warm-up step to enhance fine-tuning on new classes and rapidly converge the new weights.

The iterative training approach may be prone to overfitting as the model is re-trained multiple times on repetitive data. For this reason, we use a decaying dropout rate to tackle the small data size at the beginning of the annotation. However, overfitting is not totally unfavorable for our use case as the goal of the incremental process is somehow to mimic the annotator behavior and not train a final model for production. Ideally, if the dataset used is composed of similar documents, the closer the model gets to the fed documents, the fewer corrections are needed, but this does not apply if the documents are from entirely different domains. To investigate this, we evaluate the model performance throughout the annotation phase against a test set compared to a traditionally trained model. Results of this analysis are reported in Sect. 4.

3.5 Framework Selected

Many frameworks can be used to assist the annotation process, as long as they support a continuous learning strategy. For this reason, the tool was built in a modular way, so that any other model that supports the training features described above can be integrated. The specific ones we selected were chosen only for our initial investigation of the strategy, as comparing frameworks is not the focus of this study.

Hugging Face. To perform NER, we use a BERT-based Transformer model. BERT [7] is a pre-trained transformer network [24], which sets for various NLP tasks new state-of-the-art results. It was trained on a large corpus in a self-supervised fashion using a masked language modeling objective. This enables the model to learn an internal representation of the languages in the training set that can then be used to extract features useful for downstream tasks. We fine-tune the model on the NER task by adding a token classification head on top of the hidden-states output. Our work is based on the implementation distributed by Hugging Face [13]. However, we modified the original trainer implementation to add new classes to the model architecture on the fly without the need to retrain the model from scratch.

Breds. For the SRE task, we base our work on BREDS [3], an adaptation of Snowball [21] algorithm that uses word embeddings to compute the similarity between phrases. It is a bootstrapping approach that iteratively expands a set of initial seeds by automatically generating extraction patterns. We chose this method as bootstrapping approaches do not require a large labeled dataset and can easily scale to other relations by adding new patterns or new seeds. Additionally, this method fits the mental model of investigators that usually have examples expressing a known or unknown relation and aim to find similar seeds and/or discover the nature of the relation. We improved the original BREDS pipeline to expand the extraction to non-verb mediated relations.

3.6 Experimental Setup

In addition to developing a new corpus of general and crime-related entities and relations between them, this study aims to determine how to best address this task using a semi-automatic annotation tool. To assess its validity, we perform two different experiments.

Experiment 1. Seven annotators with a variety of backgrounds participated in the study. Each user was asked to curate documents manually and using the semi-automatic approach. Both experiments were done using the same annotation tool. To address the proficiency bias, half of the annotators started with the manual mode and the other half began with the semi-automatic mode. For each document they worked with, the total annotation time and editing (adding, removing) actions were saved. Finally, annotators reported their general satisfaction with both experiments by filling a questionnaire. By assisting curators with automated annotations, we expect their work to be considerably reduced in time and complexity since they have to correct previous annotations rather than create them from scratch. However, due to time constraints, this experiment was performed on only a subset of the dataset. The goal was to get an effort measurement and assess the feasibility of the study. Additionally, we ask an expert annotator to manually label the data used in this experiment to evaluate the quality of the annotations.

Experiment 2. In this experiment, only one annotator was recruited to label the whole dataset. The annotator had been involved in the creation of the local manually annotated corpus and had experience annotating named entities and relations. During the annotation, we trained two different evolutive models, one every time a new document is reviewed and the second one every time ten new documents are corrected, to assess the impact of the updates on the model's performance. We are also interested in knowing how far these incremental models will be, performance-wise, from the final model trained once on the whole corpus. We suspect that the second approach will be more accurate as it is less prone to overfitting.

Before running these experiments, we started by annotating a couple of documents manually with domain experts to get familiar with the task and refine the annotation guidelines. Then, we retrained NLP models on these documents. Finally, once the accuracy of the system became stable, we started the experiments.

Dataset. The dataset used consists of real, non-confidential, and anonymized documents collected from the internal database of CSCI. The documents were randomly extracted to avoid bias and have a large representation of the knowledge database. It consists of several texts, including crime reports and complaints.

Annotation Scheme. The annotation scheme was first developed after inspecting, with domain experts, the entities and relations of interest. It was further enriched after a first manual annotation campaign. Special cases encountered at this stage, helped adjust the defined guidelines. For instance, some modus operandi texts did not specify precisely what the infraction is, but it is an information that can be inferred from other elements of the text. For example, the words: 'rummage' and 'break-in' indicate a possible theft. These elements were therefore marked as crime elements (CELM).

The final annotation scheme for Named Entities consists of regular entities such as PER, ORG, GPE, DATE, TIME, MONEY, EVENT, etc. but also specific domain entities such as LEO (law enforcement officer name, including titles), DRUG, WEAPON, CRIME (infractions), and CELM (words or expressions referring to an infraction). The final annotation scheme for Semantic Relations is summarized in Table 1.

Table 1. Types and sub-types of relations in the annotation scheme.

Relation label	Sub-types
PER-PER	Familial and social relations, aliases, criminal action
PER-OBJ	NORP (nationality), DATE (date of birth, date of death), GPE (place of birth, place of death), ADDRESS (place of residence), PROFESSION (title), CRIME (victim, assailant)
PROFESSION-OBJ	ORG (Organization affiliation), GPE (place of work)
ORG-GPE	Physical location
DATE-TIME	Timeline
CRIME-OBJ	DATE (crime date), TIME (crime time), GPE (crime location), MONEY (damage)
EVENT-OBJ	DATE (event date), GPE (event location)

Evaluation Process.

Metrics. To evaluate the model's performance, we compute the P (Precision), R (Recall) and F1-score metrics by comparing the golden standard annotations with the output of the automatic system.

Incremental NER Models. An additional evaluation method is used to compare the different approaches used for training evolutive models against the vanilla model, i.e., the original pre-trained model.

The utility and difficulty of recognizing some types varies. Therefore, we go beyond simple token-level performance and evaluate each entity type recognized in the corpus. We define the accuracy ratio as

$$ratio = \frac{correct - incorrect}{correct + incorrect} \tag{1}$$

where #correct represents the total number of correct predictions and #incorrect, the total number of incorrect predictions.

- A positive ratio means that the model is overall making correct predictions.
- A ratio of 1 means that all the model predictions are correct.
- A negative ratio means that the model is overall making incorrect predictions.
- A ratio of -1 means that all the model's predictions are incorrect.

- A ratio of 0 means that the model is balanced.

The ratio is computed every time a new document is reviewed and corrected by a human annotator. The values are saved and plotted in an accumulative ratio graph. This curve enables to better visualize the global trend of the model performance evolution over the annotation campaign.

4 Results and Discussion

4.1 Dataset

Following the semi-automatic approach, we create a labeled dataset for NER and SRE using the annotation scheme described in Sect. 3.6. The data was annotated with the help of a domain specialist to ensure the annotation guideline followed was concordant with the user's needs and requirements. The generated corpus consists of 3063 documents, 348503 tokens, 16780 sentences, 27416 entities and 5182 relation tuples in total.

4.2 Annotation Time and Effort

Table 2 shows the averaged annotation time and number of actions according to each method. The annotation time is approximately two times shorter than that of Manual, which indicates an improvement linked to the use of our approach. During the experimentation, we noticed that the annotation time decreased as annotators got more familiar and experienced with the task. However, the total annotation time decreased even more when using pre-annotated documents. From these observations, we can conclude that the annotation becomes faster with the curation assistance. This is further confirmed with the analysis on the number of correction actions performed in both settings.

Table 2. Comparison of annotation time and number of actions for the two annotation modes

Method	Averaged time per sentence (seconds)	Number of actions per sentence
Manual	23.61	15
Semi-automatic	10.27	8

4.3 Annotation Quality

Manual Inspection. We evaluate the curations generated by the different annotators with respect to a golden standard manually generated by an expert annotator. The results, reported in Table 3, indicate that annotations are, on average, more consistent with the presence of pre-annotations. Therefore, the overall annotation quality is higher in these conditions as annotators seem to make fewer errors. A possible explanation is that the automatic task performs relatively well on easy tasks such as detecting dates or times, and the other complicated ones are left for the human. Therefore, their focus is reduced to the essential and complex cases, making the annotator less prone to make errors.

Training Data for the Automatic Model. To further validate the quality of the semi-automatic process on a larger set of data, we train a final model using the generated corpus during the second experimentation. We split the data into a training set (90% of the total data) and a test set (10% of the total data) and obtain a Precision of 88%, a Recall of 86% and an F1-score of 87% for the NER task.

Table 3. Averaged annotation quality in terms of P, R and F1 for the two annotation modes

Method	Precision	Recall	F1-score
Manual	82%	71%	76%
Semi-automatic	80%	85%	82%

In order to have a fair evaluation of our model, we validate the model performance on a fully human-annotated dataset. We use the CoNLL-2003 dataset [22], as gold standard and achieve an F-score of 91.7% which validates the quality of the generated corpus.

4.4 Annotator Feedback

At the end of the experimentation, annotators were asked to assess their satisfaction with the tool. Most annotators agreed that the user interface functionalities made the process more pleasant. They especially appreciated the automatic boundary snapping functionality during token selection. It was generally observed that annotators were comfortable and rapidly got familiar with the tool. They also reported that less manual look-up was required. Overall ratings of the tool were positive except for some negative comments focusing primarily on difficulties understanding the feedback process in general and details of exactly how the automatic algorithms operated.

4.5 Incremental Models' Performance

Table 4 compares the performance of incremental models to a traditionally trained model. The results show that the iterative models were able to overcome overfitting and generalize well. The final model has a higher F1-score, but the distance between these systems is not significant. This was also observed during the annotation. The auxiliary model's predictions were fairly accurate, and the human annotator added only a few modifications. This achieved our goal of switching from an active annotation mode to a reviewing mode. These findings can be explained by the high regularisation used over the iterative models to prevent them from overfitting.

We perform another evaluation to closely analyze the accuracy evolution of the iterative models throughout the experimentation. Figures 1 and 2 show the accumulative

Table 4. Models performance scores in terms of Precision, Recall and F1-score

Model	Training set			Test set		
	Precision	Recall	F1-score	Precision	Recall	F1-score
1by1	89.05%	87.58%	88%	83.38%	82.3%	82.84%
10by10	89.89%	87.47%	88.67%	84.44%	82.56%	83.49%
All (baseline)	90.38%	87.59%	88.96%	88.44%	86.56%	87.49%

accuracy ratio, in percentage, of some entity classes. The training iterations represent the number of documents manually reviewed.

We compare the performance of the incremental models on the new entities added in Fig. 1. The graphs show that both models could learn new entities over the iterations as the curve is increasing steadily until it reaches a stable point. It can also be seen that the training size has a significant impact on model learning. There is a general trend of increasing accuracy the more documents are labeled. This observation was also noticed during the experimentation. Indeed, after annotating over 500 documents, the models were able to output correct predictions and tag these new entities correctly. This significantly improved the annotation time as it reduced the number of corrections required. Overall, both models' performance was similar as seen for a couple of classes such as CELM. However, there was a noticeable difference in predicting the tags: CRIME, ADDRESS, DRUG, and PERIOD. For these entities, the 10 by10 model prediction was more accurate. A possible reason could be the noisy steps introduced by the frequent updates on the 1by1 model. Updating the model each time a modification is performed could add a noisy gradient signal as observed when comparing Stochastic Gradient Descent with Mini-Batch Gradient Descent algorithms.

In Fig. 2, we use the vanilla model as a baseline and compare it to the iterative models on only the old set of entities recognized by the original model. It can seem surprising that the vanilla model performed poorly on old entities, i.e. entities trained to detect on a large corpus of documents. This is due to the fact that we changed the definition of these entities slightly by including tokens in the tags that were not considered before. For example, we include the postcode of the city in the GPE definition and also the person title in PER. The gap between the vanilla model and the iterative models shows that these models could learn and adapt to the updated entities' definitions. Overall, we notice that the 10 by10 model achieves higher accuracy compared to the vanilla baseline and 1by1 model.

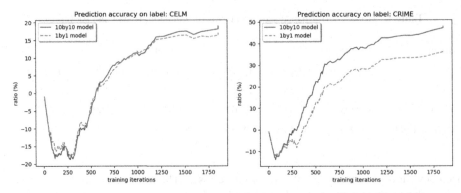

Fig. 1. Percentage of the accumulative ratio of correct predictions on new entities

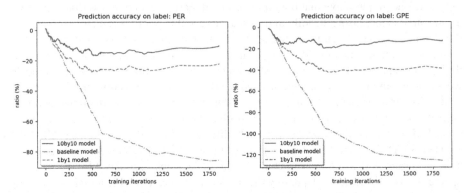

Fig. 2. Percentage of the accumulative ratio of correct predictions on old entities

5   Conclusion

This paper presents a semi-automatic annotation tool based on an iterative learning process to reduce human intervention. We evaluate the effectiveness of our method on two NLP tasks that perform NER and SRE for general and criminal entities and relations between them. The proposed method helped reduce the annotation time and number of actions performed by more than 50%, compared to manual curation, and improve the corpus quality. Using the generated dataset, with new annotated classes, we achieve a final F1-score of 87% and 81% for NER and SRE tasks respectively. These findings can have many implications as the underlying method can be applied to other multimedia applications and be of great use for large-scale annotation campaigns.

There are other areas in which we can further evaluate and enhance the performance of the system. Further experimental investigations are needed to assess the impact of incremental learning approaches against traditional semi-automatic methods at annotation quality levels. Due to time constraints, it was not possible to do these experiments as part of the current work. Another interesting study is to find the optimal trade-off interval value for incremental models. This paper showed that a low training frequency could add a noisy gradient element and disrupt the training. Meanwhile, choosing a high value would not rapidly convey the knowledge introduced by the manual reviewing. Additional work has to investigate the optimal hyper-parameter tuning strategy to train evolutive models.

Acknowledgement. This research has been funded with support from the European Commission under the H2020-EU.3.7.1 and H2020-EU.3.7.8 project with Grant Agreement 833276. This publication reflects the views only of the authors, and the European Commission cannot be held responsible for any use which may be made of the information contained therein.

References

1. Akpinar, M.Y., Oral, B., Engin, D., Emekligil, E., Arslan, S., Eryigit, G.: A semi-automatic annotation interface for named entity and relation annotation on document images. In: 2019 4th International Conference on Computer Science and Engineering (UBMK), pp. 47–52 (2019). https://doi.org/10.1109/UBMK.2019.8907209
2. Alex, B., Grover, C., Shen, R., Kabadjov, M.A.: Agile corpus annotation in practice: an overview of manual and automatic annotation of CVs. In: Linguistic Annotation Workshop (2010)
3. Batista, D.S., Martins, B., Silva, M.J.: Semi-supervised bootstrapping of relationship extractors with distributional semantics. In: EMNLP (2015). https://doi.org/10.18653/v1/D15-1056
4. Bianco, S., Ciocca, G., Napoletano, P., Schettini, R.: An interactive tool for manual, semi-automatic and automatic video annotation. Comput. Vis. Image Underst. **131**, 88–99 (2015). https://doi.org/10.1016/j.cviu.2014.06.015
5. Canito, A., Marreiros, G., Corchado, J.M.: Automatic document annotation with data mining algorithms. In: Rocha, Á., Adeli, H., Reis, L., Costanzo, S. (eds.) New Knowledge in Information Systems and Technologies, vol. 930, pp. 68–76. Springer, Cham (2019). https://doi.org/10.1007/978-3-030-16181-1_7
6. Cano, C., Labarga, A., Blanco, A., Peshkin, L.: Collaborative semi-automatic annotation of the biomedical literature. In: 2011 11th International Conference on Intelligent Systems Design and Applications, pp. 1213–1217 (2011). https://doi.org/10.1109/ISDA.2011.6121824
7. Devlin, J., Chang, M., Lee, K., Toutanova, K.: BERT: pre-training of deep bidirectional transformers for language understanding. NAACL (2019)
8. French, R.M.: Catastrophic forgetting in connectionist networks. Trends Cogn. Sci. **3**, 128–135 (1999). https://doi.org/10.1016/S1364-6613(99)01294-2
9. Ganchev, K., Pereira, F.C., Mandel, M.A., Carroll, S., White, P.S.: Semi-automated named entity annotation. In: Proceedings of the Linguistic Annotation Workshop (LAW 2007), pp. 53–56. Association for Computational Linguistics (2007)
10. Goodfellow, I.J., Mirza, M., Da, X., Courville, A.C., Bengio, Y.: An empirical investigation of catastrophic forgetting in gradient-based neural networks. CoRR https://arxiv.org/abs/1312.6211 (2014)
11. Halike, A., Abiderexiti, K., Yibulayin, T.: Semi-automatic corpus expansion and extraction of uyghur-named entities and relations based on a hybrid method. Information **11**, 31 (2020). https://doi.org/10.3390/info11010031
12. Hoxha, K., Baxhaku, A.: An automatically generated annotated corpus for Albanian named entity recognition. Cybern. Inf. Technol. **18**(1), 95–108 (2018). https://doi.org/10.2478/cait-2018-0009

13. Hugging face – the AI community building the future. https://huggingface.co/. Accessed 17 Jun 2021

14. Komiya, K., Suzuki, M., Iwakura, T., Sasaki, M., Shinnou, H.: Comparison of annotating methods for named entity corpora. ACM Trans. Asian Low-Resour. Lang. Inf. Process. **17**(4), Article 34 (2016). https://doi.org/10.1145/3218820

15. Kulkarni, S., Nath, S.S., Pandian, B.: Enterprise information portal: a new paradigm in resource discovery (2003)

16. Laclavik, M., Hluchý, L., Seleng, M., Ciglan, M.: Ontea: platform for pattern based automated semantic annotation. Comput. Inform. **28**, 555–579 (2009)

17. Li, J., Sun, A., Han, J., Li, C.: A survey on deep learning for named entity recognition. IEEE Trans. Knowl. Data Eng. (2018). https://doi.org/10.1109/TKDE.2020.2981314

18. Li, Z., Hoiem, D.: Learning without forgetting. In: Leibe, B., Matas, J., Sebe, N., Welling, M. (eds.) ECCV 2016. LNCS, vol. 9908, pp. 614–629. Springer, Cham (2016). https://doi.org/10.1007/978-3-319-46493-0_37

19. Liu, W., Dumais, S.T., Sun, Y., Zhang, H., Czerwinski, M., Field, B.A.: Semi-automatic image annotation. In: Interact (2001)

20. Pawar, S., Palshikar, G.K., Bhattacharyya, P.: Relation extraction: a survey. ArXiv https://arxiv.org/abs/1712.05191 (2017)

21. Porter, M.F.: Snowball: a language for stemming algorithms (2001)

22. Sang, E.T., Meulder, F.D.: Introduction to the CoNLL-2003 shared task: language-independent named entity recognition. In: CoNLL (2003). https://doi.org/10.3115/1119176.1119195

23. Teixeira, J.: Automatic generation of a training set for NER on Portuguese journalistic text (2011)

24. Vaswani, A., et al.: Attention is all you need. ArXiv https://arxiv.org/abs/1706.03762 (2017)

Residual Stress Prediction of Welded Joints Using Gradient Boosting Regression

Sachin Bhardwaj[1], Arvind Keprate[2(✉)], and R. M. C. Ratnayake[1]

[1] Department of Mechanical and Structural Engineering and Material Science, University of Stavanger, Stavanger, Norway

[2] Department of Mechanical, Electronics and Chemical Engineering, Oslo Metropolitan University, Oslo, Norway

Arvind.keprate@oslomet.no

Abstract. Welding residual stress (WRS) estimation is highly nonlinear process due to its association with high thermal gradients generated during welding. Accurate and fast estimation of welding induced residual stresses in critical weld geometries of offshore structures, piping components etc., becomes important from structural integrity perspective. Fitness for services (FFS) codes like API 579, BS7910 recommend residual stress profiles are mainly based on three approaches, out of which nonlinear finite element modelling (FEM) results coupled with residual stress experimental measurement, have been found to be most conservative and realistic. The residual stress estimation from thermo mechanical FEM models is computationally expensive as it involves a large degree of interactions between thermal, mechanical, metallurgical and phase transformations etc. The destructive and non-destructive measurement techniques also carry a large amount of uncertainly due to lack of standardization and interpretation variability of measurement results. To mitigate the aforementioned challenges, response surface models (RSMs) have been proposed in this study, for the estimation of WRS at a significant confidence. This paper examines the applicability of 12 different Response Surface Models (RSMs) for estimating WRS. The training and testing data is generated using FEM, Abaqus - 2D weld interface (AWI) plug-in. To compare the accuracy of the RSMs, three metrics, namely, Root Mean Square Error (RMSE), Maximum Absolute Error (AAE), and Explained Variance Score (EVS) are used. An illustrative case study to demonstrate the applicability of the response surface model to predict WRS is also presented.

Keywords: Welding residual stress · Response surface model · Gradient boosting regressor

F. Sanfilippo et al. (Eds.): INTAP 2021, CCIS 1616, pp. 45–57, 2022.
https://doi.org/10.1007/978-3-031-10525-8_4

1 Introduction

Residual stresses are defined as internal self-balanced stresses, which are inherently present in the material without the application of external load. Residual stress acts in three distinct length scales [17] defined as type I (long range macro stresses), type II (grain dimension inter-granular stresses) and type III (sub grain or atomic scale stresses), where type I are often used in practice for maintaining structural integrity of welded joints. Residual stresses estimation has always been a subject of interest for designers, manufacturers, and integrity engineers as harmful tensile residual stress have been found to accelerate crack propagation in welded joints. Accurate estimation of stress intensity factor due to residual stresses can further help in better prediction of remaining fatigue life of welded joints while using fracture mechanics procedures of welded joints. In various defect assessment procedures of fitness for service codes (FFS) like BS 7910, API-579 [8, 15], welding residual stresses (WRS) profiles for distances away from weld toe or welds placed at close proximity like critical offshore brace joints, piping's welds etc. are not available [4] often leading to conservative assessment. Challenges due to harmful tensile residual stress at distance away from welds have been well documented in [1] causing failures due to stress corrosion cracking in welded austenitic steel piping's of nuclear plants.

Finite Element Methods (FEM) is still considered a fast and inexpensive method for determining residual stresses. However, due to the multi physics phenomenon of complex fluid and thermo dynamics associated with the weld pool during melting, coupled with the global thermo-mechanical behavior of the weld, FEM consumes a large amount of computational time. Consequently, to overcome the aforementioned shortcomings of FEM, Response Surface Models (RSMs) may be used to closely predict the WRS for any values of dimensional parameters for these weld joints. Previously, authors have used RSM to predict Stress Intensity Factor (SIF) for assessing fatigue degradation of offshore piping [10, 11]. Thus, the main objective of this manuscript is to predict WRS of welded joints using RSMs. Different Machine learning (ML) algorithms are trained on the training dataset (obtained from the Abaqus simulation) and compared to each other based on the metrics such as RMSE, MAE, EVS. K-fold cross validation is used to for dividing the dataset into training and testing. Finally, the most accurate algorithm is used to estimate the WRS values for the test dataset.

The remainder of the paper is structured as follows: In Sect. 2, the manuscript discusses the uncertainty associated with FEM simulation of WRS and various other methods to evaluate it. Thereafter in Sect. 3, a small discussion regarding the RSM is presented. Subsequently, in Sect. 4, an illustrative case study is presented. Finally, the paper is concluded in Sect. 5.

2 Uncertainty in Estimation of Welding Induced Residual Stress

To estimate WRS various FEM based numerical methods are available [5] which often consumes large computational time as welding process involves a complex interaction between thermal, mechanical, phase transformations, metallurgical a shown in Fig. 1 [12]. FEM model of welds involves many parameters, such as 2D or 3D approaches, heat source calibration, filler, parent metal temperature dependent properties, heat loss consideration, efficiency of welding process, phase transformations, constraint conditions, etc. These models are able to estimate long-range type-1 residual stresses [17] at the macro level, as they follow a continuum mechanics approach. Weld modeling can be dealt with at a complex fluid and thermo dynamics level, where conservation of mass and momentum of various parameters are considered in thermal modeling. Hence, to conservatively model complex residual stress distribution during welding, improve heat source calibration based on analytical models, isotropic hardening models where mixed hardening models are not available and the use of annealing transitional temperature ranges are adopted [5].

However, in general applications, the structural mechanics approach of sequentially coupled thermal and thermo-mechanical method is employed to model single and multi-pass welds. 2D axisymmetric models have been used in past due its time saving, however 3D models are well known to capture realistic welding conditions which consumes more computational time. Various other, simplified thermo elastic plastic time saving technique like sub-structing, block dumping [3], inherent strain method [16] have been known to reduce large computational time for WRS estimation. In recent times, various machine learning based predictive models [2] have also gained popularity in estimating WRS but relies heavily on accuracy of input numerical and experimental data and training and testing of developed algorithms.

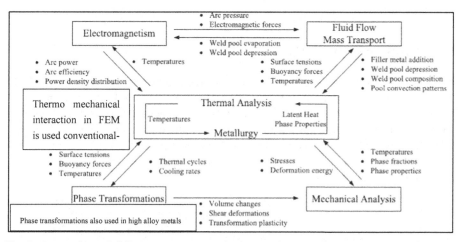

Fig. 1. Interactions of different parameters and processes in arc welding of ferritic steel adapted from [7]

3 Response Surface Modeling

As discussed in Sect. 1, the main purpose of RSMs is to act as a replacement to the computationally expensive and/or time-consuming simulations, without compromising the accuracy of the output. In total, 12 regression algorithms, namely, multi li-near regression (MLR), least absolute shrinkage and selection operation (LASSO), Ridge, Bayesian Ridge, Support Vector Machine (SVM), k-nearest neighbor (kNN), Tree, Random Forest, Bagging, AdaBoost, Gaussian Process Regression (GPR) and Gradient Boosting Regression (GBR), have been used to predict the value of Residual Stress in the weld. The mathematical details of a few of the aforementioned regression algorithms have been discussed by the authors in [10, 11]. As will be shown in the next section, that GBR is the most accurate algorithm amongst the aforementioned algorithms to predict WRS.

GBR is a generalization of gradient boosting and involves three elements, namely, a loss function (which needs to be optimized), a weak learner (used for making predictions) and an additive model (to add weak learners to minimize the loss function) [9]. The principal idea behind this algorithm is to construct the new base-learners to be maximally correlated with the negative gradient of the loss function, associated with the whole ensemble [9]. The loss functions applied can be arbitrary, but if the error function is the classic squared loss, then the learning procedure would result in consecutive error-fitting. Furthermore, the prediction accuracy of GBR also depends upon the hyperparameter selection such as the number of estimators, learning rate etc., which shall be discussed in the next section.

4 Illustrative Case Study

In this manuscript, the single bead-on-plate analysis of the European Network Task Group, NeT Task [13] Group 1, has been analyzed on type 316L steel, as shown in Fig. 5, by performing a thermo-mechanical analysis in Abaqus using a 2D weld interface (AWI) plug-in. The single bead was modeled using dimensions from weld macrography and temperature-dependent physical and tensile material properties referenced from [6]. Due to symmetry, with respect to the weld section centerline, half symmetry was used to reduce the model size (Fig. 2).

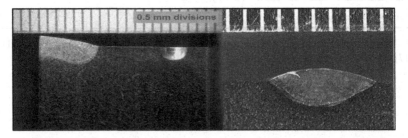

Fig. 2. Single bead mid-length macrograph of net specimen adopted from [13]

4.1 Abaqus 2D Weld Modeler Interface (AWI)

The 2D weld modeler is a plug-in for Abaqus CAE, compatible with its 2017 version. This plug-in imports the basic geometry, having materials, sections assigned, and parts meshed with no imposed boundary conditions. It can automatically generate and define weld passes, by facilitating easy assignment of the weld bead sequence, which is very effective in the modeling of multi-pass welds. In the pass control section of this plug-in, the time required to ramp up the heating cycle to melting and the hold time can be inserted for each pass. Similarly, the cooling time can be inserted, accordingly. Surface film conditions and radiation heat transfer properties can be assigned simultaneously. Subsequently, AWI generates thermal and mechanical models, which can be edited to assign mesh elements and related boundary condition. The model change feature allows AWI to activate and deactivate weld beads in torch hold and pause step and controls the amount of heat transferred to the model, to avoid overheating. In mechanical analysis, torch temperature is capped, avoiding excessively large thermal strains. The annealing temperature can be set in material properties, to avoid a large accumulation of plastic strains.

4.2 Finite Element Modeling

A 4-node linear heat transfer quadrilateral DC2D4 element was used in the thermal analysis, along with 4-node bilinear generalized plane strain quadrilateral CPEG4 element in the mechanical model. A total of 2497 elements were created for the entire model. A generalized plain strain CPEG4 element was used in the mechanical model, as it has been demonstrated to give higher accuracy results, compared to those of plane strain element. An annealing temperature of 1200 °C was used in the modeling, to avoid the accumulation of plastic strain, and elastic perfectly plastic conditions was used in the analysis.

4.3 Thermal and Mechanical Model in AWI

In the Abaqus AWI plug-in, torch hold time is calculated as shown in Tables 1 and 2, from linear 2D heat input approximation [14]. Welding parameters are referenced from [6] for the linear heat input Q (J/mm) calculation. Ramp and hold time were used in the thermal model, followed by convective cooling as thermal boundary condition. To remove rigid body motions and to introduce symmetry conditions in the 2D model, appropriate boundary conditions were employed in the mechanical model. Contour plots of nodal temperature distribution and longitudinal stresses are shown in Fig. 3.

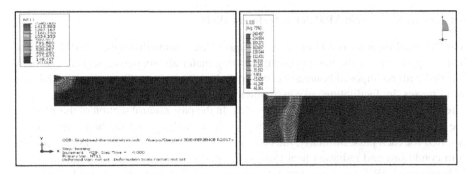

Fig. 3. Nodal temperature & longitudinal stresses distribution in Abaqus

4.4   Data Preparation and Model Evaluation

Two different data sets corresponding to Longitudinal Stress (LS) and Transverse Stress (TS) generated from FEM are used to train and test the performance of different RSMs. The dataset is shown in Table 1 and Table 2. The values of the following input parameters "current, voltage and traveling speed" are referred from the cases study presented in [13], while the input parameters "heat input to the metal, Length of weld pool, Hold time" are analytically derived. A correlation matrix for the training dataset is shown in Figs. 4 and 5. It can be seen from Fig. 4, that LS has a strong negative correlation with the parameter "Distance from center of weld", while in Fig. 5, TS has a positive correlation with the same parameter, which is in agreement with the physical observations due to the fact that stresses perpendicular to the weld are more deleterious to structural integrity due to its loading direction. In order to gain maximum advantage of the predictive power of the machine learning algorithms, scaling of the data using Standard Scaler function of Sckitlearn library was performed. Thereafter, a ML pipeline consisting of all the algorithms was created in order to prevent data leakage. Since, we had limited number of data, therefore K-fold cross validation technique (10 folds and 10 repeats) was used to evaluate different ML models. In order to compare the accuracy of the regression algorithms, three metrics, namely, Root Mean Square Error (RMSE), Mean Absolute Error (MAE), and Explained Variance Score (EVS) are used. Mathematically, these are written as:

$$RMSE = \sqrt{\frac{\left(\sum_{i=1}^{n}(y_i - \hat{y}_i)^2\right)}{n}}$$

$$MAE = \frac{\sum_{i=1}^{n}|y_i - \hat{y}_i|}{n} \tag{1}$$

$$EVS = 1 - \frac{Var(y_i - \hat{y}_i)}{Var(y_i)}$$

Table 1. FEM based training data set input

S.no	Current (amps)	Voltage (V)	Traveling speed (v) (mm/s)	Heat input to the metal (J/mm)	Length of weld pool (mm)	Hold time (sec) = l/v
1	202.73	9.03	2.49	552.24	4.34	1.74
2	218.66	7.55	2.61	475.21	4.02	1.54
3	207.41	10.01	2.51	621.10	4.80	1.91
4	213.71	7.62	2.66	459.03	4.73	1.78
5	206.88	9.35	2.65	548.10	4.18	1.58
6	212.46	8.55	2.48	549.44	4.15	1.67
7	211.64	8.40	2.68	498.30	4.41	1.65
8	217.23	9.89	2.44	660.48	4.44	1.82
9	212.71	9.21	2.41	610.94	4.31	1.79
10	204.06	9.03	2.30	600.35	4.03	1.75
11	216.44	9.33	2.53	599.32	4.44	1.76

Table 2. FEM based testing data set input and output

S.no	Current (amps)	Voltage (V)	Traveling speed (v) (mm/s)	Heat input to the metal (J/mm)	Length of weld pool (mm)	Hold time (sec) = l/v
1	203.51	8.13	2.65	467.70	4.59	1.73
3	219.46	8.70	2.55	561.05	4.00	1.57
4	207.97	9.13	2.37	600.95	4.34	1.83
5	215.55	7.88	2.62	485.59	4.64	1.77

4.5 Result Discussion

The regression model which has lowest value of RMSE and MAE and for which EVS are closer to 1 is the most accurate model. The value of the three metrics for 12 algorithms for the analysis has been shown in Table 3. The collective time taken by all 12 algorithms for training and making predictions was less than 2 min, and for GBR, the time taken was 45 s. From Table 3 it is seen that Gradient Boosting Regression (GBR) is the most accurate algorithm as it has lowest errors (i.e. RMSE, MAE) and EVS closest to 1. The value of various hyperparameters for GBR used in the case study are learning rate =

0.5, number of estimators = 200 (as seen from Fig. 6). The value of RS obtained from FEM and GBR on the validation data set is shown in Fig. 7. As can be seen from Fig. 7 that there are very few outliers and in general the trend between the actual and predicted Longitudinal RS and Transverse RS is almost linear, thus indicating good prediction accuracy of the GBR. Thereafter authors used the trained GBR to predict the value of Longitudinal and Transverse RS on the test dataset (shown in Table 2) the results of which are presented in Figs. 8, 9, 10 and 11, which clearly depict that GBR is able to predict the WRS with significantly higher accuracy.

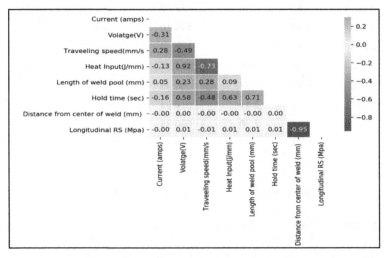

Fig. 4. Correlation matrix for longitudinal RS

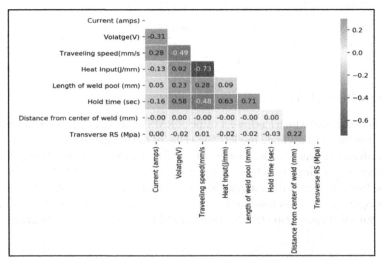

Fig. 5. Correlation matrix for transverse RS

Table 3. Different RSMs comparison for longitudinal & transverse RS

RSM	RMSE		MAE		EVS	
	Long	Trans	Long	Trans	Long	Trans
MLR	58.1	39.7	48.2	30.2	0.881	−0.173
LASSO	56.7	39.5	46.9	30.0	0.885	−0.148
Ridge	61.9	39.1	49.1	29.7	0.844	−0.13
BayesRidge	56.9	36.5	46.9	28.0	0.883	−0.001
SVM	46.0	29.1	37.9	20.5	0.915	0.353
kNN	61.7	19.3	49.8	16.3	0.848	0.72
Tree	13.3	22.3	8.3	15.7	0.995	0.661
RandomForest	4.0	2.6	2.1	1.9	0.996	0.995
Bagging	4.1	2.7	2.1	1.9	0.998	0.994
AdaBoost	4.0	6.6	2.7	4.8	0.998	0.966
GPR	41.7	15.0	31.5	9.7	0.921	0.87
GBR	4.0	1.3	2.0	0.9	0.999	0.999

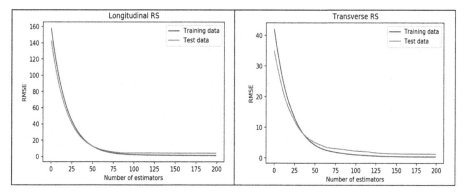

Fig. 6. Estimator selection for GBR

The Gradient boosting regression model used in this case study for predicting the nonlinear pattern of WRS is an attempt to highlight the application of ML in structural integrity world. Welding input parameters used for given case study are limited in range hence expected outcomes from GBR and FEM models have a better correlation. Training of these regression models from wider range of input parameters having varying weld geometries in combination with outputs of various experimental & numerical methods (considering non linearities associated with welding) will be way forward.

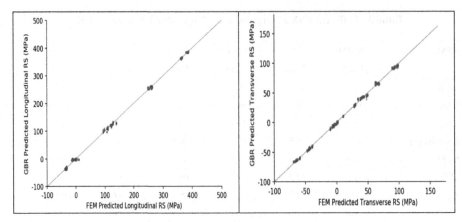

Fig. 7. RS predicted by FEM and GBR for test data set

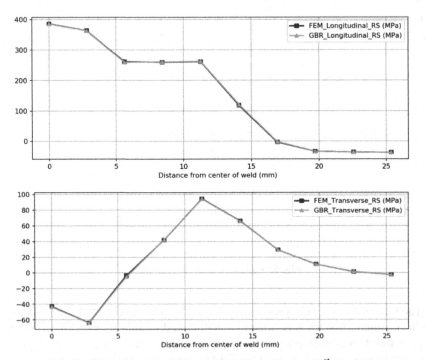

Fig. 8. RS predicted by FEM and GBR for test data set (1st Test Set)

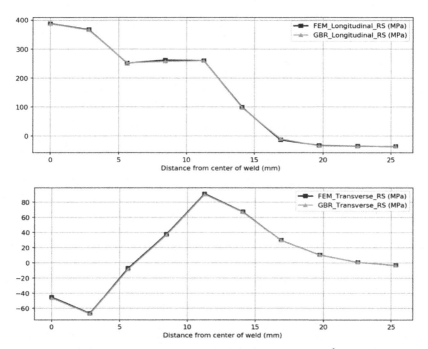

Fig. 9. RS predicted by FEM and GBR for test data set (2nd Test Set)

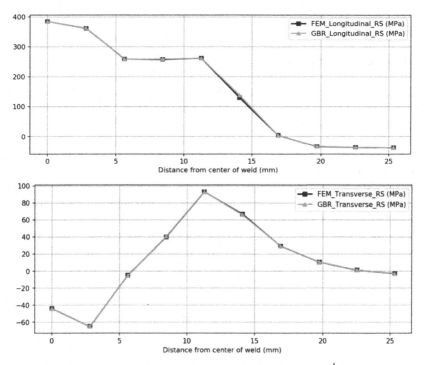

Fig. 10. RS predicted by FEM and GBR for test data set (3rd Test Set)

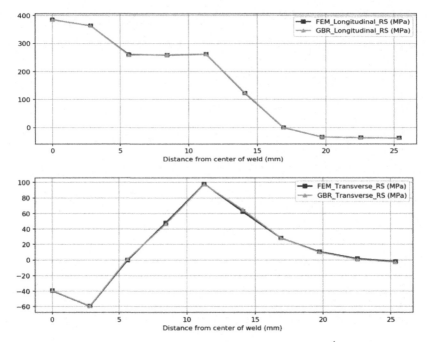

Fig. 11. RS predicted by FEM and GBR for test data set (4th Test Set)

5   Conclusion

The main conclusion of the paper is as follows:

- Welding residual stresses (WRS) estimation away from weld center becomes important from structural integrity aspect especially in constrained geometries of offshore jackets and piping's welds.
- Longitudinal stresses (LS) equal or more than yield magnitude of material in plastic zone formed adjacent to fusion zone can help in determining full field WRS profile from weld center till they fully vanish.
- Transverse stresses (TS) distribution estimation away from weld center can help in SIF determination due to WRS and help in efficient determination of crack propagation rates used in fracture mechanics procedures.
- Gradient Boosting Regressor accurately predicted the WRS in the longitudinal and transverse direction on the test dataset. The time taken for training and testing the GBR model was 45 s which in comparison to FEM is quite fast the FEM simulations took approximately 30 min.
- The trained GBR may be used as an alternative to FEM for predicting WRS in similar problems without compromising the accuracy, nevertheless saving simulation time.

References

1. Bhardwaj, S., Ratnayake, R.M.C.: Challenges due to welds fabricated at a close proximity on offshore structures, pipelines, and piping: state of the art. In: ASME 2020 39th International Conference on Ocean, Offshore and Arctic Engineering (2020)
2. Bhardwaj, S., et al.: Machine learning approach for estimating residual stresses in girth welds of topside piping. In: ASME 2020 39th International Conference on Ocean, Offshore and Arctic Engineering (2020)
3. Bhatti, A.A., Barsoum, Z., Khurshid, M.: Development of a finite element simulation framework for the prediction of residual stresses in large welded structures. Comput. Struct. **133**, 1–11 (2014)
4. Dong, P., et al.: On residual stress prescriptions for fitness for service assessment of pipe girth welds. Int. J. Press. Vessels Pip. **123–124**, 19–29 (2014)
5. Dong, P.: Residual stresses and distortions in welded structures: a perspective for engineering applications. Sci. Technol. Weld. Joining **10**(4), 389–398 (2005)
6. Ficquet, X., et al.: Measurement and prediction of residual stress in a bead-on-plate weld benchmark specimen. Int. J. Press. Vessels Pip. **86**(1), 20–30 (2009)
7. Francis, J.A., Bhadeshia, H.K.D.H., Withers, P.J.: Welding residual stresses in ferritic power plant steels. Mater. Sci. Technol. **23**(9), 1009–1020 (2007)
8. Institute, A.P., API RP 579-1/ASME FFS-1. Houston, TX: American Petroleum Institute; USA, August 2007 (2007)
9. Brownlee, J.: A gentle introduction to the gradient boosting algorithm for machine learning (2020). http://machinelearningmastery.com/gentle-introduction-gradient-boosting-algorithm-machine-learning/. Accessed 30 Aug 2021
10. Keprate, A., Ratnayake, R.M.: Using gradient boosting regressor to predict stress intensity factor of a crack propagating in small bore piping (2017)
11. Keprate, A., Ratnayake, R.M.C., Sankararaman, S.: Comparing different metamodelling approaches to predict stress intensity factor of a semi-elliptic crack. In: ASME 2017 36th International Conference on Ocean, Offshore and Arctic Engineering (2017)
12. Mirzaee-Sisan, A., Wu, G.: Residual stress in pipeline girth welds- a review of recent data and modelling. Int. J. Press. Vessels Pip. **169**, 142–152 (2019)
13. Smith, M.C., et al.: A review of the NeT Task Group 1 residual stress measurement and analysis round robin on a single weld bead-on-plate specimen. Int. J. Press. Vessels Pip. **120–121**, 93–140 (2014)
14. Song, S., Pei, X., Dong, P.: An analytical interpretation of welding linear heat input for 2D residual stress models. In: ASME 2015 Pressure Vessels and Piping Conference (2015)
15. Standard, B.: BS 7910 Guide to methods for assessing the acceptability of flaws in metallic structures, UK (2019)
16. Ueda, Y., Murakawa, H., Ma, N.: Introduction to measurement and prediction of residual stresses with the help of inherent strains. In: Ueda, Y., Murakawa, H., Ma, N. (eds.) Welding Deformation and Residual Stress Prevention, pp. 35–53. Butterworth-Heinemann, Boston (2012)
17. Withers, P.J., Bhadeshia, H.K.D.H.: Residual stress. Part 2 – Nature and origins. Mater. Sci. Technol. **17**(4), 366–375 (2001)

A Novel Group Teaching Optimization Algorithm Based Artificial Neural Network for Classification

Syed Kumayl Raza Moosavi[1]([✉]), Hassaan Bin Younis[1], Muhammad Hamza Zafar[2], Malik Naveed Akhter[1], Shahzaib Farooq Hadi[1], and Haider Ali[3]

[1] National University of Sciences and Technology, Islamabad, Pakistan
moosavi7@hotmail.com
[2] Capital University of Science and Technology, Islamabad, Pakistan
[3] Northwestern Polytechnical University, Xian, China

Abstract. Traditional techniques of training Artificial Neural Networks (ANNs) i.e. the Back Propagation algorithm (BPA), have high computational time and number of iterations and hence have been improved over the years with the induction of meta-heuristic algorithms that introduce randomness into the training process but even they have been seen to be prone to falling into local minima cost solutions at high dimensional search space and/or have low convergence rate. To cater for the inefficiencies of training such an ANN, a novel neural network classifier is presented in this paper using the simulation of the group teaching mechanism to update weights and biases of the neural network. The proposed network, the group teaching optimization algorithm based neural network (GTOA-NN) consists of an input layer, a single hidden layer of 10 neurons, and an output layer. Two University of California Irvine (UCI) database sample datasets have been used as benchmark for this study, namely 'Iris' and 'Blood Transfusion Service Center', for which the training accuracy is 97% and 77.9559% whereas the testing accuracy is 98% and 83.5341% respectively. Comparative analysis with PSO-NN and GWO-NN unveil that the proposed GTOA-NN outperforms by 0.4% and 4% in training accuracy and 2.6% and 6.8% in testing accuracy respectively.

Keywords: Meta-heuristic · Neural network · Intelligent control system · Group teaching optimization algorithm · Classification

1 Introduction

System's complexity affects its accuracy. Many researchers have proposed different models by imitating human learning capability and intelligence. Most common among them are fuzzy logic [1], expert system [2], artificial neural networks [3] and adaptive control [4]. Expert systems are incapable to cater for imperfections due to general complexities as they are centered on expert experiences instead of real time statistics. Fuzzy logic and neural networks are among intelligent systems to handle complexities.

Artificial Neural Networks (ANNs) simulate human behavior of processing information. As of now, the field of artificial intelligence is centered on the combination of

F. Sanfilippo et al. (Eds.): INTAP 2021, CCIS 1616, pp. 58–70, 2022.
https://doi.org/10.1007/978-3-031-10525-8_5

intelligent identification and decision making strategies. Subsequently, the utilization of ANN in various fields of engineering has become a center of focus. In the field of pattern classification, ANNs have shown impeccable performance in terms of adjusting themselves to the data without any explicit information. Basic utilized classification methods primarily incorporate Naive Based approach (NB) [5], Support Vector Machine (SVM) [6], Radial Basis Function Neural Network (RBF-NN) etc.

ANNs address non-linearity better than other models. Hand writing identification [7], product assessment [8], fault recognition [9] and medical findings [10] are some of the fields in which ANNs are contributing. Back propagation algorithm (BPA) based neural networks are perhaps the most abundantly applicable and developed ANN model but a major drawback in this model is that the training speed is slower than anticipated. The training process of neural networks contribute majorly to the complexity of model. In addition to it, structure of the network impacts the execution remarkably. Accordingly, to decide the ideal weights and organization of an ANN is a tough ask.

With an aim to beat afore-mentioned shortcoming of redundant ANN and enhance the efficiency of ANN, a multi-input novel approach is proposed that uses Group Teaching Optimization Algorithm [11] based classifier to optimize neural network.

2   Related Work

Many researchers have proposed their methods using ANNs in different applications. Liu et al. [4] presented ANN based technique to calculate the unknown mass of a car body approximately using adaptive control scheme for a quarter car model. ANNs show better performance during learning as compared to the traditional classification methods. Neural networks mostly used are based upon the BP algorithm. This method consists of two processes: forward propagation of information and back propagation of error. While network is trained, variations are constantly monitored and weights are converged towards relative error function gradient until the stopping condition is met. The major limitations of BP based ANNs include falling into local minima or maxima and slower speed.

In order to overcome these shortcomings, many researchers have proposed their models while transforming the formation, applying different activation functions and refining weight updation methodology. Zhang et al. [12] presented a model to overcome the weaknesses in BP neural networks. In this model, multiple-input feed-forward neural network activated by Chebyshev polynomials of Class 2 was used. Zhang et al. [13, 14] also proposed methods to optimize activation functions using linear independent polynomials or orthogonal polynomials. Han et al. [15] merged Adaptive PSO with Radial Basis Function Neural Network (RBF-NN) for optimization of neural network constraints. Sanz et al. [16] presented a hybrid Hopefield Network Genetic Algorithm based model to handle Terminal Assignment (TA) problem in situations where greedy heuristic based techniques are no longer valid. Ren et al. [17] introduced Particle Swarm Optimization (PSO) based BP neural network combined with comprehensive parameter selection to calculate wind speed forecasting. Khadse et al. [18] proposed conjugate gradient back propagation based approach for classification of voltage sag and swell detection in real time power quality calculation using ANN. Zhang et al. [19] provided relatively simpler connection between forward and backward stages via unified two-stage orthogonal least squares methods. Da et al. [20] presented improved PSO combining simulated annealing algorithm and conventional PSO to avoid local optimum. Li et al. [21] presented super-resolution mapping of wetland inundation from remote sensing imagery through integration of BP neural network and genetic algorithm. Mavrovouniotis et al. [22] trained neural network through ant colony optimization algorithm for pattern classifications. Younis et al. [23] used RBF-NN to predict fatigue crack growth rate in aircraft aluminum alloys. Zafar et al. [24] presented a model containing MPPT control of PV systems under partial shading and complex partial shading using a meta-heuristic algorithm namely; the Group Teaching Optimization Algorithm (GTOA). Meta-heuristic algorithms also have many applications in the field of renewable energy [25–30].

3   Group Teaching Optimization Algorithm Based Neural Network (GTOANN)

Before discussing the implementation of GTOA on an ANN, basic idea of GTOA is introduced. The algorithm mimics group teaching mechanism. The target is to improve knowledge of the whole class. The entire class differs from each other depending upon the abilities. To apply group teaching technique for optimization of the algorithm, a certain population is assumed. Decision variables and fitness function depend upon the students, courses offered and acquaintance of students for the offered courses. Keeping in view, the generality, a simple model is designed based upon the following rules:

- Students of the class are primarily segregated on the basis of ability to fetch knowledge. Larger is the difference between ability to accept knowledge, more difficult is to formulate the teaching plan
- A good teacher is the one who pays more attention to the students who have poorer acceptance tendency as compared to the students with brighter students
- It is considered for a good student to self-learn during his free time by interacting with other students and vice versa
- A good instructor allocation is pivotal in improving knowledge of the students

The algorithm consists of four phases. It starts with teacher allocation phase, followed by grouping phase, then the teacher phase and finally the student phase. These phases are briefly explained and illustrated in Fig. 1.

3.1   Grouping Phase

Assuming that the knowledge of whole class lies in normal distribution, it is mathematically represented as:

$$(x) = \frac{1}{\sqrt{2\pi}\delta} e^{\frac{-(x-u)^2}{2\delta^2}} \tag{1}$$

where x represents the value for which function of normal distribution is needed. δ and u represents the standard deviation and mean knowledge respectively. A large value of δ means greater difference between knowledge of students. A good teacher is the one who improves the knowledge of students and reduces standard deviation.

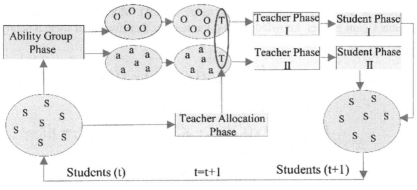

S= Students   a= Average Student   T= Teacher   O= Outstanding Group

Fig. 1. Phases of GTOANN

3.2 Teacher Phase

This phase corresponds to the second rule, which is that the teacher transfers knowledge to one student. On the basis of that, different teaching plans are made for average and brilliant students. Keeping this in view, this phase is further sub-divided into two categories.

Teacher Phase I. Based upon the stronger capability of taking information, an instructor teaches the brilliant section of the class. Moreover, teacher aims to increase average comprehension of whole class keeping in view the difference in abilities of absorbing information. Thus, the ability of brilliant student of gaining knowledge is given by.

$$x^{t+1}_{teacher.i} = x^t_i + a \times \left(T^t - F \times \left(b \times M^t + c \times x^t_i\right)\right), \tag{2}$$

where

$$M^t = \frac{1}{N}\sum x^t_i, \tag{3}$$

and

$$b + c = 1. \tag{4}$$

t represents the number of iterations, N is number of students, x^t_i represents the student's knowledge i at time t. T^t represents the knowledge of teacher at time t. F is a factor to decide efficiency of teacher, $x^{t+1}_{teacher.i}$ is the knowledge of student i at time t after gaining knowledge from instructor. a, b and c are randomly selected values between 0 and 1.

Teacher Phase II. Good teacher pays more attention to the students having poor ability of fetching knowledge according to second rule. Thus, knowledge of average group is represented by:

$$x^{t+1}_{teacher.i} = x^t_i + 2 \times d \times \left(T^t - x^t_i\right), \tag{5}$$

where d is the random number in the range of [0,1]. Moreover, some of the students cannot gain enough knowledge from the teacher therefore their mental acuity is represented using Eq. (6).

$$
x_{teacher.i}^{t+1} = \begin{cases} x_{teacher.i}^{t+1}, & f\left(x_{teacher.i}^{t+1}\right) < f\left(x_i^t\right) \\ x_i^t, & f\left(x_{teacher.i}^{t+1}\right) \geq f\left(x_i^t\right) \end{cases}
\tag{6}
$$

$$
x_{student.i}^{t+1} = \begin{cases} x_{teacher.i}^{t+1} + e(x_{teacher.i}^{t+1} - x_{teacher.j}^{t+1}) + g(x_{teacher.i}^{t+1} - x_i^t), \\ \qquad for f(x_{teacher.i}^{t+1}) < f(x_{teacher.j}^{t+1}) \\ x_{teacher.i}^{t+1} - e(x_{teacher.i}^{t+1} - x_{teacher.j}^{t+1}) + g(x_{teacher.i}^{t+1} - x_i^t), \\ \qquad for f(x_{teacher.i}^{t+1}) \geq f(x_{teacher.j}^{t+1}) \end{cases}
\tag{7}
$$

$$
T^t = \begin{cases} x_{first}^t, & f\left(x_{first}^t\right) \leq f\left(\frac{x_{first}^t + x_{second}^t + x_{third}^t}{3}\right) \\ \frac{x_{first}^t + x_{second}^t + x_{third}^t}{3}, & f\left(x_{first}^t\right) \leq f\left(\frac{x_{first}^t + x_{second}^t + x_{third}^t}{3}\right) \end{cases}
\tag{8}
$$

3.3 Student Phase

Student phase is based upon the third rule. In their free time, students can enhance his/her information either through self-learning or by interaction with other classmates. It can mathematically be represented by Eq. (7) where e and g are values within the range [0,1]. $x_{teacher.i}^{t+1}$ is the student's knowledge i through learning by interacting with other students whereas, $x_{teacher.j}^{t+1}$ represents comprehension of student j at time t, after gaining from mentor. $j \in \{1, 2, \ldots, i-1, i+1, \ldots, N\}$. Moreover, a student may not be able to enhance his information by interacting with fellow students. Mathematically this weakness of the student is represented as:

$$
x_i^{t+1} = \begin{cases} x_{teacher.i}^{t+1}, & f\left(x_{teacher.i}^{t+1} < f\left(x_{student.i}^{t+1}\right)\right) \\ x_{student.i}^{t+1}, & f\left(x_{teacher.i}^{t+1} \geq f\left(x_{student.i}^{t+1}\right)\right) \end{cases}
\tag{9}
$$

3.4 Teacher Allocation Phase

In order to enhance the comprehension of whole class, allocation of a good teacher is crucial during learning phase. This process is explained in Eq. (8) where x_{first}^t, x_{second}^t and x_{third}^t are best students on first, second and third spots respectively. Outstanding and average group of the class must share same teacher for the algorithm to converge rapidly. A pseudo code for GTOA, to get an optimum solution is shown in Fig. 2.

initialize the random population $X_i = (i=1, 2, ..., n)$
evaluate fitness of all particles
find g_{best} and arrange in descending order on fitness bases
while *(iteration< max_iteration)*

> *Calculate the teacher T using Eq. (8) by selecting best three particles.*
> *Divide the population in two groups in outstanding group X_{best} and others in average group X_{avg}.*
> *For X_{best}, the teacher phase is calculated using Eq. (2), Eq. (6).*
> *For X_{avg}, teacher phase is implemented using Eq. (5) and Eq. (6).*
> *After that, create a new population in X_{best}.*
> *Student phase is conducted using Eq. (7) and Eq. (9).*
> *Create a new population of X_{avg}.*
> *X_{best} and X_{avg} constructs a new population.*

evaluate the new construct population
update g_{best}
end while
return g_{best}

Fig. 2. Pseudo code of the proposed GTOANN

4   Design GTOANN and Theoretical Analysis

For the design of an ANN, a three layered network, as seen in Fig. 3, is constructed which contains an input layer, a hidden layer and output layer.

The connections between the layers are made such that every neuron in the input layer is connected with each neuron in the hidden layer and each neuron in the hidden layer is further connected with all neurons in the output layer. A conversion function for tuning the inputs into desired form of outputs are also utilized in the neural network, called the activation function. Lastly the comparison between desired output and predicted neural network output i.e. the cost function is the result that needs to be minimized for an efficient neural network classifier.

For the construction of GTOA based NN, randomly assigned weights and biases are incorporated into the network initially. Two-thirds of a sample dataset are marked as the training dataset and are fed into the network. The output generated by the network, predicted output, and the desired output are fed to the algorithm which in turn optimizes the weights and biases of the neural network so that the cost function is minimized. This training scheme is depicted as a flowchart in Fig. 4.

It is pertinent to mention that number of hidden layer neurons have a great influence on overall efficiency of network. Smaller number of neurons effects the learning capability of network, ultimately effecting the accuracy of the training phase. Consequently, if the number of hidden layer neurons is large, it results in forming the overfitting phenomenon and increases complexity of the network. Therefore, optimum value of intermediate layer neurons is quite crucial. On the basis of trial and error, 10 neurons were chosen to converge the network into its optimum solution. With neurons less than 10, the training dataset ended up with inadequate accuracy while with neurons more than

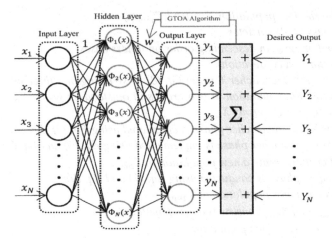

Fig. 3. Proposed structure of GTOA-NN

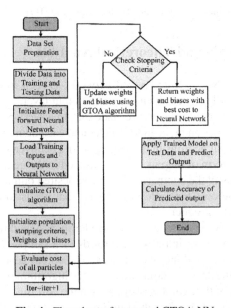

Fig. 4. Flowchart of proposed GTOA-NN

10, the training accuracy improved but prediction of any outliers on the testing dataset were inaccurate and hence testing accuracy was insufficient.

Secondly, a suitable activation function needs to be acquired. The activation function determines the strength the neuron will produce and receive. In [31], a comparison was performed between the four activation function as given by (10), (11), (12) and (13). It concluded that the sigmoid function substantially outperforms the other activation functions, therefore for the purposes of this study the sigmoid activation function is utilized.

$$\breve{a}_i = ax_i + b \qquad \text{Linear Func.} \tag{10}$$

$$\breve{a}_i = \frac{1}{1 + e^{-x_i}} \qquad \text{Sigmoid Func.} \tag{11}$$

$$\breve{a}_i = \frac{e^{x_i} - e^{-x_i}}{e^{x_i} + e^{-x_i}} \qquad \text{Hyberbolic Tan.Func.} \tag{12}$$

$$\breve{a}_i = \exp\left[-\frac{1}{2\sigma^2}\|n_i - m_i\|^2\right] \qquad \text{Gaussian Func.} \tag{13}$$

In [32], a popular cost function namely; Normal Mean Square Error (NMSE) is used for a neural network training algorithm, therefore it is chosen for the purpose of this study as well.

5   Results

Two University of California Irvine (UCI) database sample datasets were chosen as the benchmark for the proposed GTOA-NN classifier, details of which are tabulated as Table 1. 'Iris' dataset contains 3 classes of 50 instances each, where each class refers to a type of iris plant and 'Blood Transfusion Service Center (BTSC)' dataset, which is the donor list database from the BTSC of Hsin-Chu City in Taiwan. Division of the datasets was made such that the training sample came to two-thirds of the complete matrix will the remaining became the testing dataset. Using the NN determined in the previous chapter a population size of 100 particles was chosen for the GTOA and the stopping criteria was chosen to be 50 iterations which provided sufficiently high accuracy. In contrast, increasing the number of iterations would result in overfitting of the ANN. GTOA's tuning parameter i.e. efficiency of teacher F, is set at 0.8.

Table 1. Details of datasets.

Dataset	Number of attributes	Number of classes	Number of instances
Iris	4	3	150
Blood transfusion service center	4	2	748

Table 2. Comparison of classification for training data.

Dataset	Training accuracy (%)		
	PSONN	GWONN	GTOANN
Iris	97	89	97
Blood transfusion service center	77.1543	77.5551	77.9559
Average rank	87.0772	83.2776	87.4780

Table 3. Comparison of classification for testing data.

Dataset	Testing accuracy (%)		
	PSONN	GWONN	GTOANN
Iris	96	92	98
Blood transfusion service center	80.3213	75.9036	83.5341
Average rank	88.1607	83.9518	90.7671

To further reaffirm the advantages of the GTOANN classifier a comparison analysis was performed with two other swarm based multi-input algorithms for neural network weights updation namely, particle swarm optimization [33] based neural network (PSO-NN) and grey wolf optimization [34] based neural network (GWO-NN). For the comparison experiment, same number of iterations and population size were selected. For PSO the tuning parameter C1 and C2 are set at 1.5 and for GWO the parameter 'a' is set at 2. The error graphs of training the two abovementioned datasets can be seen in Fig. 5 which makes known that the overall cost is minimized further for the proposed GTOA-NN as compared to other designed ANNs.

With the minimized cost prediction at 50 iterations each, the accuracy of the trained models is tested for both the training dataset and the testing dataset. Results of the comparison are depicted in Table 2. and Table 3. It can be seen that GTOA-NN exhibits higher accuracy. This is so, primarily because GTOA is very effective in optimization of

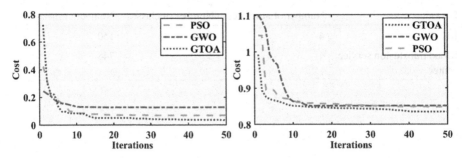

Fig. 5. Cost vs iterations for Iris (Left) and BTSC (Right) dataset.

complex mathematical problems due to the nature of algorithm in improving knowledge of the whole class of students.

Figure 6 and Fig. 7 show scatter plots of the true outputs of each dataset and its predicted output from the four NNs against two features of the dataset. This further clarifies the superiority of the GTOA-NN. For PSO, convergence becomes challenging for a high-dimensional state space because the randomness causes the solution to move

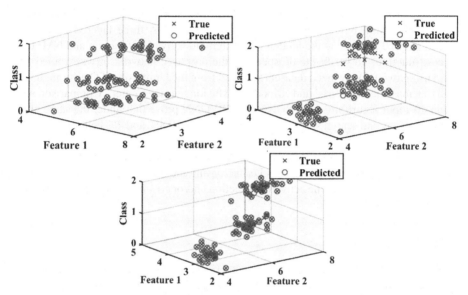

Fig. 6. Scatter plot for Iris testing dataset – GTOA (Left), GWO (Right), PSO (Bottom).

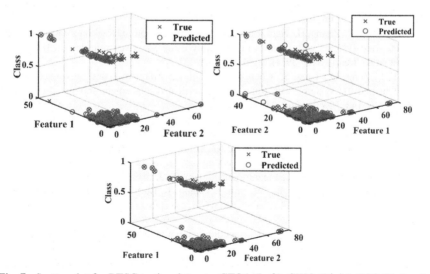

Fig. 7. Scatter plot for BTSC testing dataset – GTOA (Left), GWO (Right), PSO (Bottom).

rather unevenly. Whereas in the case of GWO, although the heuristics of the algorithm ensures fast cost minimization i.e. at fewer number of iterations, the parameter 'a' which is decreasing with the increase in number of iterations, causes the algorithm to converge at a local minima solution.

6 Conclusion

This paper proposed a novel neural network classifier namely the Group Teaching Optimization algorithm based Neural network (GTOA-NN). A three layered network is utilized with 10 neurons at the hidden layer, sigmoid activation function and NMSE as the cost function. To verify the prospects of the proposed network, it was trained and tested using two varying sized datasets acquired from the University of California Irvine (UCI) database namely, 'Iris' and 'Blood Transfusion Service Center'. Comparison with two multi-input algorithms i.e. PSONN and GWONN prove that under the same number of iterations and search space, GTOA-NN performs 0.4% and 4% better for training accuracies and 2.6% and 6.8% better for testing accuracies respectively. It is possible to examine further multi-faceted datasets using this neural network classification technique subject to change in the preliminaries i.e. increasing the number of neurons, widening the search space, changing the activation function and/or cost function depending on the problem in question, etc.

References

1. Liu, L., Liu, Y.-J., Tong, S.: Fuzzy based multi-error constraint control for switched nonlinear systems and its applications. IEEE Trans. Fuzzy Syst. **27**, 1519–1531 (2018)
2. Dong, Z., Zhao, J., Duan, J., Wang, M., Wang, H.: Research on agricultural machinery fault diagnosis system based on expert system. In: Proceedings of 2nd IEEE Advanced Information Management, Communicates, Electronics and Automation Control Conference (IMCEC), pp. 2057–2060, May 2018
3. Liu, L., Wang, Z., Zhang, H.: Neural-network-based robust optimal tracking control for MIMO discrete-time systems with unknown uncertainty using adaptive critic design. IEEE Trans. Neural Netw. Learn. Syst. **29**(4), 1239–1251 (2017)
4. Liu, Y.-J., Zeng, Q., Tong, S., Chen, C.L.P., Liu, L.: Adaptive neural network control for active suspension systems with time-varying vertical displacement and speed constraints. IEEE Trans. Ind. Electron. **66**, 9458–9466 (2019)
5. Rennie, J.D.M., Shih, L., Teevan, J., Karger, D.R.: Tackling the poor assumptions of Naive Bayes text classifiers. In: Proceedings of the 20th International Conference on Machine Learning (ICML), pp. 616–623. AAAI Press, Menlo Park (2003)
6. Liu, X., Tang, J.: Mass classification in mammograms using selected geometry and texture features, and a new SVM-based feature selection method. IEEE Syst. J. **8**(3), 910–920 (2014)
7. Xiao, X., Jin, L., Yang, Y., Yang, W., Sun, J., Chang, T.: Building fast and compact convolutional neural networks for offline handwritten Chinese character recognition. Pattern Recogn. **72**, 72–81 (2017)
8. Ko, K.W., Cho, H.S.: Solder joints inspection using a neural network and fuzzy rule-based classification method. IEEE Trans. Electron. Packag. Manuf. **23**(2), 93–103 (2000)
9. Cheng, Y., Zhao, H.: Fault detection and diagnosis for railway switching points using fuzzy neural network. In: Proceedings of 10th IEEE Conference on Industrial Electronics and Applications (ICIEA), pp. 860–865, June 2015

10. Yao, C., et al.: A convolutional neural network model for online medical guidance. IEEE Access **4**, 4094–4103 (2016)
11. Zhang, Y., Jin, Z.: Group teaching optimization algorithm: a novel metaheuristic method for solving global optimization problems. Expert Syst. Appl. **148**, 113246 (2020)
12. Zhang, Y., Yu, X., Guo, D., Yin, Y., Zhang, Z.: Weights and structure determination of multiple-input feed-forward neural network activated by Chebyshev polynomials of Class 2 via cross-validation. Neural Comput. Appl. **25**(7–8), 1761–1770 (2014). https://doi.org/10.1007/s00 521-014-1667-0
13. Zhang, Y., Yin, Y., Guo, D., Yu, X., Xiao, L.: Cross-validation based weights and structure determination of Chebyshev-polynomial neural networks for pattern classification. Pattern Recognit. **47**(10), 3414–3428 (2014)
14. Zhang, Y., Chen, D., Jin, L., Wang, Y., Luo, F.: Twice-pruning aided WASD neuronet of Bernoulli-polynomial type with extension to robust classification. In: Proceedings of 11th IEEE International Conference on Dependable, Autonomic and Secure Computing (DASC), pp. 334–339, December 2013
15. Han, H.G., Lu, W., Hou, Y., Qiao, J.F.: An adaptive-PSO-based selforganizing RBF neural network. IEEE Trans. Neural Netw. Learn. Syst. **29**(1), 104–117 (2018)
16. Salcedo-Sanz, S., Yao, X.: A hybrid hopfield network-genetic algorithm approach for the terminal assignment problem. IEEE Trans. Syst. Man Cybern. Part B Cybern. **34**(6), 2343–2353 (2004)
17. Ren, C., An, N., Wang, J., Li, L., Hu, B., Shang, D.: Optimal parameters selection for BP neural network based on particle swarm optimization: a case study of wind speed forecasting. Knowl. Based Syst. **56**, 226–239 (2014)
18. Khadse, C.B., Chaudhari, M.A., Borghate, V.B.: Conjugate gradient back-propagation based artificial neural network for real time power quality assessment. Int. J. Electr. Power Energy Syst. **82**, 197–206 (2016)
19. Zhang, L., Li, K., Bai, E.W., Irwin, G.W.: Two-stage orthogonal least squares methods for neural network construction. IEEE Trans. Neural Netw. Learn. Syst. **26**(8), 1608–1621 (2015)
20. Da, Y., Xiurun, G.: An improved PSO-based ANN with simulated annealing technique. Neurocomputing **63**, 527–533 (2005)
21. Li, L., Chen, Y., Xu, T., Liu, R., Shi, K., Huang, C.: Super-resolution mapping of wetland inundation from remote sensing imagery based on integration of back-propagation neural network and genetic algorithm. Remote Sens. Environ. **164**, 142–154 (2015)
22. Mavrovouniotis, M., Yang, S.: Training neural networks with ant colony optimization algorithms for pattern classification. Soft Comput. **19**(6), 1511–1522 (2015)
23. Younis, H.B., et al.: Prediction of fatigue crack growth rate in aircraft aluminum alloys using radial basis function neural network. In: 2018 Tenth International Conference on Advanced Computational Intelligence (ICACI). IEEE (2018)
24. Zafar, M.H., et al.: Group teaching optimization algorithm based MPPT control of PV systems under partial shading and complex partial shading. Electronics **9**(11), 1962 (2020)
25. Zafar, M.H., Khan, U.A., Khan, N.M.: A sparrow search optimization algorithm based MPPT control of PV system to harvest energy under uniform and non-uniform irradiance. In: 2021 International Conference on Emerging Power Technologies (ICEPT), pp. 1–6. IEEE (2021)
26. Mirza, A.F., et al.: High-efficiency hybrid PV-TEG system with intelligent control to harvest maximum energy under various non-static operating conditions. J. Clean. Prod. **320**, 128643 (2021)
27. Khan, N.M., Khan, U.A., Zafar, M.H.: Maximum power point tracking of PV system under uniform irradiance and partial shading conditions using machine learning algorithm trained by sailfish optimizer. In: 2021 4th International Conference on Energy Conservation and Efficiency (ICECE). IEEE (2021)

28. Zafar, M.H., Khan, U.A., Khan, N.M.: Hybrid grey wolf optimizer sine cosine algorithm based maximum power point tracking control of PV systems under uniform irradiance and partial shading condition. In: 2021 4th International Conference on Energy Conservation and Efficiency (ICECE). IEEE (2021)

29. Zafar, M.H., et al.: A novel meta-heuristic optimization algorithm based MPPT control technique for PV systems under complex partial shading condition. Sustain. Energy Technol. Assess. **47**, 101367 (2021)

30. Zafar, M.H., et al.: Bio-inspired optimization algorithms based maximum power point tracking technique for photovoltaic systems under partial shading and complex partial shading conditions. J. Clean. Prod. **309**, 127279 (2021)

31. Shenouda, E.A.A.: A quantitative comparison of different MLP activation functions in classification. In: Wang, J., Yi, Z., Zurada, J.M., Lu, B.L., Yin, H. (eds.) Advances in Neural Networks, vol. 3971, pp. 849–857. Springer, Heidelberg (2006). https://doi.org/10.1007/117 59966_125

32. Moosavi, S.K.R., Zafar, M.H., Akhter, M.N., Hadi, S.F., Khan, N.M., Sanfilippo, F.: A novel artificial neural network (ANN) using the mayfly algorithm for classification. In: 2021 International Conference on Digital Futures and Transformative Technologies (ICoDT2), pp. 1–6. IEEE (2021)

33. Wang, D., Tan, D., Liu, L.: Particle swarm optimization algorithm: an overview. Soft. Comput. **22**(2), 387–408 (2017). https://doi.org/10.1007/s00500-016-2474-6

34. Mirjalili, S., Mirjalili, S.M., Lewis, A.: Grey wolf optimizer. Adv. Eng. Softw. **69**, 46–61 (2014)

On the Effects of Properties
of the Minibatch in Reinforcement
Learning

Eivind Bøhn[1(✉)], Signe Moe[1,2], and Tor Arne Johansen[2]

[1] Department of Mathematics and Cybernetics, SINTEF, Oslo, Norway
{eivind.bohn,signe.moe}@sintef.no
[2] Department of Engineering Cybernetics, NTNU, Trondheim, Norway
{signe.moe,tor.arne.johansen}@ntnu.no

Abstract. Neural networks are typically trained on large amounts of data using a gradient descent optimization algorithm. With large quantities of data it is infeasible to calculate the gradient over the entire dataset, and the gradient is therefore estimated over smaller minibatches of data. Conventional wisdom in deep learning dictates that best performance is achieved when each minibatch is representative of the whole dataset, which is typically approximated by uniform random sampling from the dataset. In deep reinforcement learning the agent being optimized and the data are intimately linked, as the agent often chooses its own traversal of the problem space (and therefore data generation), and further the objective is not necessarily to perform optimally over the whole problem space but rather to identify the high rewarding regions and how to reach them. In this paper we hypothesize that one can train specifically for subregions of the problem space by constructing minibatches with data exclusively from this subregion, or conversely that one can avoid catastrophic forgetting by ensuring that each minibatch is representative of the whole dataset. We further investigate the effects of applying such a strategy throughout the training process in the offline reinforcement learning setting. We find that specific training in this sense is not possible with the suggested approach, and that simple random uniform sampling performs comparable or better than the suggested approach in all cases tested.

1 Introduction

Deep learning (DL) is a field of machine learning (ML) encompassing methods for training artificial neural networks (ANNs) to perform tasks such as classification and regression. These networks are typically trained in an iterative fashion with gradient descent methods. To generalize well to the networks' production environment, a large and diverse training dataset is needed. With large datasets it is generally preferable to estimate the gradient over smaller minibatches, i.e.

This work was financed by grants from the Research Council of Norway (PhD Scholarships at SINTEF grant no. 272402, and NTNU AMOS grant no. 223254).

F. Sanfilippo et al. (Eds.): INTAP 2021, CCIS 1616, pp. 71–80, 2022.
https://doi.org/10.1007/978-3-031-10525-8_6

subsets of the whole datasets, as this allows more iterations of improvements in the same amount of time as calculating the true gradient over the entire dataset, while still yielding sufficient accuracy for consistent improvements over time [2]. This algorithm is called stochastic gradient descent (SGD) [8], which also has the added benefit of introducing some noise in the optimization process which can help avoid getting stuck in local minima of the loss function.

For the trained model to be consistent it is typically assumed that each sample in the training set and in the minibatches are i.i.d, and this is usually achieved with the simple random sampling (SRS) scheme, where every sample is drawn without replacement with uniform probability [2]. Since the aim of SGD is to yield the true gradient over the whole training set *in expectation*, conventional wisdom dictates that best performance is achieved when each minibatch is representative of the whole dataset.

One of the main benefits of the class of off-policy reinforcement learning (RL) algorithms are their superior sample efficiency—due to them storing the agent's experiences in a replay buffer which constitutes the training dataset of the problem—from which minibatches are sampled *with* replacement. Also there is typically a marked difference in the informativeness of different experience samples. For instance, some samples may correspond to typical events that already are highly represented in the data and therefore sampled and learned from often, while other samples may represent rare highly rewarding events that the agent should learn how to achieve more often.

This paper investigates whether faster convergence or better asymptotic performance can be achieved for off-policy RL methods by ensuring a certain state space distribution of the gradient descent minibatches. Specifically, we first explore whether specific training in RL is possible with this approach, i.e. training to learn subtasks or improve performance in subregions of the state space without deteriorating performance in other tasks and regions. We then explore how specializing minibatches into subregions and subtasks compare to conventional SRS and to ensuring that each minibatch is general and representative of the whole dataset, on their effects on the convergence rate and asymptotic performance of the learning process in RL. We will use the offline RL setting [9] to investigate these questions, as it better isolates the effects we are looking at than online RL.

The rest of the paper is organized as follows. Section 2 presents related approaches in modifying the sampling strategy in deep learning optimization algorithms. Section 3 then presents the requisite RL theory and presents the SGD algorithm. In Sect. 4, the methodology proposed in this work is evaluated in a regular deep learning setting on the MNIST dataset as a pedagogical example to gain some insights. Section 5 outlines the methodology used in this work and details the experiments performed. Section 6 presents the results of these experiments and discusses the methodology and claims of the paper in light of these results and concludes the paper, presenting the author's thoughts on further work in this area.

2   Related Work

Curriculum learning (CL) is a an alternative approach to the problem of achieving better convergence speed by selecting data samples for training. The concept of CL is based on starting with the easy parts and gradually increasing the difficulty as the trainee improves. In the DL setting this amounts to identifying the data samples that are easier to learn and serve these to the neural network (NN) first. Thus the CL approach requires either some expert domain knowledge to ascertain the difficulty of different data points, or requires first processing the data points with the model being trained to use self supervised curriculum methods. CL in reinforcement learning is often applied at the level of designing experiments [4,11], starting with giving the agent easier instances of the environment or episodes with favorable conditions, rather than using it as a method of sampling from the experience replay buffer like the approach in this paper.

Several previous works have noted the inadequacies of uniform SRS and the room for improvements. In [14], the authors suggest performing stratified sampling from clusters designed to minimize the in-cluster gradient variance, which in turn accelerates the convergence of minibatch SGD. Recently, [12] suggested a similar scheme called typicality sampling in which the dataset is divided into two: one group which is typical for the dataset—in the sense that the samples are highly representative of the whole dataset and contribute the most to the true gradient—while the other group is the rest of the dataset. Minibatches are constructed by SRS in each group. The authors show that this scheme reduces the variance of each minibatch gradient wrt. the true gradient, and further that the method achieves a linear convergence speed in expectation. Both of these methods require reconstructing the clusters and groups at each iteration, but they both include approximate versions of the methods that are shown empirically to outperform standard SGD on several datasets.

Prioritized experience replay (PER) [13] is an attempt at improving on the standard SRS scheme in RL. The idea in PER is that the more "surprising" an experience is, the more there is to learn from it. Samples are drawn with a non-uniform probability based on the "surprise" metric, which is typically the temporal difference (TD) error. PER shows clear improvements over uniform SRS in sample efficiency, and was found in [7] to be the single most important contribution to the then state of the art (SOTA) algorithm on the Atari-game suite, Rainbow, which combined several advancements in RL.

3   Background Theory

3.1   Reinforcement Learning

RL is a machine learning framework to compute optimal plans for sequential decision making problems framed as Markov decision processes (MDPs). The process is defined by a tuple $\langle \mathcal{S}, s_0, \mathcal{A}, R, \mathcal{T}, \gamma, \rangle$, where $\mathcal{S}$ is a set of states and s_0 is the distribution of initial states, $\mathcal{A}$ is a set of actions, $R(s, a)$ is a reward function, $\mathcal{T}$ is a discrete time state transition function describing transitions between states as a function of actions, and $\gamma \in [0, 1)$ is a discount factor, reflecting the relative importance of immediate and subsequent rewards. In the episodic setting we define the return, $R(\tau) = \sum_{(s_t, a_t) \sim \tau} \gamma^t R(s_t, a_t)$ as the sum of rewards over a sequence of states and actions, $\tau = (s_1, a_1, s_2, a_2, \ldots, s_T, a_T)$, where T is the episode length and $\sim$ denotes that the states and actions are distributed according to the sequence τ. The RL objective can be stated as finding a policy π, i.e. a function generating actions from states, that maximizes the return over the states and actions in the environment: $\max_\theta J(\theta) = \mathbb{E}_{\tau \sim T(s_0, \pi_\theta)}[R(\tau)]$. Here θ denotes the parameterization of the policy.

Deep Determinstic Policy Gradient (DDPG). DDPG [10] is an off-policy actor-critic RL algorithm employing function approximation for the key components, the policy π and the state-action value function Q, typically implemented as neural networks. Samples are collected by using a stochastic version of the policy π^b—typically obtained by adding independent Gaussian noise to the output of the policy (2)—and are then added to a replay buffer $\mathcal{D}$. The agent is trained by estimating the action-value function of the policy $Q^\pi(s, a) = \mathbb{E}_{\tau \sim \pi}[R(\tau) \mid s_i = s, \ a_i = a]$, which estimates the value of being in state s_i, taking action a_i and from then on always acting according to the policy π. This action-value function therefore offers guidance on how to improve the current policy π, by differentiating the action-value function wrt. the actions as in (1) with the objective function (3):

$$\pi(s) = \arg\max_a Q(s, a) \tag{1}$$

$$\pi^b(s) = \pi(s) + \mathcal{N}(\mu, \sigma) \tag{2}$$

$$\mathcal{L}^\pi(\theta) = \max_\theta \mathbb{E}_{s \sim \mathcal{D}}[Q_{\theta^Q}(s, \pi_\theta(s))] \tag{3}$$

where θ^Q is the parameterization of the Q-function. The Q-function is trained to satisfy the 1-step Bellman optimality equation over mini-batches $\mathcal{B}$ drawn from the replay buffer $\mathcal{D}$.

$$y_t = R(s_t, a_t) + \gamma Q_{\theta^Q}(s_{t+1}, \pi_\theta(s_{t+1})) \tag{4}$$

$$\mathcal{L}^Q(\theta^Q) = \mathbb{E}_{(s_t, a_t, s_{t+1}) \sim \mathcal{B}}\left[(y_t - Q_{\theta^Q}(s_t, a_t))^2\right] \tag{5}$$

3.2   Stochastic Gradient Descent

The objective functions in Sect. 3.1 are typically optimized with some variant of SGD. The parameters η of the objective $\mathcal{L}$ are updated by performing a step of gradient descent of length α along the gradient estimated over the minibatch of samples $\mathcal{B}$ according to:

$$\eta = \eta - \alpha \nabla_\eta \mathcal{L} \tag{6}$$

$$\mathcal{L} = \sum_{i \in \mathcal{B}} \ell(x_i) \tag{7}$$

Here, ℓ is the objective evaluated at a single data sample x_i. In true SGD the gradient is estimated over a single data sample, while the mini-batch variant estimates the gradient over a larger batch of data points. The data points in the mini-batch are usually assumed to be i.i.d. In RL however data samples are temporally correlated as they are generated in sequences of interaction with the environment with a likelihood that depends on the generating function π. To alleviate this temporal correlation, off-policy RL algorithms gather the data samples in a replay buffer and then sample independently of the time dimension from this buffer.

4   Looking at MNIST: A Motivating Example

To develop some intuition and understanding in a more controlled environment we will first look at how the distribution of samples in the mini-batch affects performance in regular deep learning. We use the MNIST dataset, consisting of 70000 images of handwritten digits, commonly used to test image processing algorithms for classification purposes. To make the comparison to reinforcement learning more straightforward, a simple multilayer perceptron (MLP) is used consisting of two hidden dense layers with 512 units. We test two cases, one where we use the whole dataset and the distribution over digits is uniform, and one unbalanced case where the distribution is uneven as shown in Fig. 1b. Each data sample is grouped based on its label, and each batch contains only images of one digit in the single sampling strategy or a distribution proportional to that of the whole dataset in the proportional strategy.

This experiment confirms the conventional wisdom: having each batch be representative of the whole dataset yields the best performance, and random sampling performs very similar if not identically to this. Specializing each batch into only one digit performs considerably worse than the other two alternatives. Interestingly this performance gap shrinks when the dataset is unbalanced. This suggest that if one cares more about performance in certain aspects or subregions of the data space, that specializing might have the hypothesized effect, which is promising for the reinforcement learning setting.

5   Reinforcement Learning

We will look at the offline RL setting [9], in which the agent is exclusively trained on data that already been collected by another policy, and the agent has no interaction with the environment of its own. This setting makes clustering the data easier, makes comparisons to regular deep learning more straightforward,

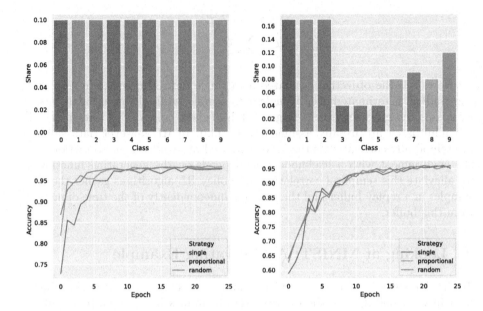

Fig. 1. Validation accuracy on the MNIST dataset for the three sampling strategies on the balanced dataset on the left and the uneven dataset on the right.

and isolates the effects that we are investigating to a larger degree than online RL.

To further facilitate clustering of the data we have focused on the two environments MountainCarContinuous-v0 and Pendulum-v0 who both feature a low dimensional state space, consisting of two and three dimensions respectively. To see if the insights garnered from low dimensional problems are applicable to higher dimensional problems we also conduct the same experiments on the Walker2d-v3 environment.

5.1 Data and Clustering

We adopt the "final"-strategy from [6] to obtain the datasets, i.e. train a regular RL agent with high exploration noise $\mathcal{N}(0, 0.5)$ for $[100k, 100k, 1m]$ time steps for each environment Pendulum, MountainCarContinuous and Walker2d, respectively and save all experiences from the training process. This strategy should ensure sufficient coverage of the state and action spaces making offline learning possible, even for algorithms such as twin delayed DDPG (TD3) which are not specifically designed for the offline RL setting [1]. We use the default hyperparameters of TD3 from [5] except for the learning rate which we halve to 0.0005.

We employ three different sampling strategies: (1) "single", meaning all data in a minibatch come from the same cluster, (2) "proportional", meaning each minibatch has the same distribution over clusters as the whole dataset, and (3) "default", corresponding to normal SRS without clustering of data.

For simplicity we have chosen to use the K-means clustering algorithm. The number of clusters was set individually for each environment based on the size of the state space aiming at a similar homogenity in the clusters among the environments. The state spaces of the environments and clusters estimated from the datasets are shown in Fig. 2. We did experiment with more advanced clustering algorithms such as DBSCAN [3], but found similar results, and therefore preferred the simpler K-means algorithm.

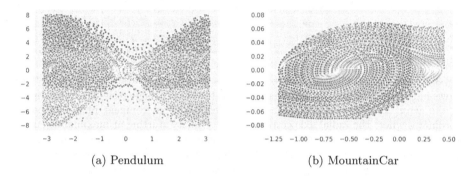

(a) Pendulum   (b) MountainCar

Fig. 2. The state spaces and clusters of the different environments for the datasets used in the experiments. The Walker2d environment is not shown here due to its high dimensionality.

5.2 Specific Training

To test whether specific training is possible, we take a model that has been trained such that it is able to complete the task set forth by the environment, train it further with data only from a specific subset of the state space, and look at whether behaviour is changed in this region but not other regions. Figure 3 shows the results of these experiments, in state space transition plots. Although we can see that behaviour is most greatly impacted for the data trained on, there are also significant changes in behaviour in other parts of the state space.

6 Results, Discussions and Conclusion

Considering that specific training does not seem to work as hypothesized, one should not expect that specializing minibatches should give increased performance. Indeed, Fig. 4 and 5 shows that in general the single sampling strategy has a much slower learning curve than the other two strategies and a worse asymptotic performance in most cases Notably, for the Pendulum environment the single strategy is unable to find a solution to the problem for 4 of 5 seeds,

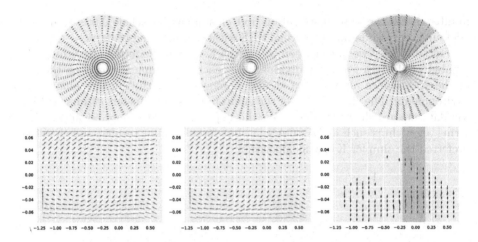

Fig. 3. Results of specific training experiments visualized in state space plots. The arrows indicates the direction and magnitude of the state change resulting from applying the actor action in the given state. The Pendulum environment plot is in polar coordinates where the radial axis corresponds to velocity starting at maximal negative velocity, while the angular axis corresponds to the angle of the pendulum. Left) Before specific training, Middle) After specific training, Right) The difference in state transitions before and after specific training. The shaded region corresponds to the training data used for this experiment. Again, the Walker2d environment is omitted due to its high dimensionality.

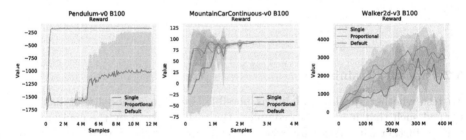

Fig. 4. The learning curves of the different sampling techniques with minibatches of size 100.

while the other strategies solve the problem within very few samples. Interestingly, the SRS technique performs equal or better than ensuring that each minibatch is representative of the whole dataset for both batch sizes and in all environments.

With smaller minibatch size, the single sampling strategy has less of a performance gap, although the performance order between the approaches is maintained. This might be because with smaller minibatches, the updates make less drastic changes to the actor and Q-networks, and each strategy therefore becomes more similar to each other.

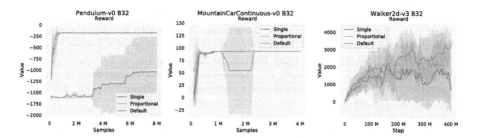

Fig. 5. The learning curves for the different sampling techniques with minibatches of size 32.

These results suggest that it is important when training NNs in RL that the NNs continually train on diverse data. Since NNs typically employ a global loss function and uses non-local activation functions in its layers, there is no mechanism to constrain the changes to the output to be local in the neighborhood of the input. This means that even if the training minibatch only contains data from one region, there is no guarantee that the agent does not change behaviour for other inputs. Furthermore, having diverse data in the minibatches might be important to avoid catastrophic forgetting, i.e. unlearning useful primitives and behaviour that the NN previously has showcased when it is trained to improve at new tasks and data.

Finding some way to ensure that the behaviour RL agents are modified locally could be important to allow for learning of specific primitives and to avoid catastrophic forgetting. Some techniques to achieve this has been proposed, such as dividing the state space and assigning a separate agent to each part, but such an approach introduces edge effects on the borders of the division and in general more complexity. Developing a way to achieve this with a single agent is therefore an interesting prospect.

While we found that specializing minibatches into state space clusters did not improve performance in RL, there are several other properties one can design the minibatches to have, which might have more positive effects. For instance, one can look into how the ratio of imagined data from hindsight experience replay (HER) or simulated data through a world model to real data affects performance, or the mix of on-policy and off-policy data. This is left for future research.

References

1. Agarwal, R., Schuurmans, D., Norouzi, M.: An optimistic perspective on offline reinforcement learning. In: International Conference on Machine Learning (2020)
2. Bottou, L., Curtis, F.E., Nocedal, J.: Optimization methods for large-scale machine learning. SIAM Rev. **60**(2), 223–311 (2018). https://doi.org/10.1137/16M1080173
3. Ester, M., Kriegel, H.P., Sander, J., Xu, X., et al.: A density-based algorithm for discovering clusters in large spatial databases with noise. In: KDD, vol. 96, pp. 226–231 (1996)

4. Florensa, C., Held, D., Geng, X., Abbeel, P.: Automatic goal generation for reinforcement learning agents. In: Dy, J., Krause, A. (eds.) Proceedings of the 35th International Conference on Machine Learning. Proceedings of Machine Learning Research, vol. 80, pp. 1515–1528. PMLR, 10–15 July 2018

5. Fujimoto, S., Hoof, H., Meger, D.: Addressing function approximation error in actor-critic methods. In: International Conference on Machine Learning, pp. 1587–1596. PMLR (2018)

6. Fujimoto, S., Meger, D., Precup, D.: Off-policy deep reinforcement learning without exploration. In: International Conference on Machine Learning, pp. 2052–2062. PMLR (2019)

7. Hessel, M., et al.: Rainbow: combining improvements in deep reinforcement learning. In: Thirty-Second AAAI Conference on Artificial Intelligence (2018)

8. Kiefer, J., Wolfowitz, J.: Stochastic estimation of the maximum of a regression function. Ann. Math. Statist. 23(3), 462–466 (1952). https://doi.org/10.1214/aoms/1177729392

9. Levine, S., Kumar, A., Tucker, G., Fu, J.: Offline reinforcement learning: tutorial, review, and perspectives on open problems. arXiv preprint arXiv:2005.01643

10. Lillicrap, T.P., et al.: Continuous control with deep reinforcement learning. In: 4th International Conference on Learning Representations, ICLR 2016, September 2015

11. Matiisen, T., Oliver, A., Cohen, T., Schulman, J.: Teacher-student curriculum learning. IEEE Trans. Neural Netw. Learn. Syst. (2019). https://doi.org/10.1109/TNNLS.2019.2934906

12. Peng, X., Li, L., Wang, F.Y.: Accelerating minibatch stochastic gradient descent using typicality sampling. IEEE Trans. Neural Netw. Learn. Syst. 31(11), 4649–4659 (2019)

13. Schaul, T., Quan, J., Antonoglou, I., Silver, D.: Prioritized experience replay. arXiv preprint arXiv:1511.05952, February 2015

14. Zhao, P., Zhang, T.: Accelerating minibatch stochastic gradient descent using stratified sampling. arXiv preprint arXiv:1405.3080, May 2014

A Novel Migration Simulation and Prediction Tool

Georgios Stavropoulos[1,2(✉)], Ilias Iliopoulos[1], Nikolaos Gevrekis[1], Konstantinos Moustakas[2], and Dimitrios Tzovaras[1]

[1] Information Technologies Institute, Centre for Research and Technology Hellas, 57001 Thessaloniki, Greece
stavrop@iti.gr

[2] Department of Electrical and Computer Engineer, Polytechnic Faculty, University of Patras, Rio Campus, 26504 Patras, Greece

Abstract. Throughout history, people have migrated from one place to another. People try to reach European shores for different reasons and through different channels. The "European migration crisis" is still ongoing and more than 34,000 migrants and refugees have died trying to get to Europe since 1993. Migrants look for legal ways, but also risk their lives to escape from political oppression, war, and poverty, as well as to reunite with family and benefit from entrepreneurship and education. Reliable prediction of migration flows is crucial for better allocation of resources at the borders and ultimately, from a humanitarian point of view, for the benefit of the migrants. Yet, to date, there are no accurate largescale studies that can reliably predict new migrants arriving in Europe. The purpose of ITFLOWS H2020 project is to provide accurate migration predictions; to equip practitioners and policy makers involved in various stages migration management with adequate methods via the EuMigraTool (EMT); and to propose solutions for reducing potential conflict/tensions between migrants and EU citizens, by considering a wide range of human factors and using multiple sources of information. In this paper, a machine learning framework, capable of making promising predictions, focusing in the case of mixed migration from Syria to Greece, is proposed as an initial implementation of the EMT.

Keywords: Big data · Simulation · Migration · Prediction

1 Introduction

1.1 Motivation

Back in 2015, more than one million people crossed into Europe. Many of them took huge risks and embarked on dangerous journeys to escape conflict and find a better life. But the sudden influx of people sparked a crisis - both humanitarian and political - as Europe struggled to respond. Thousands died attempting to reach its shores and, while some countries opened their arms, others erected fences and closed their borders. The EU is committed to finding effective ways forward. Amongst other considerations, the

F. Sanfilippo et al. (Eds.): INTAP 2021, CCIS 1616, pp. 81–92, 2022.
https://doi.org/10.1007/978-3-031-10525-8_7

EU and its Member States have repeatedly pointed out the need for a comprehensive approach to migration and security [1], as both the anticipation and the actual arrival of an initially irregular migrant in EU territory requires appropriate policy decisions by national and EU authorities, and efficient operational actions by border authorities, NGOs, and municipalities. Hence, two major challenges have been recently recognized by the EU Commission: 1. The reliable prediction of migration movements [2]; and 2. The specific management of migration, particularly the arrival, reception, settlement of asylum seekers, and the successful integration of refugees [3]. Reliable prediction of migrants is crucial for better allocation of resources at the borders and ultimately, from a humanitarian point of view, for the experience of the migrants. Yet, to date, there are no accurate large-scale studies that can reliably predict new migrants arriving in Europe [4].

The main issue is a lack of cohesion between the tools and data platforms in the field of migration and asylum in Europe, with numerous international, national, and nongovernmental organizations gathering data on migratory movements, the number of refugees and available resources, but doing it independently from each other and with limited scope. The data is scattered, existing information is not analysed in its entirety and in addition, there is a dearth of real-time information to anticipate a variety of headwind drivers of migration, such as conflict, weather and climatic conditions, or political upheaval. Therefore, policy designs in migration, asylum and integration management often lack appropriate foresight. ITFLOWS project aims to provide accurate migration predictions and to propose solutions for reducing potential conflict/tensions between migrants and EU citizens via the EuMigraTool (EMT).

The overall impact of EMT is envisaged to be the following: For practitioners, the immediate benefit of more accurate foresight and research-backed predictions will allow better coordination amongst the various actors and stakeholders engaging in the management of migration flows across the European regions. These are first responders, border authorities, law-enforcement agencies, search and rescue NGOs, as well as field operatives engaging in hotspots and registration points. For policy makers, ITFLOWS will lay the ground for research-based policy recommendations that could help design future EU policies in the field of mixed migration management and, particularly, asylum and integration. It will thus provide a picture of how the near future will look in terms of all relevant stages of migration, while using these informative predictions to signal the necessity for new or reformed immigration and integration policies.

1.2 Related Work

Most data-driven approaches for prediction so far have focused solely on one specific country of origin or destination in each study. For instance, predictions have been made on the Haitian migration to the United States [5 , 6] and the US/Mexico border [7]. There are also models predicting forced displacement trends from Mali, African Central Africa, Burundi [8] and South Sudan [9].

In Europe, some countries, such as the United Kingdom [10] and Sweden [11], are using their own individual models to forecast the number of migrants arriving in their territories but each of them uses different data sources and timeframes for prediction [12]. Similarly, some early warning models have been able to predict which countries have the potential to create refugee outflows [13] but they have not included movements driven primarily by environmental causes, such as natural disasters [14], weather changes [15], or other unexpected conditions. Finally, a very promising effort was made by the Conflict Forecast Project [16] where data on conflict histories together with a corpus of over 4 million newspaper articles were used in a combination of unsupervised and supervised machine learning to predict conflict at the monthly level in over 190 countries.

ITFLOWS' EMT aims to provide utilize multi-disciplinary data sources to provide a large-scope model, that will be able to cover multiple areas/countries as a global view, while at the same time providing dedicated small-scale models targeting specific origin and destination countries. This way, stakeholders will be able to focus on their areas of interest and utilize various state-of-the-art algorithms and data sources to run simulations and get predictions on migration flows from specific origin countries as well as potential tensions in destination countries. With the ITFLOWS' EMT, practitioners will be able to better achieve their goals in managing migration flows and better allocate their resources, while migrants will benefit from better procedures and receival in their settlement areas. Although, as mentioned above, EMT targets global coverage, the present work focuses on a specific case (namely Syria-Greece), as the ITFLOWS project is still in an early development stage.

1.3 Inspiration

The present work is inspired by the recent works of the UNHCR Jetson Project [17] and the Somalia case. According to them, the most influential (independent, x) variables – and therefore the datasets collected – to understand forced displacement and the push-pull factors of population movement in Somalia are:

- **Violent conflict**: is defined in ACLED codebook – which is one of the main violent conflict data sources in the region. They used two main variables from this data source: the sum of violent incidents per month per region and the number of fatalities (deaths) per month per region. ACLED is the only data source for Jetson with a public API.
- **Climate & Weather anomalies**: climate and weather predictive analytics is a rigorous science with many meteorology and environmentally based methods. To keep the experiment as simple as possible they analysed two main variables: *rain patterns* and *river levels.*
- **Market prices**: were suggested to be included in this experiment by refugees themselves via key informant interviews. They highlighted the importance of two commodities for their livelihoods: water drum prices and [local] goat market prices, this latter being a proxy for movement. This is because refugees stated that goats are a sensitive product to extreme weather conditions.

In the examined case of Syria-Greece migration prediction, features are built accordingly and applied to a machine learning framework similar to the project's Experiment #1, where forced displacement is predicted one month in advance.

2   Data Sources and Forecast Methodology

2.1   Data Sources

ITFLOWS uses Big Data sources to measure migration intentions and provide accurate predictions of recent flows. The choice of indicators requires a clear understanding of the various actors connected, their demographics and behavioural characteristics. This is presented visually through a network graph in Fig. 1. The project accesses a vast collection of different datasets regarding asylum seekers (UNHCR, HDX, FRONTEX, IOM etc.), demographic/socioeconomic indicators for both origin and destination countries (most notably EUROSTAT, WORLDBANK etc.) as well as climate change indicators (EMDAT, ECMWF etc.) and features indicating the presence of violence or disaster in general, (Armed Conflict Location & Event Data project, GDELT etc.). Since every prediction case requires a tailored collection of features to rely on, a thorough analysis was conducted for the Syria-Greece case to find the best fit of features for the model.

Fig. 1. Visual presentation of the network graph.

Syria-Greece Case: Understanding migration dynamics and drivers is inherently complex. At the individual level as well as at a national level, circumstances differ from person to person. Existing research strongly suggests that human migration is considered as a possible adaptive response to risks associated with climate change [18], violence [17] as well as demographic/socioeconomic indicators [19]. Therefore, all the prementioned datasets were explored and representative features were created with them. The most important databases for the model are the Emergency Events Database (EMDAT), the Armed Conflict Location & Event Data project (ACLED), UNHCR's Operation Portal of Refugee Situations, the Humanitarian Data Exchange (HDX) database and the WORLDBANK dataset.

2.2   Data Processing and Features Extraction

Since the goal is to develop a machine learning model capable of producing reliable and unbiased predictions, it is extremely important that enough data are provided to the algorithms. Hence, a prediction on a monthly basis was selected, and yearly features were converted to monthly ones without the use of interpolation. A careful examination of the data led to i) the following time window of training: February 2016–August 2020 and ii) the following prediction and target variables.

More than 300 indicators (both demographic and socioeconomic) of the WORLD-BANK dataset were inspected, as far as correlation with the target variable and data suitability are concerned, and 25 of them (the ones with the highest absolute value correlation) were provided as input to the model. Since correlation is not causation, different groupings and subgroupings of the features were used to avoid any omitted variables bias. The best results were achieved using features FEAT_1 and FEAT_2 of the Table 1. Since immigration seems to be not only an event-driven (wars, disasters, coups etc.) response but also a gradually developing phenomenon (economic crisis, climate change, political upheaval etc.), different time lags were tested on the independent variables (last 250 days, last 100 days etc.) to provide the models with such intuitions.

2.3   Model Specifications

The target variable is a numerical one which makes the prediction of it a problem of regression. Therefore, various regressors were examined to find the best fit for the model including SVR, Lasso, Ridge, Random Forests, Decision Tree and Linear Regression (without penalization). The metric used for each model's performance evaluation is the coefficient of determination R^2.

$$R = 1 - \frac{RSS}{TSS}$$

RSS: Sum of square of residuals.
   TSS: Total sum of squares.
   R square is a good measure of how much variability in the dependent variable can be explained by the model.

Train-Test Split.   Since the task is a time series regression, randomly shuffling the data was not a choice. After a lot of experimentation with all the models, a 75/25 percent split of the data was selected for training and testing, respectively, leading to the following prediction timespan: July 2019–August 2020.

Table 1. Final set of features used for the prediction of monthly sea and land arrivals at Greece from Syria.

Feature Name	Dataset	Description	Type	Freq	Var
NUM_NAT_DIS_200	EMDAT	Number of Natural Disasters during the last 200 days.	Disasters	Monthly	Pred.
NUM_NAT_DIS_100	EMDAT	Number of Natural Disasters during the last 100 days.	Disasters	Monthly	Pred.
NUM_BATTLES_250	ACLED	Number of battles, explosions, or remote violence during the last 250 days.	Violence	Monthly	Pred.
TOT_AFFECTED_200	EMDAT	Number of people affected by feature No1.	Disasters	Monthly	Pred.
TOT_DEATHS_200	EMDAT	Number of deaths caused by feature No1.	Disasters	Monthly	Pred.
TOT_AFFECTED_100	EMDAT	Number of people affected by feature No2.	Disasters	Monthly	Pred.
TOT_DEATHS_100	EMDAT	Number of deaths caused by feature No2.	Disasters	Monthly	Pred.
TOT_FAT_250	ACLED	Total fatalities of feature No3.	Violence	Monthly	Pred.

(*continued*)

Table 1. (*continued*)

Feature Name	Dataset	Description	Type	Freq	Var
NUM_PROT_RIOT_VAL_250	ACLED	Number of civilian violence (protests, riots etc.) during the last 250 days.	Violence	Monthly	Pred.
TOT_FAT_PROT_250	ACLED	Total fatalities of feature No9.	Violence	Monthly	Pred.
ASYLUM_APL_SYRIANS	HDX	Total asylum applications from Syrian civilians during that year.	Refugee	Yearly	Pred.
FROM_SYRIA	UNHCR	Sea and land arrivals to Greece from Syria.	Refugee	Monthly	Target
LAST_INCOMING	UNHCR	Last month's sea and land arrivals to Greece from Syria.	Refugee	Monthly	Pred.
FEAT_1	WORLDBANK	Net official development assistance and official aid received (current US$)	Economy	Yearly	Pred.
FEAT_2	WORLDBANK	Population ages 20 -24, female (% of female population)	Economy	Yearly	Pred.

Table 2. Correlation of violence and disaster features with the target variable (Pearson).

Feature name	Correlation (Pearson)
TOT_AFFECTED_200	0.012276
TOT_DEATHS_200	0.063775
NUM_NAT_DIS_100	0.474577
TOT_AFFECTED_100	−0.062395
TOT_DEATHS_100	−0.024254
NUM_NAT_DIS_100	−0.062368
NUM_BATTLES_250	−0.218147
TOT_FAT_250	−0.185228
NUM_PROT_RIOT_VAL_250	−0.289228
TOT_FAT_PROT_250	−0.258253
LAST_INCOMING	0.881505

Correlation is not causation. However, when it comes to linear regression it provides helpful intuition on the predictive power of the features. For that reason, the features having the least significant correlation (TOT_AFFECTED_200, TOT_DEATHS_200, TOT_AFFECTED_100, TOT_DEATHS_100) with the target variable as shown in Table 2 were excluded (only for the linear regressors, not the decision trees).

For comparison purposes, a base performance was established using only last month's sea and land arrivals as input to a Ridge Regressor which achieved a basic $R^2 = 0.5514$. Any performance worse than that helped refine the feature extraction process. The adjusted R squared metric, which penalizes you when you add an independent variable with insignificant impact to the model (in contrast to R squared), was also used as a guide for comparing a model's performance on different predictors. This decision improved the performance of the linear regressors significantly and led the model to optimal performance as shown in the Results section.

3 Results

The best pipeline, of the ones tested, achieved a promising $R^2 = 0.6812$ when predicting monthly sea and land arrivals of Syrians to Greece. This pipeline consists of a standardization step and a Ridge Regressor with strict penalization (alpha = 6). The input features to the final model are the following (Table 3 and Fig. 2):

It is interesting that although migration is heavily tied to unemployment and labour, there was no economic indicator (of the ones available) that improved the model's performance significantly. Such observation makes sense for the case of Syria since the country has suffered extreme violence and war the latest years, generating refugees and not so many emigrants.

For comparison purposes, the next best-performing model is the Lasso Regressor achieving $R^2 = 0.6162$ (Fig. 3).

Table 3. Best fit of features of the final model.

Feature name	Description
NUM_NAT_DIS_250	Number of natural disasters last 200 days
NUM_NAT_DIS_100	Number of natural disasters last 100 days
NUM_BATTLES_250	Number of battles last 250 days
TOT_FAT_50	Total fatalities of battles last 250 days
NUM_PROT_RIOT_VAL_250	Number of civilian violence (riots etc.) last 250 days
TOT_FAT_250	Total fatalities during civilian violence last 250 days
LAST_INCOMING	Total sea and land arrivals last month
ASYLUM_APL_SYRIANS	Total applications filled by Syrians for EU countries last month
FEAT_1	Net official development assistance and official aid received (current US$) Syria
FEAT_2	Population ages 20–24, female (% of female population) Syria

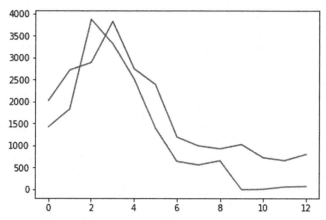

Fig. 2. Plot of the model's predictions (green) vs the real values (blue) [Ridge]. Vertical axis denotes number of migrants arriving by land or sea, while the horizontal axis denotes time in months (July 2019–August 2020) (Color figure online)

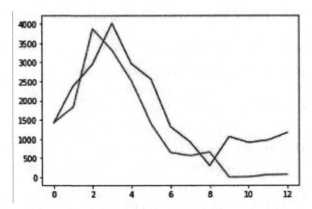

Fig. 3. Plot of the model's predictions (green) vs the real values (blue) [Lasso]. Vertical axis denotes number of migrants arriving by land or sea, while the horizontal axis denotes time in months (July 2019–August 2020) (Color figure online)

4 Conclusion/Future Work

Undoubtedly, there is much room for improvement when it comes to not only predicting accurately but also providing the end user (of the EMT tool) with valuable intel on the predicted migrant flows (age, sex etc.). GDELT is one of the most promising databases available and one of the main datasets for this project is the *Global Quotation Graph,* or GQG in short. GDELT is a project constructing catalogues for human societal-scale behaviours and beliefs from countries all around the world. The database works in almost real time and is one of the highest resolution inventories of the media systems of the non-Western world. It is described as a key for developing technology that studies the worlds society. GQG compiles quoted statements from news all around the world. It scans monitored articles by GDELT and creates a list of quoted statements, providing enough context (before and after the quote) to allow users to distinguish speaker identity. The dataset covers 152 languages from all over the world with some minor limitations and most of them are translated to English. It is updated every minute but is generated for public use only every 15 min [20-22].

Downloaded content and reports from this dataset will be used as input in an LDA model for topic modelling. The main goal is to detect violence and various other topics (like immigration, terror, economic crisis etc.) on the national press of the destination countries, which might provide the model with helpful predictive intuition on the country's generated migrant flows.

Apart from the Syria-Greece case, ITFLOWS project emphasizes in analysing the countries shown in Table 4 in their respective way to forecast migrant flows. The aims to include more data in the model like climate change and topic shares from the LDA as well as data found through GDELT and mainly GQG. That way the forecast can be more accurate and comprehensive.

Table 4. List of countries of origin and destination countries, listed in alphabetical order with no relation between countries in the same row.

Countries of origin	Destination countries
Afghanistan	France
Eritrea	Germany
Iraq	Greece
Mali	Italy
Morocco	Netherlands
Nigeria	Poland
Syria	Spain
Venezuela	Sweden

Acknowledgment. This work is co-funded by the European Union (EU) within the ITFLOWS project under Grant Agreement number 882986. The ITFLOWS project is part of the EU Framework Program for Research and Innovation Horizon 2020.

References s

1. Frontex, Risk Analysis for 2019, Frontex (2019). ISBN: 978-92-9471-315-5
2. JRC Science Hub, The Future of Migration in the European Union: Future scenarios and tools to stimulate forward-looking discussions, Luxembourg: Publications Office of the European Union (2018). ISBN 978-92-79-90207-9
3. European Commission, Eurobarometer survey 469 on the integration of immigrants in the European Union, 13 April 2018
4. Buettner, T., Muenz, R.: Comperative analysis of international migration in population projections, Knomad Working Paper 10 (2016)
5. Shellman, S.M., Stewart, B.M.: Predicting risk factors associated with forced migration: an early warning model of Haitian flight. Civ. Wars **9**, 174–199 (2007)
6. Lu, X., Bengtsson, L., Holme, P.: Predictability of population displacement after the 2010 Haiti earthquake, 17 July 2012
7. National Research Council, Model-Based Approach to Estimating Migration Flows, in Chapter 6 of Options for Estimating Illegal Entries at the U.S.-Mexico Border, pp. 93–144. The National Academies Press, Washington, DC (2013)
8. Suleimenova, D., Bell, D., Groen, D.: A generalized simulation development approach for predicting refugee destinations. Sci. Rep. **7**, 13377 (2017)
9. Campos, C.V., Suleimenova, D., Groen, D.: A coupled food security and refugee movement model for the South Sudan conflict. In: Computational Science, vol. 11540, pp. 725–732. Springer, Cham (2019). https://doi.org/10.1007/978-3-030-22750-0_71
10. Disney, G., Wisniowski, A., Fordter, J.J., Smith, P.W.F., Bijak, J.: Evaluation of existing migration forecasting methods and models. Report for the Migration Advisory Committee, ESRC Centre for Population Change, University of Southampton (2015)
11. Swedish Migration Agency, Prediction of Migration Flows. Migration Algorithms (2018). ISBN: 978-91-7016-907-6

12. OECD, Migration Policy Debates, OECD/EASO, no. 16, pp. 1–9 May 2018
13. Martineau, J.S.: Red flags: a model for the early warning of refugee outflows. J. Immigr. Refug. Stud. **8**, 135–157 (2010)
14. Ahmed, M.N., et al.: A multi-scale approach to data-driven mass migration analysis (2016)
15. Johnson, S.: Predicting migration flow through Europe (2016). https://medium.com/@Simon_B_Johnson/predicting-migrationflow-through-europe-3b93b0482fcd
16. Hannes, F.M., Christopher, R.: The hard problem of prediction for conflict prevention, CEPR Discussion Paper No. DP13748, May 2019
17. Jetson Project, UNHCR. https://jetson.unhcr.org/
18. McLeman, R., Smit, B.: Migration as an adaptation to climate change. Clim. Change **76**, 31–53 (2006). https://doi.org/10.1007/s10584-005-9000-7
19. Dövényi, Z., Farkas, M.: Migration to Europe and its demographic background, Központi Statisztikai Hivatal (2018)
20. GDELT. https://www.gdeltproject.org/#downloading. Accessed 05 2021
21. GDELT. https://www.gdeltproject.org/data.html#documentation. Accessed 05 2021
22. GDELT. https://blog.gdeltproject.org/announcing-theglobal-geographic-graph/. Accessed 05 2021

Development Environment for Software-Defined Smart City Networks

Filip Holik$^{(\boxtimes)}$ (iD)

Norwegian University of Science and Technology, 2815 Gjøvik, Norway
`filip.holik@ntnu.no`

Abstract. Smart cities are becoming the key technology as more and more people are attracted to living in urban environments. Increased number of inhabitants and current issues such as pandemic restrictions, terrorist threats, global warming and limited resources require maximum effectivity in all areas of city operations. To support these dynamic demands, software-based approaches for network management are being used. They provide programmability, which allows implementation of almost any functionality, but is dependent on quality of the developed application. To ensure the best possible quality, developers need an environment on which they can develop and test the application effectively. Such an environment should be as close to a real network as possible, but as easy to use as an emulated network.

This paper describes a method for creating a flexible and inexpensive practical environment for developing and testing applications for software-defined smart city networks. The paper analyzes four relevant open source controllers, compares their features and suitability for smart city applications; and provides a guideline for creating inexpensive SDN capable switches from general purpose single board Raspberry Pi computers. The presented environment can be deployed easily, but its hardware nature allows real performance measurements and utilization of IoT-based nodes and sensors. This is verified in an use case smart city topology.

Keywords: SDN controllers · Smart city · Software-defined networks · Software switch · Raspberry Pi

1 Introduction

Smart city is a concept for enhancing current mega cities by innovative technologies from information and communication fields with the goal of improving every aspect of the city's operations. This includes economy, transportation, safety, waste and resources managements, and many others. The smart city market is steadily growing with investments increasing about 20% every year and expected to reach almost 200 billion U.S. dollars in 2023 [26]. Recent pandemic

F. Sanfilippo et al. (Eds.): INTAP 2021, CCIS 1616, pp. 93–104, 2022.
https://doi.org/10.1007/978-3-031-10525-8_8

events and their negative impact on the economy might lead to an assumption that these expanses will be reduced, but the opposite is more likely true. Smart cities will be more important than ever, as their functionalities might significantly help with enforcing quarantine restrictions, support contact tracing, and check social distancing. The increased effectiveness of all city's operations plays an even greater role in these demanding situations.

Growth of smart cities puts requirements on corresponding underlying technologies, especially on communication networks. These networks must cope with stringent requirements on performance, reliability, scalability and security, which can change significantly based on dynamically fluctuating city needs. From this perspective, the static concept of traditional networking is ineffective and outdated. Only innovative software-based approaches such as software-defined networks (SDN) can cope with these dynamic conditions effectively.

SDN is a network concept of physical separation of forwarding and control layers on a networking device. While the forwarding layer is left on the device, the control layer is placed on a centralized element called the SDN controller. The controller provides management of the entire network and can be extended with custom made applications - for example to fit specifically smart city scenarios.

Functionality of SDN is based on the quality of its control application. Development of these applications is a demanding task, especially in complex and large scale networks such as smart cities. These networks are spread across vast areas and must remain fully functional, which eliminates the possibility of pre-deployment testing. SDN applications must therefore be developed and tested on dedicated, often only emulated networks. While this approach is quick and simple, it does not provide practical insight into the network operations. On the other hand, use of real networking devices only for development is expensive, time consuming and inflexible. The approach described in this paper combines the advantages of both approaches.

2   Related Work

SDN is widely accepted as a suitable technology for demanding smart city networks and a lot of research work has been done in this area [5–8,11,16,18,25,28]. Authors in [8] summarized the main advantages of SDN in smart cities: intelligence, scalability and integration; and limitations of traditional networks: users identification based on IP addresses, problematic security and ineffective mobility management. Further research proved that SDN is capable of handling real-time applications, including in problematic areas such as wireless sensor networks [7,11].

Activities towards real world deployment and practical verification are emerging. A large scale integration of SDN, cloud and IoT devices was tested on 8 million inhabitants Guadalajara smart city [5]. An emulated multi-tenant network corresponding to a virtual smart city of Poznan, integrated metro scale IoT network, cloud orchestrator and the SDN controller in [18].

Most of the research work in the area of SDN controllers comparison is focused either on security [2,27] or performance [21,22,29,30]. The most relevant comparison of Rosemary, Ryu, OpenDayLight and ONOS summarized basic features of these controllers, but the main focus of the work was on security comparison using the STRIDE (Spoof, Tamper, Repudiate, Information Disclose, DoS and Elevate) model [2]. Software reliability of 10 different versions of the ONOS controller was analyzed in [27]. Performance comparison work targeted mostly outdated or experimental controllers [21,22,30]. The most advanced open source controllers - OpenDaylight and ONOS - were compared only in [29], where authors performed tests in 5 different scenarios. In most of these scenarios, the ONOS controller achieved slightly higher performance.

The idea of creating an SDN-enabled switch from a single board computer by installation of a software switch is not new and was first researched in [13]. Authors installed Open vSwitch (2.0.90), which supported OpenFlow 1.0, into the first model of Raspberry Pi and tested its performance. Despite this software and hardware, the measured performance was comparable with 1 Gbps net-FPGA (Field Programmable Gate Arrays), which costs approximately 30 times as much as the Raspberry Pi. The following paper [12] analyzed a stack of four Raspberry Pi devices controlled by the ONOS controller. This work was followed by several other papers [1,3,4,15] implementing more recent versions of Open vSwitch and using newly emerging Raspberry Pi models. None of the mentioned work considered use of the created environment for practical development of SDN applications for scenarios such as smart cities. The closest work in this area is providing QoS in IoT networks on 4-port switches made from Raspberry Pi 3 devices [17].

3   Open Source SDN Controllers

The key component of a software-defined network is a controller, which manages all connected devices, provides networking functions, collects traffic statistics and has interfaces for remote control and advanced applications integration. SDN controllers can be classified into open source and commercial. This section describes features of the four most relevant open source controllers for smart city scenarios.

3.1   Ryu

Ryu [24] is one of the simpler SDN controllers and has only basic functions. It is written in Python and uses module structure for various networking functionalities. These modules are placed in separated Python files and their use has to be specified during each controller launch via the *ryu-manager* command. The controller has extensive documentation, which contains examples of code implementation and format of OpenFlow messages in JSON. The community also provides a freely accessible Ryu book [23], which explains several modules and describes process of developing custom applications.

The controller is ideal for anyone starting with general SDN development. It has a relatively shallow learning curve and the strict module separation allows safe and quick development of custom functionality. It is also suitable for quick establishment of network connectivity and for testing specific functions.

In the area of smart cities, the controller is missing advanced features and it is therefore not recommended for these deployments. Applications developed for this controller would have to be migrated into more suitable controllers before the real deployment.

3.2 Floodlight

Floodlight controller [9] provides a compromise between the simplest and most advanced controllers. It has clear documentation, straightforward installation, basic configuration, but also provides GUI and supports even advanced features including high availability. The controller is written in Java and uses similar modular architecture as more advanced controllers.

The controller provides a set of extensible Representational State Transfer (REST) APIs and the notification event system. The APIs can be used by external applications to get and set the state of the controller, and to allow modules to subscribe to events triggered by the controller using the Java Event Listener.

Floodlight supports basic features necessary for every smart city deployment - namely GUI and high availability. It does not have more advanced features such as security, support of legacy devices, or ability to dynamically adjust modules while running, but this fact is compensated by its relative simplicity and low hardware requirements. Unfortunately, the controller lacks in frequency of updates, which would address security and other issues.

The controller is ideal for new developers learning to work with SDN, but using a near-realistic environment. Developed applications can also be used in real scenarios. However, for development of more advanced commercial applications, which would be used in real smart city scenarios, use of more advanced controllers is recommended.

3.3 OpenDaylight

OpenDaylight [20] is the most widespread open source SDN controller and it is defined as "a modular open platform for customizing and automating networks of any size and scale". OpenDaylight is written in Java and it is being used as a base for many commercial controllers, which extend its functionality.

Use of OpenDaylight controller requires significantly more resources than previous controllers - in terms of hardware, knowledge, installation and initial configuration. Developing custom applications is even more demanding as the controller has a complex architecture. Moreover, the official documentation is not nearly as user friendly and complete as in previous controllers, and described features are often relevant only for older versions of the controller.

OpenDaylight is an ideal controller for real smart city scenarios. It can reliably monitor and control large scale networks with a high number of connected nodes. The controller is focused on security and reliability and allows configuration changes or installation of a new functionality without a need for restarting the controller. The controller is also in active development and new major versions are regularly released every 6 months with minor updates available as needed. The fact that it is widely used as a base for commercial controllers proves its suitability for real world use.

3.4 Open Networking Operating System

Open Networking Operating System (ONOS) [19] is a similar controller to Open-Daylight, but its main focus is on resiliency, scalability and deployment in production environments.

ONOS provides a slightly more detailed documentation than OpenDaylight, but it is still not so well structured and complete as in the case of Ryu or Floodlight. Use of the controller requires similar resources as in the case of OpenDaylight.

ONOS is the second analyzed controller, which is ideal for real smart city deployments. It is similar to OpenDaylight, but offers several unique features. It is slightly more oriented towards resiliency and it is the only controller which supports individual removal of functionalities even during the controller operations. Its functionalities can be also installed and activated without a need of restarting the controller. New versions are being released in approximately 3 month intervals with incremental updates available if needed.

3.5 Summary of Controllers Features

Table 1 summarizes supported features of each of the analyzed controllers. It includes only features which are officially supplied with the controller. Other features provided by independent developers and communities can be additionally installed.

4 Custom SDN-Enabled Switches

The second key component of SDN are forwarding devices, which are connected to the controller. They are being called switches, although they support all ISO/OSI layers and not only layer 2 forwarding. They can have the following forms:

1. Traditional switch with optional OpenFlow support (limited features)
2. Software switch (slow performance)
3. Specifically developed OpenFlow device (full features)

Hardware networking devices supporting the OpenFlow protocol are relatively expensive and their use only for development purposes might not be economically sustainable. Use of software devices is much more efficient method, but it does not allow practical verification and native connection of specific hardware IoT sensors and nodes. A solution using advantages of both approaches is to create an SDN-enabled device from a cheap generic single board computer with an integrated software switch.

Table 1. Features of compared SDN controllers

Functionality/Controller	RYU	FLT	ODL	ONOS
Basic functionality (L2, L3, STP, VLANs, ACL, FW)	✓	✓	✓	✓
GUI (S = secure)	-	✓	S	S
Dynamic routing (M = MPLS)	-	-	✓	M
Virtualization, OpenStack	-	✓	✓	✓
Fault tolerance	-	✓	✓	✓
Quality of Service (QoS)	✓	✓	✓	-
L2 link aggregation	✓	-	✓	-
Intent networking	-	-	✓	✓
Service Function Chaining	-	-	✓	✓
YANG Management	-	-	✓	✓
Virtual Private Network (VPN)	-	-	✓	-
Dynamic Host Configuration Protocol (DHCP)	-	✓	-	✓
Load-balancing	-	✓	-	✓
ISP support	-	-	-	✓
CAPWAC	-	-	✓	-
Performance monitoring	-	✓	-	✓
Machine-to-machine communication	-	-	✓	-
Legacy device support	-	-	✓	✓
Device drivers	-	-	✓	✓
Controllers cooperation	-	-	✓	-

4.1   Required Components

To create a custom SDN-enabled device from a single board computer, two components are required:

1. Software switch - the most widespread being Open vSwitch (OVS). It is an open source multilayer software switch written in C language. It is flexible, universal and supports various management protocols including OpenFlow. OVS can be deployed either as a software switch (for example in virtualized data center environments) or in a hardware device.
2. Hardware computer - can have form of a single board computer based on the ARM (Advanced RISC Machine) architecture. The most widespread type of this computer is Raspberry Pi. It has several models, which differs in size, performance and connectivity options as summarized in Table 2.

4.2   Installation

There are two methods of installation of Open vSwitch on the Raspberry devices default operating system - Raspbian:

Table 2. Comparison of Raspberry Pi models

Model	Release date	Price (USD)	CPU (GHz)	RAM (MB)	Ports	USB
B	02/2012	25	1×0.7	512	1FE	2
A+	11/2014	20	1×0.7	256	-	1
B+	07/2014	25	1×0.7	512	1FE	4
Zero	11/2015	5	1×0.7	512	-	0
2B	02/2015	35	4×0.9	1024	1FE	4
3B	02/2016	35	4×1.2	1024	1FE	4
3B+	03/2018	35	4×1.4	1024	1GbE	4
3A+	11/2018	25	4×1.4	512	-	1
4B	01/2019	35/45/55	4×1.5	1024/2048/4096	1GbE	4
4B	05/2020	75	4×1.5	8192	1GbE	4

1. Installation from Raspbian repository - it is the easiest method of installation as it requires only a single command: *sudo apt-get install openvswitch-switch.* The main disadvantage of this method is that the repository might not include the most recent version of OVS (at the time of writing this paper, only version 2.3, which supports only OpenFlow 1.3 and older, was available).
2. Installation with Debian packages - the most up to date source code can be downloaded from Github [10]. This version already supports OpenFlow 1.4. The following commands show the installation. The last component will also perform initial configuration of the switch and sets it to automatic startup upon the system's boot.

```
# 1. Download the source code
git clone https://github.com/openvswitch/ovs.git
# 2. Compilation (requires build-essential and fakeroot tools)
#    X = the number of threads, which the compilation can use
DEB_BUILD_OPTIONS='parallel=X' fakeroot debian/rules binary
# 3. Installation of Dynamic Kernel Module Support (DKMS)
sudo apt-get install dkms
# 4. Compiled kernel package installation
sudo dpkg -i openvswitch-datapath-dkms_2.5.2-1_all.deb
# 5. Installation of a package for generation of unique IDs
sudo apt-get install uuid-runtime
# 6. Order-dependent installation of user-space packages
sudo dpkg -i openvswitch-common_2.5.2-1_armhf.deb
sudo dpkg -i openvswitch-switch_2.5.2-1_armhf.deb
```

4.3 SDN Configuration

Installed and configured OVS can be integrated with SDN. This requires establishing communication between the controller and the device. Two modes of this communication are available:

1. Unsecured communication - the basic form of connection uses standard TCP and can be setup with the following commands.

```
# 1. Create a virtual switch with a name S-NAME
sudo ovs-vsctl add-br S-NAME
# 2. Configure IP and TCP port (default 6653) of the controller
sudo ovs-vsctl set-controller S-NAME tcp:IP:PORT
# 3. Create a virtual interface in the /etc/dhcpd.conf
interface S-NAME
static ip_address = IP/PREFIX
# 4. Apply the configuration (or reboot the device)
sudo /etc/init.d/dhcpcd reload
# 5. Assign the physical interface to the virtual switch
sudo ovs-vsctl add-port S-NAME INT-NAME
```

2. Secured communication - this form uses TLS for encryption and it requires use of private keys and certificates. The required files can be generated by the OpenFlow public key infrastructure management utility, which can be managed by the *ovs-pki* command. Files generated on the device then have to be transferred to the controller. The procedure of how to load these files will vary based on the controller.

```
# 1. Create certification authorities
sudo ovs-pki init
# 2. Create private key and certificate for the controller
sudo ovs-pki req+sign C-NAME controller
# 3. Create private key and certificate for the switch
sudo ovs-pki req+sign S-NAME switch
# 4. Set the required files for the TLS configuration
sudo ovs-vsctl set-ssl
/home/S-NAME-privkey.pem
/home/S-NAME-cert.pem
/home/controllerca/cacert.pem
# 5. Enable TLS
sudo ovs-vsctl set-controller S-NAME ssl:IP:PORT
```

5   Use Case Verification

Installation and configuration of switches and controllers were verified on a topology simulating a small smart city as shown in Fig. 1. Three Raspberry Pi 3B devices were used as SDN-enabled switches. The same platform cannot be used to host SDN controllers due to the different architecture (ARM vs x86-64) and low CPU performance. To make the use case environment as efficient as possible, a NUC8i7BEH mini-PC [14] was used for the SDN controller. Such a device is relatively cheap (around 800 USD depending on RAM and SSD configuration), has sufficient performance and low energy consumption. It is therefore ideal for this role.

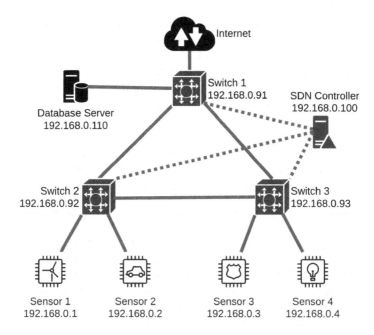

Fig. 1. Use case verification topology

5.1 Controllers Analysis

Four controllers from Sect. 3 were installed into separate virtual machines in order to test their performance - especially various RAM configurations. The main motivation was to determine the minimal amount for stable run of the controller. Results are presented in Table 3 together with approximate startup times and controllers support to launch modules.

Table 3. Controllers performance analysis

Controller	Minimum RAM	Startup time*	Support of modules launch
Ryu	256 MiB	<30 s	At start (manually)
Floodlight	256 MiB	<20 s	At start (configuration file)
OpenDaylight	4096 MiB	<20 s	Dynamic start at run
ONOS	4096 MiB	<20 s	Dynamic start/stop at run

* Measured time is just approximate as it is highly dependent on the network topology size, the controller performance and its current load.

Results show that Ryu and Floodlight have very low memory requirements and can run on practically any device. On the other hand, OpenDaylight and ONOS require a device with at least 4 GiB of RAM even in the smallest network topologies. Startup times do not vary significantly between the controllers and should not play a role in the controller selection process.

In environments where the network should correspond to real smart cities, only OpenDaylight and ONOS are recommended as they are the only ones allowing to start new modules while the controller is running (and in the case of ONOS also stop and remove them).

5.2   Deployment Findings

The verification revealed the need to use specific features, which are summarized below to make any future deployment testing more effective.

1. Port numbers - the OVS device uses integer labeling. A specific port can be found with the following command:
   ```
   sudo ovs-ofctl dump-ports DEVICE-NAME INTERFACE-NAME
   ```
2. Datapath ID - is an identification number, which the controller uses to recognize connected devices. By default, the device's MAC address of the interface leading to the controller is used. This address can be configured with the following command (sets the MAC address to 1):
   ```
   sudo ovs-vsctl set bridge DEVICE-NAME
      other-config:hwaddr=00:00:00:00:00:01
   ```
3. Time synchronization - encrypted communication and use of certificates require synchronized time between the controller and devices. In this case, it is necessary to ensure the time synchronization, for example by the Precision Time Protocol (PTP). A time difference can lead to the following error:
   ```
   SSLError: [SSL: SSLV3_ALERT_BAD_CERTIFICATE]
   ```

6   Conclusions

The paper described issues of developing SDN applications for smart city scenarios. In two main sections, the topic of creating a practical and cost-effective environment for these scenarios was researched. Presented information was verified and tested on an use case topology of a small scale smart city network.

The analysis of four open source controllers summarized their key features and included recommendations for the most effective utilization of each controller in smart city networks. Ryu controller was recommended only for learning purposes and quick verification of connectivity as its deployment in smart cities is not feasible due to lack of features. Floodlight controller was identified as a compromise between simple Ryu and more advanced controllers. While it can be used for development and testing of smart city applications, its usage in real networks was also not recommended.

OpenDaylight and ONOS were identified as similarly advanced open source controllers. They require significantly more effort to deploy and manage, but because of supported features, they can be safely used in real world smart city networks. The final choice from these two controllers depends on the target application. OpenDaylight supports more functionalities while ONOS offers slightly higher performance and is more flexible in terms of controlling running features.

The presented approach for creating an SDN-enabled switch from a Raspberry Pi device can be used to quickly create an environment suitable for practical development testing not limited only to smart city scenarios.

References

1. Alipio, M., Udarbe, G., Medina, N., Balba, M.: Demonstration of quality of service mechanism in an OpenFlow testbed, pp. 443–447 (2016). https://doi.org/10.1109/IMCEC.2016.7867251
2. Arbettu, R., Khondoker, R., Bayarou, K., Weber, F.: Security analysis of OpenDaylight, ONOS, Rosemary and Ryu SDN controllers, pp. 37–44 (2016). https://doi.org/10.1109/NETWKS.2016.7751150
3. Ariman, M., Seçinti, G., Erel, M., Canberk, B.: Software defined wireless network testbed using Raspberry Pi of switches with routing add-on. In: 2015 IEEE Conference on Network Function Virtualization and Software Defined Network (NFV-SDN), pp. 20–21 (2015)
4. Babayigit, B., Karakaya, S., Ulu, B.: An implementation of software defined network with Raspberry Pi. In: 2018 26th Signal Processing and Communications Applications Conference (SIU), pp. 1–4 (2018)
5. Cedillo-Elias, E., Orizaga Trejo, J.A., Larios-Rosillo, V., Arellano, L.: Smart Government infrastructure based in SDN networks: the case of Guadalajara metropolitan area, pp. 1–4 (2018). https://doi.org/10.1109/ISC2.2018.8656801
6. Chakrabarty, S., Engels, D.W.: A secure IoT architecture for Smart Cities. In: 2016 13th IEEE Annual Consumer Communications Networking Conference (CCNC), pp. 812–813 (2016)
7. Din, S., Rathore, M.M., Ahmad, A., Paul, A., Khan, M.: SDIoT: software defined internet of thing to analyze big data in Smart Cities. In: 2017 IEEE 42nd Conference on Local Computer Networks Workshops (LCN Workshops), pp. 175–182 (2017)
8. Fekih, A., Gaied, S., Yousef, H.: A comparative study of content-centric and software defined networks in smart cities. In: 2017 International Conference on Smart, Monitored and Controlled Cities (SM2C), pp. 147–151 (2017)
9. Floodlight community: Floodlight controller (2018). https://floodlight.atlassian.net/wiki/spaces/floodlightcontroller/overview. Accessed 25 Aug 2021
10. GitHub: Open vSwitch (2021). https://github.com/openvswitch/ovs. Accessed 25 Aug 2021
11. Hakiri, A., Gokhale, A.: Work-in-progress: towards real-time smart city communications using software defined wireless mesh networking. In: 2018 IEEE Real-Time Systems Symposium (RTSS), pp. 177–180 (2018)
12. Han, S., Lee, S.: Implementing SDN and network-hypervisor based programmable network using Pi stack switch. In: 2015 International Conference on Information and Communication Technology Convergence (ICTC), pp. 579–581 (2015)
13. Hyunmin, K., Jaebeom, K., Young-Bae, K.: Developing a cost-effective OpenFlow testbed for small-scale Software Defined Networking, pp. 758–761 (2014). https://doi.org/10.1109/ICACT.2014.6779064

14. Intel: Intel® NUC Kit NUC8i7BEH with 8th Generation Intel® Core™ Processors (2021). https://www.intel.com/content/www/us/en/products/sku/126140/intel-nuc-kit-nuc8i7beh/specifications.html. Accessed 25 Aug 2021
15. Jaramillo, A.C., Alcivar, R., Pesantez, J., Ponguillo, R.: Cost effective test-bed for comparison of SDN network and traditional network. In: 2018 IEEE 37th International Performance Computing and Communications Conference (IPCCC), pp. 1–2 (2018)
16. Munir, M.S., Abedin, S.F., Alam, M.G.R., Tran, N.H., Hong, C.S.: Intelligent service fulfillment for software defined networks in smart city. In: 2018 International Conference on Information Networking (ICOIN), pp. 516–521 (2018)
17. Nguyen, Q.H., Ha Do, N., Le, H.: Development of a QoS provisioning capable cost-effective SDN-based switch for IoT communication. In: 2018 International Conference on Advanced Technologies for Communications (ATC), pp. 220–225 (2018)
18. Ogrodowczyk, L., Belter, B., LeClerc, M.: IoT ecosystem over programmable SDN infrastructure for Smart City applications. In: 2016 Fifth European Workshop on Software-Defined Networks (EWSDN), pp. 49–51 (2016)
19. Open Networking Foundation: Open Network Operating System (2020). https://www.opennetworking.org/onos/. Accessed 25 Aug 2021
20. OpenDaylight Project: OpenDaylight (2018). https://www.opendaylight.org/. Accessed 25 Aug 2021
21. Priyadarsini, M., Bera, P., Bampal, R.: Performance analysis of software defined network controller architecture-a simulation based survey, pp. 1929–1935 (2017). https://doi.org/10.1109/WiSPNET.2017.8300097
22. Rastogi, A., Bais, A.: Comparative analysis of software defined networking (SDN) controllers—in terms of traffic handling capabilities, pp. 1–6 (2016). https://doi.org/10.1109/INMIC.2016.7840116
23. RYU project team: RYU SDN Framework (2016). https://osrg.github.io/ryu-book/en/Ryubook.pdf. Accessed 24 Aug 2021
24. Ryu SDN Framework Community: Component-based software defined networking framework (2017). https://ryu-sdn.org/. Accessed 24 Aug 2021
25. Saqib, M., Khan, F.Z., Ahmed, M., Mehmood, R.M.: A critical review on security approaches to software-defined wireless sensor networking. Int. J. Distrib. Sen. Netw. **15**(12) (2019). https://doi.org/10.1177/1550147719889906
26. Statista: Technology spending into smart city initiatives worldwide from 2018 to 2023 (2020). https://www.statista.com/statistics/884092/worldwide-spending-smart-city-initiatives/. Accessed 24 Aug 2021
27. Vizarreta, P., et al.: An empirical study of software reliability in SDN controllers, pp. 1–9 (2017). https://doi.org/10.23919/CNSM.2017.8256002
28. Wang, S., Gomez, K.M., Sithamparanathan, K., Zanna, P.: Software defined network security framework for IoT based smart home and city applications. In: 2019 13th International Conference on Signal Processing and Communication Systems (ICSPCS), pp. 1–8 (2019)
29. Yamei, F., Qing, L., Qi, H.: Research and comparative analysis of performance test on SDN controller, pp. 207–210 (2016). https://doi.org/10.1109/CCI.2016.7778909
30. Zhao, Y., Iannone, L., Riguidel, M.: On the performance of SDN controllers: a reality check. In: 2015 IEEE Conference on Network Function Virtualization and Software Defined Network (NFV-SDN), pp. 79–85 (2015)

Robotics

Branch-Manoeuvring Capable Pipe Cleaning Robot for Aquaponic Systems

Kristian Muri Knausgård[1]([✉]) [iD], Siv Lene Gangenes Skar[2] [iD],
Filippo Sanfilippo[1] [iD], Albert Buldenko[1], Henning Lindheim[1], Jakob Lunde[1],
Eligijus Sukarevicius[1], and Kjell G. Robbersmyr[1]

[1] Top Research Centre Mechatronics (TRCM), University of Agder (UiA),
4879 Grimstad, Norway
kristianmk@ieee.org
[2] Norwegian Institute of Bioeconomy Research, NIBIO Landvik,
4886 Grimstad, Norway

Abstract. Aquaponic systems are engineered ecosystems combining aquaculture and plant production. Nutrient rich water is continuously circulating through the system from aquaculture tanks. A biofilter with nitrifying bacteria breaks down fish metabolism ammonia into nitrite and nitrate, which plants and makes the aquaculture wastewater into valued organic fertiliser for the plants, containing essential macro and micro elements. At the same time, the plants are cleaning the water by absorbing ammonia from the fish tanks before it reaches dangerous levels for the aquatic animals. In principle, the only external input is energy, mainly in the form of light and heat, but fish food is also commonly provided. Growing fish food is potentially feasible in a closed loop system, hence aquaponic systems can possibly be an important source of proteins and other important nutrition when, for example, colonising other planets in the future. Fully autonomous aquaponic systems are currently not available. This work aims at minimising manual labour related to cleaning pipes for water transport. The cleaning process must be friendly to both plants and aquatic animals. Hence, in this work, pure mechanical cleaning is adopted. A novel belt-driven continuum robot capable of travelling through small/medium diameter pipes and manoeuvring branches and bends, is designed and tested. The robot is modular and can be extended with different cleaning modules through an interface providing CAN-bus network and electric power. The flexible continuum modules of the robot are characterised. Experimental results demonstrate that the robot is able to travel through pipes with diameters varying from 50 mm to 75 mm, and also capable of handling T-branches of up to 90°.

Keywords: Autonomous aquaponics · Urban agriculture · Pipe cleaning · Continuum robots · Space colonisation

This work is part of the project *Smart integrated multitrophic city food production systems -a water and energy saving approach for global urbanisation* (CITYFOOD), which has received funding from the Horizon 2020 - JPI-Urban Europe, Belmont Forum and National Funding Organisations, grant agreement No 726744.

F. Sanfilippo et al. (Eds.): INTAP 2021, CCIS 1616, pp. 107–118, 2022.
https://doi.org/10.1007/978-3-031-10525-8_9

| a) Plant section | b) Fish tanks | c) Bio filter | d) Pipes system |

Fig. 1. NIBIO Living Lab aquaponic system.

1   Introduction

The potential of integrated aqua-agriculture systems (IAAC) for large commercial and smaller urban applications to contribute to sustainable development is promising. IAAC, like aquaponic circular-food-production-systems, can help solving the Food-Water-Energy Nexus challenge [29]. In aquaponic systems (Fig. 1), fish excrement and fish feed remnants are composted and provides the plant crops with nitrogen, phosphorus and other essential nutrients. Elements that the plants absorb. This is a win-win situation since fishes do not tolerate some of these nutrients in large amount. As a result, the water can be reused and recycled for the fish production site, and a huge amount of water can be saved, coupled with an organic way of producing healthy and sustainable food.

When producing aquatic animals on-land together with plant production in water cultivation, floating trays are used to support the plants. Plant roots are hanging underneath these trays, directly into the fish wastewater. In this way plants are, partly through bacteria/biofilter, cleaning the water and removing ammonia from the fish tanks before it reaches dangerous levels for the aquatic animals. Water is continuously circulating through the system, and nutritious water is used as fertiliser for the plants. To give the optimal crop nutrition level, the water stream flowing from the aquaculture fish tanks can be controlled. In principle, the only external inputs are replacement of evaporated water and energy, mainly in the form of artificial grow light and heat, together with fish feed. Recirculated land-based aqua-agriculture food production systems may be possible in completely closed loops, hence aquaponic systems could be an important source to produce proteins and other important nutrition to people in urban areas or when for example colonising other planets in the future [2, 26].

Fully automatic and autonomous aquaponic systems are currently not available [32]. This work aims on removing some of the manual labour related to cleaning small and medium diameter pipes for water transport, to reduce man hours used on cleaning the system parts and therefore reducing costs. Due to the nutritious water circulating in an aquaponic system, microorganism such as algae and bacteria growth [7] leads to the need of regular cleaning of especially fish tanks and water transporting pipes. Cleaning has to be eco-friendly to both

Fig. 2. Digital Mock-Up (DMU) of modular pipe cleaning robot with cleaning module as payload.

plants and aquatic animals, hence the decision taken to use pure mechanical cleaning for this project. A novel belt-driven continuum robot capable of travelling through small and medium diameter pipes and manoeuvring branches and bends is designed and tested.

This paper is organised as follows. The need for developing a pipe-cleaning robot is motivated in Sect. 2. A brief review of related continuum-robot research is given in Sect. 3. In Sect. 4, the main contributions of this work are presented, including robot concept development and detailed design of key components. In Sect. 5, preliminary results are outlined. Finally, conclusions and future works are discussed in Sect. 6.

2   Robotic Pipe Cleaning and The Need of Novel Solutions

Robotic pipe cleaning is an active research area, and a number of different principles and solutions was found during the initial phase of the project. However, to include a larger number of principles and prior art in the literature study, it was decided to include pipe inspection robots and some other robots capable of locomoting through narrow passages in general. This section is therefore not limited to pipes and pipe cleaning.

The existing research and technology will be presented and briefly discussed in the light of aquaponic-specific requirements given for this pipe-cleaning task. Firstly the robot must be capable of travelling small and varying diameter pipes with T-branches and bends, secondly the robot must be produced in bio-compatible materials to avoid contamination of the closed-loop aquaponic system. As a final requirement, the robot must be modular, to be extendable for future tasks, for example swimming and cleaning the main fish farming tanks in addition to pipes.

Existing pipe travelling robots can be divided into traditional- and non-conventional locomotion variants [19]. Traditional designs include belt driven, wheel driven, and fluid propulsion with propellers or other thruster designs. The non-conventional category is a bag for everything else, such as clamp-and-pull-designs, smart balls, inchworm-mimicking designs [19], and other bio-inspired concepts like legged robots, peristaltic earth-worm-like robots [28] and snake robots as presented in Sect. 3 (Continuum Robots).

An example of traditional locomotion is the cylindrical elastic crawler mechanism for pipe inspection developed by Fukunaga and Nagase [17]. This amoeba-inspired tracked crawler design consists of a plastic screw inside a cylindrical outer shell, with multiple belts symmetrically positioned perpendicular to the shell, giving propulsion in longitudinal direction. The belts are directly driven by the screw, resulting in identical velocity on all belts, working similar to a locking differential in a car. In addition to the size-benefit of having only one motor, the synchronised movement is also expected to improve traction under slippery conditions. This robot is as a consequence not steerable, and therefore on its own not suitable for manoeuvring pipe branches. The original design from [17] is able to travel through pipes ranging from 30 mm to 100 mm in diameter.

Few existing pipe cleaning robots are found to be modular and steerable. One of the few existing modular and steerable designs is made for inspecting urban gas pipes, but is not suitable for pipe diameters below 160 mm [5]. The aquaponics pipe cleaning task is demanding when it comes to the small and varying diameter of pipes, T-branches and bends, and bio-compatibility. Due to the lack of available existing solutions viable for small diameter pipes, it was decided to develop a new, novel pipe cleaning robot concept. This concept is combining conventional crawling-belt propulsion modules with continuum robot elements for bending and steering. The pipe-crawling module design is strongly influenced by ground-breaking work of Fukunaga et al. on amoeba inspired propulsion [9,17,18], and inherits the ability to passively handle a sufficiently large span of pipe diameters. Continuum robots is a large research field on its own, and the next section will give an overview of important developments as seen by the authors.

3   Continuum Robots

The term continuum manipulator was first introduced in [3,4,21]. Continuum robots are continuously curving manipulators. They do not exhibit rigid linkages and distinct rotational joints. Instead, the structures bend continuously along their length due to elastic deformation and create motion by generating smooth curves, much like animal tentacles, or arms of an octopus, or tongues [14]. This notion is analogous to the continuous morphological manipulator described in [4], which is a snake/hyper-redundant robot idea pushed to its logical extreme. Namely, this group of robots has backbone architectures that have been pushed to their limits, with their number of joints tending to infinity and with their link lengths tending to zero [31].

Since the early 1960 s, several designs of continuum robots have been proposed. One of the first implementation was the *Tensor Arm*, which was presented in [1], based on the original *Orm* concept of Leifer and Scheinman [22]. The *Tensor Arm* foreshadowed several later designs by having a flexible backbone bent by remotely powered tendons. However, synchronization of the inputs to exploit the robot's shapes proved challenging until the 1990 s. Successively, experts like Shigeo Hirose [10] have made significant contributions to the field of continuum robotics.

How to actuate (bend and possibly extend/contract) the backbone is one of the most important design concerns of this type of robots. Actuation of continuum manipulators can either be intrinsic to the structure (e.g., pneumatic or hydraulic [8,13]) or extrinsic through mechanical transmission (e.g., tendons [16,20]).

The structure design of continuum robots can also be approximated by adopting a modular approach. In this perspective, our research group recently introduced *Serpens*, a low-cost, open-source and highly-compliant multi-purpose modular snake robot with series elastic actuator (SEA) [24,25]. Even though the proposed prototype was validated for achieving perception-driven obstacle-aided locomotion [23], it was not specifically designed to navigate pipes. Regarding robotic systems specifically designed for in-pipe inspection, recent works have proven the potential of multi-link robots to adapt to pipes with different diameters. For example, the design of an inspection robot with passive adaptation ability, which is used to inspect small size water supply pipeline was presented in [12,35].

However, to the best of our knowledge, it is still an open challenge to build continuum robots capable of being resilient to uncertain environments, such as travelling through small and medium diameter pipes and manoeuvring through different debris and branches.

4   Pipe Cleaning Robot Design and Development

For proof-of-concept, a robot consisting of two belt-driven propulsion modules, a continuum bending actuator module, and the main computer module was designed. A digital mock-up is shown in Fig. 2. This design is resulting from a systematic and top-down product development process, breaking down top level functions into more manageable pieces, potentially in an iterative fashion, and then identifying technologies and solutions for fulfilling each derived function. Similar top-down design methods can be applied for both product development and systems engineering in general [6,30]. A simplified breakdown structure for the top-level function of cleaning pipes in an operating aquaponic facility is shown in Table 1.

The continuum bending actuator module consists of two spine-style flexible actuators. One of the flexible actuators, resulting from the iterative design process is depicted in Fig. 3. This can be considered an adaption and improvement of the design shown in [34]. In the design process multiple other variants were explored. Including a spineless flexible rubber structure and a vertebra spine-like variant mimicking human body [36]. These first variants did not behave

Fig. 3. Continuum bending module for pipe cleaning robot, detail with metal tension spring backbone visible inside the 3D-printed outer spring structure. Monofilament nylon strings for actuation.

Fig. 4. Translation module assembly.

well from a control system point of view, as motions ended up to be unpredictable due to the flexibility in all axis, and difficulty in controlling tension for the vertebra variant. A different principle, in the form of a spring actuator completely 3D-printed including a centre compression spring was also explored. This version was also too flexible in the longitudinal axis, due to the compression spring. Therefor this was replaced with a tension spring. However, printing tension springs requires too fine tolerances for a viable spring to be printed, and the fifth and final version therefore ended up with a metal tension spring backbone inside the actuated 3D-printed outer spring structure. The last version is the only tested configuration that behaved sufficiently well to be controllable and therefore applicable for the pipe robot steering function.

A key technology for implementing the propulsion concept inspired by [9], is production of bio-compatible and durable belts. A food-grade silicone material was selected for this purpose, and custom molds designed and 3D printed for belt molding and splicing/gluing (Fig. 5). A housing and waterproofable motor compartment was designed for the propulsion module. The prototype is 3D printed in non-waterproof ABS plastic, but with the possibility of gaskets in essential locations for later stage underwater tests. A complete translation module is shown in Fig. 4.

Table 1. Top-down design approach with one top level function.

Top level function	Cleaning aquaponic water pipes				
Derived functions	Move robot	Navigate	Detect bends, junctions, and obstacles	Clean pipe	Avoid harming fish
Explored solutions	Fluid propulsion (propellers)	Acoustic	Force feedback	Passive brush	Passive safety
	Wheels	Odometry	Computer vision	Active brush	Active safety (Fish detecting AI [15])
	Belts	Inertial	Acoustic		
	Non-conventional	Pre-loaded map or SLAM			

The module interface is standardised at mechanical, electrical and logical level. This enables the robot to be quickly re-organised in different configurations and potentially with new modules. At the electrical and logic level, power is available for computers and actuators, while CAN-bus [11] is used for information flow. The module interface is shown in Fig. 6.

5 Testing and Verification

Propulsion and bending modules was tested and verified separately during development. The final assembly was then tested at system level, to verify if the requirements of crawling through both straight pipes and manoeuvring bends and T-junctions could be fulfilled.

The belt propulsion module design is shown to be viable, and able to provide necessary power and traction for pipe crawling by running the translation module

Fig. 5. Bio compatible silicone belts.

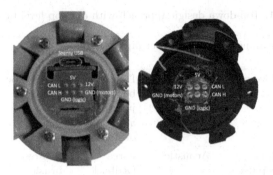

Fig. 6. Pipe cleaning robot electrical module interface.

assembly (Fig. 4) through a set of acrylic pipes. Friction between belts and the main propulsion screw is identified to be an issue with this design while running in air. Water immersion is expected to reduce this problem. Visible wear and tear on the belts was however more or less eliminated with lubrication, and food-grade lubrication is readily available if necessary. No further testing was performed on propulsion module-level.

Table 2. Monofilament nylon string pulled distance vs applied pulling force.

Step number	Force [N]	Measured pulled distance [mm]
0	0.00	0.0
1	1.01	1.0
2	2.02	2.0
3	3.03	2.9
4	4.04	4.0
5	5.05	5.3
6	6.06	8.0
7	7.07	12.0
8	8.08	19.0
9	9.09	21.0
10	10.10	23.5
11	11.11	25.2
12	12.12	28.0

Testing of the spring-based continuum actuators shows this design to be viable with improvements to durability. The nylon monofilament lines selected was susceptible to damage from sharp edges on the 3D-printed springs, an issue that still is not solved for long term use. It was also observed that the nylon lines

Fig. 7. Bending module with speckle pattern ready for Digital Image Correlation (DIC) measurements.

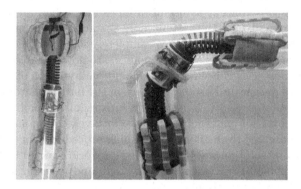

Fig. 8. Robot prototype manoeuvring through straight acrylic pipe and a 90° T-junction.

lost some tension over time, but not to such extent that it posed a problem, and this issue was not looked into further. The modules overall perform well, and are expected to be closed-loop controllable using similar methods as developed for the universal joint-spine robot in [33]. The relation between force applied to one of the nylon strings and the deflection of the actuator was measured using Digital Image Correlation (DIC) with Vic-3D from Correlated Solutions Inc. This measurement method requires a speckle pattern to be used on the object under test. A flexible actuator module with speckle pattern is shown in Fig. 7. A reference measurement was first taken during no-load conditions. Then tension was increased in twelve steps of 1.01 N using small weights of approximately 101 g each. Results from this initial load test are summarised in Table 2. For each of the steps, the deflection was also measured using the DIC equipment, such that the raw data from this test is force versus pulled string distance, and deflection since last measurement. Based on the measured deflections and applied force, a relation between bending angle α resulting from a given string pull force input f_n can be calculated.

System level testing was performed in a dry but otherwise representative environment, consisting of acrylic pipes for observability. In the first test, the robot is crawling through a straight acrylic tube as shown in Fig. 8. As a final check of the manoeuvring capability, the robot was manually steered through a 90° T-junction, as shown in the same figure. No control system was developed for the characterised bending actuator, so these tests are open-loop only.

6   Concluding Remarks

Producing fish and vegetables together, in a fully automatic aquaponic system, is potentially achievable. Fish and vegetables are valuable sources for proteins among other nutritious human diets, also if or when colonising distant planets [2]. Today we see this concept as useful in cities and urban areas where space comes at a premium. To get the system more sustainable, automation is necessary due to expensive man hours. Today, completely self-contained circular aqua-agriculture production systems e.g. aquaponics, are not available on the market [32]. One of the obstacles concerns cleaning and maintenance of the IAAC systems. Microbes like algae and bacteria thrives in the nutritious water circulating in these IAAC systems, and it is necessary with regular cleaning of fish tanks and water transportation pipes in particular. Both vegetation and aquatic creatures, must be protected throughout the cleaning procedure. For these reasons, a mechanical cleaning solution was proposed in this work. A novel belt-driven continuum robot capable of travelling through small and medium diameter pipes, was proposed. The robot is modular, and is ready to be expanded with for example various cleaning modules through a combined interface providing CAN-bus network and electric power. Preliminary experimental results were presented to illustrate the potential of the proposed design. The presented results include a one degree-of-freedom characterisation of the continuum actuator for steering, as a starting point for closed loop control system development. The robot is demonstrated capable of moving through pipes with a varying diameter from 50 mm to 75 mm, and is able to handle T-branches up to 90° as demonstrated in Fig. 8.

As future work, the design of reliable control algorithms for the proposed robot will be investigated. Also a battery-module including inductive charging is planned, to make the concept even more suitable for underwater use. Another important area for improvement is software modularity and interfaces. Usage of micro-ROS [27] and similar light-weight frameworks will be explored. The current low-level software architecture of the robot must be supplemented with functionality for route planning and guidance, navigation, and control (GNC). This would make it possible to extend the robot capabilities towards autonomous operations in sustainable, circular food production facilities.

References

1. Anderson, V.C.: Tensor arm manipulator design. Trans. ASME **67**, 1–12 (1967)
2. Brown, L., et al.: Aquatic invertebrate protein sources for long-duration space travel. Life Sci. Space Res. **28**, 1–10 (2021)
3. Chirikjian, G.S.: A continuum approach to hyper-redundant manipulator dynamics. In: Proceeding of the IEEE/RSJ International Conference on Intelligent Robots and Systems (IROS 1993), vol. 2, pp. 1059–1066 (1993)
4. Chirikjian, G.: Theory and applications of hyper-redundant robotic mechanisms. Ph. D thesis, Department of Applied Mechanics, California Institute of Technology (1992)
5. Choi, H., Ryew, S.: Robotic system with active steering capability for internal inspection of urban gas pipelines. Mechatronics **12**(5), 713–736 (2002)
6. Clark, J.O.: System of systems engineering and family of systems engineering from a standards, v-model, and dual-v model perspective. In: 2009 3rd Annual IEEE Systems Conference, pp. 381–387 (2009)
7. Eck, M., et al.: Exploring bacterial communities in aquaponic systems. Water **11**(2), 260 (2019)
8. Eder, M., Karl, M., Knoll, A., Riesner, S.: Continuum worm-like robotic mechanism with decentral control architecture. In: Proceeding of the IEEE International Conference on Automation Science and Engineering (CASE), pp. 866–871 (2014)
9. Fukunaga, F., Nagase, J.Y.: Cylindrical elastic crawler mechanism for pipe inspection inspired by amoeba locomotion. In: 2016 6th IEEE International Conference on Biomedical Robotics and Biomechatronics (BioRob), pp. 424–429 (2016)
10. Hirose, S.: Biologically inspired robots. Snake-Like Locomotors and Manipulators (1993)
11. ISO: Road vehicles - Controller area network (CAN) - Part 1: Data link layer and physical signalling. Standard, International Organization for Standardization, Geneva, CH (2015)
12. Kakogawa, A., Ma, S.: A multi-link in-pipe inspection robot composed of active and passive compliant joints. In: Proceeding of the IEEE/RSJ International Conference on Intelligent Robots and Systems (IROS), pp. 6472–6478 (2020)
13. Kang, R., Guo, Y., Chen, L., Branson, D.T., Dai, J.S.: Design of a pneumatic muscle based continuum robot with embedded tendons. IEEE/ASME Trans. Mechatron. **22**(2), 751–761 (2016)
14. Kier, W.M., Smith, K.K.: Tongues, tentacles and trunks: the biomechanics of movement in muscular-hydrostats. Zool. J. Linnean Soc. **83**(4), 307–324 (1985)
15. Knausgård, K.M., et al.: Temperate fish detection and classification: a deep learning based approach. Appl. Intell. **52**, 1–14 (2021). https://doi.org/10.1007/s10489-020-02154-9
16. Li, M., Kang, R., Geng, S., Guglielmino, E.: Design and control of a tendon-driven continuum robot. Trans. Inst. Measur. Control **40**(11), 3263–3272 (2018)
17. y. Nagase, J., Fukunaga, F.: Development of a novel crawler mechanism for pipe inspection. In: IECON 2016–42nd Annual Conference of the IEEE Industrial Electronics Society, pp. 5873–5878 (2016)
18. y. Nagase, J., Suzumori, K., Saga, N.: Cylindrical crawler unit based on worm rack mechanism for rescue robot. In: 2012 19th International Conference on Mechatronics and Machine Vision in Practice (M2VIP), pp. 218–221 (2012)
19. Ogai, H., Bhattacharya, B.: Pipe Inspection Robots for Structural Health and Condition Monitoring. ISCASE, vol. 89. Springer, New Delhi (2018). https://doi.org/10.1007/978-81-322-3751-8

20. Oliver-Butler, K., Till, J., Rucker, C.: Continuum robot stiffness under external loads and prescribed tendon displacements. IEEE Trans. Robotics **35**(2), 403–419 (2019)
21. Robinson, G., Davies, J.B.C.: Continuum robots-a state of the art. In: Proceeding of the IEEE International Conference on Robotics and Automation (ICRA), vol. 4, pp. 2849–2854. IEEE (1999)
22. Roth, B., Rastegar, J., Scheinman, V.: On the design of computer controlled manipulators. In: On Theory and Practice of Robots and Manipulators. ICMS, vol. 201, pp. 93–113. Springer, Vienna (1974). https://doi.org/10.1007/978-3-7091-2993-7_7
23. Sanfilippo, F., Azpiazu, J., Marafioti, G., Transeth, A.A., Stavdahl, Ø., Liljebäck, P.: Perception-driven obstacle-aided locomotion for snake robots: the state of the art, challenges and possibilities. Appl. Sci. **7**(4), 336 (2017)
24. Sanfilippo, F., Helgerud, E., Stadheim, P.A., Aronsen, S.L.: Serpens: a highly compliant low-cost ros-based snake robot with series elastic actuators, stereoscopic vision and a screw-less assembly mechanism. Appl. Sci. **9**(3), 396 (2019)
25. Sanfilippo, F., Helgerud, E., Stadheim, P.A., Aronsen, S.L.: Serpens, a low-cost snake robot with series elastic torque-controlled actuators and a screw-less assembly mechanism. In: Proceeding of the IEEE 5th International Conference on Control, Automation and Robotics (ICCAR), Beijing, China, pp. 133–139 (2019)
26. Skar, S., et al.: Urban agriculture as a keystone contribution towards securing sustainable and healthy development for cities in the future. Blue-Green Syst. **2**(1), 1–27 (2020)
27. Staschulat, J., Lange, R., Dasari, D.N.: Budget-based real-time executor for micro-ros. CoRR abs/2105.05590 (2021). https://arxiv.org/abs/2105.05590
28. Tanise, Y., Taniguchi, K., Yamazaki, S., Kamata, M., Yamada, Y., Nakamura, T.: Development of an air duct cleaning robot for housing based on peristaltic crawling motion. In: 2017 IEEE International Conference on Advanced Intelligent Mechatronics (AIM), pp. 1267–1272 (2017). https://doi.org/10.1109/AIM.2017.8014192
29. Thorarinsdottir, R.: Aquaponics guidelines. Technical report. University of Iceland (2015). https://doi.org/10.13140/RG.2.1.4975.6880
30. Ulrich, K.T.: Product Design and Development, 7th edn. McGraw-Hill Higher Education, New York (2019)
31. Walker, I.D., Choset, H., Chirikjian, G.S.: Snake-like and continuum robots. In: Siciliano, B., Khatib, O. (eds.) Springer Handbook of Robotics, pp. 481–498. Springer, Cham (2016). https://doi.org/10.1007/978-3-319-32552-1_20
32. Yanes, A.R., Martinez, P., Ahmad, R.: Towards automated aquaponics: a review on monitoring, IoT, and smart systems. J. Cleaner Prod. **263**, 121571 (2020)
33. Yeshmukhametov, A., Koganezawa, K., Seidakhmet, A., Yamamoto, Y.: Wire-tension feedback control for continuum manipulator to improve load manipulability feature. In: 2020 IEEE/ASME International Conference on Advanced Intelligent Mechatronics (AIM), pp. 460–465 (2020)
34. Yoon, H.S., Yi, B.J.: A 4-DOF flexible continuum robot using a spring backbone. In: 2009 International Conference on Mechatronics and Automation, pp. 1249–1254 (2009). https://doi.org/10.1109/ICMA.2009.5246612
35. Yuan, Z., Yuan, J., Ma, S.: Design and implementation of a pipeline inspection robot with camera image compensation. In: Proceeding of the IEEE/RSJ International Conference on Intelligent Robots and Systems (IROS), pp. 6398–6403 (2020)
36. Zhou, Y., Asplund, L., Tsai, C.C., Georgilas, I., Tourassis, V.: From the human spine to hyperredundant robots: The ermis mechanism. ISRN Robotics (2013)

A Multi-modal Auditory-Visual-Tactile e-Learning Framework

Filippo Sanfilippo[1]([✉]), Tomas Blažauskas[2], Martynas Girdžiūna[2], Airidas Janonis[2], Eligijus Kiudys[2], and Gionata Salvietti[3]

[1] University of Agder (UiA), Grimstad, Jon Lilletuns vei 9, 4879 Grimstad, Norway
`filippo.sanfilippo@uia.no`
[2] Kaunas University of Technology, Studentu str. 50, 51368 Kaunas, Lithuania
[3] University of Siena, 53100 Siena, Italy

Abstract. With a high number of countries closing learning institutions due to the restrictions in response to the COVID-19 pandemic, over 80% of the world's students was not attending school. As a response to this challenge, many educational institutions are increasing their efforts to utilise various educational technologies and provide remote learning opportunities. One of the biggest drawbacks of the majority of these existing solutions is limited support for hands-on laboratory work and practical experiences. This is especially relevant to science, technology, engineering, and mathematics (STEM) departments, which must continuously develop their laboratories and pedagogical tools to provide their students with effective study plans. To facilitate a safe, digital access to laboratories, a novel haptic-enabled framework for hands-on e-Learning is introduced in this work. The framework enables a fully-immersive tactile, auditory, and visual experience. This is achieved by combining virtual reality (VR) tools, with a novel wearable haptic device, which is designed by augmenting a low-cost commercial off-the-shelf (COTS) controller with vibrotactile actuators. For this purpose, the Unity game engine and the Valve Knuckles EV3 controllers are adopted. To demonstrate the potential of the proposed framework, a human subject study is presented. Results suggest that the proposed haptic-enabled framework improves the student engagement and illusion of presence.

Keywords: E-learning · VR · Haptics

1 Introduction

E-Learning courses and contents have been dramatically boosted by the Covid-19 pandemic although many universities and higher education institutions were already starting providing on-line contents. Most probably, all the experiences gained during the period of mobility restrictions will represent a step change in

This work is supported by the European Union through the Erasmus+ Program under Grant 2020-1-NO01-KA203-076540, project title "AugmentedWearEdu", https://augmentedwearedu.uia.no/.

the world of learning, with effects that may potentially rest also when the sanitary emergency will be finished. E-Learning brings several possibilities in terms of interaction for the students, enlargement of possible users and design of specific contents [3]. However, there are many aspects of a "in presence" lecturing that cannot be delivered "at home". Among all, physically attending a lecture is an experience involving all the human senses beside the auditory and visual channels typically used for e-Learning. As an example, several medicine classes are held in practical labs, where students not only listen to the teacher, but can also physically interact with dummy reproduction of organs or ex-vivo experiments. In these examples, the sense of touch plays a fundamental role and is at the bases of the whole learning process. Several other examples can be identified in other disciplines with a similar predominant role of tactile experiences. This is especially true for science, technology, engineering, and mathematics (STEM) education. In the last two decades, the field of Haptics has introduced a possible digitisation of the sense of touch [9]. Starting from complex and cumbersome desktop haptic interfaces, in the last few years many research groups have proposed wearable haptic interfaces, which enable a multi contact interaction with virtual or remote objects [16,19]. This opens up to the opportunity of a new generation of e-Learning contents that includes tactile experience. The main roadblock toward the spreading of this technology is the current cost or complexity of the proposed solutions, that must also include a reliable hand tracking system [4]. To achieve a possible large spread of solutions allowing the developments of tactile contents, it is necessary to develop systems with a reduced cost by using commercially available off-the-shelf (COTS) components.

In this perspective, our research group earlier presented a low-cost platform for a fully immersive haptic, audio, and visual experience to allow researchers for including haptic capabilities in a more adaptable, interactive, and transparent manner to their applications [23]. This is made feasible by a pair of haptic gloves that uses vibrotactile actuators and open-source electronics. A Leap Motion sensor [28] tracks hand and finger motions, while a head-mounted 3D display provides intuitive visual stereoscopic feedback. Using a headset with a built-in microphone provides an extra bidirectional audio channel. The Unity cross-platform 3D environment [29] is chosen to properly integrate these aspects. Successively, a new prototyping iteration was implemented aiming at improving the robustness of the proposed framework [24]. To demonstrate the potential of the redesigned framework, two human subject studies in virtual reality (VR) were considered. Results proved that the proposed haptic-enabled framework provides good rendering performance and a realistic illusion of presence. These studies demonstrate that it is possible to fabricate immersive tools that are economical, customisable, and fast to fabricate.

In line with these same designing guidelines, this paper introduces an innovative haptic-enabled architecture for hands-on e-Learning. This is accomplished by integrating VR tools with a novel wearable haptic device created by adding vibrating actuators to a COTS controller. To achieve this, the Unity gaming engine [29] and the Valve Knuckles EV3 [30] controllers are employed. A human subject study is conducted to show the possibilities of the proposed framework.

The paper is organised as it follows. A review of the related research work is given in Sect. 2. In Sect. 3, the proposed framework architecture is presented. The considered human subject study is described in Sect. 4. In Sect. 5, simulation results are outlined. Finally, conclusions and future works are discussed in Sect. 6.

2   Related Research Work

The majority of haptic devices that are currently available on the market cannot be considered fully wearable. Interfaces like those of the *sigma.x*, *omega.x* and *delta.x* series (Force Dimension) or the *Phantom Premium* (3D Systems, Inc.) are usually accurate, and able to provide a wide range of forces. In literature, they are called "grounded" interfaces, as their base is fixed to the ground [19]. The pursuit of more wearable haptic technologies lead researchers to the development and design of exoskeletons, a type of haptic interface which is grounded to the body [13]. Even if exoskeletons can be considered wearable haptic systems, they are often quite heavy and cumbersome, reducing their applicability and effectiveness. This is why, in recent years, research efforts in the field of haptics focused on the development of a new generation of wearable haptic interfaces. Haptic thimbles [14,21], haptic rings [15,18], and haptic armbands [2], have been successfully applied in different applications, ranging from teleoperation and VR or augmented reality (AR) to human guidance. The key feature enabling wearability of such devices is that the grounding of the system is coincident with the point of application of the stimulus. As a consequence, the haptic interface is only capable of providing cutaneous cues that indent and stretch the skin [7], and not kinaesthetic cues, i.e., stimuli that act on skeleton, muscles, and joints [10]. Wearable haptic interfaces, providing only cutaneous stimuli, do not exhibit any unstable behaviour due, for instance, to the presence of communication delay in the closed haptic loop [17]. As a consequence, the haptic loop with wearable tactile interfaces results to be intrinsically stable.

Regarding the application of haptics for e-Learning, a multimodal haptic simulator was presented in [8]. The haptic simulator helps student comprehension of complex ideas (e.g., physics topics) and has the potential to supplement or replace traditional laboratory training with an interactive interface that improves motivation, retention, and intellectual stimulation. A review and early pilot test of haptic tooling to support design practice, within a distance learning curriculum was recently presented in [5]. However, most of these works still adopt relatively expensive haptic devices that are yet not available to the vast majority of students. Hence, our research group recently presented a novel perspective for a sustainable integration of virtual and augmented reality (VR/AR) with haptic wearables into STEM education to achieve multi-sensory learning [22]. To the best of our knowledge, a low-cost and open framework for a fully-immersive haptic, audio and visual experience is still missing for e-Learning laboratory skills and student engagement.

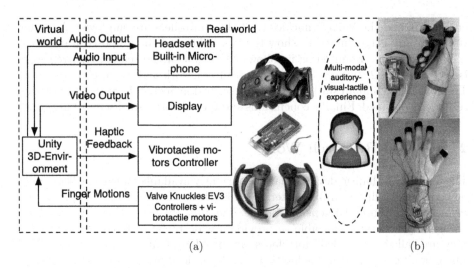

(a)   (b)

Fig. 1. The proposed framework: (a) the framework architecture, (b) the Valve Knuckles EV3 controllers augmented with vibrotactile motors.

3   Framework Architecture

The proposed framework architecture, encompassing software, hardware, and multi-modal rendering strategies, is described in this section.

3.1   Software Architecture

The framework architecture is depicted in Fig. 1-a. In the following, the key elements of the system are presented.

The primary components of the proposed framework are the COTS Valve Knuckles EV3 controllers. These controllers combine complex sensor inputs to track hand position, finger position, motion, and pressure to determine user intent. We have equipped these controllers with precise shaft-less vibrotactile motors embedded on the outer shell, as shown in Fig. 1-b. Distinctive haptic feedback patterns may be communicated to the user via these motors, accurately simulating virtual finger collisions. The controller for the motors is implemented on an *Arduino Mega* board [1]. The *Arduino* is an open-source electronics prototyping platform that uses flexible, user-friendly hardware and software. A variety of libraries are provided by *Arduino* to make programming the microcontroller easier. As a result, software development and, by extension, hardware development are simplified, cutting down on the time it takes to prototype a system. The choice of adopting an *Arduino* board makes the motor controller simple to maintain and allows for the addition of new features in the future. The Valve Knuckles EV3 controllers, which are augmented with vibrotactile motors, represent a significant advance when compared to similar COTS devices since they are easy to obtain by just using simple additional components, and they are

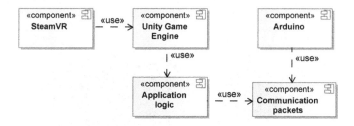

Fig. 2. The components diagram of the proposed system.

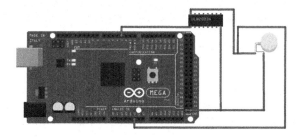

Fig. 3. The control circuit for one vibrotactile actuator.

resilient and low-cost. The *SteamVR* application programming interface (API) is then used for the integration with the visualisation environment.

The *Unity* cross-platform 3D-environment [29] is chosen as middleware for the integration of all framework components. The HTC VIVE Pro VR headset is adopted to provide the user with realistic visual feedback (a common computer monitor can also be used to lower the cost) and with a bidirectional audio channel to enhance the user experience.

Based on the Unified Modeling Language (UML), a component diagram is shown in Fig. 2.

3.2 Hardware Implementation

One of the embedded vibrotactile actuators and the corresponding control circuit is shown in Fig. 3. The motors are driven by a ULN2003 stepper motor driver module. Three 1,5 V AA alkaline batteries are used to power the circuit for a total of 4,5 V.

3.3 Multi-modal Rendering Strategies

For the collision detection, finger ray casting is adopted [11], as shown in Fig. 4. For the i-th finger, a ray is casted, from the finger tip, in the forward direction, against all object colliders in the scene when within a length t, which is the distance tolerance. This makes it possible to calculate d_i, which is the distance value of the representative i-th contact.

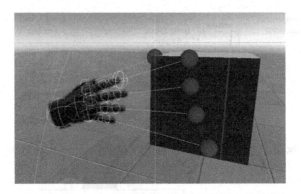

Fig. 4. The implementation of finger ray casting for collision detection.

Based on [24], the tactile rendering system employs a force calculation paradigm in which the amount of force exhibited is related to the penetration depth or separation distance [12]. The i-th force F_i is given by:

$$F_i = k(t - d_i) - k_v v_i, \tag{1}$$

where v_i is the i-th approaching velocity. While, k and k_v are stiffness and damping constants, respectively. The force is then rendered by using a Pulse Width Modulation (PWM) signal, where the duty cycle of the i-th vibration actuator, D_i, is proportional to the force to be rendered normalised between the specific actuator range, as shown by the following equation:

$$D_i = \frac{\alpha F_i - F_{min}}{F_{max} - F_{min}}, \tag{2}$$

where α is a scaling factor. While, F_{min} and F_{max} are the minimum and maximum renderisable forces, respectively.

Furthermore, auditory rendering is obtained by generating a sound feedback with a pitch that is proportional to the force to be rendered normalised between the specific frequency range. The i-th pitch frequency, f_i, is calculated according to the following equation:

$$f_i = f_{min} \frac{\beta(F_i - F_{min})(f_{max} - f_{min})}{F_{max} - F_{min}}, \tag{3}$$

where β is a scaling factor. While, f_{min} and f_{max} are the minimum and maximum renderisable frequencies, respectively.

Similarly, visual rendering is achieved for the collision points by generating a colour feedback with a wavelength that is proportional to the force to be rendered normalised between the specific wavelength range (visible spectrum). The i-th wavelength, λ_i, is calculated according to the following equation:

$$\lambda_i = f_{min} \frac{\gamma(F_i - F_{min})(\lambda_{max} - \lambda_{min})}{F_{max} - F_{min}}, \tag{4}$$

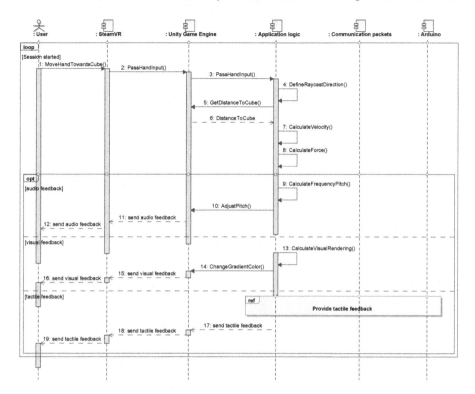

Fig. 5. A sequence diagram depicting the interaction with a virtual object.

where γ is a scaling factor. While, λ_{min} and λ_{max} are the minimum and maximum renderisable wavelengths, respectively.

The multi-modal rendering is achieved by simultaneously combining auditory, visual and tactile rendering together, as depicted in the sequence diagram shown in Fig. 5. When a finger moves towards an interactive virtual object (i.e., within the distance tolerance), the SteamVR component detects this movement and sends the corresponding input signal towards the main application logic component. When this signal is received, the application logic component defines the direction in which the ray cast should be drawn. According to the interactive collision, the Unity Game Engine provides the distance between the finger tip and the colliding virtual object on the corresponding casted ray. After successfully determining the distance of collision, the application logic component estimates the velocity at which the finger is moved towards the colliding object. Consequently, the force is calculated and the corresponding tactile feedback is rendered. To render the audio feedback, the application logic calculates the required frequency level, then adjusts the pitch according to the calculation and renders the audio feedback through the virtual reality headset. Visual feedback is rendered in a similar manner - the system calculates the required wavelength, which is then displayed to the user.

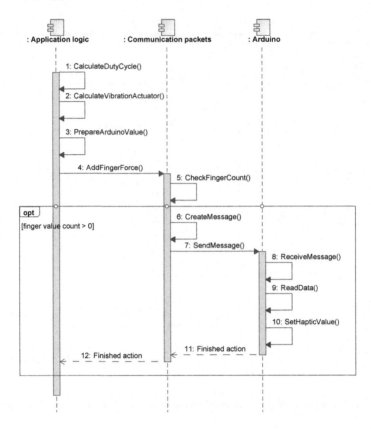

Fig. 6. A sequence diagram of the procedure for rendering of tactile feedback.

As shown in the detailed sequence diagram of Fig. 6, to render tactile feedback, the application logic component calculates the duty cycles to be sent to the motors. These values are prepared to be sent to the Arduino through communication packets component. When the values are sent through communication packets, the system checks how many fingers should receive the feedback. If there are no fingers in contact, the system does not send any signals to the Arduino. Otherwise, if there is at least one finger in contact, the communication packets component creates a message, which is then sent to the Arduino. The Arduino simply actuated the received values to the motors. Consequently, the tactile feedback is perceived by the user.

4   Human Subject Study

To demonstrate the potential of the proposed framework, a case study is presented. In particular, an educational approach to the recycling and disposal of domestic waste is considered. The aim is to increase both academic and public awareness for this process. Recycling includes a series of activities consisting of collecting any kind of recyclable materials that would otherwise be considered waste, sorting and processing them into raw materials. In the considered case study, we focus on the sorting procedure. As shown in Fig. 7, a simulated scene is created including two main interactive stations: 1) a counter where unsorted waste items are laid up; 2) a sorting counter with allocated/marked collecting regions for paper, glass and plastic materials. The underlying idea is that the user would learn how to properly sort out home waste by participating into a multi-modal auditory-visual-tactile experience. A game-based learning and gamification approach is adopted to promote user engagement and motivation. The goal is to sort all waste materials in the shortest time possible. From a grasping perspective, waste objects composed of shape primitives like cuboids, cylinders and spheres are considered. This is relevant because it makes it possible to assess grasping procedures that could potentially be generalised to different types of objects [25–27].

A number of human subjects is selected for this study. In particular, 10 persons participate to this preliminary study. Each participant is first asked to familiarise with the simulation environment and successively is asked to perform the following test sequences: a) sorting materials by using only visual feedback; b) sorting materials by using auditory and visual feedback; c) sorting materials by using a combined auditory, visual and tactile feedback.

For each test, a timer is started when the user first touch any of the waste objects. The timer is stopped when all the waste objects are properly sorted. Moreover, a user survey is conducted immediately after the test session. In particular, the Igroup Presence Questionnaire (IPQ) [20] is considered. The IPQ test is a scale for measuring the sense of presence experienced in a virtual environment (VE). The current version of the IPQ has three sub-scales and one additional general item not belonging to a sub-scale. The three sub-scales, which can be regarded as independent factors, include: a) spatial presence - the sense of being physically present in the VE; b) involvement - measuring the attention devoted to the VE and the involvement experienced; c) experienced realism - measuring the subjective experience of realism in the VE. The additional general item assesses the "sense of being there", and has high loadings on all three factors, with an especially strong loading on spatial presence.

5   Simulations and Experimental Results

Figure 7 depicts the scene of one human subject sorting materials by using a combined auditory, visual and tactile feedback. A video depicting the entire experiment is available on-line at https://youtu.be/izcScavUGbo. The IPQ survey results for the multi-modal rendered experience are shown in Fig. 8. These results are very promising regarding spatial presence and realism, while involvement is relatively well perceived on average.

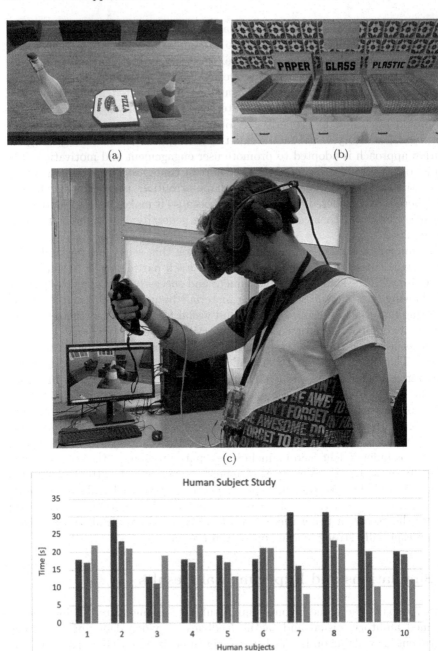

Fig. 7. The results of the conducted human subject study: (a) the objects to be sorted, (b) the sorting baskets, (c) a human subject sorting objects by using the combined auditory, visual and tactile feedback, (d) the time distribution for the selected test sequences.

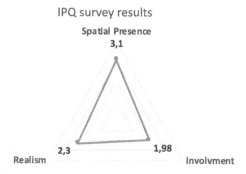

Fig. 8. The IPQ survey results for the multi-modal rendered experience.

6   Conclusions and Future Work

This study introduced an innovative haptic-enabled framework for hands-on e-Learning to offer safe, digital access to laboratories. A fully immersive tactile, auditory, and visual experience is achievable thanks to the proposed framework. This is accomplished by merging virtual reality (VR) tools with a novel wearable haptic device created by supplementing a low-cost commercial off-the-shelf (COTS) controller with vibrotactile actuators. The Unity gaming engine and the Valve Knuckles EV3 controllers are used for this purpose. A human subject research was performed to validate the developed framework. The considered haptic-enabled framework boosts student engagement and the perception of spatial presence, realism and involvement.

As future work, the proposed framework could be used to develop teaching modules and to test the concept with engineering students in an experimental setting [6]. This would make it possible to evaluate the applicability of the concept on a larger and practical scale.

Acknowledgements. The authors gratefully acknowledge the contribution of Romas Šleževičius.

References

1. Arduino (2021). http://arduino.cc/. Accessed 6 May 2021
2. Baldi, T.L., Scheggi, S., Aggravi, M., Prattichizzo, D.: Haptic guidance in dynamic environments using optimal reciprocal collision avoidance. IEEE Robot. Autom. Lett. **3**(1), 265–272 (2017)
3. Beetham, H., Sharpe, R.: Rethinking Pedagogy for a Digital Age: Designing and Delivering e-Learning. Routledge (2007)
4. Bortone, I., et al.: Wearable haptics and immersive virtual reality rehabilitation training in children with neuromotor impairments. IEEE Trans. Neural Syst. Rehabil. Eng. **26**(7), 1469–1478 (2018)

5. Bowers, L.J.: Touching creativity; a review and early pilot test of haptic tooling to support design practice, within a distance learning curriculum. Open Learn. J. Open Dist. e-Learn. **34**(1), 6–18 (2019)
6. Callaghan, M., Harkin, J., Scibilia, G., Sanfilippo, F., McCusker, K., Wilson, S.: Experiential based learning in 3D virtual worlds: visualization and data integration in second life. In: Proceedings of the Remote Engineering and Virtual Instrumentation (REV 2008) Conference (2008)
7. Chinello, F., Malvezzi, M., Pacchierotti, C., Prattichizzo, D.: Design and development of a 3RRS wearable fingertip cutaneous device. In: Proceedings of the IEEE International Conference on Advanced Intelligent Mechatronics (AIM), pp. 293–298 (2015)
8. Hamza-Lup, F.G., Adams, M.: Feel the pressure: e-learning systems with haptic feedback. In: Proceedings of the Symposium on Haptic Interfaces for Virtual Environment and Teleoperator Systems, pp. 445–450. IEEE (2008)
9. Hannaford, B., Okamura, A.M.: Haptics. In: Siciliano, B., Khatib, O. (eds.) Springer Handbook of Robotics, pp. 1063–1084. Springer, Cham (2016). https://doi.org/10.1007/978-3-319-32552-1_42
10. Hayward, V., Astley, O.R., Cruz-Hernandez, M., Grant, D., Robles-De-La-Torre, G.: Haptic interfaces and devices. Sens. Rev. (2004)
11. Höll, M., Oberweger, M., Arth, C., Lepetit, V.: Efficient physics-based implementation for realistic hand-object interaction in virtual reality. In: Proceedings of the IEEE Conference on Virtual Reality and 3D User Interfaces (VR), pp. 175–182 (2018)
12. Kim, Y.J., Otaduy, M.A., Lin, M.C., Manocha, D.: Six-degree-of-freedom haptic rendering using incremental and localized computations. Presence Teleoper. Virtual Environ. **12**(3), 277–295 (2003)
13. Leonardis, D., et al.: An EMG-controlled robotic hand exoskeleton for bilateral rehabilitation. IEEE Trans. Haptics **8**(2), 140–151 (2015)
14. Leonardis, D., Solazzi, M., Bortone, I., Frisoli, A.: A wearable fingertip haptic device with 3 DoF asymmetric 3-RSR kinematics. In: Proceedings of the IEEE World Haptics Conference (WHC), pp. 388–393 (2015)
15. Maisto, M., Pacchierotti, C., Chinello, F., Salvietti, G., De Luca, A., Prattichizzo, D.: Evaluation of wearable haptic systems for the fingers in augmented reality applications. IEEE Trans. Haptics **10**(4), 511–522 (2017)
16. Meli, L., Salvietti, G., Gioioso, G., Malvezzi, M., Prattichizzo, D.: Multi-contact bilateral telemanipulation using wearable haptics. In: Proceedings of IEEE/RSJ International Conference on Intelligent Robots and Systems, Deajeon, Korea, pp. 1431–1436 (2016)
17. Pacchierotti, C., Meli, L., Chinello, F., Malvezzi, M., Prattichizzo, D.: Cutaneous haptic feedback to ensure the stability of robotic teleoperation systems. Int. J. Robot. Res. **34**(14), 1773–1787 (2015)
18. Pacchierotti, C., Salvietti, G., Hussain, I., Meli, L., Prattichizzo, D.: The hRing: a wearable haptic device to avoid occlusions in hand tracking. In: Proceedings of the IEEE Haptics Symposium (HAPTICS), pp. 134–139 (2016)
19. Pacchierotti, C., Sinclair, S., Solazzi, M., Frisoli, A., Hayward, V., Prattichizzo, D.: Wearable haptic systems for the fingertip and the hand: taxonomy, review, and perspectives. IEEE Trans. Haptics **10**(4), 580–600 (2017)
20. Panahi, S.M., Fathi, A.A., Azad, F.P., Montazer, G.A.: Reliability and validity of Igroup presence questionnaire (IPQ) (2009)

21. Prattichizzo, D., Chinello, F., Pacchierotti, C., Malvezzi, M.: Towards wearability in fingertip haptics: a 3-DoF wearable device for cutaneous force feedback. IEEE Trans. Haptics **6**(4), 506–516 (2013)
22. Sanfilippo, F., et al.: A perspective review on integrating VR/AR with haptics into stem education for multi-sensory learning. Robotics **11**(2), 41 (2022)
23. Sanfilippo, F., Hatledal, L.I., Pettersen, K.: A fully-immersive hapto-audio-visual framework for remote touch. In: Proceedings of the 11th IEEE International Conference on Innovations in Information Technology (IIT 2015), Dubai, United Arab Emirates (2015)
24. Sanfilippo, F., Pacchierotti, C.: A low-cost multi-modal auditory-visual-tactile framework for remote touch. In: Proceedings of the 3rd International Conference on Information and Computer Technologies (ICICT), pp. 213–218. IEEE (2020)
25. Sanfilippo, F., Salvietti, G., Zhang, H., Hildre, H.P., Prattichizzo, D.: Efficient modular grasping: an iterative approach. In: Proceedings of the 4th IEEE RAS & EMBS International Conference on Biomedical Robotics and Biomechatronics (BioRob), pp. 1281–1286 (2012)
26. Sanfilippo, F., Zhang, H., Pettersen, K.Y.: The new architecture of ModGrasp for mind-controlled low-cost sensorised modular hands. In: Proceedings of the IEEE International Conference on Industrial Technology (ICIT), pp. 524–529 (2015)
27. Sanfilippo, F., Zhang, H., Pettersen, K.Y., Salvietti, G., Prattichizzo, D.: Mod-Grasp: an open-source rapid-prototyping framework for designing low-cost sensorised modular hands. In: Proceedings of the 5th IEEE RAS/EMBS International Conference on Biomedical Robotics and Biomechatronics, pp. 951–957 (2014)
28. Leap Motion Controller (2021). https://www.ultraleap.com/product/leap-motion-controller/. Accessed 6 May 2021
29. Unity Real-Time Development Platform (2021). https://unity.com/. Accessed 6 May 2021
30. Valve Knuckles EV3 (2021). https://www.valvesoftware.com/en/index/controllers. Accessed 6 May 2021

A Perspective on Intervention Approaches for Children with Autism Spectrum Disorder

Saishashank Balaji[1]([✉]) [iD], Filippo Sanfilippo[1] [iD], Martin W. Gerdes[1] [iD], and Domenico Prattichizzo[2]

[1] University of Agder (UiA), Grimstad, Norway
saishashank.balaji@uia.no
[2] University of Siena, 53100 Siena, Italy

Abstract. Autism spectrum disorder (ASD) is a neurodevelopmental disorder that affects 1 in 160 children globally. Autism is characterised by abnormalities in communication, social interactions and behavioural challenges. Sensory processing difficulties affect two-thirds of children with autism. This causes anxiety and typically leads to repetitive behaviour referred to as problem behaviours. Stereotypy and aggression are some of the most frequently observed problem behaviours. Behavioural interventions may help manage symptoms and develop cognitive skills, thus promoting a child's participation in social activities. A growing body of literature suggests that technological advancements in mobile health (mHealth) systems can be utilised to develop various intervention modalities. The central goal is to help children with ASD adapt to their surroundings by managing their problem behaviours. A promising possibility is to monitor physiological signals with wearable sensors to anticipate the onset of problem behaviour and provide intervention through wearable assistive devices. This paper presents a new perspective to manage problem behaviour and concept guidelines for a potential mHealth framework to deliver vibrotactile and thermal stimuli for sensory-based intervention.

Keywords: Autism · Wearable devices · Vibrotactile intervention · Thermal intervention · mHealth

1 Introduction

ASD is one of the most common childhood disorders (1 in 160) [17]. Autism is a neurodevelopmental disorder that results in significant psychological, emotional, and behavioural difficulties. Autism is further considered a pervasive disorder that can cause sensory-perceptual anomalies, such as a hypersensitivity to contact with other people. Children with ASD may also have sensory integration

This research is funded by the Top Research Centre Mechatronics (TRCM), University of Agder (UiA), Norway.

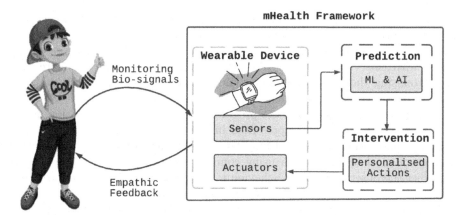

Fig. 1. The underlying idea of adopting wearable technology based interventions.

difficulties in processing the visual, auditory, kinaesthetic, tactile, and olfactory sensory systems [9]. Sensory integration is the ability to process and regulate sensory stimuli in the surroundings for adaptive functioning. A behavioural meltdown may occur due to overwhelming external stimuli, resulting in a temporary loss of control. This loss of control usually leads to repetitive, distracting behaviour known as stereotypical motor movements or stereotypy [8]; often expressed verbally (e.g., shouting, crying), and/or physically (e.g., kicking, lashing out, biting). Physical aggression is particularly debilitating as it may happen suddenly and without notice, and sometimes even long after the effect of the stressor (external stimuli). This unpredictability makes it difficult for them to participate in social activities. These individuals have a hard time understanding the social world and interpreting it, thus resulting in diminished situational awareness. This acts as a barrier to accessing essential services such as access to healthcare, education, and employment for individuals on the spectrum. Management of these challenges requires some form of behavioural therapy. Therapeutics for autism incorporate a multidisciplinary approach. It includes a combination of psychological and behavioural therapies, speech therapy, educational interventions, and psycho-pharmacological treatments.

This work focuses on non-pharmacological treatments (evidence-based therapies) using wearable and mobile technologies that support optimal outcomes for children with autism. Wearable technology-based interventions provide a promising option for improving sensory integration in autistic children. The underlying concept is as shown in Fig. 1. The use of assistive technologies in ASD can be helpful in communication, cognition, and sensory integration. These technologies can be used in various ways, such as an agent for motivating pedagogy or an alternative and augmentative communication device that mainly focuses on social interactions for autistics.

In a review by Wali & Sanfilippo [54], the prevailing implementation, as well as the research challenges of supporting technology for individuals with autism, were presented; the study highlights both therapeutic and technological solutions. In another study by Sanfilippo et al. [43,44]; a prototype of an integrated wearable health sensor monitoring system with haptic feedback was presented. In line with this viewpoint, our research team presented a novel architecture for customising the surrounding environment using information from multiple sensory channels to increase situational awareness [45].

The objective for this work is to provide fresh insights on intervention mechanisms based on the evidence presented in the existing literature on wearable assistive devices and digital health systems. A promising approach is monitoring physiological biosignal data using commercially available wearable devices to predict the onset of problem behaviours using machine learning and artificial intelligence models, to provide proactive behavioural intervention.

We seek to stimulate global efforts towards the development of wearable intervention technologies for delivering empathic vibrotactile and thermal stimulus as intervention. This paper is not a systematic literature review but rather a new perspective on the current state of the art in wearable behavioural intervention technologies and our research aspirations for a proactive intervention framework. This work includes a background on psycho-physiological aspects of problem behaviours (aggression, stereotypy, anxiety). We focus on wearable and mobile technologies for intervention, particularly devices that augment the sensory functions of kinaesthetic and tactile somatosensory systems. This paper is divided into two sections; the first section looks into the existing intervention approaches; the second section presents the guidelines for the mHealth framework.

2   Intervention Approaches

2.1   Visual and Auditory

Virtual reality (VR) has evolved as a tool for cognitive behavioural therapy in treating psychological disorders, and it has been proven to help individuals cope with stressful situations. Studies [12,14] show vision-based techniques have been used for cognitive training. Visual learning methods are suitable for children with autism, as they may aid in sensorimotor integration and social communication. The benefits of employing VR therapies, such as computer-based representations of reality, to help people with autism practice demanding social interactions in a less anxiety-inducing environment are noteworthy. With advancements in VR glasses and mounted displays, point of view scenarios are utilised to develop safe environments for visual intervention. Studies [42,52] have found improved results in sensorimotor accuracy when virtual reality and kinaesthetic methods are used together with no short term negative consequences. Researchers that have used VR together with cognitive behavioural therapy have shown improvements across social communication, overcoming fear, and reduced stereotypes [11,32].

Studies have demonstrated that individuals with autism prefer auditory stimuli to other types of stimuli. A study by Hall L et al. [24] has reported improvements in children's behaviour related to sensory processing and visual-motor delays. They reported that when an auditory stimulus is presented, children interact for a more extended period. Gee et al. [20] has demonstrated that negative and stimming behaviours have decreased in a participant who was provided sound-based intervention combined with occupational therapy for 10 weeks. This intervention technique has shown that it reduces auditory sensory over-responsivity.

2.2 Vibrotactile Prompting

Tactile (sense of touch) processing difficulties are among the most frequently reported sensory complaints in ASD patients. Tactile empathy is the ability to perceive and interpret emotions through touch. The perception of touch is essential for laying the foundation for social connection, communication, and other behaviours. Touch and pressure generating modalities are widely used as non-pharmacological therapeutics in the management of sensory hypersensitivity in autistics. Deep pressure stimulation (DPS) is a form of tactile stimulation that uses weighted blankets, vests, and vibrotactile devices to help reduce anxiety in children with hyposensitivity. DPS is regarded as an evidence-based intervention mechanism for reducing stress and creating a sense of relaxation. In empirical studies [19,41] the effects of DPS on problem behaviour are fairly promising. A study by Bestbier et al. [7] has shown that deep pressure touch has immediate effects on the somatosensory response and benefits the population.

Prompting is a method of making individuals execute desired behaviour by providing additional stimuli (prompts). Taylor et al. [49] in their study used vibrational prompts at routine intervals to maximize verbal initiations in children. Anglesea et al. [4] in their research employed vibrational prompts at variable intervals (range of 10–30 s) to prompt participants to bite at each vibration, resulting in reduced rapid eating for all three participants. Safety skills were targeted in research by Taylor et al. [48], to successfully train three participants to request support while they were lost in a group environment. Anson et al. [5] compared their prompting approach to verbal and gestural prompting and found that the discreet, non-intrusive tactile prompt was as effective as the more conventional prompting method.

Studies [23,29,36] have shown that apparent haptic movements could potentially help with social communication. This motion is observed when two stimuli are presented in alternation at a relatively high frequency. Apparent haptic motions create the illusion of continuous motion, this resembles the sense of touch and could be a relaxing stimulus based on the individual's sensitivity to touch [27].

2.3   Wearable Assistive Devices and Applications

With constant improvements in technological and functional design applications of wearable assistive devices, real-time feedback of physiological biomarkers is becoming a reality. This has enabled affect sensing for monitoring emotional state and valence of individuals. Various studies have utilised wearable sensors and smartwatches for affect/emotion recognition [3,22,28,47,56]. A feasibility study by Di Palma et al. [13] identified a correlation between children's physiological responses and their engagement in cognitive tasks using wearable devices. Another research by Daniel et al. [10] has reported the support among children for the usability of wearable devices for affect sensing. Studies have also explored the possibility of using wearable devices for emotional regulation and behavioural interventions. Torrado et al. [50] in their study, reported that children recovered from mild episodes of stress when using smartwatches for interaction. Voss et al. [53] utilised Google glass as a digital intervention to improve socialisation in children with autism. They reported a 4.58-point average gain on the Vineland Adaptive Behaviour Scale involving 71 participants.

While researchers have examined the various uses of wearable devices, only a few have looked at the possibility of employing wearable assistive devices for behavioural and cognitive intervention. Table 1, presents a few of the selected wearable sensors and solutions that are available commercially. This table does not review all the devices/prototypes in this area of research. However, it focuses more on wearable sensors and assistive devices for behavioural intervention and highlights the design gaps. Current intervention approaches are reactive, i.e., behavioural intervention is only delivered when physical symptoms of problem behaviour are observed. We believe there is little evidence of existing work that combines prediction science and intervention mechanisms for problem behaviours.

3   Guidelines for mHealth Framework

3.1   Motivation

Intervention approaches within the gamut of behavioural and developmental interventions have become the primary method for treating children with autism to promote social, adaptive and behavioural functioning. There are many potential uses of affect sensing for individuals with autism. These include developing physiological and behavioural measures to classify emotional states associated with preclinical symptoms of problem behaviour and monitoring physiological and behavioural reactions to tailor treatment to an individual. Evidence [30,35,46] suggests that problem behaviour causes physiological changes preceding the onset of an emotional meltdown episode. Researchers have shown success in utilising the changes in the physiological state by monitoring biomarkers to predict emotional state [22,26,28,37]. Even though wearable and digital intervention solutions need more evidence-based research and clinical trials, studies have shown such solutions are accepted amongst most individuals.

Table 1. Overview of selected wearable sensors and intervention solutions for autism.

Ref.	Form factor	Biomarkers	Intervention method	Type	Description
Emotibit [1]	Wristband	HR, HRV, EDA, RR, SpO2	–	Open-source prototype	Real-time monitoring of biomarkers
E4 [15]	Wristband	HR, HRV, EDA, ST	–	Commercial device (research grade)	A research-grade wearable device for real-time physiological data acquisition
PulseOn OHR [40]	Wristband	HR, HRV, Acc	–	Commercial device	Arrhythmia detection and analysis software
ViSi Mobile System [16]	Wristband with electrodes	HR, HRV, ST	–	Commercial device (clinical use)	Monitoring vitals for arrhythmia and fall detection
AIO Sleeve [2]	Arm sleeve	HR, HRV	–	Commercial device	Monitors stress in real-time
My Feel Sensor [34]	Wristband	HR, EDA, ST	In-app alert	Commercial device	Monitors biomarkers throughout the day and learns to recognize your emotional patterns
Awake Labs [6]	Smartwatch	HR, EDA	In-app alert	Commercial Device	Stress and anxiety management
Moodmetric Smart Ring [33]	Ring	EDA	In-app alert	Commercial device	It helps to identify personal stress triggers
Pip [39]	Fingertip Sensor	EDA	In-app alert	Commercial device	Looks for variations in EDA using fingertip sensors to monitor stress
Touchpoints Europe [51]	Wristband	–	Alternating tactile simulation	Commercial device	Produces bi-lateral vibrations for calming
Feelzing [18]	Ear patch	–	Neuro-stimulation	Commercial device	Uses a proprietary waveform to stimulate the nervous system

We suggest integrating promising intervention approaches with affect/emotion prediction, thus enabling proactive just-in-time solutions for managing problem behaviours. We present concept guidelines in this section for a potential mHealth framework. This is divided into two parts. First, it predicts the probability of a meltdown antecedent to the occurrence of the episode. Based on this prediction, the second part delivers vibrotactile and thermal feedback as stimuli for managing problem behaviours.

3.2 Background

Sensory and attention abnormalities of stimuli are an important area of study in autism psychophysiology. It is known that abnormalities in physiological arousal underlie behavioural issues in autism; Several researchers have hypothesized that abnormalities in physiological reactivity may underlie emotional meltdowns and arousals [25]. Arousal is a type of emotion that occurs when the autonomic nervous system (ANS) is actuated. The ANS is a division of the nervous system that controls many organic functions, and is critical to maintaining homeostasis; it is a dynamic equilibrium in which continuous changes occur, yet relatively uniform conditions prevail. Among various neurophysiological traits in autism, the role of ANS has gained more attention. The ANS is one of the body's major systems for maintaining homeostasis. It has two main branches: the sympathetic nervous system (SNS) and the parasympathetic nervous system (PNS). The SNS and PNS work together to maintain homeostasis. Individuals are sympathetic-predominant when facing a challenge or stress, whereas parasympathetic activity increases during resting and relaxation. The SNS is dominant in emergencies; it triggers pervasive and dramatic changes in the body, including heart rate (HR) acceleration, elevated electrodermal activity (EDA), bronchiole dilation, dopamine release and blood pressure enhancement. The PNS contains cholinergic fibres that produce enzymes that control the contractility of smooth muscles and slow HR.

3.3   Sensing Using Viable Biomarkers

As mentioned above, when the system is regulated by sympathetic behaviour, the HR is increased. When the parasympathetic system actively modulates sympathetic activity, the HR declines towards a resting rate. Another physiological signal for assessing an individual's anxiety is assessing electrodermal function. An increase in EDA reflects SNS activation, while stable and decreasing EDA indicates PNS activity. Psychophysiological functionality may also be assessed by heart rate variability (HRV), which is a marker of autonomic cardiovascular activity and is generally accepted as a good predictor of the relationship between psychological and physiological processes. Preliminary research suggests that cardiovascular reactivity can be used to characterise anxiety [21]. As sympathetic and parasympathetic modulations control heart functions, HRV is widely accepted and convenient in measuring the signal of autonomic function; its variability can reflect autonomic activity.

HRV measures the beat-to-beat variation in heart rate and reflects the interplay between sympathetic and parasympathetic systems. Greater variability in the beat-to-beat rhythm indicates a balance between sympathetic and parasympathetic contributions and is predictive of an overall good mental health. HRV has also been used to investigate physiological differences in generalised anxiety disorder, social anxiety, post-traumatic stress disorder, and panic disorder. While EDA is not a direct measure of sensory processing, it is a reliable measure of SNS arousal. Activation of the SNS results in the secretion of sweat, which conducts electricity, from eccrine sweat glands throughout the body. Eccrine sweat glands are only innervated by the sympathetic branch of the ANS, so increases in EDA can be, in part, attributed to increases in physiological arousal.

3.4   A Novel Approach to Proactive Intervention

Based on the hypothesis that physiological changes occur prior to the occurrence of a problem behaviour, this work lays the groundwork for developing user-centered proactive wearable intervention device. This device will potentially reduce the impact of problem behaviour by predicting an emotional meltdown prior to its occurrence in individuals with ASD. We present guidelines for the design of an mHealth framework for delivering empathic vibrotactile and thermal feedback. As previously stated, the framework is divided into two parts: (a) Prediction of problem behaviour by monitoring biomarkers using wearable sensors; (b) Intervention by delivering vibrotactile and thermal feedbacks as a stimulus using a novel wearable assistive device.

Prediction: The ability to assess changes in emotional valence during a meltdown without interfering with everyday routines could revolutionize behavioural healthcare. Researchers [30,35] have studied the practicality of employing wearable biosensors for affect sensing in autistics using data obtained from participants in artificial environments that replicate problem behaviour. While these findings are intriguing, previous research in this field has relied on contrived experimental conditions and activities. In our work, we plan to conduct data collection in naturalistic environments, such as in schools and therapy sessions. This information will be used to develop prediction models based on time-series analysis of the biomarker data (HR, HRV, EDA). The prediction model will subsequently be used to detect problem behaviours using biomarkers in real-time using a wearable open source commercial-off-the-shelf sensor. We plan on exploring two methods for developing the prediction algorithm: statistical and ML. Statistical methods such as Bayesian non-parametric clustering and the non-homogeneous Poisson point process are a few methods we plan to implement. Machine learning models such as support vector machines, linear regression classifiers, principal component analysis and other pattern recognition algorithms will be utilized. Furthermore, deep neural networks for time series classification is also a possible approach to consider for developing a prediction algorithm.

Intervention: Existing research provides some evidence that the tactile prompt can increase verbal initiation in children [5]. However, a hypothesis that has not yet been tested is whether incorporating a tactile stimulus as an intervention mechanism regulates problem behaviours. Based on this hypothesis, the ultimate goal of our research is to develop a real-time automated prediction system that parents, teachers, and caregivers may utilize to deliver just-in-time intervention for children with autism. C-Tactile (CT) afferents are low-threshold mechanoreceptive units found in lower densities in glabrous human hand skin [55]. The axons of CT afferents are unmyelinated, which means there is no insulation around them, as found in the wrists and arms. Taking advantage of this, we will design, test and validate a novel wearable device that stimulates CT afferent neurons to provide empathic tactile feedback. Mechanical/haptic actuators such as eccentric rotating mass, linear resonant actuators, and piezoelectric vibrational actuators are possible elements that could generate vibrotactile motions that mimic the sense of touch and pressure. Studies [31,38] have shown that the proprioception of warmth can also help reduce stress and anxiety in the general population, but this hypothesis has not yet been studied in individuals with autism. Thus, combining thermal stimuli with tactile stimuli might be beneficial to render thermo-tactile feedback as a stimulus. We can achieve this by integrating flexible thermal pads and other Peltier elements in the design of the wearable device prototype.

4   Conclusion and Future Work

Many studies looked into the relationship between physiology and psychology in autism, only a few have looked into predicting problem behaviours using biomarkers in autistics. There is lack of sufficient literature integrating prediction and intervention mechanisms for problem behaviour in children with autism. This paper presents a guideline for the use of physiological biomarkers to predict problem behaviours and render empathic vibrotactile feedback for behavioural intervention. This research project relies on the hypothesis that stimulating the somatosensory system reduces stress/anxiety, thereby reducing the effect of problem behaviours. Noticeably, there is overwhelming evidence suggesting that physiological signals can be used as indicators of certain psychological states of humans. Biomarkers such as heart rate, heart rate variability, and electrodermal activity have been shown in studies to be extremely useful in detecting aggression, emotional distress, and stereotypy. There is a need to develop solutions targeting problem behavior in individuals to improve sensory integration for situational awareness in autistics. It will be interesting to combine prediction algorithms and intervention approaches, especially focusing on the use of wearable devices for empathic auditory-visual-tactile feedback and contribute towards the design, implementation and validation of a proactive framework.

References

1. EmotiBit: wearable biometric sensing for any project. https://www.emotibit.com/. Accessed 30 Apr 2021
2. (2021). https://komodotec.com/stress/. Accessed 30 Aug 2021
3. Amiri, A.M., et al.: WearSense: detecting autism stereotypic behaviors through smartwatches. In: Healthcare, vol. 5, p. 11. Multidisciplinary Digital Publishing Institute (2017)
4. Anglesea, M.M., Hoch, H., Taylor, B.A.: Reducing rapid eating in teenagers with autism: use of a pager prompt. J. Appl. Behav. Anal. **41**(1), 107–111 (2008)
5. Anson, H.M., Todd, J.T., Cassaretto, K.J.: Replacing overt verbal and gestural prompts with unobtrusive covert tactile prompting for students with autism. Behav. Res. Methods **40**(4), 1106–1110 (2008)
6. (2021). https://www.awakelabs.com/. Accessed 30 Aug 2021
7. Bestbier, L., Williams, T.I.: The immediate effects of deep pressure on young people with autism and severe intellectual difficulties: demonstrating individual differences. Occup. Ther. Int. **2017** (2017)
8. Bodfish, J.W., Symons, F.J., Parker, D.E., Lewis, M.H.: Varieties of repetitive behavior in autism: comparisons to mental retardation. J. Autism Dev. Disord. **30**(3), 237–243 (2000)

9. Bogdashina, O.: Sensory Perceptual Issues in Autism and Asperger Syndrome: Different Sensory Experiences-different Perceptual Worlds. Jessica Kingsley Publishers, London (2016)

10. Daniels, J., et al.: Feasibility testing of a wearable behavioral aid for social learning in children with autism. Appl. Clin. Inform. 9(01), 129–140 (2018)

11. De Luca, R., et al.: Innovative use of virtual reality in autism spectrum disorder: a case-study. Appl. Neuropsychol. Child 10(1), 90–100 (2021)

12. Dechsling, A., et al.: Virtual reality and naturalistic developmental behavioral interventions for children with autism spectrum disorder. Res. Dev. Disabil. 111, 103885 (2021)

13. Di Palma, S., et al.: Monitoring of autonomic response to sociocognitive tasks during treatment in children with autism spectrum disorders by wearable technologies: a feasibility study. Comput. Biol. Med. 85, 143–152 (2017)

14. Didehbani, N., Allen, T., Kandalaft, M., Krawczyk, D., Chapman, S.: Virtual reality social cognition training for children with high functioning autism. Comput. Hum. Behav. 62, 703–711 (2016)

15. (2021). https://www.empatica.com/research/e4/. Accessed 30 Aug 2021

16. (2021). https://www.soterawireless.com/. Accessed 30 Aug 2021

17. Elsabbagh, M., et al.: Global prevalence of autism and other pervasive developmental disorders. Autism Res. 5(3), 160–179 (2012)

18. (2021). https://feelzing.com/. Accessed 30 Aug 2021

19. Fertel-Daly, D., Bedell, G., Hinojosa, J.: Effects of a weighted vest on attention to task and self-stimulatory behaviors in preschoolers with pervasive developmental disorders. Am. J. Occup. Ther. 55(6), 629–640 (2001)

20. Gee, B.M., Thompson, K., St John, H.: Efficacy of a sound-based intervention with a child with an autism spectrum disorder and auditory sensory over-responsivity. Occup. Ther. Int. 21(1), 12–20 (2014)

21. Goodwin, M.S., et al.: Cardiovascular arousal in individuals with autism. Focus Autism Other Dev. Disabil. 21(2), 100–123 (2006)

22. Goodwin, M.S., Mazefsky, C.A., Ioannidis, S., Erdogmus, D., Siegel, M.: Predicting aggression to others in youth with autism using a wearable biosensor. Autism Res. 12(8), 1286–1296 (2019)

23. Hachisu, T., Suzuki, K.: Smart bracelets to represent directions of social touch with tactile apparent motion. In: Kajimoto, H., Lee, D., Kim, S.-Y., Konyo, M., Kyung, K.-U. (eds.) AsiaHaptics 2018. LNEE, vol. 535, pp. 155–157. Springer, Singapore (2019). https://doi.org/10.1007/978-981-13-3194-7_34

24. Hall, L., Case-Smith, J.: The effect of sound-based intervention on children with sensory processing disorders and visual-motor delays. Am. J. Occup. Ther. 61(2), 209–215 (2007)

25. Hutt, C., Hutt, S., Lee, D., Ounsted, C.: Arousal and childhood autism. Nature 204(4961), 908–909 (1964)

26. Imbiriba, T., Cumpanasoiu, D.C., Heathers, J., Ioannidis, S., Erdoğmuş, D., Goodwin, M.S.: Biosensor prediction of aggression in youth with autism using kernel-based methods. In: Proceedings of the 13th ACM International Conference on PErvasive Technologies Related to Assistive Environments, pp. 1–6 (2020)

27. Kuehn, E.: Research into our sense of touch leads to new treatments for autism. Luettu 15, 2018 (2016)

28. Kushki, A., Puli, A.S.R.: Anxiety detection in different user states. US Patent App. 16/276,208, 20 August 2020

29. Lacôte, I., Pacchierotti, C., Babel, M., Marchal, M., Gueorguiev, D.: Generating apparent haptic motion for assistive devices. In: WHC 2021-IEEE World Haptics Conference (2021)
30. Lydon, S., Healy, O., Dwyer, M.: An examination of heart rate during challenging behavior in autism spectrum disorder. J. Dev. Phys. Disabil. **25**(1), 149–170 (2013)
31. Maeda, T., Kurahashi, T.: TherModule: wearable and modular thermal feedback system based on a wireless platform. In: Proceedings of the 10th Augmented Human International Conference 2019, pp. 1–8 (2019)
32. Maskey, M., Lowry, J., Rodgers, J., McConachie, H., Parr, J.R.: Reducing specific phobia/fear in young people with autism spectrum disorders (ASDs) through a virtual reality environment intervention. PLoS One **9**(7), e100374 (2014)
33. (2021). https://moodmetric.com/. Accessed 30 Aug 2021
34. (2021). https://www.myfeel.co/. Accessed 30 Aug 2021
35. Nuske, H.J., et al.: Heart rate increase predicts challenging behavior episodes in preschoolers with autism. Stress **22**(3), 303–311 (2019)
36. Ogrinc, M., Farkhatdinov, I., Walker, R., Burdet, E.: Sensory integration of apparent motion speed and vibration magnitude. IEEE Trans. Haptics **11**(3), 455–463 (2017)
37. Özdenizci, O., et al.: Time-series prediction of proximal aggression onset in minimally-verbal youth with autism spectrum disorder using physiological biosignals. In: Proceedings of the 40th Annual International Conference of the IEEE Engineering in Medicine and Biology Society (EMBC), pp. 5745–5748. IEEE (2018)
38. Peiris, R.L., Feng, Y.L., Chan, L., Minamizawa, K.: ThermalBracelet: exploring thermal haptic feedback around the wrist. In: Proceedings of the 2019 CHI Conference on Human Factors in Computing Systems, pp. 1–11 (2019)
39. (2021). https://thepip.com/en-eu/. Accessed 30 Aug 2021
40. (2021). https://pulseon.com/tech/ohr-tracker. Accessed 30 Aug 2021
41. Quigley, S.P., Peterson, L., Frieder, J.E., Peterson, S.: Effects of a weighted vest on problem behaviors during functional analyses in children with pervasive developmental disorders. Res. Autism Spectr. Disord. **5**(1), 529–538 (2011)
42. Sahin, N.T., Keshav, N.U., Salisbury, J.P., Vahabzadeh, A.: Safety and lack of negative effects of wearable augmented-reality social communication aid for children and adults with autism. J. Clin. Med. **7**(8), 188 (2018)
43. Sanfilippo, F., Pacchierotti, C.: A wearable haptic system for the health monitoring of elderly people in smart cities. Int. J. Online Eng. **14**(08), 1–15 (2018)
44. Sanfilippo, F., Pettersen, K.Y.: A sensor fusion wearable health-monitoring system with haptic feedback. In: Proceedings of the 11th International conference on innovations in information technology (IIT), pp. 262–266. IEEE (2015)
45. Sanfilippo, F., Raja, K.: A multi-sensor system for enhancing situational awareness and stress management for people with ASD in the workplace and in everyday life. In: Proceedings of the 52nd Hawaii International Conference on System Sciences (HICSS 2019), Maui, Hawaii, United States of America, pp. 4079–4086 (2019)
46. Sarabadani, S., Schudlo, L.C., Samadani, A.A., Kushski, A.: Physiological detection of affective states in children with autism spectrum disorder. IEEE Trans. Affect. Comput. **11**(4), 588–600 (2018)
47. Simm, W., et al.: Anxiety and autism: towards personalized digital health. In: Proceedings of the 2016 CHI Conference on Human Factors in Computing Systems, pp. 1270–1281 (2016)
48. Taylor, B.A., Hughes, C.E., Richard, E., Hoch, H., Coello, A.R.: Teaching teenagers with autism to seek assistance when lost. J. Appl. Behav. Anal. **37**(1), 79–82 (2004)

49. Taylor, B.A., Levin, L.: Teaching a student with autism to make verbal initiations: effects of a tactile prompt. J. Appl. Behav. Anal. **31**(4), 651–654 (1998)
50. Torrado, J.C., Gomez, J., Montoro, G.: Emotional self-regulation of individuals with autism spectrum disorders: smartwatches for monitoring and interaction. Sensors **17**(6), 1359 (2017)
51. (2021). https://www.touchpointeurope.com/pages/autism. Accessed 30 Aug 2021
52. Valori, I., Bayramova, R., McKenna-Plumley, P.E., Farroni, T.: Sensorimotor research utilising immersive virtual reality: a pilot study with children and adults with autism spectrum disorders. Brain Sci. **10**(5), 259 (2020)
53. Voss, C., et al.: Effect of wearable digital intervention for improving socialization in children with autism spectrum disorder: a randomized clinical trial. JAMA Pediatr. **173**(5), 446–454 (2019)
54. Wali, L.J., Sanfilippo, F.: A review of the state-of-the-art of assistive technology for people with ASD in the workplace and in everyday life. In: Pappas, I.O., Mikalef, P., Dwivedi, Y.K., Jaccheri, L., Krogstie, J., Mäntymäki, M. (eds.) I3E 2019. LNCS, vol. 11701, pp. 520–532. Springer, Cham (2019). https://doi.org/10.1007/978-3-030-29374-1_42
55. Watkins, R.H., Dione, M., Ackerley, R., Backlund Wasling, H., Wessberg, J., Löken, L.S.: Evidence for sparse C-tactile afferent innervation of glabrous human hand skin. J. Neurophysiol. **125**(1), 232–237 (2021)
56. Williams, M.A., Roseway, A., O'dowd, C., Czerwinski, M., Morris, M.R.: SWARM: an actuated wearable for mediating affect. In: Proceedings of the Ninth International Conference on Tangible, Embedded, and Embodied Interaction, pp. 293–300 (2015)

A Framework for Hazard Identification of a Collaborative Plug&Produce System

Bassam Massouh[✉], Sudha Ramasamy, Bo Svensson, and Fredrik Danielsson

Department of Engineering Science, University West, Trollhättan, Sweden
bassam.massouh@hv.se

Abstract. Plug&Produce systems accept reconfiguration and have the attribute of physical and logical flexibility. To implement the Plug&Produce system in a manufacturing plant, there is a need to assure that the system is safe. The process of risk assessment provides information that is used to implement the proper safety measures to ensure human and machine safety. An important step in the risk assessment process is hazard identification. Hazard identification of Plug&Produce system is unique as the hazard identification method provided in the safety standards do not consider system flexibility. In this paper, a framework for hazard identification of a collaborative Plug&Produce system is presented. A study case that includes a collaborative Plug&Produce system is presented and the framework is applied to identify the system's hazards. Also, the generalisation of the framework application is discussed.

Keywords: Plug&Produce · Collaborative robots · Risk assessment · Hazard identification

1 Introduction

Reconfigurable manufacturing systems (RMS) are designed for rapid change in the structure to adjust the production output within the same part family in response to the requirements [13]. The concept of Plug&Produce system is built upon the concept of RMS. A Plug&Produce system has the capability of instant and automatic physical reconfiguration, and the capability to adapt intelligent control logic. Plug&Produce possess the attributes of logical flexibility and physical flexibility. Logical flexibility refers to system ability for facilitated replanning, reprograming, and rescheduling. Also, physical flexibility refers to system ability for facilitated change in the layout, machines, and material handling devices. A human worker can be considered as the most flexibles component of the manufacturing system and the involvement of human worker in the manufacturing system add flexibility to the system. A collaborative operation is an industrial operation performed by humans and robots working side by side and collaborating to achieve the task. The collaborative work between the human and the robots raises safety challenges.

To realize the industrial application of the Plug&Produce system, it is required to assure that the system is complying with safety standards. To ensure the safety of the

© The Author(s), under exclusive license to Springer Nature Switzerland AG 2022
F. Sanfilippo et al. (Eds.): INTAP 2021, CCIS 1616, pp. 144–155, 2022.
https://doi.org/10.1007/978-3-031-10525-8_12

system according to standards, risk assessment is needed to be performed and to perform risk assessment, it is required to identify the hazards. Hazard identification process must consider the flexibility of the system and the possibility of system reconfiguration. The safety standards can be used to assess the safety of a flexible system. However, the existing standards do not consider flexibility.

In this study, a framework, to identify the hazards of a collaborative Plug&Produce system, is presented. The study discusses risk assessment according to standards and describes the process of hazard identification within the risk assessment. Then the study discusses hazard identification for collaborative operations and hazard identification for Plug&Produce systems. A framework for hazard identification of collaborative Plug&Produce system is derived. A collaborative Plug&Produce system with several reconfiguration scenarios is presented as a study case and the framework is applied to identify the hazard of the system in the presented study case. Also, the generalisation of the framework application is discussed.

2   Background

2.1   Plug&Produce Systems

Modern manufacturing systems have some critical requirements such as short lead-time, a high variety of products, and fluctuating production volumes with low production costs. To meet the requirements several strategies are developed based on the reconfigurable manufacturing concept [5]. The concept of Plug&Produce is inspired by the concept of Plug and Play in the computer world. It is described as an agile manufacturing system that accepts reconfiguration in a short time and has distributed control system over the manufacturing devices [2]. One framework for the Plug&Produce considers the system as a system of several self-aware and modular production process modules with a distributed control strategy based on a multi agent system [4]. New devices plugged into the Plug&Produce system are identified automatically and instantly allowing for making changes in the system in a short time [3].

A Plug&Produce system contains resources, and resources have skills. To achieve the production goals, the system generates process plans. A process plan is a sequence of skills that are utilised to achieve the goal. The skills are utilised without specifying the resource which allows the system to achieve the goal if resources are changed [4].

2.2   Collaborative Robot System

The objective of collaborative robots is to combine the repetitive skills of the robots with the cognitive skills and abilities of the human. A collaborative robot system is a system designed in a way that the operator and the robot share the workspace. The robot is a component in the collaborative robot system and the associated cell layout is designed to eliminate the hazard. The operational characteristics of the collaborative robot system are different from the traditional robot systems. In collaborative operations, the operator can be in proximity with the robot while the actuators of the system are powered [20].

Human-Robot Collaboration opens new possibilities for industries and adds additional flexibility to industrial production. New robotic applications are enabled by a human-robot collaboration including robot assistance in welding tasks and assembly processes, human assistance and ergonomic support and machine tending and material handling [14, 21].

Plug&Produce systems allow quick and easy adaptation of collaborative operations in the manufacturing processes. The modular integration of collaborative operations within Plug&Produce allows achieving the collaborative operation goals regardless of the participating resources [16, 22].

2.3 Safety Standards

The standard ISO 12100 gives an overview of the basic principles and methodology for hazard identification, risk assessment and risk reduction. The standard also defines basic terms that are related to risk assessment. Harm is defined as physical injury or damage to health. Hazard is defined as the potential source of harm. Risk is defined as the combination of the probability of occurrence of the hazard that generates the harm and the severity of the harm [17].

The standard ISO 10218 specifies the requirements and provide a guideline for safe design and use of industrial robots, and describes the hazards associated with robots and provides requirements to eliminate the hazards. The standards provide definitions for terms. Collaborative operation is defined as the state in which specifically designed robots work in collaboration with a human operator within the same defined workspace. The collaborative workspace is a workspace within the safeguarded zone in which the human and the robot perform the collaborative operation [18].

The standard ISO 14121 gives a guideline to conduct a risk assessment in accordance with ISO 12100 and provides tools and methods to achieve the actions included in the risk assessment. It also provides examples of measures to reduce risks [19].

The standard ISO 15066 specifies the safety requirements for collaborative robot systems and the work environment. It provides a guideline for hazard identification, risk assessment and risk reduction associated with collaborative robot systems [20].

ISO 10218 and ISO 15066 identify four collaborative methods. Safety-rated monitored stop, Hand guiding, Speed and separation monitoring and Power and force limiting [18, 20].

Safety-rated monitored stop includes that the operator performs manual tasks inside a collaborative area, which is an operative space shared between the human and the robot. Inside such a collaborative area, both the human and the robot can work, but not at the same time since the latter is not allowed to move if the operator occupies this shared space. In the hand guiding method, the operator can teach the robot positions by moving the robot without the need of an intermediate interface, e.g., robot teach pendant.The speed and separation monitoring method allows the human presence within the robot's space through safety-rated monitoring sensors.The power and force limiting collaborative method prescribe the limitation of motor power and force so that a human worker can work side-by-side with the robot.

The current collaborative methods given by the standards are similar to traditional automation and don't support the implementation of an intelligent collaborative system.

A new type of collaborative method named deliberation in planning and acting is proposed, in which the robot and the operator deliberate and execute an agreed-upon plan [10].

There is a possibility to change between operational modes, the collaborative, and non-collaborative modes. When the collaborative mode is activated, it is indicated clearly to the operator with light indicators. The sensory system is adjusted to allow the human presence in the collaborative workspace without causing a safety stop. Robot speed at the collaborative mode is adjusted to ensure human safety according to the performed risk assessment [9].

3   Risk Assessment and Hazard Identification

The process of risk assessment provides information that is used to implement the proper safety measures to ensure human and machine safety. The general strategy for risk assessment is provided in ISO 12100 and a practical guideline for achieving the risk assessment activities is provided in ISO 14121. The procedure of a system risk assessment includes the following actions, in the order given:

1. Determine the limits of the machinery, which includes the limitation of the machine in space and defining the intended use and reasonably foreseeable misuse.
2. Identify the hazards and the associated hazardous situations.
3. Estimate the risk for each identified hazard.
4. Evaluate the risk and decide the need for risk reduction.

The objective of determining the limitation of the machine is to have a clear description of the machine properties, the use and possible misuse and the environment in which the machine will be operated and maintained. The objective is achieved by an examination of the functions of the machine and the tasks associated with the use of the machine.

The objective of hazard identification is to list all hazards and hazards associated situations which allow describing the hazard scenario. Hazard identification methods must consider the human interaction with machines during the entire life cycle of the machine, the possible operating conditions and modes of the machine, and the unexpected behaviour of the operator or reasonably foreseeable misuse of the machine.

Risk estimation is the process to understand the nature of the risk and determine its magnitude which results from combining the consequences and their likelihood. It starts by addressing the severity of the harm. There are levels of severity of harm. It combines the level of severity with the probability of occurrence of the harm. The combination leads to determine the level of the risk.

Risk evaluation is the process of comparing the results of risk estimation with applied protective measures to determine if the hazardous situation requires further risk reduction. Also, to determine if the risk reduction has been achieved without introducing new hazards or raise the level of other risks.

3.1 Hazard Identification of Collaborative Robot System

Standard ISO 15066 defines risk assessment for a collaborative robot system, as the need to identify the hazards and estimate the risk of a collaborative robot system so the proper risk reduction methods measures are implemented. The hazard identification process of collaborative robot operation in a collaborative robot system considers the robot-related hazards such as robot characteristics, robot contact conditions and the proximity of the operator to the robot. Also, it considers the hazard related to the robot system including the end-effector and workpiece hazard and operator location with respect to hazardous fixtures. To identify the hazards of a collaborative operation, the collaborative operation is divided into several tasks, each task is allocated to the robot or the human operator and allocated to a workspace. Each task is then analysed to identify the hazards [20].

Task-based hazard identification of collaborative operations is discussed in [6–8]. The safety design of the collaborative robot system focuses on individual hazards within the collaborative workspace rather than keeping the operator away from the hazardous zone [11].

3.2 Hazard Identification for Plug&Produce Systems

Risk assessment of Plug&Produce comprises of determining the limit of the machines, hazard identification, risk estimation and risk evaluation. The modularity feature of the Plug&Produce system makes the procedure of risk assessment specific. The Plug&Produce system is modular and consists of several process modules, and each process module can be considered as a system itself.

A system of systems consists of several autonomous systems. A Plug&Produce system can be considered a system of systems [1]. Two types of hazards are identified in the system of systems. The two types of hazards are single system hazards and emergent hazards [12, 15]. Relative to the Plug&Produce concept, the single system hazards are associated with hazards of a single module while the emergent hazards are associated with the hazards that are generated when several modules are configured in the Plug&Produce system. According to [15], emerging hazards can be subdivided into reconfiguration hazards, integration hazards and interoperability hazards.

1. Integration hazards: can be subcategorized into interface hazards, proximity hazards, resources hazards.

- Interface hazard: a hazard in which the module transfers a hazard source to another dependent or cooperative module.
- Proximity hazard: a hazard in one module caused by close physical proximity to another module.
- Resource hazard: a hazard resulted from insufficient shared resources or resources conflict.

2. Reconfiguration hazards: results from a change in the system configuration from one configuration to another.
3. Interoperability hazard: it occurs when data of one module is miss interpreted by another module.

4   Hazard Identification of Collaborative Plug&Produce System

Hazard identification of collaborative robot systems is discussed in Sect. 3.1, and hazard identification of Plug&Produce system is discussed in Sect. 3.2. Based on findings Sects. 3.1 and 3.2, the hazard identification of a collaborative Plug&Produce system is discussed.

The risk assessment of the collaborative Plug&Produce system includes the steps of identifying the machine limitation, hazard identification, risk estimation and risk evaluation. In this study, identifying the use of process modules is considered as identifying machine limitations.

The step of hazard identification of collaborative Plug&Produce is unique due to the flexibility of the system both in hardware and control structure. The safety standards can be used to assess the safety of a flexible system. However, the existing standards do not consider flexibility. Hazard identification process must consider the flexibility of the system and the possibility of system reconfiguration. Plug&Produce system reconfiguration means that process modules are added or removed from the system, or the position of process modules and the layout of the physical system is changed. Also, in a Plug&Produce system, the objective could be changed. Hence, the use of the same process module is changed.

4.1   Hazard Identification Framework

To address the unique hazard identification process of the collaborative Plug&Produce system, a framework for hazard identification is proposed. Also, a study case of a collaborative Plug&Produce system is presented. The framework is applied to identify the hazard of the collaborative Plug&Produce system described in the study case. The framework includes the following steps:

1. Determine the use of each process module.
2. Identify the hazard of each module and the associated hazards situations for every use of the module.
3. Identify the emerging hazards for every foreseen reconfiguration.

4.2   Study Case

To demonstrate the proposed hazard identification framework, a Plug&Produce cell is presented in this study case. Figure 1 shows the presented Plug&Produce cell. The cell consists of an industrial robot in the centre of the cell and several positions for Plug&Produce process modules. Two process modules are included in the cell and the cell can be configured differently. The yellow circle estimates the collaborative workspace. Process module 1, shown in Fig. 2, includes an inherently safe designed collaborative robot and a surface space. Process module 2, shown in Fig. 3, includes an industrial robot and a surface space. When process module 1 is configured in the system, the shared accessible collaborative workspace is indicated to the operator, and the worker understands that it is safe to be in the shared collaborative workspace.

In the presented Plug&Produce system, three foreseen reconfigurations can be identified. The reconfigurations are:

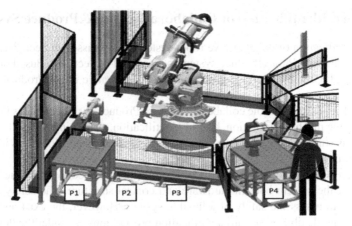

Fig. 1. Plug&Produce cell

Fig. 2. Module 1 includes an inherently safe designed collaborative robot

Fig. 3. Module 2 includes an industrial robot

1. Reconfiguration1: change of the use of the collaborative process module

Module 1 is used to perform two collaborative operations. the use of the collaborative module changes based on the produced part. The first collaborative operation is assembly, and the second collaborative operation is grinding. The first operation contains the following steps:

- The industrial robot in the centre of the cell carries a workpiece and place it on the table of the collaborative module.
- The operator prepares a part.
- The collaborative robot picks the part and places it in its intended position in the workpiece.

Also, the cell produces another product using the second collaborative operation. The part that the operator prepares, needs grinding performed by the collaborative robot. The worker then picks the finished part and place it in position in the workpiece. The second operation contains the following steps:

- The industrial robot in the centre of the cell carries a workpiece and places it on the table of the collaborative module.
- The operator prepares a part.
- The collaborative robot performs grinding on the part.
- The worker picks the part and places it in position.

2. Reconfiguration2: change the location of the collaborative module.

The second configuration is the change position of module 1 i.e., the change of the cell layout so the collaborative module is in a different position. The collaborative module location is changed from position 4 indicated in the figure by P4 to position 2 indicated on the figure by P2.

3. Reconfiguration3: change the collaborative module with a different module.

The third reconfiguration is to change module 1 with module 2. The assembly operation objective does not change. However, the assembly operation is not collaborative. The operator does not participate in the assembly operation. The operator job of preparing the parts is done outside of the robot workspace and then a batch of the prepared parts is brought to the processing module to achieve the assembly operation.

4.3 Hazard Identification of the Study Case

The first two steps in the framework are to identify the use of the process modules and to identify the associated hazards. Table 1 presents the identified hazards for module 1, Table 2 presents identified hazards for module 2. The modules have defined uses, and the hazards associated with assembly operation are different depending on the module that is used to perform the assembly. Module 1 includes a robot that is safe inherently designed, so the power and force of the robot's motor are limited to element the hazard of collision between the robot and the worker body.

The third step is to identify the emerging hazards from every foreseen reconfiguration of the system. Table 3 lists the identified emerging hazards of every foreseen reconfiguration.

Table 1. Module 1 identified hazards

Module 1					
Module use	Life cycle	Task	Hazard zone	Hazard	Hazardous situation
Assembly	Operation	Pick & Place	Shared workspace with the worker	Head or body injury	Worker in the shared workspace and the contact with the part carried by the robot happens due to loss of part control
Griding	Operation	Grinding the surface	Shared workspace with the worker	Head or body injury	The grinding wheel bursts and parts of the grinding wheel hits the worker
				Eye injuries	Debris from the grinding operation flies and reach the operator's eyes
				Body part burn	Grinding results in heat and contact with hot material causes burn

Table 2. Module 2 identified hazards

Module 2					
Module use	Life cycle	Task	Hazard zone	Hazard	Hazardous situation
Assembly	Operation	Pick & Place	Shared workspace with the worker	Head or body injury	Worker in the shared workspace and the contact with the part carried by the robot happens due to loss of part control
		Pick & Place	Shared workspace with the worker	Head or body injury	Worker in the shared workspace and the contact with robot happens due to robot movement

Table 3. Identified emerging hazards

Reconfiguration	Emerging hazard type	Hazard	Hazardous situation
Reconfiguration1	Resource hazard	Body or head injury	The use of a process module with a high power load becomes included in the system which causes electricity overload. The system shut down unexpectedly and in an unsafe manner
Reconfiguration2	Proximity hazard	Body or head injury	Module 1 and module 2 become in proximity and the contact between the robot in module 2 and the operator happens due to the robot movement
Reconfiguration3	Interoperability hazard	Body or head injury	The human faultily interprets the indicators that the workspace is not collaborative, and contact happens due to the robot movement

5 Conclusion

Plug&Produce systems have physical and logical flexibility. Including collaborative operations in the Plug&Produce system increases flexibility. Guidelines provided in safety standards can be used for hazard identification of collaborative Plug&Produce system. However, safety standards do not consider flexibility. The hazard identification of the highly flexible collaborative Plug&Produce is unique. A framework to identify the hazards of a collaborative Plug&Produce system is proposed in this paper. The framework is used to identify the hazards of a collaborative Plug&Produce cell presented in a study case. The generalisation of the framework is then discussed. The generalisation of the framework is faced with challenges. These challenges are related to the extended effort needed to identify all emerging hazards due to many possible reconfigurations of the system. Also, due to the complexity of identifying the hazards of such a highly flexible system, there is a need to verify that all hazards are identified.

A possible improvement to the framework is to automatically identify the hazards. Information that can be used to identify the hazards such as the functional and the physical attribute of the process module along with the use of the module are stored in a database. A software that is programmed to perform the proposed framework for hazard identification, uses the stored hazard-related information and automatically identifies all the hazards. The software is programmed with a verification method to ensure all hazards are identified. The development of the verification method for hazard identification and the development of the software for automatic hazard identification is an interesting topic for future research.

Acknowledgement. This work is a part of the project named SafeAgain funded by the KK-stiftelsen foundation.

References

1. Aitken, J.M., Alexander, R., Kelly, T.: A risk modelling approach for a communicating system of systems. In: 2011 IEEE International System Conference SysCon 2011 – Proceedings, pp. 442–447 (2011). https://doi.org/10.1109/SYSCON.2011.5929099
2. Arai, T., Aiyama, Y., Maeda, Y., Sugi, M., Ota, J.: Agile assembly system by 'Plug and Produce.' CIRP Ann. – Manuf. Technol. **49**, 1–4 (2000). https://doi.org/10.1016/S0007-850 6(07)62883-2
3. Bennulf, M., Danielsson, F., Svensson, B.: Identification of resources and parts in a Plug and Produce system using OPC UA. Procedia Manuf. **38**, 858–865 (2019). https://doi.org/10. 1016/j.promfg.2020.01.167
4. Bennulf, M., Danielsson, F., Svensson, B., Lennartson, B.: Goal-oriented process plans in a multi-agent system for Plug & Produce. IEEE Trans. Ind. Inform. 1 (2020). https://doi.org/ 10.1109/tii.2020.2994032
5. Bi, Z.M., Lang, S.Y.T., Shen, W., Wang, L.: Reconfigurable manufacturing systems: the state of the art. Int. J. Prod. Res. **46**, 967–992 (2008). https://doi.org/10.1080/00207540600905646
6. Gopinath, V., Johansen, K.: Risk assessment process for collaborative assembly - a job safety analysis approach. Procedia CIRP **44**, 199–203 (2016). https://doi.org/10.1016/j.procir.2016. 02.334

7. Gopinath, V., Johansen, K., Gustafsson, Å., Axelsson, S.: Collaborative assembly on a continuously moving line - an automotive case study. Procedia Manuf. **17**, 985–992 (2018). https://doi.org/10.1016/j.promfg.2018.10.105

8. Gopinath, V., Johansen, K., Ölvander, J.: Risk assessment for collaborative operation: a case study on hand-guided industrial robots. In: Risk Assess (2018). https://doi.org/10.5772/intechopen.70607

9. Gopinath, V., Ore, F., Grahn, S., Johansen, K.: Safety-focussed design of collaborative assembly station with large industrial robots. Procedia Manuf. **25**, 503–510 (2018). https://doi.org/10.1016/j.promfg.2018.06.124

10. Hanna, A., Bengtsson, K., Götvall, P.L., Ekström, M.: Towards safe human robot collaboration - risk assessment of intelligent automation. In: IEEE International Conference on Emerging Technologies and Factory Automation, ETFA 2020-September, pp. 424–431 (2020). https://doi.org/10.1109/ETFA46521.2020.9212127

11. Hull, T., Minarcin, M.A.: Considerations in collaborative robot system designs and safeguarding. SAE Int. J. Mater. Manuf. **9**, 545–551 (2016). https://doi.org/10.4271/2016-01-0340

12. Koo, C.H., Schröck, S., Vorderer, M., Richter, J., Verl, A.: A model-based and software-assisted safety assessment concept for reconfigurable PnP-systems. Procedia CIRP **93**, 359–364 (2020). https://doi.org/10.1016/j.procir.2020.03.076

13. El Maraghy, H.A.: Flexible and reconfigurable manufacturing systems paradigms. Flex. Serv. Manuf. J. **17**, 261–276 (2006). https://doi.org/10.1007/s10696-006-9028-7

14. Matheson, E., Minto, R., Zampieri, E.G.G., Faccio, M., Rosati, G.: Human-robot collaboration in manufacturing applications: a review. Robotics **8**, 1–25 (2019). https://doi.org/10.3390/robotics8040100

15. Redmond, P.J., Michael, J.B., Shebalin, P.V.: Interface hazard analysis for system of systems. In: 2008 IEEE International Conference on System of Systems Engineering, SoSE 2008 (2008). https://doi.org/10.1109/SYSOSE.2008.4724202

16. Schou, C., Madsen, O.: A plug and produce framework for industrial collaborative robots. Int. J. Adv. Robot. Syst. **14**, 1–10 (2017). https://doi.org/10.1177/1729881417717472

17. SIS (Swedish Standards Institute): Safety of machinery - general principles for design - Risk assessment and risk reduction (ISO 12100:2010) (2010)

18. SIS (Swedish Standards Institute): Robots and robotic devices – Safety requirements for industrial robots – Part 1: Robots (ISO 10218-1:2011) (2011)

19. SIS (Swedish Standards Institute): Safety of machinery – Risk assessment – Part 2: Practical guidance and examples of methods (ISO 14121-2:2012, IDT) (2015)

20. SIS (Swedish Standards Institute): Robots and robotic devices – Collaborative robots, (ISO/TS 15066:2016, IDT) (2016)

21. Thomas, C., Matthias, B., Kuhlenkötter, B.: Human - robot collaboration – new applications in industrial robotics. In: International Conference on Competitive Manufacturing, pp. 293–299 (2016)

22. Wojtynek, M., Steil, J.J., Wrede, S.: Plug, plan and produce as enabler for easy workcell setup and collaborative robot programming in smart factories. KI - Künstliche Intelligenz **33**(2), 151–161 (2019). https://doi.org/10.1007/s13218-019-00595-0

ML and AI for Intelligent Health, Applications of Intelligent Technologies in Emergency Management

Future Perspectives on Automated Machine Learning in Biomedical Signal Processing

Luis Miguel Lopez-Ramos[1,2(✉)] ⓘ

[1] SFI Offshore Mechatronics Center, University of Agder, Grimstad, Norway
luis.m.lopez.ramos@gmail.com
[2] Department of ICT, University of Agder, Grimstad, Norway

Abstract. Recent developemnts in Machine Learning (ML) and Signal Processing (SP) are of paramount importance for the advancement of artificial intelligence in the health sector. The implications of these enabling technologies encompass several broad fields from mathematics to product development in connection with the practitioners and patients. This paper aims at guiding researchers and entrepreneurs in the journey from basic research to application of data-driven technology for the health sector. Two key topics related to automatization of data processing, namely sparsity-based processing, and automated ML, are introduced and discussed in relation to biomedical SP. The discussed topics are exemplified in the context of cardiac signal processing.

Keywords: Signal processing · Biomedical engineering · Interpretability · Machine learning · Automated machine learning · Autonomous information management

1 Introduction

Machine learning (ML) algorithms play a key role in recent technological advances to improve clinical care, design new medicines, and reduce healthcare costs [38]. Predictive algorithms are part of the core of enhanced diagnosis, automated treatments, and systematic understanding of disease progression [1]. Under the umbrella term of Artificial intelligence (AI), many different technologies are applied and continuously evolved to increase the quality of computer-aided patient care, monitoring [35], and healthcare system management [7].

In the recent past, the main limitation of data-driven information systems was the scarcity of training data sets. Nowadays we live in an era of data deluge where information systems are generally more limited by the speed at which data are processed. The development of algorithms to efficiently implement *Big-data* analytics [19,32] has raised a lot of interest in the last years in many sectors,

The work in this paper was supported by the SFI Offshore Mechatronics grant 237896/O30.

F. Sanfilippo et al. (Eds.): INTAP 2021, CCIS 1616, pp. 159–170, 2022.
https://doi.org/10.1007/978-3-031-10525-8_13

including healthcare. In this context, the availability of enormous amounts of information stems from the rapid and systematic digitalization of hard copies of patient records [30], and the capability of new equipment to easily store data from medical imaging (e.g., magnetic resonance imaging (MRI) [9]) and biomedical signals such as electrocardiography (ECG) [19] and electroencephalography (EEG) [41].

An increased capability to store and process large amounts of data at a practical speed allows to have access to data from large numbers of patients[1], but it also allows to store signal data with a high resolution, and reducing the negative impact of compression algorithms. The analysis of signals with high resolution and high dimensionality [40] is subject to a great deal of research activity, where the recent advances in ML are rapidly incorporated and exploited.

Signal processing (SP) is the enabling technology for the transformation and interpretation of real-world sources of information in many forms such as electrical potentials, pressure, light or, more generally, anything that can be measured by a sensor or user interface. Signals are different from bulk data in the fact that they are defined on structured domains, such as time, space (in the case of images or volumetric signals), or graphs (in the case of, e.g. epidemiological [8] or point-cloud data [29]). Whereas SP extracts knowledge from information considering its structure, biomedical SP focuses on physiological activities ranging from gene and protein sequences, to neural and cardiac rhythms or images from tissues and organs [6].

Recent mathematical developments in statistical SP (SSP) are a rigorous foundation for signal interpretation [28,31] beyond mere prediction of outcomes, enabling theoretical performance bounds [42], or interpretation of numerical parameters of trained models [23], a simple but prototypical example being regression analysis [37]. Interpretability [17], explainability [33], and adaptation to diverse tasks [16] are desirable properties of ML and SP algorithms, especially when they are part of critical systems such as biomedical signal monitoring and decision-making [34,36]. Modern SP research seeks continuous improvement in terms of adaptivity of signal refining algorithms [5], and accuracy of pathology classification [18]. The main technical challenges in this context are related to the computational complexity [3] and the need for large and representative datasets [2] for the algorithms to be applicable in a wide range of patients and clinical cases.

The vision that this paper aims to put forth is that the design of SP algorithms must be based on rigorous formulation of optimization problems and judiciously chosen figures of merit [24]. In other words, algorithm design is based on rigorously applied mathematics and, as a consequence, engineers and practitioners with a focus on applied healthcare need to be aware of the implications of the mathematical models underlying their tools. With the correct formula-

---

[1] It is worth noting that the legal and ethical challenges associated with the automated analysis of personal sensitive data are equally important and closely associated with the technical challenges, motivating the inter-disciplinarity between both research areas.

tion, application of novel optimization methods has demonstrated the potential to reduce the computational and large sample requirements [13] of current SP techniques. Much of the research effort consists in carefully analyzing the problem formulations and data structures to find the mathematical properties that allow to reduce computation times by orders of magnitude [4].

When such a breakthrough is achieved, the convention of what is an "intractable" technical problem is challenged because some problems become tractable, creating opportunities for development at more advanced levels of technology readiness which ultimately lead to novel products with a direct societal impact. An example of such a breakthrough in the recent past has given rise to the rapid growth of mobile communications in the last few years. Future advances of data-driven biomedical processing and eHealth will stem not only from the surrounding technology but also from basic research and algorithmic foundations.

Overview. The goal of this paper is to explain more in detail the interrelation between the research topics relevant to the development of new solutions for biomedical signal and data processing, and how this can have an impact in making biomedical applications accessible to a broader sector of the world population (democratization and reduction of the technological gap). Specifically, several topics in mathematics, computation, ML theory, SP/data analysis, and biomedical applications will be discussed in depth (Fig. 1).

2   From Mathematical Formulas to Data-Driven Biomedical Applications

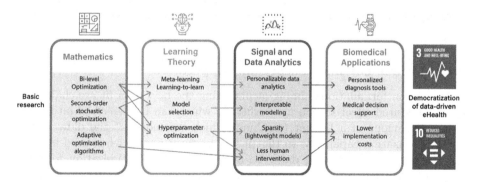

Fig. 1. Summary of the key research topics that, in view of the author, will enable innovation in Biomedical SP research in the near future.

2.1   Mathematical Foundations of Signal Processing and Machine Learning

Optimization: Finding Models with Good Data Fit. Optimization theory underpins the design and performance analysis of adaptive mechanisms in many applications in science and engineering. The best known applications of optimization formulations are in engineering system design in areas such as telecommunications, mechatronics, and computational physics. However, optimization formulations are of paramount importance in SP and in ML, regardless of whether it is to optimize parameters in neural network (NN) architectures or other types of machines aimed at learning from data. With the rigorous formulation of optimization problems where data-fit cost functions are optimized, together with recently developed and powerful optimization algorithms, modern applications such as artificial vision, speech processing, network planning, logistics, search engines, and biomedical engineering enjoy advancements in capabilities that were only achievable by humans in the recent past. Moreover, technical tasks that are less visible but still fundamental, such as dimensionality reduction, data representations, feature extraction, statistical modelling, resource allocation, etc. directly benefit from research advances in optimization theory.

Statistics: Reasoning Under Uncertainty. For various reasons ranging from the natural randomness in life science to more technical challenges, data acquired in biomedical contexts will suffer from uncertainty. More specifically, equipment imperfections, the preference for less invasive measurement methods, or even radiation dose reduction, make the available data noisy or even cause data misses. Many datasets contain bad or missing data, and the need of imputing (inferring) some data entries from the rest of the available data becomes larger as the number of variables and/or data points grow. Also, noise is unavoidable in any physical data acquisition system, and SP research continuously provides with novel techniques to mitigate the effect of noise using the structure underlying the data.

2.2   Machine Learning Theory and Applications

Optimization formulations aiming at obtaining the best data fit are challenged by an undesired effect known as overfitting, which can be described intuitively as the behaviour of a learner (machine) which "memorizes" the data with a low generalization capability, so that it will perform poorly when used in cases not covered by the training data. To avoid overfitting, optimization formulations in ML are often regularized, meaning that they are modified to express a priori information about the desired properties, and/or promote simple solutions. Adding a penalty (regularization) function based on application-dependent information is common practice, and it involves a slight increase of the number of parameters to learn (hyperparameters) but current methods suffer a large increase in computational complexity to control the intensity of the regularization and find a balance between data fit and model simplicity. Procedures to systematically adjust hyperparameters have only recently been proposed (see, e.g. [11,20] and references therein), and they have not been fully analysed yet despite their importance.

Hyperparameter optimization is a task directly related to meta-learning techniques. In a nutshell, meta-learning is a more ample learning paradigm that aims beyond learning specific tasks from given datasets. It is about enabling machines to learn new tasks by reusing previous experience, rather than considering each new task in isolation [10] Meta-learning systems are trained by being exposed to a large number of tasks and then their ability to learn new tasks is exploited. Initial experiments consisted in training with images of a large number of classes and few training images in each class. After training the meta-learning system, a small number of images of a new class (unknown by the trained system) were given and the agent was required to learn how to classify images of the new class.

More recently, meta-learning (and more specifically, model-agnostic meta-learning, MAML [10]) has shown the power to produce personalized data analysis tools as reported in [39]. Besides, meta-learning has proven to enhance the clinical risk prediction with limited electronic health records [43]. The latter two results motivate further studies to exploit the potential of meta-learning in biomedical signal processing.

Meta-learning and hyperparameter optimization rely heavily on bi-level optimization [11] because there are two optimizations at play: a) the learning of a specific task (which corresponds to classic ML), and b) the "learning-to-learn" (specific to meta-learning). Several techniques are available for bi-level optimization, and some of them use second-order information (Hessian) of the first task (a.k.a. inner objective). In ML applications though, due to the high dimensionality, models are conventionally optimized through first-order stochastic methods, and second-order information is often not available. Recent development of second-order stochastic optimization have a clear potential to extract the necessary second-order information for the bi-level optimization problems that may arise in biomedical ML and SP formulations.

2.3   Signal and Data Processing

Recent advances in SP are based on ML and optimization algorithms. Empirical risk minimization (fitting a model to the available data) is not always enough though, as it does not take into account the problems associated with excessive complexity of the models. Section 3 will further elaborate on a set of techniques for promoting simple models, known as sparsity-aware signal processing.

2.4   Biomedical Applications

One of the multiple knowledge needs in biomedical engineering and eHealth is related to the efficiency of the data processing algorithms. Improvements in such efficiency have an economic meaning but, more importantly, direct benefits for individual and public health. For the reasons argued above, aiming this research action at developing interpretable SIP algorithms specifically for biomedical/eHealth applications has a huge potential to turn recent mathematical developments into a direct and tangible benefit for the society.

The aforementioned results in Meta-learning [39,43] motivate future studies where meta-learning is used to produce a system for personalized clinical risk prediction tool, but no research work has addressed this task yet.

Cardiac Pathologies. In order to focus our discussion on a specific example, Sect. 5 will focus on biomedical SP in cardiology. The classification of cardiac pathologies from electrocardiographic (ECG) signals will be discussed. The widespread use of ECG recordings relies heavily on the development of SIP tools for denoising and interference suppression, feature extraction, and diagnosis of cardiac diseases.

3   Sparsity: Automated Simplicity

Sparse data structures can be easily compressed as they contain many zero entries. Sparsity is discussed and exploited in many fields of mathematics: mainly to improve the efficiency at solving large systems of equations. In sparse data, having the information concentrated in a few data entries helps interpretability. Data structures such as vectors, matrices, tensors, graphs and neural networks, the sparser they are, the more efficiently they can be stored and processed, because all the zero entries do not need to be written/loaded in memory.

One of the most relevant aspects of sparsity is that, apart from being useful for mathematical procedures, it can be enforced in the data structures that are obtained by inference algorithms that are present in engineering, statistics, measurement equipment, data analytics, and network science. The ability of the aforementioned algorithms to obtain data representations that (apart from accurately describing the data) are as sparse as possible, has a direct impact on the scalability of the data-processing systems.

Lengthy descriptions are generally not human-readable, and patients and doctors need to access the available information at different levels of detail. One of the advantages of sparsity-aware SP is that it is naturally endowed with the ability to regulate the level of detail of a model inferred from data.

Natural signals can often be processed in a way such that relevant information lies in a few points of the signal domain (e.g., frequencies), as opposed to complex representations that are not human-readable. To this end, sparsity-aware SP algorithms can detect the structure that enhances interpretability using recent mathematical advances to exploit sparsity in signals of natural or technical origin. This is important in health-related applications as health issues are generally explained by a restricted set of variables [27].

Sparsity-aware signal processing uses recent advances in mathematical optimization and statistics to exploit sparsity in signals and networks in both natural and technical contexts.

The recent mathematical developments in statistical learning with sparsity [12] are a rigorous foundation for interpretation of sparse vectors of coefficients when performing, e.g., a regression analysis. In order to discover a sparse structure (which is also associated with good generalization of ML models), regularization is a critical element. If this is realized correctly, the impact in the application side will be huge.

Optimization formulations are often regularized to promote simple solutions such as sparse structures, i.e., where information is concentrated in a few entries while most of the rest are zero. Sparsity, as a form of simplicity, is one of the key features for interpretability. However, sparsity-promoting penalties are sensitive to hyperparameters.

Recent developments in sparsity from a rigorous mathematical point of view [14] characterize the properties of statistical learning with sparsity. Beyond the mathematical analysis, engineering researchers and practitioners are actively finding new ways to exploit sparsity to improve the applicability and impact of their algorithms.

4   Automated Machine Learning (AutoML)

Adaptation to diverse tasks is a desirable property of ML algorithms. In this context, the recently developed paradigm of automated machine learning (AutoML) [15] is leading to a higher degree of autonomous information management as it allows to adjust ML models with reduced human intervention.

In the context of AutoML, learning-to-learn techniques [10] allow to tailor ML model training for specific classes of problems, to process data even more efficiently than traditional ML approaches. It is natural therefore to expect future research aiming at using these tools to bring personalization of data analysis to tackle the diversity of health-related needs across individuals and population groups. Recent works about meta-learning (learning general features for classes of tasks) have motivated increased interest for bi-level optimization techniques. Additionally, algorithms that automatically optimize hyperparameters [20] have a huge potential for developing SP algorithms.

The meta-learning framework breaks the "one machine-one task" pattern present in ML, one of the obstacles towards a general AI. Instead of processing one dataset associated with one task, a meta-learning algorithm processes a collection of datasets (related to a class of tasks) extracting general information useful for learning a new task of the same class with a minimal amount of data. Meta-learning is related to transfer learning, with the additional advantage that it can extract general information pertaining a class of tasks. This is particularly useful when many of the tasks have a small amount of data associated.

Conventional ML approaches aim at training a single classifier from the data from multiple patients, trying to minimize the prediction error averaged over the whole set of patients represented in the dataset. This generally produces one-size-fits-all models that apply the same rules to all signals regardless of the patient. However, signal patterns may have different meanings if they are produced by different underlying clinical conditions. Consequently, patients with minoritarian clinical conditions may be affected by larger misclassification rates.

On the other hand, a meta-learning approach formalizes signal classification for each patient as a separate task, removing the constraint of using a single classifier aimed at all patients. The output of a meta-learning algorithm is a learning entity that can use patient-specific training data to complete their training and improve the classification accuracy for each individual. An example of such an entity is a computer program consisting of: i) a deep neural network (DNN) with specific initial neural weights, and ii) a training algorithm. The specific initial weights are determined using data from all patients in the dataset using model-agnostic meta-learning (MAML) and the training is completed for each patient by running a few learning epochs with the patient-specific data. The result is a personalized classifier for each patient, leading to a higher overall accuracy. Alternative meta-learning approaches aim at automatically designing the training algorithm to maximize the capacity of learning from the data of a single patient.

5   Cardiac Signal Enhancement and Interpretation

The external ECG is traditionally obtained non-invasively by attaching a set of electrodes to the chest and limbs, although alternative wearable and wireless devices to acquire ECG have been recently developed [25]. On the other hand, intracavitary or intracardiac ECGs (referred to as electrograms (EGMs)) are obtained by setting one or more electrodes in direct contact with the inner surface of the heart; this technique is used for the identification of ventricular tachycardias and classification of other types of arrhythmias. The processing of EGMs has the additional associated challenge of using a multivariate signal, and the exploitation of its spatio-temporal correlations is a currently active research field. However, currently existing algorithms lack the scalability required to process a large set of time series while limiting the model complexity.

A typical ECG SP pipeline is compound of several processing blocks, including 5 fundamental steps: filtering to remove noise and interferences, waveform delineation, feature extraction, ECG compression, and classification of the patient's status. In the context of ECG denoising, the spectral properties (frequencies) of the signal are the main features used to identify and separate the different components (QRS complex, P-wave, T-wave, noise, and artifacts). For instance, baseline wander and power line interference have strong structure that can be exploited to filter them out. On the other hand, electrode noise and electromyographic noise have frequential components that overlap the characteristic frequencies of some of the waveforms of interest [21]. The frequency overlap between some types of noise and the signals of interest calls for the development of nonlinear SP algorithms, which have not been analysed as much as linear time invariant (LTI) systems and are object of current research.

The properties of LTI filters allow further development into adaptive filtering algorithms. Adaptive filters are solutions where the filter's configuration (response coefficients) varies with time depending on the input data, which is particularly useful when the noise is nonstationary. LTI and adaptive filters have been proposed and compared for the removal of different types of noise and artifacts in cardiac signals. Their flexibility and applicability motivate further research in adaptive nonlinear filtering and extended Kalman filtering [26,44]. Surprisingly, the benefits of hyper-parameter optimization and meta-learning in the context of univariate or multivariate adaptive filters have not been studied yet.

Denoising and classification of ECG can also be designed via regression-based methods. These can be further divided into parametric and nonparametric (fully data-driven) methods. Parametric methods based on wavelets express the signal as the addition of many instances of "basic waveforms" (called wavelets because of their short duration), and its main advantages are their flexibility and interpretability. In this basis, a complex and long ECG can be expressed by listing the location and shape of the wavelets in a sparse data structure. A few recent works (see [22] and references therein) have developed sparse regression techniques where each coefficient corresponds to a heartbeat, which enjoys high interpretability. However, such a method has only been tested on synthetic data and its adaptation to real signals requires its hyperparameters to be optimized.

The use of sparsity-aware SP appears also in the detection of atrial fibrillation, a pathology of high risk that is also a high-complexity electrical pattern in the heart [27].

6   Conclusion

Signal processing algorithms are designed to extract knowledge from biomedical information, based on rigorous mathematical formulations and with a solid practical motivation. The interpretability of the information structures produced by ML algorithms is valuable when they are applied to biomedical signals and patient records, and this motivates future research in sparsity-aware signal processing. Future research will aim at improving the efficiency and learning capability of the aforementioned SP techniques. Researchers and innovation-oriented business face the challenge of identifying specific biomedical practical problems where the newly developed schemes can bring a qualitative improvement. The resulting algorithms will be a key piece in medical equipment software and end-user eHealth applications, with the aim of making them more dynamic and easily re-programmable. An important step in this process is to demonstrate the usability and reduced need for human intervention of the newly developed algorithms and product prototypes.

Acknowledgement. The author wants to thank Ayan Chatterjee, Martin Wulf Gerdes, David Luengo, and Baltasar Beferull-Lozano for fruitful discussions during the preparation of this survey.

References

1. Advisory, K.: Living in an AI world 2020 report: healthcare insiders. https:// advisory.kpmg.us/content/dam/advisory/en/pdfs/2020/healthcare-living-in-an-ai-world.pdf. Accessed 21 June 2021
2. Bellazzi, R.: Big data and biomedical informatics: a challenging opportunity. Yearb. Med. Inform. **9**(1), 8 (2014)
3. Blanco-Velasco, M., Cruz-Roldán, F., López-Ferreras, F., Bravo-Santos, A., Martinez-Munoz, D.: A low computational complexity algorithm for ECG signal compression. Med. Eng. Phys. **26**(7), 553–568 (2004)
4. Boyd, S., Boyd, S.P., Vandenberghe, L.: Convex Optimization. Cambridge University Press, Cambridge (2004)
5. Chandrakar, C., Kowar, M.: Denoising ECG signals using adaptive filter algorithm. Int. J. Soft Comput. Eng. (IJSCE) **2**(1), 120–123 (2012)
6. Chang, H.H., Moura, J.M.: Biomedical signal processing. Biomed. Eng. Design Handb. **2**, 559–579 (2010)
7. Chen, M., Decary, M.: Artificial intelligence in healthcare: an essential guide for health leaders. In: Healthcare Management Forum, vol. 33, pp. 10–18. SAGE Publications Sage CA, Los Angeles (2020)
8. Cutura, G., Li, B., Swami, A., Segarra, S.: Deep demixing: reconstructing the evolution of epidemics using graph neural networks. arXiv preprint arXiv:2011.09583 (2020)
9. Edupuganti, V., Mardani, M., Vasanawala, S., Pauly, J.: Uncertainty quantification in deep MRI reconstruction. IEEE Trans. Med. Imaging **40**(1), 239–250 (2020)
10. Finn, C., Abbeel, P., Levine, S.: Model-agnostic meta-learning for fast adaptation of deep networks. In: International Conference on Machine Learning, pp. 1126–1135. PMLR (2017)
11. Franceschi, L., Frasconi, P., Salzo, S., Grazzi, R., Pontil, M.: Bilevel programming for hyperparameter optimization and meta-learning. In: International Conference on Machine Learning, pp. 1568–1577. PMLR (2018)
12. Friedman, J., Hastie, T., Tibshirani, R., et al.: The Elements of Statistical Learning. Springer Series in Statistics, vol. 1. Springer, New York (2001)
13. Guo, F., Qian, G.: Sample-efficiency-optimized auxiliary particle filter. In: 2005 IEEE/SP 13th Workshop on Statistical Signal Processing, pp. 393–398. IEEE (2005)
14. Hastie, T., Tibshirani, R., Wainwright, M.: Statistical Learning with Sparsity: The Lasso and Generalizations. Chapman and Hall/CRC (2019)
15. Hutter, F., Kotthoff, L., Vanschoren, J.: Automated Machine Learning: Methods, Systems, Challenges. Springer, Heidelberg (2019). https://doi.org/10.1007/978-3-030-05318-5
16. Javanmardi, M., Tasdizen, T.: Domain adaptation for biomedical image segmentation using adversarial training. In: 2018 IEEE 15th International Symposium on Biomedical Imaging (ISBI 2018), pp. 554–558. IEEE (2018)
17. Kumar, R., Srivastava, R., Srivastava, S.: Detection and classification of cancer from microscopic biopsy images using clinically significant and biologically interpretable features. J. Med. Eng. **2015** (2015)
18. Lillo-Castellano, J., et al.: Symmetrical compression distance for arrhythmia discrimination in cloud-based big-data services. IEEE J. Biomed. Health Inform. **19**(4), 1253–1263 (2015)

19. Lillo-Castellano, J.M., Mora-Jiménez, I., Moreno-González, R., Montserrat-García-de Pablo, M., García-Alberola, A., Rojo-Álvarez, J.L.: Big-data analytics for arrhythmia classification using data compression and kernel methods. In: 2015 Computing in Cardiology Conference (CinC), pp. 661–664. IEEE (2015)

20. Lopez-Ramos, L.M., Beferull-Lozano, B.: Online hyperparameter search interleaved with proximal parameter updates. In: 2020 28th European Signal Processing Conference (EUSIPCO), pp. 2085–2089. IEEE (2021)

21. Luengo, D., Oses, D., Trigano, T.: Digital signal processing of ECG and PCG signals (2021)

22. Luengo, D., Vía, J., Trigano, T.: Efficient iteratively reweighted lasso algorithm for cross-products penalized sparse solutions. In: 2020 28th European Signal Processing Conference (EUSIPCO), pp. 2045–2049. IEEE (2021)

23. Luo, W., et al.: Guidelines for developing and reporting machine learning predictive models in biomedical research: a multidisciplinary view. J. Med. Internet Res. **18**(12), e323 (2016)

24. Luo, Z.Q., Yu, W.: An introduction to convex optimization for communications and signal processing. IEEE J. Sel. Areas Commun. **24**(8), 1426–1438 (2006)

25. Majumder, S., Chen, L., Marinov, O., Chen, C.H., Mondal, T., Deen, M.J.: Non-contact wearable wireless ECG systems for long-term monitoring. IEEE Rev. Biomed. Eng. **11**, 306–321 (2018)

26. Mneimneh, M., Yaz, E., Johnson, M., Povinelli, R.: An adaptive Kalman filter for removing baseline wandering in ECG signals. In: 2006 Computers in Cardiology, pp. 253–256. IEEE (2006)

27. Monzón, S., Trigano, T., Luengo, D., Artes-Rodriguez, A.: Sparse spectral analysis of atrial fibrillation electrograms. In: 2012 IEEE International Workshop on Machine Learning for Signal Processing, pp. 1–6. IEEE (2012)

28. Nguyen, Q.T.: Contributions to statistical signal processing with applications in biomedical engineering. Ph.D. thesis, Télécom Bretagne, Université de Bretagne Occidentale (2012)

29. Ortega, A., Frossard, P., Kovačević, J., Moura, J.M., Vandergheynst, P.: Graph signal processing: overview, challenges, and applications. Proc. IEEE **106**(5), 808–828 (2018)

30. Raghupathi, W., Raghupathi, V.: Big data analytics in healthcare: promise and potential. Health Inf. Sci. Syst. **2**(1), 1–10 (2014)

31. Shiavi, R.: Introduction to Applied Statistical Signal Analysis: Guide to Biomedical and Electrical Engineering Applications. Elsevier, Amsterdam (2010)

32. Slavakis, K., Giannakis, G.B., Mateos, G.: Modeling and optimization for big data analytics:(statistical) learning tools for our era of data deluge. IEEE Signal Process. Mag. **31**(5), 18–31 (2014)

33. Tjoa, E., Guan, C.: A survey on explainable artificial intelligence (XAI): toward medical XAI. IEEE Trans. Neural Netw. Learn. Syst. **32**, 4793–4813 (2020)

34. Tsao, H.Y., Chan, P.Y., Su, E.C.Y.: Predicting diabetic retinopathy and identifying interpretable biomedical features using machine learning algorithms. BMC Bioinform. **19**(9), 111–121 (2018)

35. Uckun, S.: Intelligent system in patient monitoring and therapy management. Int. J. Clin. Monit. Comput. **11**(4), 241–253 (1994). https://doi.org/10.1007/BF01139876

36. Valdes, G., Luna, J.M., Eaton, E., Simone, C.B., Ungar, L.H., Solberg, T.D.: MediBoost: a patient stratification tool for interpretable decision making in the era of precision medicine. Sci. Rep. **6**(1), 1–8 (2016)

37. Vittinghoff, E., Glidden, D.V., Shiboski, S.C., McCulloch, C.E.: Regression Methods in Biostatistics: Linear, Logistic, Survival, and Repeated Measures Models. Springer, Heidelberg (2006)
38. Weintraub, K.: Giving medicine a dose of AI. https://www.technologyreview.com/2019/04/24/135725/giving-medicine-a-dose-of-ai/. Accessed 21 June 2021
39. Wijekoon, A., Wiratunga, N.: Personalised meta-learning for human activity recognition with few-data. In: Bramer, M., Ellis, R. (eds.) SGAI 2020. LNCS (LNAI), vol. 12498, pp. 79–93. Springer, Cham (2020). https://doi.org/10.1007/978-3-030-63799-6_6
40. Xie, H.B., Zhou, P., Guo, T., Sivakumar, B., Zhang, X., Dokos, S.: Multiscale two-directional two-dimensional principal component analysis and its application to high-dimensional biomedical signal classification. IEEE Trans. Biomed. Eng. **63**(7), 1416–1425 (2015)
41. Yang, F., Elmer, J., Zadorozhny, V.I.: SmartPrognosis: automatic ensemble classification for quantitative EEG analysis in patients resuscitated from cardiac arrest. Knowl.-Based Syst. **212**, 106579 (2021)
42. Yazdanfar, S., Yang, C., Sarunic, M.V., Izatt, J.A.: Frequency estimation precision in doppler optical coherence tomography using the Cramer-Rao lower bound. Opt. Express **13**(2), 410–416 (2005)
43. Zhang, X.S., Tang, F., Dodge, H.H., Zhou, J., Wang, F.: MetaPred: meta-learning for clinical risk prediction with limited patient electronic health records. In: Proceedings of the 25th ACM SIGKDD International Conference on Knowledge Discovery & Data Mining, pp. 2487–2495 (2019)
44. Ziarani, A.K., Konrad, A.: A nonlinear adaptive method of elimination of power line interference in ECG signals. IEEE Trans. Biomed. Eng. **49**(6), 540–547 (2002)

DeepFireNet - A Light-Weight Neural Network for Fire-Smoke Detection

Muhammad Mubeen[1][(✉)], Muhammad Asad Arshed[2], and Hafiz Abdul Rehman[1] [iD]

[1] Comsats University Islamabad, Lahore Campus, Islamabad, Pakistan
mubeenmeo344@gmail.com
[2] The Islamia University of Bahawalpur, Bahawalpur, Pakistan

Abstract. From the visual scenes, detection of smoke and fire is a challenging task and many approaches have been proposed for the classification of smoke and fire. However, an intelligent image-based system for fire and smoke detection is crucial to prevent large-scale fire events in the world. Rule-based conventional algorithms are not very sufficient to perform these types of detections in real-world due to manual feature engineering and other issues like complex images, similar intensities, variations in objects shape and size, etc. To overcome these issues, DeepFireNet model is proposed. DeepFireNet model performs automatic feature engineering as it is totally based convolutional neural networks (CNN). A generalized dataset is collected and then DeepFireNet model is trained on the raw pixels of the images belonging to the fire and smoke category. The proposed method outperforms, when it is compared with the state-of-the-art methods like AlexNet, Squeeze Net, and Fire Detection Model. The proposed method is achieved an accuracy of 92.33% on an open-source dataset named 'DeepQuestAI'. As the proposed CNN is very simple and straight forward, due to simplicity and a smaller number of layers in the network, DeepFireNet is a lightweight model and could easily deployed in hand carry devices like mobile phones, and Raspberry Pi.

Keywords: Deep learning · Convolutional neural network · Fire detection · Smoke detection

1 Introduction

To avoid large-scale damages and property loss due to fire events, fire and smoke detection at early stages is necessary. Several tools and algorithms have been proposed for the detection of fire and smoke using traditional methods, and in most cases expensive fire and smoke sensors is required in fire and smoke detection. The main disadvantage of the traditional methods is that the installed sensors can only detect fire or smoke in very limited area. Furthermore, these sensors are unable to provide sufficient information about the fire area, area localization and direction [7, 11]. To overcome the issues found in traditional methods, many AI based deep learning solutions have been proposed. These models can detect fire and smoke where these are installed. Chen et al. [2] proposed a method for smoke detection. To conclude pixels that each pixel represents smoke or not, and diffusion & chromatically based rule used. Toreyin et al. [13] were used clue

© The Author(s), under exclusive license to Springer Nature Switzerland AG 2022
F. Sanfilippo et al. (Eds.): INTAP 2021, CCIS 1616, pp. 171–181, 2022.
https://doi.org/10.1007/978-3-031-10525-8_14

and motion features for the detection of fire and flame. Mueller et al. [10], propose a video-based optical flow method to detect fire and non-fire motion. To measure the dimensions of the flame GIS-based reality method was proposed by Bugaric et al. [1]. The above-mentioned methods are used to create rule-based algorithms that depend on expert knowledge. The huge diversity can be found among features of fire and smoke due to color, texture and due to these diversities obtaining an effective accuracy is a challenging task. To overcome the above issue of feature extraction, many deep learning algorithms are best to extract features of smoke and fire images. CNN is best to achieve an effective result in visual problems, only a few studies have been published with CNN in terms of fire and smoke detection. Two joined deep CNNs proposed by Zhang et al. [15] for detection of fire in image dataset. In this method firstly image is tested if the fire is detected in this image, then other classifiers detect the exact location of a fire in the particular image.

The advancements of computer vision and image processing techniques can be used to overcome problems faced in classification of fire and smoke. Video based fire detection technologies can cover more areas for fire detection and fast responses. Deep neural network solutions perform very well concerning traditional algorithms. As described above CNN is the deep convolutional neural network, which can be used to solve several problems with modern solutions. Image classification, object detection, object localization and instance segmentation in machine learning and computer vision are some common issues solved using deep learning. In this study, deep convolutional neural network (DCNN) based solution is proposed to solve image classification problem. This problem is from multi-class classification domain as there are more than two classes to predict.

2 Background

In recent years, many methods are proposed for fire and smoke detection. Jian Zhang et al. [12] used Deep Convolutional Neural Network to take the advantages of neural networks to train the model for smoke detection. In this study 2D images and corresponding annotations used for training, the proposed method automatically extracts the features from the given image. The proposed method used the AlexNet model and change the output layers to 2 classes, one for smoke images and the second class for non-smoke images. In their proposed method total number of layers was 8 (5- convolutional layers), 4 sets of datasets were used for training and testing, and finally got the average accuracy alarm rate 99.56% and false alarm rate 44%. Frizzi [4] proposed a method that used CNN which performs feature extraction and classification in the same architecture. CNN consists of different layers with a combination of convolutional layers and fully connected layers. They used a dropout rate of 0.5 to prevent the model from overfitting. In their dataset, they were considered simple 2D RGB images for training and testing for 3 classes (fire, smoke, and no-fire). The number of samples in the considered dataset was 1427 samples of fire images, 1758 smoke images samples, and 2399 negative images to train the model. After training, they achieved 97% accuracy on the testing dataset. They applied a sliding window of 12×12 on the last feature map to detect fire and smoke. Angelo Genovese et al. [5] proposed an image processing system based on computational intelligence techniques for fire and smoke detection. Their proposed method provides an affordable system that consumes low power and minimum computational resources. As the smoke predicts the possibility of fire so they mainly focus on the detection of smoke to make this system responsive and affordable for inexpensive platforms. The proposed method was designed to handle 320x240 images at the rate of 7 FPS, which makes it run faster. For the accomplishment of this task first, they performed feature extraction and then performs classification on two classes (fire, not fire). The feature extraction process mainly focuses on the below following things: • Moving Region Detection • Smoke Color Analysis • Rising Region Detection • Perimeter Disorder Analysis • Growing Region Detection • Perimeter Disorder Analysis Finally, after training, they achieved a 1.97% True positive rate and 98% True negative rate on 7FPS. Yin et al. [14] proposed a method that based on deep normalization and convolutional neural network of 14 layers for automatic feature extraction and classification for fire and smoke detection from images. To improve the performance of traditional convolutional neural networks they replaced the convolutional layers with normalized convolutional neural layers. For the prevention of overfitting because of the imbalanced dataset, they generated more training samples from the original dataset by using intelligent image enhancement techniques in their study. They used a total of 10712 images for training from which 2254 images of fire and 8363 of non-fire. Finally, in their study, they achieved 97% True alarm rates and 60% false alarm rate. Yong-Tae Lee et al. [9] proposed a method in which aerial images are considered for fire and smoke detection. In their study, they were considered unmanned vehicle images (UAV) due to the expensiveness of manned vehicles like aero planes in terms of fire monitoring, images taken from satellite can't be used for early fire detection due to low temporal resolution and low spatial resolution. For UAV images they used deep convolutional neural networks for wildfire detection. In their study, a total of 23053 images were used for training from which 10985 images were of 'fire' and 12068 images of 'non-fire'. Experiments on different convolutional neural networks performed for significant results achievements in terms of training time consumption, and out of them modified GoogLeNet they were able to achieve 99% accuracy for fire detection with 3 h training time.

Literature review shows that CNNs are the more powerful solutions for fire and smoke detection like problems but still there exists some shortcomings in the studies discussed above. First, current algorithms based on machine learning, required features to learn the problem and solution. In machine learning manual features engineering made these methods dependents on features extraction and selection techniques. The second problem is that the datasets are used in mostly studies contains images full of fire and lack of images having view of early stage of fire. However, in real life fire and smoke images are totally different for early stage of fire and covers a small area as compared with later stage images. The third problem is that mostly studies are worked on binary classification and omit the images contains smoke, which is a strong factor in initiating any big fire events. However, in the early stage of fire, smoke and flame only covered a small area of the image.

Most of the proposed approaches are for detecting smoke and fire from images but as described above all these have some limitations. The advancements of computer vision and image processing techniques can be used to overcome problems faced in classification of fire and smoke. Video based fire detection technologies can cover more areas for fire detection and fast responses. Deep neural network solutions perform very well concerning traditional algorithms. As described above CNN is the deep convolutional neural network, which can be used to solve several problems with modern solutions. Image classification, object detection, object localization and instance segmentation in machine learning and computer vision are some common issues solved using deep learning. In this study, deep convolutional neural network (DCNN) based solution is proposed to solve image classification problem. This problem is from multi-class classification domain as there are more than two classes to predict. In other words, it separates different objects in the image or video and returns classes around objects. The pros of CNN based solutions is that these can automatically extract and learn useful and effective features from the fire and smoke images, thus the cons of manual features engineering dropped successfully. The dataset is used in this study contains images with early stage of fire images with later stages of fire also and thus generalize the solution for most conditions. The dataset is contained images belongs to three classes, fire, smoke and neutral. Images in the dataset are taken using several cameras from different fire scenes and labels are assigned to each image from predefined set of classes. Image labeling is kind easy in such problems as human eye can easily classify the images into corresponding classes. The proposed method is a deep convolutional neural network model named DeepFireNet for image classification. The key points of our proposed model are, DeepFireNet can automatically leant and extract the features from the images and makes automatic classification into predetermined number of classes. A dataset named 'DeepQuestAI' that we have considered contains 2D images with corresponding classes (fire, smoke and neutral) (Table 1).

Table 1. Literature review

Study	No. of images	Purpose	Classes	Algorithm	Evaluation	
					TAR	FAR
Jian Zhang et al. [12] 2017	24217	Classification	Fire, non-fire	AlexNet	Acc. 99%	44%
Eric Moreau et al. [4] 2016	27919	Classification	Fire, smoke, non-fire	Sliding technique, FCN	Acc. 97%	–
Genovese et al. [5] 2011	–	Classification	Fire, non-fire	Comp. intelligence	1.97%	–
Yin et al. [14] 2017	24217	Classification	Fire, non-fire	CNN	97%	60%
Lee et al. [9] 2017	23053	Classification	Fire, non-fire	GoogLeNet	Acc. 99%	–

3   Convolutional Neural Network (CNN)

A convolutional neural network was first introduced by Fukushima [8] derived a hier-archical neural network inspired by Hubel's research work [3]. CNN is a deep learning algorithm that takes in an image as input and assigns importance such as weights/biases to different scenes or objects in the images. CNN performs automatic classification on given images. Mostly in other classification algorithms, we need some pre-processing techniques for better classification, but there is especially no need to pre-process the given image. CNN automatically performs features extraction from a given image and then automatically performs image classification in output classifiers layers in given classes. A convolutional neural network consists of different types of layers to perform different tasks. Further details are given in the below following sections.

3.1   Convolutional Layers

Convolutional layers are the basic building blocks for Convolutional neural networks. Convolutional layers are the image convolution of the previous layers. The weights of the filters determine the convolutional filter. As the number of filters increases in a convolutional layer, more features extracted from the image and get the details of image content in more depth. We also specify the padding methods like 'zero paddings', 'the same padding' to control image border pixels.

3.2   Pooling Layers

Pooling layers subsample the input. We often perform pooling after each convolutional layer. There are different methods for performing pooling such as choosing maximum, linear combinations, or taking an average. The most commonly used pooling technique is MaxPooling (2 $\times$ 2) shown in Fig. 1.

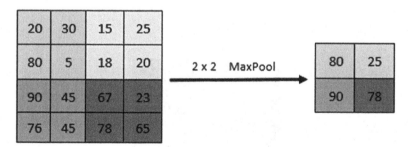

Fig. 1. MaxPooling (2 $\times$ 2)

3.3   Fully Connected Layers

Finally, after applying some convolutional and pooling layers, we used fully connected layers for high-level reasoning in the neural network. We specify the number of classes in the output layer that we required as output results. In the neural network, every layer detects some specific features from the original data provided in the form of an image. Features detected by the first layer in the network can easily be recognized and interpreted. The features extracted by middle layers are difficult to recognize because of more abstract features. The last layer can classify the features selected from all previous layers in the network.

4   Methodology

4.1   Dataset

Open-source dataset downloaded from DeepQuestAI GitHub repository and we have considered 3000 2D images for our DeepFireNet model and 100 images for each class used for testing (100*3), 700 images for each class used to train the model (700*3). The dataset contains images for the following classes (Fig. 2 and Table 2).

Table 2. Images used in experiments

Number of smoke images	Number of fire images	Number of neutral images	Purposes for
100	100	100	Testing
200	200	200	Validation
700	700	700	Training

- Fire
- Smoke
- Neutral

Fig. 2. Smoke, fire, neutral

We have resized all images to 255*255. In this study, we were considered three classes and trained our model on three classes.

4.2 DeepFireNet Model Design

We have designed a DeepFireNet model in which there were total two convolutional layers with filters 32 and 64 are used to convolve image features automatically. As we know that overfitting is a common problem in deep learning-based problems, to avoid overfitting we have used dropout of 0.1–0.3. To extract features in more depth we have to down sample the image, for this propose a MaxPooling layer is used. A flatten layer to create vector of features extracted from the image through convolutional layers, and then one fully connected layer is used with 64 number of filters. A rectified linear unit (ReLU) activation function is used in this model with all convolutional layers except the last layer. Finally, the last fully connected layer is used with sigmoid function to obtain required output labels (fire, smoke, neutral). Figure 3 is the graphical representation of our proposed model. The network is simple and the number of layers was less than other proposed models that our model is effective in terms of memory consumption and speed.

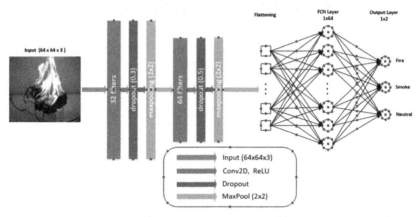

Fig. 3. DeepFireNet framework

5 Experiments

5.1 Training and Accuracy

To train the DeepFireNet model, we use the system with 32 GB RAM, 1 TB disk drive, 3.2 GHz processor speed, CUDA 10.1 version with 12 GB NVIDIA GPU. A batch size of 64 was used for training and testing, an Adam optimizer was used to optimize the loss weights to improve training performance, and the initial learning rate was set to 0.001. The number of epochs set to 200 for training and model weights were to be saved automatically after each epoch based on the increment in validation accuracy during training (Table 3).

Results achieved by our proposed model are represented in Fig. 4. The validation score of our proposed model is 90 ± 4.

The accuracy and loss in terms of training and testing are displayed in Fig. 4. Figure 5 is represented confusion matrix of DeepFireNet model.

Table 3. Hyperparameters fine tuning

Learning rate	Batch size	Dropout	No. of epochs	Accuracy	Loss
0.001	32	0.01	300	86%	1%
0.002	64	0.02	250	88%	2%
0.01	64	0.005	200	90%	0.1%
0.01	**64**	**0.01**	**200**	**92.33%**	**0.01%**
0.01	128	0.002	150	89%	4%

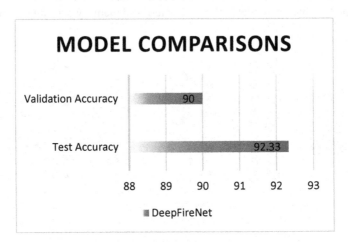

Fig. 4. DeepFireNet model results

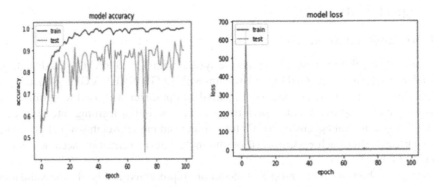

Fig. 5. Accuracy and loss

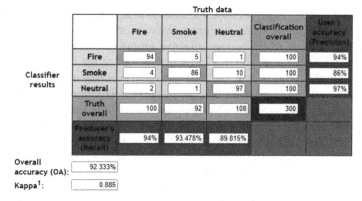

Fig. 6. DeepFireNet confusion matrix

5.2 DeepFireNet

For the robustness of our model, we have presented a detailed comparison of different fire detection models with our proposed DeepFireNet. Our proposed model achieved the highest accuracy than other pioneered models (Fire Detection, Squeeze Net, and AlexNet) [6].

Figure 6 result shows that DeepFireNet performs well than other well-known models in terms of test accuracy and due to the minimum number of layers our model is not complex as other models (Fig. 7).

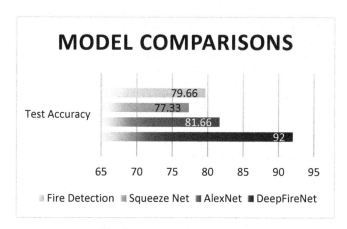

Fig. 7. DeepFireNet robustness

6 Conclusion

In this paper, we have introduced the DeepFireNet model for fire detection and compared it to existing convolutional neural network models. The comparison of fire detection was performed on the same images' dataset. The aim was to design a lightweight fire detection CNN-based model with the highest accuracy. We showed that even with a small number of images our proposed model is quite effective for the detection and classification of fire images. Our modal size is (376.4 kb) which is half of the baseline modal (683.1 kB) proposed by J. Gotthans et al. [6]. The measured accuracy of our proposed model DeepFireNet was 92.33% and in the base study, the presented accuracy of AlexNet was 81.66%, Fire Detection and Squeeze Net accuracy was 79.66% and 77.33% respectively. In terms of execution time, our proposed model based on fewer network layers than other models due to its execution time of DeepFireNet was less than other CNN models. In the future, we have planned to work on the video dataset for fire detection and also locating the location 92.33 90 88 89 90 91 92 93 Test Accuracy Validation Accuracy MODEL COMPARISONS DeepFireNet 92 81.66 77.33 79.66 65 70 75 80 85 90 95 Test Accuracy MODEL COMPARISONS Fire Detection Squeeze Net AlexNet DeepFireNet of the fire in video frames. The concept of transfer learning may be used to improve the modal performance but may also extend the size of the modal.

References

1. Bugaric, M., Jakovcevic, T., Stipanicev, D.: Computer vision based measurement of wildfire smoke dynamics. Adv. Electr. Comput. Eng. **15**(1), 55–62 (2015). https://doi.org/10.4316/AECE.2015.01008
2. Chen, T.H., Yin, Y.H., Huang, S.F., Ye, Y.T.: The smoke detection for early fire-alarming system based on video processing. In: Intelligent Information Hiding and Multimedia Signal Processing, pp. 427–430 (2006). https://doi.org/10.1109/IIH-MSP.2006.265033
3. Hubel, D.H., Wiesel, T.N.: Ferrier lecture: functional architecture of macaque monkey visual cortex. Proc. R. Soc. Lond. Biol. Sci. **198**(1130), 1–59 (1977)
4. Frizzi, S., Kaabi, R., Bouchouicha, M., Ginoux, J.M., Moreau, E., Fnaiech, F.: Convolutional neural network for video fire and smoke detection. In: IECON Proceedings (Industrial Electronics Conference), pp. 877–882 (2016). https://doi.org/10.1109/IECON.2016.7793196
5. Genovese, A., Labati, R.D., Piuri, V., Scotti, F.: Wildfire smoke detection using computational intelligence techniques. In: IEEE International Conference on Computational Intelligence for Measurement Systems and Applications Proceedings, pp. 34–39 (2011). https://doi.org/10.1109/CIMSA.2011.6059930
6. Gotthans, J., Gotthans, T., Marsalek, R.:Deep convolutional neural network for fire detection. In: 2020 30th International Conference Radioelektronika (RADIOELEKTRONIKA), Bratislava, Slovakia, pp. 1–6 (2020). https://doi.org/10.1109/RADIOELEKTRONIKA49387.2020.9092344
7. Zhang, J., Li, W., Yin, Z., Liu, S., Guo, X.: Forest fire detection system based on wireless sensor network. In: 2009 4th IEEE Conference on Industrial Electronics and Applications, ICIEA 2009, pp. 520–523 (2009). https://doi.org/10.1109/ICIEA.2009.5138260
8. Fukushima, K.: Neocognitron: a self-organizing neural network model for a mechanism of pattern recognition unaffected by shift in position. Biol. Cybern. **36**(4), 193–202 (1980)
9. Lee, W., Kim, S., Lee, Y.T., Lee, H.W., Choi, M.: Deep neural networks for wild fire detection with unmanned aerial vehicle. In: 2017 IEEE International Conference on Consumer Electronics, ICCE 2017, pp. 252–253 (2017). https://doi.org/10.1109/ICCE.2017.7889305
10. Mueller, M., Karasev, P., Kolesov, I., Tannenbaum, A.: Optical flow estimation for flame detection in videos. IEEE Trans. Image Process. **22**(7), 2786–2797 (2013). https://doi.org/10.1109/TCSVT.2015.2392531

11. Chen, T.H., Yin, Y.H., Huang, S.F., Ye, Y.T.: The smoke detection for early fire-alarming system base on video processing. In: Proceedings of 2006 International Conference on Intelligent. Information Hiding and Multimedia Signal Processing, IIH-MSP 2006, pp. 427–430 (2006). https://doi.org/10.1109/IIH-MSP.2006.265033
12. Tao, C., Zhang, J., Wang, P.: Smoke detection based on deep convolutional neural networks. In: Proceedings - 2016 International Conference on Industrial Informatics - Computing Technology, Intelligent Technology, Industrial Information Integration, ICIICII 2016, pp. 150–153 (2017). https://doi.org/10.1109/ICIICII.2016.0045
13. Töreyin, B.U., Dedeoğlu, Y., Güdükbay, U., Cetin, A.E.: Computer vision based method for real-time fire and flame detection. Pattern Recogn. Lett. **27**(1), 49–58 (2006). https://doi.org/10.1016/j.patrec.2005.06.015
14. Yin, Z., Wan, B., Yuan, F., Xia, X., Shi, J.: A deep normalization and convolutional neural network for image smoke detection. IEEE Access **5**, 18429–18438 (2017). https://doi.org/10.1109/ACCESS.2017.2747399
15. Zhang, Q., Xu, J., Xu, L., Guo, H.: Deep convolutional neural networks for forest fire detection. In: Proceedings of the 2016 International Forum on Management, Education and Information Technology Application. Atlantis Press (2016)

Smart Electrical Energy Systems, AI and ML in Security

THD Reduction Comparison of Three Phase SPPS via Conventional RC and Novel PRESH Controller

Uma Yadav$^{(\boxtimes)}$, Anju Gupta, and Rajesh Kumar Ahuja

J C Bose University of Science and Technology YMCA, Faridabad, India
er.yadavuma11@gmail.com

Abstract. The proposed paper aims to analyze the THD (Total Harmonic Distortion) of a three-phase SPPS (Solar Photovoltaic Power System) and a comparison of THD analysis is done via conventional RC (Resonant Current) and the Novel PRESH (PRES + RESH) Controller. Presently, to eliminate the harmonics from three phase SPPS, various filters and controllers have already been proposed, but they either result in having THD on the higher side or make the system bulky. These techniques fail to eliminate the harmonic when the reference waveform gets distorted from its original position. The Novel PRESH Controller proposed here is a combination of PRES (Proportional Resonant) and RESH (Resonant Harmonic) controllers where inverter current is used as input to a compensator of lower forward gain instead of applying the difference between reference current signal and grid current as in conventional RC controller. The proposed controller can also overcome the problem of distorted reference waveform. An Experimental Setup is designed for investigating the Novel PRESH controller in terms of THD mitigation and a comparison is made with the conventional RC controller with the help of BP (Bode Plot) to show that the proposed Novel PRESH controller can tackle the distorted reference waveform in a reliable manner. Furthermore, to show that the THD obtained through the help of the Novel PRESH Controller is much lower than that of a conventional RC controller and under the limit as defined by IEEE standards 519 and 1547.

Keywords: SPPS · PRESH · PRES · RESH · THD · RC

1 Introduction

Solar Photovoltaic Power System (SPPS) can be connected to grid using converter [14, 23]. The converter used here will ensure flow of power from SPPS to grid. SPPS can also be connected with other local load, energy storage [9, 15, 17]. The power quality of grid mainly depends upon voltage, frequency, harmonic, etc. [7, 11, 20, 28]. In order to have good power-factor and minimum line losses the harmonic content of grid connected solar photovoltaic system should be as low as to 1%. Photo-Voltaic system should have low current harmonic distortion so that all other equipment connected to grid do not face any adverse effects. Acc. to IEEE standard 519 and 1547, THD (Total Harmonic Distortion) is

© The Author(s), under exclusive license to Springer Nature Switzerland AG 2022
F. Sanfilippo et al. (Eds.): INTAP 2021, CCIS 1616, pp. 185–196, 2022.
https://doi.org/10.1007/978-3-031-10525-8_15

kept below 5% [21]. Generally, for reducing current harmonic of SPPS, earlier technique developed are through: lead-lag [8], modified PI [3, 30], repetitive [22, 34], dead-beat [12], PR controller [13, 29, 33], shunt filter [4, 10, 25–27], PRES Controller [2, 16]. Common technique adopted before for eliminating harmonics among researcher was to make use of resonant current controller [13, 29, 33]. This controller makes use of proportional resonant and resonant compensator. The function of duo is to keep track of fundamental reference current signal and for attenuating the current harmonics. With normal condition, this controller as referred in reference [13, 33] work perfectly, but when abnormal condition arises, this compensator performance deteriorates resulting in increase of current harmonic distortion. The simplest technique for eliminating the current harmonic is by engaging the PRES [2, 16] because of its modularity. In PRES controller, K_P (Proportional gain) is added with resonant path which is set at desired frequency. Several advanced techniques for mitigating the harmonic have been discussed in details [1, 18, 19]. These control techniques make use of separately generated current reference by the help of positive and negative sequence component. Phase locked loop Algorithm as discussed in [16] and [5, 19] does not get affect from the voltage harmonic, inter-harmonic and imbalance conditions. But these control techniques are complex and have high computational loading problem. The alternative for these techniques is achieved through [24, 31, 32] where Resonant Harmonic Controller is incorporated in series with Proportional resonant controller.

The presented paper at first will discuss the design procedure of Novel PRESH controller along with its implementation in grid tied SPPS. In second step, a comparison is done in THD reduction for three phase SPPS via conventional RC and Novel PRESH controller. For eliminating the higher order harmonic, Novel PRESH controller make use of PRES controller which is connected in parallel with RESH controller instead of conventional series connection as discussed in [1, 32]. The analysis of Conventional RC and Novel PRESH controller is done through the help of bode plot analysis.

Novelty and Originality of the proposed research paper are as:

- Earlier technique develops for reducing current harmonics among researcher were lag-lead controller [8], modified PI controller [3, 30], repetitive controller [22, 34], dead beat controller [12], PR controller [13, 29, 33],shunt filter [4, 10, 25–27], suffer certain drawback as indicated:
- Standard PI controller, can't track ac current reference.
- [3, 12, 13, 22, 29, 30, 33, 34], shows very poor response in tracking sinusoidal reference as well as while rejecting the disturbances.
- [13, 29, 33] can't use with present day Grid Connection as there is need of digital implementation of controller for rejecting the harmonic.
- [4, 10, 25–27], Elimination of harmonic through the use of shunt filter becomes an old technique as their inability in eliminating the harmonic as per IEEE reference 519 and 1547.
- Design algorithm of Novel PRESH (Proportional Resonant Harmonic) controller is discussed where inverter current is used as input to compensator of lower forward gain instead of applying the difference of reference current signal and grid current as that in conventional RC controller.

- Comparison between Conventional RC and designed Novel PRESH controller is done in term of THD mitigation, to show that designed Novel PRESH controller can tackle even if reference waveform is distorted one and also to show that THD obtained by Novel PRESH controller is far less than conventional RC controller.

The proposed paper is carved out in the following manner: Sect. 2 will discuss about three phase grid tied solar photovoltaic power system (SPPS), Sect. 3 will deal with design algorithm of Novel PRESH controller, Sect. 4 will deal with THD analysis of Novel PRESH controller in term of Bode-Plot analysis and harmonic mitigation followed by conclusion.

2   Three Phase SPPS

Figure 1 represent the three phase SPPS having Photovoltaic module/array, a capacitor Cdc and a 3- phase voltage source inverter connected with three phase grid having voltages as Vga, Vgb and Vgc.

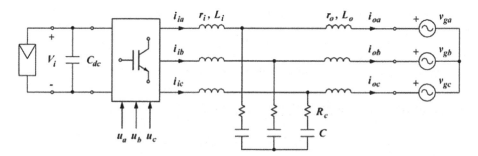

Fig. 1. Three phase solar photovoltaic power system (SPPS)

For reducing the high frequency switching harmonic, L-C-L filter is employed and for attenuating the peak magnitude of L-C-L filter at resonance frequency and damping resistor is made to connect in series with capacitor.

2.1   Open Loop Mode (OLM)l of 3-phase SPPS

Average model of 3-phase SPPS is shown by below Fig.

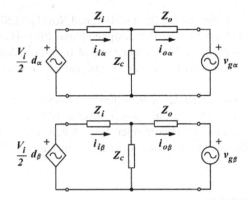

Fig. 2. Average circuit model (ACM) of three phase grid tied SPP

Input to this model is V_i which is a dc link voltage, grid voltage is denoted as V_g and control input d whose value varies from -1 to $+1$.

$$-1 \leq d_\alpha \leq +1 \tag{1}$$

$$-1 \leq d\beta \leq +1 \tag{2}$$

Inverter current is indicated by i_i whereas grid current is indicated by i_o.

3   Designing of Novel PRESH Controller

3.1   Conventional RC Controller in Three Phase SPPS

Figure 3 shows a Conventional RC controller. Where, $H_1(s)$ is PRES (Proportional Resonant) controller and $H_2(s)$ is RESH (Resonant Harmonic) Controller.

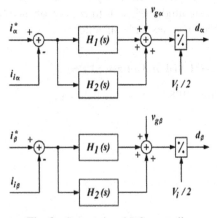

Fig. 3. Conventional RC controller

The difference of input current and reference current i.e. error is processed through proportional controller and resonant controller. Generally, inverter current is used in place of grid current so as to increase the robustness of the system and to reduce the requirement of current sensor. Dc link voltage and voltage of grid are used here as a forwarded signal so as to improve the system dynamic. By engaging this forwarded signal, system capability in rejecting external disturbances also gets enhanced [6, 10].

Following equation can be derived from Fig. 3 as:

$$d_\alpha = \frac{2}{V_i}\left[v_{g\alpha} + (H_1(s) + H_2(s))\left(i_\alpha^* - i_{i\alpha}\right)\right]H_d(s) \tag{3}$$

$$d_\beta = \frac{2}{V_i}\left[v_{g\beta} + (H_1(s) + H_2(s))\left(i_\beta^* - i_{i\beta}\right)\right]H_d(s) \tag{4}$$

Here, d_α, d_β are the control input which can take value from -1 to $+1$, and V_g is the voltage of grid and $H_d(s)$ is transfer function of model having time delay as T_d.

For control processing time delay T_d, transfer function is given as

$$H_d(s) = e^{-T_d s} \tag{5}$$

The parameter used in the transfer function of above compensator is shown by Table 1, along with list of value used in the work. Table 1 also contain the detail parameter of three phase SPPS used here.

Table 1. Parameters of three phase SPPS.

Symbol	Quantity	Nominal Value
P_m	Maximum output power	3.2 KW
f_s	Switching frequency	10 KHz
$V_{i, OC}$	Open Circuit PV array output Voltage	750 V
$I_{i, SC}$	Short circuit PV array output current	5.4 A
$V_{i, MP}$	Maximum power PV output voltage	650 V
$I_{i, MP}$	Maximum Power PV output current	4.9 A
L_i	Inverter side Inductance	6.9 mH
R_i	Inverter side resistance	0.27 Ω
C	Filter Capacitor	680 nF
R_c	Filter damping resistance	6.8 Ω
L_o	Grid side inductance	2.1 mH
R_o	Grid side resistance	0.14 Ω
V_d	Grid Voltage (rms, phase to neutral)	200 V
f_o	Grid frequency	50 Hz
K_p	Proportional gain	60 Ω
K_{s1}	Fundamental integral gain	300 Ω s²
K_{in}	n-harmonic integral gain	300 Ω s²
ϵ_1	Fundamental damping factor	0.01
ϵ_n	n-harmonics damping factor	0.01
N	Selected harmonics to be attenuated	5,7,11,13
T_d	Control Processing delay time	100 μs

4   Novel PRESH in Three Phase SPPS

4.1   1st Step: Design Control Configuration of Novel PRESH Controller

In this Novel PRESH controller, shown by Fig. 4, inverter current is used as input to compensator of lower forward gain instead of applying the difference of reference current signal and grid current.

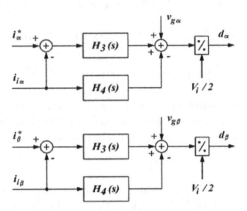

Fig. 4. Proposed PRESH controller

Transfer functions of PRESH controller are obtained as:

$$H_3(s) = \frac{k_{i1} 2\xi_1 \omega_o s}{s^2 + 2\xi_1 \omega_o s + \omega_o^2} \tag{6}$$

$$H_4(s) = k_p + \sum_n \frac{k_{in} 2\xi_n (n\omega_o) s}{s^2 + 2\xi_n (n\omega_o) s + (n\omega_o)^2} \tag{7}$$

4.2   2nd Step: Closed-Loop Transfer Function of Novel PRESH Controller

From Fig. 4, control input of Novel PRESH controller can be written as

$$d_\alpha = \frac{2}{V_i} \left[v_{g\alpha} + H_3(s)(i_\alpha^* - i_{i\alpha}) - H_4(s)i_{i\alpha} \right] H_d(s) \tag{8}$$

$$d_\beta = \frac{2}{V_i} \left[v_{g\beta} + H_3(s)\left(i_\beta^* - i_{i\beta}\right) - H_4(s)i_{i\beta} \right] H_d(s) \tag{9}$$

By substituting Eq. (8) and (9) in Fig. 2 so as to obtain closed loop transfer function of Novel PRESH controller, we get:

$$T(s) = (Z_c(s) + Z_o(s))G_i(s)(H_3(s) + H_4(s)) \times H_d(s) \tag{10}$$

$$G_r(s) = \frac{Z_c(s)G_i(s)H_3(s)H_d(s)}{1 + T(s)} \tag{11}$$

$$G_g(s) = -\frac{G_i(s)(Z_i(s) + (H_3(s) + H_4(s))H_d(s))}{1 + T(s)} \tag{12}$$

5   Analysis of Novel PRESH Controller

5.1   Bode Plot Analysis of Novel PRESH Controller

Bode Plot figure of PRES and RESH controller used in proposed PRESH Controller is indicated by Fig. 5.

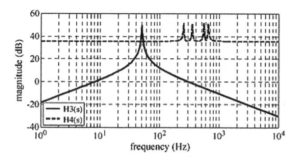

Fig. 5. BP figure of PRES & RESH controller used in proposed novel PRESH controller

Bode-Plot of transfer function for proposed Novel PRESH controller is indicated by Fig. 6. All the value taken for case study of Novel PRESH controller is indicated in Table 1.

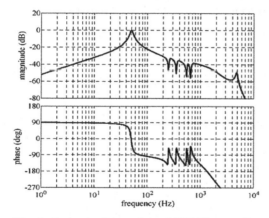

Fig. 6. Bode-plot figure of novel PRESH controller

From the above figure it is clear that, transfer function of proposed Novel PRESH controller has behavior similar to band pass filter. At, selected harmonic frequency i.e. 250, 350, 550 and 650 Hz, dip in magnitude diagram can be seen. Thus, by using this proposed Novel PRESH controller, tracking of fundamental component of signal can be expected even if reference waveform is distorted one.

5.2 THD Analysis of PRES Controller in Three Phase SPPS

Experimental Setup of 3-Phase GTSPPS for testing of proposed PRESH Controller is shown by Fig. 7.

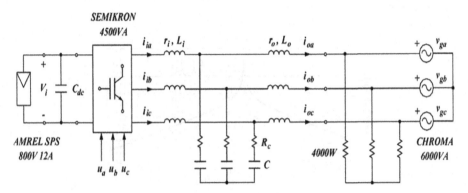

Fig. 7. Experimental set up of three phase SPPS for novel PRESH controller testing

It makes use of dc source connected with PV array, an inverter, programmable chroma and others. Here load taken is 4KW resistive in nature. This load presence is mandatory in the proposed experimental setup as ac source can't absorb the active power injected.

Further, it also includes standard external control loop and internal control loop along with modulator represented by Fig. 8 and Fig. 9 respectively.

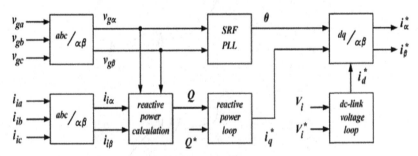

Fig. 8. External control loop

The proposed novel PRESH Controller of this paper is tested with high voltage disturbances of the grid and the waveform of various parameter used is shown by Fig. 10, and the THD measures are listed in Table 2. To simulate a difficult practical scenario, different voltage harmonic contents were programmed into the ac source for each grid phase. When the Novel PRESH compensator is activated, the conventional resonant current (RC) control performs better. Indeed, in this instance, the present THD is much decreased, and all measurements are far below the 5% limit. The suggested control further minimises harmonic distortion and lowers the existing THD to near-zero values.

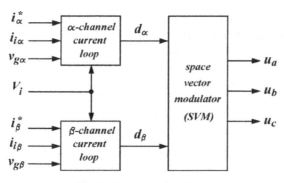

Fig. 9. Internal control loop

The last series of tests examines a grid with voltage harmonics and imbalances, where magnitudes and phases are given in per unit and degrees, respectively. The experimental measurements are shown in Fig. 10 and Table 2. Take note that the current has increased as a result of the grid voltage decrease. Essentially, the voltage control loop has increased the amplitude of the current reference signals in order to keep the injection of active power constant, while conventional control provides poor results. The novel PRESH controller presented here achieves excellent performance. The present THD is quite low, comparable to the value recorded when there is no voltage imbalance on the grid. This property is due to the proposed control's capacity to remove the harmonics present in the existing reference signals.

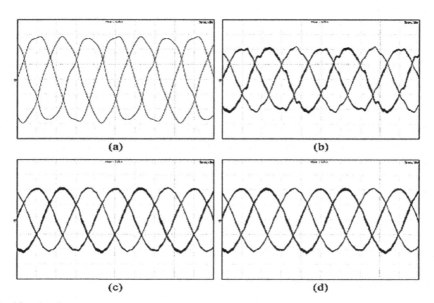

Fig. 10. Simulation result for grid condition with high voltage THD (a) grid voltage (b) standard control without resonant harmonic controller (c) standard control with resonant harmonic controller (d) proposed novel PRESH controller

Harmonic distortion thus calculated is depicted by Table 2 comparing the THD without controller and with proposed controller of the system.

From Table 2, it is cleared that standard control gives very poor performance when resonant harmonic controller is not engaged however, the performance improves a bit after engaging the resonant harmonic controller.

The Proposed Novel PRESH controller reduces the current harmonic distortion well below to 5% which is as per IEEE standard 519 and 1547.

Table 2. THD under different control technique

Control technique	Vga	Vgb	Vgc	I_{oa}	Iob	Ioc
Conventional control without resonant harmonic controller	4.0	4.5	7.5	3.6	3.4	5.7
Conventional control with resonant harmonic controller	3.7	4.7	7.8	1.8	1.8	2.3
Novel PRESH controller	3.8	4.8	7.8	0.9	0.92	0.945

From Table 2, it is cleared that standard control gives very poor performance when resonant harmonic controller is not engaged however, the performance improves a bit after engaging the resonant harmonic controller.

The Proposed Novel PRESH controller reduces the current harmonic distortion well below to 5% which is as per IEEE standard 519 and 1547.

6   Conclusions

The presented paper discusses the design algorithm and performance anlaysis in term of THD and harmonic mitigation along with bode plot analysis of Novel PRESH (PRES + RESH) controller Interfaced with three phase SPPS (Solar Photovoltaic Power System).

Implementation of Phase Locked Loop is done in an effective manner, for synchronizing the SPPS with grid voltage. Further, identification of indirect mechanism is done that was responsible in generating the current harmonic from abnormal grid condition in standard resonant current controller. The proposed Novel PRESH controller overcome this problem by connecting in a different configuration as explained by using case study. Thus, able to track the fundamental component even if abnormal condition arises.

References

1. Alhafadhi, L., The, J.: Advances in reduction of total harmonic distortion in solar photovoltaic systems: a literature review. Int. J. Energy Res. **44**, 1–16 (2019)
2. Althobaiti, M., Armstrong, M., Elgendy, M.A., Mulolani, F.: Three-phase grid connected PV inverters using the proportional resonance controller. In: 2016 IEEE 16th International Conference on Environment and Electrical Engineering (EEEIC), Florence, Italy, pp. 1–6 (2016)
3. Blanco, C., Tardelli, F., Reigosa, D., Zanchetta, P., Briz, F.: Design of a cooperative voltage harmonic compensation strategy for islanded microgrids combining virtual admittance and repetitive controller. IEEE Trans. Ind. Appl. **55**(1), 680–688 (2019)

4. Campanhol, L.B.G., Silva, S.A.O., Sampaio, L.P., Azauri, A.O.: A grid-connected photovoltaic power system with active power injection, reactive power compensation and harmonic filtering. In: Proceedings of COBEP, pp. 642–649 (2013)
5. Castilla, M., Miret, J., Matas, J., Garcia de Vicuna, L., Guerrero, J.M.: Linear current control scheme with series resonant harmonic compensator for single-phase grid-connected photovoltaic inverters. IEEE Trans. Ind. Electron. **55**(7), 2724–2733 (2008)
6. Cavalcanti, M.C., de Oliveira, K.C., de Farias, A.M., Neves, F.A., Azevedo, G.M., Camboim, F.C.: Modulation techniques to eliminate leakage currents in transformerless three-phase photovoltaic systems. IEEE Trans. Ind. Electron. **57**(4), 1360–1368 (2010)
7. Cordova-Garcia, J., Wang, X., Xie, D., Zhao, Y., Zuo, L.: Control of communications-dependent cascading failures in power grids. IEEE Trans. Smart Grid **10**(5), 5021–5031 (2019)
8. Faiz, M.T., Khan, M.M., Jianming, X., Habib, S., Tang, H.: Double feed-forward compensation based true damping of Inductor-capacitor-Induxtor type grid tied lainverter. In: 2018 IEEE International Conference on Industrial Technology (ICIT), pp. 788–793 (2018)
9. Guerrero, J.M., Vasquez, J.C., Matas, J., Garcia de Vicuna, L., Castilla, M.: Hierarchical control of droop-controlled ac and dc microgrids—a general approach toward standardization. IEEE Trans. Ind. Electron. **58**(1), 158–172 (2011)
10. He, J., Li, Y.W., Blaabjerg, F., Wang, X.: Active harmonic filtering using current-controlled, grid-connected DG units with closed-loop power control. IEEE Trans. Power Electron. **29**, 642–653 (2013)
11. IEEE Standard for Distributed Resources With Electric Power Systems, IEEE15471, (2008)
12. Khomsi, C., Bouzid, M., Jelassi, K., Champenois, G.: Harmonic current conpensation in a single-phase grid connected photovoltaic system supplying nonlinear load. In: 2018 9th International Renewable Energy Congress (IREC), pp. 1–6 (2018)
13. Kuo, Y.S., Lin, J.Y., Tang, J.C., Hsieh, J.G.: Lead-lag compensator design based on vector margin and steady-state error of the step response via particle swarm optimization. In: 2016 International Conference on Fuzzy Theory and Its Applications (iFuzzy), pp. 1–6 (2016)
14. Lumei, K.: Design and analysis of a three-phase grid-connected solar PV inverter with proportional-integral controller. In: 2020 IEEE International Conference for Innovation in Technology (INOCON), pp. 1–5 (2020)
15. Marańda, W.: Analysis of self-consumption of energy from grid-connected photovoltaic system for various load scenarios with short-term buffering. SN Appl. Sci. **1**(5), 1–10 (2019). https://doi.org/10.1007/s42452-019-0432-5
16. Padula, A.S., Agnoletto, E.J., Neves, R.V.A., Magossi, R.F.Q., Machado, R.Q., Oliveira, V.A.: Partial harmonic current distortion mitigation in microgrids using proportional resonant controller. In: 2019 18th European Control Conference (ECC), Naples, Italy, pp. 435-440 (2019)
17. Phannil, N., Jettanasen, C., Ngaopitakkul, A.: Power quality analysis of grid connected solar power inverter. In: 2017 IEEE 3rd International Future Energy Electronics Conference and ECCE Asia (IFEEC 2017 - ECCE Asia), pp. 1508–1513 (2017)
18. Prasad, P.S., Parimi, A.M.: Harmonic mitigation in grid connected and islanded microgrid via adaptive virtual impedance. In: 2020 IEEE International Conference on Power Electronics, Smart Grid and Renewable Energy (PESGRE2020), Cochin, India, pp. 1–6 (2020)
19. Rodriguez, P., Timbus, A.V., Teodorescu, R., Liserre, M., Blaabjerg, F.: Flexible active power control of distributed power generation systems during grid faults. IEEE Trans. Ind. Electron. **54**(5), 2583–2592 (2007)
20. Sharma, S., Gupta, A., Yadav, U.: Simulation of grid connected solar power system and harmonic reduction. J. Power Electron. Devices **4**(2), 1–11 (2018)
21. Shetty, D., Prabhu, N.: Ziegler-Nichols method based VAR current controller for static compensator. Energy Procedia **117**, 543–550 (2017)

22. da Silva, J.N., Filho, A.J.S., Fernandes, D.A., Tahim, A.P.N., da Silva, E.R.C., Costa, F.F.: A discrete current controller for 1-phase grid-tied inverters. In: 2017 Brazilian Power Electronics Conference (COBEP), p. 1–6 (2017)

23. Singh, A.K., Kumar, S., Singh, B.: Solar PV energy generation system interfaced to three phase grid with improved power quality. IEEE Trans. Ind. Electron. **67**(5), 3798–3808 (2020)

24. Stojic, D.: Digital resonant controller based on modified tustin discretization method. Adv. Electr. Comput. Eng. **16**(4), 83–88 (2016)

25. Trinh, Q., Lee, H.: An advanced current control strategy for three-phase shunt active power filters. IEEE Trans. Ind. Electron. **60**(12), 5400–5410 (2013)

26. Yadav, U., Gupta, A.: Current harmonic mitigation in grid tied solar photovoltaic system via PRES. In: 2020 5th IEEE International Conference on Recent Advances and Innovations in Engineering (ICRAIE), Jaipur, India, pp. 1–5 (2020)

27. Yadav, U., Gupta, A., Ahuja, R.: Robust control design procedure and simulation of PRES controller having phase-locked loop (PLL) control technique in grid-tied converter. In: 2020 3rd International Seminar on Research of Information Technology and Intelligent Systems (ISRITI), Yogakarta, Indonesia, pp. 445–450 (2020)

28. Yadav, U., Gupta, A., Ahuja, R.: Analysis of CPG control strategies using APC for single phase grid tied SPPS. Mater. Today Proc. (2021) https://doi.org/10.1016/j.matpr.2021.05.195

29. Yadav, U., Gupta, A., Rai, H.K., Bhalla, D.K.: Mitigation of harmonic current in grid connected solar power system. In: Muzammil, M., Chandra, A., Kankar, P.K., Kumar, H. (eds.) Recent Advances in Mechanical Engineering, pp. 605–610. Springer, Singapore (2021). https://doi.org/10.1007/978-981-15-8704-7_74

30. Yang, Y., Zhou, K., Wang, H., Blaabjerg, F.: Analysis and mitigation of dead-time harmonics in the single-phase full-bridge PWM converter with repetitive controllers. IEEE Trans. Ind. Appl. **54**(5), 5343–5354 (2018)

31. Yazdani, A., Iravani, R.: Voltage-Sourced Converters in Power Systems: Modeling, Control, and Applications. Wiley, Hoboken (2009).Chapter 7

32. Yepes, A.G., Freijedo, F.D., Doval-Gandoy, J., Lopez, O., Malvar, J., Fernandez-Comesana, P.: Effects of discretization methods on the performance of resonant controllers. IEEE Trans. Power Electron. **25**(7), 1692–1712 (2010)

33. Youcefa, B.E., Massoum, A., Barkat, S., Bella, S., Wira, P.: DPC method for grid connected photovoltaic system acts as a shunt active power filter implemented with processor in the loop. In: 2018 International Conference on Electrical Sciences and Technologies in Maghreb (CISTEM) (2018)

34. Zhou, K., Blaabjerg, F., Wang, D., Yang, Y.: Periodic Control of PEC, IET (2016)

Artificial Neural Network (ANN) Trained by a Novel Arithmetic Optimization Algorithm (AOA) for Short Term Forecasting of Wind Power

Muhammad Hamza Zafar[1], Noman Mujeeb Khan[1], Syed Kumayl Raza Moosavi[2], Majad Mansoor[3], Adeel Feroz Mirza[3], and Naureen Akhtar[4(✉)]

[1] Capital University of Science and Technology, Islamabad 44000, Pakistan
[2] National University of Sciences and Technology, Islamabad 44000, Pakistan
[3] University of Science and Technology of China, Heifi 230027, China
[4] Department of Engineering Sciences, University of Agder, 4879 Grimstad, Norway
naureen.akhtar@uia.no

Abstract. Stochastic nature of wind power with a high amount of non-linearity makes it very difficult to predict wind power production in real time which has a high impact in the renewable energy industry. The uncertainty of wind power makes it challenging to integrate it with the power grid. As a solution, an early short term forecasting of the wind flow significantly improves the wind power generation. For this purpose, a novel arithmetic optimization algorithm is used to train an artificial neural network for short term wind power prediction. Effective exploration and exploitation behavior of the algorithm due to embedded arithmetic operators for updating the weights and biases train the neural network. To validate the performance of the proposed technique, well-known techniques are compared using a case study on wind power in Turkey for the winter and summer season as a benchmark. The proposed method has shown better prediction performance as compared to the existing techniques. AOANN achieves up to 94.87% and 97.18% less training error and up to 96.42% and 83.64% less testing error in winter and summer seasons respectively.

Keywords: Bio-inspired neural network · Intelligent control system · Arithmetic optimization algorithm · Wind power · Regression

1 Introduction

The euphoria of living in a society that is technologically advanced is compelling. However, this advancement has exponentially risen the demand of energy as well. Heavy reliance of the modern world on power has sky-rocketed the demand for energy globally. Conventional energy resources such as oil, gas and coal are not only fatal for living things but they are also hazardous to the environment. Now, more than ever, the need for alternate resources of energy have grown rapidly. Sources of energy such as wind, solar, and bio-gas, on the other hand, being clean and in-exhaustible provide a reliable alternate

© The Author(s), under exclusive license to Springer Nature Switzerland AG 2022
F. Sanfilippo et al. (Eds.): INTAP 2021, CCIS 1616, pp. 197–209, 2022.
https://doi.org/10.1007/978-3-031-10525-8_16

solution. These sources neither produce green gases nor can they be depleted. Amongst the mentioned alternate energy sources, wind energy is one of the fastest growing technological field. A single wind turbine can generate up-to several Mega Watt's (MW) of power. Wind power however is intermittent in nature i.e. it is dependent upon the weather conditions. This dependency poses certain challenges ranging from the cost of to the dispatching of wind power from power grid stations. Moreover, the intermittency of wind power has adverse effects on the stable operation of wind turbines. The non-stable operation of wind turbine hinders the large scale integration of wind power due to voltage and frequency fluctuations. Therefore a balance is required between power generation and transmission. For this purpose wind power prediction plays a vital role in smooth and cost effective operation of wind turbines.

In order to extract the maximum power out of the wind power systems, many researches have been conducted in recent years. Typically, two classification models can be found in literature for the prediction of wind power; the physical model and the statistical model. Physical models are excellent in terms of long term power prediction. However they suffer from low precision. Statistical models have the ability to correlate between wind power and corresponding input variables such as meteorological data.

Physical models, also known as deterministic models are dependent upon the numerical weather conditions, that is these models use equations of atmospheric motions in order to calculate what meteorological measurements will be in the future. These models are comprised of several features namely climate, terrain, or atmospheric condition etcetera and wind power is predicted via one of these features.

Physical models predict the power in two stages; first the wind speed is predicted and then it is then converted into electrical power. Physical models have shown promising long term prediction results, however they suffer from certain drawbacks as well such as being costly, and difficult to design which renders them unsuitable for predicting wind power.

To overcome the shortcomings of a physical model for wind power prediction, statistical models have been gaining much popularity among many researchers. Statistical models make use of training datasets in order to predict wind power. [1] utilizes the least squares support vector machine to predict wind power and in order to improve the prediction results, an optimization technique known as gravitational search (GS) procedure is implemented.

In some cases, datasets contain missing data. To overcome such flaws [2] introduced a Gaussian regression process and performed multiple imputations for wind power prediction. The process included an expectation-maximization procedure for estimating mixture components of the data distribution for handling the missing data. [3] used a hybrid model to produce better wind prediction results.

The trend of wind flow is captured using a wind power curve. This trend is adjusted using data-driven schemes which have a few inherent problems i.e. increased complexity and longer prediction time.

With the popularity and success in the domain of machine learning (ML), ML algorithms have gained significant recognition among researchers. K-nearest neighbors (KNN) [4] is an ML algorithm that uses multiple features of a meteorological input data. [16] uses a robust algorithm that utilizes genetic programming based ensemble of neural networks to predict wind power on short term basis. Support vector machine (SVM) technique used in [5] finds a co-relation between wind speed and power by altering the invalid initial measurements. However, SVM does not have the ability to predict wind power for a long term basis. In [6] a hybrid of SVM uses a combination of wavelet transform and SVM to produce exceptional results. Another modified version of SVM uses a combination of autoregressive moving average (ARMA) model, support vector machine (SVM) prediction and particle swarm optimization (PSO), called a hybrid PSO-SVM-ARMA [7], is employed to improve the prediction results significantly. In [8], K-Means-long short-term memory (K-Means-LSTM) network model is employed that is capable of handling the time dependencies on a time series data which makes it superior than a back-propagation based neural network and a support vector machine model.

In retrospect, meta-heuristic algorithms have shown great promise in recent decades in terms of data prediction. For example in [9] a swarm based meta-heuristic algorithm namely; the mayfly algorithm was employed to train an Artificial Neural Network for data prediction.

2 Meta Heuristic Algorithms

Meta-heuristic algorithms possess excellent capabilities in terms of locating the global minimum cost solutions. Literature survey shows a wide variety of such algorithms, therefore, they can be split into two distinct categories:

2.1 Single Agent Based

Single Agent Based (SAB) algorithms make use of single agent or a single candidate in order to locate the minimum solution. Examples of SAB Algorithms include Simulated Annealing (SA) [10], Greedy randomized adaptive search (GRAP) [11]. This single agents are improved within the search space until an optimum solution is achieved.

2.2 Multi-agent Based

One of the most obvious problems associated with the SAB is that it is limited in its searching capabilities since a single agent can only search limited number of instances for finding the desired results. This drawback of single agent technique renders it ineffective when it comes to multi-faceted data prediction. In order to mitigate this problem, multi-agent based (MAB) algorithms are utilized.

Multi-agents have a tendency to find the global minimum via learning from each other's position whilst utilizing a complex network of relations. Group Teaching Optimization Algorithm (GTOA) [12], swarm intelligence algorithms such as Particle Swarm Optimization (PSO) [13], the Grey Wolf Optimization (GWO) [14], the Grasshopper Algorithm (GHO) [15], the Firefly Algorithm [16], Barnacle optimization algorithm (BMO) [17] are some of the algorithms that make use of multi-agents. Multiagent optimization algorithms also have application in the field of renewable energy [18–23].

The use of these multi-agent based algorithms can also be seen in the field of deep learning. Updation of weights and biases of an ANN is accomplished through the use of such heuristic algorithms. Several algorithms have already been employed for the purpose of optimizing a neural network but since it can never be certified that a single algorithm is most suitable for every problem, more and more algorithms are introduced every day. In this perspective, a novel, multi-agent based, arithmetic optimization algorithm [24] has been chosen as the focus of this research for the purposes of training an ANN, namely the Arithmetic Optimization Algorithm based Neural Network (AOANN). The effective exploration and exploitation capability of AOA, with few number of tuning parameters and random numbers, make it efficient for minimization of the cost function during the training of neural network.

3 Arithmetic Optimization Algorithm (AOA)

In this paper the arithmetic optimization algorithm is used to train the feed forward neural network. This algorithm is also a population based optimization algorithm which uses arithmetic operators to update the position without calculating their derivatives. Arithmetic is a basic part of number theory but also the important part of modern mathematics. Traditional arithmetic operators are used to in the study which are addition, subtraction, multiplication, and division. The inspiration for AOA comes from the use of these arithmetic operators in solving arithmetic problems. The proposed algorithm is explained as under.

3.1 Initialization

The initialized set of candidate solutions (D), which are generated randomly are presented in (1).

$$
D = \begin{bmatrix} d_{1,1} & \cdots & d_{1,j} \\ d_{2,1} & & \vdots \\ \cdots & \ddots & \vdots \\ d_{N-1,1} & & d_{N-1,j} \\ d_{N,1} & \cdots & d_{N,j} \end{bmatrix}
\tag{1}
$$

At the start of AOA, it first needs to select the search phase i.e. exploitation or exploration. This is achieved by the math optimizer coefficient (MOA) function calculation using (2).

$$
MOA = Min + it \times \left(\frac{Max - Min}{Max\_it} \right)
\tag{2}
$$

where Max and Min are the maximum and minimum value of MOA predefined at the initialization. it is the current iteration while Max_it represents the maximum number of iterations. If $r_1 >$ MOA then exploration phase occurs else the exploitation phase is followed. r_1 is a random number selected within the range [0,1].

3.2 Exploration Phase

In the arithmetic operators, high distributed values can be achieved by using multiplication M or division D operator in mathematical calculations. This leads to the exploration search mechanism. Due to high dispersion created by D and M operator, it is difficult to approach target but in exploitation phase S and A operator will be reach the desired targets more precisely as depicted in Fig. 1.

In the exploration phase, updating of position occurs using (3) with D and M operators.

$$d_{i,j}(it+1) = \begin{cases} best(d_j) \div (MOP + \varepsilon) \times ((UB - LB) \times \mu + LB), & r_2 > 0.5 \\ best(d_j) \times (MOP) \times ((UB - LB) \times \mu + LB), & otherwise \end{cases} \quad (3)$$

where $best(d_j)$ is the global minima position, UB and LB are the upper and lower boundary search space, ε is a small value, r_2 is a random value in the range [0,1] and μ is a control parameter which is used to adjust the search process. MOP is the math optimization probability whose value will be updated using (4).

$$MOP(it) = 1 - \frac{it^{1/\alpha}}{Max\_it^{1/\alpha}} \quad (4)$$

where α is a sensitive parameter and defines the accuracy of the exploration and exploitation phase over the course of the iterative process.

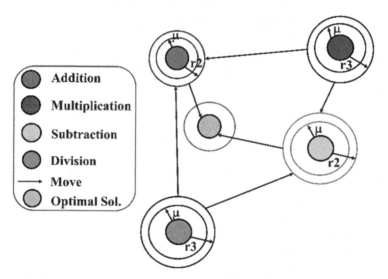

Fig. 1. Position updation of math operators in search of optimal solution.

3.3 Exploitation Phase

In the arithmetic operators, high dense results are produced using the addition A and subtraction S operator which is the exploitation mechanism since S and A cause low dispersion which leads to the target value.

The condition of exploitation phase is also related to the MOA. The subtraction searching strategy and the addition searching strategy are used to search deeply on the dense regions which is modeled in (5).

$$d_{i,j}(it) = \begin{cases} best(d_j) - MOP \times ((UB - LB) \times \mu + LB), & r_3 > 0.5 \\ best(d_j) + MOP \times ((UB - LB) \times \mu + LB), & otherwise \end{cases} \tag{5}$$

This mechanism is modeled for deep search. The subtraction S mechanism will be implemented if $r_3 > 0.5$, where r_3 is the random number between [0,1]. If $r_3 \leq MOA$ then addition A will perform the required task. The most important parameter is μ which needs to be carefully adjusted for the best stochastic process.

3.4 Pseudo Code

The pseudo code of AOA algorithm is shown in Fig. 2. Since every solution updates its position according to the best extracted result, MOA increases linearly from 0.2 to 0.9.

> **initialize** *the AOA parameters, that is,* μ, α
> **initialize** *the random population* $d_i = \{1,2,3,\cdots,N\}$
>   **while***(it<max_it)*
>   *calculate fitness of every solution*
>   *update value of MOA and MOP using (2) and (4)*
>   *generate random number* r_1, r_2, r_3
>   **if** $r_1 > MOA$
>   **if** $r_2 > 0.5$
>   *update position using the first rule in (3)*
>   **else**
>   *update position using the second rule in (3)*
>   **end if**
>   **if** $r_3 > 0.5$
>   *update position using the first rule in (5)*
>   **else**
>   *update position using the second rule in (5)*
>   **end if**
>   **end if**
>   *it=it+1*
>   **end while**
> **Return** *the best solution* d

Fig. 2. Pseudo code of the proposed AOANN for short term wind forecasting updation.

4 Design of AOA-NN

In this paper a 3 layer neural network, that is, input, hidden, and output layer is proposed. The hidden layer contains 10 neurons. The proposed structure of NN is shown in Fig. 3. As shown, the AOA algorithm is used to update the weights and biases of the NN.

The input vector contains the instances of N input features and the corresponding output y_i. The AOA-NN is implemented in the MATLAB 2018a. The flowchart for updating the weights and the biases are shown in Fig. 4.

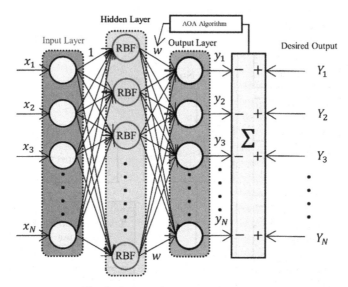

Fig. 3. Proposed structure of AOA-NN.

4.1 Neural Network Design

Figure 3 depicts the structure that is used to design the neural network. Selection for the number of neurons is paramount as it effectively determines the networks high efficiency and less computational time. Neural networks with low number of neurons and hidden layers may not be able to predict the output very efficiently. On the other hand, with high number of neurons and hidden layers results are highly efficient but the computational complexity would increase just as much. Therefore, the right set of variables are required for highest order of accuracy.

4.2 Activation Function

In order to effectively train and test the neural network model, the right activation function for the hidden layer is required. For classification of dataset, the sigmoid function is suitable as shown in (6)

$$\hat{a}_i = \frac{1}{1 + e^{-x_i}} \tag{6}$$

but since wind power prediction is a regression problem, the neural network will predict continuous values. Therefore, the activation function used for this problem is radial basis function as shown in (7) and (8).

$$h(x) = e^{-\left(\frac{(x-c)^2}{r^2}\right)} \tag{7}$$

$$y(x) = \sum_{j=1}^{N} w_j h_j(x) \tag{8}$$

where $h(x)$ is the function for the hidden layer and $y(x)$ is the predicted output.

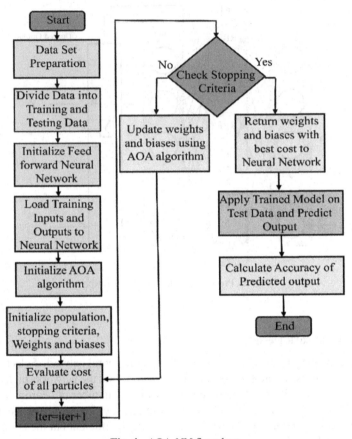

Fig. 4. AOA-NN flowchart.

4.3 Fitness Function

In optimization problems the most important part is the definition of the cost function which is also known as a fitness function. The weights and the biases of the neural network needs to be updated in such a way that the cost function is minimized in the training process. When the cost function is minimized, the latest updated weights and the biases will give the best relation between input and output. The fitness function ($F.F.i$) chosen for the neural network is the normalized mean square error presented in (9).

$$F.F.i = \frac{1}{N} \sum_{j-1}^{N} \left(Y_j - Y_j^n\right)^2 \tag{9}$$

where Y_j is the true output while Y_j^n is the predicted output.

5 Results and Discussions

In this section the training and testing results of models are discussed. The algorithms used for the comparative analysis employ 50 multi-agents and are trained for 50 iterations each. Back-propagation algorithms based on the gradient descent technique require iterations at around 10,000, therefore, the comparison of AOANN is made with PSONN, GWONN and BMONN which are similar meta-heuristic techniques. The statistical analysis, training error and testing error suggest the superior performance of the proposed technique.

5.1 Preparation of Dataset

In wind turbine system, SCADA systems are utilized to record the wind direction, the wind speed and power generated by the wind turbine [25]. The dataset taken is of wind turbine located in Turkey through SCADA systems with 10 *min* intervals. The dataset is also available at [26].

5.2 Forecasting of Wind Power

Comparison is made with true wind power and predicted wind power by all four techniques. The data is divided into training and testing by ratio of 67% and 33% respectively. Firstly, all techniques are trained on training dataset with optimally tuned parameters. Then proposed method and other comparative techniques are tested on the testing dataset. Table 1 and Table 2 shows the minimum error achieved by all techniques during the training and testing process which clearly indicate that the proposed technique achieves less error as compared to the other techniques. The training accuracies for the winter season are illustrated in Fig. 5 (a) which show that the AOA based NN effectively minimizes cost function in less epochs comparatively. Figure 6(a) show that the wind power is highly non-linear and varies greatly in 48 h for the winter season. The power predicted by the AOANN is close to the actual curve. This shows that AOANN is highly effective for the prediction of the highly volatile wind power dataset. The robustness of the proposed technique can also be verified from Fig. 6 (b) which show the relative error generated by the proposed technique to being far less as compared to other techniques. The relative error is calculated by

$$R.E.(\%) = \left(\frac{Y - Y'}{Y'}\right)100\% \qquad (10)$$

where Y is the actual value and Y' is predicted value.

The Vectoral map in Fig. 7(a) shows that the summer season in Turkey has larger variations in wind torrents due to strong winds. The performance of proposed technique is also compared for the summer season. Figure 5 (b) shows comparison of cost achieved w.r.t. epochs by competing techniques and corresponding power prediction is presented in Fig. 7 (a). The power in summer season is highly non-linear but still AOANN achieves closer prediction to the actual value. The performance of proposed techniques in summer season can also be validated by the relative error shown in Fig. 7 (b).

Table 1. Comparison of NMSE of training data.

Technique	Training error	
	Winter	Summer
AOANN	0.0061	0.0040
BMONN	0.01760	0.0165
GWONN	0.0794	0.2196
PSONN	0.1191	0.1419

Table 2. Comparison of NMSE of testing data

Technique	Testing error	
	Winter	Summer
AOANN	0.0172	0.0705
BMONN	0.0855	0.1261
GWONN	0.4140	0.8016
PSONN	0.4812	2.262

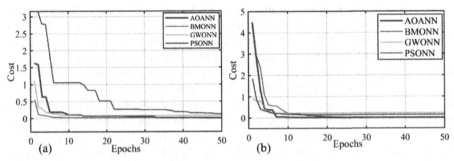

Fig. 5. (a) Cost vs epochs for training in winter season (b) cost vs epochs for training in summer season.

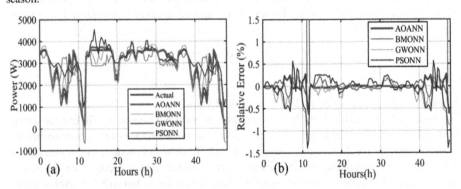

Fig. 6. (a) Comparison of prediction of wind power during winter season (b) relative error comparison for winter season

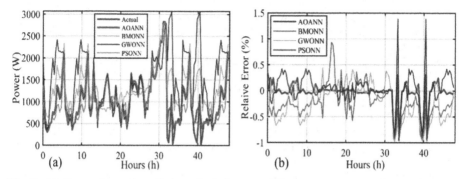

Fig. 7. (a) Comparison of prediction of wind power during summer season (b) relative error comparison for summer season

6 Conclusion

This paper presents a novel implementation of AOANN based forecasting of wind power production. The objective of the study was to improve efficiency of the wind energy conversion system of wind turbines and stability of grid connected operations. The random and intermittent nature of wind leads to a non-linear wind power production, which in turn leads to difficulty in achieving precise prediction and MPPT control. AOANN based prediction model of the wind power production is put into comparison with recently developed meta-heuristic techniques i.e., PSONN, GWONN and BMONN. Training error, testing error, wind power prediction, relative error and efficiency parameters are the parameters utilized for the comparative analysis. To check the performance of the proposed technique in real time, the model is applied on summer and winter weather conditions of Turkey. The statistical study validate the superior performance of the proposed technique for short term wind power prediction. Future study involves the training of deep neural networks with meta heuristic algorithms for complex datasets such as hybrid pv-wind power prediction.

References

1. Yuan, X., Chen, C., Yuan, Y., Huang, Y., Tan, Q.: Short-term wind power prediction based on LSSVM–GSA model. Energy Convers. Manage. **101**, 393–401 (2015)
2. Liu, T., Wei, H., Zhang, K.: Wind power prediction with missing data using Gaussian process regression and multiple imputation. Appl. Soft Comput. **71**, 905–916 (2018)
3. Yan, J., Ouyang, T.: Advanced wind power prediction based on data-driven error correction. Energy Convers. Manage. **180**, 302–311 (2019)
4. Yesilbudak, M., Sagiroglu, S., Colak, I.: A novel implementation of kNN classifier based on multi-tupled meteorological input data for wind power prediction. Energy Convers. Manage. **135**, 434–444 (2017)
5. Zameer, A., Arshad, J., Khan, A., Raja, M.A.Z.: Intelligent and robust prediction of short term wind power using genetic programming based ensemble of neural networks. Energy Convers. Manage. **134**, 361–372 (2017)

6. Liu, Y., Shi, J., Yang, Y., Lee, W.J.: Short-term wind-power prediction based on wavelet transform–support vector machine and statistic-characteristics analysis. IEEE Trans. Ind. Appl. **48**(4), 1136–1141 (2012)

7. Wang, Y., Wang, D., Tang, Y.: Clustered hybrid wind power prediction model based on ARMA, PSO-SVM, and clustering methods. IEEE Access **8**, 17071–17079 (2020)

8. Zhou, B., Ma, X., Luo, Y., Yang, D.: Wind power prediction based on LSTM networks and nonparametric kernel density estimation. IEEE Access **7**, 165279–165292 (2019)

9. Moosavi, S.K.R., Zafar, M.H., Akhter, M.N., Hadi, S.F., Khan, N.M., Sanfilippo, F.: A novel artificial neural network (ANN) using the mayfly algorithm for classification. In: 2021 International Conference on Digital Futures and Transformative Technologies (ICoDT2), pp. 1–6. IEEE (2021)

10. Fatollahi-Fard, A.M., Govindan, K., Hajiaghaei-Keshteli, M., Ahmadi, A.: A green home health care supply chain: new modified simulated annealing algorithms. J. Clean. Prod. **240**, 118200 (2019)

11. Exposito-Marquez, A., Exposito-Izquierdo, C., Brito-Santana, J., Moreno-Pérez, J.A.: Greedy randomized adaptive search procedure to design waste collection routes in La Palma. Comput. Ind. Eng. **137**, 106047 (2019)

12. Zafar, M.H., et al.: Group teaching optimization algorithm based MPPT control of PV systems under partial shading and complex partial shading. Electronics **9**(11), 1962 (2020)

13. Wang, D., Tan, D., Liu, L.: Particle swarm optimization algorithm: an overview. Soft. Comput. **22**(2), 387–408 (2017). https://doi.org/10.1007/s00500-016-2474-6

14. Mirjalili, S., Mirjalili, S.M., Lewis, A.: Grey wolf optimizer. Adv. Eng. Softw. **69**, 46–61 (2014)

15. Mirjalili, S.Z., Mirjalili, S., Saremi, S., Faris, H., Aljarah, I.: Grasshopper optimization algorithm for multi-objective optimization problems. Appl. Intell. **48**(4), 805–820 (2017). https://doi.org/10.1007/s10489-017-1019-8

16. Gandomi, A.H., Yang, X.S., Talatahari, S., Alavi, A.H.: Firefly algorithm with chaos. Commun. Nonlinear Sci. Numer. Simul. **18**(1), 89–98 (2013)

17. Sulaiman, M.H., Mustaffa, Z., Saari, M.M., Daniyal, H.: Barnacles mating optimizer: a new bio-inspired algorithm for solving engineering optimization problems. Eng. Appl. Artif. Intell. **87**, 103330 (2020)

18. Zafar, M.H., Khan, U.A., Khan, N.M.: A sparrow search optimization algorithm based MPPT control of PV system to harvest energy under uniform and non-uniform irradiance. In: 2021 International Conference on Emerging Power Technologies (ICEPT), pp. 1–6. IEEE (2021)

19. Mirza, A.F., Mansoor, M., Zerbakht, K., Javed, M.Y., Zafar, M.H., Khan, N.M.: High-efficiency hybrid PV-TEG system with intelligent control to harvest maximum energy under various non-static operating conditions. J. Clean. Prod. **320**, 128643 (2021)

20. Khan, N.M., Khan, U.A., Zafar, M.H.: Maximum power point tracking of PV system under uniform irradiance and partial shading conditions using machine learning algorithm trained by sailfish optimizer. In: 2021 4th International Conference on Energy Conservation and Efficiency (ICECE), pp. 1–6. IEEE (2021)

21. Zafar, M.H., Khan, U.A., Khan, N.M.: Hybrid grey wolf optimizer sine cosine algorithm based maximum power point tracking control of PV systems under uniform irradiance and partial shading condition. In: 2021 4th International Conference on Energy Conservation and Efficiency (ICECE), pp. 1–6. IEEE (2021)

22. Zafar, M.H., et al.: A novel meta-heuristic optimization algorithm based MPPT control technique for PV systems under complex partial shading condition. Sustain. Energy Technol. Assess. **47**, 101367 (2021)

23. Zafar, M.H., Khan, N.M., Mirza, A.F., Mansoor, M.: Bio-inspired optimization algorithms based maximum power point tracking technique for photovoltaic systems under partial shading and complex partial shading conditions. J. Clean. Prod. **309**, 127279 (2021)

24. Abualigah, L., Diabat, A., Mirjalili, S., Abd Elaziz, M., Gandomi, A.H.: The arithmetic optimization algorithm. Comput. Methods Appl. Mech. Eng. **376**, 113609 (2021)
25. Şahin, S., Türkeş, M.: Assessing wind energy potential of Turkey via vectoral map of prevailing wind and mean wind of Turkey. Theoret. Appl. Climatol. **141**(3–4), 1351–1366 (2020). https://doi.org/10.1007/s00704-020-03276-3
26. https://www.kaggle.com/berkerisen/wind-turbine-scada-dataset

Bode Plot Analysis of PRES and Novel PRESH Controller Interfaced with Three Phase GTSPPS

Uma Yadav[✉], Anju Gupta, and Rajesh Kumar Ahuja

J C Bose University of Science and Technology YMCA, Faridabad, India
er.yadavuma11@gmail.com

Abstract. The presented research paper deals with design algorithm and its Analysis on BP (Bode Plot) of PRES and Novel PRESH (PRES + RESH) controller Interfaced with three phase GTSPPS (Grid-Tied Solar Photovoltaic Power System) and its simulation on MATLAB. Presently, for eliminating the harmonic from three phase SPPS, various filters and controllers have already been proposed but it either resulted in increase of computational load or made the system bulky. The proposed research paper will discuss the design procedure of two controller helpful in mitigating the THD of three phase SPPS near to 1% and thus satisfying the IEEE standard 519 and 1547. PRES controller is suitable in eliminating the THD when grid does not suffer any abnormal condition whereas Novel PRESH controller can be incorporated when grid suffers from abnormal condition. Further, the difference between two techniques will be discussed with its digital implementation.

Keywords: GTSPPS · PRESH · PRES · RESH · THD · Bode plot

1 Introduction

In order to grid-tied solar photovoltaic power system (GTSPPS), converters [3, 6, 7, 11, 14, 19, 21, 24] must be used. The converter used in this case will guarantee that electricity is transferred from SPPS to the grid. Other local loads, such as energy storage, may be linked to the SPPS system. [4, 15, 35]. The voltage, frequency, harmonics, and other characteristics of the grid's power quality [1, 12, 16] are the most important factors. If you want a solar PV system that is linked to the grid to have excellent power factor and minimal line losses, the harmonic content of the system should be as low as 1 percent. The current harmonic distortion of a photovoltaic system should be kept to a minimum so that no detrimental effects are experienced by any other equipment connected to the grid. [33] According to IEEE standards 519 and 1547, THD (Total Harmonic Distortion) should be maintained below 5%. In general, previous techniques established for removing the harmonics of SPPS current include: lead-lag [27], modified PI [13, 20], repetitive [28, 30], dead-beat [36], PR controller [5, 9, 34], shunt filter [8, 18, 26, 29], PRES Controller [12, 17, 22, 23, 31, 32]. The use of resonant current controllers [9, 34] was a common method for reducing harmonics that researchers used in the past. It makes use of proportional resonant and resonant compensator in order to achieve its results. The duo's primary purpose is to maintain track of the fundamental reference current signal

F. Sanfilippo et al. (Eds.): INTAP 2021, CCIS 1616, pp. 210–222, 2022.
https://doi.org/10.1007/978-3-031-10525-8_17

while attenuating the current harmonics in the process. Because of its modularity, the controller described in references [9, 34] performs flawlessly under normal conditions. However, when abnormal conditions arise, the compensator's performance deteriorates, resulting in an increase in current harmonic distortion. The simplest technique for eliminating current harmonic distortion is to engage the PRES. PRES controllers include the addition of K_P (Proportional gain), which is used in conjunction with a resonant route that is tuned to the desired frequency. In today's environment, it is necessary to digitally apply it in order to improve the entire system's efficiency and therefore its effectiveness. The concept of Proportional Resonant Controller is presented in [12, 17, 22, 23, 31, 32]. The first section of this article will describe the algorithms of PRES and Novel PRESH Controller. The examination of both controllers is carried out with the assistance of a graph as well as a bode plot analysis. The performance analysis of the PRES and Novel PRESH controllers will be shown in the second phase. Instead of the usual series connection described in [10, 25], the PRES compensator is linked in parallel with the RESH controller to form a Novel PRESH controller, which effectively eliminates the higher order harmonic. Novel PRESH controller presented in this article for comparison with PRES controller has the major benefit of demonstrating that even when the reference waveform is distorted, this controller can deal with it in a highly dependable way, which is not true of PRES controller.

The following are examples of novelness and originality in the suggested research paper:

Researchers have previously developed a method for decreasing current harmonics, but it had a latency.

There are certain disadvantages to the lead controller [27], the modified PI controller [13, 20], the repetitive controller [28, 30], the dead beat controller [36], the PR controller [9, 34], and the shunt filter [5], which are as follows:

The standard PI controller is incapable of tracking the alternating current reference.

Especially in terms of following sinusoidal reference as well as rejecting disturbances, [13, 20] has extremely poor responsiveness.

[9, 34] It is not possible to use with the current Grid Connection because the rejection of harmonics necessitates the use of a digital version of the controller.

IEEE standard 519 and 1547 state that the usage of a shunt filter for harmonic elimination has become an outdated method due to the filter's failure to eliminate harmonic interference.

The implementation of the PRES (Proportional Resonant) controller in digital form will be shown in this article in order to keep up with the current situation.

This paper presents a method for designing a PRESH (Proportional Resonant Harmonic) controller, in which the PRES controller is linked in parallel with the RESH (Resonant Harmonic) controller, rather than in series, as is conventionally done.

PRES and PRESH controllers are addressed in terms of harmonic mitigation with minimal computational burden, as opposed to conventional controller design, in terms of performance analysis.

Following is the outline for the suggested paper: Sect. 1 Introduction, A three phase grid tied solar photovoltaic power system (GTSPPS) will be discussed in Sect. 2. Section 3 will deal with the design algorithm of the digital PRES and PRESH controllers, and Sect. 4 will deal with the performance analysis of the PRES and Novel PRESH controllers in terms of Bode-Plot, followed by the conclusion.

2 Grid-Tied Three Phase Solar Photovoltaic Power System

Figure 1 represent the three phase GTSPPS having Photovoltaic module/array, a capacitor C_{dc} and a 3-phase voltage source inverter connected with three phase grid having voltages as V_{ga}, V_{gb} and V_{gc}.

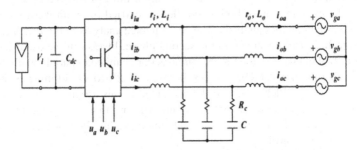

Fig. 1. Grid-tied solar photovoltaic power system (GTSPPS)

For reducing the high frequency switching harmonic, L-C-L filter is employed and for attenuating the peak magnitude of L-C-L filter at resonance frequency and damping resistor is made to connect in series with capacitor.

Average model of 3-phase GTSPPS is shown by below Fig.

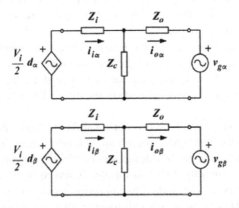

Fig. 2. Average circuit model (ACM) of three phase grid tied SPPS

Input to this model is V_i which is a dc link voltage, grid voltage is denoted as V_g and control input d whose value varies from −1 to + 1.

$$-1 \leq d_\alpha \leq +1 \tag{1}$$

$$-1 \leq d\beta \leq +1 \tag{2}$$

Inverter current is indicated by i_i whereas grid current is indicated by i_o.

The parameter used in the transfer function of above compensator is shown by Table 1, along with list of value used in the work. Table 1 also contain the detail parameter of three phase GTSPPS used here.

Table 1. Parameters of three phase SPPS

Symbol	Quantity	Nominal Value
P_m	Maximum output power	3.2 KW
f_i	Switching frequency	10 KHz
$V_{i,OC}$	Open Circuit PV array output Voltage	750 V
$I_{i,SC}$	Short circuit PV array output current	5.4 A
$V_{i,MP}$	Maximum power PV output voltage	650 V
$I_{i,MP}$	Maximum Power PV output current	4.9 A
L_i	Inverter side Inductance	6.9 mH
R_i	Inverter side resistance	0.27 Ω
C	Filter Capacitor	680 nF
R_c	Filter damping resistance	6.8 Ω
L_o	Grid side inductance	2.1 mH
R_o	Grid side resistance	0.14 Ω
V_g	Grid Voltage (rms, phase to neutral)	200 V
f_o	Grid frequency	50 Hz
K_p	Proportional gain	60 Ω
K_{i1}	Fundamental integral gain	300 Ω s²
K_{in}	n-harmonic integral gain	300 Ω s²
ϵ_1	Fundamental damping factor	0.01
ϵ_n	n-harmonics damping factor	0.01
N	Selected harmonics to be attenuated	5,7,11,13
T_d	Control Processing delay time	100 μs

3 Design Algorithm of PRES and PRESH

3.1 Design Algorithm of PRES

Proportional Resonant/PRES Controller is represented by Fig. 3. PRES controller is added by using inductor (Linv) with the having a resistance (Rinv) which is denoted by (Rg). Grid resistance and inductance are denoted by Rg and Lg respectively. Current and voltage sensed by inverter output is sent back to control block. Here, reference signal is compared with inverter current output. The controller output is used as input of inverter via PWM. PWM modulator make use of carrier wave having an amplitude as 1. The reference signal used here is sinusoidal in nature and is kept in synchronization with grid voltage with the help of PLL (Phase Locked Loop). PRES controller make use of K_P and resonant gain (K_i). The resonant path consists of K_i and filter.

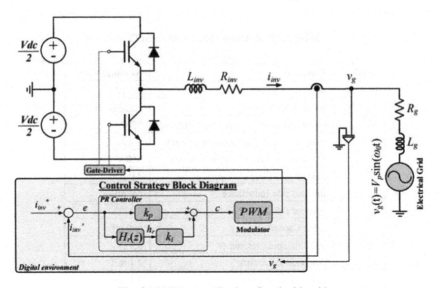

Fig. 3. PRES controller interfaced with grid

Transfer Function of resonant path in Z-domain analysis is given by Eq. (3).

$$H_r(z) = \frac{b_0 + b_1 z^{-1} + b_2 z^{-2}}{a_0 + a_1 z^{-1} + a_2 z^{-2}} \tag{3}$$

where, $a_0, a_1, a_2, b_0, b_1, b_2$ are constant. For PRES controller design, value of K_P, K_i, $a_0, a_1, a_2, b_0, b_1, b_2$ is needed. Different steps are there in designing of digital PRES controller which are elaborated as:

1st Step: Defining various System parameter of System.

The first step is defining system parameter. Table 2, consist of the different system parameter in term of their symbol and SI unit. Resonant frequency, makes the controller to go into zero steady state error condition.

2nd Step: Computing K_P and K_i.

For calculating the proportional gain (K_P) and resonant gain (K_i) of PRES controller Eq. (2) and (3) of have been used and is given by (4) and (5) equation. Here $\in$ is the damping factor.

$$K_P = \frac{(2\in +1)\sqrt{(2\in +1)}\omega_r L_{inv} - R_{inv}}{0.5 V_{dc}} \frac{1}{H_i} \tag{4}$$

$$k_i = \frac{\omega_r^2 L_{inv}\left[(2\epsilon + 1)^2 - 1\right]}{V_{dc}} \frac{1}{H_i} \tag{5}$$

3rd Step: Finding resonant filter (R.F) constant.

For computing the value of a_0, a_1, a_2, b_0, b_1, b_2 of T.F of R.F obtained in Z-domain reference has been taken from [38]. Values of a_0, a_1, a_2, b_0, b_1, b_2 obtained are given by Eq. (6) to (12):

$$a_0 = 1 \tag{6}$$

$$a_1 = -2e^{-0.5B_r T_a}\cos(T_a\sqrt{\omega_r^2 - 0.25B_r^2}) \tag{7}$$

$$a_2 = e^{-B_r T_a} \tag{8}$$

$$b_0 = K_r B_r T_a \tag{9}$$

$$b_1 = [-K_r B_r e^{-0.5B_r T_a}\cos(T_a\sqrt{\omega_r^2 - 0.25B_r^2} - C]T_a) \tag{10}$$

Here, B_r is resonant angular bandwidth and C is the constant and is given by.

$$C = \frac{0.5k_r B_r^2}{\sqrt{\omega_r^2 - 0.25B_r^2}}e^{-0.5B_r T_a}\sin(T_a\sqrt{\omega_r^2 - 0.25B_r^2}) \tag{11}$$

Table 2. Different system parameters

System Parameters	Symbol	SI Unit
Inverter Inductance	L_{inv}	H
Inverter Resistance	R_{inv}	Ω
Total DC Link Voltage at Inverter	V_{dc}	V
Switching Frequency	f_{sw}	Hz
Current Sensor Gain	H_i	A/A
Nominal Power of Inverter	P_{inv}	W
Frequency	f_a	Hz
Angular Frequency	ω_a	rad/sec
Period	$T_a = 1/f_a$	sec
Grid Voltage (Peak)	V_p	V
Frequency of Grid	f_g	Hz
Grid Angular frequency	$\omega_g = 2\pi f_g$	rad/sec

$$b_2 = 0 \qquad (12)$$

Value chosen for system parameter while designing PRES controller is depicted by Table 3.

Table 3. System parameter of designed PRES controller

System Parameter	Symbol	Chosen value
Proportional gain	Kp	0.827435088693
Resonant gain	Ki	234.028059558628
B_0 coefficient	b_0	$3.14159265355 \times 10^{-4}$
B_1 coefficient	b_1	$-3.14159265354 \times 10^{-4}$
B_2 coefficient	b_2	0
A_0 coefficient	a_0	1
A_1 coefficient	a_1	-1.999528003284
A_2 coefficient	a_2	0.999685890075

Table 4. Value chosen for case study

System Parameters	Symbol	SI Unit
Inverter Inductance	L_{inv}	10 mH
Inverter Resistance	R_{inv}	0.495 mΩ
DC Link Voltage at Inverter	V_{dc}	450V
Switching Frequency	f_{sw}	30 KHz
Current Sensor Gain	H_i	0.1A/A
Inverter Nominal Power	P_{inv}	1500 W
Frequency	f_a	30kHz
Angular Frequency	ω_a	1.88×10^5 rad/sec
Time Period	$T_a = 1/f_a$	33.33μsec
Grid Peak Voltage	V_p	180V
Frequency (Grid)	f_g	60Hz
Angular frequency of grid	$\omega_g = 2\pi f_g$	377rad/sec
Inductance of Grid	L_g	100μH
Resistance of Grid	R_g	0.1mΩ
Resonant Frequency	F_r	60Hz
Resonant Angular frequency	ω_x	377rad/sec
Resonant Bandwidth	B_a	1.50 Hz

Further for case study of PRES controller, value chosen are depicted in the Table 4. For verifying the design of Proportional Resonant controller, frequency plane is used. Further, by making use of it, z domain analysis can be done in s-domain.

$$Z = \frac{1 + \left(\frac{T_a}{2}\right)\omega}{1 - \left(\frac{T_a}{2}\right)\omega} \tag{13}$$

Frequency of both planes can be related through Eq. (14) as given:

$$V = \frac{2}{T_a} \tan \frac{\omega T_a}{2} \tag{14}$$

Resonant filter is plotted into w-plane and is given by Eq. (15).

$$H_r(w) = H_r(z)|_z = \frac{1 + \left(\frac{T_a}{2}\right)\omega}{1 - \left(\frac{T_a}{2}\right)\omega} \tag{15}$$

Resonant filter magnitude and phase function can be given as:

$$Mag_{Hr}(v) = 20 \log|H_r(w)|$$
$$Phase_{Hr}(v) = Arg|H_r(w)|$$

4   Design Procedure of Novel PRESH Controller

The main purpose of PRESH controller is to achieve lower current harmonic distortion even if grid current experiences the abnormal conditions.

1st step: Control Configuration of Novel PRESH controller.

In this Novel PRESH controller, shown by Fig. 4, inverter current is used as input to compensator of lower forward gain instead of applying the difference of reference current signal and grid current.

Where, $H_3(s)$ is PRES (Proportional Resonant) controller and $H_4(s)$ is RESH (Resonant Harmonic) Controller. Transfer functions of PRESH controller are obtained as:

$$H_3(s) = \frac{k_{i1} 2\xi_1 \omega_o s}{s^2 + 2\xi_1 \omega_o s + \omega_o^2} \tag{16}$$

$$H_4(s) = k_p + \sum_n \frac{k_{in} 2\xi_n(n\omega_o)s}{s^2 + 2\xi_n(n\omega_o)s + (n\omega_o)^2} \tag{17}$$

2nd step: Closed-Loop Transfer Function of Novel PRESH controller.

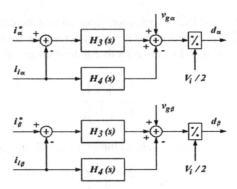

Fig. 4. Proposed Novel PRESH controller

Here, d_α, d_β are the control input which can take value from -1 to $+1$, and V_g is the voltage of grid and $H_d(s)$ is transfer function of model. From Fig. 4, control input of Novel PRESH controller can be written as:

$$d_\alpha = \frac{2}{V_i}\left[v_{g\alpha} + H_3(s)\left(i_\alpha^* - i_{i\alpha}\right) - H_4(s)i_{i\alpha}\right]H_d(s) \tag{18}$$

$$d_\beta = \frac{2}{V_i}\left[v_{g\beta} + H_3(s)\left(i_\beta^* - i_{i\beta}\right) - H_4(s)i_{i\beta}\right]H_d(s) \tag{19}$$

By substituting Eq. (18) and (19) in Fig. 2 so as to obtain closed loop transfer function of Novel PRESH controller, we get:

$$T(s) = (Z_c(s) + Z_o(s))G_i(s)(H_3(s) + H_4(s)) \\ \times H_d(s) \tag{20}$$

$$G_r(s) = \frac{Z_c(s)G_i(s)H_3(s)H_d(s)}{1 + T(s)} \tag{21}$$

$$G_g(s) = -\frac{G_i(s)(Z_i(s) + (H_3(s) + H_4(s))H_d(s))}{1 + T(s)} \tag{22}$$

5 Analysis of Novel PRES and PRESH Controller

5.1 Bode Plot Analysis of Digitally Implemented Novel PRES Controller

Proportional Resonant controller transfer function is represented by $TF_{PRES}(z)$:

$$k_p + k_i H_r(z) = k_p + k_i \frac{b_0 + b_1 z^{-1} + b_2 z^{-2}}{a_0 + a_1 z^{-1} + a_2 z^{-2}} \tag{23}$$

For obtaining the magnitude response of PRES controller take log of $TF_{PRES}(z)$ and is shown by Fig. 5.

From above bode-plot, highest amplification of 47 DB occurs at 60 Hz. For obtaining the phase response of PRES controller take argument of $TFPRES(z)$ and is shown by Fig. 6. For low and high frequencies, phase obtained is zero and obtained phase shift is similar to resonant filter.

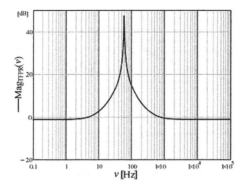

Fig. 5. Proposed PRES controller – magnitude response

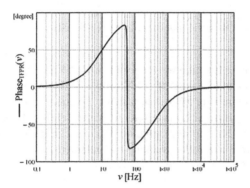

Fig. 6. Proposed PRES controller – phase response

5.2 Bode Plot Analysis of Novel PRES Controller

Bode Plot figure of PRES and RESH controller used in proposed Novel PRESH Controller is indicated by Fig. 7.

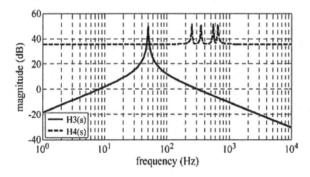

Fig. 7. BP figure of PRES & RESH controller used in proposed novel PRESH controller

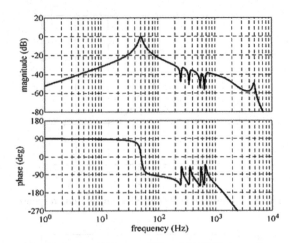

Fig. 8. Bode-plot figure of Novel PRESH controller

Bode-Plot of transfer function for proposed Novel PRESH controller is indicated by Fig. 8. All the value taken for case study of Novel PRESH controller is indicated in Table 1. From the above figure it is clear that, transfer function of proposed Novel PRESH controller has behavior similar to band pass filter. At, selected harmonic frequency i.e. 250, 350, 550 and 650 Hz, dip in magnitude diagram can be seen. Thus, by using this proposed Novel PRESH controller, tracking of fundamental component of signal can be expected even if reference waveform is distorted one.

6 Conclusions

The given paper discussed the design methodology and performance analysis of PRES and Novel PRESH (PRES + RESH) controllers interfaced with three phase GTSPPS in terms of THD and harmonic mitigation, as well as bode plot analysis (Grid Tied Solar Photovoltaic Power System). PLL (Phase Locked Loop) is used effectively to synchronise the GTSPPS with the grid voltage. Additionally, the suggested study takes use of frequency analysis to demonstrate the proposed controller's correctness. Additionally, a case study is being conducted to demonstrate the proposed controller's design process. Additionally, an indirect mechanism is identified that was responsible for the generation of current harmonics in a conventional resonant current controller due to aberrant grid conditions. The Novel PRESH controller circumvents this issue by connecting in a unique configuration, as shown in the case study. As a result, the basic component can be tracked even in the event of an aberrant situation. PRES & Novel PRESH controllers will be used to analyse the performance of three phase SPPS. The emphasis will also be on lowering the current harmonic distortion of grid-connected converters and maintaining a THD of less than 1% even when abnormal grid conditions occur.

References

1. 2002 National Electrical Code. National Fire Protection Association, Inc., Quincy, MA (2002)
2. Althobaiti, Armstrong, M., Elgendy, M.A., Mulolani, F.: Three-phase grid connected PV inverters using the proportional resonance controller. In: 2016 IEEE 16th International Conference on Environment and Electrical Engineering (EEEIC), Florence, Italy, pp. 1–6 (2016)
3. Araujo, S.V., Zacharias, P., Mallwitz, R.: Highly efficient single-phase transformerless inverters for grid-connected photovoltaic systems. IEEE Trans. Ind. Electron. **57**(9), 3118–3128 (Sep. 2010)
4. Balaguer, I.J., Lei, Q., Yang, S., Supatti, U., Peng, F.Z.: Control for grid-connected and intentional islanding operations of distributed power generation. IEEE Trans. Ind. Electron. **58**(1), 147–157 (2011)
5. Blaabjerg, F., Teodorescu, R., Liserre, M., Timbus, A.V.: Overview of control and grid synchronization for distributed power generation systems. IEEE Trans. Ind. Electron. **53**(5), 1398–1409 (Oct. 2006)
6. Bratcu, A., Munteanu, I., Bacha, S., Picault, D., Raison, B.: Cascaded dc–dc converter photovoltaic systems: power optimization issues. IEEE Trans. Ind. Electron. **58**(2), 403–411 (2011)
7. Cacciato, M., Consoli, A., Attanasio, R., Gennaro, F.: Soft-switching converter with HF transformer for grid-connected photovoltaic systems. IEEE Trans. Ind. Electron. **57**(5), 1678–1686 (May 2010)
8. Campanhol, L.B.G., Silva, S.A.O., Sampaio, L.P., Junior, A.A.O.: A grid-connected photovoltaic power system with active power injection, reactive power compensation and harmonic filtering. In: Proceedings of COBEP, pp. 642–649 (2013)
9. Castilla, M., Miret, J., Matas, J., Garcia de Vicuna, L., Guerrero, J.M.: Control design guidelines for single-phase grid-connected photovoltaic inverters with damped resonant harmonics compensators. IEEE Trans. Ind. Electron. **56**(11), 4492–4501 (2009)
10. Castilla, M., Miret, J., Matas, J., Garcia de Vicuna, L., Guerrero, J.M.: Linear current control scheme with series resonant harmonic compensator for single-phase grid-connected photovoltaic inverters. IEEE Trans. Ind. Electron. **55**(7), 2724–2733 (2008)
11. Cavalcanti, M.C., de Oliveira, K., C., Farias de A. M., Neves F. A., Azevedo G. M., and Camboim F. C.,: Modulation techniques to eliminate leakage currents in transformerless three-phase photovoltaic systems. IEEE Trans. Ind. Electron. **57**(4), 1360–1368 (2010)
12. Characteristics of the Utility Interface for Photovoltaic (PV) Systems, IEC61727, December 2004
13. Faiz, M.T., Khan, M.M., Jianming, X., Habib, S., Tang, H.: Double feed-forward compensation based true damping of Inductor-capacitor-Induxtor type grid tied lainverter. In: 2018 IEEE International Conference on Industrial Technology (ICIT), pp. 788–793 (2018)
14. Figueres, E., Garcerá, G., Sandia, J., González-Espin, F., Rubio, J.C.: Sensitivity study of the dynamics of three-phase photovoltaic inverters with an LCL grid filter. IEEE Trans. Ind. Electron. **56**(3), 706–717 (2009)
15. Guerrero, J.M., Vasquez, J.C., Matas, J., Garcia de Vicuna, L., Castilla, M.: Hierarchical control of droop-controlled ac and dc microgrids—a general approach toward standardization. IEEE Trans. Ind. Electron. **58**(1), 158–172 (2011)
16. IEEE standard for interconnecting distributed resources with electric power systems. IEEE15471 (2008)
17. Jeong, H.-G., Kim, G.-S., Lee, K.-B.: Second-order harmonic reduction technique for photovoltaic power conditioning systems using a proportional-resonant controller. Energies **6**, 79–96 (2013)

18. He, J., Li, Y.W., Blaabjerg, F., Wang, X.: Active harmonic filtering using current-controlled, grid-connected DG units with closed-loop power control. IEEE Trans. Power Electron. **29**(2), 642–653 (2013)
19. Kadri, R., Gaubert, J.P., Champenois, G.: An improved maximum power point tracking for photovoltaic grid-connected inverter based-on voltage oriented control. IEEE Trans. Ind. Electron. **58**(1), 66–75 (2011)
20. Kuo, Y.S., Lin, J.Y., Tang, J.C., Hsieh, J.G.: Lead-lag compensator design based on vector margin and steady-state error of the step response via particle swarm optimization. In: 2016 International Conference on Fuzzy Theory and Its Applications (iFuzzy), pp. 1–6 (2016)
21. Mai, Q., Shan, M., Liu, L., Guerrero, J.M.: A novel improved variable step-size incremental-resistance MPPT method for PV systems. IEEE Trans. Ind. Electron. **58**(6), 2427–2434 (2011)
22. Padula, A.S., Agnoletto, E.J., Neves, R.V.A., Magossi, R.F.Q., Machado, R.Q., Oliveira, V.A.: Partial harmonic current distortion mitigation in microgrids using proportional resonant controller. In: 2019 18th European Control Conference (ECC), Naples, Italy, pp. 435-440 (2019)
23. Prasad, P.S., Parimi, A.M.: Harmonic mitigation in grid connected and islanded microgrid via adaptive virtual impedance. In: 2020 IEEE International Conference on Power Electronics, Smart Grid and Renewable Energy (PESGRE2020), Cochin, India, pp. 1–6 (2020)
24. Rahim, N.A., Chaniago, K., Selvaraj, J.: Single-phase sevenlevel grid-connected inverter for photovoltaic system. IEEE Trans. Ind. Electron. **58**(6), 2435–2443 (2011)
25. Rodríguez, P., Luna, A., Candela, I., Mujal, R., Teodorescu, R., Blaabjerg, F.: Multiresonant frequency-locked loop for grid synchronization of power converters under distorted grid conditions. IEEE Trans. Ind. Electron. **58**(1), 127–138 (2010)
26. Salmeron, P., Litran, S.: Improvement of the electric power quality using series active and shunt passive filters. IEEE Trans. Power Delivery **25**(2), 1058–1067 (2010)
27. Shetty, D., Prabhu, N.: Ziegler-Nichols method based VAR current controller for static compensator. Energy Procedia **117**, 543–550 (2017)
28. da Silva, J.N., Filho, A.J.S., Fernandes, D.A., Tahim, A.P.N., da Silva, E.R.C., Costa, F.F.: A discrete current controller for 1-phase grid-tied inverters. In: 2017 Brazilian Power Electronics Conference (COBEP), pp. 1–6 (2017)
29. Trinh, Q., Lee, H.: An advanced current control strategy for three-phase shunt active power filters. IEEE Trans. Industr. Electron. **60**(12), 5400–5410 (2013)
30. Wang, L., Ertugrul, N., Kolhe, M.: Evaluation of died beat CC for grid tied converters. In: IEEE PES Innovative Smart Grid Technologies, pp. 1–7 (2012)
31. Yadav, U., Gupta, A.: Current harmonic mitigation in grid tied solar photovoltaic system via PRES. In: 2020 5th IEEE International Conference on Recent Advances and Innovations in Engineering (ICRAIE), Jaipur, India, pp. 1–5 (2020)
32. Yadav, U., Gupta, A., Ahuja Kr, R.: Robust control design procedure and simulation of pres controller having phase-locked loop (PLL) control technique in grid-tied converter. In: 2020 3rd International Seminar on Research of Information Technology and Intelligent Systems (ISRITI) yogakarta, Indonesia, pp. 445-450 (2020)
33. Yadav, U., Gupta, A., Ahuja, R.K.: Analysis of CPG control strategies using APC for single phase grid tied SPPS. Material Today Proceeding. https://doi.org/10.1016/j.matpr.2021.05.195, (https://www.sciencedirect.com/science/article/pii/S2214785321037718)
34. Yadav, U., Gupta, A., Rai, H.K., Bhalla, D.K.: Mitigation of Harmonic Current in Grid-Connected Solar Power System. In: Muzammil, M., Chandra, A., Kankar, P.K., Kumar, H. (eds.) Recent Advances in Mechanical Engineering. LNME, pp. 605–610. Springer, Singapore (2021). https://doi.org/10.1007/978-981-15-8704-7_74
35. Yuen, C., Oudalov, A., Timbus, A.: The provision of frequency control reserves from multiple microgrids. IEEE Trans. Ind. Electron. **58**(1), 173–183 (2011)
36. Zhou, K., Blaabjerg, F., Wang, D., Yang, Y.: Periodic control of PEC, IET (2016)

Energy Tracing and Blockchain Technology: A Primary Review

Paul K. Wan$^{(\boxtimes)}$ and Lizhen Huang

Norwegian University of Science and Technology, Teknologivegen 22,
2815 Gjøvik, Norway
{paul.k.wan,Lizhen.huang}@ntnu.no

Abstract. Reducing greenhouse emission is a mission for many organizations. Since road transportation is a major contributor of CO_2 emission, there is a shift towards electric vehicles (EV) rather than fuel vehicles due to zero CO_2 emission during operation stage. With the gradual shift towards EV, the demand for electricity would also increase. Thus, it is important to move our attention on how electricity is generated because the provenance of electricity supply is closely linked to climate change. Energy system is a complex resulting in difficulty to truly verify the claims of only using green energy source to generate electricity. Blockchain technology caught the attention of researchers to adapt this technology to trace the end-to-end process of products. The purpose of this paper is to identify the current state-of-art focusing on energy tracing and blockchain in academic and commercial sector. From our search, we identified one literature and one commercial project that focus on energy tracing. Effort focusing on energy tracing remain small. One of the reasons is the electricity is a non-physical attribute matter which makes tracing of the source challenging. The volatility of renewable energy source (RES) such as wind and solar power farms, along with complex energy distribution system, makes tracing harder. Current work on energy tracing remain scarce and more work should focus on this section to prevent rebound effect of carbon emission due to the lack of a transparent carbon footprint.

Keywords: Energy tracing · Blockchain · Rebound effect · Electric vehicles

1 Introduction

1.1 Background

Moving towards greener energy is a part of the strategy in reducing greenhouse gas emission. This has been a challenge for various international bodies. The

---

Supported by Norwegian University of Science and technology's Digital Transformation Project: Trust and transparency in digital society through blockchain technology.

F. Sanfilippo et al. (Eds.): INTAP 2021, CCIS 1616, pp. 223–231, 2022.
https://doi.org/10.1007/978-3-031-10525-8_18

European Union Commission has put in place legislation to reduce emissions by at least 40% by 2030, as part of the EU's 2030 climate and energy framework [9]. Nations outside of EU also committed to bring down the greenhouse emission to a pledge target. For example, the Norwegian government pledges to be a carbon neutral country by 2050 and Canada pledges to cut carbon emissions by 30% by 2030 [24,31].

Road transportation contributed of greenhouse gas emission up to 70% compared to other mode of transportation [10]. Similarly, the energy demand for road transportation is the highest compared to other types. To combat climate change, there is now a gradual shift towards electric vehicles (EV) from fossil fuel types because fossil fuels-based vehicles inevitably emits CO_2. EV is a greener mode of transportation because of the zero-carbon emission during the operation phase. Therefore, it is now important to move our attention to production stage on how electricity is generated.

With the current trend of shifting towards a greener world, the reliance of non-renewable energy, particularly fossil fuel, is reducing. Offices, residential area, manufacturing plant and soon, more vehicles rely on electricity. Electricity is generated from different types of energy source to sustain our daily lives. Different types of energy source have different impact on climate change. For example, renewable energy sources like solar power has less negative impact on climate change than fossil fuels.

Owing to the complex distribution of electricity generated from different energy sources, it is challenging to truly verify the provenance of the electricity. There is an extensive research on using blockchain as a digital tool to track the provenance of product and food throughout the entire supply chain. However, the focus on the provenance of the electricity remains little. This paper is to draw a clearer picture of the current state-of-art the electricity tracing in the energy sector. To answer this, a systematic literature review is executed to answer the following two research tasks (RT).

RT1: What is the state-of-art?
RT2: What are the barriers and potential future work?

2   Related Work

2.1   Electricity

Things are now more electrified than before. For example, the shift to EV from fuel-based vehicle. Therefore, it is important to understand how electricity is generated because it is closely related to climate change. Electricity is the delivery of energy resulted from a series of transmission across multiple grid levels and the interplay of numerous entities across several connected infrastructures [5].

Electricity can be generated from two types of sources: (1) Renewable energy sources (RES) such as solar, wind and hydro and (2) Non-renewable sources like fossil fuels. For example, in a fossil fuel plant, electricity is generated through the conversion of heat energy to electricity while hydropower converts kinetic energy

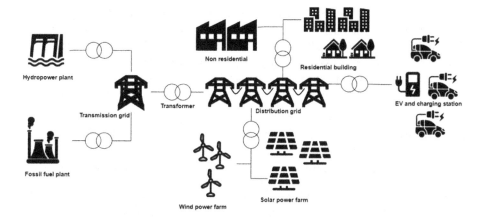

Fig. 1. Layout of general electricity network.

to electricity. The generated electricity is then transmitted through a series grid then to final consumer as shown in Fig 1. Both these energy sources generate electricity to support daily lives, but each have different impact on the climate. A life cycle assessment done by [27], they encouraged electricity derived from hydropower power plant to be heavily utilized because it does not use utilize fossil fuel to generate electricity throughout the life cycle.

Energy markets is already highly complex and with the increasing share of renewable energy sources such as wind and solar power plants only serve to amplify this complexity [5]. Today, there are claims on only utilizing only green energy sources to generate electricity. The deeper question is how we can know the source and trace the electricity that we use. A lot of work has mentioned on how blockchain can enhance the traceability of product within a complex supply chain [28].

2.2 Blockchain

Blockchain technology is a distributed ledger that contains replicated and synchronized digital data. This technology has the potential in enhancing traceability and transparency owing to how blockchain stores data structure. All valid transactions are recorded in a block format, and each block is linked with a time stamp and hash references forming a chain of blocks [6]. The data storage structure ensures that information and data are stored in a tamper-evident environment [11] because any attempt to alter information breaks the hash reference and thus makes it obvious to the other members of the network. This way, a hash reference creates a tamper-evident environment that maintains and ensures data integrity. Blockchain technology can store events chronologically which enhance the traceability.

Blockchain has caught the attention of sectors like food [19] and pharmaceutical [18] sectors to ensure end-to-end traceability and the product integrity. With the similar interest, this technology can potentially shed some light in energy tracing. However, the current focus in tracing the provenance of electricity using blockchain remain unclear. This is an important key as things are electrified, it is crucial to for user to know the degree of "greenness" of the electricity source. To answer this, we will perform a systematic literature review on blockchain and energy tracing to have a clearer picture of the current state-of-art.

3   Methodology

3.1   Search Requirement

In our search, we include academic, commercial and startup projects. Literature included mainly literature from: published work reports and application descriptions of a commercial project, revealing the core idea of the project from both private and public sectors are collected.

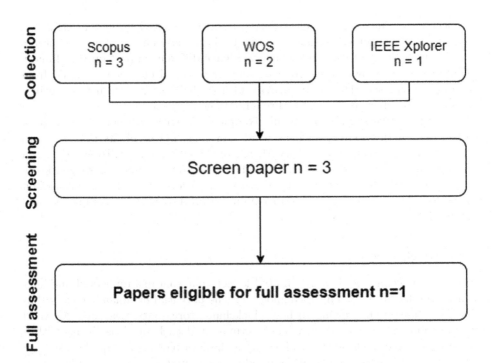

Fig. 2. Summary flow of systematic literature review.

The review of material starts as early as in 2008, since the term blockchain was firstly introduced, until May 2021 prior to the submission of this paper. Material collection was carried out through various databases (Scopus, IEEE Xplorer digital library and Web of science) to gather widest possible samples.

Only English papers were included, with no restrictions on the year or country of publication. We excluded general views, no full paper, and conference abstracts.

In order to capture blockchain technology specifically within the energy tracing, and to be as comprehensive as possible, generic keywords we used the following:

- (blockchain) AND ("Energy tracing")
- (blockchain) AND ("Energy tracking").

3.2 Material Collection and Analysis

We initially collected a total of 6 papers (3 from Scopus, 2 from Web-of-Science and 1 from IEEE Xplorer Library). After a thorough screening based on our systematic literature flow as shown in Fig. 2, there is only 1 paper that fits our criteria. Similar, from our search in the commercial sphere, there is only one commercial project focusing in energy tracing using blockchain technology.

Table 1. Summary of the collected material

Author	Type	Scope	Approach	Comments
Yang et al.	Academic	Electric vehicle	Display Green Pass and checking Green Pass on the blockchain	Certification is difficult to justify the sourceof electricity generation
Iberdrola Group	Commercial project	Green energy certificate	To guarantee, in real time, that the energy supplied and consumed is 100% renewable	The framework is not explained

Table 1 gives a summary of the collected material. There is one published literature which focused on blockchain-based energy tracing in electric vehicles (EV). Yang, et al. [30] published their work on energy tracing method for electric vehicles charging consumption in relation to the type and source of energy. They designed a platform which integrates the power trading centre, power dispatching centre, local power operators and EV user using blockchain. Green pass is stored on blockchain for checking to ensure to check the renewable transaction. However, electricity generation is from a mix of different energy source; therefore, a certified green pass may be difficult to justify the origin of energy source.

Iberdrola Group [16], a company in Spain, is working on to certify the source of green energy generated wind farms in Spain. They have begun a pilot project based on using blockchain to guarantee, in real time, that the energy supplied and consumed is 100% renewable. Using this technology, they have managed to link plants where electricity is produced to specific points of consumption, allowing the source of the energy to be traced. This increases transparency and ultimately encourages the use of renewable energy. However, the framework is not explained in details.

4   Finding and Discussion

4.1   RT1: What is the State-of-Art

After internet of Energy (IoE), blockchain has emerged as a popular technology in the energy sector by integrating blockchain to can result in a more secure, fast, transparent and low-cost operation solution [20]. There are eight [3–5,12,13,17,20,25] systematic literature review published on blockchain-based within the energy sector. Andoni, et al. [4] reviewed and mapped out 140 blockchain commercial and research initiatives on the challenges and opportunities of the applications of blockchain for energy industries. They pointed some of the potential impacts are sharing resources for EV charging and significantly improve auditing and regulatory compliance. However, they did not mention on the tracing of the electricity and the energy source in most their work.

Ante, et al. [5] pointed out in their literature review that energy management in smart grids such as peer-to-peer trading is the potential emerging fields within the energy sector using blockchain. This is due to what blockchain can offer; immutable timestamped transaction which makes trading easier and less complex. Private oil and gas company like Shell [8] also envision the potential of blockchain in renewable energy source tracking which could change relationship between how energy is produced and consumed and transform the way companies collaborate and interact to accelerate the development of low-carbon energy.

Energy tracing is important because without a transparent energy footprint, rebound effect of carbon emission may occur. The increase in the use of electricity, particularly EV. This is important for user to know what types of energy source generated electricity. Since the operation stage are now relying on electricity, the generation stage becomes the main focus in order to meet the energy demand. If the energy source are not generated from renewable energy source like hydropower and solar energy, it could potentially result in increasing production of energy source to meet the demand which leads to an increase of rebound effect of CO_2 emission [14].

Digitalization can help to decarbonise future energy system for example in both tracing EV consumption and energy management system. Becour is private firm that focuses on tracking of renewable energy with the goal of increasing transparency of the energy market accelerate the shift away from fossil-based production [7]. Petrusic and Janjic [23] proposed a novel charging system to track the origin of the energy for the charging of EV in multiples systems using multicriteria algorithm. However, both the work did not mention blockchain technology as digital tool to enhance tracking. This could be due to the nature of electricity is difficult to trace.

4.2   RT2: What Are the Barriers and Potential Future Work

Unlike physical object tracking like food and diamond, electricity is a non-physical attribute making it challenging to trace the origin. The concept of tracking the provenance of food is easier as current approach is assigned unique identifier to the physical product but that is not for the case for electricity tracing. The fact that, energy flow is highly dynamic, which makes electricity more challenging to trace from energy source of the electricity then to final consumer. The current approach in ensuring the use of green energy source is by trading of green certificate. Owing to the immutable nature of blockchain, researchers have suggested this technology can store and trace the green certificate which guarantees the electricity is generated from green energy. However, electricity is highly dynamic which make green certificate difficult to truly reflect the origin of the energy source.

Another barrier in tracing electricity is because electricity is generated from a mix of different energy sources in order to provide sufficient electricity. Unlike Norway almost 100% of the electricity production come from renewable energy sources (RES) [22], most of the other countries have a diverse energy mix to generate electricity. For example, in the US about 80% of the electricity is produced from fossil fuels and about 11% is from RES [1]. RES is a better alternative compared to fossil fuels when it comes the greenhouse emission, but its volatile supply of energy only serves to amplify this complexity which in turns makes tracing of energy harder. Batteries can be an alternative to store energy from RES during good weather condition, but it faces issues such as reduction in power quality and increased of energy loses during charging [21].

Apart from electricity consumption in EV, the electricity consumption in building sector dominates approximately 30% of the global annual greenhouse gases emission [26]. And in the entire life span of a building, the operational stage has the largest share of carbon emission [15,29]. The International Energy Agency [2] reported that in the operational stage, up to approximately 50% of the energy supplied is utilized for space heating and cooling purposes in the OECD countries. Therefore, the types of energy supply to both residential and non-residential building for activities like heating and cooling is important to prevent greenwashing and rebound effect of CO_2 emission.

5 Conclusion

Blockchain has emerged as a popular technology in the energy sector due to various benefits such as secure, transparent, and low-cost operation solution offered by blockchain. However, the focus on the energy tracing remains very limited. The energy source for electricity generation is closely connected to carbon emission. It is important to place a strong focus in tracing the energy source since things are more electrified than before. From our search, only 2 items of literature focus on energy tracing. Current method of trading green energy certificate may not truly reflect how the energy source since electricity is highly dynamic. This work highlights the need to focus on energy tracing. With the benefits offer by blockchain, particularly in terms of traceability, it potentially can reduce some complexity and open up new types of services in the energy market for a more transparent green energy trading. Although from our search, there are not many relevant literature and commercial project focusing on energy tracing at this stage, yet. Nonetheless, it is vital to understand the entire end-to-end of electricity generation to consumption in order to have a positive impact on climate change.

References

1. U.S. Energy Information Administration: U.S. energy facts explained. https://www.eia.gov/energyexplained/us-energy-facts/
2. International Energy Agency: Coming in from the cold: Improving district heating policy in transition economies. Report (2004)
3. Ahl, A., Yarime, M., Tanaka, K., Sagawa, D.: Review of blockchain-based distributed energy: implications for institutional development. Renew. Sustain. Energy Rev. **107**, 200–211 (2019). https://doi.org/10.1016/j.rser.2019.03.002, https://www.scopus.com/inward/record.uri?eid=2-s2.0-85062647769
4. Andoni, M., et al.: Blockchain technology in the energy sector: a systematic review of challenges and opportunities. Renew. Sustain. Energy Rev. **100**, 143–174 (2019). https://doi.org/10.1016/j.rser.2018.10.014
5. Ante, L., Steinmetz, F., Fiedler, I.: Blockchain and energy: a bibliometric analysis and review. Renew. Sustain. Energy Rev. **137**, 110597 (2021). https://doi.org/10.1016/j.rser.2020.110597
6. Antonopoulos, A.M.: Mastering Bitcoin: Unlocking Digital Cryptocurrencies. O'Reilly Media, Newton (2015)
7. Becour: What we do. https://becour.com/what-we-do/
8. Brink, S.: How can blockchain support the energy transition? https://www.shell.com/energy-and-innovation/digitalisation/news-room/blockchain-building-trust-to-enable-the-energy-transition.html
9. European Comission: Progress made in cutting emission. https://ec.europa.eu/clima/policies/strategies/progress_en#tab-0-0
10. European Comission: A European strategy for plastics in a circular economy. https://ec.europa.eu/clima/eu-action/climate-strategies-targets/progress-made-cutting-emissions_en#tab-0-0
11. Drescher, D.: Blockchain Basics?: A Non-technical Introduction in 25 Steps. Apress, New York (2017)
12. Erturk, E., Lopez, D., Yu, W.Y.: Benefits and risks of using blockchain in smart energy: a literature review. Contemp. Manag. Res. **15**(3), 205–225 (2019). https://doi.org/10.7903/cmr.19650
13. Golosova, J., Romanovs, A., Kunicina, N.: Review of the blockchain technology in the energy sector. In: Proceedings of the 7th IEEE Workshop on Advances in Information, Electronic and Electrical Engineering, AIEEE 2019, vol. 2019-November (2019). https://doi.org/10.1109/AIEEE48629.2019.8977128
14. Grant, D., Jorgenson, A.K., Longhofer, W.: How organizational and global factors condition the effects of energy efficiency on CO2 emission rebounds among the world's power plants. Energy Policy **94**, 89–93 (2016). https://doi.org/10.1016/j.enpol.2016.03.053
15. Huang, L., Liu, Y., Krigsvoll, G., Johansen, F.: Life cycle assessment and life cycle cost of university dormitories in the southeast china: case study of the university town of fuzhou. J. Clean. Prod. **173**, 151–159 (2018). https://doi.org/10.1016/j.jclepro.2017.06.021

16. Iberdrola: How can blockchain be used to certify the source of green energy. https://becour.com/what-we-do/
17. Johanning, S., Bruckner, T.: Blockchain-based peer-to-peer energy trade: a critical review of disruptive potential. In: International Conference on the European Energy Market, EEM, vol. 2019-September. https://doi.org/10.1109/EEM.2019.8916268
18. Leal, F., et al.: Smart pharmaceutical manufacturing: ensuring end-to-end traceability and data integrity in medicine production. **24** (2021). https://doi.org/10.1016/j.bdr.2020.100172
19. Loke, K.S., Ann, O.C.: Food traceability and prevention of location fraud using blockchain, vol. 2020-December (2020). https://doi.org/10.1109/R10-HTC49770.2020.9356999
20. Miglani, A., Kumar, N., Chamola, V., Zeadally, S.: Blockchain for internet of energy management: review, solutions, and challenges. Comput. Commun. **151**, 395–418 (2020). https://doi.org/10.1016/j.comcom.2020.01.014
21. Nichoals, M., Hall, D.: Lessons learned on early electric vehicle fast-charging deployments. White Paper for the International Council on Clean Transportation (2018)
22. Statistics Norway: Electricity. https://www.ssb.no/en/energi-og-industri/energi/statistikk/elektrisitet
23. Petrusic, A., Janjic, A.: Article renewable energy tracking and optimization in a hybrid electric vehicle charging station. **11**(1), 1–17 (2020). https://doi.org/10.3390/app11010245
24. Reuters: Norway seeks to be carbon neutral by 2050. https://www.reuters.com/article/us-globalwarming-norway/norway-seeks-to-be-carbon-neutral-by-2050-idUSL1929214720070419
25. Salian, A., Shah, S., Shah, J., Samdani, K.: Review of blockchain enabled decentralized energy trading mechanisms. In: 2019 IEEE International Conference on System, Computation, Automation and Networking, ICSCAN 2019. https://doi.org/10.1109/ICSCAN.2019.8878731
26. SBCI, U.: Sustainable buildings climate initiative, buildings and climate change (2009)
27. Siddiqui, O., Dincer, I.: Comparative assessment of the environmental impacts of nuclear, wind and hydro-electric power plants in ontario: a life cycle assessment. J. Clean. Prod. **164**, 848–860 (2017). https://doi.org/10.1016/j.jclepro.2017.06.237
28. Wan, P.K., Huang, L., Holtskog, H.: Blockchain-enabled information sharing within a supply chain: a systematic literature review. IEEE Access **8**, 49645–49656 (2020)
29. Weiler, V., Harter, H., Eicker, U.: Life cycle assessment of buildings and city quarters comparing demolition and reconstruction with refurbishment. Energy and Build. **134**, 319–328 (2017). https://doi.org/10.1016/j.enbuild.2016.11.004
30. Yang, Y., Peng, D., Wang, W., Zhang, X.: pp. 2622–2627 (2020). https://doi.org/10.1109/iSPEC50848.2020.9350999
31. Zimonjic, P., McDiarmid, M.: Canada set to meet Paris climate commitments under plan to be announced friday. https://www.cbc.ca/news/politics/carbon-emissions-climate-deal-ministers-1.3888060

Emulation of IEC 60870-5-104 Communication in Digital Secondary Substations

Filip Holik$^{(\boxtimes)}$ [iD], Doney Abraham[iD], and Sule Yildirim Yayilgan[iD]

Norwegian University of Science and Technology, 2815 Gjøvik, Norway
filip.holik@ntnu.no

Abstract. This paper describes two methods of emulation of digital secondary substations and their communication to the control center via the IEC 60870-5-104 protocol. The first method describes use of Mininet network emulator, which omits certain minor networking features, but can create the topology very efficiently. The second method describes use of virtual machines, which can be interconnected to achieve the full functionality including router devices and VPN connections.

An open source library libIEC60870-5 is used for communication between substations and the control center. The library is analyzed and compared to real traffic provided by Norwegian National Smart Grid Laboratory. Based on found differences, the paper provides information of how to modify the library in order to create messages identical to the real traffic. These messages can be used to verify the substation behavior, or for security penetration testing by creating messages with spoofed temperature or multimeter sensor values.

Keywords: Communication emulation · Digital secondary substations · IEC 60870-5-104 · libIEC60870-5 · Smart grid

1 Introduction

Digital transformation of electricity grid continues as more areas are being updated in order to support smart grids. One of the most important elements in an electricity distribution network to undergo this transformation was digital substations (DS). It brought advantages such as effective real-time monitoring, higher resiliency, infrastructure simplification and cost reductions. The same process is now reaching secondary substations.

These secondary substations have much smaller scope in terms of transformed voltage, number of equipment and served area; but on the other hand, their number is an order of higher magnitude. Their digital transformation is therefore essential in order to create resilient and efficient smart grid [10].

This work was funded by the Research Council of Norway, Innovation Project for the Industrial Sector - ENERGIX program, project number 296381 (Security of supply in smartgrids with interacting digital systems).

F. Sanfilippo et al. (Eds.): INTAP 2021, CCIS 1616, pp. 232–243, 2022.
https://doi.org/10.1007/978-3-031-10525-8_19

The main contribution of this paper is to propose and analyze methods to develop a model of a digital secondary substation (DSS) using real data communication. The term *emulation* is used for this method. Unlike *simulation* which simplifies the behavior. Emulated traffic uses real-like messages which can be appropriately recognized and handled by all networking devices. Such a model can then be used for behavior analysis and to verify security, which is one of the most important research question as the DSS different structure means new challenges and brings unexpected issues. Especially considering that these substations are enclosed in a single relatively compact block and therefore much easier to access by an attacker than DS with several access restriction techniques.

1.1   Digital Secondary Substations

Digital secondary substations (DSS) are transforming medium voltage to low voltage and are therefore most often located between DS and energy consumption (additional transformers can scale the voltage even further) [10]. DSS network topology is very simple when compared to DS as it is shown in Fig. 1.

The topology contains one gateway router connected to a remote terminal unit (RTU), which connects several transformer temperature sensors (TTS), low-voltage switchboard multimeters (LSM) and a door sensor. These devices can be connected via various protocols such as Modbus and the RTU acts as an interface between these protocols and communication to the control center realized by the IEC 60870-5-104 protocol (IEC104) [3]. No time-critical messages are being used to protect the grid function and the communication part within the DSS does not provide redundancy as in the case of a DS [10].

The connection out of the substation is typically redundant and is realized over a public network of an ISP. VPN is being used for encryption. The connection can use optic fiber or some form of wireless communication (most often cellular).

2   Related Work

Current work in the area of emulation approaches of DSS communication is very limited. To our best knowledge, only the work [13] presents a relevant model of limited parts of the communication between SCADA and RTU. Authors used Mininet for network emulation and Scapy tool for generation of selected IEC104 messages. Authors are working on extending the work to cover the entire IEC104 protocol and they are planning to publish the framework as open-source.

The only other relevant research is focused on the IEC104 protocol itself. Its behavior in terms of data flows, distribution of different message types and traffic frequency was analyzed in [7]. Description of communication scenarios with traffic measurements was analyzed in [9]. Protocol's security aspects were researched in [1,12]. Authors in [1] proposed a multivariate Intrusion Detection System for anomalies detection which can signalize a Man-in-the-Middle attack

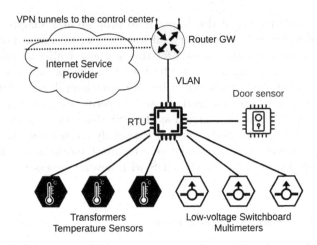

Fig. 1. Topology of a digital secondary substation

as the protocol does not use any encryption. Paper [12] proposes a Coloured Petri Net threat model and risk assessment for four types of attacks (ordered from the most to the least dangerous): unauthorized access, Denial of Service, Man-in-the-Middle, and traffic analysis.

The lack of further research confirms the importance and usefulness of emulation models described in this work.

3   The IEC 60870-5-104 Protocol

The IEC 60870-5-104 protocol (IEC104) [3] is mostly used for communication between the control center and DS (both primary and secondary) and is therefore build on top of a reliable TCP communication.

3.1   Message Types

The protocol uses the *Type* field to define three basic types of messages [4]:

1. Type U (0x03) - a fixed length message used for communication control. It has three subtypes: START (for connection initialization), STOP (for connection termination) and TEST (for verification of an active connection).
2. Type I (0x00) - a variable length message used for data transfer. It contains a payload in form of an Application Service Data Unit (ASDU).
3. Type S (0x01) - a fixed length message used for supervision and sending of acknowledgments.

3.2 Application Service Data Unit (ASDU)

ASDU contains payload of type I messages. The structure can vary based on the data type which is defined in the *TypeID* field. ASDU can be divided based on the communication direction [4]:

1. From control to monitors - includes two types of messages with the same *TypeID* (C_XX_XX_X): process information and system information. Process information includes single and double commands, step positions and set points. System information includes interrogation commands, reset, test, read and time synchronization.
2. From monitors to control - also includes process information (M_XX_XX_X) such as status values, measurements, step positions, etc.; and system information (M_EI_NA_1).
3. Bidirectional - includes control direction parameters (P_XX_XX_X) for modifying deadbands and a type for file transfers (F_XX_XX_X).

4 Emulation of Digital Secondary Substations Topology

This section describes two methods for creating an emulated topology of a DSS. For illustration purposes, examples show topologies of two DSS and a simplified control center.

4.1 Mininet Emulation

Mininet [8] is an open-source tool for creating a virtual network, which can contain hosts (end devices), switches and software-defined network controllers. Mininet uses a lightweight virtualization where all devices share the kernel with the host system. For this reason, Mininet is available only for Linux-based operating systems. This requirement can be avoided by installing Mininet within a Linux-based virtual machine (VM). This also allows an easy export of the entire model - including the DSS topology, the libIEC60870-5 library and any other software tools. This method is recommended and shown in Fig. 2.

Figure 2 also shows mapping of DSS equipment to Mininet elements. RTU and routers are represented by switches, while sensors are represented by hosts.

The main advantage of the Mininet approach is low demand on computational resources [5]. Even a network topology with hundreds of devices can easily run on an average laptop. The modeled system can also be easily exported in form of a Python script. A script for this topology is provided on GitHub [2].

The main disadvantage of Mininet is simplification of certain aspects, mostly the inability to emulate the router functionality. Another problem is VLAN configuration on software switches. Solutions to these issues are described below.

Routing Simulation. Routing can be ignored if all the topology devices are located within the same subnet. If the routing behavior is required, it can be simulated with the use of software-defined networking (SDN). An SDN controller can instruct switches of how to handle incoming messages.

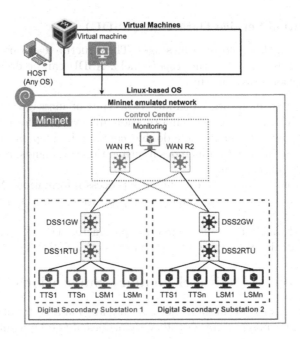

Fig. 2. Mininet emulation of digital secondary substations

VLAN Configuration. Mininet does not support VLAN configuration commands for software switches. Configuration must be set outside the Mininet environment. The following example shows assignment of VLAN 10 to port 1 on switch 1:

```
sudo ovs-vsctl set port S1-eth1 tag=10
```

4.2 Full Emulation

This approach uses virtual machines for emulation of RTUs, routers and the monitoring control center host. Each device is implemented in one virtual machine and a virtual network is created for their interconnection. A hosting platform for this approach can use any virtualization tool (Oracle VM VirtualBox, VMware Workstation, OpenStack, etc.). Oracle VM VirtualBox [11] was used in this work. The emulation schema is shown in Fig. 3. Sensor and multimeter devices are omitted from VMs as they would unnecessary increase the topology complexity. Their messages are generated by the RTU (on the figure shown with dash lines).

The main advantage of this approach is a possibility to fully emulate routers, which can be implemented as Linux-based hosts with appropriate tools, or as general boxes with router operating systems (for example pfSense, VyOS, OpenWrt and its variants). In case of the DSS emulation, these routers have to be configured with the following features:

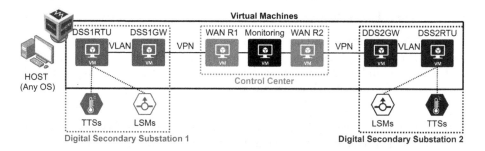

Fig. 3. Full emulation of digital secondary substations

– Routing - to provide connectivity, routers must have information about remote networks. This can be achieved by setting up a dynamic routing protocol (for example OSPF or BGP) or by static routing configuration.
– VLAN - a dedicated VLAN has to be created on the gateway router and assigned to the interface leading to the RTU.
– VPN - to emulate encrypted communication between DSS routers and a WAN routers, a site-to-site IPsec VPN must be set up.

The main disadvantage of full emulation are significantly more demanding computational resources as each device uses full virtualization. This approach is therefore more suitable for smaller topologies.

Network Emulation. The network emulation varies based on the used virtualization technology. In Oracle VM VirtualBox, the *internal network adapter* option should be used to interconnect neighboring devices (for example the RTU to the router gateway). Name of the network must be the same on both devices. These interfaces then have to be configured within virtual machines (to set up theirs IP addresses, network masks and default gateways).

Optionally, an additional network adapter can be used for administration (*host-only adapter*) or for external access (*NAT*). The host-only network can be configured under the *File/Host Network Manager*, where an IP address of the host and a DHCP server can be set.

5 Communication Emulation

The library libIEC60870-5 [6] is used for communication emulation in both emulation methods. The library is written in C language and supports all major operating systems including Linux, macOS and Windows. This library must be installed on end nodes which varies based on the used emulation method. In both methods, the library can be downloaded from the official webpage [6].

5.1 Library Installation

Mininet Emulation. End nodes (hosts) in the Mininet tool share the file system with the host linux-based operating system. The library must therefore be downloaded and decompressed only on the host system. All the Mininet hosts will then be able to access and use the library.

Full Emulation. Emulated end nodes (RTUs and the control center) must use a supported operating system of the libIEC61850 library. This operating system should be lightweight, well documented and up to date. The library must be separately downloaded and decompressed on each emulated device.

5.2 Library Launch

The library contains an *examples* folder with pre-prepared scripts for emulating the traffic. To launch these scripts, executable files must be firstly created with the *make* tool. This tool can be simply launched with the command `make` executed either separately for each script file, or for the entire library in the root folder.

5.3 Devices Emulation

Sensors and Multimeters Scripts. In a real network, RTUs create TCP/IP messages based on data received from the grid sensors. The `simple_server.c` script can be used to generate these messages. The script will start listening for a client connection on the default TCP port 2404. When a client connects, the script will start sending IEC104 messages. The following command starts the script (must be launched from the library folder):

```
sudo ./lib60870-C/examples/cs104_server/simple_server
```

Control Center Scripts. A control center can be simulated by collecting the messages generated in substations. The `simple_client.c` script can be used. The following command starts the script (with up to two optional parameters for IP address and PORT number - they must correspond to the server):

```
sudo ./lib60870-C/examples/cs104_client/simple_client IP PORT
```

6   Library Evaluation

The topology presented in Fig. 3 was implemented according to the description in Sect. 5. The IEC104 traffic was then transmitted and analyzed by the Wireshark tool [15]. Emulated traffic was compared to real traffic provided by Norwegian National Smart Grid Laboratory [14]. This traffic is stated as "real traffic".

6.1 Default Script Analysis

Default library scripts (cs104_client/server) have a fixed sequence of messages, but the total number of sent messages can vary based on the synchronization mechanism and cycle sleep times. The entire communication takes around 9 s. A detailed time analysis and comparison of traffic was not conducted as IEC104 messages are not time critical (they use slower TCP) and they serve mostly for monitoring and control. Emulation of real latency on the WAN would not be possible as it varies case by case and in time. The following list shows the sequence:

1. Connection establishment - U messages (ACT and CON) are exchanged.
2. M_ME_NB_1 I messages are being sent with an S message acknowledgment returned after every 8th message. Messages contain a single scaled value element (starts with a value which is increased by 1 in every consequent message).
3. C_IC_NA_1 messages - Act and ActCon are exchanged.
4. M_ME_NB_1 I message is sent, but with "Inrogen" *CauseTx* instead of "Per/Cyc" and with 3 measured values elements (-1, 23 and 2300).
5. M_SP_NA_1 I message with two single-point information elements (0x01 and 0x00) is sent.
6. M_SP_NA_1 I message with eight single-point information elements (alternating 0x01 and 0x00) is sent.
7. M_BO_NA_1 I message with 32-bits string of value 0xaaaa0000 is sent.
8. C_IC_NA_1 I ActTerm interrogation message is sent.
9. M_ME_NB_1 I messages are sent in one second intervals. An S message acknowledgment is sent after the first message. Messages continue with the sequentially increasing single scaled value.
10. TCP closes the connection (FIN, ACK).

Real Traffic Behavior. Real data traffic is exchanged based on a polling mechanism. Typically, an S message (can be accompanied by an I message) is sent to the monitoring device and the device then sends a measurement I message back. Transmission is not bounded by time as it runs indefinitely.

6.2 Messages Analysis

Both real traffic and default library scripts use all types of messages - U, I and S. The U, S, and control I messages are identical as they have the same format and same values. The only difference between real traffic and library scripts are monitoring I messages, which use different *TypeIDs*. Default library scripts use M_ME_NB_1 (measured scaled values), and M_BO_NA_1 (bitstring values), which were not present in the real traffic. The only common monitoring messages were M_SP_NA_1 (single-point information).

The following messages are transmitted by the real traffic, but they are not present in the default library scripts:

1. M_ME_NC_1 - short floating point number.
2. M_ME_TF_1 - short floating point number with a CP56 timestamp.
3. M_SP_TB_1 - single-point information with a CP56 timestamp.
4. M_IT_TB_1 - integrated totals with a CP56 timestamp.

The following section describes how to emulate these messages (and the common M_SP_NA_1 message) by modification of the default library scripts.

6.3   Real Traffic Messages Emulation

This section describes modifications of the default library script in order to create messages equal to the real traffic. The complete script is provided on GitHub [2].

The following code explains how to create and send a message and it is therefore common for all following specific messages.

```
/* Create an ASDU */
CS101_ASDU newAsdu = CS101_ASDU_create(alParams, false,
    CS101_COT_INTERROGATED_BY_STATION, 0, 1, false, false);

/* Create an Information Object and add it into the ASDU */
io = (InformationObject) ... // Varies based on the message type
CS101_ASDU_addInformationObject(newAsdu, io);

/* Send the message and deallocate */
InformationObject_destroy(io);
IMasterConnection_sendASDU(connection, newAsdu);
CS101_ASDU_destroy(newAsdu);
```

1. M_ME_NC_1. One of the real traffic messages has short floating point number of value 29.25 and IOA of 3. The following command shows an example of how to reproduce an equal message using the library. Important variables (IOA and the value) are shown in blue.

```
io = (InformationObject) MeasuredValueShort_create(NULL,
    3, 29.25, IEC60870_QUALITY_GOOD);
```

2. M_ME_TF_1. Includes the same information as in the case of M_ME_NC_1 messages, but adds the CP56Time2a timestamp. The current timestamp in miliseconds can be generated by calling the function Hal_getTimeInMs() located in the file: /src/hal/time/unix/time.c.

Another difference is that the real traffic uses "Spont" (3) *CauseTx* while the library uses "Inrogen" (20) by default. This can be changed by replacing the ASDU function parameter. All of the available parameters are listed in the file: /src/iec60870/cs101/cs101_asdu.c.

The following commands show, how to recreate the message:

```
/* Create the timestamp */
CP56Time2a timestamp = CP56Time2a_createFromMsTimestamp(NULL,
   Hal_getTimeInMs());

/* Create the ASDU with "Spont" CauseTx */
newAsdu = CS101_ASDU_create(alParams, false,
   CS101_COT_SPONTANEOUS, 0, 1, false, false);

io = (InformationObject)
   MeasuredValueShortWithCP56Time2a_create(NULL, 3, 29.25,
   IEC60870_QUALITY_GOOD, timestamp);
```

3. M_SP_TB_1. Uses the same CP56Time2a timestamp and "Spont" CauseTx. The following command shows the information object creation (with IOA 11).

```
io = (InformationObject) SinglePointWithCP56Time2a_create(NULL,
   11, false, IEC60870_QUALITY_GOOD,timestamp);
```

4. M_IT_TB_1. Uses the timestamp and data values formatted as "binary counter". The library implements *BinaryCounterReading* class located in the file: /src/iec60870/cs101/cs101_bcr.c. The following commands show how to create a binary counter object and insert it into the information object with IOA 9:

```
/* BCR parameters: self, value, SQ, CY, CA, IV */
BinaryCounterReading bcr = BinaryCounterReading_create(NULL, 0,
   10, false, false, false);

io = (InformationObject)
   IntegratedTotalsWithCP56Time2a_create(NULL, 9, bcr,timestamp);
```

5. M_SP_NA_1. This message is created in the default library script, with 8 IOAs. The following command shows the modification needed to emulate the real traffic (IOA 10, SIQ 0x00):

```
CS101_ASDU_addInformationObject(newAsdu, io = (InformationObject)
   SinglePointInformation_create(NULL, 10, false,
   IEC60870_QUALITY_GOOD));
```

6.4   Discussion

The aforementioned library script modifications can create identical messages to real traffic. This has been proven by comparing the traffic in the Wireshark tool. Figure 4 shows comparison of M_ME_TF_1 messages - real traffic and emulated

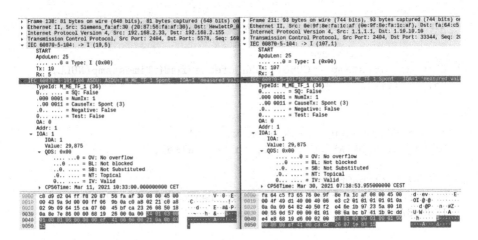

Fig. 4. Comparison of real (left part) and emulated (right part) traffic

using the script. It can be seen that the IEC104 messages contain same values except in variable fields such as Tx, Rx (depends on previously sent messages) and the timestamp.

These results show that the libIEC60870-5 library has a potential to create messages unrecognizable from real DSS messages. This fact can be used for various verifications before an expensive deployment within a real DSS. It also demonstrate how easily messages can be injected by an attacker if an access to a DSS is gained. Injection of messages with specific values can damage the grid equipment and can cause a local blackout.

The only limitation of the presented script is the need of Tx and Rx fields modification to correspond to the legitimate traffic in case of an attack simulation where the control center should not detect any suspicious activity.

7   Conclusion

The analysis of the libIEC60870-5 library has shown that the tool can be used to easily recreate messages with values corresponding to the real DSS or to purposefully create messages with a potential to cause damage. This can be used to verify security mechanisms or to test any other communication behavior without a need to use a real DSS network.

The paper did not cover any performance measurements as these are irrelevant in DSS. IEC104 messages are mostly used for monitoring purposes and not for real-time grid adjustments as is the case of GOOSE messages in DS. In our future work, we would like to target emulation of these messages including theirs performance comparison.

References

1. Grammatikis, P.R., Sarigiannidis, P., Sarigiannidis, A., Margounakis, D., Tsiakalos, A., Efstathopoulos, G.: An anomaly detection mechanism for IEC 60870-5-104. In: 2020 9th International Conference on Modern Circuits and Systems Technologies (MOCAST), pp. 1–4, September 2020. https://doi.org/10.1109/MOCAST49295.2020.9200285
2. Holik, F.: DSS (2021). https://github.com/filipholik/DSS. Accessed 26 Aug 2021
3. IEC 60870-5-104:2006 (2016). https://webstore.iec.ch/publication/25035. Accessed 01 Mar 2021
4. Introduction to the IEC 60870-5-104 standard (2021). https://www.ensotest.com/iec-60870-5-104/introduction-to-the-iec-60870-5-104-standard/. Accessed 22 Mar 2021
5. Lantz, B., Heller, B., McKeown, N.: A network in a laptop: rapid prototyping for software-defined networks, p. 19 (2010). https://doi.org/10.1145/1868447.1868466
6. libIEC61850/lib60870-5 (2020). https://libiec61850.com/libiec61850/about/. Accessed 01 Mar 2021
7. Mai, K., Qin, X., Ortiz Silva, N., Cardenas, A.A.: IEC 60870–5-104 network characterization of a large-scale operational power grid. In: 2019 IEEE Security and Privacy Workshops (SPW), pp. 236–241, May 2019. https://doi.org/10.1109/SPW.2019.00051
8. Mininet (2018). http://mininet.org/. Accessed 25 Feb 2021
9. Musil, P., Mlynek, P.: Overview of communication scenarios for IEC 60870-5-104 substation model. In: 2020 21st International Scientific Conference on Electric Power Engineering (EPE), pp. 1–4, October 2020. https://doi.org/10.1109/EPE51172.2020.9269173
10. Omerovic, A., Vefsnmo, H., Gjerde, O., Ravndal, S.T., Kvinnesland, A.: An industrial trial of an approach to identification and modelling of cybersecurity risks in the context of digital secondary substations. In: Kallel, S., Cuppens, F., Cuppens-Boulahia, N., Hadj Kacem, A. (eds.) CRiSIS 2019. LNCS, vol. 12026, pp. 17–33. Springer, Cham (2020). https://doi.org/10.1007/978-3-030-41568-6_2
11. Oracle VM VirtualBox (2021). https://www.virtualbox.org/, last accessed 05 Mar 2021
12. Radoglou-Grammatikis, P., Sarigiannidis, P., Giannoulakis, I., Kafetzakis, E., Panaousis, E.: Attacking IEC-60870-5-104 SCADA systems. In: 2019 IEEE World Congress on Services (SERVICES), vol. 2642–939X, pp. 41–46, July 2019. https://doi.org/10.1109/SERVICES.2019.00022
13. Salazar, L., Ortiz, N., Qin, X., Cardenas, A.A.: Towards a high-fidelity network emulation of IEC 104 SCADA systems. In: Proceedings of the 2020 Joint Workshop on CPS; IoT Security and Privacy, CPSIOTSEC 2020, pp. 3–12. Association for Computing Machinery, New York (2020). https://doi.org/10.1145/3411498.3419969
14. Smart Grid Laboratory - SINTEF (2017). https://www.sintef.no/en/all-laboratories/smartgridlaboratory/. Accessed 15 Mar 2021
15. Wireshark (2021). https://www.wireshark.org/. Accessed 15 Mar 2021

ML and AI for Sensing Technologies, Social Media Analytics

Point Cloud Instance Segmentation for Automatic Electric Vehicle Battery Disassembly

Henrik Brådland[1,2](✉) ⓘ, Martin Choux[1] ⓘ,
and Linga Reddy Cenkeramaddi[2] ⓘ

[1] Department of Engineering Sciences, University of Agder, Kristiansand, Norway
henrikbraadland@hotmail.com
[2] Department of Information and Communication Technology, University of Agder,
Kristiansand, Norway

Abstract. This paper describes a novel design based on recent 3D perception methods for capturing point clouds and segmenting instances of cabling found on electric vehicle battery packs. The use of cutting-edge perception algorithm architectures, such as graph-based and voxel-based convolution, in industrial autonomous lithium-ion battery pack disassembly is investigated. The proposed approach focuses on the challenge of getting a desirable representation of any battery pack using an industrial robot in conjunction with a high-end structured light camera, with "end-to-end" and "model-free" as design constraints. The proposed design employs self-captured datasets comprised of several battery packs that have been captured and labeled. Following that, the datasets are used to create a perception system. Based on the results, graph-based deep-learning algorithms have been shown to be capable of being scaled up to $50,000$ inputs while still exhibiting strong performance in terms of accuracy and processing time. The results show that an instance segmenting system can be implemented in less than two seconds. Using off-the-shelf hardware, we demonstrate that a 3D perception system is industrially viable and competitive as compared to a 2D perception system (The different algorithms studied in this article are implemented in Python and can be obtained through the following link: https://github.com/HenrikBradland-Nor/intap21).

Keywords: Graph CNN · Part segmentation · Large point clouds · Structured-light camera

1 Introduction

With expected 120 GWh/year automotive battery capacity available for repurposing or recycling by 2030 [3], the need for automation in Lithium-Ion Battery (LIB) disassembly is increasing. One challenge yet to be solved, is to develop a perception system able to cope with the large variations in LIB packs and hence based on a model-free approach. With this objective the authors in article [4]

F. Sanfilippo et al. (Eds.): INTAP 2021, CCIS 1616, pp. 247–258, 2022.
https://doi.org/10.1007/978-3-031-10525-8_20

developed a perception system, based on a high resolution 3D camera, able to detect the main components inside a LIB pack within 5 s. However, flexible and entangled parts, as for example electrical wires, were not recognised mainly due to the fact that only 2D images where used by the detection algorithm whereas the depth information was added in a second step to estimate the pose. In contrast, object detection algorithms based on point cloud semantic segmentation (PCSS) directly process the 3D data which extends their capabilities.

For most recent studies the preferred method for PCSS are based in majority on the PointNet [11] where Multi-Layer Perceptron (MLP) is used to approximate per-point local features for each point, that are later classified by another MLP. The most promising methods are Graph Neural Networks (GNNs) like SPG [7], DGCNN [17] and RGCNN [15], which show excellent performance [22]. These methods are mostly applied towards LiDAR-based point clouds of outdoor environments, e.g. Airborn LiDAR Scanning or self-driven cars, or indoors RGB-D based data [22]. At the time of writing, there exists no known data-sets for disassembling EV battery pack, one needs hence to be generated.

Most work on PCSS of objects is done on small point clouds, commonly in the range of 2000–4000 points per point cloud [17, 19, 22, 23]. However with modern sensors, the resolution of real-world data gets vastly larger, and can easily go over one million points. Therefore, there is still work to be done in order to connect the models in a real-world environment. In addition, deep learning-based algorithms for PCSS or instance segmentation of point clouds are commonly only compared by accuracy and not by processing time. This is probably a result of the field of deep learning on point cloud being quite fresh [9, 22]. Several promising algorithms, rooted in different concepts, still need to be tested and compared with a focus not only on classification performance but also on forward processing time.

This paper aims at first presenting what algorithms based on PCSS are the most suitable for electrical wire detection in EV battery packs both in term of accuracy and processing time, and second to validate if such algorithms can be used on large point cloud (50 000 points or more) generated by high resolution 3D cameras and consequently be industrially viable as an alternative to the more traditional 2D equivalent. The proposed design of the instance segmentation algorithms is presented and the results are validated through experiments conducted on two different automotive battery packs.

2   Material and Methods

2.1   System Work-Flow

The overall workflow of the proposed perception system is illustrated in Fig. 1, starting from a raw point cloud and with final output the instance segmentation.

Filtering and Downsampling. Classification algorithms do not perform well on noisy and bias raw data as in Fig. 1a [8]. The point cloud needs first to be filtered to remove invalid points, background, and redundant points and second, to be downsized since a state-of-the-art HDR 3D camera provides over two million points, which is magnitudes more than what most algorithms are designed

(a) The raw point cloud.   (b) The point cloud is filtered and downsampled.   (c) The points are assigned a semantic value.   (d) Clusters are formed.

Fig. 1. The workings of the perception system.

to work on (Commonly <10, 000) [19, 22]. In order to ensure a fast and non-bias downsampling of the output, a hybrid solution is selected where first a voxel-grid is applied to remove redundant points and performing the majority of the downsampling, followed by a random reduction filter to reach the desired size. After this operation the data take a grid-like shape with some empty squares as shown in Fig. 1b.

Semantic Segmentation. The second step so-called semantic segmentation aims to label the points in the downsampled point cloud as shown in Fig. 1c. This step is likely to be the most time-consuming part of the pipeline as most popular techniques have a high time complexity. Voxel grid-based methods grow cubical with respect to the resolution [11] and graph-based, in the best case, grows quadratic [21]. More novel and traditional approaches like Random Forrest, SVM and PointNet have drastically lower time complexities [11]. Nevertheless, the novel approaches are outperformed by more complex ones in the large benchmarks [19,20]. Since boosting algorithms have also been used for PCSS of point clouds derived from outdoor areal data with promising results [10,18], gradient boosting is therefore also included in our proposed methods. In the above mentioned benchmarks accuracy is the metric of choice, rather than time usage. A novelty in this paper is to present a comparison of time complexity or forward time versus accuracy across the following six promising architectures implemented and tested on large point clouds:

1. Random Forest (RF)
2. Support-Vector Machines (SVM)
3. Gradient boosting [6]
4. PointNet [11] (Pointnett++, is excluded as it is shown to have a vastly poorer time usage than DGCNN [16])
5. Dynamic Graph CNN (DGCNN) [17]
6. VoxelNet [24] (replication of SEGCloud [14])

In some of the chosen algorithms, only a subset of the points are labelled in order to reduce computational time. Inspired by SEGCloud [14], Mask-MCNet [23] and Point-GNN [13], trilinear interpolation, is proposed to transfer the learned label back to the original filtered point cloud. Trilinear interpolation allows the data to be a weighted average of the neighbouring points, thus providing a more continuous interpolation than the alternative, k-NN.

Clustering. After the points are assigned a semantic label, they must be grouped. The clustering blocks, as shown in Fig. 1d, should form collections of points that represent cables and leave out mislabeled points. The choice of clustering algorithm is described further in Sect. 2.3.

2.2 Semantic Segmentation Algorithm

Non-deep Classifiers. Although not distinguishable, there are tendencies in the embedding of EV battery packs that there exists some combination of the nine point attributes, i.e. three colour, three positions, and three curvature features, that allows for segmentation by using a traditional classifier. The Random Forest algorithm together with the SVM with several different kernel types and gradient boosting are tested. The LightGBM version of gradient boosting is selected as it manages to train fast on large amounts of data. LightGBM runs with 1000 decision trees and a maximum 32 leafs per tree. To obtain translation and rotation invariant properties, the classifiers can not work directly on the position coordinates. Therefore they are trained on the colour and curvature features only.

Deep Learning-Based Classifiers. PointNet [11] and its successor, Point-Net + + [12], are the foundation for most deep learning-based algorithms working on point clouds [9,22]. By using a computed global representation and a point-vice representation to classify each point, the algorithms can learn both local and global features. Since PointNet is the inspiration for most deep learning-based algorithms, it becomes natural to include it in any comparison.

Graph-based neural networks is a field within neural networks that only recently gained popularity. Nevertheless, the graph-based neural networks are viewed as a promising way of processing point clouds [22]. The spatial-based GNN, Dynamic Graph CNN (DGCNN) [16], performs well on the ModelNet40 benchmark [19] with an accuracy of 92.9%. DGCNN have two core architectures that make it suitable for PCSS: The message passing method "EdgeConv" that allows for convolution-like operations while maintaining permutation inference, and the dynamic re-drawing of the graph allowing the algorithm to focus on the nodes that are difficult to distinguish. However, the formation of k-NN graphs are computationally heavy. The architecture of the PCSS version of DGCNN utilises PointNets idea of using a computed global representation together with local features to classify points by using a residual network structure, thus allowing for features related to the local neighbourhood to be forwarded while the later layers pick up features for separating similar-looking points.

A last architecture considered in this study is 3D convolutional neural networks (3D-CNN) that have the advantage of being directly transferable from the 2D equivalent as they operate on a similar grid-based structure. VoxelNet [24] presents a model where first voxel features are learned based on the containing points in their "feature learning network". This allows each voxel to learn its local features of the point clouds before the voxels are aggregated using 3D-CNN to learn global features. In the original paper, a third stage proposes regions based on the aggregated voxel features. This third stage is replaced in the present work with a trilinear interpolation layer to determine the point features from the aggregated voxels as suggested by [14,23]. The semantic value of each point is then determined by a simple three layer MLP where the 64 point features are concatenated with the three point coordinates to serve as the input. Compared to GNN, 3D-CNN is more computationally demanding, but is dependent on the number of voxels rather than the number of points. In other words, a good embedding from points to voxels that allows for large voxels can compensate for high time complexity.

Performance Metric. It is seen as equally important to correctly label cables (true positive) as to correctly label background (true negative). False positives can lead to the formation of false clusters, while false negatives can lead to discontinuous clusters or too low density to form clusters. Accuracy is used as the performance metric because it represents the classification of both positive and negative observations. The disadvantage of the accuracy metric is its sensitivity to unbalanced data sets. The second performance metric is the forward time which is defined to not include the time of prepossessing of the data, only the semantic segmentation.

Training. The data sets used in this paper, are highly unbalanced. This is counteracted by training on balanced subsets extracted from each point cloud. All the positive samples are directly transferred to the new subset, while the negative samples are randomly sampled to preserve the natural variance in the features of the background points. The inputs are all normalised, except for training the DGCNN where the original coordinates are preserved to not interfere with the forming of the graphs. The non-deep learning-based algorithms are directly fitted to the data.

To overcome the memory limitation of the GPU (8 GB), the point clouds are divided into 8 smaller chunks that are individually processed. The gradients are computed based on the loss of an entire chunk, thus improving training by using mini-batches [8]. The hyperparameters used during the standard training are shown in Table 1.

The performance of PCSS is traditionally trained and compared with region-based metrics, where the mean intersection over union (mIoU) is most common [9]. EV battery cables, unlike other objects used in PCSS, are long and slim while being entangled. The boundary boxes of region-based and boundary-based loss would likely include points that are not a part of the cables, thus they are not feasible. The loss function is therefore distribution-based, hence every point is individually evaluated and compared to the ground truth. The standard cross-entropy loss is chosen as the primary loss function, as this is the standard for binary classification tasks.

2.3 Clustering

Viable clustering algorithms are DBSCAN [5] and its successor OPTICS [2]. They both work by forming cluster centres from the dense part of the data and then recursively evaluating neighbouring points to determine if they should be included or not in the current cluster. Therefore, they both work well on non-convex data. Their hyper-parameters are empirically determined.

Table 1. Base value for hyper-parameters used during training.

	DGCNN	PointNet	VoxelNet
Epochs	200	200	160
Learning rate	0.1	0.01	0.01
Scheduler type	Cosine annealing	Cosine annealing	Step ($\gamma = 0.1$)
Scheduler period	50	50	150
Momentum	0.9	-	-
Batch size	One chunk	One chunk	One chunk
Dropout probability	50%	50%	50%
Optimiser	SGD	Adam	SGD

3 Results

The aim of this section is to validate the model-free cable segmentation and to characterise its performance regarding time and accuracy. Two different battery packs serve as the case study.

Hardware Setup. The experimental setup is composed of IRB4400 robot (ABB, Zürich, Switzerland), IRBT4004 track (ABB, Zürich, Switzerland), and Zivid One 3D camera (Zivid, Oslo, Norway) all connected to a PC running the Robot Operating System (ROS) as setup in article [1]. A schematic representation of the setup is showed in Fig. 2. Two battery packs - a small one from an Audi A3 e-Tron Sportback (Battery A) and a large one from a Volkswagen E-golf (Battery B) depicted in Figs. 3a and 3b - were used for the training and validation of the model-free cable segmentation.

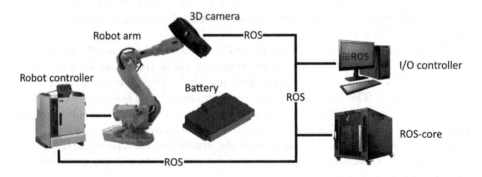

Fig. 2. Schematic diagram of the laboratory setup.

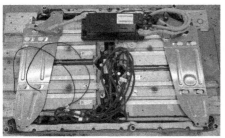

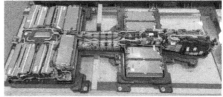

(b) The large test battery (Battery B).

(a) The small test battery (Battery A).

Fig. 3. The small and large test batteries

Performance of Classification Algorithms. Automatic disassembly of EV batteries requires an accurate and fast perception system. Assessing the accuracy and forward time of the six most promising algorithms presented and trained/fitted as described in Sect. 2.2 is therefore an important task in the design process. The data-set consists of 38 labelled point clouds split into training and validation using a 80%/20% split ratio. 22 of the point clouds are captures of battery A and battery B, while the 16 others are generated by augmenting some of the 22 original point clouds. For the two algorithms Random Forest (RF) and SVM, several versions are implemented and tested because of the lack of references on what hyper-parameters to use for PCSS. The accuracy and forward time of each algorithm are shown in Table 2 and Table 3 respectively, while they are plotted against each other in Fig. 4. The point cloud id refers to a specific point cloud in the data set also available in the previously mentioned link. Ids ending in a letter are augmented.

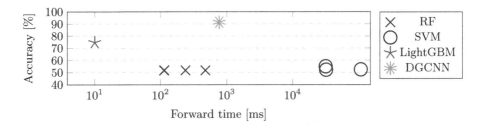

Fig. 4. Mean accuracy (Table 2) vs the log of the mean forwards time (Table 3).

Table 2. Accuracy of selected algorithms. All values in %. The accuracy of PointNet and VoxelNet is not included as the algorithms did not manage to converge.

Algorithm	Point cloud id								Mean
	3	4	13	14	40	42c	44c	45c	
RF 40	53.6	52.6	51.2	54.2	51.9	49.4	50.5	49.9	51.7
RF 100	54.4	52.7	52.4	52.9	52.7	48.7	50.1	50.1	51.8
RF 400	53.8	52.7	52.0	53.2	53.0	49.4	49.9	50.3	51.8
RF 1000	52.6	53.0	52.1	54.2	52.8	49.4	49.8	50.3	51.8
SVM Linear	57.7	54.3	52.7	52.3	50.8	49.4	50.0	50.4	52.2
SVM Polynomial	57.6	54.9	53.2	53.2	50.8	49.8	50.7	49.8	52.5
SVM Radial basis	61.9	60.7	55.3	61.3	51.1	49.4	49.5	50.4	55.0
LightGBM	81.4	85.6	77.4	87.4	92.6	50.0	50.0	73.2	74.7
DGCNN	**88.4**	**91.7**	**89.4**	**92.0**	**94.2**	**92.7**	**93.4**	**89.4**	**91.4**
PointNet	-	-	-	-	-	-	-	-	-
VoxelNet	-	-	-	-	-	-	-	-	-

Table 3. Forward time of selected algorithms performed on the test set. All values are in seconds. [1]running on CPU (AMD Ryzen 5 3600 6-Core). [2]running on GPU (NVIDIA GeForce RTX 2070).

Algorithm	Point cloud id								Mean
	3	4	13	14	40	42c	44c	45c	
RF 40[1]	.117	.105	.112	.120	.109	.113	.112	.117	.113
RF 100[1]	.119	.119	.105	.107	.116	.117	.108	.118	.114
RF 400[1]	.119	.219	.227	.108	.219	.341	.329	.332	.237
RF 1000[1]	.334	.334	.455	.218	.337	.674	.775	.675	.475
SVM Linear[1]	10.0	9.09	31.0	4.79	21.1	56.2	64.1	56.4	31.6
SVM Polynomial[1]	9.73	9.47	31.4	4.98	22.0	56.1	65.8	57.7	32.1
SVM Radial basis[1]	33.8	30.7	108	15.6	72.5	188	220	193	107
LightGBM[2]	**.013**	**0.01**	**.011**	**.010**	**.009**	**.009**	**.010**	**.011**	**.010**
DGCNN[2]	.791	.844	.750	.716	.737	.758	.786	.773	.769
PointNet[2]	.075	.090	.093	.073	.073	.074	.072	.075	.078
VoxelNet[2]	22.6	24.5	24.8	22.6	21.6	21.7	22.2	22.5	22.8

Finally, the results of the PCSS are compared to the ground truth in Fig. 5 for both batteries.

From the results shown in Table 2 it is clear that the traditional classifiers (random forest and SVM) do not manage to provide any reliable results as none of them performs sufficiently better than a pure guess (50%) on the augmented point clouds 42c, 44c and 45c. The SVM algorithms performed marginally better

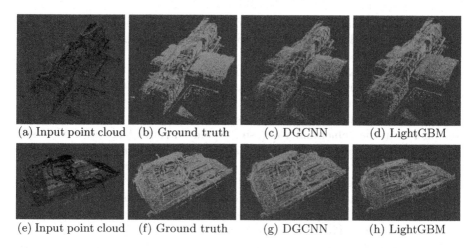

(a) Input point cloud   (b) Ground truth   (c) DGCNN   (d) LightGBM

(e) Input point cloud   (f) Ground truth   (g) DGCNN   (h) LightGBM

Fig. 5. The result of the PCSS of battery A (point cloud nr. 3) and battery B (point cloud nr. 45c).

than the random forest but are also seen as week classifiers. From the three implementations of SVM, the radial basis-based one performs notably better on test point cloud 3, 4 and 14. This is likely to be a consequence of the simpler geometry of battery A. On the other side, all three implementations of SVM show extremely poor time usage with time upwards of several minutes.

The boosting algorithm, LightGBM, shows surprisingly good performance both within accuracy and forward time. With accuracy up towards 90% and an average forward time of 10 [ms], the algorithm clearly outperforms the traditional classifiers, thus showing the potential of boosting-based algorithms. Nevertheless, the algorithm fails to generalise on the augmented versions of the data 42c and 44c.

Finding the correct hyperparameters for training turned difficult as no other known projects are working on point clouds of the same size. For the DGCNN algorithm, increasing the original value for k in [16] from $k = 20$ to $k = 100$, to then include a larger amount of features showed to help. As shown in Fig. 4 DGCNN outclasses the other algorithms in term of accuracy, generalises well on the augmented versions, and performs within an acceptable forward time.

4   Discussion

The fact that neither the boosting algorithm nor the traditional classifiers manage to generalise supports the idea of PointNet [11] saying that the semantic value of any single point depends on more than the point features alone. Thus to classify any point, one needs knowledge about the global features in combination with the local features. In other words, a point cloud is more than the sum of its parts.

Initially, the binary cross-entropy loss function was used, as described in Sect. 2.2. The model did not manage to learn due to the extreme value of the loss function.

Although the loss is averaged over the entire chunk, at least one point will be too strong of an influence due to the exponential nature of the binary cross-entropy loss function.

Conversely, the mean square error loss function acting in a quadratic way, do not suffer from the vulnerability of a single point having a large error while still punishing wrong guesses progressively harder in a non-linear way. Although the mean square error loss function is most commonly used in regression problems, it showed a good effect when applied in this work.

Neither the PointNet model nor the VoxelNet model managed to converge to a useful result even if a comprehensive amount of hyper-parameters were tested, as shown in Table 4. This is an indication that the algorithms are intended for smaller point clouds.

When training on chunks rather than the entire point cloud, the global feature vector might not be able to provide a good representation for PointNet. The VoxelNet algorithm is an attempt to reconstruct SEGCloud, but its training is based on the hyper-parameters of the original VoxelNet algorithm. This might be a source of error as the original VoxelNet algorithm is trained with a region-based loss function rather than a distribution-based one.

On the other side, a solution to PointNet is to produce a global feature vector before the point cloud is divided into chunks. Thereby allowing the algorithm to have a proper representation of the entire point cloud when performing PCSS. The SEGCloud algorithm could be reconstructed with another backbone than VoxelNet. It is not certain that another backbone would enhance the performance, but it is a possible source of error. Neither to say, a larger training set might have helped on improving the results.

The quality of the PCSS must also be evaluated by visual inspection. As shown in Fig. 5, the LightGBM algorithm does not manage to distinguish the orange panels from the orange cables in all cases. Also when looking at Table 2 LightGBM seems to overfitt on the test set rather than generalising as it performs poorly on the augmented data. Nevertheless, the LightGBM shows an impressive forward time and outperforming all the other algorithms. With a larger and more diverse data set, the LightGBM algorithm might work in an industrial setting. In case of only limited variations between battery packs, the LightGBM could with a sufficient amount of training data in combination with more engineered features possibly be viable in an industrial setting.

Table 4. The following configurations were tested when attempting to make PointNet and VoxelNet converge to satisfying performance.

Parameter	Values
Learning rate	0.1, 0.01, 0.001
Batch size	16, 32, 512, 1024, One chunk
Number of epochs	200, 300, 500
Loss function	BCE, MSE, Focal-Loss, NLLL
Output layer activation function	Soft-Max, Log Soft-Max, Sigmoid, Tanh
Scheduler type	Cosine annealing, step ($\gamma = 0.9$)
Scheduler period	30, 50, 200
Solver	SGD, Adam

From a time perspective, a perception system consisting of a combination of a PCSS and a clustering system is well within the time requirements and is therefore viable for industrial applications. If using DGCNN and for example DBSCAN for the clustering algorithm, the total time usage is 1.1 s for the large battery. With additional prepossessing and filtering added, the total time will not exceed two seconds. Depending on the application, this might allow for the usage of larger point clouds as it would be beneficial for the classification algorithms.

5   Conclusion

This paper presented a comparison between the most promising algorithms for instance segmentation of point clouds applied to classify components inside an end-of-life electrical vehicle battery pack. As the clustering algorithm has been shown to consume more time than the semantic segmentation algorithms, the PCSS-cluster approach is preferred over the cluster-class approach.

The proposed paper demonstrated that it is possible to extend the DGCNN algorithm to large point clouds (50,000 points) while still exhibiting strong performance in terms of accuracy and processing time. The results show that an instance segmenting system can be implemented with a forward time of less than two seconds. Furthermore, the poor performance of traditional classifiers and the success of DGCNN point to PointNet-based architectures that embed local and global features as a promising method of performing PCSS.

Using off-the-shelf hardware, this study has shown that a 3D perception system is industrially viable and competitive compared to its 2D perception counterpart.

References

1. Aalerud, A., Dybedal, J., Ujkani, E., Hovland, G.: Industrial environment mapping using distributed static 3D sensor nodes. In: 2018 14th IEEE/ASME International Conference on Mechatronic and Embedded Systems and Applications, MESA 2018 (2018). https://doi.org/10.1109/MESA.2018.8449203
2. Ankerst, M., Breunig, M.M., Kriegel, H.P., Sander, J.: OPTICS: ordering points to identify the clustering structure. ACM SIGMOD Rec. **28**(2), 49–60 (1999)
3. Awan, A.: Batteries: an essential technology to electrify road transport, pp. 185–219. International Energy Agency, June 2020
4. Choux, M., Marti Bigorra, E., Tyapin, I.: Task planner for robotic disassembly of electric vehicle battery pack. Metals **11**(3), 387 (2021)
5. Ester, M., Kriegel, H.P., Sander, J., Xu, X., et al.: A density-based algorithm for discovering clusters in large spatial databases with noise. In: KDD, vol. 96, pp. 226–231 (1996)
6. Ke, G., et al.: LightGBM: a highly efficient gradient boosting decision tree. In: Advances in Neural Information Processing Systems (NIPS), pp. 3147–3155 (2017)
7. Landrieu, L., Simonovsky, M.: Large-scale point cloud semantic segmentation with superpoint graphs (2018)

8. LeCun, Y.A., Bottou, L., Orr, G.B., Müller, K.-R.: Efficient BackProp. In: Montavon, G., Orr, G.B., Müller, K.-R. (eds.) Neural Networks: Tricks of the Trade. LNCS, vol. 7700, pp. 9–48. Springer, Heidelberg (2012). https://doi.org/10.1007/978-3-642-35289-8_3

9. Liu, W., Sun, J., Li, W., Hu, T., Wang, P.: Deep learning on point clouds and its application: a survey. Sensors (Switzerland) **19**(19), 1–22 (2019). https://doi.org/10.3390/s19194188

10. Lodha, S.K., Fitzpatrick, D.M., Helmbold, D.P.: Aerial lidar data classification using AdaBoost. In: Proceedings 6th International Conference on 3-D Digital Imaging and Modeling, 3DIM 2007, pp. 435–442 (2007). https://doi.org/10.1109/3DIM.2007.10

11. Qi, C.R., Su, H., Mo, K., Guibas, L.J.: PointNet: deep learning on point sets for 3D classification and segmentation. In: Proceedings - 2016 4th International Conference on 3D Vision, 3DV 2016, pp. 601–610 (2016). https://doi.org/10.1109/3DV.2016.68

12. Qi, C.R., Yi, L., Su, H., Guibas, L.J.: PointNet++: deep hierarchical feature learning on point sets in a metric space. In: Advances in Neural Information Processing Systems, pp. 5100–5109 (2017)

13. Shi, W., Rajkumar, R.R.: Point-GNN: graph neural network for 3D object detection in a point cloud. arXiv, pp. 1711–1719 (2020)

14. Tchapmi, L., Choy, C., Armeni, I., Young Gwak, J., Savares, S.: SEGCloud: semantic segmentation of 3D point clouds (2017)

15. Te, G., Hu, W., Guo, Z., Zheng, A.: RGCNN: regularized graph CNN for point cloud segmentation (2018)

16. Wang, Y.U.E., Sun, Y., Liu, Z., Sarma, S.E., Bronstein, M.M., Solomon, J.M.: Dynamic graph CNN for learning on point clouds **1**(1) (2019)

17. Wang, Y., Sun, Y., Liu, Z., Sarma, S.E., Bronstein, M.M., Solomon, J.M.: Dynamic graph CNN for learning on point clouds (2019)

18. Wang, Z., et al.: A multiscale and hierarchical feature extraction method for terrestrial laser scanning point cloud classification. IEEE Trans. Geosci. Remote Sens. **53**(5), 2409–2425 (2015). https://doi.org/10.1109/TGRS.2014.2359951

19. Wu, Z., et al.: 3D ShapeNets: a deep representation for volumetric shapes. https://modelnet.cs.princeton.edu/download.html. Accessed 05 Oct 2021

20. Wu, Z., et al.: 3D ShapeNets: a deep representation for volumetric shapes. In: Proceedings of the IEEE Conference on Computer Vision and Pattern Recognition, pp. 1912–1920 (2015)

21. Wu, Z., Pan, S., Chen, F., Long, G., Zhang, C., Yu, P.S.: A comprehensive survey on graph neural networks. arXiv, pp. 1–22 (2019). https://doi.org/10.1109/tnnls.2020.2978386

22. Xie, Y., Tian, J., Zhu, X.X.: Linking points with labels in 3D: a review of point cloud semantic segmentation. IEEE Geosci. Remote Sens. Mag. **8**, 38–59 (2020). https://doi.org/10.1109/MGRS.2019.2937630

23. Zanjani, F.G., et al.: Mask-MCNet: tooth instance segmentation in 3D point clouds of intra-oral scans. Neurocomputing (2021). https://doi.org/10.1016/j.neucom.2020.06.145

24. Zhou, Y., Tuzel, O.: VoxelNet: end-to-end learning for point cloud based 3D object detection. Comput. Educ. J. **6**(3), 46–48 (2018)

Radar-Based Passive Step Counter and Its Comparison with a Wrist-Worn Physical Activity Tracker

Muhammad Muaaz$^{(\boxtimes)}$, Sahil Waqar, and Matthias Pätzold

Faculty of Engineering and Science, University of Agder,
P.O.Box 509, 4898 Grimstad, Norway
{muhammad.muaaz,sahil.waqar,matthias.paetzold}@uia.no

Abstract. Inspired by novel applications of radio-frequency sensing in healthcare, smart homes, rehabilitation, and augmented reality, we present an FMCW radar-based passive step counter. If a person walks or performs other activities, the individual body segments, such as head, torso, legs, arms, and feet, move at different radial speeds. Owing to the Doppler effect, the individual body segments in motion cause distinct Doppler shifts that can be used to recognize and analyze the performed activities. We compute the time-variant Doppler spectrogram of a walking activity of a person and extract the high energy Doppler components that mainly describe the torso movements during walking. From the computed Doppler spectrogram, we then compute the mean Doppler shift. To detect and count steps, we apply the peak detection algorithm to the mean Doppler shift. Our approach is evaluated using a walking activity data set. We have used ground truths and a commercially available wrist-worn human activity tracker to validate the results of our approach. Our results show that our system is capable of passively counting 97.71%–98.51% steps within a 12 m range. Therefore, our proposed system can be used as a passive step counter in indoor environments. Besides, it can also contribute to indoor localization and human tracking applications.

Keywords: FMCW radar · Mean doppler shift · Peak detection · Spectrogram · Step counting

1 Introduction

The World Health Organization (WHO) statistics[1] on obesity and overweight reveal that 1.9 billion individuals, 18 years and above, were overweight in 2016. Out of these, 34.2% were obese. Research has shown that the obese people are at higher risk for various diseases and health conditions including hypertension, type 2 diabetes, coronary heart disease, mental illness, sleep disorders, and low quality of life [20]. Regular physical exercise, especially walking, and a healthy

---

[1] https://www.who.int/news-room/fact-sheets/detail/obesity-and-overweight.

F. Sanfilippo et al. (Eds.): INTAP 2021, CCIS 1616, pp. 259–272, 2022.
https://doi.org/10.1007/978-3-031-10525-8_21

diet are among the best ways to treat obesity. Walking is one of the simplest forms of physical activity that can easily be carried out in indoor and outdoor settings. Long term studies have found evidence that regular counselling, step goals, and pedometer-based interventions are useful to increase and maintain walking levels among low active Scottish individuals [10]. Another study [5] reports that pedometer users tend to walk approximately one mile (or 2000 steps) more compared to people who do not use pedometers. According to [23], in WHO European region, people spend just about 90% of their time in indoor environments. Out of which approximately 60% time is spent at home.

The widely available and commonly used pedometers are body-worn and consist of sensors such as accelerometers and gyroscopes. These sensors record the acceleration and variation in orientation due to the walking activity and process the recorded data to count the steps of the user. Moreover, many people use their smartphones with built-in pedometers to count their steps. People need to wear these pedometers all the time for continuously registering their steps, which may be uncomfortable for some people in-home settings. As studies have shown [5, 10] the pedometers act as a motivational tool for increasing physical activity. Therefore, to promote an active life-style in indoor environments, there is a need to develop a user-friendly step counting system that can unobtrusively count steps of users in-home settings. In addition to that a passive step counter can also contribute in developing more robust indoor human tracking and localization solutions.

Compared to vision and wearable sensing modalities, the radio-frequency (RF) sensing modality has emerged as an attractive alternative in a lot of applications, such as human activity recognition (HAR) [9, 11], gesture recognition [21], vital signs monitoring [22], and security and surveillance [12]. There exist various reasons that have led to the wide acceptance of RF-sensing in human-centric applications. First and foremost, RF sensing is truly unobtrusive in nature, which means users do not need to wear or carry additional sensors. Moreover, the RF-sensing modality is far more privacy-preserving compared to other available sensing methods such as vision, wearable, and acoustics. In addition to that, the RF sensing can operate in poor lighting conditions, see-through obstacles and its performance is not affected by anthropocentric variations and changes in the environment. Within the context of RF sensing, Wi-Fi and frequency modulated continuous wave (FMCW) radars are commonly used for perceiving human activities. Although Wi-Fi is ubiquitous and low-cost, it offers a lower bandwidth, which results in a lower spatial resolution and therefore Wi-Fi-based activity recognition methods struggle in recognizing fine-grained human activities. On the other hand, FMCW radars generally enjoy much larger bandwidth, which results in higher spatial resolution and thus they can effectively be employed to identify fine-grained human activities with higher precision and accuracy [18]. Besides, FMCW radars are also capable of identifying the range and speed (or Doppler frequencies) of the target. These properties are the key enablers that have led to the wide adoption of FMCW radars for the aforementioned applications compared to Wi-Fi, continuous wave, and ultra-wide-band pulse radars.

As we know, the electromagnetic waves emitted by the FMCW radar reflect off both static and moving objects present in the environment. Owing to the Doppler effect, different movements of a moving object result in distinct Doppler shift patterns [8]. Various studies have demonstrated that these distinct Doppler shift patterns can effectively be exploited to not only discern humans [7,19], animals [3], and vehicles [13,15] but also to recognize different human activities [9, 11,16,18], such as walking, sitting, standing, running, jumping, etc.

In this paper, we investigate the novel idea of using Doppler shifts caused by a walking person to count the number of steps and provide preliminary results. As we know, the human walk is cyclic in nature and during each step-to-step transition, the moving body segments exhibit repetitive cycles of movements. Thus, a cyclic gait pattern will manifest itself in velocities (or cyclic Doppler variations) of the body segments. We first process the recorded RF sensing data of a walking activity to reduce the noise impact, and then we compute the spectrogram of the data. The spectrogram shows the time-variant micro-Doppler patterns associated with movements of different human body segments, such as torso and legs. Next, we compute the time-variant mean Doppler shift from the spectrogram. Finally, we apply a peak (or valley) detection algorithm to detect and count the number of steps. We use a human walking activity data set to evaluate our approach. We use ground truths to validate the results of our approach. Besides, we also use an accelerometer-based wrist-worn step counter to compare the performance of our radar-based step counter with an existing off-the-shelf step-counter.

Our results show that the proposed step-counter can count 97.71%–98.51% steps in a 12 m range. Note that, to accurately count the number steps, it is crucial to first identify when a person is walking. This information can be obtained using a HAR recognition system developed in our previous works [16–18], which is able of recognizing the walking activity with almost 100% precision and recall. This work enable us to combine HAR and passive step counter to develop a solution that is not only able to recognize human activities but also capable of implicitly counting the steps.

The rest of the paper is organized as follows. In Sect. 2, we describe the basic principle of FMCW radar systems, explain the various steps of radar signal processing, and present expressions for computing spectrogram and mean Doppler shift. The details of our experimental setup and data collection process are given in Sect. 3. The results of our approach are presented in Sect. 4. The limitations of this work are presented in Sect. 5. Finally, in Sect. 6, we conclude this work and present its future outlook.

2 System Description and Radar Signal Processing

In this work, we have used an FMCW radar system as an RF sensor to capture the micro-Doppler effects caused by a walking person. The FMCW radar uses a synthesizer to generate a frequency modulated (FM) electromagnetic wave (known as chirp), which is transmitted in the environment via a transmit antenna

T_x [22]. The instantaneous frequency of the chirp changes linearly over a fixed time period (know as sweep time T_{sw}) by a modulating signal [6]. The transmitted signal $s_{T_x}(t')$ can be expressed as [1]

$$s_{T_x}(t') = \exp[j2\pi(f_0 t' + \frac{\alpha}{2}t'^2)] \qquad (1)$$

where f_0 indicates the start frequency, α is the chirp rate, and t' denotes the fast-time. The chirp rate is expressed as $\alpha = (f_1 - f_0)/T_{sw}$, where f_1 stands for the stop frequency. The bandwidth B of the radar is the difference between the stop frequency f_1 and the start frequency f_0, i.e., $B = f_1 - f_0$. The transmitted wave reflects from different static and moving scatterers that are present in the environment, as shown in Fig. 1. The reflected electromagnetic wave is received by the receive antenna R_x with a time delay $\tau = 2R/c$, where R is the distance of the scatterer from the radar and c is the speed of light [22]. The received electromagnetic wave $s_{R_x}(t')$ that is reflected from a single scatterer is a τ delayed version of the transmitted signal [1]

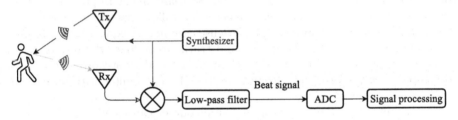

Fig. 1. A block diagram of an FMCW radar system.

$$s_{R_x}(t') = a \exp[j2\pi(f_0(t' - \tau) + \frac{\alpha}{2}(t' - \tau)^2)] \qquad (2)$$

where symbol a in (2) represents the amplitude, which depends on the physical properties of the system, such as the transmission losses and the radar cross-section of the scatterer. As per the principle of the FMCW radar, the transmitted signal $s_{T_x}(t')$ and the received $s_{R_x}(t')$ signal are mixed together and passed through a low pass filter to obtain the so-called beat (or intermediate frequency) signal which can expressed as [1,22]

$$s_b(t') = a \exp[j(2\pi\alpha\tau t' + 2\pi f_0\tau)] = a \exp[j(2\pi f_b' t' + \psi)] \qquad (3)$$

where f_b' is the beat frequency and ψ is the phase of the beat signal. The beat signal is then sampled by an analog to digital converter (ADC). The output of ADC is stored in an $n \times m$ matrix s_b, where n denotes the number of samples per sweep (or fast-time data) and m represents the number of transmitted sweeps (or chirps). For the following discussion, we consider the beat signal s_b as a function of fast-time t' and slow-time t, such as $s_b(t', t)$. As shown in (3), the fundamental frequency of a single point moving scatterer is present at $f_b' = \alpha\tau$. Therefore, we can obtain the range information of a scatterer by computing the fast Fourier transform (FFT) of the beat $s_b(t', t)$ with respect to fast-time data, i.e.,

$$S_b(f_b, t) = \int_0^{T_{sw}} s_b(t', t) exp[-j2\pi f_b t']dt'. \tag{4}$$

The Doppler frequency of the moving scatterer is estimated over a series of continuously transmitted sweeps (or chirps). The result obtained after applying the FFT according to (4), undergoes an additional FFT (known as the Doppler FFT), which is applied on the windowed range profile along the slow-time, i.e.,

$$X(f_b, f, t) = \int_{-\infty}^{\infty} S_b(f_b, t)W_r(x - t)exp[-j2\pi f x]dx \tag{5}$$

where $W_r(\cdot)$ indicates the rectangular window function, x is the running time, and f denotes the Doppler frequency. The short-time Fourier transform (STFT) of the range profile provides us with the range and Doppler information of the moving scatterer. To obtain the time-variant Doppler frequencies, we agglomerate the range information as follows

$$X(f, t) = \int_0^{f_{b,\max}} X(f_b, f, t)df_b \tag{6}$$

where $f_{b,\max}$ denotes the maximum beat frequency that an FMCW radar can resolve [14]. In the next step, we compute the spectrogram $S(f, t)$, which is defined in [4] as the absolute square of $X(f, t)$, i.e.,

$$S(f, t) = |X(f, t)|^2. \tag{7}$$

The spectrogram presents the time-varying micro-Doppler signature of the moving scatterer. Finally, the time-variant mean Doppler shift $B_f(t)$ is computed as

$$B_f(t) = \frac{\int_{-\infty}^{\infty} f S(f, t)df}{\int_{-\infty}^{\infty} S(f, t)df}. \tag{8}$$

3   Experimental Setup and Data Collection

In this work, we considered an indoor environment, where we used the Ancortek SDR-KIT2400T2R4 [2] (SDR-KIT) as shown in Fig. 2 to collect RF sensing data. The SDR-KIT is a software-defined FMCW radar that operates in the K-band

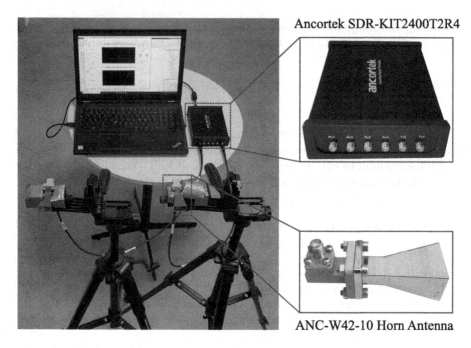

Ancortek SDR-KIT2400T2R4

ANC-W42-10 Horn Antenna

Fig. 2. Hardware setup for collecting radar-sensing data in the presence of a walking person.

within 24–26 GHz. The SDR-KIT consists of two transmit and four receive units where two T_x and four R_x antennas can be connected.

Within the scope of this work, we only used a single transmit and a single receive unit. The T_x and R_x antennas were connected to the SDR-KIT using 1 m RF cables. We attached the T_x and R_x antennas to two separate tripods and set the height of both antennas to 110 cm from the floor. The SDR-KIT is connected to a laptop using a universal serial bus cable. The laptop runs a program that provides a graphical user interface (GUI) to interact with the SDR-KIT. Using the GUI, the users can set different parameters of the radar and issue commands to start and stop recording the data. The recorded data are in the form of ADC samples and stored on the laptop. We placed our hardware setup in a corridor as shown in Fig. 3. We used the co-located[2] antenna configuration, and set the bandwidth B, centre carrier frequency f_0, and sweep time T_{sw} to 250 MHz, 24.125 GHz, 1 ms, respectively.

We collected walking activity data from two participants. For the first participant, we recorded walking activity data in two separate sessions. In the first session, we asked the participant to walk in front of the T_x and R_x antennas from Point A to Point B, as shown in Figs. 3. The distance from Point A to Point B was 8 m, where the participant needed to take exactly 10 steps at a normal walk

---

[2] By co-located antenna configuration, we mean that the T_x and R_x antennas were placed close to each other, as can be seen in Fig. 3.

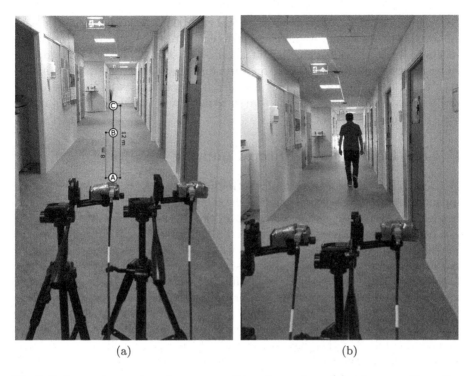

(a)   (b)

Fig. 3. Indoor radar sensing of a person walking along a floor: (a) antenna configuration and (b) walking activity.

pace to cover this distance. The participant walked in total 150 times from Point A to Point B and 150 times back from Point B to Point A. This actually provides us the ground truth, as we know, the participant took 3000 steps while walking back and forth between points A and B. For the second session, we asked the participant to walk from Point A to Point C, which are shown in Fig. 3(a). The distance from Point A to Point C was 12 m. To walk 12 m distance, the participant needed to take exactly 15 steps at a normal walking speed. In the second session, the participant again walked 3,000 steps, by walking 100 times in each direction. In each session, the data corresponding to each walk were stored in a separate file to keep the size of each data file manageable. This means, we stored the walking RF data in 300 files in the first session and in 200 files in the second session.

For the second participant, the walking activity data was recorded only in a single session. Just like the first participant, the second participant walk 12 m from Point A to Point C. To walk 12 m distance, the second participant needed to take exactly 17 steps and walked 59 times back and forth between points A and C. The data corresponding to each walk was stored in a separate file. This means, the second participant took a total of $1,003^3$ steps while walking back and forth between Points A and C. Also, to compare the results of our approach with commercially available activity trackers, we asked the participants to wear a Garmin Forerunner 935 watch on the non-dominant wrists to register the steps taken during data recording sessions. The watch uses its internal 3-axis acceleromter to measure dynamic arm movement and translates each complete arm swing into two steps.

4   Step Detection and Step Counting Results

We processed each recorded walking activity data file. At first, we removed the impact of ambient noise by subtracting the sample mean from the raw radar data. Besides, the mean subtraction also removes the contributions of fixed scatterers to a certain extent. Moreover, we applied a high-pass filter to fully remove the contributions of fixed scatterers, such as walls, ceiling, and furniture. Thereafter, we estimated the range of the moving scatterers by computing the range-FFT as presented in (4). From the range-profile (see Fig. 4), we can observe that the person was first standing still for the first three seconds at a distance of 2.4 m distance from the radar, and then the person started walking away from the radar's T_x and R_x antennas. The person walked for 6.5 s and covered a distance of approximately 8 m. The last five seconds of the range-profile plot show that the person stood still at a distance of 10.24 m.

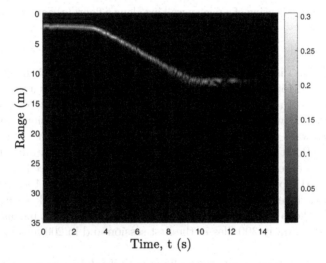

Fig. 4. The measured range profile of an 8 m long walking activity performed by the first participant.

---

[3] Note that, our goal is to compare the total number of steps taken by a participant in reality with the total number of steps recorded by the wrist-worn activity tracker and the proposed radar-based step counter. Therefore, each participant does not need to take the same number of steps.

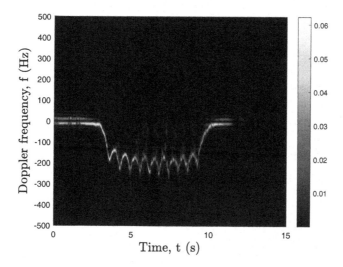

Fig. 5. The spectrogram of an 8 m long walking activity performed by the first participant. Note that, the negative Doppler shift is due to the fact that participant was walking away from the away from the co-located T_x and R_x antennas.

The range-profile is useful for determining how the distance of a walking person changes over time. However, the number of steps cannot directly be counted from the range profile. We use the spectrogram method to extract the micro-Doppler signature of the walking activity from the range profile, as presented in (5)—(7). The spectrogram of the walking activity is shown in Fig. 5, which gives an impression of the micro-Doppler signatures associated with different limbs in motion during the walking activity. The negative frequencies in the micro-Doppler signatures are due to the fact that the person is walking away from the T_x and R_x antennas of the radar.

The high energy component of the spectrogram (see Fig. 5) can be associated with the micro-Doppler signature of the repetitive movement of the torso. Whereas, the low energy components are due to the movements of the feet, legs, and arms. We threshold the spectrogram to remove these low energy components and then compute the time-variant mean Doppler shift (see Fig. 6) by using (8). The minima of the time-variant mean Doppler shift coincides with the steps of the person. If the person is walking towards the T_x and R_x antennas of the radar, the Doppler shift will be positive and each peak of the mean Doppler shift will indicate a step of the person.

We apply the Matlab's "findpeaks" algorithm to detect the peaks of the time-variant mean Doppler shifts that correspond to the steps. By default, the "findpeaks" peak detection algorithm will detect all peaks of the mean Doppler shift. Therefore, to prune peaks that do not correspond to the true steps, we set the four parameters of the "findpeaks" algorithm, i.e., minimum peak height, minimum peak separation, minimum peak prominence, and minimum peak height difference to 20, 0.005, 15, 0.001, respectively. We use the exhaus-

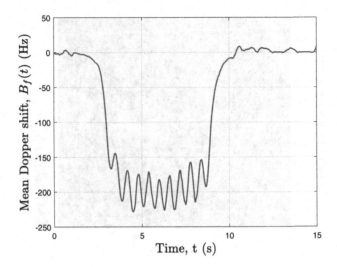

Fig. 6. The time-variant mean Doppler shift of a person walking away from the co-located T_x and R_x antennas.

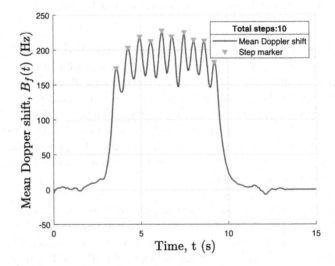

Fig. 7. The steps identified by the peak detection algorithm for the case that the person walks towards the co-located T_x and R_x antennas. Each identified step is marked by the ▼ symbol.

tive grid search approach to optimize the aforementioned parameters of the peak detection algorithm. As shown in Fig. 7, the peak detection algorithm is able to correctly identify steps in the time-variant mean Doppler shift. We iterate over all recorded walking activity data files and accumulate the identified steps in each file. The results of our approach are presented in Table 1.

Table 1. A comparison of the step-count results of the garmin forerunner 935 activity tracker and our FMCW radar-based approach.

Session	Walking distance	True step count	Steps counted by the garmin forerunner 935	Steps counted using the proposed approach
Results of participant 1				
1	8 m	3000	2880 (96.00%)	2948 (98.27%)
2	12 m	3000	2975 (99.17%)	2955 (98.51%)
Results of participant 2				
1	12 m	1003	939 (93.61%)	980 (97.71%)

For the first participant's 8 m walking scenario, both the Garmin Forerunner 935 activity tracker and the FMCW radar were not able to count all steps. In this case, our FMCW-radar-based approach registered a total of 2948 steps out of the 3000 steps, which are 2.27% more compared to the Garmin 935 activity tracker. For the 8 m walks, our FMCW-radar-based approach and the Garmin 935 activity tracker under-reported 1.73% and 4.0% steps, respectively.

For the first participant's 12 m walking scenario, the step count accuracy of the Garmin 935 activity tracker is 99.17%, whereas the accuracy of our FMCW-radar-based system is 98.51%. We can observe a 3.17% improvement in the accuracy of the Garmin 935 activity tracker for 12 m walks compared to 8 m walks. Whereas, we do not notice a significant change in the performance of our FMCW-radar-based step counter. The radar-based-system performs slightly (0.24%) better for 12 m walks compared to 8 m walks. This is due to the reason that a very slowly taken step does not result in a significant-peak of the time-variant mean Doppler shift. Thus, it cannot be detected as a step by the peak detection algorithm. Such extremely slow steps may occur either at the beginning or at the end of a walk. As, there are fewer start and stop steps in the 12 m walks compared to the 8 m walks, it is therefore plausible that the peak detection algorithm made slightly fewer errors for 12 m walks.

Similarly, upon analysing the step counting results of the second participant, we notice that our radar-based step counter reported a total of 980 steps. Whereas the Garmin 935 activity tracker reported a total of 935 steps. Moreover, we also observe that the step counting accuracy of the Garmin 935 activity tracker significantly varies not only from scenario to scenario but also from person to person. On the contrary, our radar-based step counter reports very similar results for both participants. Note that, for both participants, we used the same thresholds for the "findpeaks" algorithm as mentioned earlier in this section.

5   Limitations

Based on the preliminary results (see Table 1), we argue that the radar-based step counter devised in this work can potentially be used for indoor settings step counting applications. However, there are some limitations. Currently, the proposed system can only count the number of steps of a single person walking back and forth in front of the co-located T_x and R_x antennas. To achieve orientation independence, in future, we will use a distributive multiple-input multiple-output (MIMO) radar system. During the experiments, the participants were asked to walk at their routine-life normal walking speeds. In our future work, we will analyse the influence of fast and slow walking speeds on the devised approach.

6   Conclusion and Future Work

In this paper, we proposed an RF-based system to passively count human steps. Our system uses an FMCW radar for its capability to estimate the range and Doppler information of a moving person. We used the spectrogram approach to compute the time-variant mean Doppler shift and then applied a peak detection algorithm to detect and count the steps taken by a person. To evaluate our approach, we used a 24 GHz FMCW radar to record the measurements while a person was walking in front of the T_x and R_x antennas of the radar. We used ground-truths to validate the results of our system. Besides, as a reference, we also used an accelerometer-based wrist-worn physical step counter to compare the performance of our system with one off-the-shelf step counters. The experimental results show that the overall step counting accuracy of our system ranges from 97.71%–98.51% if the walking activity is performed within a range of 12 m. The comparative analysis of the results of our system and the wrist-worn activity tracker (used in this work) demonstrates the reliability of our RF-sensing system. Therefore, our system can potentially be used as an in-home passive step counter and for indoor localization. In future, we will further analyze the Doppler shifts to determine gait stability of walking persons. Besides, we will integrate the step counter developed in this work with our previously developed human activity recognition system, such that our indoor human activity recognition system can implicitly count human steps.

Acknowledgement. This work has been carried out within the scope of the CareWell project funded by the Research Council of Norway (300638/O70).

References

1. Alizadeh, M., Shaker, G., Almeida, J.C.M.D., Morita, P.P., Safavi-Naeini, S.: Remote monitoring of human vital signs using mm-Wave FMCW radar. IEEE Access **7**, 54958–54968 (2019)
2. Ancortek Inc: SDR 2400T2R4 K-Band — Two-Channel Tx/Four-Channel Rx — Kit or Embedded (2020). https://ancortek.com/wp-content/uploads/2020/05/SDR-2400AD2-Datasheet.pdf

3. Anderson, M.G., Rogers, R.L.: Micro-Doppler analysis of multiple frequency continuous wave radar signatures. In: Radar Sensor Technology XI, vol. 6547, p. 65470A. International Society for Optics and Photonics (2007)

4. Boashash, B.: Time-Frequency Signal Analysis and Processing: A Comprehensive Reference. Academic Press, Cambridge (2015)

5. Bravata, D.M., et al.: Using pedometers to increase physical activity and improve health: a systematic review. Jama **298**(19), 2296–2304 (2007)

6. Brooker, G.M.: Understanding millimetre wave FMCW radars. In: 1st International Conference on Sensing Technology, pp. 152–157 (2005)

7. Cao, P., Xia, W., Ye, M., Zhang, J., Zhou, J.: Radar-ID: human identification based on radar micro-doppler signatures using deep convolutional neural networks. IET Radar Sonar Navig. **12**(7), 729–734 (2018)

8. Chen, V.C.: The Micro-Doppler Effect in Radar. Artech House, Norwood (2019)

9. Erol, B., Amin, M.G.: Radar data cube processing for human activity recognition using multisubspace learning. IEEE Trans. Aerosp. Electron. Syst. **55**(6), 3617–3628 (2019)

10. Fitzsimons, C.F., Baker, G., Gray, S.R., Nimmo, M.A., Mutrie, N.: Does physical activity counselling enhance the effects of a pedometer-based intervention over the long-term: 12-month findings from the walking for wellbeing in the west study. BMC Public Health **12**(1), 1–12 (2012). https://doi.org/10.1186/1471-2458-12-206

11. Hernangómez, R., Santra, A., Stańczak, S.: Human activity classification with frequency modulated continuous wave radar using deep convolutional neural networks. In: 2019 International Radar Conference (RADAR), pp. 1–6. IEEE (2019)

12. Jin, Y., Kim, B., Kim, S., Lee, J.: Design and implementation of FMCW surveillance radar based on dual chirps. Elektronika Ir Elektrotechnika **24**(6), 60–66 (2018)

13. Li, Y., Du, L., Liu, H.: Hierarchical classification of moving vehicles based on empirical mode decomposition of micro-doppler signatures. IEEE Trans. Geosci. Remote Sens. **51**(5), 3001–3013 (2012)

14. Mota, A., Hoogeboom, P., Ligthart, L.P.: Signal processing for FMCW SAR. IEEE Trans. Geosci. Remote Sens. **45**(11), 3519–3532 (2007)

15. Molchanov, P., Totsky, A., Astola, J., Egiazarian, K., Leshchenko, S., Rosa-Zurera, M.: Aerial target classification by micro-doppler signatures and bicoherence-based features. In: 2012 9th European Radar Conference, pp. 214–217. IEEE (2012)

16. Muaaz, M., Chelli, A., Abdelgawwad, A.A., Mallofré, A.C., Pätzold, M.: WiWeHAR: multimodal human activity recognition using Wi-Fi and wearable sensing modalities. IEEE Access **8**, 164453–164470 (2020)

17. Muaaz, M., Chelli, A., Gerdes, M.W., Pätzold, M.: Wi-Sense: a passive human activity recognition system using Wi-Fi and convolutional neural network and its integration in health information systems. Ann. Telecommun. **77**, 163–175 (2021). https://doi.org/10.1007/s12243-021-00865-9

18. Muaaz, M., Chelli, A., Pätzold, M.: WiHAR: from Wi-Fi channel state information to unobtrusive human activity recognition. In: 2020 IEEE 91st Vehicular Technology Conference (VTC2020-Spring), pp. 1–7. IEEE (2020)

19. Qiao, X., Shan, T., Tao, R.: Human identification based on radar micro-Doppler signatures separation. Electron. Lett. **56**(4), 195–196 (2020)

20. U.S. Department of Health and Human services: Clinical guidelines on the identification, evaluation, and treatment of overweight and obesity in adults. Technical report, National Institutes of Health (1998)

21. Wang, Y., Ren, A., Zhou, M., Wang, W., Yang, X.: A novel detection and recognition method for continuous hand gesture using FMCW radar. IEEE Access **8**, 167264–167275 (2020)
22. Wang, Y., Wang, W., Zhou, M., Ren, A., Tian, Z.: Remote monitoring of human vital signs based on 77-GHz mm-wave FMCW radar. Sensors **20**(10), 2999 (2020)
23. World Health Organization: Combined or multiple exposure to health stressors in indoor built environments. Technical report, World Health Organization: Regional Office for Europe (2013)

Principles for the Arrangement of Social Media Listening Practices in Crisis Management

Lucia Castro Herrera$^{(\boxtimes)}$, Tim A. Majchrzak, and Devinder Thapa

University of Agder, Kristiansand, Norway
{lucia.c.herrera,timam,devinder.thapa}@uia.no

Abstract. Social media listening is used to support the need for information throughout the crisis management life-cycle with emphasis on the phases of response and recovery. The academic literature illustrates that the adoption and implementation of social media listening in crisis management happens through improvisation using trial and error. Moreover, previous studies argue that to integrate social media as a source of information, implementation strategies need to look beyond the acquisition of sophisticated technologies. Additional resources, capabilities, and the fundamental characteristics of the environment where social media listening takes place play a role in the arrangement of social media listening practices. Therefore, by performing an analysis of existing knowledge that address this phenomenon, we propose preliminary guiding principles that support the arrangement of practices of social media listening as a vehicle to fulfill information needs. This study contributes to the systematization of social media practices in crisis management.

Keywords: Social media · Social media listening · Crisis management · Principles

1 Introduction

Social media is increasingly used as an informal source of information in crisis management [42,48] and the integration to existing crisis management practices remains a challenge [17,47]. These practices are emerging in an improvised manner [15], either from top-down initiatives, where managers believe in the relevance of social media; or bottom-up approaches, where the scarcity of information, mainly during the early onset of crises, creates an immediate need for alternative and readily available sources of information [36,48]. Social media listening is therefore the arrangement of tasks performed by human and technical entities that use social media as a source of information to meet information requirements that help meeting objectives in crisis management. Social media listening is also known as monitoring, surveillance or intelligence. However, this article makes use of the term listening as it is closely related to the term practitioners use.

© The Author(s), under exclusive license to Springer Nature Switzerland AG 2022
F. Sanfilippo et al. (Eds.): INTAP 2021, CCIS 1616, pp. 273–286, 2022.
https://doi.org/10.1007/978-3-031-10525-8_22

Social media is a widely researched topic with an extensive body of knowledge that focuses on explaining and addressing existing challenges from a social, organizational, technical, and sociotechnical angles [43]. Efforts in improving the status quo are focused on prioritizing technology-based solutions as the means to achieve objectives as opposed to considering the phenomenon from an inclusive sociotechnical perspective [17,21]. However, such studies advocate for the need of this perspective. In this regard, we integrate the fragmented literature to organize knowledge regarding the emergence, adoption and improvement of practices in crisis management. We argue that existing knowledge works as a starting point for the formulation of principles that aim to guide the arrangement of social media listening practices in crisis management. Social media listening is used to support the need for information throughout the crisis management life-cycle with emphasis on the phases of response and recovery. The academic literature illustrates that the adoption and implementation of social media listening in crisis management happens through improvisation using trial and error. Moreover, previous studies argue that to integrate social media as a source of information, implementation strategies need to look beyond the acquisition of sophisticated technologies. Additional resources, capabilities, and the fundamental characteristics of the environment where social media listening takes place play a role in the arrangement of social media listening practices. Therefore, by performing an analysis of existing knowledge that address this phenomenon, we propose preliminary guiding principles that support the arrangement of practices of social media listening as a vehicle to fulfill information needs. This study contributes to the systematization of social media practices in crisis management.

We formulate guiding principles that stem from the identification of the core features of social media listening practices. These principles are derived from studies that look at views from stakeholders, namely users, implementers, decision makers, researchers, designers and developers [12]. These stakeholders influence the enactment of social media listening practices. Thus, we seek to answer the following research question:

What are the principles that could guide the arrangement and improvement of the practice of social media listening for crisis management?

Practices of social media listening keep on evolving while knowledge is captured as a static snapshot in time. By formulating guiding principles from the literature, we aim to motivate the transcendence of knowledge in the dimensions of temporality and space that change as practices are enacted [40].

The remainder of the paper is structured as follows: Sect. 2 provides conceptual and theoretical underpinnings of the practice of social media listening. Section 3 describes the methodology used in this study; Sect. 4 formulates and describes the guiding principles. Section 5 presents a general discussion and future research avenues. Finally, Sect. 6 concludes.

2 Conceptual and Theoretical Underpinnings

In this section we discuss the concept of imbrication to theorize the practices of social media listening in crisis management.

Understood from a sociotechnical perspective, the social media listening practice could be defined as the recursive shaping of information [5,33] that results from searching, extracting, classifying and analyzing publicly available data shaped by the environment living in social media platforms to satisfy the requirements for information necessary to realize objectives during the management of crises [16]. Thus, practice fulfills objectives by performing tasks from extraction of data to reporting of information found in social media conversations.

In crisis management the importance of monitoring social media in crises is unquestionable [42,49] but technological, environmental and organizational challenges are limitations that keep practitioners away from fully realize the potential of social media as a source of information [47]. Entities in social media listening are entangled without predefined boundaries [35] that focus on the fulfillment of objectives throughout the crisis management life-cycle, namely: preparedness, response, recovery, mitigation and prevention [8]. In meeting objectives, practices are enacted through arrangements of physical, social and technical entities [2]. Therefore, discerning whether actions are performed by human abilities or material automation is difficult. In addition, the context in which crisis occur is uncertain, unfamiliar, complex, volatile, and rapidly changing [5,19]. In social media listening, technical entities (i.e., software, artificial intelligence, social media platforms) are not passive agents controlled by users, instead, they count with agency and capabilities that contribute to shape realities [34]. Human intervention and guidance are a necessary part of the process as the objectives in crisis management deal protecting essential human needs such as security, food and shelter [30] that are hardly understood by technical entities. Moreover, skepticism and lack of trust towards new processes and technology capabilities still present in the field [48] exacerbate the challenge to fully integrate social media into crisis management processes. Using social media data as a source of information is attractive but involves the adoption or change in established sociotechnical routines such as attributes of technology, training, context, and additional resources that crisis management organizations have adopted without a systematic approach for over a decade [42]. Therefore, an initial step towards systematization of social media listening practices is the formulation of guiding principles.

For the purposes of our study, when proposing guiding principles, results necessary to analytically separate entities that take place in practice [16,28] even though we recognize that all practices are co-constituted by the social and the material and that relations emerge dynamically in practice [2]. We do so by relying on the metaphor of imbrication [24] where the interlocking of material and social agencies forms an infrastructure that allows the fulfillment of tasks. Imbrication suggests the social and the material form an integrated structure while retaining their properties despite their mutual dependance for the assembly and perpetuation of a practice [24,28].

Agency is understood as the capability of doing, the capacity of action [11]. Human agency is characterized by intentionality or the ability to form and realize one's goals [25]. Material agency refers to non-human entities' capacity to act without human intervention [25]. Technologies exercise their agency through the things they do without human control [25]. The space between social and

material agencies is where possibilities and limitations are constructed, negotiated and decided on. It is in this trading zone where agencies converse and,
therefore, imbrications occur [26]. With imbrication, human and non-human entities are interdependent but maintain their distinct attributes when conforming
and performing practices [22,24].

Crisis management is a dynamic and cyclical process of imbrications that
interact, change and emerge during each crisis and pre-established protocols.
Pre-existing imbrications are the starting point for subsequent ones [24]; the
iterative process of the intertwining of agencies produces the attributes of practices of social media [18]. These attributes are not static, but evolve through
time, calling for an adaptation from established routines [27]. While imbrications
can be undone and remade [28]. As the structure of imbrications strengthens
through time, repetitive interlocking is more challenging to influence because
of the dependencies created with other imbrications [18]. Which can explain
the barriers and challenges in arranging social media in crisis management
organizations.

From this perspective, social media listening is recognized as a unit with a
continuous flow of action in constant state of development. Thus, our guiding
principles take place in that trading zone where attributes of practice are defined.
In crisis management, social media listening contributes to fulfill a need for information throughout the crisis-lifecycle with focus on the response phase [43]. At
the same time, the information outputs from social media listening may contribute to decision making [7]. The literature illustrates that social media listening is used mostly as a reactive mechanism to an urgent and instantaneous need
for information [10,36]. However, it has the potential to serve as a preemptive
avenue that complements crisis management operations [17].

3   Methodology

Our formulations are routed in a systematic literature review [32] that analyzed
multidisciplinary studies involving sociotechnical features of social media use
in crisis management. The process, summarized in Table 1, started with a scope
definition and a formulation of Boolean operators to search for relevant literature
in five academic databases. Then the process continued with a series of iterative
steps involving manual and automated processing of the literature to select the
final 109 out of 1,699 articles for analysis.

With the concept of imbrication in mind, and with the aim to help practitioners in crisis management to take advantage of social media listening, we
formulate guiding principles that focus on flexibility, cyclical routines, and coordination aspects that standout in the literature.

Inspired by Gregor, Chandra Kruse and Seidel [12] and Halabi, Sabiescu,
David, Vannini and Nemer [13], we turned their points of discussion into our
approach where descriptive knowledge [40] based on previous experiences with
social media in crisis management informs the arrangement and improvement
of current and future practices. Therefore, we analyzed our data and formulated key principles following the aim, context or boundary condition, means

Table 1. Summary of process for systematic literature review

Parameter	Description
Boolean search	("social media" AND (listening OR analytics OR monitoring OR "situational awareness" OR "situation aware*" OR intelligence OR surveillance OR "sense making" OR sensemaking OR sensor*)) AND (practice* OR process* OR operation* OR network OR ecosystem OR component* OR system) AND (crisis OR crises OR emergency OR emergencies OR disaster* OR pandemic)
Databases	– ProQuest – Web of Science – Scopus – AIS Library – IEEE Xplore
Literature	Peer-reviewed journals and conference proceedings.
Language	English
Automated steps	– Filtering irrelevant fields of study – Fusing the literature – Removing of duplicates
Manual inclusion criteria	– The article should talk directly about social media use as an information source – The article should involve stakeholders from the crisis management field – Articles describing recounts of practice, organizational configurations or improvisational experiences
Manual exclusion criteria	– Articles proposing methods for information extraction without validation with crisis management practitioners – Absence of practice experience
Coding approach	Inductive that brough pattern identification

of achievement, and justification structure proposed by Gregor, Chandra Kruse and Seidel [12]. Finally, we outlined a plan for further validation and testing routed on empirical data.

4 Guiding Principles for the Arrangement of Social Media Listening

We abord our formulations from the perspective of implementers and enactors, leveraging Gregor, Chandra Kruse and Seidel [12] terminology, concerned with adopting and taking advantage of the full potential of insights from social media data in crisis management. As mentioned before, we structured our principles using the aim, context or boundary condition, means of achievement, and justification structure and the identification of actors illustrated on Table 2. We

Table 2. Actors in social media listening practices for crisis management

Actors	Instance
Implementer	Decision makers, process, and technology solution designers
User	Decision makers, population affected by a crisis, population that receives services from the organization that enacts social media listening
Enactor	Those performing social media listening activities (i.e., analysists, information officers, digital volunteers)
Theorizer	The research team, existing research, and future interview objects

aim to understand and frame the benefits and challenges of practice adoption, integration, implementation, and perception of social media listening practices in different organizational, technical, and environmental contexts.

The context in which crisis management operates is characterized by unpredictability and rapid decision making where enactors act with incomplete information that becomes available as crisis events unfold [48]. We thus propose and discuss the following principles to guide the arrangement of ractices.

Principle 1: Knowledge, Familiarity, and Craft. To perform social media listening practices and facilitate the information gathering, analysis and reporting of findings to decision makers, access to knowledge and techniques that foster expertise in social media analytics and crisis management operations should be secured and encouraged. Because practice is strengthened by the increased human and artificial ability to navigate social media platforms through text and multimedia queries [4] and the understanding and experience in managing and responding to crises [44,48].

Social media listening obtains a perceived snapshot of events by connecting experiences illustrated through text and multimedia data enclosed in a social media platform [4]. The extraction and analysis of that data is only possible by a combination of objectives and information requitements [20], big data processing technologies [19], and knowledge on how to manipulate technologies and recurring crisis response [44]. The lack of knowledge, experience [1], and reluctance to adopt or improve current information seeking and reporting practices [10] makes social media driven insights a missed opportunity as crises become more frequent.

Principle 2: Cyclicality. When crises are noticed, whether through social media or other mechanisms, managed, and mitigated to allow systems to rapidly adapt from non-crisis to crisis management and vice versa, implementers need to set the conditions and priorities that guide the shift and continuity of response operations throughout the duration of the crisis. Defined strategies and roles in crisis and non-crisis periods are the starting point to allow for continuity of the enablers operations as activities flow throughout the areas of preparedness, response, recovery, and mitigation. Because objectives and focus changes when transitioning through the crisis management life-cycle. Priorities shift towards saving lives, damage assessments, casualties, basic needs, response capacity, and sentiment.

In social media, shift in crisis management is evidenced as a behavior change where authorities shift from providing situational awareness to extracting situational awareness and content shifts to safety and response themes [37]. Established protocols will seek to enhance capacity in trying to continuously understand the situation. Operation centers are examples where cyclical operations are exercised throughout the life-cycle of crisis management [41]. Response protocols are studied and exercised during non-crisis periods. Dedicated social media and digital information management roles are created to continuously monitor social media for disruptions, assess reputational risk, or find opportunities to engage with local communities in preparedness, prevention, and mitigation [29,38]. Crisis management is in constant change as it learns through each cyclical enactment and all crises are different in nature.

Principle 3: Spontaneous Coordination. For information requirements to be fulfilled by enactors during early crisis response, systems should allow for flexibility and rapid integration where improvisation and spontaneous coordination is accepted within the parameters of meeting concrete objectives of crisis management and response. Because speed is the main objective in decision making during the first 48 h of a crisis where numerous unknowns exist and pressure to act is latent [48]. Empowering social media listening practices to act outside the established protocols encourages agility.

Practice studies indicate that during the first 48 h of a crisis impact, decision-making is performed on the spot and by-passing established protocols. Information requirements are both dynamic and static [3,46], the dynamic information requirements that result from unexpected developments demand speed in action that leads to alternative means of response and organization that emerges from spontaneous coordination either from a top-down or bottom-up initiative [9,10].

Principle 4: Collaboration and Relationships. To increase the enactors capacity, man-power and technical resources, when crises emerge and evolve, decision makers and enactors should establish a network of contacts or known trusted organizations that can be easily integrated/embedded in the organizational structure. Because initial demands for information and workforce exhaustion, demands, and criticality [45] affect the continuous flow of information during crisis response. Rigid command and control structures of response agencies contribute to increase the burthen on the workforce [48].

As crisis events unfold, stakeholders meet both online and offline. Collaboration patterns are observed in social media platforms by sharing and resharing information and guiding affected communities towards available services [23]. However, lack of awareness of social media presence of key stakeholders, influencers, and other drivers of information results in delayed flows of information and missed opportunities for online collaboration [9]. Moreover, demands for information require the temporary increase of capacity that can be filled with additional resources such as digital volunteers [10], reserve staff [29] or alliances (personal or formal) with organizations with similar objectives [48]. Much of these relationships emerge from personal contacts and networks of professionals made during non-crisis times and maintained through meetings and collaboration [36, 48]. Synergy between technical tasks and social-relational activities is needed [14]. Cooperation and alignment with digital volunteers and other stakeholders at the local, national, and international level ensures common understanding and operationality [10].

Principle 5: Inter-Organization Expansion and Contraction (Operations and Systems). Processes, systems, and organizations should be aligned beforehand to technological, organizational, and structural attributes to facilitate the fulfillment of information requirements throughout the crisis life-cycle [3]. This is done by encouraging implementers and enablers to actively and transparently establish relationships, share system and process specifications and protocols; establish formal collaboration agreements; and conduct simulations during non-crisis periods. Such measurements strengthen collaboration routines that grow expand with each crisis event [6].

Technological, organizational and structural attributes defined as, outcomes, principles, community, action, social fabric, infrastructure, services and governance, are some of the considerations that need to be defined and negotiated before a crisis occurs and strengthened through time [3]. Moreover, considerations such as collaborative work, geographic dispersion, backchannel conversations and trusted networks are some mechanisms that influence the orchestration of operations under a collaboration scheme [6].

Principle 6: Preempting and Foresight. For decision makers and designers to develop and implement a social media listening system for situational awareness [37], two-way conversations [20] or early warning [14] to provide information that impacts decision making in the management of crisis, ensure that human and technical resources and infrastructure are considered, available, and in place before crisis periods. Because of the nature of crisis management, during a crisis immediate demands and objectives are prioritized leaving research, implementation, process improvement, training, and design solutions on stand-by until crises are stabilized.

Most social media analytics tools are designed during non-crisis periods, based on historical data from past crises [42]. In addition, studies indicate that barriers of adoption of social media in crisis management are resources, availability, knowledge and experience with both crises and technology [44, 47]. Therefore, during non-crisis times enactors could be introduced and acquire the necessary knowledge about their systems and the social media environment that represents the community and context they work with [38]. This knowledge includes on one hand, testing new technologies in collaboration with developers and theorizers [39]. On the other hand, leveraging drills and simulations of potential crisis scenarios foments the capacity of reaction in a timely manner [31].

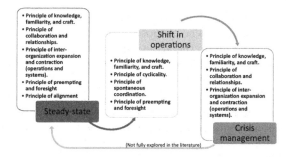

Fig. 1. Mapping principles to the social media listening cycle

Principle 7: Alignment. For social media to be integrated into crisis management tasks and systems at an organizational and operational level as an authoritative source of information, implementers could enable fusion methodologies and architectures that integrate various information sources with organization wide systems and infrastructures. Because social media listening practices are performed in isolation and are considered a non-authoritative data source that complements traditional sources such as physical and remote sensors and context or event specific warning systems [9].

Social media listening practices reach validation when integrated with current and established operating systems organization wide [9]. Triangulation, verification, and management of uncertainty allows information to be perceived from different angles [10]. However, studies of social media practices show that a specific set of systems are used for specific functions in a determined context, diminishing the value of permanently integrating social media-based systems [17].

5   Discussion and Future Work

We identified principles for the arrangement of practices of social media listening in crisis management. In doing so, we conducted a systematic literature review and identified seven principles. These principles are aimed as guidance for mangers, decision makers, enablers, and system designers in strategizing the enhancement of information gathering and analysis in crisis management organizations. We contribute to the existing crisis management knowledge by mapping these principles to the cycle of practices of social media listening for crisis management [15]. For example, the principles aim for cyclicality and their applicability varies depending on the social media listening cycle [15]. This cycle is inclusive of the general crisis life-cycle phases of preparedness, response, recovery and mitigation [8]. The practice shifts between steady-state or non-crisis, shift in operations and back to a new normal after the crisis. Figure 1 presents the cyclicality approach of the practice of social media listening and we relate the principles proposed in this paper.

In addition, we have theorized practices of social media listening through the imbrication lens to dynamically explain an ever-transforming practice through time and space. Entities maintained their agency while coming together to meet crisis management objectives. The proposed principles aim to strengthen already existing imbrications and invite the arrangement of new ones by encouraging the performance of the social media listening practice with other sources of information. Moreover, these principles aim at the sustainability of practices with suggestions that influence social media listening and the parallel practices that converge in decision making and future action. Our formulations explore trust and flexibility as enablers of continuous imbrication where the degree of intertwining in social media listening could be dictated by the learned relationship that morphs within the cyclical nature of crisis management.

Our suggested guiding principles emerged from the collective analysis and pattern generalization of previous experiences in using social media as a source of information. This is a first step towards generalizing and integrating a knowledge base for the arrangement of practices that shows the maturity of processes in crisis management. Considering these principles would save time and resources for managers wanting to establish or review their social media listening capabilities. Managers or analysists interested in social media listening can rely on past experiences and know what to expect. Reducing the need for improvisation in the arrangement of the practice.

The limitations of the principles rest in their conceptual in nature that calls for empirical validation. In addition, the applicability of the principles to diverse contexts of operation both geographical and organizational could be questionable as research in social media for crisis management is mostly performed in areas with high-connectivity and access to research resources [43]. Moreover, the proposed principles are mostly focused on the preparedness, response and recovery phases of crisis management. Given that the step from crisis management to non-crisis has not been fully explored in the academic literature, we haven't formulated principles for that step which could be part of future analyses. We emphasize the preliminary nature of our results because of the absence of a verification, validation and decomposition steps that could enhance the usefulness of the principles for implementers and users alike. These limitations suggest avenues for future research.

Finally, the prescriptive nature of the principles suggests that the arrangement of practices could be designed, and prescriptive knowledge can emerge from past experiences. Previous approaches to designing with a focus on practice include Bjørn and Østerlund [2], where practices are considered as a set of boundings and design interventions influence and reconfigure existing and new boundings follow practices proposed; and Leonardi and Rodriguez-Lluesma [28], who leverage the concept of imbrication to maneuver design propositions where social and material entities converge while preserving their agency and properties. Both approaches focus on introducing artifacts and fostering innovation. Future work will contribute to the design knowledge from a cyclical and rapidly changing practice perspective such as crisis management.

6   Concluding Remarks

In this paper, seven guiding principles for the arrangement of social media listening practices were identified through a review of the academic literature and grounded in the concept of imbrication [24]. Our formulations act as a road map to advance constantly evolving practices and reduce the need to improvise under crisis contexts where rapid decision making and action are essential for societal security. In addition, we mapped the principles to the different stages of social media listening practices to evidence the cyclicality of the practice and opportunities for future studies. The conceptual nature of the proposed principles calls for further validation and study using empirical data that could result in additional principles and illustrate the trading zones that occur while social media practices navigate through the crisis management life cycle [8]. Methods such as interviews with stakeholders could be used to gain insights into how practices are arranged. Then, workshops with subject matter experts could validate the combined guiding principles. In addition, simulations could serve as observation platforms for rapid analysis of interventions in practice. Moreover, further analysis could include the performance of practices during extended crisis scenarios such as the current COVID-19 pandemic, that poses new challenges and conditions to social media listening in crisis management.

References

1. Anson, S., Watson, H., Wadhwa, K., Metz, K.: Analysing social media data for disaster preparedness: understanding the opportunities and barriers faced by humanitarian actors. Int. J. Disaster Risk Reduction **21**, 131–139 (2017)
2. Bjørn, P., Østerlund, C.: Sociomaterial-design beyond healthcare. In: Sociomaterial-Design. CSCW, pp. 97–102. Springer, Cham (2014). https://doi.org/10.1007/978-3-319-12607-4_9
3. Bunker, D., Ehnis, C., Levine, L., Babar, A., Sleigh, A.: When worlds collide: Alignment of information systems (is) incompatibilities abstract for effective disaster recovery. In: 24th AMCIS, pp. 1–10 (2018)
4. Burns, R.: Rethinking big data in digital humanitarianism: practices, epistemologies, and social relations. GeoJournal **80**(4), 477–490 (2014). https://doi.org/10.1007/s10708-014-9599-x
5. Bénaben, F., Lauras, M., Truptil, S., Salatgé, N.: A metamodel for knowledge management in crisis management. In: 49th HICSS, pp. 126–135 (2016)
6. Cobb, C., McCarthy, T., Perkins, A., Bharadwaj, A., Comis, J., Do, B., Starbird, K.: Designing for the deluge: understanding and supporting the distributed, collaborative work of crisis volunteers. In: 17th ACM, pp. 888–899 (2014)
7. Coche, J., Rodriguez, G.R., Montarnal, A., Tapia, A., Benaben, F.: Social media processing in crisis response: an attempt to shift from data to information exploitation. In: 54th HICSS, pp. 2285–2294 (2021)
8. Coppola, D.P.: Introduction to International Disaster Management. Elsevier (2006)
9. Ehnis, C., Bunker, D.: Repertoires of collaboration: incorporation of social media help requests into the common operating picture. Behav. Inf. Technol. **39**(3), 343–359 (2020)

10. Fathi, R., Thom, D., Koch, S., Ertl, T., Fiedrich, F.: VOST: a case study in voluntary digital participation for collaborative emergency management. In: Information Processing and Management, pp. 1–25 (2019)
11. Giddens, A.: The Constitution of Society: Outline of the Theory of Structuration. University of California Press, Berkeley (1984)
12. Gregor, S., Chandra Kruse, L., Seidel, S.: Research perspectives: the anatomy of a design principle. J. Assoc. Inf. Syst. **21**(6), 1622–1652 (2020)
13. Halabi, A., Sabiescu, A., David, S., Vannini, S., Nemer, D.: From exploration to design: Aligning intentionality in community informatics projects. J. Commun. Inf. **11**(3) (2015)
14. Henriksen, H.J., Roberts, M.J., van der Keur, P., Harjanne, A., Egilson, D., Alfonso, L.: Participatory early warning and monitoring systems: a Nordic framework for web-based flood risk management. Int. J. Disaster Risk Reduction **31**, 1295–1306 (2018)
15. Herrera, L.C.: Configuring social media listening practices in crisis managment. In: 18th ISCRAM (2021)
16. Herrera, L.C., Majchrzak, T.A., Thapa, D.: Ecosystem of social media listening practices for crisis management. In: I3E2021 (Forthcoming) (2021)
17. Hiltz, S.R., Hughes, A.L., Imran, M., Plotnick, L., Power, R., Turoff, M.: Exploring the usefulness and feasibility of software requirements for social media use in emergency management. Int. J. Disaster Risk Reduction **42**, 1–14 (2020)
18. Holeman, I., Barrett, M.: Insights from an ICT4D initiative in Kenya's immunization program: designing for the emergence of sociomaterial practices. J. Assoc. Inf. Syst. **18**(12), 2 (2017)
19. Imran, M., Castillo, C., Diaz, F., Vieweg, S.: Processing social media messages in mass emergency: a survey. ACM CSUR **47**(4), 1–38 (2015)
20. Kaufhold, M.A., Rupp, N., Reuter, C., Amelunxen, C.: 112. social: design and evaluation of a mobile crisis app for bidirectional communication between emergency services and citizens. In: 26th ECIS (2018)
21. Kaufhold, M.A., Rupp, N., Reuter, C., Habdank, M.: Mitigating information overload in social media during conflicts and crises: design and evaluation of a cross-platform alerting system. Behav. Inf. Technol. **39**(3), 319–342 (2020)
22. Kautz, K., Jensen, T.B.: Sociomateriality at the royal court of is: a jester's monologue. Inf. Organ. **23**(1), 15–27 (2013)
23. Lambert, A.: Disaster data assemblages: five perspectives on social media and communities in response and recovery. In: The 49th HICSS, pp. 2237–2245 (2016)
24. Leonardi, P.M.: When flexible routines meet flexible technologies: affordance, constraint, and the imbrication of human and material agencies. MIS Q. **35**(1), 147–167 (2011)
25. Leonardi, P.M.: Materiality, Sociomateriality, and Socio-Technical Systems: What Do These Terms Mean? How are They Related? Do We Need Them?, pp. 25–48. Oxford University Press, Oxford (2012)
26. Leonardi, P.M.: Theoretical foundations for the study of sociomateriality. Inf. Organ. **23**(2), 59–76 (2013)
27. Leonardi, P.M., Nardi, B.A., Kallinikos, J.: Materiality and organizing: social interaction in a technological world. Oxford University Press on demand (2012)
28. Leonardi, P.M., Rodriguez-Lluesma, C.: Sociomateriality as a lens for design. Scand. J. Inf. Syst. **24**(2), 79–88 (2012)
29. Markenson, D., Howe, L.: American red cross digital operations center (DigiDoc): an essential emergency management tool for the digital age. Dis. Med. Public Health Preparedness **8**(5), 445–451 (2014)

30. Maslow, A.H.: A theory of human motivation. Psychol. Rev. **50**(4), 370–396 (1943)
31. Meesters, K., van Beek, L., Van de Walle, B.: #help. the reality of social media use in crisis response: lessons from a realistic crisis exercise. In: 49th HICSS, pp. 116–125 (2016)
32. Okoli, C.: A guide to conducting a standalone systematic literature review. Commun. Assoc. Inf. Syst. **37**(1), 1–43 (2015)
33. Orlikowski, W.J.: Sociomaterial practices: exploring technology at work. Organ. Stud. **28**(9), 1435–1448 (2007)
34. Orlikowski, W.J.: The sociomateriality of organisational life: considering technology in management research. Camb. J. Econ. **34**(1), 125–141 (2009)
35. Orlikowski, W.J., Scott, S.V.: Sociomateriality: challenging the separation of technology, work and organization. Acad. Manag. Ann. **2**(1), 433–474 (2008)
36. Petersen, L., Fallou, L., Havârneanu, G., Reilly, P., Serafinelli, E., Bossu, R.: November 2015 Paris terrorist attacks and social media use: preliminary findings from authorities, critical infrastructure operators and journalists. In: 15th ISCRAM, pp. 629–638 (2018)
37. Pogrebnyakov, N., Maldonado, E.: Didn't roger that: social media message complexity and situational awareness of emergency responders. IJIM **40**, 166–174 (2018)
38. Power, R., Kibell, J.: The social media intelligence analyst for emergency management. In: 50th HICSS (2017)
39. Power, R., Robinson, B., Wise, C., Cameron, M.: Information integration for emergency management: recent CSIRO case studies. In: 20th International Congress on Modeling and Simulation, pp. 2061–2067 (2013)
40. Purao, S., Kruse, L.C., Maedche, A.: The origins of design principles: where do... they all come from? In: Hofmann, S., Müller, O., Rossi, M. (eds.) DESRIST 2020. LNCS, vol. 12388, pp. 183–194. Springer, Cham (2020). https://doi.org/10.1007/978-3-030-64823-7_17
41. Purohit, H., Castillo, C., Imran, M., Pandey, R.: Ranking of social media alerts with workload bounds in emergency operation centers. In: IEEE/WIC/ACM International Conference on Web Intelligence, pp. 206–213 (2018)
42. Reuter, C., Hughes, A.L., Kaufhold, M.A.: Social media in crisis management: an evaluation and analysis of crisis informatics research. Int. J. Hum.-Comput. Interact. **34**(4), 280–294 (2018)
43. Reuter, C., Kaufhold, M.A.: Fifteen years of social media in emergencies: a retrospective review and future directions for crisis informatics. J. Contingencies Crisis Manag. **26**(1), 41–57 (2018)
44. Reuter, C., Kaufhold, M.A., Spahr, F., Spielhofer, T., Hahne, A.S.: Emergency service staff and social media - a comparative empirical study of the attitude by emergency services staff in europe in 2014 and 2017. Int. J. Disaster Risk Reduction **46**, 1–14 (2020)
45. Santos, J.R., Herrera, L.C., Yu, K.D.S., Pagsuyoin, S.A.T., Tan, R.R.: State of the art in risk analysis of workforce criticality influencing disaster preparedness for interdependent systems. Risk Anal. **34**(6), 1056–1068 (2014)
46. Steen-Tveit, K.: Identifying information requirements for improving the common operational picture in multi-agency operations. In: 17th ISCRAM (2020)
47. Stieglitz, S., Mirbabaie, M., Fromm, J., Melzer, S.: The adoption of social media analytics for crisis management-challenges and opportunities. In: 26th ECIS 4 (2018)

48. Tapia, A.H., Moore, K.: Good enough is good enough: overcoming disaster response organizations' slow social media data adoption. Comput Support. Coop Work **23**(4), 483–512 (2014)
49. Vieweg, S., Hughes, A.L., Starbird, K., Palen, L.: Microblogging during two natural hazards events: what twitter may contribute to situational awareness. In: SIGCHI, pp. 1079–1088 (2010)

AMUSED: An Annotation Framework of Multimodal Social Media Data

Gautam Kishore Shahi[1(✉)] and Tim A. Majchrzak[2]

[1] University of Duisburg-Essen, Duisburg, Germany
gautam.shahi@uni-due.de
[2] University of Agder, Kristiansand, Norway
timam@uia.no

Abstract. Social media has become popular among users for social interaction and news sources. Users spread misinformation in multiple data formats. However, systematic studying of social media phenomena has been challenging due to the lack of labelled data. This paper presents a semi-automated annotation framework AMUSED for gathering multilingual multimodal annotated data from social networking sites. The framework is designed to mitigate the workload in collecting and annotating social media data by cohesively combining machines and humans in the data collection process. AMUSED detects links to social media posts from a given list of news articles and then downloads the data from the respective social networking sites and labels them. The framework gathers the annotated data from multiple platforms like Twitter, YouTube, and Reddit. For the use case, we have implemented the framework for collecting COVID-19 misinformation data from different social media sites and have categorised 8,077 fact-checked articles into four different classes of misinformation.

Keywords: Data annotation · Social media · Misinformation · News articles · Fact-checking · COVID-19

1 Introduction

With the increasing popularity of social media platforms, there has been an increase in the number of social media users, thus making social media an integral part of our lives. They play an essential role in making communication easier and more accessible. Over the past few years, the horizon of social media platforms have expanded from being just an entertainment source to now becoming a means of important information sharing. Organisations and individuals use social media to browse and share critical information. This has become especially true during the COVID-19 pandemic; since social media platforms receive tremendous attention from users [24,39]. Several statistical or computational studies have been conducted using social media data for analysing public discourse [5]. Braun and Tarleton [5] conducted a study to analyse public discourse on social media sites and news organisations. Data gathering and its annotation are challenging and financially expensive [19].

© The Author(s), under exclusive license to Springer Nature Switzerland AG 2022
F. Sanfilippo et al. (Eds.): INTAP 2021, CCIS 1616, pp. 287–299, 2022.
https://doi.org/10.1007/978-3-031-10525-8_23

Social media data analytic research poses challenges in data collection, data sampling, data annotation, quality of data, and bias in data [17]. Researchers annotate social media data to research hate speech, misinformation, online mental health, etc. Data annotation is the process of assigning a category to data. For a machine learning model, labelled data sets are required to understand input patterns [30]. To build a supervised or semi-supervised model on social media data, researchers face two primary challenges, timely data collection and data annotation [37]. Timely data collection is essential because some platforms either restrict data access or the post itself is deleted by Social Networking Sites (SNSs) or by the user [38]. Another problem stands with data annotation; it is conducted either in an in-house fashion (within a lab or an organisation) or by using a crowdsourcing tool (like Amazon Mechanical Turk (AMT)) [4]. Both approaches require a fair amount of effort to write annotation guidelines along. There is also a chance of wrongly labelled data leading to bias [10].

We propose a semi-automatic framework for data annotation from SNSs to solve timely data collection and annotation. AMUSED gathers labelled data from different social media platforms in multiple formats (text, image, video). It can get annotated data on social issues like misinformation, hate speech or other critical social scenarios. In addition to that, the framework AMUSED resolves bias in the data (wrong label assigned by annotator). Our contribution is to provide a semi-automatic approach for collecting labelled data from different social media sites in multiple languages and data formats. Our framework can be applied in many application domains for which it typically is hard to gather data, for instance, misinformation, mob lynching, etc.

This paper is structured as follows; in Sect. 2 we discuss the background of our work. We then present the work method of AMUSED in Sect. 3, in Sect. 4 we give details on the implementation of AMUSED based on a case study and emphasise the obtained results in Sect. 5. We discuss our observations in Sect. 6 and draw a conclusion in Sect. 7.

2   Background

The following section describes the background on data annotation, types of data on social media, and the problems of current annotation techniques.

2.1   Data Annotation

the current research on social media data are typically restricted to a few SNSs and a few languages. Moreover, obtained results are published with limited amounts of data. There are multiple reasons for these limitations; one of the key reasons is the shortage of annotated data for the research [2,28,42]. Chapman et al. highlight the problem of getting labelled data for Natural Language Processing (NLP) related tasks [8]. A study is conducted on data quality and the role of annotators in the performance of machine learning models. With poor data, it is hard to build a generalisable classifier [15].

Researchers are dependent on in-house or crowd-based data annotation. The current annotation technique is dependent on the background expertise of the annotators. Recently, Alam et al. used a crowd-based annotation technique and asked people to volunteer for data annotation, but there is no significant success in getting a large number of labelled data [3]. Finding past data on an incident like mob lynching is challenging because of data restrictions by SNSs. It requires looking at many posts and news articles, leading to much manual work. In addition, billions of SNSs are sampled from a few thousand posts for data annotation by different sampling methods, leading to sampling bias.

Hiring an annotator with background expertise in a domain with in-house data annotation is challenging. Another issue is the development of a *codebook* with a proper explanation [13]. The entire process is financially expensive, and time-consuming [12]. The problem with crowd-based annotation tools like AMT is that the low cost may result in the wrong labelling of data. Many annotators may bypass, perform the job improperly, use robots, or answer randomly [14,29]. For crowd-based, maintaining annotation quality is complicated. Moreover, maintaining a good agreement between multiple annotators is tedious. Also, writing a good codebook requires domain knowledge and consultation from experts.

Since the emergence of social media as a news resource [7], people use this resource very differently. They may share news, state a personal opinion or commit a social crime in the form of hate speech or cyberbullying [23]. The COVID-19 pandemic arguably has led to a surge in the spread of misinformation [34]. Nowadays, journalists cover common issues like misinformation, mob lynching, and hate speech; they also link social media posts in news articles [11]. Social media platforms restrict users when fetching data; for example, a user deletes tweets on Twitter or videos on YouTube. Without on-time crawling, a sufficient amount of data is lost. Second, if the volume of data is high, data sampling based on several criteria like keyword, date, location etc., is needed. The sampling degrades data quality by excluding a significant amount of data. For example, if we sample data using hateful keywords for hate speech, we might lose many hate speech tweets that do not contain hateful words. On the other hand, SNSs are available in multiple languages, but much research is limited to English. Data annotation for under-resourced languages is difficult due to the lack of experienced annotators.

Social media posts mentioned in the news articles can be used to solve the mentioned data collection problem and their annotation. Labelling social media is then done based on the news article's contents. To get a reliable label, the credibility of the news source must be considered [22]. For example, a professional news website registered with the International Fact-Checking Network should, generally, be rather creditable[1]. A similar approach is proposed in some of the latest studies on fake news [20,21,25,26,36].

---

[1] https://www.poynter.org/ifcn-covid-19-misinformation/.

2.2   Data on Social Networking Sites

Every day, billions of posts containing images, text, and videos are shared on social media sites such as Facebook, Twitter, YouTube, and Instagram [1]. Social Media sites allow users to create and view posts in multiple formats. Data are available in different formats, and each SNS apply restriction on data crawling. For instance, Facebook allows crawling data only related to public posts and groups.

Giglietto et al. discuss the requirement of multimodal data for the study of social phenomenon [16]. Almost every SNS allows users to create or respond to the social media post in *text*. But each SNS has a different restriction on the length of the text. The content and the writing style change due to different restriction imposed by different SNS. *Images* are also common across different social media platforms. However, most of the platforms have restrictions on the size of the image. Some platforms like YouTube are primarily focused on *video*, whereas some are multimodal like Twitter. Furthermore, there are restrictions in terms of the allowed duration for videos. This influences the characteristics of usage.

3   Method

In the due process of gathering the annotated data, AMUSED consists of 9 steps. Notice that, although AMUSED is used to collect data for COVID-19 misinformation, it proposes very generic steps, which make it applicable to build any other domain, hate speech, mob lynching etc. Figure 1 shows the steps involved in the AMUSED methodology, and they are discussed below:

Step 1: Domain Identification. The first step is the identification of the domain in which we want to gather the data. A domain could focus on a particular public discourse. For example, a domain could be *fake news in the US election*, or *hate speech*. Domain selection helps to find the relevant data sources.

Step 2: Data Source. Data sources comprise news websites that mention a particular topic. For example, many news websites have a separate section that discusses any upcoming/ongoing/past election related topics or other ongoing issues.

Step 3: Web scraping. AMUSED then crawls all news articles from news websites using a Python-based crawler. We fetch details such as the published date, author, location, and news content (see Table 1).

Step 4: Language Identification. After getting the details from the news articles, we identify their language. We use ISO 639-1[2] for naming the language. We can further filter articles and apply a language-specific model for finding insights based on the language.

Step 5: Social Media Link. From the crawled data, we fetch the anchor tag <a> mentioned in the news content. We then filter the hyperlinks to identify social media platforms and fetch unique identifiers to the posts.

---

[2] https://en.Wikipedia.org/wiki/List_of_ISO_6391_codes.

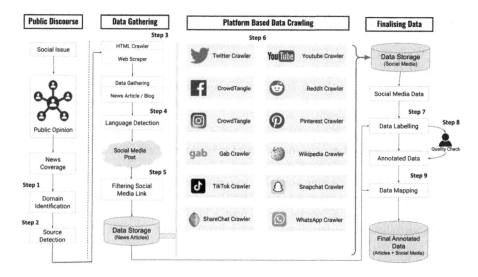

Fig. 1. AMUSED: an annotation framework for multimodal social media data

Table 1. Description of attributes and their examples

Element	Definition
News_ID	Unique identifying ID of each news articles. We use an acronym for news source and the number to identify a news articles
	Example: *PY9*
Newssource_URL	Unique identifier pointing to the news articles
	Example: https://factcheck.afp.com/video-actually-shows-anti-government-protest-belarus
News_Title	The title of the news article
	Example: *A video shows a rally against coronavirus restrictions in the British capital of London*
Published_date	Date when an article published in online media
	Example: *01 September 2020*
News_Class	Each news articles published the fact check article with a class like false, true, misleading. We store it in the class column
	Example: *False*
Published-By	The name of the news websites
	Example: *AFP, TheQuint*
Country	Country where the news article is published
	Example: *Australia*
Language	Language used for news article
	Example: *English*

Step 6: Social Media Data Crawling. We now fetch the data from the respective social media platform. For this purpose, we built a crawler for each social media platform because each platform has different crawling criteria and

parameters. We use the unique identifiers obtained from the previous step. For *Twitter* we used a Python crawler using Tweepy[3], which crawls all details about a Tweet. We collect text, time, likes, retweets, and user details such as name, location, and follower count [31]. Similarly, we build our crawler for other platforms. Due to the data restriction from Facebook and Instagram, we use Crowdtangle to fetch data from Facebook and Instagram, but it only gives numerical data like likes and followers [40].

Step 7: Data Labelling. We assign labels to the social media data based on the label assigned to the news articles by journalists. Often news articles categorise a social media post, for example, a social media post like hate speech or misinformation. We assign the label to social media posts as a class mentioned in the news article as a class described by the journalist. For example, suppose a news article *a* containing social media post *s* has been published by a journalist *j*, and journalist *j* has described the social media post *s* to be misinformation. In that case, We label the social media post *s* as misinformation. It will ease the workload by getting the number of social media posts checked by a journalist.

Step 8: Human Verification. To check the correctness, a human verifies the assigned label to the social media post. A human verifies the label of the collected data. If the label is wrongly assigned, then data is removed from the corpus. This step assures that the collected social media post contains the relevant post and correctly given label.

Step 9: Data Enrichment. We finally merge the social media data with the details from the news articles. It helps to accumulate extra information, which might allow for further analysis.

4   Implementation: A Case Study on Misinformation

While our framework allows for general application, understanding its merits is best possible by applying it to a specific domain. AMUSED can be helpful for several domains, but news companies are quite active in the domain of misinformation, especially during a crisis. *Misinformation*, often yet imprecisely referred to as a piece of information that is shared unintentionally or by mistake, without knowing the truthfulness of the content [32]. There is an increasing amount of misinformation in the media, social media, and other web sources; this has become a topic of much research attention [44]. Currently, more than 100 fact-checking websites are working to tackle the problem of misinformation [9].

People have spread vast amounts of misinformation during the COVID-19 pandemic and elections and disasters [18]. Due to the lack of labelled data, it is challenging to analyse the misinformation properly. As a case study, we apply the AMUSED for data annotation for COVID-19 misinformation, following the steps illustrated in the prior section.

Step 1: Domain Identification. Out of several possible application domains, we consider the spread of misinformation in the context of COVID-19. Misinformation likely worsens the negative effects of the pandemic [34]. The director of

---

[3] https://www.tweepy.org/.

the World Health Organization (WHO) considers that we are not only fighting a pandemic but also an *infodemic* [41,43]. One of the fundamental problems is the lack of sufficient corpus related to pandemic [32].

Step 2: Data Sources. For data source, we analysed multiple fact-checking websites and decided to use *Poynter* and *Snopes*. We choose Poynter because it has a central data hub that collects data from more than 98 fact-checking websites. While Snopes is not integrated with Poynter but has more than 300 fact-checked articles on COVID-19.

Step 3: Web Scraping. In this step, we fetched all the news articles from Poynter and Snopes. We used a python-based crawler for content scrapping and stored them in a database.

Step 4: Language Detection. We collected data in multiple languages like English, German, and Hindi. To identify the language of the news article, we used langdetect[4], a Python-based library to detect the language of the news articles. We used the textual content of news articles to detect their language.

Step 5: Social Media Link. In the next step, while performing HTML crawling, we filtered the URLs from the parsed tree of the DOM (Document Object Model). We analysed the URL pattern from different SNSs and applied keyword-based filtering from all hyperlinks in the DOM. For instance, Twitter follows a URL pattern https://twitter.com/user_name/status/tweetid for each tweet. So, in the collection of hyperlinks, we searched for the keyword "twitter.com" and "status". This assures that we have collected the hyperlink referring to the tweet as shown in Fig. 2.

Similarly, we followed the approach for other social media platforms, Facebook and Instagram, in our case. In the next step, we used the regex code to filter the unique ID for each social media post.

Step 6: Social Media Data Crawling. Using the unique identifier of each social media post, we build a Python-based program for crawling data from respective social media platforms. The summary is given in Table 2.

Table 2. Summary of data collected using AMUSED framework

Platform	Posts	Unique	Text	Image	Text+Image	Video
Facebook	5,799	3,200	1167	567	1,006	460
Instagram	385	197	-	106	41	52
Pinterest	5	3	-	3	0	0
Reddit	67	33	16	10	7	0
TikTok	43	18	-	-	-	18
Twitter	3,142	1,758	1300	116	143	199
Wikipedia	393	176	106	34	20	16
YouTube	2,087	916	-	-	-	916

---

[4] https://pypi.org/project/langdetect/.

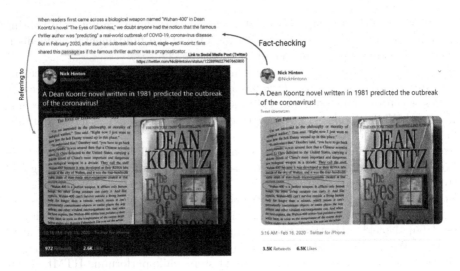

Fig. 2. An Illustration of data collection from social media platform (Twitter) from a news article [32]

Step 7: Data Labelling. For data labelling, we used the label assigned in the news articles, then we mapped the social media post with their respective news article and assigned the label to the social media post. For example, a Tweet extracted from a news article is mapped to the class of the news article as shown in Fig. 3.

Fig. 3. An Illustration for annotation of social media posting using the label mentioned in the news article.

Step 8: Human Verification. We manually checked each social media post to assess the correctness of the process. We provided the annotators with all necessary information about the class mapping and asked them to verify it. For example, as illustrated in Fig. 3, a human reads the news article using the newssource_URL and verifies the label assigned to the tweet. For COVID-19 misinformation, we checked the annotation by randomly choosing 100 social media posts from each social media platform and verifying the label assigned to the social media post and the label mentioned in the news articles. We measured the inter-coder reliability using Cohen's kappa and got a value of 0.86, which

Table 3. Summary of COVID-19 misinformation posts collected.

SM platform	False	Partially false	Other	True
Facebook	2,776	325	94	6
Instagram	166	28	2	1
Reddit	21	9	2	1
Twitter	1,318	234	50	13
Wikipedia	154	18	3	1
YouTube	739	164	13	0

is a good agreement. We further normalised the data label into *false, partially false, true* and *others* using the class definitions mentioned in [32,33].

Step 9: Data Enrichment. We then enriched the data by providing extra information about the social media post. The first step is merging the social media post with the respective news article, and it includes additional information like textual content, news source, and author. The detailed analysis of the collected data is discussed in the result section.

5   Results

For the use case of COVID-19 Misinformation, we identified Poynter and Snopes as the data source, and we collected data from different social media platforms. Overall, we collected 8,077 fact-checked news articles from 105 countries in 40 languages. Around 51% of news articles linked their content to social media websites. We then cleaned the hyperlinks collected using the AMUSED framework and filtered the social media posts by removing duplicates using unique identifiers.

Table 3 presents the class distribution of these posts from different SNSs; most of the social media posts are from Facebook and Twitter, followed by YouTube, Wikipedia and Instagram. There are very few posts from Pinterest (3), WhatsApp (23), Tiktok (25), or Reddit (43). Misinformation also follows the COVID-19 situation in many countries because the number of social media posts also decreased after June 2020. The possible reason could be that the spread of misinformation is reduced or that fact-checking websites are not focusing on this issue as much as they did during the early stages.

6   Discussion

Our study highlighted the process of fetching labelled social media posts from fact-checked news articles. Usually, fact-checking websites links social media posts from multiple social media platforms. We tried to gather data from various social media platforms, but we found the maximum number of links belonged to Facebook, Twitter, and YouTube. There are a few unique posts from Reddit (21), and TikTok (9), which show that fact-checker mainly focuses on analysing content from Facebook, Twitter, and YouTube. This situation proposes the need for further studies on Twitter, YouTube, and Facebook and proposes requirements for fact-checking on WhatsApp and TikTok.

Surprisingly there are only three unique posts from Pinterest, and there are no data available from Gab, ShareChat, and Snapchat. However, Gab is well known for harmful content, and people in their regional languages use ShareChat. Many people use Wikipedia as a reliable source of information, but there are 393 links from Wikipedia. Hence, the overall fact-checking websites are limited to trending social media platforms like Twitter or Facebook. In contrast, social media platforms like Gab and TikTok are infamous for malformation, or misinformation [6]. WhatsApp is an instant messaging app used among friends or groups of people. So, we only found some hyperlink which links to the public WhatsApp group, which is in contrast to the findings by Kazemi et al. that misinformation is widely shared on WhatsApp [20]. To increase the visibility of fact-checked articles, a journalist can also use schema.org vocabulary along with the Microdata, RDFa, or JSON-LD formats to add details about Misinformation to the news articles [35].

AMUSED requires some effort but still is beneficial compared to random data annotation because we need to annotate thousands of social media posts. Another aspect is the diversity of social media posts on different social media platforms. News articles often mention Facebook, Twitter, and YouTube, yet there were no mentions of Instagram, Pinterest, Gab, and Tiktok. This calls for a need to speculate the reasons behind it, as the more the platforms are available for research, the better the study of the propagation of misinformation turns out to be. Such a cross-platform study would be particularly insightful with contemporary topics such as misinformation on COVID-19 and would turn into better classification models [27,30].

We also analysed the multimodality of data on social media platforms; the number of social media posts is shown in Table 2. We further classify the misinformation into four different categories, as discussed in step 8. In terms of multimodality, there is more misinformation as text than video or image on each platform except YouTube. Thus, in Table 3 we present the textual misinformation into four different categories. Apart from text, the misinformation is also shared as image, video or embedding format like image-text.

While applying the AMUSED framework to the misinformation on COVID-19 data, we found that misinformation spreads across multiple source platforms, mainly circulated on Facebook, Twitter, and YouTube. Our finding suggests concentrating mitigation efforts on these platforms.

7   Conclusion and Future Work

This paper presented a semi-automatic framework for social media data annotation. The framework can be applied to several domains, such as misinformation, mob lynching, or online abuse. We also used a Python-based crawler for different social media websites as part of the framework. As a case study, we implemented the proposed framework for collecting misinformation posts related to COVID-19. After data labelling, the labels were cross-checked by a human, ensuring a two-step verification of data annotation. We also enriched the social media posts by mapping them to news articles to gather more information about them. The advantage of the data enrichment process was that it provides additional information for the social media post. The framework can be used to gather annotated data for other domains from multiple social media sites for further analysis.

Having put forward the multiple advantages of the proposed framework, we now shed light on some limitations of the framework. First and foremost is that we presently do not address the multiple (possibly contradicting) labels assigned by different fact-checkers over the same claim. Another limitation is that the data providers do not follow the structure of the web page; in this case, they may assign some wrong labels to crawled data. As a result, for future work, we propose extending the framework for evaluating annotated data on multiple vast ranges of topics, such as hate speech and mob lynching.

Lastly, we conclude by bringing to attention that the proposed framework, AMUSED, will decrease the labour cost for the data annotation process and save invaluable time in the process. Moreover, a major by-product of the proposed framework is that the annotation quality of the data increases manifold due to the fact that the data is crawled from news articles published by an expert journalist.

References

1. Aggarwal, C.C.: An introduction to social network data analytics. In: Aggarwal, C. (ed.) Social Network Data Analytics, pp. 1–15. Springer, Heidelberg (2011). https://doi.org/10.1007/978-1-4419-8462-3_1
2. Ahmed, S., Pasquier, M., Qadah, G.: Key issues in conducting sentiment analysis on Arabic social media text. In: 2013 9th International Conference on Innovations in Information Technology (IIT), pp. 72–77. IEEE (2013)
3. Alam, F., et al.: Fighting the Covid-19 infodemic in social media: a holistic perspective and a call to arms. arXiv preprint arXiv:2007.07996 (2020)
4. Aroyo, L., Welty, C.: Truth is a lie: crowd truth and the seven myths of human annotation. AI Mag. **36**(1), 15–24 (2015)
5. Braun, J., Gillespie, T.: Hosting the public discourse, hosting the public: when online news and social media converge. J. Pract. **5**(4), 383–398 (2011)
6. Brennen, J.S., Simon, F., Howard, S.N., Nielsen, R.K.: Types, sources, and claims of Covid-19 misinformation. Reuters Inst. **7**, 3–1 (2020)
7. Caumont, A.: 12 trends shaping digital news. Pew Res. Center **16** (2013)
8. Chapman, W.W., Nadkarni, P.M., Hirschman, L., D'avolio, L.W., Savova, G.K., Uzuner, O.: Overcoming barriers to NLP for clinical text: the role of shared tasks and the need for additional creative solutions (2011)
9. Cherubini, F., Graves, L.: The rise of fact-checking sites in Europe. Reuters Institute for the Study of Journalism, University of Oxford (2016). http://reutersinsfitute.polifics.ox.ac.uk/our-research/rise-fact-checking-sites-europe
10. Cook, P., Stevenson, S.: Automatically identifying changes in the semantic orientation of words. In: LREC (2010)

11. Cui, X., Liu, Y.: How does online news curate linked sources? A content analysis of three online news media. Journalism **18**(7), 852–870 (2017)
12. Duchenne, O., Laptev, I., Sivic, J., Bach, F., Ponce, J.: Automatic annotation of human actions in video. In: 2009 IEEE 12th International Conference on Computer Vision, pp. 1491–1498. IEEE (2009)
13. Forbush, T.B., Shen, S., South, B.R., DuValla, S.L.: What a catch! traits that define good annotators. Stud. Health Technol. Inform. **192**, 1213–1213 (2013)
14. Fort, K., Adda, G., Cohen, K.B.: Amazon mechanical Turk: gold mine or coal mine? Comput. Linguist. **37**(2), 413–420 (2011)
15. Geiger, R.S., et al.: Garbage in, garbage out? Do machine learning application papers in social computing report where human-labeled training data comes from? In: Proceedings of the 2020 Conference on Fairness, Accountability, and Transparency, pp. 325–336 (2020)
16. Giglietto, F., Rossi, L., Bennato, D.: The open laboratory: limits and possibilities of using Facebook, Twitter, and YouTube as a research data source. J. Technol. Hum. Serv. **30**(3–4), 145–159 (2012)
17. Grant-Muller, S.M., Gal-Tzur, A., Minkov, E., Nocera, S., Kuflik, T., Shoor, I.: Enhancing transport data collection through social media sources: methods, challenges and opportunities for textual data. IET Intell. Transp. Syst. **9**(4), 407–417 (2014)
18. Gupta, A., Lamba, H., Kumaraguru, P., Joshi, A.: Faking sandy: characterizing and identifying fake images on Twitter during hurricane sandy. In: Proceedings of the 22nd International Conference on World Wide Web, pp. 729–736 (2013)
19. Haertel, R.A.: Practical cost-conscious active learning for data annotation in annotator-initiated environments. Brigham Young University-Provo (2013)
20. Kazemi, A., Garimella, K., Shahi, G.K., Gaffney, D., Hale, S.A.: Research note: tiplines to uncover misinformation on encrypted platforms: a case study of the 2019 Indian general election on WhatsApp. Harvard Kennedy School Misinformation Review (2022)
21. Köhler, J., Shahi, G.K., Struß, J.M., Wiegand, M., Siegel, M., Mandl, T.: Overview of the CLEF-2022 CheckThat! lab task 3 on fake news detection. In: Working Notes of CLEF 2022–Conference and Labs of the Evaluation Forum, CLEF 2022, Bologna, Italy (2022)
22. Kohring, M., Matthes, J.: Trust in news media: development and validation of a multidimensional scale. Commun. Res. **34**(2), 231–252 (2007)
23. Mandl, T., et al.: Overview of the HASOC track at FIRE 2020: hate speech and offensive content identification in Indo-European languages. In: Mehta, P., Mandl, T., Majumder, P., Mitra, M. (eds.) Working Notes of FIRE 2020. CEUR Workshop Proceedings, vol. 2826, pp. 87–111. CEUR-WS.org (2020)
24. McGahan, C., Katsion, J.: Secondary communication crisis: social media news information. Liberty University Research Week (2021)
25. Nakov, P., et al.: Overview of the CLEF-2021 CheckThat! lab on detecting check-worthy claims, previously fact-checked claims, and fake news. In: Proceedings of the 12th International Conference of the CLEF Association: Information Access Evaluation Meets Multiliguality, Multimodality, and Visualization, CLEF 2021, Bucharest, Romania (2021)
26. Nakov, P., et al.: The CLEF-2021 CheckThat! lab on detecting check-worthy claims, previously fact-checked claims, and fake news. In: Hiemstra, D., Moens, M.-F., Mothe, J., Perego, R., Potthast, M., Sebastiani, F. (eds.) ECIR 2021. LNCS, vol. 12657, pp. 639–649. Springer, Cham (2021). https://doi.org/10.1007/978-3-030-72240-1_75

27. Nandini, D., Capecci, E., Koefoed, L., Laña, I., Shahi, G.K., Kasabov, N.: Modelling and analysis of temporal gene expression data using spiking neural networks. In: Cheng, L., Leung, A.C.S., Ozawa, S. (eds.) ICONIP 2018. LNCS, vol. 11301, pp. 571–581. Springer, Cham (2018). https://doi.org/10.1007/978-3-030-04167-0_52

28. Röchert, D., Shahi, G.K., Neubaum, G., Ross, B., Stieglitz, S.: The networked context of Covid-19 misinformation: informational homogeneity on YouTube at the beginning of the pandemic. Online Soc. Netw. Media **26**, 100164 (2021)

29. Sabou, M., Bontcheva, K., Derczynski, L., Scharl, A.: Corpus annotation through crowdsourcing: towards best practice guidelines. In: LREC, pp. 859–866 (2014)

30. Shahi, G.K., Bilbao, I., Capecci, E., Nandini, D., Choukri, M., Kasabov, N.: Analysis, classification and marker discovery of gene expression data with evolving spiking neural networks. In: Cheng, L., Leung, A.C.S., Ozawa, S. (eds.) ICONIP 2018. LNCS, vol. 11305, pp. 517–527. Springer, Cham (2018). https://doi.org/10.1007/978-3-030-04221-9_46

31. Shahi, G.K., Clausen, S., Stieglitz, S.: Who shapes crisis communication on Twitter? An analysis of German influencers during the Covid-19 pandemic. In: Proceedings of the 55th Hawaii International Conference on System Sciences (2022)

32. Shahi, G.K., Dirkson, A., Majchrzak, T.A.: An exploratory study of Covid-19 misinformation on Twitter. Online Soc. Netw. Media 100104 (2021)

33. Shahi, G.K., Majchrzak, T.A.: Exploring the spread of Covid-19 misinformation on Twitter. Technical report (2021)

34. Shahi, G.K., Nandini, D.: FakeCovid - a multilingual cross-domain fact check news dataset for Covid-19. In: Workshop Proceedings of the 14th International AAAI Conference on Web and Social Media (2020). http://workshop-proceedings.icwsm.org/pdf/2020_14.pdf

35. Shahi, G.K., Nandini, D., Kumari, S.: Inducing schema.org markup from natural language context. Kalpa Publ. Comput. **10**, 38–42 (2019)

36. Shahi, G.K., Struß, J.M., Mandl, T.: Overview of the CLEF-2021 CheckThat! lab task 3 on fake news detection. Working Notes of CLEF (2021)

37. Shu, K., Sliva, A., Wang, S., Tang, J., Liu, H.: Fake news detection on social media: a data mining perspective. ACM SIGKDD Explor. Newsl. **19**(1), 22–36 (2017)

38. Stieglitz, S., Mirbabaie, M., Ross, B., Neuberger, C.: Social media analytics-challenges in topic discovery, data collection, and data preparation. Int. J. Inf. Manag. **39**, 156–168 (2018)

39. Talwar, S., Dhir, A., Kaur, P., Zafar, N., Alrasheedy, M.: Why do people share fake news? Associations between the dark side of social media use and fake news sharing behavior. J. Retail. Consum. Serv. **51**, 72–82 (2019)

40. Team, C: CrowdTangle. Facebook, Menlo Park, California, United States (2020)

41. The Guardian: The WHO v coronavirus: why it can't handle the pandemic (2020). https://www.theguardian.com/news/2020/apr/10/world-health-organization-who-v-coronavirus-why-it-cant-handle-pandemic

42. Thorson, K., et al.: YouTube, Twitter and the occupy movement: connecting content and circulation practices. Inf. Commun. Soc. **16**(3), 421–451 (2013)

43. Zarocostas, J.: World report how to fight an infodemic. Lancet **395**, 676 (2020). https://doi.org/10.1016/S0140-6736(20)30461-X

44. Zhou, X., Zafarani, R.: Fake news: a survey of research, detection methods, and opportunities. CoRR abs/1812.00315 (2018). http://arxiv.org/abs/1812.00315

ML in Energy Sectors and Materials

An Evaluation of Predictor Variables for Photovoltaic Power Forecasting

Lennard Visser[1]([✉])[iD], Tarel AlSkaif[2][iD], and Wilfried van Sark[1][iD]

[1] Copernicus Institute of Sustainable Development, Utrecht University,
Princetonlaan 8a, 3584 CB Utrecht, The Netherlands
l.r.visser@uu.nl

[2] Information Technology Group, Wageningen University and Research,
Hollandseweg 1, 6706 KN Wageningen, The Netherlands

Abstract. Accurate forecasts of the electric power generation by solar Photovoltaic (PV) systems are essential to support their vast increasing integration. This study evaluates the interdependence of 14 predictor variables and their importance to machine learning models that forecast the day-ahead PV power production. To this purpose, we use two feature selection models to rank the predictor variables and accordingly, examine the performance change of two forecast models when a growing number of variables is considered. The study is performed using 3 years of data for Utrecht, the Netherlands. The results show the most important variables for PV power forecasting and identifies how many top variables should be considered to achieve an optimal forecast performance accuracy. Additionally, the best forecast model performance is found when only a few predictor variables are considered, including a created variable that estimates the PV power output based on technical system characteristics and physical relations.

Keywords: Photovoltaics · Solar power forecasting · Predictor variables · Machine learning · Weather forecasts

1 Introduction

In recent years, we have experienced a rapid growth of the installed capacity of solar Photovoltaic (PV) systems. Moreover, this growth is foreseen to last during this decade, which will lead to an expected increase from an installed solar PV capacity of 760 GWp in 2020 [8] to 1,800 GWp in 2025 [11]. Due to the variable nature of power generation from PV systems, forecast models are deemed essential for effective integration in the electricity system, and subsequently, facilitate a high PV penetration level [13].

Artificial intelligence and particularly Machine Learning (ML) have already proven its value to solar forecasting in several studies [3,15,17]. Especially those studies that have utilized ML models to post-process numerical weather predictions (NWPs) have found acceptable forecast results, where the obtained accuracy results from the high local climate dependency.

However, the importance and contribution of the various predictor variables, which usually include meteorological variables, to forecast the PV power output are rarely studied. Instead, most studies select few predictor variables, lacking any substantial argumentation concerning their in- or excludance. Besides, the focus of literature related to PV power forecasting has been on the models, and particularly the model performance. An exemption to this concerns a study that assessed the importance of several predictor variables for estimating the PV power output [2]. In this study the interdependence of nine meteorological variables was studied as well as their individual contribution to the ML models that estimate the power output of PV systems in two different climate regions. Similar work related to establishing the importance of predictor variables for forecasting is unknown to the authors.

In this paper we set a first step in describing the importance and contribution of different predictor variables for day-ahead solar power forecasting. Subsequently, we provide insight into the most important predictor variables. We firstly assess the dependency of the PV power output per predictor variable and examine the interdependence among the predictor variables. Thereafter, we quantify the contribution of the various predictor variables on the model forecast performance.

This paper is organized as follows. The following Sect. 2 presents the methods. The data collection and assessment of the variable interdependence are discussed in Sects. 3. Next, Sect. 4 presents the results. Conclusions and recommendations are given in Sect. 5.

2 Methods

2.1 Feature Selection Method

In the present study Recursive Feature Elimination (RFE) is used to select and rank the most important predictor variables for PV power forecasting. RFE is a wrapper-based feature selection method that deploys a regression or machine learning model in its core to rank the most important variables. This is accomplished by an iterative process, where the model is fitted to the variables in the training data set after which the least contributing variables are removed. The number of iterations needed depends on the step size (i.e. the number of variables that are removed in one iteration), the desired number of variables and the number of variables present in the data set. Since we aim to rank the variables, we continue this process until we have found the most important variable with a step size of one [6,16]. Furthermore, in this study two different models are used to define the variable ranking, namely a Multivariate Linear Regression (MLR) and Random Forest regression (RF) model. Moreover, in MLR the importance of a variable is per iteration set to be equal to the (regression) coefficient. Since RF is an ensemble regression model [4], the variable importance is based on the Mean Decrease Impurity (MDI). In short, the MDI is established by considering the relative contribution of all the splits for which a specific variable is responsible with respect to the overall model accuracy [6,16].

2.2 Forecast Models

Three different models that forecast the PV power output are considered in this study. For simplicity reasons, the two models selected for feature selection (MLR and RF), are also considered for forecasting. Training data is used to set the parameters and in case of RF also to find the optimal hyper-parameters through k-fold cross-validation [4,15]. In addition, in this study we include the Hay-Davies transposition model as a benchmark [7,12]. Moreover, this transposition model directly estimates the PV power output based on the technical properties of the PV system as well as a number of weather variables. These variables include the Global Horizontal Irradiance (GHI), the Direct Normal Irradiance (DNI), Diffuse Horizontal Irradiance (DHI), Ambient Temperature (AT), Wind Speed (WS) and Surface Pressure (SP). Since predictions of these variables can be obtained (see Sect. 3.1), it presents an alternative forecast approach.

Furthermore, the performance of the forecast models is examined by the Mean Absolute Error (MAE). To quantify these results independently of the PV system size, the MAE is expressed in percentages considering the installed capacity of the system.

3   Data Description and Analysis

3.1 Data Collection

Power measurements of a rooftop PV system present the target variable and are collected from January 2014 until December 2016. The PV system is located in Utrecht, the Netherlands, with an approximate (GDPR compliant) latitude and longitude of 52.1° and 5.1°. Moreover, the PV system has an installed capacity of 2295 Wp. The system is oriented due south (180°) with a tilt angle of 38°. By means of averaging one-minute power measurements, hourly production values are obtained [15].

Furthermore, part of the predictor variables concern historical weather predictions. These are collected for the same period. The weather predictions are generated by the High Resolution Forecast Configuration (HRES) of the Integrated Forecast System (IFS) developed by the European Centre for Medium-Range Weather Forecasts (ECMWF) [5]. These variables include: Ambient and Dewpoint Temperature (AT and DT); Global Horizontal Irradiance (GHI); Surface Pressure (SP); Total, Low, Mid and High cloud cover (TCC, LCC, MCC and HCC); and the zonal and meridonal wind vector components. The latter two variables are merely retrieved to estimate the Wind Speed (WS). These variables are collected as it is well-known that they affect the power production of a solar PV system either directly or indirectly [7,10,12]. To comply with the requirements and generate day-ahead PV power forecasts, the retrieved weather predictions are characterized by a 12 h lead time, a 36 h time horizon, an hourly temporal resolution and a daily update rate.

Besides, a number of additional predictor variables are either retrieved or created. Firstly, the estimated GHI under clear sky conditions according to the

Ineichen-Perez model, i.e. Clear Sky Irradiance (CSI) [9]. Secondly, the DIRINT model is used to decompose the predicted GHI into its two components, DNI and DHI [10,12]. Lastly, since we can estimate the PV power output by means of a transposition model (see Sect. 2.2), we include the expected or transposed PV (T-PVP) power output as an additional predictor variable.

Furthermore, since power is only generated during daytime, nighttime values are discarded from the data set. Besides, in case of any missing values in the data set, the respective timestamp is removed from the data set. Next, the data set is split into a train and test set, whereas the former comprises two years of data (2014–2015) and the latter one (2016). In addition, all variables in the training set have been normalized to obtain only values between 0 and 1. Finally, the test set has been normalized using the data characteristics of the train set.

3.2   Data Analysis

To provide insights into the predictor and target variables, in this section first Pearson correlation is applied to define the cross-correlation amongst the predictor and target variables. The resulting correlation coefficient between a pair of variables is a measure of their linear dependence. The correlation is calculated over the combined train and test period.

The dependency of the target variable (PV power, PVP) on the predictor variables are illustrated by the most left row in Fig. 1a. The strongest positive correlations for the PV power production is found for T-PVP and GHI, where correlations values of 0.85 and 0.82 are obtained respectively. This shows the dependency of PV power production on the predicted GHI and T-PVP, indicating that a higher predicted value results in an increasing PV power production. Next, a strong positive correlation for PVP is found with CSI (0.68), DNI (0.63) and DHI (0.60). On the other hand, the strongest negative correlations for PV are found for TCC (-0.27), MCC (-0.23), LCC (-0.23) and HCC (-0.17). This negative relation is simply explained as a higher cloud cover rate will decrease the solar irradiance and therefore result in a lower PV power output. Nevertheless, the reason for the limited extend of the negative correlation can be found in the little effect of the cloud cover rate on the PVP during early and late hours, where the PV power production is also low under a clear sky.

Besides, Fig. 1a presents the interdependence amongst the predictor variables. From the figure a strong positive correlation between GHI and T-PVP can be observed (0.94). This values shows the high dependency of T-PVP on GHI, as explained in Sect. 2.2. Strong positive correlations are also found among the predicted DT and AT (0.88), and the predicted GHI and CSI (0.81). In this study, the strongest yet relative limited negative correlations are found for LCC, MCC and TCC with DNI ($-0.45, -0.40, -0.48$). Similarly, a negative correlation is found between T and SP (-0.42).

In this study, a Principal Component Analysis (PCA) is used to further assess the interdependence amongst the predictor variables. In a PCA, the input variables are decomposed and transformed into a new feature subspace. These

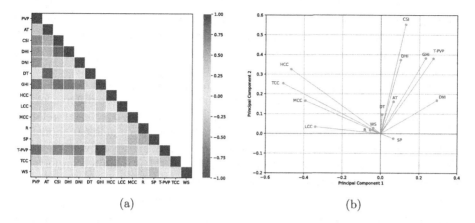

(a)   (b)

Fig. 1. Interdependence of the predictor and target variables, presented by the (a) cross correlation (best viewed in color) and (b) biplot of the first and second principal components. (Color figure online)

constructed features, i.e. Principal Components (PCs), are uncorrelated to each other, while holding information from all input variables [1,14].

Figure 1b depicts a biplot representation of the predictor variables. Moreover, the figure marks the contribution of each predictor variables to the first two principal components, which are orthogonal to each other. Figure 1b confirms the correlation values obtained and depicted in Fig. 1a. Moreover, it presents a high positive correlation between HCC and TCC, which have a high contribution to the first PC. Similarly, a high positive correlation is found between GHI and T-PVP, as well as DHI and CSI, which all have a high contribution to the second PC. In addition, Fig. 1b shows a negative correlation between SP and WS, which have a small contribution to the first two PCs. A negative correlation is also found for DNI with LCC, MCC and TCC.

4   Results and Discussions

4.1   Predictor Variable Importance

An overview of the most important variables for day-ahead PV power forecasting is given in Table 1. Both recursive selection algorithms, MLR and RF, have indicated the T-PVP variable as the top predictor variable. In contrast to the others, this variable was constructed based on knowledge on the operation of this PV system. Moreover, the variables describes the expected output of a PV system by its physical dependency on the GHI, DNI, DHI, WS, AT and SP, while also considering the systems' characteristics, e.g. tilt angle and orientation. Consequently, this shows the added value of develop and include predictor variables based on expert knowledge. Furthermore, from Table 1 it is striking that the 4 CC variables are marked of limited importance in both selection algorithms. This is due to the relative low negative correlation found between the CC variables and PV power output (see Sect. 3.2). Besides, the information presented by the CC variables is partly captured by the GHI, after all an increased cloud cover rate will reduce the GHI.

On the other hand, notable differences in the importance of the AT, DT, GHI, DNI and R variables can be observed from Table 1. These differences are explained by the model type, i.e. the MLR model relies on a linear relation between the predictor and target variables, while RF is a nonlinear model. A good example of this concerns GHI, which is due to its high positive correlation with T-PVP and the linear nature of the MLR model, has a limited importance as scored by the MLR model.

Table 1. Top predictor variables per selection method, where rank 1 presents the most important variable.

Rank	1	2	3	4	5	6	7
MLR selection	T-PVP	AT	DT	CSI	GHI	SP	DNI
RF selection	T-PVP	GHI	SP	CSI	AT	TCC	R
Rank	8	9	10	11	12	13	14
MLR selection	TCC	DHI	WS	R	MCC	LCC	HCC
RF selection	WS	DHI	DT	LCC	MCC	DNI	HCC

4.2   Forecast Performance

Figure 2 presents the forecast performance in terms of the MAE for a varying number of included variables. Moreover, the variables in Fig. 2a are based on the MLR selection model, whereas the variables in Fig. 2b come from the RF model. In general, both figures show a trend of an improving forecast, i.e. reduced MAE, with an increasing number of variables. However, some remarkable exceptions occur where the performance accuracy deteriorates with an added variable. In addition, after including 4 and 6 variables for MLR and RF, respectively, and considering their respective selection models the performances are barely found to improve with additional variables. Consequently, an optimal model performance is found by selecting the top 4 and 6 variables in case of MLR and RF. However, although the difference is limited, in the end the best forecast performances are found for both models when the RF selection model is considered. Moreover, this optimum forecast performance requires the top 10 variables in case of the MLR forecast model and 12 for the RF forecast model.

Furthermore, the poor performance of the MLR model compared to the transposition model is outstanding, especially when we keep in mind that the MLR model is fed with this exact information through the T-PVP variable. From Fig. 2, we find that in this study the best forecast performance is obtained for the RF model. Moreover, at least 6 and 8 variables are needed to outperform the Transposition model in case of considering the RF and MLR selection models, respectively. Most remarkably, in both cases the TCC variable turns out to be the missing variable in order to outperform the transposition model. Considering this significant performance improvement because of TCC, this raises the question if earlier adoption of this feature would have improved the model performance at an earlier stage (i.e., for less features).

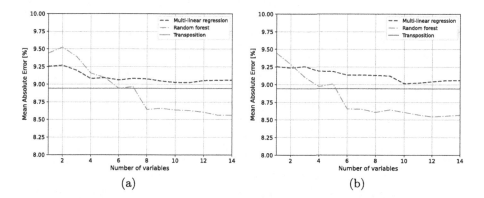

Fig. 2. Forecasting model performance according to n top ranked predictor variables, (a) MLR selection and (b) RF selection. The results for the Transposition model are independent of the number of variables selected (see Sect. 2.2).

5   Conclusion and Outlook

In this study, we have assessed the interdependence of 14 predictor variables and their value when utilized for PV power forecasting. The latter is reached by ranking the importance of the respective variables by two feature selection models and evaluating their contribution to the performance of two forecast models. Firstly, this study finds the RF forecast model to outperform the MLR and Transposition, if provided with an adequate selection of predictor variables. Furthermore, the results show the value of including expert knowledge within the operation of ML models to forecast the PV power production, as the top rated variable is the constructed expected power output based on the Transposition model.

In future work we will extend this study by assessing the importance of predictor variables for other locations located in different climate regions. In addition, we will create and consider an increasing number of predictor variables. Finally, by examining the forecast model performance for different data subsets that in- and exclude the created variables i.e. T-PVP, we will quantify the value of expert knowledge in PV power forecasting.

Acknowledgements. This work is part of the eNErgy intrAneTs (NEAT: ESI-BiDa 647.003.002) project, which is funded by the Dutch Research Council NWO in the framework of the Energy Systems Integration & Big Data programme.

References

1. AlSkaif, T., Dev, S., Visser, L., Hossari, M., van Sark, W.: On the interdependence and importance of meteorological variables for photovoltaic output power estimation. In: 2019 IEEE 46th Photovoltaic Specialists Conference (PVSC), pp. 2117–2120. IEEE (2019)
2. AlSkaif, T., Dev, S., Visser, L., Hossari, M., van Sark, W.: A systematic analysis of meteorological variables for PV output power estimation. Renewable Energy **153**, 12–22 (2020)
3. Antonanzas, J., Osorio, N., Escobar, R., Urraca, R., Martinez-de Pison, F., Antonanzas-Torres, F.: Review of photovoltaic power forecasting. Sol. Energy **136**, 78–111 (2016)
4. Breiman, L.: Random forests. Mach. Learn. **45**(1), 5–32 (2001). https://doi.org/10.1023/a:1010933404324
5. ECMWF: European Centre for Medium-range Weather Forecasts, ECMWF (2020). https://www.ecmwf.int/en/forecasts/datasets/archive-datasets
6. Guyon, I., Gunn, S., Nikravesh, M., Zadeh, L.A.: Feature Extraction: Foundations and Applications, vol. 207. Springer (2008)
7. Hay, J.E.: Calculating solar radiation for inclined surfaces: practical approaches. Renewable Energy **3**(4–5), 373–380 (1993)
8. IEA: Snapshot of global PV markets 2021. Technical report, International Energy Agency (2021). https://iea-pvps.org/snapshot-reports/snapshot-2021/
9. Ineichen, P., Perez, R.: A new airmass independent formulation for the Linke turbidity coefficient. Sol. Energy **73**(3), 151–157 (2002)
10. Ineichen, P., Perez, R., Seal, R., Maxwell, E., Zalenka, A.: Dynamic global-to-direct irradiance conversion models. ASHRAE Trans. **98**(1), 354–369 (1992)
11. Abu, D.: IRENA: Renewable capacity statistics 2020. Technical report, International Renewable Energy Agency (2021). https://www.irena.org/publications/2021/March/Renewable-Capacity-Statistics-2021
12. Lave, M., Hayes, W., Pohl, A., Hansen, C.W.: Evaluation of global horizontal irradiance to plane-of-array irradiance models at locations across the united states. IEEE J. Photovoltaics **5**(2), 597–606 (2015)
13. Lorenz, E., Scheidsteger, T., Hurka, J., Heinemann, D., Kurz, C.: Regional PV power prediction for improved grid integration. Prog. Photovoltaics Res. Appl. **19**(7), 757–771 (2011)
14. Raschka, S., Mirjalili, V.: Python machine learning: machine learning and deep learning with python. Scikit-Learn, and TensorFlow, 2nd (edn.) (2017)
15. Visser, L., AlSkaif, T., van Sark, W.: Benchmark analysis of day-ahead solar power forecasting techniques using weather predictions. In: 2019 IEEE 46th Photovoltaic Specialists Conference (PVSC), pp. 2111–2116. IEEE (2019)
16. Visser, L., AlSkaif, T., Van Sark, W.: The importance of predictor variables and feature selection in day-ahead electricity price forecasting. In: 2020 International Conference on Smart Energy Systems and Technologies (SEST), pp. 1–6. IEEE (2020)
17. Voyant, C., et al.: Machine learning methods for solar radiation forecasting: a review. Renewable Energy **105**, 569–582 (2017)

Smart Meter Data Anomaly Detection Using Variational Recurrent Autoencoders with Attention

Wenjing Dai[1], Xiufeng Liu[1(✉)], Alfred Heller[2], and Per Sieverts Nielsen[1]

[1] Department of Technology, Management and Economics,
Technical University of Denmark, 2800 Kgs Lyngby, Denmark
{weda,xiuli,pernn}@dtu.dk
[2] Niras, ØStre Havnegade 12, 9000 Aalborg, Denmark
ahr@niras.dk

Abstract. In the digitization of energy systems, sensors and smart meters are increasingly being used to monitor production, operation and demand. Detection of anomalies based on smart meter data is crucial to identify potential risks and unusual events at an early stage, which can serve as a reference for timely initiation of appropriate actions and improving management. However, smart meter data from energy systems often lack labels and contain noise and various patterns without distinctively cyclical. Meanwhile, the vague definition of anomalies in different energy scenarios and highly complex temporal correlations pose a great challenge for anomaly detection. Many traditional unsupervised anomaly detection algorithms such as cluster-based or distance-based models are not robust to noise and not fully exploit the temporal dependency in a time series as well as other dependencies amongst multiple variables (sensors). This paper proposes an unsupervised anomaly detection method based on a Variational Recurrent Autoencoder with attention mechanism. with "dirty" data from smart meters, our method pre-detects missing values and global anomalies to shrink their contribution while training. This paper makes a quantitative comparison with the VAE-based baseline approach and four other unsupervised learning methods, demonstrating its effectiveness and superiority. This paper further validates the proposed method by a real case study of detecting the anomalies of water supply temperature from an industrial heating plant.

Keywords: Anomaly detection · Variational autoencoder · Smart meter data · Attention mechanism

1   Introduction

To achieve sustainable development, effective management of production, distribution, transport and consumption of smart energy systems has become a focus for researchers and engineers [23]. As the operations of energy systems can be disrupted by various events such as equipment failures, power outages

© The Author(s), under exclusive license to Springer Nature Switzerland AG 2022
F. Sanfilippo et al. (Eds.): INTAP 2021, CCIS 1616, pp. 311–324, 2022.
https://doi.org/10.1007/978-3-031-10525-8_25

and malfunctions, energy systems have started to use Internet of Things (IoT) sensors and smart meters for monitoring and automation. Therefore, anomaly detection in smart meter data plays an important role in ensuring the healthy operation of an energy system. When performing anomaly detection, three types of anomalies are widely detected: global, contextual and collective anomalies [7]. In this paper, we mainly focus on global and contextual anomalies (defined in Sect. 3.1) from smart meter data. Global and contextual anomalies may indicate equipment failures or wrong operations. These two types of anomalies detection are needed for providing early warnings, thus reducing or avoiding economic losses. Figure 1 illustrates examples of these two types of anomalies in smart meter data.

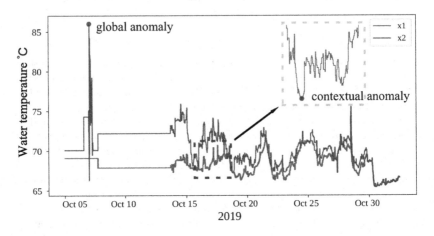

Fig. 1. A fragment of the water supply temperature data set in our paper, with global and contextual anomalies marked as red dots. (Color figure online)

However, using smart meter data to detect anomalies faces some key challenges. First, smart meter data are the time series data from production or consumption, and are characterised by different seasonal patterns and highly nonstationary. Various patterns and nonstationary data require more generic and robust anomaly detection methods. Second, smart meter data are typically of high volume, high dimensionality and lack of labeled anomalies, which necessitates the use of unsupervised or semi-supervised approaches. In addition, there are many data quality issues for the collected data, such as missing values, outliers and temporal inconsistency. How to deal with "dirty" data will affect the performance of results.

Currently, there are several algorithms for detecting anomalies in energy data, such as [6,15,22,29], but these algorithms are mainly designed to detect point anomalies and do not distinguish between global anomaly and contextual point anomaly. In addition, irregularly missing points should also be considered as anomalies, which occur very frequently in the time series of smart meters due to transmission or meter failures. It is therefore necessary to develop an effective and reliable anomaly detection model for smart energy systems.

In this paper, we propose an unsupervised anomaly detection algorithm for global and contextual anomalies in smart meter data by using variational recurrent autoencoders (VRAE) with attention. This algorithm can work without labels and takes advantage of the pre-detected global anomalies while training. It can also take advantage of the occasional labels when they are available.

- We adapt and extend VRAE models by taking into account anomaly detection for smart meter data. The proposed model is capable of detecting not only global anomalies but also contextual anomalies. Although the model is presented for smart meter data, it can also be applied to other time series with time dependency.
- We propose the method for minimising the impact of global anomalies and missing points on latent variables in the model training, using linear interpolation and an improved evidence lower bound function, which can improve the model performance.
- We evaluate the method comprehensively by comparison with other baseline methods using a synthetic data set; and present a real world case study for the proposed method.

2   Related Work

2.1   Traditional Anomaly Detection Methods

Traditional anomaly detection methods include the traditional statistical approaches, e.g., [10,16,19,33,41,43], the clustering-based approaches, e.g., [8, 42], the prediction-based approaches, e.g., [20–22], the nearest neighbour approaches, e.g. [5,16,18], the dimensionality reduction approaches, e.g. [10,32] and other complementary models. These approaches can show good performance and effectiveness for their specific applications. However, due to the wide variation of energy data such as patterns, domain expert effort is often required to select a suitable detector for a particular type of anomaly. In addition, since most existing methods have their constraints or limitations in terms of parameterisation, interpretability and generalisability, a detection framework based on ensemble learning cannot even help to achieve better results.

2.2   Unsupervised Deep Learning Models

A rich body of literature presents unsupervised learning algorithms for detecting anomalies using deep learning techniques, among many others, which include [11, 26,27,38,40]. Deep learning approaches can be further categorised into predictive models [27], VAE [1], Generative Adversarial Networks (GAN) [9] and VRNN [35]. For modeling sequential data such as time series, Recurrent Neural Networks (RNNs) show their advantage over others because of their capability to model long-term temporal dependence. RNNs (e.g. the Long and Short Term Memory (LSTM) [14] and the Gated Recurrent Unit (GRU)) introduce the so-called internal self-looping states in the network, which can accumulate information from the past. [31] combined ARIMA and LSTM to train a prediction model for energy anomaly detection. In this paper, we introduce LSTM into our neural network architecture for modeling the temporal dependence of time series.

VAE has been successfully applied in several applications for anomaly detection tasks, including [30,36,38,39]. Hollingsworth et al. [15] proposed an autoencoder-based ensemble method to detect anomalies in building energy consumption data and evaluated their performance among reconstruction ability, high-level feature quality and computation efficiency. Compared to autoencoders, the variational inference technique [12] implements the encoding of the latent space as a distribution and enables the probabilistic reconstruction of a single generated value by a probabilistic model [1]. However, in the field of smart energy, few applications have previously used generative models to detect anomalies. Existing work based on VAE is not designed for energy smart meter data and requires domain experts in detectiong different types of anomalies.

2.3   Attention Mechanism for Deep Learning Models

Attention mechanisms [3,24,37] have been introduced to obtain state-of-the-art performance when modeling sequences such as natural language processing. Attention mechanism can model the relationship regarding different positions of a single sequence or across multiple sequences to obtain representative sequences. For example, Pereira et al. [29] used weighted sum of all encoder hidden states as the attention, which are then fitted to the decoder. The attention mechanism can, therefore, tackle the weakness of processing a long sequence by neural networks. However, there are still limited attempts and their application in anomaly detection for energy time series data which exists temporal interdependency at different time positions.

3   Problem Statement and Proposed Method

3.1   Problem Statement

Given historical data of n-dimensional time series with length T, i.e. $X = (\mathbf{x}_1, \cdots, \mathbf{x}_n)^T \in \mathbb{R}^{n \times T}$, our method is capable of detecting two types of anomalies:

(a) **Global anomalies**: given an input time-series X, a global anomaly is a timestamp-value pair $\langle t, x_t \rangle$ where the observed value is far from the rest of the data.

(b) **Contextual anomalies**: given an input time-series X, a contextual anomaly is a timestamp-value pair $\langle t, x_t \rangle$ where the observed value differs significantly from its neighbours in the same context, but is not a global anomaly.

3.2   Proposed Method

Global Anomaly Detection and Labeling. Data collected from real world applications are often dirty, which require preprocessing before being used for analysis. The training process for the anomaly detection should ideally learn from "normal" data, rather than learn from abnormal data. One of challenges of unsupervised anomaly detection methods is how to minimise the impact of abnormal data as much as possible. Hence, we detect global anomalies and sequential missing points and label them as anomalies before training. We use a statistical method based on histograms of each dimension. For multivariate time series with n dimensions, we first construct a univariate histogram with k bins for each dimension. Second, the frequency of samples in each histogram (dimension) is used as a density estimate of those samples. The higher the score of a sample, the higher the probability of anomaly.

For the missing points, we categorise them into the following two categories: single missing values and sequential missing values. For single missing values, we fill them with synthetically generated values using linear interpolation. For sequential missing values, the imputation error for missing data is accumulated according to the length of the missing subsequences. As it is difficult to generate sequential data that follow their original patterns, we therefore fill these sequential missing values with zeros and label them as anomalies.

Network Architecture and Implementation. Figure 2 shows the overall neural network architecture of the proposed model. As shown in the figure, multivariate time series data come from smart meters of industries. Given multivariate time series X, we first use a sliding window with length W to segment the time series into subsequences e.g. $(x_{t-W+1}, \ldots, x_t)$. The subsequences are then used as the input of the proposed model which uses a variational auto-encoder architecture with LSTM to learn normal patterns from training data. The right side of Fig. 2 shows the detailed network structure with attention mechanism. The network structure is a variational recurrent auto-encoder which is composed of an encoder and a decoder.

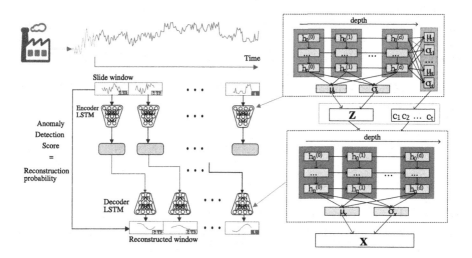

Fig. 2. The network architecture of the proposed model.

In the VRAE, the encoder compresses the input time series into the fixed-length latent representation z based on the variational distribution $q_\phi(z \mid x)$ and outputs the hidden states $\mathbf{h}_t$ as the summary of the past information until the time at t. The latent variables z are drawn from a distribution with a given prior $p_\theta(z)$, which is usually a multivariate unit with Gaussian distribution $\mathcal{N}(0, \mathbf{I})$. Here, we assume the prior distribution of the latent variables z as a multivariate normal distribution, $p_\theta(z) \sim \mathcal{N}(0, \mathbf{I})$. The outputs of the encoder are the parameters ($\boldsymbol{\mu}_z$ and $\boldsymbol{\sigma}_z$) for the posterior $q_\phi(z \mid x)$. The approximate posterior $q_\phi(z \mid x)$ of z is diagonal Gaussian $q_\phi(z \mid x) \sim \mathcal{N}\left(\boldsymbol{\mu}_\mathbf{z}, \boldsymbol{\sigma}_\mathbf{z}^2 \mathbf{I}\right)$, where the mean $\boldsymbol{\mu}_\mathbf{z}$ and the co-variance $\Sigma_\mathbf{z} = \boldsymbol{\sigma}_\mathbf{z}^2 \mathbf{I}$ are derived from the two fully connected layers ($\boldsymbol{\mu}_\mathbf{z}$ and $\boldsymbol{\sigma}_\mathbf{z}$ layers in Fig. 2) with Linear and SoftPlus activations, respectively. The latent variable $\mathbf{z}$ (chosen to be K dimensions) are then sampled from the approximate distribution with reparameterization trick, $\mathbf{z} = \boldsymbol{\mu}_\mathbf{z} + \boldsymbol{\sigma}_\mathbf{z} \cdot \boldsymbol{\epsilon}$, where $\boldsymbol{\epsilon} \sim \text{Normal}(\mathbf{0}, \mathbf{I})$ is an independent random variable used for feasible stochastic gradient descent. The decoder also uses a LSTM network to reconstruct the data from latent variable $\mathbf{z}$ through the generation distribution $p_\theta(x \mid z)$, and outputs the parameters ($\boldsymbol{\mu}_\mathbf{x}$ and $\boldsymbol{\sigma}_\mathbf{x}$) of $p_\theta(x \mid z)$.

The objective of a VAE is to maximise the evidence lower bound (ELBO), $\mathcal{L}(\theta, \phi; \mathbf{x})$, which can be written as follows:

$$
\begin{aligned}
\log p_\theta(\mathbf{x}) &\geq \mathcal{L}(\theta, \phi; \mathbf{x}) \\
&= E_{q_\phi(\mathbf{z}|\mathbf{x})}\left[\log p_\theta(\mathbf{x} \mid \mathbf{z})\right] - \mathcal{D}_{\text{KL}}\left(q_\phi(\mathbf{z} \mid \mathbf{x}) \| p_\theta(\mathbf{z})\right)
\end{aligned}
\tag{1}
$$

where the ϕ and θ are the parameters of the encoder and decoder, respectively. The first item of the right-hand side of the equation is the reconstruction loss, which can be approximated by Monte Carlo integration [1]. The second item D_{KL} is the Kullback-Leibler (KL) divergence between the approximate posterior and the prior distribution of the latent variable z.

To tackle the posterior collapse in the variational inference and the weakness in a long sequence, we additionally apply self-attention mechanism that promotes interaction between the inference model and the generative model. The attention model extracts a context vector based on all hidden states encoded from the input time series. The LSTM encoder computes all hidden states $\{\mathbf{s}_i\}_{i=1}^{T_x}$ from the input time series, while the LSTM decoder estimates the hidden state $\mathbf{h}_t$ at each time t by a recurrent function using the previous hidden state $\mathbf{h}_{t-1}$ and the context vector, denoted by:

$$
\mathbf{h}_t = f\left(\mathbf{h}_{t-1}, \mathbf{c}_t\right) \quad \text{where} \quad \mathbf{c}_t = \sum_{i=1}^{T_x} \alpha_{ti} \mathbf{s}_i
\tag{2}
$$

where $\mathbf{c}_t$ is the context vector containing the weighted sum of all source hidden states $\mathbf{s}_i$ encoded from the input time series. The attention weights, $\boldsymbol{\alpha}_t = \{\alpha_{ti}\}_{i=1}^{T_x}$, are computed by the score function of measuring the similarity between the hidden states $\mathbf{s}_t$ at time t in the encoder and all hidden states $\{\mathbf{s}_i\}_{i=1}^{T_x}$ of the last recurrent layer in the encoder. The self-attention models the relevance of each pair of the hidden states of different time instances in the encoder. Here, we use the scaled dot-product similarity [37] as the score function because of its high learning efficiency for a large input.

Due to the bypass phenomenon [4], the variational latent space may not learn much due to the powerful attention mechanism. We therefore use the variational attention mechanism to model context vectors as probability distributions. We choose the prior distribution of the context vectors c_t as the Gaussian standard distribution, i.e., $c_t \sim \text{Normal}(\mathbf{0}, \mathbf{I})$. We do the same for the latent variables. The encoder first computes the deterministic context vector $c_t = \sum_{i=1}^{T_x} \alpha_{ti} s_i$, then passes it to the linear layers to compute the parameters of the approximate posterior $q_\phi^{(a)}(c_t \mid \mathbf{x}) \sim \text{Normal}(\boldsymbol{\mu}_{c_t}, \boldsymbol{\Sigma}_{c_t}), \boldsymbol{\mu}_{c_t}$ and $\boldsymbol{\Sigma}_{c_t}$. The decoder takes the concatenation of the sampled z and the sampled c_t from their approximated posteriors as the input, and generates the parameters of $p_\theta(x \mid z)$ as the output.

3.3   Loss Function – ELBO+

With the variational attention mechanism, the variational lower bound $\mathcal{L}(\theta, \phi; \mathbf{x})$ in Eq. 1 becomes:

$$\mathcal{L}(\theta, \phi, \boldsymbol{x}) = E_{z, c \sim q_\phi(z, c \mid x)} \left[\log p_\theta(\boldsymbol{x} \mid \boldsymbol{z}, \boldsymbol{c}) \right] \\ - \mathcal{D}_{\text{KL}}(q_\phi(\boldsymbol{z}, \boldsymbol{c} \mid \boldsymbol{x}) \| p(\boldsymbol{z}, \boldsymbol{c})) \tag{3}$$

To minimise the effects of learning from abnormal data, we mitigate the contribution of global anomalies (pre-detected) and missing points by introducing a weighted vector, $\boldsymbol{\beta} = \{\beta_i\}_{i=1}^{T_x}$, to $\log p_\theta(\boldsymbol{x} \mid \boldsymbol{z}, \boldsymbol{c})$ shown in Eq. 4. If x_i is an anomaly, then $\beta_i = 0$, otherwise $\beta_i = 1$. We name this improved ELBO as ELBO+, where λ_{kl} weights the reconstruction loss and the KL loss and η_a weights the latent KL loss and the attention KL loss. The training objective is to maximise the ELBO in Eq. 4, which is the negative of the loss function for VAE. Theoretically, the anomalies present can also influence the KL losses, but the hyperparameters λ_{kl} and η_a can reduce the ratio of KL losses. We therefore do not reduce their contribution to the KL loss.

$$\mathcal{L}(\theta, \phi, \boldsymbol{x})^+ = E_{z \sim q_\phi^{(z)}(z \mid x), c_t \sim q_\phi^{(a)}(c_t \mid x)} \left[\boldsymbol{\beta} \log p_\theta(\boldsymbol{x} \mid \boldsymbol{z}, \boldsymbol{c}) \right] \\ - \lambda_{kl} \left[\mathcal{D}_{\text{KL}} \left(q_\phi^{(z)}(\boldsymbol{z} \mid \boldsymbol{x}) \| p(\boldsymbol{z}) \right) \right. \\ \left. - \eta_a \sum_{t=1}^{T} \mathcal{D}_{\text{KL}} \left(q_\phi^{(a)}(\boldsymbol{c_t} \mid \boldsymbol{x}) \| p(\boldsymbol{c_t}) \right) \right] \tag{4}$$

3.4   Anomaly Detection

Since the generative model reconstructs the input time series based on the probability distribution, it can derive different outputs according to the probability distribution. Normally, rare events (anomalies) have lower probabilities. The rarity of events can be measured by the reconstruction probability, $\log p_\theta(\boldsymbol{x} \mid \boldsymbol{z})$, which can be calculated through the Monte Carlo method.

The encoder first generates the parameters of the approximate posterior distribution $\log p_\phi(z \mid x)$ using the test data. Then, sampled latent variables (L samples) are derived from the approximate posterior distribution. The sampling strategy for latent variables takes into account the variability of the latent space in order to increase the robustness of anomaly detection. For each sample, the decoder outputs the parameters of the approximate posterior distribution $\log p_\theta(x \mid z)$. In the end, the average reconstruction probability of each sample is calculated from the output parameters, i.e.,

$$E_{z \sim q_\phi(z|x))}\left[\log p_\theta(x \mid z)\right] \approx \frac{1}{L} \sum_{l=1}^{L} \log p_\theta(x \mid \mu_l, \sigma_l) \tag{5}$$

where μ_l and σ_l are the parameters as the output from the decoder for the approximate distribution $\log p_\theta(x \mid z)$.

The reconstruction probabilities are then used as anomaly scores (between 0 and 1), which measure the strength of the anomaly of input values. We consider the observations whose anomaly score is greater than 0.5 as the contextual anomalies for the experiments in the next section. This value can be tuned as per the requirement of the problem.

4 Experiments

4.1 Data Sets and Experimental Setup

We use two data sets for the experiments, a synthetic data set generated by PyOD for the detection performance evaluation and a real smart meter data set about water supply temperature for district heating. In the real smart meter data set, we segment the time series into subsequences by a sliding window with a length of 168, and divide the subsequences into a training set, a validation set and a test set with a ratio of 75/15/10. We use PyTorch v1.6.0 to implement our algorithm and train the models via CPU i9-9900 and NVIDIA GTX 2080 Ti graphics cards with 16G RAM on Ubuntu 16.04. More details are included in appendices.

4.2 Evaluation by Comparison with Baselines

To evaluate our method, we compare it with 4 traditional methods and VAE-baseline using the synthetic data set, and use Precision (P), Recall (R) and F1 score ($F1$) as the metrics for the comparison. The comparing methods includes Cluster-based Local Outlier Factor (CBLOF) [13], K nearest Neighbors (KNN) [2], Principal component analysis (PCA) [34], One-class support vector machines (OCSVM) [28] and VAE-baseline [17]. The generated time series data by PyOD have 24,000 data points with 5 features, including 20% abnormal data points. The normal 20,000 points are used for training and 4,000 points for testing. Table 3 shows the hyperparameters used in our model.

From the results in Table 2, we can see that our method outperforms all others and are more effective for anomaly detection in terms of all three metrics. In general, the VAE-based networks have shown better performance in learning normal patterns from the train set. It also confirms that recurrent neural networks have a good capability to model long temporal dependency of time series (Table 1).

Table 1. Model hyperparameters

LSTM hidden layers	2
Units in hidden layers	218
Sequence length (W)	168
Latent dimensions	3
Training iterations	550
Learning rate	0.0001
Batch size	1024
Optimiser	Adam
λ_{kl}	0.01
η_a	0.01

Table 2. Performance on the synthetic dataset

Method	Metrics		
	P	R	$F1$
CBLOF	0.65	0.68	0.66
KNN	0.69	0.69	0.69
PCA	0.83	0.84	0.83
OCSVM	0.82	0.82	0.82
VAE-baseline	0.89	0.90	0.90
Ours	**0.95**	**0.93**	**0.94**

4.3 An Empirical Case Study

We next evaluate the proposed method by an empirical case study, which detects the "anomalies" in the water temperature time series from an industry district heating company. The data is recorded from 19/09/2019 11:05:00 to 11/08/2020 15:00:00 with 23 sensors in irregular minute-level, with a total of 220,097 observations for each time series. We align these fine-grained readings to hourly resolution by aggregation, and obtain 7,582 observations for each time series.

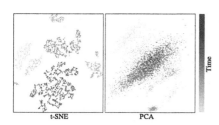

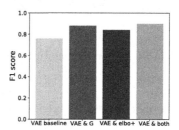

Fig. 3. Latent space visualisation of training set

Fig. 4. F1 score of different models

For visualisation purposes, we reduce the 3-dimensional latent variables of the training set to 2D and visualise them using Principal Component Analysis

(PCA) and t-distributed Stochastic Neighbour Embedding (t-SNE) [25]. Figure 3 shows the projected points of subsequences in the latent space by the dimensional reduction methods, t-SNE and PCA, respectively. The more similar subsequence are, the closer these points are placed. The color legend represents the time from the beginning (bottom) to the end (top) sequences.

Effects of ELBO+ and Pre-detected Global Anomalies. To our knowledge, minimising the impact of anomalies during training can assist the learning processing of networks. To exam the effectiveness of the pre-detected global anomalies and our modified ELBO loss function, we calculate F1 score in the test set of the real smart meter data set to compare the performance under different conditions. The F1 score is a measure of test accuracy and calculated from the precision and recall of the test. The four models are (1) VAE baseline, (2) VAE with global anomaly detection, (3) VAE with elbo+, and (4) VAE with both global anomaly detection and elbo+. Figure 4 shows that predetected global anomalies and elbo+ have a positive effect on anomaly detection and our model outperforms the VAE baseline.

From Fig. 3, the latent space has a clear tendency to group which implies there are distinct features between subsequences. Here, we gives three examples (Fig. 5) of subsequences in a time series with distinctive features. From 19/09/2019 to 12/12/2019, the transmission water temperature for district heating continuously is 74.2 °C, which is a straight line ($s1$). $s2$ is about 68.4 °C and is stationary. By contrast, $s3$ has a lower temperature and is nonstationary.

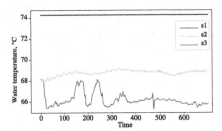 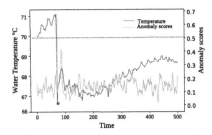

Fig. 5. Distinctive features (or patterns) in hot water temperature time series.

Fig. 6. An example of a contextual anomaly with corresponding anomaly scores.

The model outputs reconstruction probabilities of time series as anomaly scores for each point. When the anomaly score is higher than 0.5, the corresponding point is classified as an anomaly. We give an example of detected contextual anomalies in hot water temperature dataset. Figure 6 shows a contextual anomaly example and the corresponding anomaly scores of points. The red dot indicates a contextual anomalies.

5 Conclusions and Future Work

In this paper, we proposed an unsupervised anomaly detection algorithm for smart meter data using VRAE with attention mechanism. Our method can detect different types of anomalies including global and contextual anomalies. The enhanced ELBO+ function can mitigate the contribution of global anomalies and missing points. We have evaluated our method comprehensively and the results have demonstrated the effectiveness and superiority of our method. For future work, we would further improve our case study by applying a real-time architecture for online anomaly detection. We would also address dealing with concept drifts during the anomaly detection process.

Acknowledgements. The research was supported by Heat4.0 project (8090-00046A) and the project FlexSUS: Flexibility for Smart Urban Energy Systems (91352) funded by the European Union's Horizon 2020 research and innovation programme under grant agreement No 77597.

A Appendix

A.1 Data sets

We use two types of data sets for the experiments: a synthetic data set and a real smart meter data set. We use the PyOD toolkit [44] to generate synthetic data sets with anomalies. The normal data were sampled from a multivariate Gaussian distribution, while the anomalies were sampled from a uniform distribution. The generated time series data have 24,000 data points with five features, including 20% abnormal data points. The normal 20,000 points are used for training and 4,000 points for testing.

The smart meter data are the supply hot water temperature provided by a district heating company in Denmark. As there are no labels in the time series, the anomalies are detected by the unsupervised learning method. The data used are from 19/09/2019 11:05:00 to 11/08/2020 15:00:00. The time series data before 04/12/2019 09:00 have an hourly resolution, but have an irregular minute-level resolution after that time, ranging from 1 to 5 min, with a total of 220,097 observations. Therefore, we align these fine-grained readings to hourly resolution by aggregation, and obtain a total of 7,582 observations.

A.2   Experimental setup

Table 3. Model hyperparameters

LSTM hidden layers	2
Units in hidden layers	218
Sequence length (W)	168
Latent dimensions	3
Training iterations	550
Learning rate	0.0001
Batch size	1024
Optimiser	Adam
Input dimensions	5 (synthetic data), 23 (real data)
Divergence ratio λ_{kl}	0.01
Attention divergence ratio η_a	0.01

Table 3 shows the model parameters used in the experiments. We use the window size $W = 168$, as a smaller size may not be able to capture the normal patterns, while a larger size may increase the risk of overfitting. We set the latent space to 3 dimensions for visualization purposes. The encoder and decoder consist of two hidden LSTM layers, 218 units in each layer. We have tested several combinations of hyperparameters, including the number of the hidden LSTM layers, the number of hidden units in each layer, and the sequence length. However, the results do not show much difference in terms of the loss. The number of training iterations is determined based on the convergence of training loss and validation loss.

References

1. An, J., Cho, S.: Variational autoencoder based anomaly detection using reconstruction probability. Spec. Lect. IE **2**(1), 1–18 (2015)
2. Angiulli, F., Pizzuti, C.: Fast outlier detection in high dimensional spaces. In: Elomaa, T., Mannila, H., Toivonen, H. (eds.) PKDD 2002. LNCS, vol. 2431, pp. 15–27. Springer, Heidelberg (2002). https://doi.org/10.1007/3-540-45681-3_2
3. Bahdanau, D., Cho, K., Bengio, Y.: Neural machine translation by jointly learning to align and translate. arXiv preprint arXiv:1409.0473 (2014)
4. Bahuleyan, H., Mou, L., Vechtomova, O., Poupart, P.: Variational attention for sequence-to-sequence models. arXiv preprint arXiv:1712.08207 (2017)
5. Breunig, M.M., Kriegel, H.P., Ng, R.T., Sander, J.: LOF: identifying density-based local outliers. In: Proceedings of the 2000 ACM SIGMOD International Conference on Management of Data, pp. 93–104 (2000)
6. Chahla, C., Snoussi, H., Merghem, L., Esseghir, M.: A novel approach for anomaly detection in power consumption data. In: ICPRAM, pp. 483–490 (2019)
7. Chandola, V., Banerjee, A., Kumar, V.: Anomaly detection: a survey. ACM Comput. Surv. **41**(3), 1–58 (2009)

8. Chen, C., Cook, D.J.: Energy outlier detection in smart environments. In: Workshops at the Twenty-Fifth AAAI Conference on Artificial Intelligence (2011)
9. Creswell, A., White, T., Dumoulin, V., Arulkumaran, K., Sengupta, B., Bharath, A.A.: Generative adversarial networks: an overview. IEEE Sign. Process. Mag. **35**(1), 53–65 (2018)
10. Deng, J.D.: Online outlier detection of energy data streams using incremental and kernel PCA algorithms. In: 2016 IEEE 16th International Conference on Data Mining Workshops (ICDMW), pp. 390–397 (2016)
11. Fan, C., Xiao, F., Zhao, Y., Wang, J.: Analytical investigation of autoencoder-based methods for unsupervised anomaly detection in building energy data. Appl. Energy **211**, 1123–1135 (2018)
12. Goodfellow, I., Bengio, Y., Courville, A., Bengio, Y.: Deep Learning, vol. 1. MIT press, Cambridge (2016)
13. He, Z., Xu, X., Deng, S.: Discovering cluster-based local outliers. Pattern Recogn. Lett. **24**(9–10), 1641–1650 (2003)
14. Hochreiter, S., Schmidhuber, J.: Long short-term memory. Neural Comput. **9**(8), 1735–1780 (1997)
15. Hollingsworth, K., et al.: Energy anomaly detection with forecasting and deep learning. In: 2018 IEEE International Conference on Big Data (Big Data), pp. 4921–4925. IEEE (2018)
16. Jakkula, V., Cook, D.: Outlier detection in smart environment structured power datasets. In: 2010 Sixth International Conference on Intelligent Environments, pp. 29–33. IEEE (2010)
17. Kingma, D.P., Welling, M.: Auto-encoding variational bayes. arXiv preprint arXiv:1312.6114 (2013)
18. Kriegel, H.P., Kröger, P., Schubert, E., Zimek, A.: Loop: local outlier probabilities. In: Proceedings of the 18th ACM Conference on Information and Knowledge Management, pp. 1649–1652 (2009)
19. Li, X., Bowers, C.P., Schnier, T.: Classification of energy consumption in buildings with outlier detection. IEEE Trans. Ind. Electron. **57**(11), 3639–3644 (2010)
20. Liu, X., Iftikhar, N., Nielsen, P.S., Heller, A.: Online anomaly energy consumption detection using lambda architecture. In: Madria, S., Hara, T. (eds.) DaWaK 2016. LNCS, vol. 9829, pp. 193–209. Springer, Cham (2016). https://doi.org/10.1007/978-3-319-43946-4_13
21. Liu, X., Lai, Z., Wang, X., Huang, L., Nielsen, P.S.: A contextual anomaly detection framework for energy smart meter data stream. In: Yang, H., et al. (eds.) ICONIP 2020. CCIS, vol. 1333, pp. 733–742. Springer, Cham (2020). https://doi.org/10.1007/978-3-030-63823-8_83
22. Liu, X., Nielsen, P.S.: Scalable prediction-based online anomaly detection for smart meter data. Inf. Syst. **77**, 34–47 (2018)
23. Lund, H., Østergaard, P.A., Connolly, D., Mathiesen, B.V.: Smart energy and smart energy systems. Energy **137**, 556–565 (2017)
24. Luong, M.T., Pham, H., Manning, C.D.: Effective approaches to attention-based neural machine translation. arXiv preprint arXiv:1508.04025 (2015)
25. Van der Maaten, L., Hinton, G.: Visualizing data using t-SNE. J. Mach. Learn. Res. **9**(11), 2579–2605 (2008)
26. Malhotra, P., Ramakrishnan, A., Anand, G., Vig, L., Agarwal, P., Shroff, G.: Lstm-based encoder-decoder for multi-sensor anomaly detection. arXiv preprint arXiv:1607.00148 (2016)
27. Malhotra, P., Vig, L., Shroff, G., Agarwal, P.: Long short term memory networks for anomaly detection in time series. In: Proceedings, vol. 89, pp. 89–94. Presses universitaires de Louvain (2015)

28. Manevitz, L.M., Yousef, M.: One-class SVMs for document classification. J. Mach. Learn. Res. **2**(12), 139–154 (2001)
29. Pereira, J., Silveira, M.: Unsupervised anomaly detection in energy time series data using variational recurrent autoencoders with attention. In: 2018 17th IEEE International Conference on Machine Learning and Applications (ICMLA), pp. 1275–1282. IEEE (2018)
30. Pol, A.A., Berger, V., Germain, C., Cerminara, G., Pierini, M.: Anomaly detection with conditional variational autoencoders. In: 2019 18th IEEE International Conference On Machine Learning And Applications (ICMLA), pp. 1651–1657. IEEE (2019)
31. Santolamazza, A., Cesarotti, V., Introna, V.: Anomaly detection in energy consumption for condition-based maintenance of compressed air generation systems: an approach based on artificial neural networks. IFAC-PapersOnLine **51**(11), 1131–1136 (2018)
32. Schölkopf, B., Smola, A., Müller, K.R.: Nonlinear component analysis as a kernel eigenvalue problem. Neural Comput. **10**(5), 1299–1319 (1998)
33. Seem, J.E.: Using intelligent data analysis to detect abnormal energy consumption in buildings. Energy Buildings **39**(1), 52–58 (2007)
34. Shyu, M.L., Chen, S.C., Sarinnapakorn, K., Chang, L.: A novel anomaly detection scheme based on principal component classifier. Miami Univ Coral Gables FL Dept of Electrical and Computer Engineering, Technical report (2003)
35. Sölch, M., Bayer, J., Ludersdorfer, M., van der Smagt, P.: Variational inference for on-line anomaly detection in high-dimensional time series. arXiv preprint arXiv:1602.07109 (2016)
36. Su, Y., Zhao, Y., Niu, C., Liu, R., Sun, W., Pei, D.: Robust anomaly detection for multivariate time series through stochastic recurrent neural network. In: Proceedings of the 25th ACM SIGKDD International Conference on Knowledge Discovery & Data Mining, pp. 2828–2837 (2019)
37. Vaswani, A., et al.: Attention is all you need. In: Advances in neural information processing systems, pp. 5998–6008 (2017)
38. Xu, H., et al.: Unsupervised anomaly detection via variational auto-encoder for seasonal kpis in web applications. In: Proceedings of the 2018 World Wide Web Conference, pp. 187–196 (2018)
39. Zhang, C., Chen, Y.: Time series anomaly detection with variational autoencoders. arXiv preprint arXiv:1907.01702 (2019)
40. Zhang, C., et al.: A deep neural network for unsupervised anomaly detection and diagnosis in multivariate time series data. In: Proceedings of the AAAI Conference on Artificial Intelligence, vol. 33, pp. 1409–1416 (2019)
41. Zhang, Y., Chen, W., Black, J.: Anomaly detection in premise energy consumption data. In: 2011 IEEE Power and Energy Society General Meeting, pp. 1–8. IEEE (2011)
42. Zhao, J., Liu, K., Wang, W., Liu, Y.: Adaptive fuzzy clustering based anomaly data detection in energy system of steel industry. Inf. Sci. **259**, 335–345 (2014)
43. Zhao, Y., Lehman, B., Ball, R., Mosesian, J., de Palma, J.: Outlier detection rules for fault detection in solar photovoltaic arrays. In: 2013 Twenty-Eighth Annual IEEE Applied Power Electronics Conference and Exposition (APEC), pp. 2913–2920 (2013)
44. Zhao, Y., Nasrullah, Z., Li, Z.: Pyod: A python toolbox for scalable outlier detection. arXiv preprint arXiv:1901.01588 (2019)

Detecting the Linear and Non-linear Causal Links for Disturbances in the Power Grid

Odin Foldvik Eikeland[1] , Filippo Maria Bianchi[2,3] ,
Inga Setså Holmstrand[4], Sigurd Bakkejord[4], and Matteo Chiesa[1,5]

[1] Department of Physics and Technology, UiT-The Arctic University of Norway,
9037 Tromsø, Norway
[2] Department of Mathematics and Statistics, UiT-The Arctic University of Norway,
9037 Tromsø, Norway
`filippo.m.bianchi@uit.no`
[3] NORCE, The Norwegian Research Centre, 9037 Tromsø, Norway
[4] Arva Power Company, 9024 Tromsø, Norway
[5] Laboratory for Energy and NanoScience (LENS), Khalifa University of Science and Technology, Masdar Institute Campus, 127788 Abu Dhabi, United Arab Emirates

Abstract. Unscheduled power disturbances cause severe consequences for customers and grid operators. To avoid such events, it is important to identify the causes and localize the sources of the disturbances in the power distribution network. In this work, we focus on a specific power grid in the Arctic region of Northern Norway that experiences an increased frequency of failures of unspecified origin. First, we built a data set by collecting relevant meteorological data and power consumption measurements logged by power-quality meters. Then, we exploited machine-learning techniques to detect disturbances in the power supply and to identify the most significant variables that should be monitored. Specifically, we framed the problem of detecting faults as a supervised classification and used both linear and non-linear classifiers. Linear models achieved the highest classification performances and were able to predict the failures reported with a weighted F1-score of 0.79. The linear models identified the amount of flicker and wind speed of gust as the most significant variables in explaining the power disturbances. Our results could provide valuable information to the distribution system operator for implementing strategies to prevent and mitigate incoming failures.

Keywords: Energy analytics · Anomaly detection · Power quality metering · Unbalanced classification

1 Introduction

Unscheduled power distribution disruptions are often a major problem for customers and grid operators since they affect everyone connected to the power grid

F. Sanfilippo et al. (Eds.): INTAP 2021, CCIS 1616, pp. 325–336, 2022.
https://doi.org/10.1007/978-3-031-10525-8_26

from single households to large industrial players [8,16,18,27]. The distribution system operator (DSO) is contractually obliged to provide a reliable power supply and compensate customers affected by any possible power interruptions [17]. For the end-use customers, power failures might have complex and adverse socio-economic consequences in communities that are heavily reliant on the electricity supply to satisfy their needs [13,29]. To satisfy the customer's requirements, the DSOs must implement the energy management plans that account for the technology, and the infrastructure required to meet the expected demand.

In this study, we focus on a specific power grid in the Arctic region of Northern Norway where the successful transformation of the local food industries into an international company has caused a huge increase in electricity demand. The industry is characterized by fish processing activities that are highly seasonal and that require stable power quality due to the presence of many automatized machines in the production line. Even minor power disturbances in the power supply trigger significantly long interruptions since the whole production line needs to be reset. In particular, for every short-term power interruption that occurs, 40 min to 1 h might pass before resuming production.

The consequences of the power disturbances are exacerbated by the topology of the energy network under analysis, which has radial distribution. Therefore, it is important to develop strategies to increase the reliability of the power grid that ensure the growth of local industries.

One way to improve the reliability of the power distribution is to build a new power grid that can handle larger power demand. However, this is costly, time-consuming, has a huge environmental impact, and contradicts the vision of better utilizing the current electricity grid infrastructure[1] [23]. An alternative solution is to limit the failures and strengthen only the most vulnerable parts of the grid, but this requires to first identify the factors triggering power interruptions.

The identification of causing factors for failures in the power grid has proven to be a major challenge for the DSO [27]. However, the increased availability of energy-related data makes it now possible to exploit advanced data analytics techniques that allow to develop strategies to improve the reliability of the power grid [4–7,11,15,26]. Recent studies based on statistical data analysis and machine learning (ML), indicated that extreme weather conditions are often the major cause of failures in the power grid [10,19,20,22,25,28]. However, it is likely that other factors than weather conditions could affect the power quality. The impact of the increased strain on the power grid as a consequence of the increased electrification in the society were investigated in [2]. The study in [14], proposed a methodology to predict power failures by analyzing data from advanced electricity meters. The authors concluded that incipient power interruptions are easier to predict than earth failures and voltage dips. The challenge of detecting earth failures was addressed in [1], which proposed a solution to detect failures by using a specific power distribution system simulator.

Most of the studies mentioned so far are proof of concepts and the results are shown on synthetic data or benchmark power systems. In this work, we tackle

---

[1] https://www.miljodirektoratet.no/publikasjoner/2020/januar-2020/klimakur2030/.

a real-case study and we explore a wider spectrum of potential causing factors for power failures. We consider explanatory variables that are divided into two groups: meteorological and power consumption data. We exploit ML techniques to detect the power disturbances and to identify the most explanatory features among high-resolution power-quality metering data and weather variables.

This paper extends our previous study, which analyzed failure data from the year 2020 [12]. Previously, we exploited statistical and ML techniques to detect the causes of power interruptions and identified wind speed of gust and local industry activity to be the main controlling parameters. However, there were important limitations in the data collected in the 2020 failure-detection study:

1. The machinery of the local industries connected to the power grid is so sensitive to the power quality that they experience failures that are not registered in the failure-reporting system of the DSO. Since DSOs are contractually obliged to provide a reliable power supply to all their customers, is fundamental for them to gain better insight into the actual power quality to fill the gap between the customer's experiences and the DSO.
2. The resolution of data in 2020 was too low (1-hour) to get detailed information about how power consumption truly affects power quality.

To address these issues, new power quality meters were installed 19 February 2021 in the particular location of interest. These meters log data every minute, register every small voltage variations, and provide fundamental information (the specific phase where the failure is registered on, the magnitude of voltage variation, the amount of transients and flickers) about the current quality in the power grid. As shown in the experimental results, standard ML techniques for classification allow to detect most of the power disturbances, showing that high-resolution data from power quality meters in conjunction with weather data are highly informative variables to detect and localize power disturbances. Finally, by looking at the parameters of the linear classifiers, we rank the variables that are the most important in explaining the power disturbances.

2   Case Study and Reported Failures

2.1   Investigated Power Grid

The power grid analyzed in this study is a radial distribution system serving an Arctic community located approximately at (69.257°N, 17.589°E). Arva Power Company, the DSO of the power grid, has named this specific grid as SVAN22LY1 [3]. Figure 1 shows a overview of the whole SVAN22LY1 grid, indicated by green dots. The SVAN22LY1 grid spans over 60 km from south to the northernmost point and has several branches to various communities towards the north. There are 978 unique utility poles (marked by green dots in Fig. 1) that support the power lines. The black boxes in Fig. 1 represent the electric transformer stations connected to the power grids. The red lines represent a

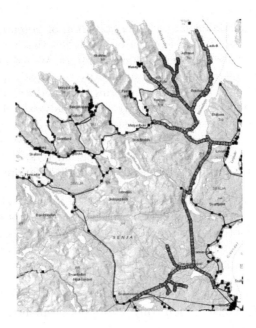

Fig. 1. The SVAN22LY1 power grid. The power is distributed towards the north from the south. Each green dot represents a unique position of a utility pole. (Color figure online)

power grid with an operating voltage of 66 kV, while the blue lines represent a power grid with an operating voltage of 22 kV. The SVAN22LY1 radial grid covered by green dots has a operating voltage of 22 kV [3]. The largest customers connected to the SVAN22LY1 grid are located at the end of the northernmost point of the radial.

The total energy demand in the Arctic community where the grid is located is dominated by the load consumption of the local industry. The industry has electrical machines that are sensitive to stable power quality and a minor disturbance in power quality could bring the production line to halt.

2.2   Reported Failures

The reported failures used in this study is logged by a power-quality (PQ) metering system. In our former study on failure detection [12], the failure data was based on a metering system that reports failures from substation monitoring. That metering system only reports events failure events when there is a power outage (90% drop in voltage magnitude from normal) on all phases in the three-phase system. However, machines are very sensitive to instabilities in the power quality and even a minor disturbance in voltage magnitude could result in production stop. Consequently, there was a mismatch between the logged failures in the substation monitoring system, and what is being experienced by the local industries.

To address this issue, in February 2021 the Arva power company installed a PQ metering system in proximity of the local industries to continuously measure the power quality. The PQ metering system reports all incidents with a voltage variation of $\pm 10\%$ from the nominal values on each phase of a three-phase system with phases A, B, C. According to the standard definition, all variations of $\pm 10\%$ from normal conditions are defined as a voltage variation and a drop larger than 10% is referred to as a voltage dip [9]. Voltage dips could provoke tripping of sensitive components such as industrial machines. For the DSO, it is fundamental to identify the causing factors for such voltage dips to implement strategies to prevent and mitigate incoming failures.

3   Methodology

To identify the causing factors for the failures in SVAN22LY1, several potentially interesting variables are collected. The variables can be divided into two groups, weather-related and power-related failures, and are described in detail in the following.

3.1   Weather Measurements

The weather variables that are considered relevant in causing power failures are: wind speed of gust, wind direction, temperature, pressure, humidity, and precipitation. Similarly to our previous study [12], the weather data are collected from areas that are more exposed to harsh weather conditions, such as hills and cliffs near the sea coast. To collect the weather-data in the Arctic region of interest, we used the AROME-Arctic weather model[2]. This model is developed by the meteorological institute of Norway (MET) and provides reanalysis of historical weather data since November 2015 with a spatial resolution of 2.5 km and a temporal resolution of 1 h. To import the variables, we use the coordinates from the weather exposed areas as input to the AROME-Arctic model.

3.2   Load Measurements

It is reasonable to assume that some types of failure are not caused by weather phenomena, but originates by external factors that influence the power flows on the grid. To model these effects, 6 different power-related variables from the largest industry connected to SVAN22LY1 are collected. The variables selected as relevant to explain power failures are: difference in frequency, voltage imbalance, difference in active and reactive power, minimum power factor, and, finally, the amount of flicker in the system. All variables are metered on three different phases (phases A, B, and C).

A *change in the power frequency* could be caused if there is an imbalance between energy production and consumption in the system. If there is a change

---

[2] https://www.met.no/en/projects/The-weather-model-AROME-Arctic.

in the power frequency (50 Hz is the normal frequency), the imbalance could cause power disturbances for the end-use customers.

Voltage imbalance is a voltage variation in the power system in which the voltage magnitudes or the phase angle between the different phases are not equal. It is believed that rapid changes (big changes within seconds/minutes) in power consumption at large industries could affect the power quality. Therefore, the *difference in active and reactive power* for each phase within each minute is computed. If the difference is large, there is a high activity at the industries, which are reported by the locals to result in larger probability for failures.

The *minimum power factor* represents the relationship between the amount of active-and reactive power in the system. If the minimum power factor is low, there is increased amount of reactive power in the system. In the end, the amount of flicker in the system are collected.

Flicker is considered as a phenomena in the power system and are closely connected to voltage fluctuations over a certain time frame [24]. A voltage fluctuation is a regular change in voltage that happens when machinery that requires a high load is starting. In addition, rapid changes in load demand could cause voltage fluctuations. If there are several start-up situations, or the load varies significantly during a given time frame, it will be measured a high amount of flicker in the system. The amount of flicker is particularly relevant in the industry considered in this study, as they have several large machines that require high loads and have a cyclical varying load pattern. In this study, the time frame of the flicker is 10-minutes, which is the standard for measuring the short-term flicker [17].

The resolution from the PQ metering system are in a 1-minute resolution with real-time logging of failures. To streamline the presentation of our findings, only the results from phase A are visualized since there are no significant differences with the observations from phases B and C.

3.3   Dataset Construction

The final dataset consist of 6 different energy-related variables and 6 different weather variables. The variables analyzed are summarized in Table 1.

Once the dataset with all variables is constructed, we model each data sample as a pair $\{\mathbf{x}, y\}$, where $\mathbf{x} \in \mathbb{R}^{12}$ is a vector containing the value of the 12 features at a given time and y is a binary label indicating if a power failure occurred ($y = 1$) or if the power grid operates at normal conditions ($y = 0$). The binary variable divides the dataset into two classes: a minority class, the failures, and a majority class, the non-failures, i.e., normal conditions.

The PQ metering system have 1-minute resolution, while the weather data have 1-hour resolution. To align the temporal resolution of the different types of variable, the power consumption data are sub-sampled by taking one sample every 60. As an alternative sub-sampling technique, we tested taking the average of the values within each batch of 60 consecutive samples of power measurements. However, the results did not change significantly and, therefore, the former sub-sampling method was used. In the final dataset, there are 90 samples with $y = 1$

Table 1. Variables analyzed to detect failures in the SVAN22LY1 power grid

Feature ID	Weather variables
1	Wind speed of gust
2	Wind direction
3	Temperature
4	Pressure
5	Humidity
6	Precipitation
	Power variables
7	Difference in frequency
8	Difference in voltage imbalance
9	Difference in active power
10	Minimum power factor
11	Difference in reactive power
12	Flicker

representing reported failure (10% drop and below in voltage magnitude), and 1,647 samples with $y = 0$ representing normal conditions without any power disturbance.

3.4   Classification Strategy

In this study, we frame the failure detection in the SVAN22LY1 grid as a classification problem and test different linear and non-linear classifiers. All models are implemented in Python with the scikit-learn library [21].

Linear Classifiers. The first linear model is a Ridge regression classifier, which first converts the target values into $\{-1, 1\}$ and then treats problem as a regression task. The second model is Logistic regression, which uses a logistic function to predict a binary variable. The third model is the Linear Support Vector Classification model (LinearSVC), which is a type of Support Vector Machine (SVM) with a linear kernel.

Due to the strong class imbalance, we configure each model to assign a class weight that is inversely proportional to the number of samples in each class. In this way, errors on the underrepresented class are penalized much more than errors on the larger class, which in our case represent the nominal condition. The linear models are configured using the default hyperparameters in the scikit-learn implementation.

One advantage of using linear classifiers is that they construct a decision boundary directly in the input space, which allow to easily interpret the decision process of the classifier. The linear models assign a weight w_i to each feature x_i in the input space: the higher w_i, the more the values of x_i impact the classification outcome. Therefore, looking at the magnitude of the weights w_i is a simple strategy to estimate the features importance for the classification task.

Non-linear Classifiers. We use three different non-linear classifiers. The first two are an SVM classifier with class weight proportional to class size, and an one-class SVM classifier. Both SVM classifiers are equipped with a radial basis kernel function. In addition, we use a Multi-layer perceptron (MLP) as the third classifier.

Non-linear models are generally more sensitive to the selection of the hyper-parameters. For the SVC classifier, we optimize the kernel width γ and the regularization parameter C, which is the weight of the L_2 penalty. For the one-class SVM, we optimize the kernel width γ and ν, a parameter that balances the training errors and the number of support vectors. Finally, for the MLP classifier we use ReLU activations, the Adam optimizer with initial learning rate $1e-3$, and batch size 200. The hyperparameters that are optimized in the MLP are the number and size of the hidden layer and the weight of the L_2 regularization term.

Model Selection and Performance Evaluation. To evaluate the model performance we first shuffle the data and then perform a stratified k-fold, with $k = 5$. In each fold, 80% of the data are used for training and the remaining 20% is used as test set. Before training the models, the input values $\mathbf{x}$ are normalized by subtracting the mean and dividing by the standard deviation computed on the training set. The training set is used to fit the model parameters by minimizing the classification loss. Once the optimization procedure has converged, its performance is evaluated on the test set. The average classification performance obtained on the 5 folds is reported as the overall performance of the classification model.

Measuring Classification Performance. The classification performance is measured by looking at the confusion matrix, which reports the following quantities: True Negatives (correctly identified non-failures), False Positives (predicted failures, while no failures happens), False Negatives (misses a failure), and finally the True Positives which is the number of failures correctly identified.

To quantify the performance with a single value we use a weighted F1 score:

$$F1 = 2 \cdot \frac{\text{precision} \cdot \text{recall}}{\text{precision} + \text{recall}} = \frac{\text{TP}}{\text{TP} + \frac{\text{FP+FN}}{2}}, \tag{1}$$

where TP, FP, and FN are the true positives, false positives, and false negatives, respectively. Due to the strong class imbalance, in this study we compute a weighted F1 score, i.e., we weight the F1-score obtained for each class by the number of samples from that class and then we compute the average.

4   Results

4.1   Classification Scores and Feature Selection

The performance achieved by each classificator are reported in Table 2 in terms of average Weighted F1 score and the average number of TN, FP, FN, and TP obtained across the 5 folds. Note that the TN, FP, FN, and TP are rounded to the closest integer.

Table 2. Classification score for different models

Classifier	TN	FP	FN	TP	Weighted F1 score
Linear					
Logistic regression	273	56	5	13	0.775
Ridge classifier	271	58	4	14	0.792
LinearSVC	272	57	5	13	0.788
Non-linear					
SVM	273	56	4	14	0.804
One-class SVM	2	327	3	15	0.591
MLP	325	3	6	12	0.793

The classification results show that there are no strong differences. The non-linear SVM classifier achieves top performance with a weighted F1 score of 0.804, followed by the MLP and the Ridge Classifier that achieve weighted F1 scores 0.793 and 0.792, respectively. Interestingly, the one-class SVM performs worse than any other model in terms of weighted F1 score, as it finds way too many FP but, on the other hand, is the model that finds the least FN on the test set. In the case study focused in this work, the main goal is to detect as many failures as possible, meaning that solutions with very few FN (missed detection of power failures) should be preferred. However, there is still a tradeoff to be made with the percentage of FP, i.e., the false alarms. Obviously, a model that classifies everything as a power failure is not useful in practice.

Finally, it interesting to notice that linear and non-linear models achieve similar performance. This suggests that the two classes are mostly linearly separable, i.e., most of the data samples can be separated reasonably well by an hyper-plane in the input features space. On the other hand, the data samples that are misclassified are likely very overlapping across the two classes and is very difficult to find a decision boundary, even if is non-linear, that can correctly separate them. The good performance of the linear models motivates the feature selection procedure discussed in the next section.

Feature Selection. As discussed in Sect. 3.4, looking at the magnitude of the weights attributed by the linear models to the input features allows us to identify the features that contribute the most to determine the correct class. In return, this can give us insights about which variables explain the most the occurrence of failures in the power grid.

Figure 2 reports the magnitude of the weights assigned to each feature after each linear model is trained. The higher the magnitude weight of a given feature, the more such a feature is important in predicting the class.

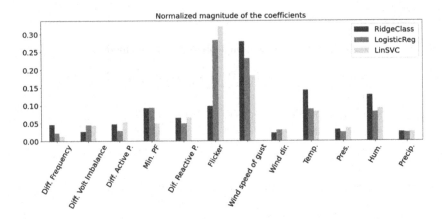

Fig. 2. Coefficients' magnitude assigned to each feature by different linear models. High magnitude indicates that the corresponding feature is important.

From Fig. 2, we observe that in each model the *Wind speed of gust* variable is always associated with a weight with large magnitude. The Linear SVC and the Logistic Regression classifiers attribute a large importance also to the *Flicker* variable, while the Ridge Regression classifiers weights the other features more uniformly and assigns weights to *Temperature* and *Humidity* that are slightly larger than the weight assigned to *Flicker*.

Overall, we can conclude that both the industry activity and the weather effects are important in discriminating between the failure and non-failure class. The most important of the power-related variables seems to be *Flicker*, while the *Wind speed of gust* is consistently the most explanatory weather-related variable according to each linear model. Our results are aligned with experiences of the DSO and the local costumers, as more failures seem to occur when there is high activity at the industries and the machines operates at full load. In addition, it has been noted that failures are more likely to occur when there is strong wind, which could create collisions in the cables of the power lines.

5   Conclusions

In this work, we tackled the problem of detecting unscheduled failures in the power grid, which have major consequences for the local industries that are experiencing an increased frequency of failures. In collaboration with the DSO, totally 12 different variables were collected (6 weather-related, and 6 energy-related).

Through a features selection procedure based on data-driven classification, we identified the variables that mostly explain the onset of power disturbances. Our results indicated that the amount of flicker and wind speed of gust as the most significant variables in explaining the power disturbances. This represents valuable information to the DSO for implementing strategies to prevent and mitigate incoming failures.

Despite the baseline classifiers used in this study managed to correctly detect most of the power failures reported (up to 75–80%), they produced several false positives. While, false positives are less critical in this particular application, more advanced classifier will be investigated in future work to improve the results, as well as strategies to interpret the decision process of non-linear classifiers.

References

1. Abusdal, G.M., Heydt, G.T., Ripegutu, A.: Utilization of advanced metering infrastructure in back-fed ground fault detection. In: 2015 IEEE Power & Energy Society General Meeting, pp. 1–5. IEEE (2015)
2. Andresen, C.A., Torsæter, B.N., Haugdal, H., Uhlen, K.: Fault detection and prediction in smart grids. In: 2018 IEEE 9th International Workshop on Applied Measurements for Power Systems (AMPS), pp. 1–6. IEEE (2018)
3. Arva Power Company, T.K.: Arva power company, troms kraft. https://www.tromskraftnett.no/hovedsiden
4. Balouji, E., Gu, I.Y., Bollen, M.H., Bagheri, A., Nazari, M.: A LSTM-based deep learning method with application to voltage dip classification. In: 2018 18th International Conference on Harmonics and Quality of Power (ICHQP), pp. 1–5 (2018). https://doi.org/10.1109/ICHQP.2018.8378893
5. Bianchi, F.M., De Santis, E., Rizzi, A., Sadeghian, A.: Short-term electric load forecasting using echo state networks and PCA decomposition. IEEE Access **3**, 1931–1943 (2015)
6. Bianchi, F.M., Maiorino, E., Kampffmeyer, M.C., Rizzi, A., Jenssen, R.: Recurrent Neural Networks for Short-term Load Forecasting: an Overview and Comparative Analysis (2017)
7. Chen, K., Hu, J., Zhang, Y., Yu, Z., He, J.: Fault location in power distribution systems via deep graph convolutional networks. IEEE J. Sel. Areas Commun. **38**(1), 119–131 (2020). https://doi.org/10.1109/JSAC.2019.2951964
8. Chiaradonna, S., Di Giandomenico, F., Masetti, G.: Analyzing the impact of failures in the electric power distribution grid. In: 2016 Seventh Latin-American Symposium on Dependable Computing (LADC), pp. 99–108. IEEE (2016)
9. Csanyi, E.: Detailed overview of power system disturbances (causes and impacts). https://electrical-engineering-portal.com/detailed-overview-of-power-system-disturbances-causes-and-impacts
10. De Caro, F., Carlini, E., Villacci, D.: Flexibility sources for enhancing the resilience of a power grid in presence of severe weather conditions. In: 2019 AEIT International Annual Conference (AEIT), pp. 1–6. IEEE (2019)
11. Ferrari, R.M.G., Parisini, T., Polycarpou, M.M.: Distributed fault detection and isolation of large-scale discrete-time nonlinear systems: an adaptive approximation approach. IEEE Trans. Autom. Control **57**(2), 275–290 (2012). https://doi.org/10.1109/TAC.2011.2164734

12. Foldvik Eikeland, O., Bianchi, F.M., Chiesa, M.: Uncovering contributing factors to interruptions in the power grid. Arxiv preprint (2021)

13. Gopinath, G.S., Meher, M.: Electricity a basic need for the human beings. In: AIP Conference Proceedings, vol. 1992, p. 040024. AIP Publishing LLC (2018)

14. Hoffmann, V., Michałowska, K., Andresen, C., Torsæter, B.N.: Incipient fault prediction in power quality monitoring (2019)

15. Khorasgani, H., Hasanzadeh, A., Farahat, A., Gupta, C.: Fault detection and isolation in industrial networks using graph convolutional neural networks. In: 2019 IEEE International Conference on Prognostics and Health Management (ICPHM), pp. 1–7 (2019). https://doi.org/10.1109/ICPHM.2019.8819403

16. Klinger, C., Owen Landeg, V.M.: Power outages, extreme events and health: a systematic review of the literature from 2011–2012. PLoS Currents, 6 (2014)

17. Lovdata, N.: Forskrift om leveringskvalitet i kraftsystemet. https://lovdata.no/dokument/SF/forskrift/2004-11-30-1557

18. Meles, T.H.: Impact of power outages on households in developing countries: evidence from Ethiopia. Energy Econ. 91, 104882 (2020)

19. Owerko, D., Gama, F., Ribeiro, A.: Predicting power outages using graph neural networks. In: 2018 IEEE Global Conference on Signal and Information Processing (GlobalSIP), pp. 743–747. IEEE (2018)

20. Panteli, M., Mancarella, P.: Influence of extreme weather and climate change on the resilience of power systems: impacts and possible mitigation strategies. Electr. Power Syst. Res. 127, 259–270 (2015)

21. Pedregosa, F., et al.: Scikit-learn: machine learning in python. J. Mach. Learn. Res. 12, 2825–2830 (2011)

22. Perera, A., Nik, V.M., Chen, D., Scartezzini, J.L., Hong, T.: Quantifying the impacts of climate change and extreme climate events on energy systems. Nat. Energy 5(2), 150–159 (2020)

23. Rubí, C.: The challenges of upgrading the power grid for a decarbonised electric future. https://informaconnect.com/the-challenges-of-upgrading-the-power-grid-for-a-decarbonised-electric-future/

24. S. Mark Halpin, A.C.: Power Electronics Handbook, 2nd (edn.), chap. 38 - Power Quality. Academic Press, Department of Electrical and Computer Engineering, Auburn University, Alabama, USA (2007)

25. Sabouhi, H., Doroudi, A., Fotuhi-Firuzabad, M., Bashiri, M.: Electrical power system resilience assessment: a comprehensive approach. IEEE Syst. J. 14(2), 2643–2652 (2019)

26. Sapountzoglou, N., Lago, J., De Schutter, B., Raison, B.: A generalizable and sensor-independent deep learning method for fault detection and location in low-voltage distribution grids. Appl. Energy 276, 115299 (2020)

27. Shuai, M., Chengzhi, W., Shiwen, Y., Hao, G., Jufang, Y., Hui, H.: Review on economic loss assessment of power outages. Procedia Comput. Sci. 130, 1158–1163 (2018)

28. Trakas, D.N., Panteli, M., Hatziargyriou, N.D., Mancarella, P.: Spatial risk analysis of power systems resilience during extreme events. Risk Anal. 39(1), 195–211 (2019)

29. Tully, S.: The human right to access electricity. Electr. J. 19(3), 30–39 (2006)

Machine Learning for PV System Operational Fault Analysis: Literature Review

Tarikua Mekashaw Zenebe$^{(\boxtimes)}$, Ole-Morten Midtgård, Steve Völler, and Ümit Cali

Norwegian University of Science and Technology, Trondheim, Norway
{tarikua.zenebe,ole-morten.midtgard,steve.voller,umit.cali}@ntnu.no

Abstract. This review paper aims to discover the research gap and assess the feasibility of a holistic approach for photovoltaic (PV) system operational fault analysis using machine learning (ML) methods. The analysis includes the detection and diagnosis of operational faults in a PV system. Even if standard protective devices are installed in PV systems, they fail to clear various faults because of low current during low mismatch levels, high impedance fault, low irradiance, etc. This failure will increase the energy loss and endanger the PV system's reliability, stability, and security. As a result of the ML method's ability to handle a non-linear relationship, distinguishing features with similar signatures, and their online application, they are getting attractive in recent years for fault detection and diagnosis (FDD) in PV systems. In this paper, a review of literature on ML-based PV system FDD methods is provided. It is found that considering their simplicity and performance accuracy, Artificial Neural networks such as Multi-layer Perceptron are the most promising approach in finding a central PV system FDD. Besides, the review paper has identified main implementation challenges and provides recommendations for future work.

Keywords: Ensemble learning · Fault detection and diagnosis · Machine learning · PV system fault · Transfer learning

Nomenclature

AC	Alternative Current
ANN	Artificial Neural Network
CNN	Convolutional Neural Network
DA	Discriminant Analysis
DC	Direct Current
DL	Deep Learning
DT	Decision Tree

Supported by NTNU.

DWT	Discrete Wavelet Transform
EL	Ensemble Learning
FDD	Fault Detection and Diagnosis
G	Irradiance at Array
$GCPVS$	Grid Connected PV System
$GFDI$	Ground Fault Detection and Interruption
I	Current
I_{MPP}	Current at Maximum Power Point
$IGBT$	Insulated Gate Bipolar Transistor
$KELM$	Kernel Based Extreme Learning Machine
$LSTM$	Long Short Term Memory
$MIMO$	Multiple Input Multiple Output
ML	Machine Learning
MLP	Multi-layer Perceptron
$MPPT$	Maximum Power Point Tracker
$OCPD$	Over Current Protection Devices
RBF	Radial Basis Function
RF	Random Forest
$SAPVS$	Stand Alone PV System
$SCADA$	Supervisory Control and Data Acquisition
SOC	State of Charge
STC	Standard Test Condition
SVM	Support Vector Machine
T	Module Temperature
TL	Transfer Learning
V	Voltage
V_{MPP}	Voltage at Maximum Power Point

1   Introduction

Owning to the various advantages PV system can provide, the global market for PV has been increasing sharply. According to [1], the cumulative globally installed capacity in 2019 increased to about 627 GW. Assuming a medium scenario where cases like COVID-19 pandemic considered, [14] estimated the total global installed PV generation capacity to exceed 1.2 TW by 2022. In addition, the price of electricity from a PV system is constantly decreasing [20]. This all shows a promise for further increase in the PV market in the coming years.

With the increase in PV system deployment for electricity production, ensuring the system's reliability, stability, and safety is crucial. However, despite the advancement in technology and implementation of standards such as the National Electric Code (NEC) article 690 [33], still, faults are problems for the efficient and effective operation of a PV system. Because there are various conditions where the protective devices fail to clear fault on time. For example, according to NEC, the fuse rating should be greater than 2.1 times the short-circuit current at standard test condition (STC) in PV system [31]. However, if line to line (LL) fault occurred at low mismatch and high impedance level, the fuse will not be able to clear the fault as the current will not be enough to blow the fuse [33]. In addition, due to the blocking diodes, which prevent the string from back-feed current, the protective devices may fail to interrupt the fault current even under STC. Moreover, these diodes may fail and lead to serious damage [12].

As mentioned in [27], the annual energy loss due to various faults might go up to 18.9%. This reported energy loss is very significant as the efficiency of a typical PV cell range between 15–21%. Unless the faults cleared on time, they might also cause additional damages to other property in case of fire. Therefore, detecting and clearing the fault on time is an indispensable solution to mitigate these losses while ensuring the reliability and security of a PV system.

Up to now, several techniques have been created for FDD in a PV system. However, the demand for techniques which is simple and cheap, can handle non-linear nature of the PV modules, can be remotely applied and can differentiate features with similar signature are the primary motivation to move to data-driven methods like that of machine learning (ML) [27] for many researchers in recent years.

If ML is used to analyze the fault in a PV system, as much as possible, there should be a holistic method that is used to detect and diagnosis at least all the most frequent and dangerous faults. Nevertheless, most of the literature focused on PV array fault. Besides, only one paper tried to implement the ML method in a programmable logic device based on the author's knowledge. Thus, this paper aim at answering the reason behind. To the best of the author's knowledge, this review paper is the first to review literature, keeping in mind the feasibility of a holistic fault analysis approach for a PV system specifically for standalone PV system (SAPVS) as well as categorizing and analyzing FDD into methods based on ML and deep learning, ensemble learning, and transfer learning.

The paper is organized as follows: After providing a summary of review papers, the first part of Sect. 2 gives detailed information about various faults commonly occurring in PV system components. Then, the second part of Sect. 2 provides a comprehensive literature review on PV FDD. Whereas, Sect. 3 presents and discuss all the findings. Finally, the paper concludes by summarizing the main findings and providing some recommendations.

2   Literature Review

Pillai et al. [33] provided a comprehensive literature review on PV faults and advanced detection techniques. The paper tried to review literature, including all PV faults. However, most of the discussion focused on PV array faults. Mellit et al. [31] presented very detailed information about PV faults, including FDD methods. But similar to [33], the main focus of the paper was on PV array faults. [40] reviewed papers on the role of artificial intelligence on modeling, sizing, control, fault diagnosis, and output estimation of PV systems. Whereas, Li et al. [24] reviewed recent work specifically applying Artificial Neural Network

(ANN) and hybrid ANN for FDD based on the fault they analyzed, the type and amount of data they used, their model's configuration, and its performance. Besides, they highlighted the major challenges and prospects of the methods. [16] is among the papers dedicated to explaining the PV system faults in a wider spectrum. Fault detection methods on grid-connected PV system (GCPVS) were studied comprehensively in [26]. Contrary to most of the review papers, the current paper focuses only on the advanced data-driven approach that of ML.

This section will discuss different PV system faults classified based on components and the various ML methods used in PV system FDD.

2.1   PV System Fault

To design an efficient and effective fault detection and diagnosis method, it is necessary to know about the character of each fault, including their protection challenges [33].

SAPVS comprises of PV array, inverter, battery, charge controller, MPPT, connection wires, and other additional protection and safety devices.

PV Array Fault. Some of the PV array faults are discussed below.

Open Circuit Fault (OC). OC fault is an unintentional disconnection of a closed-loop that results in interruption of current flow due to breakage of the cable that connects two strings, any object falling on panels, loose connection between two points, or an accidental disconnection at a current-carrying conductor [4]. In addition, broken cells, physical breakdown of cable joints, loose connections, and aged power cables near terminal may lead to OC fault [27]. Due to the presence of a bypass diode, current flow will be kept even if an OC fault occurs. In addition, it results in a substantial power loss due to the reduction in voltage in a string [27].

Line to Line Fault (LL). LL fault is an unintentional connection between lines with different potential difference [4,31,41] due to cable insulation failures, mechanical damage, water ingress, D-junction box corrosion, and hot spots caused by the back-sheet failures [31]. LL fault could lead to serious problems like fire hazards in addition to degrading PV arrays lifetime. LL fault is very hard to identify by the conventional protection devices such as Over Current Protection Devices (OCPD) that is mainly: 1) as a result of the decrease in current in cases of LL fault during high impedance and low mismatch level [31,33], 2) due to the presence of a blocking diode as it blocks back-feed current [12,33], 3) as the presence of MPPT decreases the current to optimize the power output and difficult to distinguish it from normal cases [12,33], 4) its similarity with ground fault [33], 5) as a result of low current at low irradiance values [33].

Ground Fault (GF). GF occurs when a current-carrying wire/cell/module connected with a ground accidentally. It can be detected by Ground Fault Detection and Interruption (GFDI) and Ground Fault Protection Devices in a normal scenario. However, during high impedance cases, detection is challenging as the current will be low. In addition, there are scenarios where it looks like SC fault [33]. Thus, this fault also needs an efficient method to detect and distinguish it from other faults.

Arc Fault (AF). AF is a fault where current flows in the air or dielectric outside the conductor due to loose connection. It could be a series arc in case of a connection between modules or a parallel arc in case of a closely placed conductor at different potential differences [4,31,33]. On the contrary to other faults, arc fault has little effect on the I-V or I-P characteristic of PV arrays. Nevertheless, it leads to a severe distortion in the output current and voltage waveform [33]. Arc Fault Circuit Interrupters and Arc Fault Detectors are recommended for clearing this fault. However, multiple of them have to be installed to clear the fault correctly. Moreover, when they are installed at the inverter side, they fail to protect the fault as attenuated arc signals reach them. Besides detecting arc fault, identifying which arc fault is occurring is important as the measure taken for one will increase the impact of the other [33].

Partial Shading (PS). In addition to decreasing and resulting in continuous fluctuating PV output power [4,6], PS facilitates the degradation of PV arrays [33]. Even it can lead to destruction due to fire hazards as a result of cell/module temperature increase due to the dissipated energy [27]. Furthermore, as it results in multiple peaks in I-V characteristic curve, identifying the maximum power point by MPPT will be challenging [33]. Besides, unless a time factor is used, it is hard to differentiate it from OC fault as their effect on power output characteristic has similarity [27]. Furthermore, to mitigate the problem, bypass diodes are installed at each module, but this will increase the installation cost [33].

Others. In addition to the above main PV array faults others may include degradation faults [18,34], hot spot fault [39], fault in bypass diode which could be OC or SC fault [33], and blocking diodes faults [30].

Solar Battery Fault. The battery takes around 43% of the life cycle cost of SAPVS [37]. As a result, it shall get attention, and a good working condition shall be provided. The main faults that could happen in this PV component includes external short-circuit fault [36], degradation fault [35], internal fault which could be GF and SC fault [32], overcharging (over-voltage), undercharging (under-voltage) and open circuit (total voltage to zero) [39]. The impact of those faults in a battery may range from decreasing its performance, shorten its lifetime, and increased maintenance cost to fire hazard explosion [32]. The lack of guidelines on how to select fuse and circuit breaker is mentioned in [32] as one of the main challenges in detecting internal faults. Moreover, the gradual change of current and voltage of a battery makes detecting faults on time extremely difficult.

Inverter Fault. Inverter faults may include the OC of switches, SC of switches, filter failure, and gating failure [31]. For instance, the gate failure could be an incipient fault of the Insulated Gate Bipolar Transistor (IGBT). IGBT is the most critical component in an inverter. It is also one of the main reasons for the failure of inverters. So if the incipient faults of the IGBT can be identified, the reliability of the PV system can be enhanced. Nevertheless, a procedure is needed to generate this fault to train and validate ML algorithms. Thus, Ismail et al. [21] provided the way to generate this fault.

MPPT Fault. An MPPT control system comprises various sensors to get irradiance, temperature, current, and voltage measurements and an optimization algorithm to search the maximum power point to operate the PV array and boost the PV system yield. Thus, any error in any part of the MPPT will lead to a wrong operating power point, which significantly decreases the PV system's output power. Sensor failure and lack of an efficient and effective MPPT algorithm are the most common fault in MPPT [27,29].

2.2 PV System Fault Detection and Diagnosis Methods (FDD)

In this paper, fault detection indicates the process of identifying a fault occurrence, while fault diagnosis comprises the process of finding the type of fault and localizing the occurrence. This section closely look at the literature on ML application for FDD in PV systems by classifying them into methods based on 1) machine learning and deep learning, 2) ensemble learning, and 3) transfer learning.

Methods Based on Machine Learning and Deep Learning. Similar findings and a comprehensive explanation about ML and deep learning with respective of PV application can be found in the book chapter in [30]. PV system fault has been detected and diagnosed using supervised machine learning such as Support Vector Machine (SVM), Naive Bayes (NB), k-Nearest Neighbors (KNN), Random Forest (RF), Decision Tree (DT), Discriminant Analysis (DA), Radial Basis Function (RBF), and deep learning like Multi-Layer Perceptron (MLP) and Convolutional Neural Network (CNN).

Among other works [38] used SVM with a higher classification accuracy using a climate corrected performance ratio. However, the paper fails to mention which fault has been analyzed specifically beside saying it is a fault or normal operation. Similarly Dong et al. [11] proposed an FDD method based on SVM while using available SCADA (Supervisory Control and Data Acquisition) data. In addition, as an input they used an index called anomaly detection index. However, this paper focuses only on PV string faults.

In order to analyze multiple faults Hajji et al. [17] tried to include a feature extraction and selection stage using principal component analysis. They have tested various classifiers like KNN, RF, DA, NB, DT, and SVM to classify fault in GCPVS. To evaluate the performance of the classifier, they have used additional metrics. They all have achieved an accuracy greater than 96%. In addition, the execution time of each classifier was evaluated. Relative to other papers, they have included inverters, MPPT, and DC-DC converter in addition to PV array. Nevertheless, battery fault is not analyzed.

In [23], the authors used a comparison between model and real system output to identify fault occurrence for GCPVS. First, they have tested various linear and nonlinear models of PV system. Then, they used ML techniques like KNN, DT, SVM, and MLP to identify faults such as SC, OC, degradation, and shadowing. MLP is found to be a suitable and more accurate ML algorithm. Basnet et al.[5] has used MLP, to detect and classify LL and GF in GCPVS as well. They could achieve 100% training accuracy. As input parameters, voltage, current, irradiance, average temperature of each module, and weather conditions were utilized. Despite getting a good accuracy, both papers [5, 23] application's is limited to PV array fault.

[10] is among the few papers which evaluate the ML algorithm's performance based on both accuracy and execution time. Faults like module SC, MPPT fault, OC, PS, and degradation have been detected and classified using five ML techniques: kNN, DT, SVM, and ANN. ANN resulted in higher accuracy (99.65%) even though it took longer computational time. Nevertheless, for generalization, ANN should be tested by incorporating other faults.

A cascaded Probabilistic neural network (PNN), due to its robustness to noise, has been used in [15] to detect and classify a different number of module SC and string OC faults. In addition, the result compared with a feed-forward back-propagation ANN with both noisy and noiseless data. As input features, they have utilized temperature, tilted irradiance, current (I_{MPP}), and voltage (V_{MPP}) at MPP. The training data set is generated from a validated one diode PV system model. Despite the effort made to bring a robust method, the literature focused on faults on a PV array and DC side of the GCPVS. With a similar focus on GCPVS, DT was used in [25] for detecting PS, inverter, and bypass diode failure. The authors has also used other methods for detecting and classifying these faults. They achieved an average classification accuracy of 98.7%.

A kernel-based extreme learning machine (KELM) was used in [7] to detect and classify degradation fault, OC, SC, and PS. Features that enable the identification of faults are extracted after examining their impact on I-V characteristics. Besides, the PV model was validated before using it to simulate the fault to generate a training and test data set. In addition to the simulation data, a real laboratory PV array data set has been used. In general, even if a very efficient and accurate method is devised here, the determination of I-V characteristics of the PV array in an online scenario might be problematic.

[35] is one of the few papers which has focused specifically on faults in SAPVS. They proposed a fault diagnosis method using MLP feed-forward neural network to detect and classify faults. The faults include SC of PV module, OC of PV module, and external SC of a battery where the fuse fails to clear them in low irradiance condition. Though most papers entirely focus on PV array fault, this

paper included the battery and load fault. Only electrical measurements like current and voltage are used for validation using experimental data from an existing PV system in Algeria. They have achieved 96% test and 97.8% training accuracy. Nevertheless, to consider as a valid method for complete SAPVS fault analysis, it shall be verified including the missing other faults like inverters fault, MPPT fault, and others.

Chine et al. [8] used a combination of threshold method and ML to detect and classify eight faults, including SC, bypass diode fault, OC, connection fault, shadow effect and etc. From ML, MLP and RBF have been compared. Extracted attributes like the current, voltage, and peaks from I-V characteristics were used as input. In addition to showing the method's feasibility, this is the only paper encountered that shows a prototype by implementing the ML in a Field Programmable Gate Array (FPGA). However, they used simulation data for training and testing the models. The other drawback of this paper is that they also applied threshold method which can be very much dependent on system parameters and the accuracy of the threshold limits.

The authors in [12] focused on the detection of LL fault in PV system under high impedance fault and low mismatch condition, which is one of the cases where protection devices fail to clear a fault. The authors used an SVM classifier that is resistant to model error and computational efficiency, based on the features extracted by analyzing I-V characteristics of a PV array. As the methods were validated for LL fault, further analysis is needed to apply it for multiple input and output (MIMO) cases in SAPVS. Moreover, validation is needed with real PV system data.

Instead of threshold method, Ahmad et al. [2] has used a combination of transformation for feature extraction and ML algorithm for detecting and classifying PS condition as a modular fault, DC-DC converter switch SC, inverter switch OC, inverter switch SC with LCL filter failure and gating circuit failure. They used discrete wavelet transform (DWT) due to its less computational time and complexity, as well as it enables us to work both in the time and frequency domain. Whereas the ML algorithm is MLPNN. The data set was obtained from a simulated a PV system. They can achieve an accuracy greater than 99%. However, the battery and MPPT fault is missing. Furthermore, other faults in PV array such as LL has to be checked.

[3] used a hybrid features-based support vector machine (SVM) model in order to detect and classify hot spot fault in PV array using infrared thermography as an input image for the model. The model could detect and classify with 96.8% and 92% training and testing accuracy, respectively. This paper is dedicated to one fault only. For small-scale SAPVS using this individual method will not be cost-effective.

Improper operation is one of the reasons for the short lifetime of solar batteries. In addition to the available energy from solar or demanded load, to decide whether the battery has to be charged or discharged, knowing the battery capacity accurately is a determining factor. There are various statistical estimation techniques, but recently SOC (state of charge) estimation using ML is getting attractive as it exhibits non-linear input-output characteristics. [9] presented an ML-based SOC estimation method for the most common solar battery, which is a lead-acid battery. The proposed methods are based on a feed-forward neural network, a recurrent neural network, and an adaptive neuro-fuzzy inference system. As an input feature for the model, voltage and current data were used. The findings of this paper could be used for further studying FDD methods in PV batteries. However, the paper did not mention how the training SOC data is obtained.

In [39] internal resistance effect and overcharging problem in lead-acid battery in a PV system was detected using solar radiation data estimated from satellite image analysis. The paper showed the impact of overcharging and internal resistance fault on the battery voltage and SOC. Even if the paper used the ML for estimating the solar irradiation, from the finding, there is an indication for using battery voltage to detect and classify faults in a battery. In another study in [19], the author has used a long short-term memory (LSTM) recurrent neural network for state prediction and fault prognosis for battery in an electric vehicle. This approach could also be used for solar batteries from the knowledge domain, and its finding is significantly important though its feasibility has to be checked in a solar battery.

One of the challenges in using ML, especially in analyzing inverter fault in a PV system, is the lack of methods that guide us in generating the faults in simulation as the faults do not occur frequently, but they are responsible for the majority of inverter failures. Thus, Ismail et al. [21] used a feed-forward back propagation neural network to detect SC incipient faults by first modeling a way to generate this fault for GCPVS. For using it in SAPVS, others fault has to be incorporated, and the method has to be verified for its performance for other PV system components fault.

In addition to supervised learning, unsupervised ML methods has been used in PV system FDD. In [37] an internal fault detection for solar battery using unsupervised ML algorithm based on anomaly detection method has been proposed. The intuition for using unsupervised learning is whenever it is difficult to obtain a labeled data set, which is the case in solar battery fault analysis for using ML. The internal faults investigated are SC and GF. The data set was generated using simulation of SAPVS using irradiance and temperature data from Algeria. They have used readily available current and voltage data set. As the work is only for internal fault, it is important to incorporate it/hybridize it with other methods to identify other faults in SAPVS.

Methods Based on Ensemble Learning (EL). [13], similarly to [12] the model is based on I-V characteristics and focus on LL fault at different mismatch and impedance level. However, here they used probabilistic ensemble learning model comprising of SVM, NB, and KNN. For decision, the average of all the results of the algorithm was used. They could achieve an average of 99% and 99.5% for detecting and classifying LL fault. Moreover, they have evaluated the model with simulation and experimental data set. In [22] EL method with DT,

RF, DA, etc., was used to detect PS and SC fault, but the focus is still PV array. They have used electrical parameters as input features.

Methods Based on Transfer Learning (TL). In order to detect and classify PV system faults, in [4], the concept of transfer learning has been employed by using a pre-trained AlexNetCNN for feature extraction and classification to minimize the impact of low data set in the model performance. They also proposed a deep 2-D CNN to extract 2-D scalograms generated from a PV system. The authors analyzed faults like PS, LL, OC, high-impedance series /arc fault, and faults in PS with the presence of MPPT. A detecting accuracy of 73.53% and a classification accuracy of 70.45% were achieved. They have noticed the decreasing of performance as the number of class increase. They have used deep learning in-depth and also made a comparison with classical ML models. They handled MIMO data. Though it needs to be verified, the methods they followed seem promising for SAPVS fault analysis. Even though it is only for inverter's fault in GCPVS, in [28], TL was also used to detect faults like SC, OC using ResNet with an accuracy greater than 97%.

3   Result and Discussion

As we can see from Table 1 the majority of the papers, greater than 80%, has analyzed the fault in PV array. However, faults in an inverter and a battery have also been investigated. Relatively, faults in GCPVS have got special attention than SAPVS. SC, OC, and PS in PV array are the most investigated type of fault using ML methods though faults like GF, AF, and LL, are the most severe.

Among other ML methods, SVM and MLP, in general, have been used extensively to detect and classify faults in a PV system. For evaluating the models, accuracy and confusion metrics are the most employed performance indices. However, some have utilized their own metrics and execution time. Due to ML's random nature, it is very important to report performance after conducting a reasonable number of model execution though it takes time.

Looking at the data source where the experimental PV system was installed, Algeria took the lead, China and Korea take second place. It is also very important to analyze the performance of the ML methods under different climatic and geographical conditions before utilizing them. This is because the challenge for the PV array and the battery is different depending on the geographical location. For instance, while snow is a big problem in the polar region, dust, soiling, and higher operating temperature are huge problems in the equatorial region.

Most of the papers depend on the input features which has been generated from a simulated PV system. Whereas only a few have included experimental data. This is because of the difficultly of setting up a PV system only for collecting data. Furthermore, when an available PV system exists as the environmental condition can not be controlled, it is tedious and time-consuming to generate a data set that will enable the model to acquire a generalization capacity. Irradiance, temperature, and major points from I-V characteristics are the most

Table 1. Summary of reviewed literature on PV system FDD using ML methods

Reference	Year	Methods Type	Algorithm	Data set Input data	Simulated	Real system	Fault identified Components	Faults	Comment Accuracy	Type of PV system
[28]	2021	TL	ResNet-50 CNN	I, V	✓	✗	Inverter	Norma, PS and SC	>97%	GCPVS
[22]	2021	EL	DT, RF, DA	String I, V, P, T, G	✗	✓	PV array	Norma, OC and SC	>97%	GCPVS
[18]	2021	ML	SVR, GPR	T, G, P_{peak}	✓	✓	PV array	OC, SC, LL, PS, Degradation	–	GCPVS
[38]	2020	ML	SVM	–	–	–	–	Normal and Faulty	–	–
[17]	2020	ML	KNN, RF, DA, NB, DT, SVM	–	–	–	PV array	OC, PS, Sensor	>96%	GCPVS
							Inverter	IGBT, Grid connection		
[23]	2020	ML	KNN, DT, SVM, ANN(MLP)	–	✓	✓	PV array	OC, PS, SC, Degradation	–	GCPVS
[5]	2020	ML	KNN, DT, SVM, ANN(MLP)	–	✓	✓	PV array	OC, PS, SC, Degradation	–	GCPVS
[12]	2020	ML	SVM, GA	From I-V char	✓	✗	PV array	LL	97%	–
[3]	2020	ML	SVM	Image (Infrared thermography)	✗	✓	PV array	Hotspot	>92%	SAPVS
[37]	2020	ML	Anomaly detection	–	–	–	Battery	Internal SC, GF	>99 %	SAPVS
[13]	2020	EL	SVM, NB, KNN	I-V char	✓	–	PV array	LL	>99 %	SAPVS
[4]	2020	TL	AlexNetCNN	T,G, I-V char, Boost converter $I_{max}, V_{max}, I_{max}, P_{max}$	✓	✓	PV array	LL, OC, AF, PS with MPPT	>70.45 %	SAPVS
		ML	SVM, RF, LSTM, Bi-LSTM							
[10]	2019	ML	KNN, SVM, ANN	–	–	–	PV array	Module SC, OC, PS, Degradation	99.65%(ANN)	–
							MPPT	MPPT fault		
[35]	2018	ML	MLP	I, V	✓	✓	PV array	SC, OC	>96 %	SAPVS
							Battery	External SC		
[2]	2018	ML	MLP	DWT voltage data	✓	✗	PV array	PS	>99.1%	–
							DC–DC converter	Switch SC		
							Inverter	Switch SC, OC with LCL filter failure and Gating circuit failure		
[27]	2018	ML	KNN	T, G, V_{mPP}, I_{mPP}, and P_{mPP}	✓	✓	PV array	OC, LL, PS	98.7%	GCPVS
[11]	2017	ML	SVM	SCADA data	✗	✓	PV array	PS, Hotspot	–	–
[21]	2017	ML	ANN	–	✓	✗	Inverter	SC incipient	–	GCPVS
[25]	2017	ML	DT	–	–	–	PV array	PS,By pass diode failure	>95.3 %	GCPVS
							Inverter	Failure		
[15]	2017	ML	PNN, ANN	T, G, I_{mppt}, V_{mppt}	✓	✓	PV array	Module SC, String OC	–	GCPVS
[7]	2017	ML	KELM	I-V char	✓	✓	PV array	SC, OC, PS, Degradation	–	–
[8]	2016	ML	MLP, RBF	I, V, peaks from I-V char	✓	✗	PV array	SC,bypass diode, OC, connection, PS	–	–
[39]	2014	ML	–	–	–	–	Battery	Internal resistance fault, overcharging	–	–

Note: - : Not given, ✗: Not used G: Irradiance, T: Temperature and for other abbreviations please refer to the document utilized input features in case of a fault in a PV array. In comparison, current and voltage data are used in case of a fault in a battery, inverter, MPPT, and others. Electrical and meteorological data are mostly used in ML, whereas image data are the most common input features for deep learning algorithms such as CNN. However, recently as 1-D can be transformed to 2-D data, electrical and meteorological data are also employed for deep learning algorithms in general.

Faults like arc fault that does not reflect its effect on I-V characteristics of PV arrays, a method that includes the analysis of signal waveform (some kind of transformation, for example, wavelet) which could show signal distortion effect, might be an appropriate method to capture most of the faults in a PV system. Moreover, in most papers, prepossessing of data like normalization has resulted in better accuracy. Nevertheless, whenever this is not possible deep learning models are efficient due to their capacity in extracting features automatically.

Even if major progress has been seen in the research area in using the ML method for FDD in a PV system, only one paper has implemented the ML method in prototype based on the literature review. Furthermore, so far, this method is not commercialized. Thus, the authors have identified the following main challenges.

- Training, validation, and test data set that fit at least major fault in a PV system, PV type and size are very rare to find.
- Even if most researchers have developed their own data set, most of them are simulation data. Besides, in DL-based methods, gathering the image data using a camera and drone is very expensive.
- Many measuring devices and sensors are needed due to the absence of a proper method for effective input feature selection.
- There is a lack of knowledge on how to generate rare but severe faults.
- Selection of model configurations is done with try and error.
- The model devised so far does not have the modularity and generalization capacity; as a result, ML model selection varies depending on fault type, the size, and type of input data.
- Studies that guide integrating the methods with the existing protective devices are not developed very well. Moreover, all the paper does not go in-depth on how to clear the faults. Once the fault is classified, a method and strategy are needed to coordinate it with protective devices for clearing the fault automatically and/or convey the message to the operators for solutions.
- The model's accuracy is variable as it depends on the data size, data quality, and the number of input and output features.
- For comparing ML methods based on accuracy, cost, execution time, memory usage, there are no standards or common testing platforms.

4   Conclusion and Recommendation

We found that SVM and MLP are the most utilized ML methods in recent literature. In addition, only a few literature used ensemble and transfer learning. As input features, electrical, meteorological, and image data have been used. Furthermore, the majority of ML techniques have resulted in an accuracy of greater than 90%. Besides, PV array faults such as SC, OC, and PS are the most investigated faults in a PV system. Challenges related to a data set, model configuration selection, and integration of the ML method with the existing PV system are identified. For SAPVS, it can be concluded that there is a lack of a holistic approach for critical faults in its components. Therefore, extensive research is required to see the implementation of those methods, and less investigated algorithms have to be studied. Moreover, for efficient and effective research, sharing of training, validation, and testing data set shall be encouraged.

Acknowledgements. We would like to thank our Electrical Power Engineering department at NTNU for funding this work as part of a PhD. project.

Conflict of Interest. The authors declare that they have no conflict of interest.

References

1. Snapshot of global PV markets - 2020, p. 20
2. Ahmad, S., et al.: Fault classification for single phase photovoltaic systems using machine learning techniques. In: 2018 8th IEEE India International Conference on Power Electronics (IICPE), pp. 1–6. https://doi.org/10.1109/IICPE.2018.8709463
3. Ali, M.U., et al.: A machine learning framework to identify the hotspot in photovoltaic module using infrared thermography. Sol. Energy **208**, 643–651 (2020). https://doi.org/10.1016/j.solener.2020.08.027
4. Aziz, F., et al.: A novel convolutional neural network-based approach for fault classification in photovoltaic arrays. IEEE Access **8**, 41889–41904 (1904). https://doi.org/10.1109/ACCESS.2020.2977116
5. Basnet, B., et al.: An intelligent fault detection model for fault detection in photovoltaic systems. J. Sens. **2020**, e6960328 (2020). https://doi.org/10.1155/2020/6960328
6. Bognár, A., et al.: An unsupervised method for identifying local PV shading based on AC power and regional irradiance data. Sol. Energy **174**, 1068–1077 (2018). https://doi.org/10.1016/j.solener.2018.10.007
7. Chen, Z., et al.: Intelligent fault diagnosis of photovoltaic arrays based on optimized kernel extreme learning machine and IV characteristics. Appl. Energy **204**, 912–931 (2017)
8. Chine, W., et al.: A novel fault diagnosis technique for photovoltaic systems based on artificial neural networks. Renew. Energy **90**, 501–512 (2016)
9. Cho, T.H., et al.: Comparison of intelligent methods of SOC estimation for battery of photovoltaic system, **9**(9), 8
10. Da Costa, C.H., et al.: A comparison of machine learning-based methods for fault classification in photovoltaic systems. In: 2019 IEEE PES Innovative Smart Grid Technologies Conference - Latin America (ISGT Latin America), pp. 1–6 (2019). https://doi.org/10.1109/ISGT-LA.2019.8895279
11. Dong, A., et al.: Fault diagnosis and classification in photovoltaic systems using SCADA data. In: 2017 International Conference on Sensing, Diagnostics, Prognostics, and Control (SDPC), pp. 117–122 (2017). https://doi.org/10.1109/SDPC.2017.31

12. Eskandari, A., et al.: Autonomous monitoring of line-to-line faults in photovoltaic systems by feature selection and parameter optimization of support vector machine using genetic algorithms. Appl. Sci. **10**(16), 5527 (2020). https://doi.org/10.3390/app10165527

13. Eskandari, A., et al.: Line-line fault detection and classification for photovoltaic systems using ensemble learning model based on I-V characteristics. Sol. Energy **211**, 354–365 (2020). https://doi.org/10.1016/j.solener.2020.09.071

14. Europe, S.P.: Global market outlook for solar power/2020-2024. Brussels, Belgium, Solar Power Europe (2020)

15. Garoudja, E., et al.: An enhanced machine learning based approach for failures detection and diagnosis of PV systems. Energy Convers. Manag. **151**, 496–513 (2017)

16. Ghaffarzadeh, N., Azadian, A.: A comprehensive review and performance evaluation in solar (PV) systems fault classification and fault detection techniques

17. Hajji, M., et al.: Multivariate feature extraction based supervised machine learning for fault detection and diagnosis in photovoltaic systems. https://doi.org/10.1016/j.ejcon.2020.03.004

18. Harrou, F., et al.: Monitoring of photovoltaic systems using improved kernel-based learning schemes. IEEE J. Photovoltaics **11**(3), 806–818 (2021). https://doi.org/10.1109/JPHOTOV.2021.3057169

19. Hong, J., et al.: Fault prognosis of battery system based on accurate voltage abnormity prognosis using long short-term memory neural networks. Appl. Energy **251**, 113381 (2019). https://doi.org/10.1016/j.apenergy.2019.113381

20. IRENA: Renewable power generation costs in 2018. International Renewable Energy Agency, Abu Dhabi (2019)

21. Ismail, N., et al.: Short-circuit incipient faults detection from single phase PWM inverter using artificial neural network, **10**, 10

22. Kapucu, C., et al.: A supervised ensemble learning method for fault diagnosis in photovoltaic strings. Energy **227**, 120463 (2021). https://doi.org/10.1016/j.energy.2021.120463

23. Lazzaretti, A.E., et al.: A monitoring system for online fault detection and classification in photovoltaic plants. Sensors **20**(17), 4688 (2020). https://doi.org/10.3390/s20174688

24. Li, B., et al.: Application of artificial neural networks to photovoltaic fault detection and diagnosis: a review. Renew. Sustain. Energy Rev. **138**, 110512 (2021). https://doi.org/10.1016/j.rser.2020.110512

25. Livera, A., et al.: Advanced failure detection algorithms and performance decision classification for grid-connected PV systems. https://doi.org/10.4229/EUPVSEC20172017-6BV.2.13

26. Madeti, S.R., Singh, S.N.: A comprehensive study on different types of faults and detection techniques for solar photovoltaic system. Sol. Energy **158**, 161–185 (2017). https://doi.org/10.1016/j.solener.2017.08.069

27. Madeti, S.R., Singh, S.N.: Modeling of PV system based on experimental data for fault detection using kNN method. Sol. Energy **173**, 139–151 (2018). https://doi.org/10.1016/j.solener.2018.07.038

28. Malik, A., et al.: Transfer learning-based novel fault classification technique for grid-connected PV inverter. In: Mekhilef, S., et al. (eds.) Innovations in Electrical and Electronic Engineering, pp. 217–224. Lecture Notes in Electrical Engineering, Springer. https://doi.org/10.1007/978-981-16-0749-3-16

29. Mano, M., et al.: Classification and detection of faults in grid connected photovoltaic system. Int. J. Sci. Eng. Res. **7**(4), 149–154 (2016)

30. Mellit, A.: Recent applications of artificial intelligence in fault diagnosis of photovoltaic systems. In: Mellit, A., Benghanem, M. (eds.) A Practical Guide for Advanced Methods in Solar Photovoltaic Systems, pp. 257–271. Advanced Structured Materials, Springer International Publishing. https://doi.org/10.1007/978-3-030-43473-1-13

31. Mellit, A., et al.: Fault detection and diagnosis methods for photovoltaic systems: a review. Renew. Sustain. Energy Rev. **91**, 1–17 (2018)

32. Nailen, R.L.: Battery protection-where do we stand? IEEE Trans. Ind. Appl. **27**(4), 658–667 (1991)

33. Pillai, D.S., Rajasekar, N.: A comprehensive review on protection challenges and fault diagnosis in PV systems. Renew. Sustain. Energy Rev. **91**, 18–40 (2018)

34. Sabbaghpur Arani, M., Hejazi, M.A.: The comprehensive study of electrical faults in PV arrays 2016, 1–10. https://doi.org/10.1155/2016/8712960. https://www.hindawi.com/journals/jece/2016/8712960/

35. Sabri, N., et al.: Intelligent fault supervisory system applied on stand-alone photovoltaic system. In: 2018 International Conference on Applied Smart Systems (ICASS), pp. 1–5. https://doi.org/10.1109/ICASS.2018.8651950

36. Sabri, N., et al.: Faults diagnosis in stand-alone photovoltaic system using artificial neural network. In: 2018 6th International Conference on Control Engineering & Information Technology (CEIT), pp. 1–6. IEEE (2018)

37. Sabri, N., et al.: Battery internal fault monitoring based on anomaly detection algorithm. Adv. Stat. Model. Forecast. Fault Detect. Renew. Energy Syst. 187 (2020)

38. Shin, J.H., Kim, J.O.: On-line diagnosis and fault state classification method of photovoltaic plant. Energies **13**(17), 4584 (2020). https://doi.org/10.3390/en13174584

39. Tadj, M., et al.: An innovative method based on satellite image analysis to check fault in a PV system lead-acid battery. Simul. Modell. Pract. Theory **47**, 236–247 (2014). https://doi.org/10.1016/j.simpat.2014.06.010

40. Youssef, A., et al.: The role of artificial intelligence in photo-voltaic systems design and control: a review. Renew. Sustain. Energy Rev. **78**, 72–79 (2017). https://doi.org/10.1016/j.rser.2017.04.046

41. Zhao, Y., et al.: Line-line fault analysis and protection challenges in solar photovoltaic arrays. IEEE Trans. Ind. Electr. **60**(9), 3784–3795 (2012)

Miscellaneous

An Overview of Data Based Predictive Modeling Techniques Used in Analysis of Vehicle Crash Severity

Gulshan Noorsumar$^{(\boxtimes)}$ ⓘ, Kjell G. Robbersmyr ⓘ, Svitlana Rogovchenko ⓘ, and Dmitry Vysochinskiy ⓘ

University of Agder, Jon Lilletuns vei 9, Grimstad, Norway
gulshan.noorsumar@uia.no

Abstract. Accident injury prediction is a crucial constituent to reducing fatalities linked to vehicle crashes. The vehicle development process and road safety planning includes also the injury prediction for occupants and Vulnerable Road Users (VRUs) in a vehicle crash and the identification of the factors responsible for increased traffic collision injuries. This paper reviews the different data-based prediction techniques to modeling a vehicle crash event, crash frequency and crash severity. Machine learning (ML) is a research field which has gained impetus in the recent years and is widely used in different engineering applications; including injury prediction in vehicle collisions. The paper is divided into two major sections; the first section presents an overview of the existing predictive models for estimating injury severity in a crash event to occupants and VRUs and the second section describes the applications of data-based modeling techniques to predict crash frequency in different traffic scenarios. We also discuss possible future applications of data-based modeling techniques in this domain.

Keywords: Data-based prediction models · Machine learning · Vehicle crash · Modeling and simulation · Injury prediction · Crashworthiness

1 Introduction

Road accidents have been one of the major causes of injuries and fatalities in the world. The 2015 European Commission report identifies frontal impact as the most common crash scenario leading to serious injuries, followed by side impact. This can be attributed to the different forces acting in impact scenarios in a collision [37,49]. The report also suggests further study of mechanisms and measures to mitigate occupant injuries in a crash. Researchers have developed and implemented several virtual modeling techniques to reduce impact severity in a vehicle crash. These virtual models reduce the dependence of vehicle safety on physical testing, also allowing to conduct multiple iterations to improve vehicle

Supported by University of Agder.

F. Sanfilippo et al. (Eds.): INTAP 2021, CCIS 1616, pp. 355–366, 2022.
https://doi.org/10.1007/978-3-031-10525-8_28

safety performance. Analytical modeling of crash events has replaced physical testing in the past; this applies both in the fields of vehicle design to mitigate crash injuries and in road safety planning. The vehicle development for crashworthiness has seen the emergence of analytical models like FEM (finite Element Models), LPM (Lumped Parameter Model) and MBM (Multi Body Models) [14]. These models replicate the geometrical and material details of the structure to a good extent and can be highly reliable in terms of correlation with real time crash tests. Researchers have used these models extensively to capture the vehicle crash dynamics and occupant injury characteristics in modern cars. Noorsumar et al. [38] have provided a comprehensive review of mathematical modeling techniques used to replicate vehicle crashes along with the advantages and drawbacks of each of the strategies. One of the drawbacks of these techniques is the high computational cost and the development time used in these highly complex mathematical models [28]. It is important to note that the data generated during these simulations can be used with prediction algorithms to determine crash injury severity. In road safety prediction traditionally statistical models were widely used. Researchers in the early 2000 s s used regression based statistical models to describe relationship between road accidents and driver behaviour, road conditions etc. In the past decade these models have been replaced by ML based techniques which have higher accuracy in prediction of road accidents. Figure 1 shows the flowchart of crash injury prediction in vehicle development and road safety planning,

Predictive analytics is a term used in statistical and analytics techniques, to predict future events [24]. This powerful tool is widely used in engineering to analyze current and historical data by utilizing techniques from statistics, data mining, ML and artificial intelligence. Accident crash frequency refers to the number of crashes that would occur on that segment of the road in a time period; however crash severity models explains the relationship between crash severity and contributing factors to vehicle crash such as vehicle geometry, driver behaviour and road conditions [1]. Data based modeling is an alternative to traditional modeling techniques and has proved to be successful in road planning and vehicle development.

This paper provides an overview of the applications of data-based modeling techniques in vehicle crash prediction and accident injury severity. We look at the different statistical and ML techniques and also highlight the advantages and limitations of these methodologies in crash prediction. The paper is divided into two sections; the first section deals with the data-based modeling techniques used in crashworthiness design and the second section looks at the recent techniques used in road collision prediction modeling. This paper does not review all the articles/studies in this area of research but focuses more on the existing methodologies employed by researchers and automotive companies and highlights the knowledge gaps in this area.

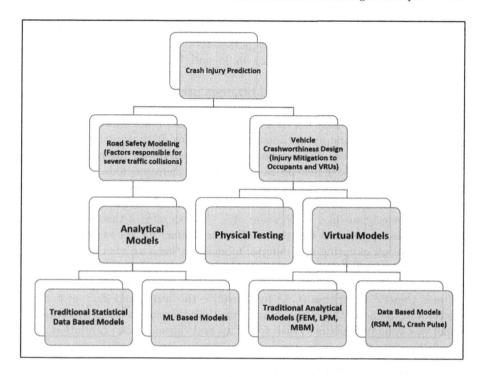

Fig. 1. Flowchart of crash injury prediction in vehicles

2 Applications of Data-Based Models in Vehicle Development to Predict Crash Severity

2.1 Parameter Identification

These problems deal with the reconstruction of unknown functions or geometric objects appearing as parameters (coefficients, right-hand sides, boundary values) in systems of differential equations [39]. Identification of parameters for mathematical models has been used in research for developing predictive models for crash loadcases. One of the earliest prediction models for vehicle front impact with LPM was [22] in 1976. A parameter study on the elastic passenger compartment indicates that the structure's capability to withstand crash increases with increasing metal thickness. This observation is in line with the basic properties of bending forces: the thickness of the structure contributes to the crashworthiness of the body. The spring and damper coefficients in LPMs and MBMs rely on robust parameter identification methodologies which support the prediction of the behaviour of a vehicle in real time crash event. Data-based methods are employed to determine the spring and damper coefficients by a number of researchers; The study in [43] uses the National Highway Transport Safety Administration (NHTSA) database to define an algorithm to predict collisions. The studies in [16] and [25] use optimization strategies to estimate crash parameters, the algorithm developed in [16] uses the force deformation data for a full frontal impact to optimize the parameters. The parameter optimization approaches are further applied in [5,29,33,34] and [7] to improve crash prediction in LPMs.

The paper by Joseph et al. [13] illustrates a parameter identification method for a thoracic impact model predicting the chest injuries. The method employs minimizing the error data between results from the mathematical model and experimental data using an optimization algorithm. It demonstrates a reasonable correlation between the curves and uses chest injury metrics to validate the mathematical model instead of real time acceleration data thereby highlighting the fact that these math based models could also support occupant protection loadcases. LPMs have been used in several studies to model occupants and pedestrians in a crash event [46], the accuracy of these models relies heavily on the spring and damper coefficients defined for the system. Parameter identification of spring and damper models has been an area of research for these occupant/pedestrian models and researchers have successfully employed optimization algorithms to predict the spring and damper values. The study in [32] uses Genetic Algorithm (GA) to determine the spring and damper parameters for a front end of the vehicle along with the occupant restraint system. This model was validated against crash test data and showed good correlation.

2.2   Optimization Techniques

Researchers have also used optimization techniques to design and develop crashworthy vehicles, however the development of optimized impact energy absorption models requires a synergy between multiple contradicting loadcases. These loadcases often have contradicting requirements; for example vehicle front end design loadcases require a stiff front end to resist against deformation in low speed impacts and a softer front end to absorb crash energy in case of a pedestrian impact. This has led researchers and vehicle safety design teams to use Multidisciplinary Design Optimization (MDO) techniques to improve the vehicle crashworthiness performance Sobiesca et al. [47] and Yang et al. [52] have developed an MDO model of a full vehicle using high performance computing (HPC) to define the design process and identify variables contributing to improved safety performance while reducing the vehicle weight, ensuring higher fuel economy for vehicles. This methodology has been used by several researchers to perform component level optimization for meeting performance [23,30]. Swamy et al. [48] used an MDO model to optimize the mass of a hood for a passenger car. This model compares the pedestrian protection performance of a hood against durability/stiffness requirements on the component level and reduces the time/effort in running multiple iterations to meet performance targets. One common aspect in all these studies is the application of simulation models, primarily LS Dyna FE models to generate data for the optimization model.

Energy absorption of the front end in a full frontal/offset impact is a critical area in accident injury research, in which optimization packages are used to optimize the crush members in a vehicle to achieve maximum crush and absorb energy. One of the earliest studies using response surface optimization algorithm to optimize tubular structures was presented in [51] in 2000; this study paved the way to several papers ([20,27,54]) utilizing this technique. Mirzae et al. [31] in 2010 used the back propagation model to map the design objectives to the variables, and Non-dominated Sorting Genetic Algorithm -II (NSGAII) [9] was applied to generate the Pareto optimal solutions. The training dataset was created using explicit ABAQUS simulation models. The results were validated against FEM data and show good correlation. Component level optimization was applied not only to passenger cars but also in ship designs to develop crashworthy structures. Jiang and Gu [21] presented a fender structure design model using FE simulation data on 196 samples to conduct parameter studies. The model uses a back propagation neural network constructed on a surrogate model to map the variables and the objective function. This is appended with a multi-objective genetic algorithm to obtain Pareto optimal solutions. The major objectives of the problem are the maximum crushing force and the specific energy absorption.

2.3   Machine Learning (ML)

ML algorithms have also been employed to predict injury severity in vehicle crashes. Omar et al. [40] introduced Recurring Neural Networks to model vehicle crash events in 1998. It was one of the first applications of Artificial Neural Network (ANN) to predict impact dynamics. The ANN was trained to correlate to FE simulations for a simple spring mass system, a simple box beam system representing the crash box in a vehicle and a Ford Taurus front impact model. In all these cases the acceleration and displacement curves showed good correlation with the FE data. This work led to future applications of ANN in the field of accident research.

3   Applications of Data-Based Models to Predict Vehicle Traffic Collisions

This section focuses on the application of data-based models used in predicting crash frequency and injury severity in traffic accidents. Crash prediction models focusing on factors influencing the increased injury severity in a crash have been of significance in the past two decades, this is primarily to reduce the increasing trend of road accidents globally. The road traffic data, social media information and injury data collected over several years has given researchers an opportunity to derive a relationship between crash severity and other factors influencing these collisions. Many of the previous studies have focused on linear regression models where the functional relationships between crash severity and related factors have been assumed linear [11]. Mussone et al. [35] have pointed that linear models suffer from use of variables with non-homogeneous distribution, the correlation among the independent variables may be greater than the acceptable levels leading to greater errors which may not be acceptable to this field (Fig. 2).

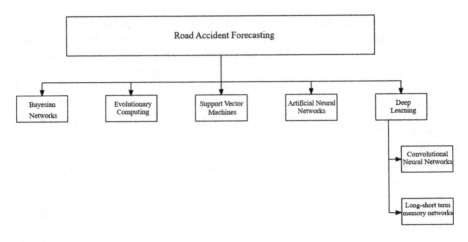

Fig. 2. Representative algorithms and methods used on road accident prediction [17]

3.1   Artificial Neural Networks (ANNs)

First used in 1960, ANNs can solve many complex analytical problems. The algorithm works by mimicking the neurological functions in the human brain, just as neurons stimulate to a real life situation. The model is trained to predict outcomes based on patterns generated by historical data. ANNs are processed in 2 steps; a linear combination of input values and then the obtained results are used as an argument for non-linear activation function [3,12,19].

ANNs are non-parametric models frequently applied to analyze road safety problems. One of the earliest studies in crash prediction using ANNs, [35,36] analyzes collisions in urban roads. The study focuses only on accidents occurring at intersections and identifies factors responsible for an accident. The paper is also very specific because it uses data only from the city of Milan. The study concluded that ANNs can be implemented to model the accident data. A recent work using ANNs in this field, by Rezaie et al. used ANN to predict variables affecting the accident severity in urban highways. They conclude that the variables such as highway width, head-on-collision, type of vehicle at fault, ignoring lateral clearance, following distance, inability to control the vehicle, violating the permissible velocity, and deviation to left by drivers are the most significant factors that increase crash severity in highways [45]. The study also highlights that feed-forward back propagation (FFBP) networks yield the best results, also pointing that any single parameter is not necessarily responsible to increase crash severity; a combination of factors might work to lead to higher crashes. Codur and Tortum [53] developed a model for highway accident prediction based on ANN, taking this as an input to the model, they included not only the basic data like driver, vehicle, time but also detailed information about the road geometry and statistics around road traffic and volume. The authors concluded that the variable degree of road curvature was a significant contributor to the increasing number of accidents on the highways. More recently [55] and [2] have proposed models using ANNs which improve the system accuracy more than a few of the existing models.

3.2 Bayesian Networks

Bayesian networks are a compact representation of a probability distribution over a set of discrete variables [42]. They are widely used models of uncertain knowledge; these networks have been used to predict vehicle crash severity. The study by Castro et al. [6] in 2016 uses bayesian networks along with the the J28 decision tree and ANN to determine the variables responsible for road accident severity.

3.3 Support Vector Machine (SVM)

SVM is an extensively used ML technique. It works under the principle of Supervised Learning that uses labeled training data to deliver input and output functions. The input and output functions are related by regression or classification functions. The data is labeled and presented in the original formulation, the data is segregated into discrete sets consistent with the training examples. The SVM is a relatively strong ML technique due to its theoretical framework. The primary intent of SVM is to minimize the error and maximize the margin by separating hyperplanes between two classes [4,10,57].

Li et al. [26] used SVMs in 2008 to predict motor vehicle crashes and compare their performance to traditional Negative Binomial Regression, SVMs were concluded to be performing better and also offering an advantage of not over-fitting the data. Xiong et al. [50] used SVMs to predict traffic collisions, this framework is based on identifying if the driver is remaining in the lane or leaving lane. The framework has an accuracy of 0.8730 which is a relatively high performance from a model. Pandhare and Shah [41] used SVM classification and logistic regression classification to classify and detect road accidents and events based on events in social media- Twitter. SVMs and Bayesian inference are combined to predict road accidents in [15].

3.4 Evolutionary Computing and Genetic Algorithms

Genetic Algorithms (GAs) tend to converge on the optimal solution and not fall in the local optimal values. GAs present their solution as a chromosome; and in medical terminology, a chromosome is composed as a set of genes, each gene is understood to be representing a particular value of a variable in a particular set of genes in a population. The solution is obtained by conducting an iterative evolutionary process; the initiation is a random set of values from the population. Like in any evolutionary process, there is crossover and mutation between each set of iterations. This process is repeated until the criteria are met or the number of iterations is completed [17]. There are several applications of this methodology in the literature, [18] conducted a study using GAs and decision trees to define a prediction model based on the accidents occurring in urban and rural roads.

3.5   Deep Learning

This is a sub-field of ML concerned with algorithms inspired by the structure and function of the brain called ANN. DL architectures such as Convolutional Neural Network (CNN) and Recurrent Neural Network (RNN) and a combination of both are used to discover hidden relationships and structures in high dimensional data. Ren et al. [44] used the deep learning method to analyze spatial and temporal data of traffic accidents in Beijing and presented a spatio-temporal correlation of the data. The authors presented a highly accurate deep learning model of accident prediction, this model can be applied to traffic accident warning systems along with other potential applications. There have been several research studies conducted in this field of research using Deep learning in the past decade, [56,58]. In [8] the authors combined CNN with long short-term memory (LSTM) to detect traffic events, the data was extracted from Twitter information, the study concluded to have outperformed previous studies with an accuracy of 0.986 and F-measure of 0.986.

4   Conclusion and Next Steps

This paper reviews the data-based models applied to develop crash and injury severity prediction models. The modeling strategies used to predict the crashworthiness of the vehicle indicate a higher preference of researchers to use optimization strategies, response surface methods and, ANNs to develop injury mitigation models. It is also observed that the use of ML techniques like Reinforcement Learning (RL), Supervised and Unsupervised Learning has very few applications in this area of research. This indicates that there is scope for researchers to employ these strategies to create prediction models. One of the reasons that we can attribute to this gap in the application is the highly non-linear complex dynamic event that most high-speed crashes are associated with. It is also tough to replicate the non-linear behaviour of materials used in a vehicle and the presence of multiple components in the vehicle. This review highlights the widespread application of optimization algorithms in parameter identification problems; these focus more on the vehicle crush and energy absorption prediction models compared to the vehicle rotations leading to pitching/yawing/rolling. There is an opportunity to use data-based models to establish a relation between vehicle acceleration and vehicle rotations along with the factors contributing to the increase of vehicle rotation about its axes in case of a crash. Most of the data sets generated in these modeling strategies have used simulation-based models, for example, LS Dyna or Pamcrash based models for non-linear dynamic impacts. This is an encouraging trend because researchers are relying more on virtual simulation methods compared to physical test data.

We also observe that data-based modeling has been applied extensively to component based modeling in passenger cars, MDO is also used to meet contradictory requirements in the vehicle like the mass of the vehicle and vehicle structural integrity. There is again scope to further use ML algorithms in this domain.

The second section of this paper reviews the prediction models used for estimating crash frequency, in other words, these models predict road traffic collisions and crash severity. It was observed that several ML based analytical techniques were employed in this domain. The use of ANNs, SVMs and, GA-based models has been predominant in the past decade to more accurately model vehicle crash severity. This trend aligns with the emergence of ML based algorithms since the year 2000; the developments in the field of computational powers have also supported this trend. We also realize that there are few models based on RL techniques and this can be a scope for future research. One of the drawbacks of these models is the dependence on data which may change over different parts of the world. It is important to create datasets that represent all types of traffic and road conditions, and validate these models against different road conditions. This would provide more robust prediction models.

It will be interesting to combine crash frequency and structural integrity/occupant injury models to improve prediction.

References

1. Abdulhafedh, A.: Road crash prediction models: different statistical modeling approaches. J. Transp. Technol. **07**(02), 190–205 (2017). https://doi.org/10.4236/jtts.2017.72014
2. Alkheder, S., Taamneh, M., Taamneh, S.: Severity prediction of traffic accident using an artificial neural network. J. Forecast. **36**(1), 100–108 (2017)
3. Assi, K., Rahman, S.M., Mansoor, U., Ratrout, N.: Predicting crash injury severity with machine learning algorithm synergized with clustering technique: a promising protocol. Accid. Anal. Prev. 17(3), 1–17 (2020). https://doi.org/10.3390/ijerph17155497, http://www.sciencepublishinggroup.com/j/acm
4. Assi, K., Rahman, S.M., Mansoor, U., Ratrout, N.: Predicting crash injury severity with machine learning algorithm synergized with clustering technique: a promising protocol. Int. J. Environm. Res. Public Health **17**(15), 1–17 (2020). https://doi.org/10.3390/ijerph17155497
5. Munyazikwiye, B.B., Vysochinskiy, D., Khadyko, M., Robbersmyr, K.G.: Prediction of Vehicle crashworthiness parameters using piecewise lumped parameters and finite element models. Designs, **2**(4), 43 (2018). https://doi.org/10.3390/designs2040043
6. Castro, Y., Kim, Y.J.: Data mining on road safety: factor assessment on vehicle accidents using classification models. Int. J. Crashworthiness **21**(2), 104–111 (2016)
7. Chang, L.Y., Mannering, F.: Analysis of injury severity and vehicle occupancy in truck- and non-truck-involved accidents. Accid. Anal. Prev. **31**(5), 579–592 (1999). https://doi.org/10.1016/S0001-4575(99)00014-7
8. Dabiri, S., Heaslip, K.: Developing a twitter-based traffic event detection model using deep learning architectures. Expert Syst. Appl. **118**, 425–439 (2019)
9. Deb, K., Pratap, A., Agarwal, S., Meyarivan, T.: A fast and elitist multiobjective genetic algorithm: NSGA-II. IEEE Trans. Evol. Comput. **6**(2), 182–197 (2002). https://doi.org/10.1109/4235.996017
10. Deka, P.C., et al.: Support vector machine applications in the field of hydrology: a review. Appl. Soft Comput. **19**, 372–386 (2014)

11. Delen, D., Sharda, R., Bessonov, M.: Identifying significant predictors of injury severity in traffic accidents using a series of artificial neural networks. Accid. Anal. Prev. **38**(3), 434–444 (2006). https://doi.org/10.1016/j.aap.2005.06.024

12. Delen, D., Tomak, L., Topuz, K., Eryarsoy, E.: Investigating injury severity risk factors in automobile crashes with predictive analytics and sensitivity analysis methods. J. Transp. Health **4**, 118–131 (2017)

13. Free, J.C., Hall, J.W., Montano, C.A.: Identification of mathematical models from impact data: application to thoracic impact. Technical report, SAE Technical Paper (1976)

14. Gandhi, U.N., Hu, S.J.: Data-based approach in modeling automobile crash. Int. J. Impact Eng. **16**(1), 95–118 (1995). https://doi.org/10.1016/0734-743X(94)E0029-U

15. Ghosh, B., Asif, M.T., Dauwels, J.: Bayesian prediction of the duration of non-recurring road incidents. In: 2016 IEEE Region 10 Conference (TENCON), pp. 87–90. IEEE (2016)

16. Graff, L., Harbrecht, H., Zimmermann, M.: On the computation of solution spaces in high dimensions. Struct. Multidiscip. Optim. **54**(4), 811–829 (2016). https://doi.org/10.1007/s00158-016-1454-x

17. Gutierrez-Osorio, C., Pedraza, C.: Modern data sources and techniques for analysis and forecast of road accidents: a review. J. Traffic Transp. Eng. (English Edition) **7**(4), 432–446 (2020)

18. Hashmienejad, S.H.A., Hasheminejad, S.M.H.: Traffic accident severity prediction using a novel multi-objective genetic algorithm. Int. J. Crashworthiness **22**(4), 425–440 (2017)

19. Hippert, H.S., Pedreira, C.E., Souza, R.C.: Neural networks for short-term load forecasting: a review and evaluation. IEEE Trans. Power Syst. **16**(1), 44–55 (2001)

20. Hou, S., Li, Q., Long, S., Yang, X., Li, W.: Design optimization of regular hexagonal thin-walled columns with crashworthiness criteria. Finite Elem. Anal. Design **43**(6–7), 555–565 (2007). https://doi.org/10.1016/j.finel.2006.12.008

21. Jiang, Z., Gu, M.: Optimization of a fender structure for the crashworthiness design. Mater. Design **31**(3), 1085–1095 (2010). https://doi.org/10.1016/j.matdes.2009.09.047

22. Kamal, M.M.: Analysis and simulation of vehicle to barrier impact. In: SAE Technical Papers. SAE International (1970). https://doi.org/10.4271/700414

23. Krishnamoorthy, R., Takla, M., Subic, A., Scott, D.: Design optimisation of passenger car hood panels for improved pedestrian protection. Adv. Mater. Res. **633**, 62–76 (2013). https://doi.org/10.4028/www.scientific.net/AMR.633.62

24. Kumar, V.L.M.: Predictive analytics: a review of trends and techniques. Int. J. Comput. Appl. **182**(1), 31–37 (2018). https://doi.org/10.5120/ijca2018917434

25. Lavinia, G.: A stochastic algorithm for the identification of solution spaces in high-dimensional design spaces (2013). https://oatd.org/oatd/record?record=oai

26. Li, X., Lord, D., Zhang, Y., Xie, Y.: Predicting motor vehicle crashes using Support Vector Machine models. Accid. Anal. Prev. **40**(4), 1611–1618 (2008). https://doi.org/10.1016/j.aap.2008.04.010

27. Liu, Y.: Crashworthiness design of multi-corner thin-walled columns. Thin-Walled Struct. **46**(12), 1329–1337 (2008). https://doi.org/10.1016/j.tws.2008.04.003

28. Lu, Q., Karimi, H.R., Robbersmyr, K.G.: A data-based approach for modeling and analysis of vehicle collision by LPV-ARMAX models. J. Appl. Math. (2013). https://doi.org/10.1155/2013/452391

29. Mentzer, S.G., Radwan, R.A., Hollowell, W.T.: The SISAME methodology for extraction of optimal lumped parameter structural crash models. SAE Technical Papers (1992). https://doi.org/10.4271/920358

30. Mercier, F., Guillon, M., Maillot, S.: Deployment of optimization studies using alternova: design of a hood inner panel for pedestrian safety performance. Ingénieurs de l'Automobile, pp. 29–46 (2012)

31. Mirzaei, M., Shakeri, M., Seddighi, M., Seyedi, S.: Using of neural network and genetic algorithm in multiobjective optimization of collapsible energy absorbers (2010)

32. Munyazikwiye, B.B., Karimi, H.R., Robbersmyr, K.G.: Application of genetic algorithm on parameter optimization of three vehicle crash scenarios. IFAC-PapersOnLine **50**(1), 3697–3701 (2017)

33. Munyazikwiye, B.B., Karimi, H.R., Robbersmyr, K.G.: A mathematical model for vehicle-occupant frontal crash using genetic algorithm. In: Proceedings - 2016 UKSim-AMSS 18th International Conference on Computer Modelling and Simulation, UKSim 2016 (April), 141–146 (2016). https://doi.org/10.1109/UKSim.2016.12

34. Munyazikwiye, B.B., Robbersmyr, K.G., Karimi, H.R.: A state-space approach to mathematical modeling and parameters identification of vehicle frontal crash. Syst. Sci. Control Eng. **2**(1), 351–361 (2014). https://doi.org/10.1080/21642583.2014.883108

35. Mussone, L., Ferrari, A., Oneta, M.: An analysis of urban collisions using an artificial intelligence model. Accid. Anal. Prev. **31**(6), 705–718 (1999). https://doi.org/10.1016/S0001-4575(99)00031-7

36. Mussone, L., Rinelli, S.: An accident analysis for urban vehicular flow. WIT Transactions on The Built Environment, vol. 26 (1970)

37. Noorsumar, G., Robbersmyr, K., Rogovchenko, S., Vysochinskiy, D.: Crash response of a repaired vehicle-influence of welding UHSS members. In: SAE Technical Papers, vol. 2020-April. SAE International (2020). https://doi.org/10.4271/2020-01-0197

38. Noorsumar, G., Rogovchenko, S., Robbersmyr, K.G., Vysochinskiy, D.: Mathematical models for assessment of vehicle crashworthiness: a review. Int. J. Crashworthiness pp. 1–15 (2021). https://doi.org/10.1080/13588265.2021.1929760, https://www.tandfonline.com/doi/full/10.1080/13588265.2021.1929760

39. Notes, L.: Parameter identification; winter school inverse problems 2005. Technical report(2005)

40. Omar, T., Eskandarian, A., Bedewi, N.: Vehicle crash modelling using recurrent neural networks. Technical Report, vol. 9 (1998)

41. Pandhare, K.R., Shah, M.A.: Real time road traffic event detection using twitter and spark. In: 2017 International Conference on Inventive Communication and Computational Technologies (ICICCT), pp. 445–449. IEEE (2017)

42. Pearl, J.: Probabilistic Reasoning in Intelligent Systems: Networks of Plausible Inference. Morgan Kaufmann Publishers Inc., San Francisco, CA, USA (1988)

43. Prasad, A.K.: CRASH3 damage algorithm reformulation for front and rear collisions. SAE Technical Papers (1990). https://doi.org/10.4271/900098

44. Ren, H., Song, Y., Wang, J., Hu, Y., Lei, J.: A deep learning approach to the citywide traffic accident risk prediction. In: 2018 21st International Conference on Intelligent Transportation Systems (ITSC), pp. 3346–3351. IEEE (2018)

45. Rezaie Moghaddam, F., Afandizadeh, S., Ziyadi, M.: Prediction of accident severity using artificial neural networks. Int. J. Civil Eng. **9**(1), 41–48 (2011)

46. Roberts, V., Robbins, D.H.: Multidimensional mathematical modeling of occupant dynamics under crash conditions. SAE Transactions, pp. 1071–1081 (1969)
47. Sobieszczanski-Sobieski, J., Kodiyalam, S., Yang, R.Y.: Optimization of car body under constraints of noise, vibration, and harshness (NVH), and crash. Struct. Multi. Optim. **22**(4), 295–306 (2001). https://doi.org/10.1007/s00158-001-0150-6, https://link.springer.com/article/10.1007/s00158-001-0150-6
48. Swamy, S., Noorsumar, G., Chidanandappa, S.: Mass optimized hood design for conflicting performances. In: SAE Technical Papers. No. November, SAE International (2019). https://doi.org/10.4271/2019-28-2546, https://www.sae.org/publications/technical-papers/content/2019-28-2546/
49. Weijermars, W., et al.: Serious road traffic injuries in Europe, lessons from the eu research project safetycube. Transp. Res. Record **2672**(32), 1–9 (2018). https://doi.org/10.1177/0361198118758055
50. Xiong, X., Chen, L., Liang, J.: A new framework of vehicle collision prediction by combining svm and hmm. IEEE Trans. Intell. Transp. Syst. **19**(3), 699–710 (2017)
51. Yamazaki, K., Han, J.: Maximization of the crushing energy absorption of cylindrical shells. Adv. Eng. Soft. **31**(6), 425–434 (2000). https://doi.org/10.1016/S0965-9978(00)00004-1
52. Yang, R.J., Gu, L., Tho, C.H., Sobieszczanski-Sobieski, J.: Multidisciplinary design optimization of a full vehicle with high performance computing. In: 19th AIAA Applied Aerodynamics Conference (2016) (2001). https://doi.org/10.2514/6.2001-1273
53. Yasin Çodur, M., Tortum, A.: An artificial neural network model for highway accident prediction: a case study of Erzurum, Turkey. PROMET-Traffic Transp. **27**(3), 217–225 (2015)
54. Zarei, H.R., Kröger, M.: Multiobjective crashworthiness optimization of circular aluminum tubes. Thin-Walled Struct. **44**(3), 301–308 (2006). https://doi.org/10.1016/j.tws.2006.03.010
55. Zhang, C., et al.: A Crash Severity Prediction Method Based on Improved Neural Network and Factor Analysis. Discret. Dyn. Nat. Soc. (2020). https://doi.org/10.1155/2020/4013185
56. Zhang, J., Li, Z., Pu, Z., Xu, C.: Comparing prediction performance for crash injury severity among various machine learning and statistical methods. IEEE Access **6**, 60079–60087 (2018). https://doi.org/10.1109/ACCESS.2018.2874979
57. Zhang, T.: An introduction to support vector machines and other kernel-based learning methods. AI Mag. **22**(2), 103–103 (2001)
58. Zhang, Z., He, Q., Gao, J., Ni, M.: A deep learning approach for detecting traffic accidents from social media data. Transp. Res. Part C Emerg. Technol. **86**, 580–596 (2018)

An Evaluation of Autonomous Car Simulators and Their Applicability for Supervised and Reinforcement Learning

Martin Holen[1]([✉]), Kristian Knausgård[2], and Morten Goodwin[1]

[1] Centre for Artificial Intelligence Research, UiA, Kristiansand, Norway
martin.holen@uia.no

[2] Top Research Centre Mechatronics, UiA, Kristiansand, Norway

Abstract. Recent advancements in the field of Machine Learning have sprouted a renewed interest in the area of autonomous cars. Companies use different techniques to develop autonomous cars, including buying several vehicles to develop Advanced Driver Assistance Systems (ADAS), while others use car simulators. Simulators for autonomous cars include a wide variety of different sensors. Some simulators come free or even open-source, while others require to pay for the simulator itself, server time, or each sensor. The quality and focus of each of these vary, with some having LIDAR scanned roads for highly realistic roads, while others have entirely natural and realistic vehicle dynamics.

This paper gives an overview of available simulators for supervised and reinforcement learning as well as their use cases.

Keywords: Autonomous cars · Machine learning · Simulation

1 Introduction

Autonomous vehicle is a field of research, in which the first attempts occurred in the 1920's [2, 23]. Though these were more simplistic implementations, more complex Neural Networks (NN) based implementations occurred in the late 1980s, ALVINN [17] in 1989, predicted the right action within 2 of its 45 units to the correct answer 90% of the time.

More recent papers include both Reinforcement Learning (RL) implementations [5, 6, 12, 22, 24, 28] as well as Supervised learning (SL) implementations [11, 25, 29]. By RL we are referring to algorithms which perform an action in an environment, and gets a reward. This reward is then used to reinforce actions with higher rewards, and penalize ones with lower rewards. While for SL we are referring to algorithms which learn by imitating data. Meaning that the algorithm attempts to find the expected output, given some data, and the difference between the expected output and the predicted output is the loss. This loss is used to guide the algorithm towards the expected outputs.

When implementing on physical vehicles, the SL method uses data collected with a human driver, while RL methods act and get rewards from its environment. The RL methods face additional costs and safety issues associated with

F. Sanfilippo et al. (Eds.): INTAP 2021, CCIS 1616, pp. 367–379, 2022.
https://doi.org/10.1007/978-3-031-10525-8_29

vehicle collisions during training. Data from humans [19], on the other hand, may not include unwanted situations during training such as the car veering off course or colliding in SL implementation. The existing disadvantages of using SL and RL on physical vehicle models for implementations lead us to simulators that support both methods of learning. If there is a lack of data for a car about to collide or drive off the road, using a simulator you can collect this data safely. Looking at RL implementations specifically, simulations are a great tool, as the vehicle can crash as many times as required for the vehicle to train.

Though one of the issues in this field of research, is which simulator to use, and which systems the researcher has to create. Some simulators may include a large variety of sensors and agents such as pedestrians [9]; other simulators focus on the vehicle dynamics, and realism [18,27]. Though overall there is a lack of an overview for each simulators' use case which we will go into more detail about; with a majority of simulators focusing on SL and some looking into RL.

2   Simulators

Among the variety of simulators, we will look at selected available ones. This includes a variety of simulators, while excluding simulators such as Nvidia drive sim, which is currently only available to those in their early access program [16].

We also exclude simulators such as summit which is an extension of Carla, the same goes for the Donkey simulator which is an extension to the self-driving car sandbox; Flow which focuses on traffic flow and does not have autonomy as its main goal; OpenAI's carracing-v0 which is a 2d top down simulator; TORCS as it does not include a simple method for interacting with the simulator; AirSim which was made as a drone simulator, which has been reworked to work for self-driving cars.

Each simulator has a set of sensors, some include the most common sensors widely used in research [21]. The level of realism for each of these implementations varies as well. One example of this is the difference between rFpro's implementations versus that of the Udacity simulator. rFpro's sensors are highly realistic with companies selling sensor models to the user, this is in stark contrast to the idealized sensors of the Udacity simulator or its modified version.

There is also a difference in how the maps look and how realistic they are. Carla includes a variety of maps with flat or sloped roads; while the rFpro implementation includes LIDAR scans of the roads, which adds potholes and bumps on the road surface increasing the realism. Some of the simulators also allow for the creation of roads based on real-world maps [15], which may suit the researchers' need compared to the pay-per-map approach used in some simulators.

2.1   Carla

CARLA is an open-source simulator for autonomous driving research made in cooperation between Intel Labs, Toyota Research Institute, and the Computer Vision Center in Barcelona [9]. It is made using the Unreal Game engine and includes a variety of actors as well as sensors when training an autonomous car. The simulator includes eight different urban maps, as well as the ability to simulate different weather conditions. This variation helps test the validity of an algorithm by changing the map or weather and seeing that the algorithm still performs the same.

The complexity can also be varied quite a lot, by controlling one or more vehicles at a time while having other actors in the environment. These other actors include traffic lights, traffic signs, vehicles, and pedestrians. The traffic lights will change according to how many vehicles are driving from each direction, while pedestrians walk around and there are traffic signs giving information to the researcher-controlled autonomous car in the environment.

In the original paper, there was a RL implementation of carla, which can be found in their github. Though it excludes the ability to train and get feedback from the environment [10].

Actors. The actors include a few sensors, traffic signs and lights, vehicles, and walkers. The sensors are placeable objects which the researcher can move; to simulate a security camera, or simply gather specific data such as segmented images. These sensors can be placed on an actor controlled by either CARLA or the researcher.

There are also spectators, which is an actor placed to give an in-game point of view over a specified location and rotation.

Then there are the traffic signs and traffic lights, the traffic signs currently include stop and yield traffic signs, while the traffic lights are an actor which the vehicle is only aware of if the vehicle is by a red light. Both are spawned using the OpenDRIVE file, and cannot be placed when the simulation has started, and the light can be changed using the API.

Unlike most other simulators CARLA includes vehicles and pedestrians. This allows the autonomous car to act in a vehicle & pedestrian-free environment until it becomes proficient at driving. The autonomous car is then tested using multiple pedestrians and vehicles. These actors can be controlled by either the simulator itself or through an algorithm programmed by the researcher.

Sensors. Carla includes a variety of sensors, which are categorized into 3 major groups [7]; namely Cameras, Detectors, and Other. For the cameras, we have a few different types, meant to handle different tasks. There is a depth-sensing camera, an RGB camera, a semantic segmentation camera as well as a DVS camera. The depth-sensing camera senses the distance to each pixel on the screen and sends it out of its object. While the RGB camera takes an image in RGB colors in its current location and rotation. The semantic segmentation camera works similarly to an RGB camera, but instead changes the color of each object it sees, so a car is one color while trees are another color. Then there is the DVS camera, which finds the change in brightness between frames and outputs those. This information can be used with an RGB camera to drive on the road and find objects which are moving, which the car may want to avoid.

We also have detectors, these detect when an event happens. The possible events are collision, lane invasion, and obstacles on the road. The collision detector detects when a vehicle crashes, which can be very useful in RL algorithms and such. Then there are the lane invasion detectors which can sense when the autonomous vehicle is changing lanes so that if the lane change is expected it can be ignored otherwise an emergency stop can occur. Lastly, we have the obstacle detector, which detects if there are any possible obstacles ahead of the parent.

We also have a variety of other sensors; like GNSS, IMU, LIDAR, Radar, RSS, Semantic LIDAR. The GNSS is a Global Navigation Satellite System, which gives the altitude latitude and longitude of the object it is placed at. An IMU or Inertial Measurement Unit, measures the linear acceleration, orientation, and includes a gyroscope that gives the angular velocity. The RADAR is a simulated radar that sends out a wave and gets back the range, angle, and velocity of the object it hits. LIDAR works quite similar to the RADAR but sends a ray outwards, sending multiple rays allows for measuring the distance to multiple objects as well as their shape. A responsibility-sensitive safety (RSS) sensor is a sensor that modifies the control safely applied to the vehicle. While the semantic LIDAR sensor which is a rotating lidar generates a 3D point cloud but with information of the object hit by the rays.

Focus. Carla is a very open simulator with a large variety of sensors, with the focus of this simulator seemingly being on creating SL based algorithms.

2.2   DYNA4

Dyna4 is a software made by Vector, their "...physical models include vehicle dynamics, power train, combustion engine, electrical motors, sensors, and traffic" [27]. These systems can be used for tasks such as creating ADAS systems, which are relevant in the development of an autonomous vehicle. To aid in the creation of an ADAS system, Dyna4 has a variety of included sensors and can use traffic simulators such as SUMO.

DYNA4 bases its physics engine on Matlab and Simulink while utilizing the graphics engine from Unity. The physical simulation of mechanics, electronics, thermodynamics, control logics, and traffic is done with MatLab and Simulink. While Unity is used for more detailed sensor simulation, Simulink includes idealized versions of the sensors. DYNA4 is split into two parts, being able to only use the MatLab/Simulink parts, with multiple OSs, while the Unity part runs on Windows only. Changing the simulation to add features is done in Simulink, and modification is easily done as DYNA4 gives access to the model states and signals.

When looking at what makes DYNA4 different, is their ability to scale the level of detail of the simulation is their main selling point. For component models there are different levels of detail, for vehicle chassis models we have a mass point, extended bicycle model, and a full vehicle dynamics model, these can be combined with other components such as a drivetrain. Choosing a simpler model indicates that there is less effort required for parameterization and computational power. When looking at the level of detail for their drivetrain architecture, we see that it starts with being able to control the torque of the wheels, up to a full simulation of the combustion engine and powertrain. They also use a variety of open standards such as ASAMs OpenDRIVE, OSI, XiL API, and MDF. The environment can also be auto-generated from OpenDRIVE files, including the road, traffic signs, lane markers, roadside objects. Their traffic model is also able to control traffic objects, these objects can be controlled with DNN or stochastic traffic simulation via SUMO. DYNA4 also includes a tire model, TMeasy, which adapts to different friction conditions. The user can set the friction coefficient of the road or the tires if it is wanted. They are also open to use any tire model, such as MFTyre or FTire and more.

As Dyna4 is meant to be used by the industry there is a cost to purchasing a license. The monetary cost of the simulation is very low for educational licenses, with industrial licensing being significantly more expensive. Educational licenses are on a per computer basis, meaning that if multiple users are developing the software at once, they need a license each.

DYNA4 also uses a continuous action space, which allows for fine control of the vehicle. While its state space can be set to continuous or discrete state space, depending on the task.

Given DYNA4's set of sensors; makes them a great tool for developing and prototyping new ADAS systems. When combining these sensors with the vehicle dynamics package vehicle control can be achieved.

Sensors. DYNA4 includes a range of available sensors like RADAR, LIDAR, Ultra-sonic, and Camera sensors. With these sensors, the vehicle can sense its surroundings, as well as the distance and speed of an object. The detail among the sensors is also varying, with both idealized as well as more detailed versions of sensors. Given their sensors, they can get both bounding boxes and features such as detected lanes as an output from their camera and radar. Their camera is not a simplistic model, taking into account the dirt and lens distortion.

Focus. DYNA4's focus seems to be on the creation of SL algorithms.

2.3 rFpro

rFpro is a simulator made with realistic physics and high visual realism. rFpro's high visual fidelity is done through ray-tracing, when using it or one of the purchased sensor models at their most realistic setting of the simulation resolution, the simulation can easily become slower than real-time. This means that there is a balance between realism and computational time [18]. The realistic physics includes a highly realistic road surface with potholes, the suspension is also simulated so that the bumps are realistic. These realistic road surfaces, which are created using extremely detailed LIDAR scans, make the simulation currently very costly. The maps also have to be purchased at a significant price, with at least one of the maps costing more than the base simulator itself [18]. As their maps are LIDAR survey scans of real roads, the validity of an algorithm can be tested on the real road while being created and trained on the simulated road.

The OS support for rFpro is currently only in Windows; though it aims for a Linux distribution sometime in the future. In regards to their API, it supports C++ for interfacing with it.

Sensors. There are a variety of sensors available for rFpro, though most of them have to be purchased at an extra cost. Purchasing the base simulator the customer gets a camera sensor included, while the rest of the sensor models have to be created or purchased from other vendors. The purchasable sensor models are simulated to high degree of accuracy. The user can create the sensor model themselves, to be as realistic as possible, simulating the sensor down to the smallest detail including error models. One example of their realistic simulation is a LIDAR which is simulated down to its UDP packets sent between the sensor and the computer.

Focus. rFpro focuses on physical modeling of the vehicle, as well as very high degree of accuracy for their sensors. And so their aim seems to be on sensor fusion as well SL based algorithms which can be moved directly from simulation to real-world.

2.4 Deepdrive

Deepdrive is an open-source autonomous car simulator, with an MIT license. It has some sensor data which can be used for the creation of path following using SL or RL-based autonomous cars. They have compatibility with Gym, docker, and more [8].

Compatibility. The Deep drive simulator works with both gym and docker. Their docker implementation uses a docker container for the environment, as well as a docker container per Deepdrive client. This allows for simple setups of clients. Their compatibility with gym, also makes them good for testing the validity of changes to their environment, such as changing the reward function for the system as any person making such changes can run a test with and without those changes with state of the art (SOA) methods such as Rainbow, PPO, DDPG and more [8].

Sensors. Deepdrive has a few sensors, namely an RGB camera, a GPS, an IMU, and some location sensors for staying in the center of the lane, and following a path [8].

Focus. Their focus seems to be on both SL, and RL, for performing tasks such as lane changing, centering the vehicle in the lane, following a path, and generalized autonomous vehicle development [8].

2.5 PGDrive

PGDrive is an open-source car simulator using RL. It has compatibility with gym, making it easy to test with the maps being procedurally generated with a few premade maps [13].

Compatibility. PGDrive is compatible with gym, which allows for testing the SOA methods such as PPO and more. Improving the reproducibility of results.

Sensors. In regards to sensors, PGDrive includes LIDAR, RGB Camera, Depth camera, birds-eye view. The sensors are adjustable with the LIDAR, RGB, and Depth Camera having "a field of view, size of film, focal length, aspect ratio, and the number of lasers" [13].

Focus. Reinforcement Learning, with procedural generation of the maps and interaction with gym environments.

2.6 Duckie Town Simulator

Unlike most other simulators, the Duckie Town simulator is a python and OpenGL-based simulator, made originally for lane keeping, but now with realistic camera distortion. Their focus is on Supervised learning with imitation learning as the currently available version of Reinforcement learning.

Sensors. It has a single sensor; an RGB camera of shape 640×480.

Focus. Duckie Town simulators focus is on SL algorithms, and lane detection more specifically.

2.7 SVL Simulator

SVL simulator is a Unity-based open simulator by LG Electronics. It allows for digital twins, making testing between the simulator and the real world simple. The simulator allows the researcher to run hardware in the loop by having two machines, one controlling the vehicle using chassis commands, and the other one hosting the environment.

Sensors. SVL includes a few sensors namely LIDAR, RADAR, Camera, IMU, GPS, and Segmentation sensors [20].

Focus. This simulator focuses on creating an environment and a set of sensors, allowing for the training of algorithms for tasks around perception, planning, and control of the autonomous vehicle [20].

2.8   MATLAB Automated Driving Toolbox

MATLAB Automated Driving Toolbox is a toolkit that helps in the design, development, and testing of ADAS systems.

With the simulator being able to control the vehicle through checkpoints, and using this to collect data. The simulator shows a cuboid simulation to the user when running the simulator, though the data collected from the environment is highly realistic.

Sensors. The simulator comes with a couple of different sensors, the camera, and Lidar. These sensors are made in a way where the labeling of their data is made simple, through a built-in toolkit. With this toolkit, the researcher can create bounding boxes and label them directly in the software. This makes the data collection process easier than manually gather the images.

There is also the implementation of real sensors, such as a Velodyne LIDAR [15].

Maps. The MATLAB software does not include a set of maps, instead having a toolkit that allows for the creation of a map using HERE HD Live Map, where the researcher marks a region of road, and then gets the corresponding map to this road. This allows for easy creation of different testing scenarios, though may lack some detail compared to other maps [15].

Focus. MATLAB Automated Drive Toolbox is a set of tools, focusing on the creation of a simulator for SL.

2.9   Udacity Simulator

Udacity is an educational organization, making courses to teach specific subjects [26]. For one of their courses, Udacity made an open simulator for an autonomous vehicle made for supervised learning algorithms. This simulator was created in Unity with two different rural maps, and a singular vehicle [4]. A modified version of the simulator support was added for RL-based autonomous vehicles. The modification is done using C#, writing the scripts and attaching them to the corresponding objects [14].

Sensors. For the modified version both the RGB camera as well as the segmentation cameras are available. The RGB camera is a simple camera attached to the vehicle, collecting photos as the vehicle drives, the segmented camera, on the other hand, is quite different, as it segments objects in the world through shaders. Lastly, there is an ideal GNSS or GPS if you wish, with which the position and rotation of the vehicle are given. These sensors are ideal sensors, with the segmented cameras giving pixel-perfect data.

Reinforcement Learning Based Systems. When training RL-based algorithms in simulations, certain things are very important to standardize. This includes a standardized method of giving rewards and penalties, which the Udacity simulator has. Another important system is the one that gives feedback for how far the RL-based algorithm has driven, achieved through checkpoints. For the modified Udacity simulation checkpoints are based on the track, some are straight and give a smaller reward, while other tracks require the vehicle to steer, granting a higher reward. To give a feedback for being off the road, a small penalty is given if the vehicle has any of its tires off the road. These systems are aimed to make the feedback standardized, making recreating results easier.

Other than the feedback, resetting the vehicle is another very important tool.

The reset is done by checking if the vehicle moves over a few hundred steps or if it is consistently off the road, if either is true the vehicle is reset and the AI algorithm is informed. These resets aim to improve the training speed of the RL algorithm steering the vehicle.

Focus. The Udacity simulator focuses on SL, while the modified version focuses on RL.

2.10   AWS DeepRacer

AWS DeepRacer is a 3D racing simulator, for training RL-based autonomous cars. The simulator focuses on performing Deep RL racing and moving these algorithms from simulation to the real-world [3]. As the simulator is very similar to that of their physical DeepRacer robot; it becomes significantly easier to move from a simulation to the real world. This allows for training in the simulator to transfer learned quite easily in the real world which is a significant advantage. The training also occurs on the AWS servers; where Amazon has a lot of available codes which aim at helping people understand not only how to run on their systems, but also how to perform RL.

The goal of the simulator map is to get around the track as fast as possible, while creating waypoints, to estimate how far the vehicle has come. After the vehicle is trained on the simulator, you can move to the real world where you can mark the road in a similar way to create a race track using tape. There is also a competition online in which each person can test the validity of their autonomous car [1].

The only sensors currently in use are either one or two 4MP cameras, which they downsize to 160×160 greyscale for performance reasons.

Reinforcement Learning. The DeepRacer Autonomous cars get feedback based on how close to the center of the track the car is. With the center of the track being a reward of 1, being off-center giving a reward of 0.5, and driving off-road giving a reward of 0. Rewarding the vehicle for driving in the middle of the track allows the car to continuously [3].

Focus. AWS DeepRacer focuses on the creation of an RL algorithm which can be transferred from their simulator to their robot.

3 Discussions

Discussing the use case of each simulator, we group them into a few different types with the main categories being Supervised learning and Reinforcement learning.

Based on our understanding we have categorized the different simulators according to their focus and compatibility Table 1.

Table 1. An overview of the simulators, their focus and their compatibility with SL and RL. *The training code is not published yet, only the validation without rewards; **There is a small number of sensors, and so it is more suited for RL.

Simulator	RL & SL	Focus
rFpro	SL	Realistic sensors and physics
Dyna4	SL	Realistic sensors and physics
Carla	Both*	Many sensors, maps, agents & some RL
AWS DeepRacer	RL	Teaching how to perform simple RL & easily transfer it to robot
MATLAB	SL	Tools for the creation of a simulator fitting the researchers needs
Udacity	Both**	Supervised Learning and Reinforcement learning
SVL	SL	Creating env & sensors for developing perception, planning and control algorithms
Donkey	SL	Racing algorithms
Duckie Town	SL	Developing lane detection algorithms
PGDrive	RL	Generate maps procedurally, standardized testing using GYM
DeepDrive	RL & SL	Developing Lane changing, path following algorithms

3.1 Supervised Learning

When looking at supervised learning there a couple of main focus points for each simulation software. The first focus is to prototype a system and move into the real world later with less focus on the realism of the sensors. The next being on creating a system that can be directly translated from the simulator to a physical vehicle.

Prototyping ADAS Systems. When prototyping ADAS systems, the main focus is on testing the efficacy of algorithms, with less focus on realistic sensors and interactions with the sensors. This leads us to simulators with idealized sensors, and preferably a large amount of them. Therefore the simulators best aimed at such a task are that of Carla, Donkey, Duckie town, and MATLAB, which have some complexity, though use idealized systems. And though it is possible to increase the realism in these sensors by coding in extra functionality it is not a default sensor. Carla has a larger set of features, while not supporting MAT-LAB or gym environments. MATLABs' implementation is more of a toolbox for creating the simulator one might want. The Donkey simulator focuses on racing for Supervised Learning algorithms using Gym. While Duckie town is a more simple implementation, which runs pure python.

Realistic ADAS. Few other implementations focus mainly on being able to move from a simulated vehicle to a real vehicle with ease. These systems may not have every sensor available at the start, and some use-cases are more difficult to train them in such as Reinforcement Learning, but their realism is significantly higher than other simulators. The three main simulators whose focus is on realism are that of rFpro and Dyna4. rFpro is more expensive than Dyna4 and SVL, though the realism in their sensor packages is higher. SVL has some features such as a digital clone which DYNA4 does not have, though DYNA4 has more vehicle dynamics in it than either of the other simulators.

3.2   Reinforcement Learning

This is one of the newer implementations on autonomous vehicles, which attempts to utilize the increased performance seen in video games such as the Atari games and multiple new highly complex game titles. In this case, having a standardized system that gives the same feedback as any other system is an advantage, and these may aim at different implementations, one being on getting from point A to point B as fast as possible. Another focus may be on the systems for giving feedback to the RL algorithm.

Racing. Focusing on driving as fast as possible on the road, is an intriguing topic, as it shows how good the vehicle is at steering and how its reaction time is. At which point does the algorithm see an obstacle and steer away from it, and is the vehicle able to not lose the grip of its tires. Here the simulator which fits best, are is AWS DeepRacer.

Generalized Autonomous Tasks. As RL-based autonomous cars are a new field of study, the systems to test and create them are not in place yet. There are therefore simulators that aim at creating these standardized systems and standardized testing. For this task, we consider PGDrive, Deepdrive & Udacity. With the PGDrive and DeepDrive having gym support, which allows for standardized testing using State of the art Algorithms, such as the stable baseline algorithms from OpenAI. Deepdrive has some focus on the feedback which can tell the distance to the center of the lane in cm. The Udacity simulator also focuses on this feedback, with more of the focus being on the ease of implementation, at the cost of the standardized testing algorithms which are easily available to those with gym for the environment interaction.

4   Conclusion

Simulators are an easy way to test algorithms for autonomous vehicles, and within the field of autonomous cars, a few simulators exist with more coming in the future. Some simulators aim to give the most realistic interaction with the vehicle and the algorithms, where the sensors act similar to those in the physical world. There are also ones that allow for prototyping and testing of the most common ADAS algorithms, focusing on more sensors, though not aiming to reach the same level of accuracy as physical sensors. Looking into the surging field of reinforcement learning-based autonomous cars, there are racers and prototyping simulators. With the racers giving feedback based solely on how quickly the car drives, while the prototyping simulator allows for the creation and testing of new feedbacks to the algorithm controlling the vehicle.

Acknowledgments. We would like to thank DYNA4 and rFpro for their time, and insights into their simulators. We would also like to thank Gabrielle Katsue Klein and Gulshan Noorsumar for their feedback on the paper.

References

1. Amazon: Developers, start your engines. https://aws.amazon.com/deepracer/#Getting_started_with_AWS_DeepRacer
2. Anschuetz, R.: A Pioneer in navigation technology. https://www.raytheon-anschuetz.com/company/history/
3. Balaji, B., et al.: DeepRacer: autonomous racing platform for experimentation with Sim2Real reinforcement learning. In: 2020 IEEE International Conference on Robotics and Automation (ICRA), pp. 2746–2754. IEEE (2020)
4. Brown, A.: Welcome to Udacity's self-driving car simulator. https://github.com/udacity/self-driving-car-sim
5. Chen, D., Zhou, B., Koltun, V., Krähenb, P., Krähenbühl, K.: Learning by cheating. In: 3rd Conference on Robot Learning (2019)
6. Codevilla, F., Müller, M., López, A., Koltun, V., Dosovitskiy, A.: End-to-end driving via conditional imitation learning (2018). https://github.com/carla-simulator/
7. Carla Community: 4th. sensors and data. https://carla.readthedocs.io/en/latest/core_sensors/
8. Deepdrive Community: Deepdrive. https://github.com/deepdrive/deepdrive
9. Dosovitskiy, A., Ros, G., Codevilla, F., Lopez, A., Koltun, V.: Carla: an open urban driving simulator. In: Conference on Robot Learning, pp. 1–16. PMLR (2017)
10. Felipe Codevilla, E.L.: Reinforcement learning in Carla. https://github.com/carla-simulator/reinforcement-learning
11. Karni, U., Ramachandran, S.S., Sivaraman, K., Veeraraghavan, A.: Development of autonomous downscaled model car using neural networks and machine learning. In: 2019 3rd International Conference on Computing Methodologies and Communication (ICCMC), pp. 1089–1094. IEEE (2019)

12. Kendall, A., et al.: Learning to drive in a day. In: 2019 International Conference on Robotics and Automation (ICRA), pp. 8248–8254. IEEE (2019)

13. Li, Q., Peng, Z., Zhang, Q., Qiu, C., Liu, C., Zhou, B.: Improving the generalization of end-to-end driving through procedural generation. arXiv preprint arXiv:2012.13681 (2020)

14. Martin Holen, K.E.S.: Udacity reinforcement learning. https://github.com/marho13/udacityReinforcement

15. MathWorks: Automated driving toolbox. https://se.mathworks.com/products/automated-driving.html

16. NVIDIA: Nvidia drive sim - powered by Omniverse. https://developer.nvidia.com/drive/drive-sim

17. Pomerleau, D.A.: ALVINN: an autonomous land vehicle in a neural network. In: Touretzky, D. (ed.) Advances in Neural Information Processing Systems, vol. 1. Morgan-Kaufmann (1989). https://proceedings.neurips.cc/paper/1988/file/812b4ba287f5ee0bc9d43bbf5bbe87fb-Paper.pdf

18. rFpro: About rFpro. https://www.rfpro.com/about/

19. Richter, S.R., Vineet, V., Roth, S., Koltun, V., Darmstadt, T.U.: Playing for data: ground truth from computer games (2016)

20. Rong, G., et al.: LGSVL simulator: a high fidelity simulator for autonomous driving. In: 2020 IEEE 23rd International Conference on Intelligent Transportation Systems (ITSC), pp. 1–6. IEEE (2020)

21. Rosique, F., Navarro, P.J., Fernández, C., Padilla, A.: A systematic review of perception system and simulators for autonomous vehicles research. Sensors **19**, 648 (2019). https://doi.org/10.3390/S19030648. https://www.mdpi.com/1424-8220/19/3/648/htmhttps://www.mdpi.com/1424-8220/19/3/648

22. Sadigh, D., Sastry, S., Seshia, S.A., Dragan, A.D.: Planning for autonomous cars that leverage effects on human actions. In: Robotics: Science and Systems, vol. 2, Ann Arbor, MI, USA (2016)

23. SENTINEL[TM]: "Phantom Auto" will Tour City, December 1926

24. Shalev-Shwartz, S., Shammah, S., Shashua, A.: Safe, multi-agent, reinforcement learning for autonomous driving. arXiv preprint arXiv:1610.03295 (2016)

25. Stavens, D.M.: Learning to Drive: Perception for Autonomous Cars. Stanford University (2011)

26. Udacity: About us. https://www.udacity.com/us

27. Vector: DYNA4 - function development in closed-loop system tests. https://www.vector.com/no/en/products/products-a-z/software/dyna4/

28. Xu, H., Gao, Y., Darrell, F.Y.T.: End-to-end learning of driving models from large-scale video datasets (2017). https://github.com/

29. Zhang, C., Liu, Y., Zhao, D., Su, Y.: RoadView: a traffic scene simulator for autonomous vehicle simulation testing. In: 2014 17th IEEE International Conference on Intelligent Transportation Systems, ITSC 2014, pp. 1160–1165, November 2014. https://doi.org/10.1109/ITSC.2014.6957844

Classification of Mechanical Fault-Excited Events Based on Frequency

Arild Bergesen Husebø[✉], Huynh Van Khang[ID], Kjell G. Robbersmyr[ID], and Andreas Klausen[ID]

Department of Engineering Sciences, University of Agder (UiA),
Jon Lilletuns vei 9, 4879 Grimstad, Norway
arild.b.husebo@uia.no

Abstract. We propose a method for classifying periodic events generated at one or multiple frequencies on any one-dimensional space. This is very useful in problems where you need to find the type of event based on observations of location, e.g. in time. For each frequency, all events are mapped into periodic axes, which are represented independently of each other. Using an expectation-maximization algorithm, we can fit distributions to the events and classify them using maximum likelihood. The proposed method is applied to two mechanical faulty cases: a defect rolling-element bearing, and a gearbox with defect teeth. We show very good classification results in cases of multiple event types of similar frequency, multiple event types of different frequencies, and combinations of the two for artificially generated events.

Keywords: Clustering · Periodic events · Condition monitoring

1 Introduction

Mechanical faults in rotating machinery usually come in the form of fatigue or wear that alters the physical shape of components over time. Examples are wear on gear teeth or cracks in the races of rolling-element bearings. During machine operation, the faults come in contact with other components, causing periodic signatures in vibration. Examples are when a broken gear tooth meshes together with teeth on a connected gear, or rolling elements passing over a crack in the bearing race. Thus, specific faults and defects in mechanical components of rotating machinery are usually associated with characteristic forcing frequencies, which can be measured using vibration sensors, e.g. accelerometers, mounted in strategic locations on the machine [4]. The characteristic frequencies can be computed analytically based on the component geometry and machine speed, e.g. the rate of which teeth on two connected gears mesh together, or the rate at which rolling elements in a bearing pass a point on a race. Diagnosis of the faults are usually performed by Fourier spectrum analysis of vibration signals or through more sophisticated methods like the envelope spectrum [12], by looking for peaks or changes at the characteristic frequencies. However, in

F. Sanfilippo et al. (Eds.): INTAP 2021, CCIS 1616, pp. 380–392, 2022.
https://doi.org/10.1007/978-3-031-10525-8_30

cases of varying machine speed, the spectrum components might be smeared [21]. The usual solution to this problem is to perform order tracking [11,13,20]. Order tracking may stretch the waveform in ways that make it less efficient for time-dependent frequency (as opposed to speed-dependent frequency) analysis like high-frequency resonance demodulation methods as in [22]. In such cases, the order tracking should be performed after signal filtering has been done, or in the case presented here, when the fault-excited events have been discretised as locations in time. From a condition monitoring perspective, the biggest drawback of frequency analysis is the inability to distinguish between two or more faults of the same characteristic forcing frequency.

Time-frequency analysis is a widely applied alternative that takes the time as well as the frequency domain into account. Its application areas contain cases where one needs to know at what time certain frequencies are most prominent, e.g. if two or more faults excite events at the same rate. Time-frequency analysis is also useful for non-stationary cases like varying speed conditions. The most common forms of time-frequency analysis methods are through the short-time Fourier transform (STFT), the continuous wavelet transform (CWT), where the Morlet wavelet is commonly selected as the mother wavelet for mechanical condition monitoring, and less common methods like the Wigner distribution function (WDF) [8]. Sophisticated techniques based on time-frequency analysis for mechanical condition monitoring are still being researched [14,23].

By analysing the time-waveform of vibration signals, it is not only possible to see when a fault-excited event occurs, e.g. the train of impulses generated when a rolling-element in a bearing passes a defect on the outer race, but also to gain a lot of information about how components interact with the defect area. This can in turn tell us about the shape of the defect [7,9,18]. Knowing the shape, e.g. size of a defect, and seeing it develop over time can give an indicator about the remaining lifetime of that component. If one is able to isolate the parts of a waveform that contain fault-excited events, this information can be found based on expected patterns modeled for different defect shapes. This is the foundation for the motivation of this paper, as will be elaborated in the following paragraphs.

Isolating fault-excited events requires locating them in time, with respect to the machine operating speed: When a machine with faulty mechanical components, e.g. rolling element bearings, is run and fault-excited impulses occur within the mechanical component, stress waves are generated. When the stress waves are reflected at interfaces with other mechanical components or the exterior, the mechanical component's resonant modes are excited [7]. In most practical cases, one resonant mode is prominent. However, the frequency or band of the resonant mode must be found and is often done so by analysis of spectral kurtosis using a kurtogram [1,2]. Vibration measurements sampled at more than twice the frequency of the resonant mode must be made. The next step consists of a popular technique in mechanical condition monitoring: envelope analysis [17]. The vibration signal is band-pass filtered at the frequency of the resonant mode, followed by computing the analytic signal whose complex modulus is the signal envelope.

The envelope should ideally contain a single peak per fault-excited response. Finally, some method of peak detection can be used to localise fault-excited impulses, which we will refer to as events.

Different components degrade at different speeds, thus an intelligent system demands knowing the type of defect in question. This is rarely a problem if there is only one defect, but when there are fault-excited events from multiple sources in the same time-waveform, it becomes hard to decide which event belongs to which defect. To solve this issue, we propose an unsupervised classification method that can classify events based on their frequency and location in relation to other events. Figure 1 illustrates the task at hand: There are two types of events generated at different frequencies. We only observe the occurrence of an event, not its type. Therefore, we want to decide the origin of our observed events.

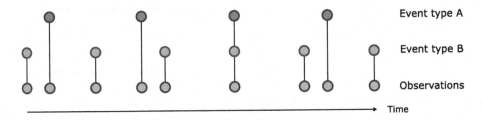

Fig. 1. Actual event types and observations

Classification is a huge topic within data science. There is a plethora of algorithms to choose from and the choice depends on the task at hand. One of the bigger categories of classification algorithms is clustering algorithms, where the main goal is to group together data that likely belong together. Common clustering techniques include k-nearest neighbours (K-NN) [5] and k-means [10]. However, for our specific application, it is desired to learn the underlying distribution of data, thus we will apply an implementation of the expectation maximization (EM) algorithm [6]. The underlying distributions provide information about variability that can be associated with mechanical phenomena like bearing roller slip or stationary shaft speed fluctuations. A similar approach has been applied to separate automated polling traffic and human-generated activity in a computer network in order to treat the two types of events separately [16]. The main contribution of this paper is that the proposed method enables differentiating fault signatures of different types in a signal for independent diagnosis in the field of mechanical condition monitoring. More information about the implementation as well as its limitations are given in Sect. 2. Two example cases with artificially generated data are explained in Sect. 3, along with classification results and discussion.

2   Event Classification

This section uses period instead of frequency for convenience. Given a period $T = f^{-1}$, we can transform events to a periodic axis w.r.t. that period using (1).

$$\phi_T(x; T) = x \bmod T \tag{1}$$

Any transformed event location falls into the interval $[0, T)$. This can be converted to radians and be represented as a point on a unit circle. For example, if x contains events generated with a period of T and a phase offset of ϕ, the transformed event locations ϕ will all lie in a cluster on that circle. The location of the cluster on the perimeter would be at ϕ radians, given by (2).

$$\phi(x; T) = 2\pi \frac{x \bmod T}{T} \tag{2}$$

The importance of having correct and accurate values for T must be stressed. Even just a slight error from the true period can lead to huge difference as the total error at location x, given in (3) where $\lfloor \rfloor$ denotes the floor function.

$$e_{\text{total}}(x; T) = e_{\text{period}} \cdot \left\lfloor \frac{x}{T} \right\rfloor \tag{3}$$

An accurate value of the period can be approximated by searching for the period T that maximizes (4), given a vector of event locations x.

$$C(T) = \left| \sum_{n=1}^{N} \exp\left\{ 2i\pi \frac{x_n}{T} \right\} \right| \tag{4}$$

Since the characteristic fault frequencies are known, a search band $T_{min} < T < T_{max}$ where the accurate value of T is expected to lie can be used to find the accurate period. Details and caveats of this method of approximating frequencies will not be discussed. Results presented in this paper use the same period as for generating the artificial data, hence it is accurate.

The number of classes and which generating period they belong to must be decided. Let the following set contain all classes $\{c_1, c_2, ...c_M\}$. Each class is also associated with a period, denoted by T_c. In many practical examples, the number of classes and their associated periods are unknown. There are many ways to solve this issue, most commonly relying on some trial and error method. However, some optimizations can be made. If the number of unique generating frequencies are known, there must be at least one class to assign every frequency. The frequencies can theoretically be found using (4), given the time of events. If the number of event classes that exist for the same frequency is known, they should all be assigned the frequency in question. If, in addition to the previous points, the probability of a specific event occurring is known, the expected number of events that will belong to a class can be estimated based on the class frequency and location of the last event. Multiple trial sets of classes can then be created and ordered after priority to optimize such a trial and error method.

However, this is not in the scope of this paper, so we assume that the set of classes is known.

The classifier is an EM algorithm that finds the components (or classes) of a mixture distribution based on data subject to a transformation dependent on the period associated with target class. Classes are represented by distributions, being part of a mixture distribution, where the probability volume must equal 1 at all times. Each class is assigned a parameter a_c that weighs the distribution according to its contribution towards the mixture, such that $\sum_{c=1}^{M} a_c = 1$.

Every class' underlying distribution is described by its respective probability density function $f_c(\phi; \boldsymbol{\theta}_c)$ and parameters $\boldsymbol{\theta}_c$. Given values for $\boldsymbol{\theta}_c$ and a_c, a membership weight for each event n in every class c, denoted as $w_{c,n}$, can be estimated using (5).

$$w_{c,n} = \frac{a_c f_c(\phi_{c,n}|\boldsymbol{\theta}_c)}{\sum_{h=1}^{M} a_h f_c(\phi_{h,n}|\boldsymbol{\theta}_h)} \tag{5}$$

This is commonly referred to as the expectation step of an EM algorithm. As long as $\sum_{c=1}^{M} a_c = 1$, $\sum_{c=1}^{M} w_{c,n} = 1$ will hold true for any event n. An expected number of events belonging to a class N_c can be represented using (6). This is used in the following maximization step.

$$N_c = \sum_{n=1}^{N} w_{c,n} \tag{6}$$

In this paper, we assume a normally distributed error on the location of every event and that each successive event location is independent of the previous one. In case of varying event period, some tracking technique must be applied. We consider the model described in (7) in the choice of distribution for our algorithm.

$$x(c, n) = nT_c + \phi_c + \epsilon_c \tag{7}$$

$x(c, n)$ is the location of event n of class c with $0 \le \phi_c < T_c$ offset. T_c is the true period between events of this class and $\epsilon_c \sim \mathcal{N}(0, \sigma_c)$ is the location error with σ_c standard deviation.

The von Mises distribution is applied as it closely approximates a wrapped normal distribution. Its parameters, μ and κ, are parameters of location and dispersion, respectively. The probability density function is given by (8), where I_0 is the modified Bessel function of order zero [15].

$$f(\phi; \mu, \kappa) = \frac{\exp\{\kappa \cos(\phi - \mu)\}}{2\pi I_0(\kappa)} \tag{8}$$

Estimation of the parameters are done in what is commonly referred to as the maximization step. For each class c, the weighted complex barycenter r_c of the transformed event locations $\phi(x_{c,n}; T_c)$, given membership weights $w_{c,n}$ found in the expectation step (5), is estimated. The estimator is shown in (9). The intuition is that events belonging to the same class will form a cluster in the complex plane. Events with higher weights have a larger impact on the barycenter, just like any weighted mean.

$$r_c = \frac{1}{N_c} \sum_{n=1}^{N} \exp \left\{ w_{c,n} \cdot j\phi(x_{c,n}; T_c) \right\} \tag{9}$$

The complex argument shown in (10) estimates the location parameter μ. This can be interpreted as the phase offset of a class.

$$\hat{\mu}_c = \mathrm{Arg}\left(r_c \right) \tag{10}$$

The dispersion parameter κ cannot be directly estimated, thus the approximation presented in [3] is applied. It is described as an approximation for the parameter of the distribution on a hypersphere, i.e. von Mises-Fisher distribution, but is more accurate in lower dimensions like the one-dimensional case of this paper. The approximation is given in (11).

$$\hat{\kappa}_c \approx \frac{2|r_c| - |r_c|^3}{1 - |r_c|^2} \tag{11}$$

$|r_c|$ denotes the complex modulus of the barycenter, i.e. $\sqrt{\mathrm{Re}(r_c)^2 + \mathrm{Im}(r_c)^2}$. We refer to the estimation of distribution parameters as the function $\theta\left(\phi_c, w_c\right)$.

Finally, new values for a_c must be estimated to update the weight of each mixture component. This is simply the expected fraction of events belonging to a class, as given in (12).

$$a_c = \frac{N_c}{N} \tag{12}$$

The mixture weights and location parameters are initialised randomly within their parameter space. The dispersion parameters are initialised to 1. Each iteration is repeated until the algorithm converges or an iteration limit is exceeded. Convergence criteria are not covered in this paper. An overview of the algorithm is given in Algorithm 1.

Some events of different frequencies may lie too close to each other to distinguish between solely based on this method. A solution to this problem is to set an upper threshold on the uncertainty of the possible outcomes of an event. That way, uncertain events can be effectively discarded. In information theory, Shannon entropy (or simply entropy) is a term representing the degree of uncertainty in the possible outcomes of a random variable [19]. It can be estimated if the probabilities of the different outcomes are known and the probability space sums to 1. Recall that the membership weight $w_{c,n}$ assigns the probability of an event n belonging to a class c. Considering an event a random variable with M possible outcomes, the entropy of that event can be estimated using (13):

$$H_n = - \sum_{c=1}^{M} w_{c,n} \cdot \log(w_{c,n}) \tag{13}$$

Algorithm 1: Classification algorithm

---

input : event locations x
classes $\{c_1, c_2, ..., c_M\}$,
periods $T_c \forall c \in \{c_1, c_2, ..., c_M\}$
output: class contribution parameters $\alpha_c \forall c \in \{c_1, c_2, ..., c_M\}$
class distribution parameters $\boldsymbol{\theta}_c \forall c \in \{c_1, c_2, ..., c_M\}$
initialize $\alpha_c, \boldsymbol{\theta}_c \forall c \in \{c_1, c_2, ..., c_M\}$;
repeat
   foreach $c \in \{c_1, c_2, ..., c_M\}$ **do**
      for $n \leftarrow 0$ **to** N **do**
         $\phi_c[n] \leftarrow \phi(x[n]; T_c)$;
         $w_c[n] \leftarrow \frac{\alpha_c f_c(\phi_c[n]|\boldsymbol{\theta}_c)}{\sum_{h=1}^{M} \alpha_h f_c(\phi_c[n]|\boldsymbol{\theta}_h)}$;
      end
      $\boldsymbol{\theta}_c \leftarrow \theta(\phi_c, w_c)$;
      $\alpha_c \leftarrow \frac{\sum_{n=1}^{N} w_c[n]}{N}$;
   end
until *convergence*;

We use the natural logarithm to achieve the results displayed in this paper. Recall that the event membership weights are estimated using a probability density function and its parameters in the expectation step of the expectation-maximization algorithm. Therefore, the entropy can not be estimated in the same manner using the aforementioned clustering methods whose clusters are not represented by probability distributions.

3 Example Cases

Two different example cases of how this method can be applied to mechanical condition monitoring are presented in this section. Artificially generated data from a defect rolling-element bearing and from gears with defect teeth are presented. The data contains the observed event locations that are directly generated according to the given conditions of the two cases. The practical step of detecting and localising the events is therefore not included.

3.1 Case A: Defect Rolling-Element Bearing

A rolling element bearing has a defect in the outer race and in the inner race, both exciting impulses when rolling elements pass over. The outer race is fixed while the inner race is connected to the shaft with a speed of 1000 rpm. Knowing the bearing geometry, dimensions and speed, the analytical frequencies of the impulses can be calculated for the considered events. The artificial data contain event locations x_n in time. They are generated according to Table 1 and based on the model given in (7). Inner race events located at x_n are discarded when $\sin(2\pi \frac{1000}{60} x_n) > -0.5$ in order to simulate the fault moving out of the load zone. An additional detection rate which randomly discards $1 - P_{\text{detection}}$ of the remaining events in that class is applied. Data is generated for a 2 s window. Applying the classification algorithm to the data gives the classifications shown in Fig. 2. Note that the shown classifications are simply based on which component having an event with the highest probability. The transformed (2) time axes are plotted against each other with respect to their associated period. The alternative axis shows the density of the mixture components resulting from the classification. An intuitive way to interpret the figure is to project the event data points onto the axes. Clusters of data points forming on one axis belongs to the associated fault type of that axis. For example, when projecting all the outer race event data points onto the x-axis, they form an outer race event cluster, here with an offset of slightly above $\frac{\pi}{2}$. The deviation from mean offset is much higher for the inner race event, which corresponds well with Table 1. The density functions describe the location distribution of all events that belong to a class, weighted by that class' contribution towards all events. Notice how events from the inner race "wraps around" the y-axis. The inner race event component density function of the cluster also consequently wraps around quite distinctively.

Table 1. Rolling-element bearing defect event generation table

Defect (c)	Frequency	T_c	ϕ_c	σ_c	$P_{\text{detection}}$
Outer race	59.7586 Hz	0.01673 s	0.00527 s	0.01	90%
Inner race	90.2714 Hz	0.01108 s	0.00912 s	0.05	90%

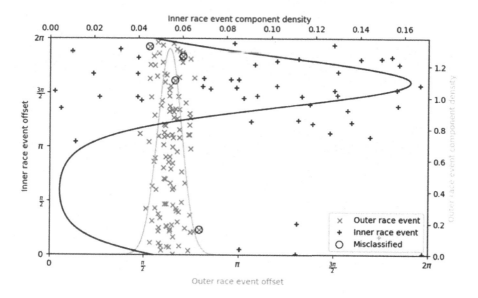

Fig. 2. Case A - Classifications and distributions (Color figure online)

This reflects the importance of using the von Mises distribution when working with large deviations in event locations. There are a few misclassifications (marked by a red circle). They are located in the area where events from the two classes intersect. These are locations where, in the time domain, events from different classes lie close to each other.

For our two-class case, the solution to (14) is plotted to show the bounds of each class.

$$\alpha_1 f_1(\phi(x[n]; T_1)|\boldsymbol{\theta}_1) = \alpha_2 f_2(\phi(x[n]; T_2)|\boldsymbol{\theta}_2) \tag{14}$$

The bounds can be seen as the solid lines in Fig. 3. The dashed line marks the entropy threshold of 0.3 and the red areas exceed this threshold. Note that the events are now marked based on their actual, true class. Due to the amount of events belonging to the outer race class compared to the inner race and the low dispersion of events within this class, the outer race class gets assigned most of the events that fall above the entropy threshold. If events located above the entropy threshold (red area) are discarded, there will be zero misclassifications. However, this comes at the cost of discarding a lot of correctly classified events, like in the intersection area. For comparison, the problem can theoretically be eliminated if the method is based on classification using fault dependent features extracted from the vibration signal waveform, although this paper addresses the problem where this is hard to impossible.

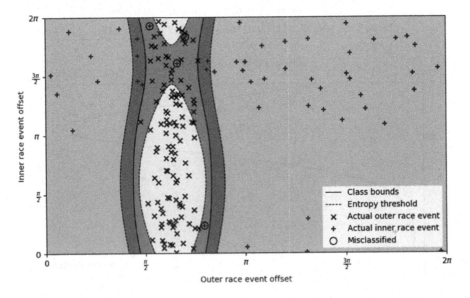

Fig. 3. Case A - Class bounds and entropy threshold (Color figure online)

3.2   Case B: Defect Gear Teeth

An input shaft and an output shaft are connected by two gears. The input gear has 64 teeth while the output gear has 48 teeth. Two teeth on the input gear are worn enough to cause noticeable amounts of backlash. One tooth on the output gear is missing. The rotational frequency of the input shaft is 7 Hz, thus the output shaft rate is $\frac{64}{48} \cdot 7\,\mathrm{Hz} \approx 9.333\,\mathrm{Hz}$. The event locations x are generated according to Table 2. Data is generated for a 5 s window.

Table 2. Gear tooth defect event generation table

Defect (c)	Frequency	T_c	ϕ_c	σ_c	$P_{\mathrm{detection}}$
Input gear tooth 1	7.000 Hz	0.14286 s	0.01786 s (Tooth 8)	0.002	20%
Input gear tooth 2	7.000 Hz	0.14286 s	0.06697 s (Tooth 30)	0.002	20%
Output gear tooth	9.333 Hz	0.10714 s	0.08928 s (Tooth 40)	0.003	90%

Figure 4 shows the classifications and their component density distributions for the second case. Notice the cluster patterns forming along both axes. This is due to the synchronicity of the involved frequencies, i.e. 4:3 gear ratio. The true input gear tooth components are similar, although the resulting dispersion parameter is higher for the first input gear tooth component. It also is noted that some of the events belonging to this class are mistaken for output gear tooth events (red circles), thus reducing the weight of that component according to (12). However, increasing the data generation time window reduces the error, making this issue seemingly more of a population size problem. An interesting effect of this approach is that if the locations or just the phases of the shafts are known, the faulty tooth can be located.

Similar to case A, the solution to (15) can be plotted for every class to get the classification bounds as shown in Fig. 5. The same upper entropy threshold of 0.3 is used.

$$\alpha_c f_c(\phi(x[n]; T_c)|\boldsymbol{\theta}_c) = \max\left(\alpha_{c'} f_{c'}(\phi(x[n]; T_{c'})|\boldsymbol{\theta}_{c'})\right), c' \in \{c_1, c_2, ..., c_M\} \setminus \{c_c\} \tag{15}$$

The figure shows that most classifications are unproblematic, except the cluster to the top left. This cluster lies close to the bounds between the input gear tooth 1 class and the output gear tooth class. As previously mentioned, these events are impossible to distinguish based solely on their location with respect to each other. However, all the misclassified events lie above the entropy threshold and would hence be discarded.

It is worth noting that the algorithm does not guarantee convergence to a global maximum. The authors have noted cases, where two clusters that are located close to each other might merge into one component, resulting in a very low weight for the second component. This in turn may lead to computational

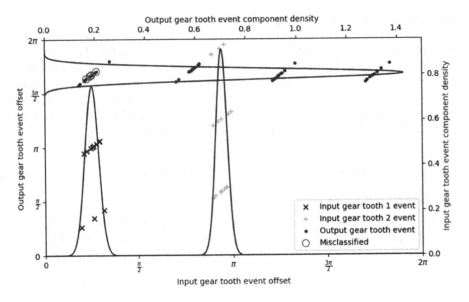

Fig. 4. Case B - Classifications and distributions (Color figure online)

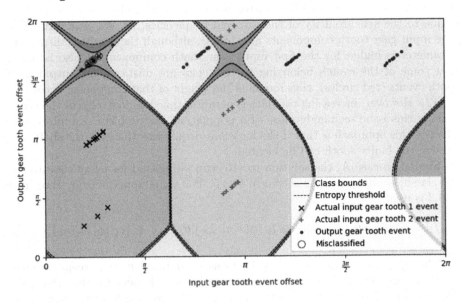

Fig. 5. Case B - Class bounds and entropy threshold

errors. In some cases, it might be required to perform multiple executions of the algorithm with different initial parameters. Other such cases may need more or new data.

4   Conclusion

A novel method to classify events based on their location and frequency of occurrence is presented in this study. The technique can be used for other applications that seek to achieve event classifications, but this paper applies it to mechanical fault-excited events from a bearing and a gearbox, showing very good results for artificial data. The clustering method uses an EM algorithm that first transforms data with respect to the frequency assigned a class. The learned mixture model consists of von Mises distributed components to account for the periodic offsets of events. The algorithm is not guaranteed to find the global maximum, and therefore problems might occur depending on the data and/or initial conditions. Another drawback is the need to specify number of classes and their associated frequencies beforehand, which is common in many classification algorithms. Finally, it is essential with correct and accurate frequencies for the method to work.

References

1. Antoni, J.: Fast computation of the kurtogram for the detection of transient faults. Mech. Syst. Sig. Process. **21**(1), 108–124 (2007). https://doi.org/10.1016/j.ymssp.2005.12.002. https://www.sciencedirect.com/science/article/pii/S0888327005002414
2. Antoni, J., Randall, R.: The spectral kurtosis: application to the vibratory surveillance and diagnostics of rotating machines. Mech. Syst. Sig. Process. **20**(2), 308–331 (2006)
3. Banerjee, A., Dhillon, I., Ghosh, J., Sra, S.: Clustering on the unit hypersphere using von Mises-Fisher distributions. J. Mach. Learn. Res. **6**, 1345–1382 (2005)
4. Choudhary, A., Goyal, D., Shimi, S.L., Akula, A.: Condition monitoring and fault diagnosis of induction motors: a review. Arch. Comput. Methods Eng. **26**(4), 1221–1238 (2019). https://doi.org/10.1007/s11831-018-9286-z
5. Cunningham, P., Delany, S.J.: k-nearest neighbour classifiers: 2nd edition (with Python examples). CoRR abs/2004.04523 (2020). https://arxiv.org/abs/2004.04523
6. Dempster, A.P., Laird, N.M., Rubin, D.B.: Maximum likelihood from incomplete data via the EM algorithm. J. Roy. Stat. Soc. Ser. B (Methodol.) **39**(1), 1–38 (1977). http://www.jstor.org/stable/2984875
7. Epps, I.: An investigation into vibrations excited by discrete faults in rolling element bearings. Ph.D. thesis, University of Canterbury, June 1991
8. Feng, Z., Liang, M., Chu, F.: Recent advances in time–frequency analysis methods for machinery fault diagnosis: a review with application examples. Mech. Syst. Sig. Process. **38**(1), 165–205 (2013). https://doi.org/10.1016/j.ymssp.2013.01.017. https://www.sciencedirect.com/science/article/pii/S088832701300071X. Condition monitoring of machines in non-stationary operations
9. Ismail, M., Klausen, A.: Multiple defect size estimation of rolling bearings using autonomous diagnosis and vibrational jerk. In: 7th World Conference on Structural Control and Monitoring (7WCSCM), China, July 2018
10. Jin, X., Han, J.: K-means clustering. In: Sammut, C., Webb, G.I. (eds.) Encyclopedia of Machine Learning, pp. 563–564. Springer, Boston (2010). https://doi.org/10.1007/978-0-387-30164-8_425

11. Klausen, A., Khang, H.V., Robbersmyr, K.G.: Multi-band identification for enhancing bearing fault detection in variable speed conditions. Mech. Syst. Sig. Process. **139**, 106422 (2020). https://doi.org/10.1016/j.ymssp.2019.106422. https://www.sciencedirect.com/science/article/pii/S0888327019306430

12. Klausen, A., Robbersmyr, K.G., Karimi, H.R.: Autonomous bearing fault diagnosis method based on envelope spectrum. IFAC-PapersOnLine **50**(1), 13378–13383 (2017). https://doi.org/10.1016/j.ifacol.2017.08.2262. https://www.sciencedirect.com/science/article/pii/S2405896317330550. 20th IFAC World Congress

13. Li, Y., Ding, K., He, G., Jiao, X.: Non-stationary vibration feature extraction method based on sparse decomposition and order tracking for gearbox fault diagnosis. Measurement **124**, 453–469 (2018). https://doi.org/10.1016/j.measurement.2018.04.063. https://www.sciencedirect.com/science/article/pii/S0263224118303440

14. Liu, Q., Wang, Y., Xu, Y.: Synchrosqueezing extracting transform and its application in bearing fault diagnosis under non-stationary conditions. Measurement **173**, 108569 (2021). https://doi.org/10.1016/j.measurement.2020.108569. https://www.sciencedirect.com/science/article/pii/S0263224120310915

15. Mardia, K.: Directional Statistics. Wiley Series in Probability and Statistics, 2nd edn. Wiley, Chichester (2000)

16. Sanna Passino, F., Heard, N.A.: Classification of periodic arrivals in event time data for filtering computer network traffic. Stat. Comput. **30**(5), 1241–1254 (2020). https://doi.org/10.1007/s11222-020-09943-9

17. Randall, R.B., Antoni, J.: Rolling element bearing diagnostics–a tutorial. Mech. Syst. Sig. Process. **25**(2), 485–520 (2011). https://doi.org/10.1016/j.ymssp.2010.07.017. https://www.sciencedirect.com/science/article/pii/S0888327010002530

18. Sawalhi, N., Randall, R.: Vibration response of spalled rolling element bearings: observations, simulations and signal processing techniques to track the spall size. Mech. Syst. Sig. Process. **25**(3), 846–870 (2011)

19. Shannon, C.E.: A mathematical theory of communication. Bell Syst. Tech. J. **27**(3), 379–423 (1948). https://doi.org/10.1002/j.1538-7305.1948.tb01338.x

20. Tang, G., Wang, Y., Huang, Y., Liu, N., He, J.: Compound bearing fault detection under varying speed conditions with virtual multichannel signals in angle domain. IEEE Trans. Instrum. Meas. **69**(8), 5535–5545 (2020). https://doi.org/10.1109/TIM.2020.2965634

21. Villa, L.F., Reñones, A., Perán, J.R., de Miguel, L.J.: Angular resampling for vibration analysis in wind turbines under non-linear speed fluctuation. Mech. Syst. Sig. Process. **25**(6), 2157–2168 (2011). https://doi.org/10.1016/j.ymssp.2011.01.022. https://www.sciencedirect.com/science/article/pii/S0888327011000677. Interdisciplinary Aspects of Vehicle Dynamics

22. Wang, W.: Early detection of gear tooth cracking using the resonance demodulation technique. Mech. Syst. Sig. Process. **15**(5), 887–903 (2001). https://doi.org/10.1006/mssp.2001.1416. https://www.sciencedirect.com/science/article/pii/S0888327001914165

23. Yu, G., Lin, T., Wang, Z., Li, Y.: Time-reassigned multisynchrosqueezing transform for bearing fault diagnosis of rotating machinery. IEEE Trans. Ind. Electron. **68**(2), 1486–1496 (2021). https://doi.org/10.1109/TIE.2020.2970571

Intelligent Technologies in the Process of Recovering Historical, Cultural, and Heritage Value in Native Communities

Ignacio Bugueño[1]([✉]) [iD], Luis García[2] [iD], and Alfonso Ehijo[1] [iD]

[1] Department of Electrical Engineering, University of Chile, Santiago, Chile
{ignacio.bugueno,alfonso.ehijo}@ing.uchile.cl
[2] Department of Design, Catholic University of Temuco, Temuco, Chile
lgarcia@uct.cl

Abstract. This paper aims to use a set of applications based on Intelligent Technologies for the testimonial recovery of native culture in South America. Artificial Intelligence (AI) algorithms and techniques (appropriately applied to the Recovery of the Intangible Cultural Heritage of the Mapuche culture) allowed us to obtain valuable results: the automatic description space for ritual dances, the automatic colourising of historical visual records, the writing of new native poems, the transferring of musical timbre, and the synthetic elaboration of an audiovisual story: from the Mapuche culture to the world. The main contribution of this work is to have combined and applied AI tools for the recovery and preservation of Mapuche cultural heritage and make it available for the rest of humanity. The dataset "trutruca" generated, together with the collection of public datasets on the artistic and cultural records of the Mapuche in Chile and Argentina, will be of great value for future research work on social aspects of Digital Heritage, such as the detection, analysis, and classification of facial and body emotions in the dances of native cultures.

Keywords: Digital Heritage · Mapuzungun · ICH · Pose · NLP

1 Introduction

Digital Heritage has been enriched by the effect of the pandemic, where a series of museums and repositories of Cultural Material have considered it necessary to digitize their contents [20] to make them available to an audience that currently is unable to access this material that enriches and expands our frontiers of knowledge. The most significant benefit of Digital Heritage is the public and global access to it. This first approach declares the general goal of this research, *"Disseminate the ICH (Inmaterial Cultural Heritage) of native peoples through new hybrid digital compositions"*, which goes beyond the documentation and

F. Sanfilippo et al. (Eds.): INTAP 2021, CCIS 1616, pp. 393–406, 2022.
https://doi.org/10.1007/978-3-031-10525-8_31

description of the heritage elements: towards a new digital/immaterial interpretation that allows us to communicate with greater diversity and effectiveness from the creation of a story.

The interest of this work is declared under the perspective of an enhancement with a conservationist naturalist approach on one of the original peoples of the Chilean territory, the Mapuche Nation People [23]. This approach is specified in the design and construction of an audiovisual story: a story that arises from and on the heritage elements recorded by some other ethnologist. This story, proposed under the framework of the 2021 Faculty of Architecture, Arts and Design (FAAD) International Workshop "Co-creating the emerging future" organised by the Catholic University of Temuco, arises mainly from the discussion opened from the observation of the registered material of this native people, native people who fight for the conservations of the natural world, its waters, its identity elements and the independence of its territory [17].

To do this, we have used a series of repositories currently available in digital format. One of the first repositories was generated by Isabel Aretz [6] in the late 1940 s,s, who recorded Mapuche music using a particular record player called "pasta recorder" [7]. We also found an exciting repository: Non-Governmental Organisation (NGO) "Ser Indígena" (Being Indigenous), created in 2001 to contribute to the visibility of the original peoples in Chile and the dissemination of their ancestral cultures [11]. One of the largest repositories of native peoples' material can be found in Memoria Chilena; this digital resource centre is made up of a multidisciplinary team that is responsible for digitalising material from the records and creating its so-called "mini-sites" that cover topics and authors, all of them make this material available to the global community [9].

2   State-of-the-Art

The integration between ICH and digital technologies defines the scope of this work; from this perspective, we find some research projects that currently carry out different approaches and extend the frontier of knowledge.

One of the rich sources of cultural heritage is the oral tradition, songs and poems, resources that provide fertile ground for exploration and experimentation in Natural Language Processing (NLP). In this area, we highlight contemporary studies linking Artificial Intelligence and expert models of learning and training. In [16,18], the result of the international collaboration between the Frontera University, the Chilean Ministry of Education and its Intercultural Bilingual Education program, and the Carnegie Mellon University with its Institute of Language Technologies and the school of computer science, all of them together form the Avenue -Mapudungun- Project team [10]. The document mentioned above describes the process carried out to train an expert model, which in the written corpus includes 200,000 transcribed and translated words. In contrast, there are 120 dialogues on Mapuche medicine in the spoken corpus, each of these dialogues lasting one hour and performed by native speakers of the -Mapuzungun- language. [19] describes the techniques to build a translator with the dataset previously created by the Avenue Project, the times of the transfer system, the transfer rules used, and other issues of definition and technical decisions in the construction of the software. Considering the millenary transcendence of Mapuche culture, it is surprising to discover that there is currently no active research work using intelligent technologies to rescue the oral and written tradition. Precisely, [1] *"presents a critical review of the current state of natural language processing in Chile and Mexico... Subsequently, the remaining problems and challenges are addressed... (1) the lack of a strategic policy that helps to establish stronger links between academia and industry and (2) the lack of a technological inclusion of the indigenous languages"*.

Similarly, if we now turn to the recovery of historical visual records, there are technically no references to computer vision applications in the digital preservation of Mapuche culture or in the search for associated patterns. Therefore, we must look to other countries and continents to find relevant work. For example, there is a speciality dedicated to the study of 3D reconstruction methods for digital preservation [2,3,15]. This paucity of proposals for the digital preservation gives us the opportunity to innovate, as we will see in this paper.

3   Recovery of Historical, Cultural, and Patrimonial Value in Native Communities

As defined in [25], *"'safeguarding' means measures aimed at ensuring the viability of the intangible cultural heritage, including the identification, documentation, research, preservation, protection, promotion, enhancement, transmission, particularly through formal and non-formal education, as well as the revitalisation of the various aspects of such heritage"*. The conservation of cultural heritage requires a panoramic view of various cultural, political and territorial aspects, which necessarily interact with each other in an active way. Similarly, the digital preservation models that emerge from cultural heritage information are a real support to the development and preservation of indigenous peoples. This safeguarding supports a diversity of cultural conservation initiatives such as education, research and tourism, among others. Therefore, we are able to connect different places and times through models that interpret or revive the elements of the past and that correspond to an earlier technological era.

The work of safeguarding the ICH [20] places value on some of the contents of the Mapuche ICH register. As discussed in [14], *"this set of traditional goods and practices that identify us as a nation or as a people is appreciated as a gift, something that we receive from the past with such symbolic prestige that it cannot be disputed. The only possible operations - preserving it, restoring it, spreading it - are the most secret base of the social simulation that holds us together"*. To achieve this scope, we use expert models under an ethical perspective of restitution of some elements that could not be captured due to the technological advances of the time when the records were taken, as well as in the prediction of some other features that, thanks to intelligent technologies, we can propose the continuity of songs or poems. Finally, the restitution and prediction of elements through digital media allow us to connect places, communities and also to generate new material that communicates the ICH of the original peoples. These new interrelations of Cultural Heritage lead to the creative act of new hybrid compositions, which are partially proposed by a mechanical or artificial intelligence, a methodological proposal that will be addressed in the following section.

4   Methodology: Design and Use of Expert Systems Based on Intelligent Technologies

The definition of a pipeline that correctly addresses the intangible historical, heritage, and cultural recovery process of Chilean native communities represents a highly complex and dimensional problem involving integrating scientific and anthropological knowledge. From the above, it is natural to propose cutting-edge technologies and expert systems based on Artificial Intelligence (as shown in Fig 1), given the incredible results that these techniques provide.

Fig. 1. Diagram of the disassembly of the ritual process [13].

However, it is essential to emphasise that not all problems need to be addressed from this perspective: multiple traditional methods adequately solve the different formulations developed. Precisely for this problem, the precariousness of audiovisual and textual data, together with their historical scarcity, promote the adoption of architectures that integrate Neural Networks (NN), Convolutional Neural Networks (CNN), Generative Adversarial Networks (GAN), among others, to recover a national intangible heritage with a global impact.

4.1   Generating a Description Space for Ritual Dances

In native communities, ritual dances correspond to a living intangible heritage associated with an activity of ethnic and cultural interest. Body movement is used as a form of expression of identity. In particular, this artistic expression employs a sequence of movements defined by a three-dimensional spatial description, together with the use of patterns specific to each culture, which may have comparatively intercultural similarity, but with an interpretation that is not invariant.

In the case of the Mapuche communities as original peoples of Chile, the traditional dances are called "pürun". Although there is a hereditary knowledge of each member regarding the symbolism of their dance, there is an interest in studying the sequences and spatial descriptions that are being executed from an anthropological perspective. In this context, we can talk about the structural analysis of the ritual dances. On the other hand, to maximise the massive use of digital technologies, multiple audiovisual records can be used as a baseline for generating 3D poses.

Our work uses a 3D human pose estimation in videos, based on the article proposed in [21], using the architecture of Fig. 2 as a reference.

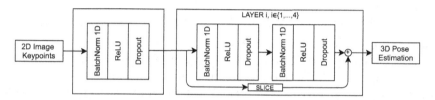

Fig. 2. 3D human pose estimation architecture used for the spatial description of ritual dances, based on [21].

This 3D pose estimation method employs temporal convolutions and semi-supervised training on 2D keypoints obtained from the input images and video frames to capture long-term information, the use of Rectified Linear Units activation function (ReLU) to avoid stagnation during the training phase, dropout to reduce overfitting, and batch normalisation to stabilise the layers of the network. This implies a high accuracy, simplicity, and efficiency model, reducing computational complexity and associated parameters, ideal for testing concepts and inferences on existing data.

Now, an important restriction of the previous model is the unitary detection of the dancer's pose, which denies using digital resources with multi-pose detection as input, resources that are also massively available. One approach that solves this challenge is [8], a model that performs a Real-time Multi-Person 2D Pose Estimation using Part Affinity Fields and has a multi-stage CNN architecture, where the first module predicts the Part Affinity Fields and the second the confidence maps, allowing simultaneous detection of the 2D Pose.

In addition to 2D pose multi-detection, the recognition of objects within an under-represented scene and the performance of the respective segmentation complement the analysis in the search for ritual dance patterns. From this perspective, Detectron2 [26] proposes the use of a Faster Region-based Convolutional Neural Networks Feature Pyramid Network architecture (Faster R-CNN FPN), composed of a Backbone Network (for the extraction of feature maps), Region Proposal Network (detection of object regions from the multi-scale features), and ROI Head (for crops and warps feature maps), which we also use in this article.

4.2   Synthetic Elaboration of an Audiovisual Story

One machine learning core is the advanced recognition of patterns to extract information that establishes relationships between sets of studies. However, this is not the only goal since the existing methods based on this premise will enable the generation and synthetic regeneration of data. Understanding that the heritage recovery process implies identifying patterns that add knowledge and value, these can be used to build a new synthetic audiovisual historical account that contributes to promoting and disseminating the cultural identity of native communities.

Colourising Historical Visual Records. One of the scientific problems with the most significant social impact is the colouring of historical images. Not only is it faced with a reliable reconstruction of precarious and low-quality visual records, but it also implies a strategic adoption to solve the lack of comparative labels that act as a reference in the training phase of advanced reconstruction systems.

Our work relies on the proposed restoration system for old images and film footage by [4], adopting as reference the architecture present in Fig. 3.

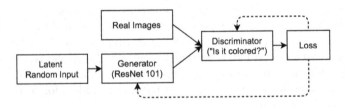

Fig. 3. DeOldify colouriser architecture used for colour restoration in visual records, based on [4,5].

DeOldify model [4] uses a NoGAN as an architecture, an approach that allows obtaining the training benefits of a GAN, dedicating the least time to direct training of the GAN itself by pre-training both the generator and discriminator. Consequently, the discriminator gap is considerably reduced, translating into a more realistic, quick, and reliable restoration of the available visual records, together with a decrease in the complexity of the training.

For a more stable model, [4] proposes using a ResNet 101 as a backbone in the generator to have an object detection system with greater consistency and accuracy, impacting a restoration with more excellent uniformity. The generator itself is called a UNet, which integrates a convolution block, an upsampling block, a Leaky ReLU for activation and batch normalisation. The model's design discriminator is built based on the convolutional layers model's design extraction of characteristics, dropout, and binary classification.

Writing New Native Poems. In native communities and even in historical cultures, the records of knowledge and cultural identity par excellence are poems, literary compositions that transfer experiences, traditions, and beliefs. There is a reassignment of meanings and definitions to language itself. As it is an artistic expression, there is no single interpretation of the meaning of the records. Moreover: there may be hidden patterns that are invisible to the authors themselves. For this reason, if one seeks to generate new cultural poems based on historical literature (or complement existing compositions), both a syntactic analysis of the language and a coherence analysis based on the culture itself must be carried out. In this way, to preserve cultural identity and adequately transfer it to new literary expressions, this work integrates an NLP Distil-GPT2 model based on [22], with architecture as shown in Fig. 4.

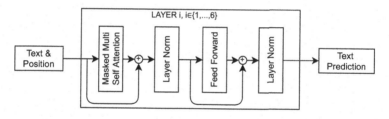

Fig. 4. Distil GPT-2 architecture used for writing new native poems, based on [22].

This NLP model is built on the English language, pre-trained under the supervision of the smaller version of a GPT-2, being on average faster than the latter. It is characterised by generating human-like output, generating synthetic texts, and being a transformer model without recurrence, with high performance. Its architecture is composed of 6 layers, each one composed of a Masked Multi Self Attention (MMSA) module, two Normalization modules, a Feed-Forward module, and two feedback loops on the output of the MMSA and the Feed Forward layer, totalling 82 M parameters. Considering that the historical texts are written in Mapudungun and Spanish, an idiomatic translation is made for Distil-GPT2, assuming the loss of meaning associated with cultural differences.

Musical Timbre Transfer: From Mapuche Culture to the World. Musical instruments are an autochthonous representation of each community, whose operation is based on the characteristic vibration of resonant systems. Although there are musical instruments that are globally taught, the musical expression of each culture is reflected through the same artistic expression. On the other hand, those not massive instruments usually have precarious and scarce digital auditory records. Therefore, detecting the patterns of these native instruments and extrapolating them as a reference model for the timbre transfer is presented as an important challenge to be addressed. Our work is based on [12] to train and construct a timbre transfer model for the trutruca, a Mapuche wind instrument.

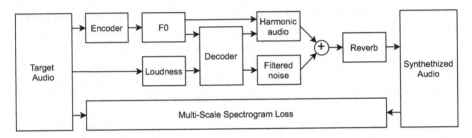

Fig. 5. DDSP architecture used for training a trutruca model timbre conversion, based on [12].

This method is characterised by using a neural network to convert a user's input into complex Digital Signal Processing controls that can produce more realistic signals, allowing the generation of a true-to-expected timbre transfer model. Its architecture shows a combination of a Harmonic Additive Synthesizer with a Subtractive Noise Synthesizer, whose output signal is run through a reverberation module to produce the final audio waveform [12]. For the design of the model associated with the trutruca, latent representation is deleted during training, as documented in Fig. 5.

5   Results

5.1   Generating a Description Space for Ritual Dances

As shown in Fig. 6, from a homemade Mapuche dance video with low pixel resolution, it is possible to estimate a 3D Pose representative of the spatial displacements described to identify sequential patterns of the culture. Although it is a controlled environment through the imposition of conditions on the scene under study (such as the simplicity of the environment and single presence of the executor of the activity), the results associated with the robustness of the estimation (despite the precariousness of the data) allow the use of this intelligent technology to be extended to non-digital communities, being aware of the scarcity of audiovisual resources available.

From [21], we can transfer the 3D points and translate them to verify the trajectories of the dance, how the dancer uses the space, and integrate him with

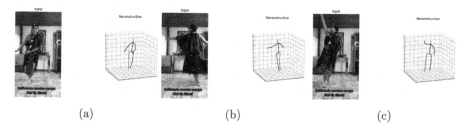

(a)   (b)   (c)

Fig. 6. 3D pose estimation based on 2D keypoints extraction from a Mapuche dance video: (a) front, (b) back, (c) side.

his body. His body, trajectory, and empty space are natural elements of the ritual, and every dance is a new and unrepeatable performance [24].

Fig. 7. Realtime multi-person 2D pose estimation based on [8].

(a)   (b)   (c)

Fig. 8. Mapuche ritual (a) dance 2D pose estimation, (b) segmentation and (c) object recognition, based on Detectron2 [26].

Other experiments in testing and obtaining the pose estimate were the use of OpenPose and Detectron2 (Fig. 7) and Detectron2 (Fig. 8); in both models, we can estimate the points of the 2D skeleton of people simultaneously, by transferring the list of points to a 3D design software, we verify that the Points are identified with good precision, but without depth, since as these models declare, they do not estimate the 3D coordinate in their architecture.

5.2   Synthetic Elaboration of an Audiovisual Story

Colourising Historical Visual Records. As shown in Fig. 9, the colourisation of the historical visual records of the native communities reaches such a level of realism that it manages to revive the history and value of each indigenous people. Although it is known that colour spaces are not descriptors of spatial depth, it is interesting to note that in the restoration process, a change in spatial perception is detected when a composition is introduced into the RGB channels.

(a)   (b)   (c)   (d)

(e)   (f)   (g)   (h)

Fig. 9. Colourization of analogue and digital historical images of Chilean native communities: (a) Mapuche woman wearing her silver ornaments, (b) and its colouring; (c) navigation system used by the ancient Mapuche Lafkenches in a lake environment, (d) and its colouring; (e) mountain landscape of Araucania, (f) and its colouring; (g) family portrait, (h) and its colouring.

In the process of colouring the Fig. 9(a), we can verify in Fig. 9(b) the certainty of the model in determining the materiality of the objects that make up the scene. In Fig. 9(c), the -wampo- is built from a single piece of traditional wood, which after burning and scraping processes with shark teeth and seashells, obtains the hollowed-out shape of a canoe. In the colorising process (Fig. 9(d)), we select a major diversity of environments to verify the way in which the model recompose the scene. In Fig. 9(f), the results are highly accurate, precisely in the way to understand the depth of field from the original scene. The last result, Fig. 9(h) it's indoor photography, where we can think about some control of illumination settings for this family portrait.

This recovery process significantly enriches the international intangible cultural heritage. The input information to the NoGAN corresponds to a limited photographic collection of historical records that are scarce both due to their age and the extinction of some communities (for example, the -selknam-). We highlight here the sensitivity of the model, not only to interpret the original colours from the black and white image but also to maintain the light sensitivity of the restored photograph. Behind this colourisation proposed by the model arises the initiative to verify at least in the sites identified from the picture the integrity of the new image.

Writing New Native Poems. The results presented in the texts attached below are high performance. The NLP model based on Distil-GPT2 not only manages to synthetically generate and complement new texts based on Mapuche poems, but it also manages to identify entities such as the -loika- (a healing bird that is part of this culture) and correctly assign attributes to it is based on the context under study. Therefore, the literary value of the intangible cultural heritage is extended through the correct identification of characteristic patterns of this community.

"El invierno su imagen y otros poemas azules", Elicura Chihuailaf, 1991 "The stars live on this ground. In this sky the water of imagination sings. Beyond the clouds that arise from these waters and these soils, our ancestors dream of us. His spirit - they say - is the full moon. The silence, your beating heart".

Natural Language Processing. "**The next step in the journey to finding our next destination is a long-term goal.** The stars live on this ground. In this sky the water of imagination sings. **The stars will live forever, as if we were living in a world without them and never, ever.** Beyond the clouds that arise from these waters and these soils our ancestors dream of us. **This is the second step of the journey we make to** His spirit the say is the full moon the silence, your beating heart".

"La loika", Huinao. G (S.f). "Why does the loika sing? if they cut down the tree where she used to sing, will have to look for a new one, singing she goes away. Why does the loika sing? If they have stolen the land where she was going to nest, she will have to look for new lands, singing she goes away. Why does the loika sing? if they do not leave her crumbs to eat, because the fruit of her forest was stolen at dawn, the loika sings for not eating. Loika, why are you singing, just to chirp? I sing for my tree, crumbs, land, for what was mine yesterday. I sing for the pain of losing it ... and because loikas will one day be lost".

Natural Language Processing. "**... There he found a small band of loikas, singing together. Do you need to hear them? It seems they couldn't sing for us, but they sang for each other. Do you need to hear their song? And how did they tell the loika that they wanted to sing it? Is the loika singing with her own voice? The loika sings for the pain of losing the land**".

Musical Timbre Transfer: From Mapuche Culture to the World

Trutruca as a Timbre Transfer Model. As previously described, using the trutruca dataset (which was generated using data augmentation techniques), we build a model that transfers the characteristic timbre of this wind instrument to a random input musical sample. Both the generated dataset and the built model are available on the website https://lgarcialara.cl.

Resynthesize Makawa to Violin Timbre. Based on the same DDSP architecture that was used in the trutruca model, a conversion of the makawa (percussion instrument) to the timbre of a violin is performed to make the retention of the audible signal patterns visible, as can be seen in Fig. 10.

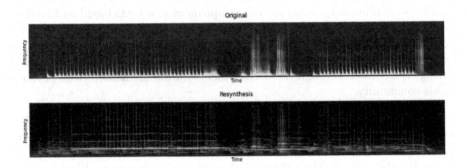

Fig. 10. Resynthesis of the -Makawa- sample to the violin timbre in the frequency and time spectrum.

Audiovisual Story. The process of recovering historical, cultural, and heritage value has implied the generation of visual, audible, and textual records, contribute considerably to the Chilean and international culture. The above leads to a proposal in which all the generated resources are combined, obtaining a historical audiovisual story that captures the essence of the communities, turning an intangible heritage into a tangible one, as shown in Fig. 11. On the website https://lgarcialara.cl are available all the audiovisual stories made from the synthetic content generated by the intelligent technologies adopted.

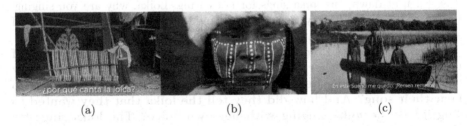

Fig. 11. The audiovisual story made from the restoration of heritage repository: image colourisation, Mapuche timbre transfer, and new native poems with NLP. From left to right, (a) Mapuche and his traditional tissue; (b) Selknam and his symmetrical face painting; (c) Mapuche on his traditional canoe (wampo).

The composition of new hybrid creations is of interest due to the interrelation between technology and ICH, this being, indeed, our starting point for experimentation. The creative act involved in the composition of a story is essential for updating these elements. A contextual setting from an up-to-date perspective presents us with a material of relevance to ICH communication.

6 Conclusions and Future Work

This paper presents an ethical use of applications based on intelligent technologies for the testimonial recovery of native culture in South America. This is a novel approach to the definition of a Digital Heritage framework. Also, we include an incipient study of dance and its description of ceremonial space through bodily measurement.

Emphasising the user's choices in image colourisation, we had the opportunity to choose specific numerical values that directly affect the result, with the decisions we made based on the human eye is essential here. The contribution made by the GTP-2 model to the prediction of poems of Mapuche origin is valuable. Indeed, it is also relevant the decision made by the designer when faced with the possibilities offered by the model, for example, when it proposes three alternatives for the continuity of the texts and the user must necessarily choose one of them. Likewise, the result generated from the recording of Mapuche songs to their representation in a graphic language in .mid format, from which we can repeat, cut, adapt, and even interpret the musical notation obtained on different instruments, is powerful. The audiovisual story created, and from which this research work arises, is a composition of greater complexity where image, musical sound, and poem are combined in a hybrid creation, the result of work proposed both by the results obtained from the expert models and the various design decisions necessary for the creation of new audiovisual productions. These results are a sensitive reading of our territory Araucanía.

Therefore, the work presented lays the foundations for research that integrate Digital Heritage, Native Communities, and Intelligent Technologies in applications such as detecting, analysing, and classifying facial emotions and body expression in ritual dances.

Acknowledgements. This work was partially funded by Internal Arts Research Fund, Catholic University of Temuco. We appreciate the collaboration of Chicahuale, B., Nova, C., Tapia, D., Cid, E., Bravo, F., Uribe, F., Inostroza, J., Pino, M., Llancafilo, N. Stehn, N., Bastias, R., Muñoz, R., Gómez, S., Manríquez, S., Díaz, S., Valderrama, V.

References

1. Aguilar, C., Acosta, O.: A critical review of the current state of natural language processing in Mexico and Chile. In: Natural Language Processing for Global and Local Business, pp. 365–389 (2021)
2. Andrade, B.T., Bellon, O.R., Silva, L., Vrubel, A: Enhancing color texture quality of 3D models for digital preservation of indigenous ceramic artworks. In: 2009 IEEE 12th International Conference on Computer Vision Workshops, ICCV Workshops, pp. 980–987. IEEE. (2009)

3. Andrade, B.T., Bellon, O.R.P., Silva, L., Vrubel, A.: Digital preservation of Brazilian indigenous artworks: generating high quality textures for 3D models. J. Cult. Herit. **13**(1), 28–39 (2012)

4. Antic, J.: DeOldify (2019). https://github.com/jantic/DeOldify

5. Antic, J., Howard, J., Manor, U.: Decrappification, deoldification, and super resolution (2019). https://www.fast.ai/2019/05/03/decrappify/

6. Aretz, I.: 1940–1941 Archives. Museo Chileno de Arte Precolombin. http://precolombino.cl/archivo/archivo-audiovisual/coleccion-isabel-aretz/. Accessed 11 Apr 2021

7. Canio, M., Pozo, G., y Juan Salva, R.: Primeras grabaciones de cantos mapuches en soporte cilindros de fonógrafo (1905 y 1907) (2014). https://revistamusicalchilena.uchile.cl/index.php/RMCH/article/view/35912

8. Cao, Z., Hidalgo, G., Simon, T., Wei, S., Sheikh, Y.: OpenPose: realtime multiperson 2D pose estimation using part affinity fields. IEEE Trans. Pattern Anal. Mach. Intell. **43**, 172–186 (2021)

9. Chilean Memory (2003). http://memoriachilena.gob.cl/. Accessed 11 Apr 2021

10. CMU, L.: Avenue Proyect (2021). https://www.cs.cmu.edu/~avenue/Chile.html. Accessed 11 Apr 2021

11. Duan, M., et al.: NGO Comunidad Ser Indígena (2020)

12. Engel, J., Hantrakul, L., Gu, C., Roberts, A.: DDSP: Differentiable Digital Signal Processing (2020). ArXiv, abs/2001.04643

13. Garcia, L.: Transcultural Technologies. Mapuche metalanguage design for new hybrid configurations (2021). https://github.com/lgarcialara/MCD2021

14. García, N.: Culturas híbridas. Estrategias para entrar y salir de la modernidad (1989)

15. Gomes, L., Bellon, O.R.P., Silva, L.: 3D reconstruction methods for digital preservation of cultural heritage: a survey. Pattern Recogn. Lett. **50**, 3–14 (2014)

16. Levin, L., et al.: Data Collection and Language Technologies for Mapudungun (2000)

17. Marimán, P., Caniuqueo, S., Levil, R., Millalen, J.: ¡... escucha, winka...!. In Anales de la Universidad de Chile, no. 13, pp. 423–431 (2006)

18. Monson, C., et al.: Data Collection and Analysis of Mapudungun Morphology for Spelling Correction (2004). https://doi.org/10.1184/R1/6604595

19. Monson, C., et al.: Building NLP systems for two resource-scarce indigenous languages: mapudungun and Quechua (2006)

20. Mudge, M., Ashley, M., Schroer, C.: A digital future for cultural heritage. In: XXI International CIPA Symposium, Athens, vol. 10 no. 1.222, p. 4779 (2007)

21. Pavllo, D., Feichtenhofer, C., Grangier, D., Auli, M.: 3D Human pose estimation in video with temporal convolutions and semi-supervised training. In: IEEE/CVF Conference on Computer Vision and Pattern Recognition (CVPR), pp. 7745–7754 (2019)

22. Radford, A., Wu, J., Child, R., Luan, D., Amodei, D., Sutskever, I.: Language models are unsupervised multitask learners (2019)

23. Soublette, G.: The Mapuche Culture (2015). https://youtu.be/N27LAd906yM. Accessed 11 Apr 2021

24. Turner, V.: The Ritual Process. Structure and Anti-Structure. Cornell Paperback. Ithaca, New York (1966)

25. UNESCO, Ethical Principles for Safeguarding Intangible Cultural Heritage (2003)

26. Wu, Y., Kirillov, A., Massa, F., Lo, W., Girshick, R.: Detectron2 (2019). https://github.com/facebookresearch/detectron2

Tensile Experiments on Adhesion Between Aluminium Profiles and Glass

Svein Olav Nyberg[✉], Kjell G. Robbersmyr, Jan Andreas Holm,
and Filippo Sanfilippo

Department of Engineering Sciences, University of Agder (UiA),
Jon Lilletuns vei 9, 4879 Grimstad, Norway
sveinon@uia.no

Abstract. In this work, the effects of the adhesion between aluminium profiles and glass are studied from a static tensile perspective. A series of stretch curves are analysed from their derivatives to find their points of float and maximum load bearing. The variable factors are glass type, and type of connection: i.e., edge adhesive, side (fugue) adhesive, and excessive fugue adhesive, for short named *fugue-edge*. The stretch data imply four quantities to analyse and compare: displacement and load respectively at float and at max load. The results are first compared factor group against factor group. With this tool, only a few significant conclusions may be found. The second comparison is by means of the more robust statistical tools of linear regression and analysis of variance (ANOVA), with conclusions about which factors are significant, and then about the size of the effect on the four variables under study. This forms the basis for a recommendations for how to obtain the strongest possible glass-frame system.

Keywords: Adhesion · Aluminium profiles · Glass · Linear regression · Analysis of variance

1 Introduction

Over the last few decades, the usage of structural adhesives in civil engineering and in the manufacturing industry has risen substantially [8]. While bonded joints have considerable benefits over traditional connections, their behaviour must be predicted taking into consideration various factors such as environmental exposure during application and service life, and adherent type. The primary issue with the mechanical performance of the metal-glass connection is the brittleness of the glass, which makes designing structural components with cooperating glass problematic. Because of this property of glass, conventional connections (such as bolted joints) are not appropriate. When compared to conventional joints, bonded joints offer a viable option since they allow consistent

This research is funded by the Top Research Centre Mechatronics (TRCM), University of Agder (UiA), Norway.

stress distribution, minimise stress concentration, and reduce junction weight. However, it is challenging to assess their nonlinear mechanical behaviour and mechanical performance under various environmental exposure circumstances.

Recent advances in the research of structural adhesives [1,5,7,9] have shown that by connecting together brittle and ductile materials (for example, glass and steel, respectively), the mechanical behaviour of the glass structure may be improved. This combination allows for the creation of a very ductile structure with high gloss and clarity. Overend et al. [10] conducted mechanical and computational modeling experiments to investigate the performance of five adhesives for load-bearing steel-glass connectors. Mechanical testing on steel-glass connections gave valuable information for choosing an adhesive (silicone).

By following these research trends, the results of an experimental campaign on glass-aluminum bonded joints are presented in this article.

The paper is organised as it follows. A review of the related research work is given in Sect. 2. The conducted experiments are described in Sect. 3. In Sect. 4, the proposed methodology is presented along with the results of the analysis. Finally, conclusions and future works are discussed in Sect. 5.

2   Related Research Work

The broad demand for lightweight, robust, and long-lasting materials in industrial applications has provided a significant push for research and development. In order to meet these criteria, it may be essential to combine elements that appear to be incompatible [2]. As a result, innovative technology processes capable of efficiently combining different materials (i.e., hybrid joint) are in great demand in the industrial sector.

Several related studies exists in the literature. For example, the durability of glass/steel bonded junctions subjected to adverse conditions was investigated in [2]. Pull-off mechanical tests were performed in this context in order to evaluate the performances evolution and damage phenomena of the bonded joints during the ageing exposition. The performance of two different adhesives were compared (i.e., epoxy and polyurethane ones). The impacts of the glass surface condition and the presence of a basalt mat layer inside the adhesive thickness were also considered. The mechanical performances were linked to the failure mechanisms that occurred. In [6], experiments were carried out to understand and anticipate the behaviour of dissimilar bonded junctions under quasi-static and impact stresses, employing composite and aluminium substrates. Following the requirements for the automobile sector, a variety of testing temperatures were examined. It was fair to assert that, when used in combination with modern crash resistant adhesives, different bonded joints can effectively be used for the construction of automotive structures, with good energy absorption capabilities under impact and no significant sacrifices in joint performance. In [11] the strength properties of aluminium/glass-fiber-reinforced laminate with an additional epoxy adhesive film inter-layer were considered. The interesting aspect of this former study is that the application of the adhesive film as an additional binding agent caused an increase in laminate elasticity. In [4], the effect of surface roughness for improving interfacial adhesion in hybrid materials with aluminium/carbon fiber reinforced epoxy composites was investigated. Various types of sanding paper and varying sanding sessions were used to regulate the roughness of the aluminium's surface. After various sanding procedures, the surface roughness of aluminium was measured using static contact angle (CA) and 3D surface scanning. The interfacial adhesion between the various alluminium surface treatments was evaluated using lap shear strength (LSS) tests. Surface treatment of aluminum in these materials has great potential for improving mechanical characteristics in aerospace, automotive, and other practical applications.

There is still a need for more accurate static tensile experiments on adhesion between aluminium profiles and glass, especially considering that, during their service life, the joining elements are exposed to various factors (e.g., ultraviolet (UV), temperature, moisture) that may affect their mechanical performance.

3   Experiments

The main objective is twofold: to test the adhesion between the glass and the adhesive, and between the aluminium profile and the adhesive.

3.1   Materials

The aluminium profile, made of ETC 5129 (anodised), has the shape as shown in Fig. 1b. The figure also shows the joint or the connection between the profile, the adhesive and the glass.

The dimensions of the glass/polycarbonate are as follows: width = 200 mm, height = 150 mm and the thickness = 6,0 mm (glass) and 5,0 mm (polycarbonate). Three factors of adhesive, and two types of glass with different types of processing of preparation were tested in combinations, as shown in Table 1. The number of samples in each group is 5, with the exception of two of these groups, which have 4.

3.2   Static Tensile Properties

The tests were performed as pure static tensile tests. A suitable test setup was developed including two fixtures to attach the test samples to the tensile testing machine. The adhesive was applied to the surfaces prescribed for each sample type in a uniform manner by the same operator. The tensile testing machine has the following designation: servo-hydraulic benchtop test machine type 804H. Figure 1a shows the clamping of the test sample in the tensile testing machine. The tests were performed by stretching the sample to fracture at a stretching speed equal of 0.02 mm/s until the frame had lost grip on the glass. The total time naturally differed between the tests. The applied load and the extension are logged, yielding the stretch curves shown in Fig. 1c.

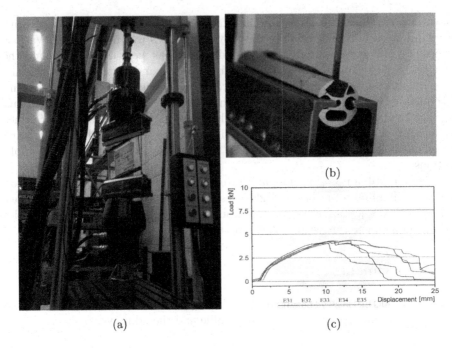

Fig. 1. Experiment illustrations: (a) machine set-up; (b) mounting profile; (c) load vs displacement curves.

4   Methodology and Results

The analysis of the load test data goes in two steps, the first of which is to extract the key points from the detailed profile of stretch data. The second is to analyse the table of key data to look for patterns.

4.1   Extracting the Key Points

The data pairs consist of load vs displacement, and a typical profile looks like Fig. 2a (close-up: Fig. 2b). The main curve (blue) is the load vs the displacement, and the secondary curve (orange) is its smoothed derivative. The float point is the first key point. It is the first point after max derivative where the derivative dips below 85% of the max derivative value. Precisely 85% is somewhat arbitrary, but it gave the least amount of disturbance due to the derivative not being absolutely smooth, all the while staying reasonably close to where visual inspection indicated the curve was tapering off. The max load is simply at max load. To find the start of the process, draw a straight line through the float point and the beginning of the rise up to it, as indicated by two open circles. The smaller full circle is then the estimated starting point. Subtract this value from the displacement values.

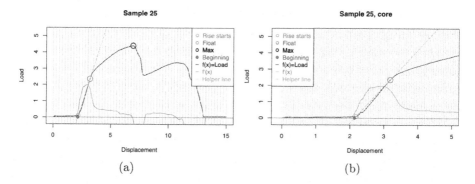

Fig. 2. Displacement-load profile: (a) individual load curve; (b) close-up. (Color figure online)

The float point and the point of max load are the most interesting sites, as they are the keys to assessing critical strength for glass-in-metal frame constructions. As such, the float point is the point before which a reversal of forces will return the adhesive back to its original shape. Both displacement and force at these points matter to these assessments. This is important to the long-term life of a construction with glass in a metal frame, such as a car, a boat or a plane. The second points of interest is the point of maximum force; that is, the force and the displacement at this point. Though this only has a one-time applicability in for instance a crash, this one time is a rather important event to plan and therefore calculate for. A possible third point of interest is on the way down from max force where the adhesive has not totally given up the glass yet, but no unique good point which could serve this function has manifested itself.

Table 1 sums up these measurement series, loaded into R (programming language) as a dataframe named tD. In this analysis, the significance levels are the conventional ones, 0.1 (.) 0.05 (∗), 0.01 (∗∗) and 0.001 (∗ ∗ ∗).

4.2 Analysis of Key Points, Take 1: Pairwise t Tests

Table 1 presents *four* different values to analyse: $y_1 =$ Displacement at float point, $y_2 =$ Load at float point, $y_3 =$ Displacement at max load, $y_4 =$ Max load.

The question is how the different factors, $x_1 =$ Glass type, (B) $x_2 =$ Edge adhesive, $x_3 =$ Fugue adhesive, and $x_4 =$ Extended fugue edge adhesive, influence the four values.

The simplest method calculates effect from grouped means and standard deviations. This is the *pairwise t test*.

Example: To see if x_1, Glass type, makes a significant difference to y_1, load at float point, write the following command in R:

```
t.test( tD[tD$x1=="PC",]$y1, tD[tD$x1=="GL",]$y1 )
```

This generates the following output:

Table 1. Raw data.

LNR	x_1 = Glass	x_2 = Edge	x_3 = Fugue	x_4 = FugueEdge	y_1 = floatDisp	y_2 = floatLoad	y_3 = topDisp	y_4 = topLoad
11	GL	1	0	0	0.913704657	1.8585	2.213804657	2.6863
12	GL	1	0	0	0.930844519	2.2858	3.491344519	3.4309
13	GL	1	0	0	0.940517524	2.3094	5.191617524	3.5782
14	GL	1	0	0	0.974659503	2.2385	4.288859503	3.4744
15	GL	1	0	0	0.83215012	1.9394	2.85085012	2.8244
21	GL	1	1	1	1.002709147	2.2316	4.500109147	3.8788
22	GL	1	1	1	1.092222408	2.5627	5.465422408	4.7325
23	GL	1	1	1	1.185509437	2.3796	4.121309437	3.9398
24	GL	1	1	1	1.046217805	2.4078	4.140617805	4.1893
25	GL	1	1	1	1.049969533	2.3598	4.782269533	4.4029
31	GL	1	1	0	0.867274823	2.1805	3.300974823	3.5172
32	GL	1	1	0	0.869963177	2.1873	5.102703177	4.0619
34	GL	1	1	0	0.80657587	2.0172	4.46102587	3.2227
35	GL	1	1	0	0.804617794	1.9478	4.439297794	3.1235
41	GL	0	1	1	1.970133284	0.40894	7.223733284	1.178
42	GL	0	1	1	2.077930748	0.4097	6.690630748	1.0124
43	GL	0	1	1	1.757843959	0.40054	8.366443959	1.5144
44	GL	0	1	1	1.826198325	0.39291	6.919598325	1.123
45	GL	0	1	1	1.586146486	0.39978	9.830146486	1.9264
51	GL	0	1	0	2.202985873	0.087738	4.819885873	0.1236
52	GL	0	1	0	1.321101477	0.069427	7.632101477	0.2533
53	GL	0	1	0	1.948846032	0.07019	4.991546032	0.16937
54	GL	0	1	0	2.807823534	0.17624	5.540623534	0.32349
61	PC	1	0	0	0.284235842	0.18311	1.181235842	0.24185
62	PC	1	0	0	0.922222222	1.0757	1.303222222	1.5747
63	PC	1	0	0	0.659016213	2.0676	0.857016213	2.2545
64	PC	1	0	0	0.637493045	2.137	0.831493045	2.4834
65	PC	1	0	0	0.769440675	1.812	0.878440675	2.0798
71	PC	1	1	1	0.624673374	1.2367	9.793673374	2.7458
72	PC	1	1	1	0.800206527	2.079	7.333206527	3.418
73	PC	1	1	1	0.757422363	1.9012	13.15342236	3.9963
74	PC	1	1	1	0.936433402	2.565	4.109433402	4.1252
75	PC	1	1	1	0.952506748	2.0248	4.698506748	3.6545
81	PC	1	1	0	0.825485636	2.4208	2.023485636	3.2433
82	PC	1	1	0	0.909353355	2.2758	3.970353355	3.125
83	PC	1	1	0	1.111201293	2.3369	2.166201293	2.9015
84	PC	1	1	0	0.344444444	0.60272	1.392444444	1.4458
85	PC	1	1	0	1.003665984	2.2247	3.762665984	3.2433
91	PC	0	1	1	0.857663302	0.25406	17.2456633	3.6919
92	PC	0	1	1	0.654478678	0.2327	18.81347868	3.6064
93	PC	0	1	1	0.490448382	0.1976	14.41844838	3.241
94	PC	0	1	1	0.619769205	0.2327	11.5007692	2.6627
95	PC	0	1	1	0.688800403	0.18768	7.852800403	1.4008
101	PC	0	1	0	1.861267134	0.080872	3.631267134	0.14114
102	PC	0	1	0	1.672033069	0.099182	4.551033069	0.2182
104	PC	0	1	0	1.097488599	0.052643	5.014488599	0.21896
105	PC	0	1	0	1.035315793	0.32501	15.20631579	3.6926

t = −3.519, df = 36.796, p-value = 0.001172
alternative hypothesis: true difference in means is not equal to 0
95 percent confidence interval: −0.7643583 −0.2057004
sample estimates:
mean of x mean of y
0.8547944 1.3398237

Here, t is the t value of the difference. The t value of a statistic is its mean divided by its standard deviation, so in other words the t value measures how many standard deviation out from 0 the mean is. The probability of the mean being this many standard deviations from 0 by accident, is the p value, and is calculated by means of the t value and the df ("degrees of freedom") in the t distribution.

In Table 1, R has designated "mean of x" to be μ_{PC}, the mean of y_1 for glass type PC, and "mean of y" to be μ_{GL}, the mean of y_1 for glass type GL.

The $size$ of the effect for factor x_1, glass type, on y_1, displacement at float, is the difference between the two means, $\Delta_{11} = \mu_{PC} - \mu_{GL} = 1.3398237 - 0.8547944 = 0.4850293$. The other important finding is the probability that this result "or worse" could have been achieved by random data. This probability is called the p-value, and is $p = 0.001172$. Its significance level is **.

Table 2 summarizes the test results by the sizes and significances for the effects of the four factors on the four values.

Table 2. The effects and significance levels of the effects in pairwise t tests.

	$x_1 =$ Glass	$x_2 =$ Edge	$x_3 =$ Fugue	$x_4 =$ FugueEdge
$y_1 =$ floatDisp	+0.485(**)	−0.614 (**)	+0.388 (**)	+0.939
$y_2 =$ floatLoad	+0.257	+1.768(***)	−0.601 (*)	−0.129
$y_3 =$ topDisp	−1.254	−4.910(***)	+4.528(***)	+4.656 (***)
$y_4 =$ topLoad	+0.076	+1.686(***)	+0.063	+0.887 (*)

This is a useful result, and $Edge$ stands out as both significant and with a large effect on all values. However, this method has its limitations, and works best if the causal effects of the factors are independent. There is no reason to make that assumption here, so instead, it is necessary to turn to a more efficient tool which does not require that assumption.

4.3 Analysis of Key Points, Take 2: Linear Regression and ANOVA

Equation 1 shows the basic linear model for y_k:

$$y_k = \beta_{k0} + \beta_{k1}x_1 + \beta_{k2}x_2 + \beta_{k3}x_3 + \beta_{k4}x_4 \tag{1}$$

Glass (type), Edge, Fugue, and FugueEdge are coded as so called $dummy$ $variables$, with the latter three explicitly set as 0 or 1 in the data frame, and the Glass type implicitly set by R itself, to GL=0 and PC=1. Equation 2 shows the results of calculating the coefficients for y_4, max load.

$$y_4 = 0.422 - 0.094x_1 + 2.088x_2 + 0.465x_3 + 1.138x_4 \tag{2}$$

R's built-in linear regression method **lm** handles these calculations by means of the command

```
mod41 = lm(y4 ~ x1 + x2 + x3 + x4, data=tD)
```

Table 3. R summary table for displacement at Max Load.

Coefficients		Estimate	Std. error	t value	$p = \Pr(> |t|)$	Sign. Lvl
(Intercept)	β_{40}	0.42158	0.45265	0.931	0.356996	
Glass,	β_{41}	−0.09397	0.27711	−0.339	0.736232	
Edge,	β_{42}	2.08825	0.31238	6.685	4.11e−08	***
Fugue,	β_{43}	0.46526	0.40594	1.146	0.258224	
FugueEdge,	β_{44}	1.13802	0.31332	3.632	0.000759	***

The command **summary(mod41)** summarizes the output from **lm** in Table 3. According to Table 3, *Edge* and *FugueEdge* are significant at any conventional level of significance.

The first column, *Coefficients*, lists the coefficients β_{4i} in the regression equation, and since these variables are dummies with values 0 and 1, the coefficients are equal to the mean difference that those particular factor make. The coefficients are therefore the equivalent to the Δ_{4i} calculated in the previous section. So β_{42}, for instance, stands for the mean effect of having adhesive on the edge as opposed to not having done it *in the presence of the other factors*. The next column, the *Std. Error*, lists the standard errors in the estimates of the coefficients.

The third column is the t value, which is sometimes called the *variability*. The variability is how many standard errors (col 2) away from 0 the estimate (col 1) is. So it is simply the value of the first column divided by the value of the second. The fourth and last column ($Pr(> |t|)$) is a probability calculation, where R uses the t distribution to find the probability that the estimate could be this many standard errors (or more) away from 0 by pure chance. $Pr(> |t|$ is also called the p-value. When the p value is small, it means that the probability of erroneously concluding the presence of an effect from that factor is correspondingly small.

So far, this sounds like means and standard deviations again, but there is a vital difference, which is that the regression takes into account *the presence of the other factors*. This is easy to see in the numbers as well, in that for instance $\Delta_{44} = 0.887$, whereas $\beta_{44} = 1.138$. The full table for the β coefficients and their significance levels, given simple linear regression, is in Table 4. Factors that were significant in Table 2 are non-significant in Table 4, and some effect sizes have changed their sign in the presence of the other factors. Since this is the more advanced analysis, it takes precedence, so in conclusion the first model with t testing was a only good first approximation.

Table 4. The effects and their significance levels in simple linear regression.

	x_0	x_1	x_2	x_3	x_4
y_1	+1.597(∗ ∗ ∗)	−0.482(∗ ∗ ∗)	−0.570(∗ ∗ ∗)	+0.224	−0.196
y_2	+0.046	−0.287 (∗)	+1.888(∗ ∗ ∗)	+0.233	+0.164
y_3	+5.572(∗ ∗ ∗)	+1.379	−3.953(∗ ∗ ∗)	+0.615	+3.648(∗ ∗ ∗)
y_4	+0.422	−0.094	+2.088(∗ ∗ ∗)	+0.465	+1.138(∗ ∗ ∗)

However, simple regression is also an approximation. One way further is to omit factors not proven to be significant. For y_4, this means a linear model omitting $x_1 = \text{Glass}$ and $x_3 = \text{Fugue}$:

```
mod42 = lm(y4 ~ x2 + x4, data=tD)
summary(mod42)
```

The summary is in Table 5. The coefficients are somewhat different, as should be expected since factors $x_1 = \text{Glass}$ and $x_3 = \text{Fugue}$ are no longer present.

Table 5. R summary table 2 for Max Load.

Coefficients	Estimate	Std. error	t value	$p = \Pr(> |t|)$	Sign. Lvl
(Intercept) β_0	0.7580	0.2726	2.781	0.00796	**
$x2 = \text{Edge } \beta_2$	1.9573	0.2891	6.769	2.49e−08	***
$x4 = \text{FugueEdge } \beta_4$	1.2854	0.2843	4.522	4.59e−05	***

A more thorough way further is to first complicate the model by looking at interactions between the factors, and only then removing the non-significant ones. To add a single interaction, like for instance between $x_1 = \text{Glass}$ and $x_2 = \text{Edge}$, modify the R command with the interaction term x1:x2:

```
mod43 = lm(y4 ~ x1 + x2 + x3 + x4 + x1:x2, data=tD)
```

To add *all* k'th order interactions, write (replace k by its value)

```
mod44 = lm(y4 ~ (x1 + x2 + x3 + x4)^k, data=tD)
```

The result of the command **summary(mod45)** would be a table of 16 rows displaying the effects and significance levels of interactions on par with the factors on their own. The interesting result in that table is that the conventionally significant factors are $x_2 = \text{Edge}$ (∗ ∗ ∗), $x_4 = \text{FugueEdge}$ (∗) and $x_1 : x_2$ (∗). Glass itself is highly non-significant with a p-value of 0.940.

Since the interaction terms soak up some of the variation, both the coefficients and the p-values change somewhat from those of the simple regression.

To proceed, note that the p-values are the likelihood that the coefficients in question actually differ from 0, *given the model*. The next logical step is to consider the model itself, more precisely the likelihood that the model captures as much variability as it does.

Data has variability, and the variability may be classed into two types: variability explained by the model, and variability unexplained by the model. Adding a new explanatory factor will explain more, and thus increase the part explained by the model. The tool ANOVA (Analysis Of Variance) analyses the contribution by the added factor (or interaction of factors).

ANOVA can compare just two models, or it can look at an entire hierarchy of models, built from the bottom and up. The simplest is Type I ANOVA (R command: **anova**), and is the easiest to understand. It is however, dependent on the order in which the factors are entered, so it is not the best. Type II ANOVA (R command: **Anova**, found in the R library *car*) does not have this problem.

The analysis of the models for y_4 uses Type II. Table 6 summarizes the results of the R command **Anova(mod45)**.

Table 6. R's ANOVA table for the factors explaining Max Load.

Coefficient	Sum Sq	Df	F value	Pr(> F)	Sign. Lvl
Edge	40.065	1	68.1300	6.502e−10	***
Fugue	2.292	1	3.8980	0.0558445	
FugueEdge	11.545	1	19.6320	8.055e−05	***
Glass	0.121	1	0.2051	0.6532458	
Edge:Fugue		0			
Edge:FugueEdge	1.222	1	2.0783	0.1578147	
Edge:Glass	8.346	1	14.1929	0.0005746	***
Fugue:FugueEdge		0			
Fugue:Glass	0.720	1	1.2248	0.2755654	
FugueEdge:Glass	0.321	1	0.5458	0.4647200	
Edge:Fugue:FugueEdge		0			
Edge:Fugue:Glass		0			
Edge:FugueEdge:Glass	0.257	1	0.4370	0.5126844	
Fugue:FugueEdge:Glass		0			
Edge:Fugue:FugueEdge:Glass		0			
Residuals	21.758	37			

In Table 6 the first column is Sum Sq, meaning *Sum of square deviations*. It sums the squares of the improvement in prediction for each coefficient added, as more coefficients are added through progressing down the list. The Df is *degrees of freedom*. The F value is calculated from the Sum Sq and Df, and Pr($¿$F) is the probability of getting an F value that large, or larger.

Both the ANOVA table and the summary table display the curious effect that *glass type* seems to be non-significant when considered on its own, but not when interacting with the factor of edge adhesive! This is, however, not difficult to interpret, since this means that glass type does not matter *when averaged for the presence and non-presence of edge adhesive*, but that one type of glass boosts the effect of edge adhesive whereas the other glass type diminishes it. Table 7 shows the effect of Edge+Glass+Glass:Edge.

Table 7. Glass and Edge interaction term.

	No Edge adhesive	Edge adhesive
GL	$0 + 0 + 0 = 0$	$3.0524 + 0 + 0 = 3.26389$
PC	$0 + 1.2500 + 0 = 1.2500$	$3.0524 + 1.2500 − 2.1649 = 2.1375$

But first, which is the better choice? It is in general a bad idea to include an interaction of factors without including the factors, so if glass:edge is in, so is glass itself. For the other factors, choose generously at a significance level of 0.1 for a final model for the max load of

mod4Final = lm(y4 ~ x1 + x2 + x4 + x1:x2, data=tD)

The final linear formula for the factors is then in Eq. 3

$$y_4 = 0.141 + 1.250x_1 + 3.052x_2 + 1.271x_4 - 2.165x_1x_2 \tag{3}$$

4.4 The Other 3 Values and Summary

The other analyses proceed in the same way, by looking at interactions as well as the factors themselves, and then pruning down as far as possible. The resulting formulas for the sizes of the effects of the conventionally significant factors and interactions are then captured in these formulas. The significance levels (. $*$ $**$ and $* * *$) are written below their respective coefficients:

$$y_1 = 2.137 - 0.787x_1 - 1.284x_2 - 0.346x_4 + 0.707x_1x_2 - 0.288x_1x_4 + 0.622x_2x_4$$
$$\quad\;\; * * * \quad\;\; * * * \quad\;\; * * * \quad\;\; * \quad\;\; * * * \quad\;\; . \quad\;\; * * *$$

$$y_2 = 0.053 - 0.290x_1 + 1.883x_2 + 0.319x_3$$
$$\quad\;\; * \quad\;\; * * * \quad\;\; .$$

$$y_3 = 6.201 + 1.195x_1 - 2.476x_2 + 1.241x_4 - 3.201x_1x_2 + 5.093x_1x_4$$
$$\quad\;\; * * * \quad\;\; * \quad\;\; * \quad\;\; * * $$

$$y_4 = 0.141 + 1.250x_1 + 3.052x_2 + 1.271x_4 - 2.165x_1x_2$$
$$\quad\;\; * * \quad\;\; * * * \quad\;\; * * * \quad\;\; * * *$$

Two factors were present to explain all four values: $x_1 =$ Glass type, and $x_2 =$ Edge adhesive. Of these, x_2 was by far both the most significant *and* the one with the greatest effect. Among the remaining two, $x_3 =$ Fugue, was the least significant, and $x_4 =$ FugueEdge (extended fugue adhesive) mattered only for the value of the max load, beyond the float point. However, in interaction with glass type, x_4 did have a strong effect on the displacements (y_1 and y_3).

5   Concluding Remarks

This paper investigated the effects of adhesion between aluminium profiles and glass from a static tensile standpoint, with view to applying these insights to calculations of structural strength. The key elements under study were the displacement and loads at two critical points to strength calculations. The key takeaway result is that the edge adhesive is the most important contributor to both points, and that the glass type makes an appreciable difference to the adhesion as well. Theoretically, this paper looked at two different forms of statistical analysis, pairwise t-tests, and regression analysis with ANOVA. The latter is by far the more robust and detailed tool, and reversed some conclusions from the simpler t-test, most notably when the t-test concluded that the presence of fugue adhesive was a key contributor to both points of structural strength. The regression analysis also showed that the effect of "fugue edge" depends on glass type and on edge adhesive. As future work, intelligent optimisation and machine learning (ML) techniques [3] may be applied to better understand the considered process.

Acknowledgements. The authors want to thank Geir Horst Soøraker and Arne Skjølingstad at Ertec AS for producing the test samples and for valuable discussions.

References

1. Bedon, C., Louter, C.: Structural glass beams with embedded GFRP, CFRP or steel reinforcement rods: comparative experimental, analytical and numerical investigations. J. Build. Eng. **22**, 227–241 (2019)
2. Fiore, V., et al.: Pull-off adhesion of hybrid glass-steel adhesive joints in salt fog environment. J. Adhes. Sci. Technol. **30**(19), 2157–2174 (2016)
3. Hatledal, L.I., Sanfilippo, F., Zhang, H.: JIOP: a Java intelligent optimisation and machine learning framework. In: Proceedings of the 28th European Conference on Modelling and Simulation (ECMS), Brescia, Italy, pp. 101–107 (2014)
4. Kwon, D.J., et al.: Comparison of interfacial adhesion of hybrid materials of aluminum/carbon fiber reinforced epoxy composites with different surface roughness. Compos. B Eng. **170**, 11–18 (2019)
5. Louter, C., Belis, J., Bos, F., Veer, F.: Reinforced glass beams composed of annealed, heat-strengthened and fully tempered glass. In: Challenging Glass 3, pp. 691–702. IOS Press (2012)
6. Machado, J., Nunes, P., Marques, E., da Silva, L.F.: Adhesive joints using aluminium and CFRP substrates tested at low and high temperatures under quasi-static and impact conditions for the automotive industry. Compos. B Eng. **158**, 102–116 (2019)
7. Machalická, K., Eliášová, M.: Adhesive joints in glass structures: effects of various materials in the connection, thickness of the adhesive layer, and ageing. Int. J. Adhes. Adhes. **72**, 10–22 (2017)
8. Marchione, F., Munafò, P.: Experimental strength evaluation of glass/aluminum double-lap adhesive joints. J. Build. Eng. **30**, 101284 (2020)
9. Martens, K., Caspeele, R., Belis, J.: Load-carrying behaviour of interrupted statically indeterminate reinforced laminated glass beams. Glass Struct. Eng. **1**(1), 81–94 (2016). https://doi.org/10.1007/s40940-016-0017-2
10. Overend, M., Jin, Q., Watson, J.: The selection and performance of adhesives for a steel-glass connection. Int. J. Adhes. Adhes. **31**(7), 587–597 (2011)
11. Trzepiecinski, T., Kubit, A., Kudelski, R., Kwolek, P., Obłój, A.: Strength properties of aluminium/glass-fiber-reinforced laminate with additional epoxy adhesive film interlayer. Int. J. Adhes. Adhes. **85**, 29–36 (2018)

Machine Learning for Capacity Utilization Along the Routes of an Urban Freight Service

Mandar V. Tabib[1]([✉]), Jon Kåre Stene[2], Adil Rasheed[1], Ove Langeland[3], and Frants Gundersen[3]

[1] SINTEF Digital, Mathematics and Cybernetics, Trondheim, Norway
`mandar.tabib@sintef.no`
[2] Kolonial As, Oslo, Norway
[3] Transportøkonomisk Institutt, Oslo, Norway

Abstract. A machine-learning based methodology has been developed to investigate its applicability in enhancing capacity utilization of freight services. Freight services employ vehicles for picking and delivering goods from and to retailers, and better utilization of freight capacity can save fuel, time and encourage environment friendly operations. The methodology developed here involves identifying the regions in the map where the services are expected to experience lower freight capacity and have good opportunity to enhance this capacity by considering the presence of nearby retailer density. For this, we compare ability of various machine learning models for (a) predicting the weight of freight in the van along various stops in its given freight route, and for (b) predicting the freight traffic counts of vehicles at a location. The data used for this work involves all the freight routes used by a commercial company for freight transport in the Oslo city in a given month along with corresponding freight weight data, as well as data on location of all the retailers in the city. The ML methods compared are Artificial Neural network, Support Vector Machine (SVM), Random forest and linear regression using cross-validation and learning curves. The random forest model performs better than most models for our data, and is used to predict freight weight at stops along new unseen routes. In unseen test scenario (new unseen freight routes), the ML-based methodology is able to predict two out of actual seven best locations for enhancing capacity utilization, thus showing its usefulness. The challenges lies in enhancing accuracy of ML models as the prediction of freight weight is expected to be dependent on input features that are not easy to measure (for example, unseen traffic congestion, local demand/supply changes, etc.). The scope and challenges encountered in this work can help in outlining future work with focus on relevant data acquisition and for integrating the proposed methodology in vehicle route optimization tools.

Keywords: Machine learning · Freight · Capacity · Transport

© The Author(s), under exclusive license to Springer Nature Switzerland AG 2022
F. Sanfilippo et al. (Eds.): INTAP 2021, CCIS 1616, pp. 419–432, 2022.
https://doi.org/10.1007/978-3-031-10525-8_33

1   Introduction

An efficient utilization of freight capacity will lead to cost-saving as well as better environment [15]. Road freight transport in urban areas is growing due to increasing frequencies of delivery transports which are caused by e-Commerce, home delivery schemes and the reduction of storage in central urban area [13]. To manage this freight transport intelligently, use of Machine learning and AI has been gaining ground [3]. However, the focus for use of AI/ML have been mostly in areas such as freight demand forecast [10], freight asset maintenance and transportation management [3], vehicle trajectory prediction [11], vehicular arrival time prediction, and freight flow and traffic prediction [6]. There have been only limited literature on prediction of freight weight (or volume) along the freight route. Like, [2] have presented a method for route and freight estimation, where for freight estimation, they have used a simplistic method based on averaging of the consignments on the historical known trips for the estimated route. The authors have suggested scope for improvement as their freight estimation is applied only for ordered and known freight type. These simplistic methods might not be able to predict for a new route locations involving freight pick up and drops where historical data is not available. Then, there are works like the yearly railway freight volume prediction [9] and the yearly shipping port freight volume prediction [8] at a port (just one location), and such works are again much different than a vehicle-based freight transport along multiple stops involving pickups and drops of freight (as has been studied in our work here). In research literature, there has so far been no machine-learning based work on predicting freight weights at different stops along the freight-vehicle routes.

In this context, our proposed work here employs a ML based methodology involving real operational data from commercial freight operators. Here, machine learning (ML) algorithm is used to predict the expected freight-weight along a given route and identify regions where the vehicular capacity can be gained (in this case by looking at proximity to nearby retail business operators who would want to use the freight delivery system).

The main objectives of this work are: to study the scope and challenges in using machine-learning based approach as a means to enhance freight capacity in a realistic set-up involving freight pick-up and drop scenarios at multiple stops in the freight route. The next section describes the methodology.

2   Methodology

The aim is to find stop locations in a potential freight-delivery routes that has scope for better capacity utilization. It involves predicting those stop-locations where: (a) the utilization capacity of vans will be low (in other words, the vans will be predicted to have lower freight weight along such stops), and where (b) the nearby retailer density is high, so there is scope for improving the van capacity at these stops as more retailers can be sought for delivery/transportation of goods. To do this we need information on expected frequency of visit of vans at all stops in the routes and expected freight weight of a van along the route.

Hence, we first develop separate machine learning models for predicting: (a) expected freight weights of the van at a give stop location depending upon where the location is on a given van's delivery route, and (b) expected traffic count (frequency) at a given location. The models are trained using the dataset provided by a commercial freight delivery service. The dataset is divided into training, validation and test set as described later in Sect. 3. However, during testing of methodology on unseen test freight data, the frequency count of vans passing through all stop locations is known to us from the data itself so we have used only the freight weight machine learning model in the methodology testing below. It has an added advantage that the freight weight prediction would not be dependent on errors from ML based prediction of frequency count. The overall methodology is described below in the following steps. The inputs provided to the methodology are new freight routes, retailer data set and trained machine learning models.

Step 1 → First predict the "freight weight" at various stop locations in the freight route using the "trained machine learning weight estimation model". Also obtain the frequency of visits of vans at these various stop locations (here, we can also employ the second ML model to predict the freight traffic count if the frequency count is not available from dataset). Then, obtain the "summed capacity" at all stops, i.e. the summation of freight weights for all vans stopping at a stop location. Then compute the ratio of "summed capacity" to the total frequency of visits by vans for each stop location in the freight routes. Now save "list" of location coordinates that has the least ratio of summed capacity to frequency of visit in ascending order. So, in step 1, we obtain the stop locations in freight routes that have lower freight weights despite being visited quite often by the vans.

Step 2 → In this step, we look at proximity of all stop locations to the retailers. So we identify a parameter R, where R is the radius in km from the given stop location. Then,

(a) For each of the lowest capacity location i in the list in Step 1, we find sum of square of its distance from all the retail shops within a given radius R (say 0.5 km). Here, the radius R is a parameter. Call this distance D_i.

(b) Find the number of retail stations within radius R Kms for each coordinate i. Call it N_i. Then, obtain the ratio D_i/N_i (i.e. sum of distance to number of retail shops for each lowest capacity location i). Now sort in ascending order of this ratio and select the top 7 location coordinates i pertaining to the least ratio. These location coordinates are regions where scope of capacity enhancement lies as the proximity to retailers is high and freight weight of vans is low.

Step 3: Comparison with test data → On the test data that is unseen by the trained machine learning models, we compare the locations "predicted" by the above machine learning based methodology with "actual" locations in the test dataset that have potential for enhancing the capacity. This gives an indication of scope and challenges with above methodology.

In the next section, we discuss about the development of machine learning models and the data-set used in this study.

3   Machine Learning Model Development and Data Characteristics

The information on datasets used in this work is provided below.

3.1   Dataset

Figure 1 shows (a) all the locations along freight routes operated by vans of a commercial freight transport business, and (b) all Retailer locations in the city. Here Retailers refers to all business units that might be interested in availing of freight services for transport of their goods. The details of three datasets are given below:

Freight weight data: This data-set is used for developing a ML model for predicting freight-weight in Step 1 of methodology. This dataset involves about 2223 trips of the freight delivery vans across the Oslo city during a month, with about 56272 total number of stops for loading/unloading of freights during all these trips. Out of the 56272 stops, about 8227 are unique stop locations (as seen in Fig. 1-a) that gets visited repeatedly. Here, at each stop location in a given freight-delivery trip - the data-set has corresponding measured values of the van freight weight (which is the dependent variable) along with the given stop number in the trip, the time of visit and location coordinates of visit, as well as time spent by van at the given location. For any given freight trip, the first location is the first stop number. On average, each journey have about 25 stops (stop numbers). The independent features in the regression model are: location of stop, stop number in the journey, time of visit, day of visit.

Traffic count data-set: The data-set used for developing ML model for traffic count involves traffic count data (number of visit by the traffic at a given location) at different locations (about 101661 number of observations) and it has been collected over a period of one year in Oslo city. This machine learning model could also be used in Step 1 if required. The machine learning is used to relate each observation (i.e. each traffic count) with known independent variables such as station location represented by distance from centre, lane direction, month, time, weekday and weather conditions (wind speed, temperature, precipitation).

Retailer dataset: The retail dataset has list of about 40000 retailers spread across Oslo city with their latitude and longitude coordinates. The methodology described in Sect. 2 uses this spatial coordinates of retailers to find distance from freight stop location to determine number of retailers within distance R Kms. Next, we include a small note on preprocessing done on data before it is ready for machine learning model.

3.2   Data Treatment

The above datasets are preprocessed for missing value, outliers, multi-collinearity and redundancy. The freight-weight and traffic count dataset have been subjected to feature engineering, feature scaling and data standardization. The feature variables are categorized into either cyclic variables (example - hours, wind direction, weekday), or as categorical nominal variables (like, month in traffic count data), and rest as continuous variables. The categorical variables are subjected to the "one-hot encoding" procedure, while the cyclic ordinal variables like "hours" are also transformed into two newer variables in order to preserve relevant information (like '23' and '0' h are close to each other and not far from each other). For a 24 h clock, this is achieved through following transformation: $x = sin(2 * \pi * hour/24), y = cos(2 * \pi * hour/24)$. Next, we discuss about split of data into training, validation and test data for ML training.

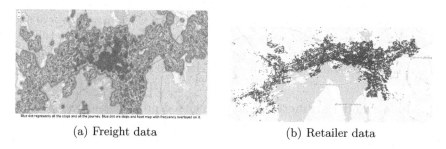

(a) Freight data   (b) Retailer data

Fig. 1. Data used in this study: Freight stop locations and Retailer locations in Oslo city.

3.3   Data Splitting: Cross-Validation and Learning Curve

Two machine learning models are developed using cross-validation and learning curve examination in order to: (a) predict the expected freight weight at each location at a given time after N number of stops in its journey, and (b) to predict the expected traffic count at each location using a vehicle data-set. Then for the methodology described in Sect. 2, the trained freight-weight machine learning model is used to predict the expected freight weight at different stops on prospective routes for a realistic case (a commercial freight operator in Oslo, Norway). These predictions will help to identify the best locations that have both: (a) locations with lower utilization of van capacity along the routes, and (b) locations where the scope of enhancing the load capacity of freight services is high based on the proximity to the retailers. The other ML model (on traffic count) can be used to predict the frequency of visit of vehicle in the above methodology, however it has not been done so in this work due to the reason outlined before but it helps to demonstrate the possibilities with the methodology and hence is included in the study. Here for both the models, four machine learning models (polynomial regressor, random forest [7], support vector machine [1,5] and artificial neural network [4,12,14]) have been compared using the cross-validation method. Cross-validation (CV) is a model validation technique for assessing the generalization ability of a machine learning algorithm to an independent data set. In our work, we split the original dataset into the 'training' and the 'test' dataset in 80:20 ratio, where the 20% test data features the unseen freight routes. For the training dataset, we have selected a $3 - foldCV$ procedure, where the 'training set' is split into 3 different smaller sets. The model prediction is learned using 2 of these 3 folds at a time (these two folds are called training set in learning curve as in Fig. 2), and the 3rd fold that is left out is used for validation (called validation set in Fig. 2). The average R2 (coefficient of determination) from the 3-fold CV is used to select the best machine learning algorithm (and the best parameter set for the method). A R2 score of 1.0 suggests a ML model with high accuracy, and a constant model that always predicts the same expected output disregarding the input features would get a R2 score of 0 and a negative score suggests a ML model with worse performance. The learning curve shows the variation of average R2 score with increasing training data and validation data and informs us about the bias-variance trade-off. Thus, it informs us about the generalization ability of a learning algorithm to unseen data.

ML Models and Parameter. The CV method provides the best parameter set by employing cross-validated "grid-search" over a parameter space for each of the four machine-learning model. The best parameter set for each model obtained from CV study are as mentioned below:

1. Random Forest. For traffic count, it is (a) Number of trees - 55 as the variance error stopped reducing further after 55 trees. For freight weight, the (a) Number of trees - 80. (b) The maximum depth of the tree that is possible is used in both cases as higher the depth, the lesser bias related errors were seen.
2. Support Vector Machine (SVM). For traffic count: RBF Kernel, $C = 100$, $\gamma = 1$, and, for the freight weight, it is: RBF Kernel, $C = 10$, $\gamma = 0.5$.
3. For Artificial Neural Network (ANN): the best ANN model was obtained with the following parameters for traffic count dataset: (a) RELU activation, (b) L2 penalty (regularization term) parameter $\alpha = 0.1$, (c) number of layers $= 3$, (d) size of each hidden layer $= 25$, and for freight weight data-set: (a) tanh activation, (b) L2 penalty (regularization term) parameter $\alpha = 1$, (c) number of layers $= 3$, (d) size of each hidden layer $= 20, 20, 20$.
4. Polynomial regression (PR) with degree 2 for both traffic count and freight weight estimation.

Next, we present results from implementation of the machine learning models.

4   Results and Discussions

Here, we discuss the performance of ML models on validation data and on unseen test data for predicting freight-weight and frequency of visit. We also compare the ML based methodology's "prediction" of best locations for capacity utilization in the test data (unseen freight routes) with the "actual" best locations from the data.

4.1   Comparison of ML Models for Traffic Count Prediction

Figure 2 compares the learning curve for the four different ML models based on the 3-fold CV data-set for predicting the traffic count (number of vehicles) on training and validation data, while Fig. 3 shows the predicted fit vs measured observation by different models for the traffic count (number of vehicles) on the hidden test data-set. The learning curve (in Fig. 2) shows that for traffic count the Random forest (RF) model reaches the highest R2 score (in range of 0.955–0.975) as length of validation data increases during CV procedure. The performance of models on both increasing training data and validation dataset is seen. RF model fit is better than other models: polynomial regression with degree 2 polynomial (which has 0.8 R2 score), SVM (around 0.85 R2 score)and ANN (0.7 R2 score). For random forest, the training score is mildly higher than the cross-validation score so a bit of over-fitting is there, but this is in acceptable limit. On the other hand, the ANN learning curve shows the least R2 score(0.7 R2 score) but there is no over-fitting. The "predicted fit vs measured observation on unseen test data" in Fig. 3 for the traffic count shows that: Random Forest provides the best fit. So considering the CV accuracy on validation data and the generalization ability on unseen test data, the random forest is performing better than SVM, ANN and polynomial regression for the traffic count.

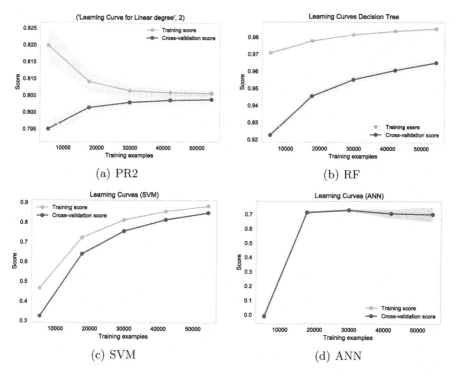

(a) PR2

(b) RF

(c) SVM

(d) ANN

Fig. 2. Learning curves for predicting traffic count based on length of training/validation data. The performances of 4 different models with accuracy (R2 scores) shown.

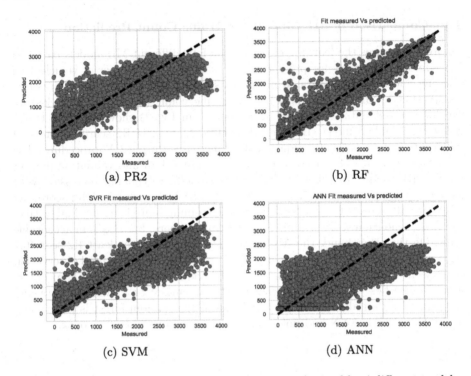

(a) PR2   (b) RF

(c) SVM   (d) ANN

Fig. 3. Test data: actual vs predicted traffic count as obtained by 4 different models.

4.2   Comparison of Models for Freight Weight Prediction

Figure 4 compares the learning curve for the four different ML models based on the 3-fold CV data-set for predicting the freight weight on training and validation data, while Fig. 5 shows the predicted fit vs measured observation by different models for the freight-weight on the hidden test data-set. The learning curve (in Fig. 4) shows that the Random forest (RF) model reaches the highest validation R2 score as compared to other models (in range of around 0.4) as the length of validation data increases during CV procedure. The RF model's validation performance is better than other models: polynomial regression with degree 2 polynomial (has 0.17 validation R2 score), SVM (around 0.35 validation R2 score) and ANN (around 0.37 validation R2 score). The "predicted fit vs measured observation on the unseen test data" in Fig. 5 also that the Random Forest provides the better fit as compared to other models (SVM, ANN, etc.). The prediction performance for all models on the unseen test data to predict freight-weight is also not high. All the models show less than satisfactory performance on both validation and test data with low R2 scores for freight-weight, indicating both high bias error (as seen from lower accuracy/R2 scores on training data) and high variance error (as seen from much lower accuracy/R2 scores on validation and test data). As compared to the ML performance on traffic count frequency predictions, the freight weight predictions by machine learn-

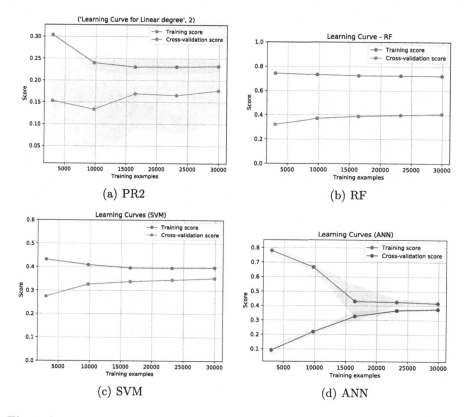

Fig. 4. Learning curves for predicting freight-weight along stops based on length of training/validation data. The performances of 4 different models with accuracy (R2 scores) shown.

ing models do not have high R2 scores (as seen by comparing Figs. 2, 3, 4 and Fig. 5). Now both traffic count and freight weight models use different data-sets and different input features. There could be some possible explanation for the low R2 scores of freight-weight, like: (a) there are independent features which are either not available or measurable, for example traffic situation, and economic factors impacting local demand/supply and operational changes resulting in change in van type for delivery. The inclusion of these difficult-to-measure features in some form can increase the explanatory power of the model to predict the freight weight and can take care of bias-related error, but currently we do not have this data in our study. Now from the error analysis in Fig. 6, the ML predicted freight-weight does seem to follow the trend at most places with errors (green line nearer to zero). Hence for the current data-set and case study, we will try to see the influence of the machine-learning predicted weight on the final results (i.e. on selecting locations/regions where scope of capacity utilization is there). We will compare the ML-based methodology predicted best locations on test routes (route data unseen by ML) with actual best locations in this test

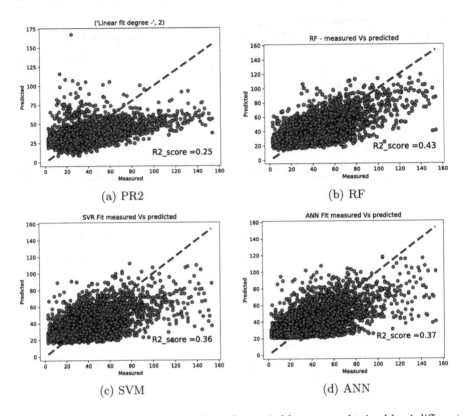

Fig. 5. Test data: actual vs predicted weight carried by van as obtained by 4 different models.

route (see Sect. 4.3). This comparison will help us to draw conclusions regarding scope and challenges of applying ML for enhancing freight-weight utilization.

4.3   Comparison: Best Locations for Enhancing Freight Weight Capacity of Vans

The realistic case-study used here involves freight-delivery services (vans) undertaking many journeys to deliver/pick up freights to retail business developers. Figure 7 illustrates the route taken for one such journey by the van. The red circle is the starting and the end point of the journey, and the black circle shows the van capacity at a given location with its radius representing the capacity. The locations with lowest capacity on this journey is noted by a text. There are about 2223 such journeys in a given month. To improve the capacity utilization, the freight-delivery services can focus on locations where vans are running with lower capacity relative to frequency of visits and where the nearby retailer density is high (i.e. high number of business retails around R kms radius from the stop location amongst all the retailer locations that were shown in the Fig. 1).

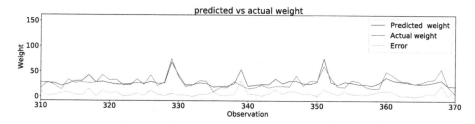

Fig. 6. Random Forest performance for freight weight prediction for each observation: actual vs ML predicted weight with error.

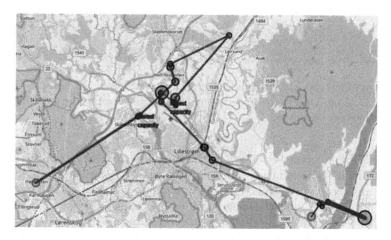

Fig. 7. Route taken for one journey by van with freight capacity represented by the line width and the radius of circle at the station.

As explained in the methodology, the machine-learning is used to "predict" the expected freight weight along the different routes using input features after being trained. The Figs. 8 shows the "actual" top 7 locations and "predicted" top 7 locations that have scope for better van capacity utilization based on test data from the month of May. The ML predicted locations (represented by black circle) and actual (represented by marker) from test data overlap at two places. In other words, ML has been able to predict two of the actual top seven locations and help to make some decisions. Thus, there is scope for improvement and there is also potential for use of the methodology for enhancing utilization of capacity of vehicles in freight route service. The benefits and challenges of the ML based methodology are summarized as below:

The benefit of using this ML based methodology is that it can help predict for new unseen freight routes provided that the ML models are well-trained with good data. The freight-delivery services then can target these predicted locations to enhance the freight-capacity of the vehicle as there are more retailers near by.

The challenges in the ML based methodology are as seen from not so high R2 scores during the freight-weight ML model fit. The results indicates that

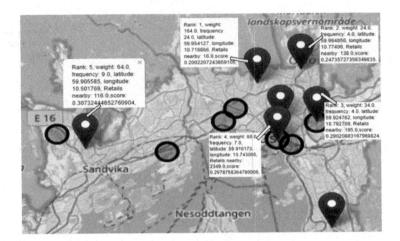

Fig. 8. Top 7 locations where freight capacity can be enhanced: ML-based methodology predicted locations (black circle) v/s actual location (marker) in the unseen test data. Two locations are common.

there could be inherent variability in the freight weight (our response variable) that is difficult to account for completely by available measurable independent feature variables. For example, difficult-to-measure variables and events like, (a) random occurrences of traffic congestion, or (b) change in local demand/supply and economic situation, or (c) change in type of van used and its capacity, can make predictions of freight weight at a given route location at a given time difficult.

From the scope and challenges that we see here, the future work can involve focused data acquisition with means to accommodate difficult-to-measure features for training ML models,integrating more statistical knowledge, and integrating the methodology with vehicle route optimization tools.

5   Conclusion

A machine learning based methodology has been developed for enhancing capacity utilization of freight services. The methodology developed here involves identifying the regions (or stop locations) in the map where the services are expected to have lower capacity along with good opportunity to enhance capacity utilization by considering the presence of retailer density. The methodology involves using machine learning based prediction of freight-weights of van along all stops in a freight routes, as well as potential for including traffic count prediction at stops in the methodology. The methodology has shown its useful to some extent by predicting some of the best locations in the test data. The challenges are there with regards to accuracy improvements of the ML model for freight-weight due to both high bias and variance errors, and the bias errors could be related to data characteristics, like: the possibility that freight-weight can be difficult to account completely by the available measurable independent feature variables. For example unaccounted difficult-to-measure features and events, like: random occurrences of traffic congestion, or variability in local demand/supply tied to economic activity, or change in van model type, such sudden changes can make predictions of freight weight at a given route location at a given time difficult. Such variables can be difficult to measure. Nevertheless, this works still helps to provide insights in what can be achieved through available data set. The scope and challenges encountered in this work should lead to future works involving focused data acquisition with means to accommodate difficult-to-measure features for enabling good training of ML models and integrating the methodology with vehicle route optimization tools.

Acknowledgment. The authors acknowledge the financial support from the Norwegian Research council's DigiMOB project (project number: 283331).

References

1. Alex, J.S., Bernhard, S.: A tutorial on support vector regression. Stat. Comput. Arch. **14**(3), 199–222 (2004)
2. Bakhtyar, S., Holmgren, J.: A data mining based method for route and freight estimation. Procedia Comput. Sci. **52**, 396–403 (2015)
3. Barua, L., Zou, B., Zhou, Y.: Machine learning for international freight transportation management: a comprehensive review. Res. Transp. Bus. Manag. **34**, 100453 (2020)
4. Bengio, Y.: Practical recommendations for gradient-based training of deep architectures. In: Montavon, G., Orr, G.B., Müller, K.-R. (eds.) Neural Networks: Tricks of the Trade. LNCS, vol. 7700, pp. 437–478. Springer, Heidelberg (2012). https://doi.org/10.1007/978-3-642-35289-8_26
5. Boser, B.E., Guyon, I.M., Vapnik, V.N.: A training algorithm for optimal margin classifiers. In: Proceedings of the Fifth Annual Workshop on Computational Learning Theory, COLT 1992, pp. 144–152. Association for Computing Machinery, New York (1992)
6. Boukerche, A., Wang, J.: Machine learning-based traffic prediction models for intelligent transportation systems. Comput. Netw. **181**, 107530 (2020)
7. Breiman, L.: Random forests. Mach. Learn. **45**(1), 5–32 (2001)
8. Gao, Y.: Forecasting of freight volume based on support vector regression optimized by genetic algorithm. In: 2009 2nd IEEE International Conference on Computer Science and Information Technology, pp. 550–553 (2009)
9. Guo, Z., Fu, J.Y.: Prediction method of railway freight volume based on genetic algorithm improved general regression neural network. J. Intell. Syst. **28**(5), 835–848 (2019)
10. Hassan, L.A.H., Mahmassani, H.S., Chen, Y.: Reinforcement learning framework for freight demand forecasting to support operational planning decisions. Transp. Res. Part E: Logist. Transp. Rev. **137**, 101926 (2020)
11. Jiang, H., Chang, L., Li, Q., Chen, D.: Trajectory prediction of vehicles based on deep learning. In: 2019 4th International Conference on Intelligent Transportation Engineering (ICITE), pp. 190–195 (2019)

12. Lecun, Y., Bengio, Y., Hinton, G.: Deep learning. Nature **521**(7553), 436–444 (2015)
13. Ruesch, M., Schmid, T., Bohne, S., Haefeli, U., Walker, D.: Freight transport with VANs: developments and measures. Transp. Res. Procedia **12**, 79–92 (2016)
14. Rumelhart, D., Hinton, G., Williams, R.: Learning representations by back-propagating errors. Nature **323**(6088), 533–536 (1986)
15. Taniguchi, E., Thompson, R., Yamada, T., Van Duin, J.: City logistics. In: Network Modelling and Intelligent Transport Systems, January 2001

Author Index

Printed in the United States
by Baker & Taylor Publisher Services